PETERSEN'S BASIC AUTO REPAIR MANUAL

INTRODUCTION

Generalization. That's the name of the game in Petersen's *Basic Auto Repair Manual,* 8th edition, because the intent of this book is to instill enough confidence in the at-home mechanic to tackle his car's innermost ailments. If we were to take you through *all* the intricacies of *all* the popular domestic cars, this book would approach 1000 pages in size. In fact, we have produced another book that *does* go into such detail. It's called Petersen's *Big Book of Auto Repair,* and it describes all the systems, subsystems and components for all U.S. cars from 1970 on. The book you're holding, though, goes into the *theory* underlying the average car's mechanical intricacies: why such and such connects to so and so, how to diagnose a strange rattle or clunk, when to suspect that your clutch needs replacing and how to understand and fix the myriad other problems that are commonplace in today's automobiles.

The two books can be used as companion volumes, or they can be used separately. This one, the *Basic Auto Repair Manual* No. 8, is exactly the primer that a do-it-yourselfer needs to understand all those hoses, lines and linkages under the hood. With it he can learn why a differential does what it does, how the mysterious typical automatic transmission functions and what to do when his engine misses and splutters. In short, he can learn about all the whats, whys, hows, wheres and whens of his car in order to better understand its care and feeding.

The confidence we mentioned earlier will come when the driveway tinkerer, interested in saving himself a few hard-earned dollars on a relatively minor repair, reads this book and learns that the complex automobile isn't really all that complex after all. Beyond that, a small set of inexpensive hand tools and the factory shop manual for his (or her) particular car are all that's needed before setting aside a few hours some Saturday morning to devote to the car's irritating quirks. The inherent pleasure that comes from knowing you fixed it yourself, and that you can very likely fix whatever else comes a cropper in the future, will make this *Basic Auto Repair Manual* one of your more prized garage "tools."

SPENCER MURRAY

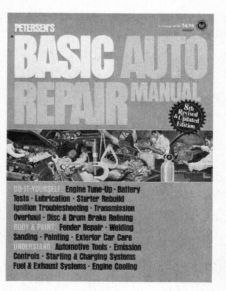

BASIC AUTO REPAIR MANUAL No. 8

Revision edited by Spencer Murray and the technical editors of Specialty Publications Division. Copyright© 1977 by Petersen Publishing Co., 8490 Sunset Blvd., Los Angeles, CA 90069. Phone: (213) 657-5100. All rights reserved. No part of this book may be reproduced without written permission. Printed in U.S.A.

COVER: Artist Chuck Ren has incorporated into his full-color rendering many of the aspects of the modern automobile that the do-it-yourselfer may involve himself with, in the interests of maintaining his car right in his own driveway. That's what this book is all about. Cover design by Al Isaacs.

Library of Congress Catalog Card Number 75-18057
ISBN 0-8227-5011-2

SPECIALTY PUBLICATIONS DIVISION

Erwin M. Rosen/Executive Editor
Spencer Murray/Senior Editor
Al Hall/Editor
Ann C. Tidwell/Managing Editor
Jay Storer/Feature Editor
Eric Rickman/Photo Editor
Richard L. Busenkell/Technical Editor
Jim Brightly/Associate Editor
Dick Fischer/Art Director
George Fukuda/Artist, Design
Angie Ullrich/Editorial Assistant

PETERSEN PUBLISHING COMPANY

R.E. Petersen/Chairman of the Board
F.R. Waingrow/President
Herb Metcalf/Senior Vice President
Philip E. Trimbach/V.P., Finance
William Porter/V.P.-Director, Circulation
Jack Thompson/Assistant Director, Circulation
T. Swift Lockard/Director, Advertising Marketing
Arthur Zarin/Director, Research
Spencer Nilson/Director, Administrative Services
Alan C. Hahn/Director, Market Development
James J. Krenek/Director, Manufacturing Services
Al Isaacs/Director, Graphics
Bob D'Olivo/Director, Photography
Maria Cox/Manager, Data Processing Services

CONTENTS

CONTENTS

282 / SUSPENSION & ALIGNMENT

294 / MANUAL STEERING

304 / POWER STEERING

306 / WHEELS & TIRES

312 / BODY & PAINT

332 / ACCESSORY FIX-IT TIPS

348 / IMPROVING FUEL ECONOMY

354 / TUNE-UP SPECIFICATIONS

370 / TROUBLESHOOTING GUIDES

The Right Tools for the Job

A mechanic without tools is like a wheel without a tire. A wheel, thankfully, is satisfied with only one tire, but a mechanic never feels that he has enough tools. Part of being a mechanic is fascination with the sight of a full toolbox, a love of all the different sockets and extensions, handles and ratchets, and even some gadgets that haven't been used for so long that it's difficult to remember what car they were designed for, or even how they work.

The best advice we can give you about buying tools is to investigate before you buy even so much as a simple pair of pliers. Get as many catalogs as possible from the tool companies, and go to the retail stores so you can see and handle the merchandise. In many cases we have seen mechanics get started with a basic set of hand tools, only to discover later that another brand was much more appealing to them. The result was they switched to the other brand, and the money spent for the original basic set was wasted. It makes no difference whether you buy Snap-On, Proto, Sears' Craftsman, Ward's Power-Kraft, Mac, or any other brand. The important thing is to know about them all before you make that necessary purchase of your basic set.

In some brands you can save a lot of money by getting a set instead of individual tools. But beware of enormous sets that include everything from thread gauges to wheel pullers, with maybe a backscratcher thrown in. After all, you may find that you like one maker's socket sets, but not his pliers. And you may go to a third manufacturer for your screwdrivers, simply because you like the way they are made. Some of the small toolmakers do an excellent job on special-purpose tools for brakes, or engines, or electrical work. In many cases they are the only source for a special tool that is just what you need.

Major brand tools are not discounted to anybody. The backyard mechanic pays the same price as the guy who works on the line at a big car dealer. Some big-city hardware stores may have a line of hand tools that they discount, but such places are hard to find, and the amount you get off is only about 10%.

The best place to find different makes of tools is at an automotive parts store. The counterman is usually out of catalogs, but you can get the address of the factory from him and write for one. Some tools, including the best hand tools available, are not sold in retail stores, but only by wagon peddlers. The peddlers usually leave their calling cards all over town at the various independent garages and car dealers. Ask your local mechanic for the phone numbers of the various wagon peddlers that call on him.

Don't ignore the mail order houses, either. Sears and Ward's have excellent tools. Incidentally, their catalog price is usually less than you would have to pay in the retail store.

For the purpose of properly selecting and using the basic hand tools for fasteners, some knowledge of those fasteners—particularly the nuts and bolts—is very important to any type of repair work. It is not only a question of the proper wrench for the nut or bolt but of the proper bolt size and how tight it should be twisted.

UNDERSTANDING FASTENERS

Fasteners vary not only in a wide range of sizes and thread count, but also in the type of material from which they are made. Increased strength for a particular assembly is not always achieved by installing a larger bolt, but very often by the specified use of a stronger bolt material. Critically stressed parts of an automobile such as the suspension, steering and structural assembly generally use nuts and bolts of a higher tensile strength than those used just to hold accessories. Sheetmetal screws, for example, may look like some of the available wood screws, but they are treated for hardness and will withstand threading into a punched hole under stresses that just twist off wood screws.

Bolt and cap screws are easily identified by distinctive markings embossed on the heads which denote the type of ma-

1. Removing a Carburetor

2. Toolboxes

BASIC BEGINNER'S TOOLS

1. Combination box- and open-end wrenches, from ⅜-in. through 1 in. in increments of 1/16-in.
2. ⅜-in.-drive socket set, with ratchet and breaker bar
3. ⅜-in-drive spark plug socket and three extensions—a short one, a long one and a flex-drive
4. Four screwdrivers—one short and one long of both the Phillips type and the regular, flat-tip type
5. Pair of slip-joint pliers
6. Pair of needle-nose pliers
7. Adjustable wrench (Crescent type)
8. Roll of mechanic's wire (cheap and very handy at times)
9. Diagonal cutting pliers
10. Small stock of sundries, such as electrical tape, WD-40 oil, engine degreaser, white-grease lube and spray-can paints
11. Ball-peen hammer
12. Two jack stands
13. Scissors jack (better than bumper jack, but not as expensive as a hydraulic jack)

OPTIONS FOR ROUTINE MAINTENANCE

1. Battery post and cable terminal cleaner
2. Drain pan for oil and water
3. Wrench for removing spin-on oil filters
4. Hand-operated grease gun
5. Antifreeze tester
6. Spray can of silicone lube, can of wheel bearing grease
7. Mechanic's creeper

OPTIONS FOR TUNE-UP WORK

1. Spark plug gap setter
2. Flat feeler gauges
3. Allen wrench for adjusting points (GM V-8's)
4. Small tube of distributor cam lube
5. Carburetor cleaner (spray can or liquid)
6. Ignition timing light
7. Wrench for distributor hold-down bolt
8. Set of small ignition wrenches
9. Hand-held dwell/tach meter
10. Combination vacuum/fuel pressure tester
11. Compression tester

OPTIONS FOR BRAKE WORK

1. Brake adjusting "spoon"
2. Offset-shank brake bleeder wrench
3. Combination remover/installer for shoe return springs
4. Wheel cylinder/master cylinder hone (must be used with an electric drill motor)
5. Combination remover/installer for hold-down springs
6. Two more jack stands

OPTIONS FOR MAJOR ENGINE WORK

1. ½-in.-drive socket set with ratchet and breaker bar, plus long, short and flex-type extensions
2. Gear puller
3. 0-100 or 0-150 ft.-lb. torque wrench (½-in.-drive)
4. Valve-spring compressor
5. Ridge remover
6. Ring compressor
7. Engine cylinder bore hone (must be used with slow-speed electric drill motor)

terial and, therefore, the tensile strength range for proper torquing. The word "torque" will continue to crop up in specifications relating to everything from spark plugs to cylinder head nuts, and is a very important function of the strength of bolts and the pieces held together by them.

Before proceeding further with torque, it is best to clarify the method of identifying fasteners by strength rating. Bolt heads are embossed with a series of lines radiating outward. Plain-headed bolts without markings are the most common to the hardware store purchaser. They are graded as 1 or 2 by the SAE (Society of Automotive Engineers), and are adequate for most accessory fastening jobs requiring only low-carbon steel strength.

Generally specified for automotive use is the SAE grade 5, noted by three embossed lines on the head and with nearly double the tensile strength of the common low-carbon, plain-headed bolt. Slightly higher in strength are the grades 6 and 7 noted by 4- and 5-line markings respectively, and topping the commercial grades is the 6-liner for use in severe stress points and on heavy-duty trucks and construction equipment.

Carriage and stove bolts are not recommended as replacement for even the lowest SAE grade of bolts, although they have their place in the fabrication of many common items. Machine screws with special heads such as flat, fillister,

round, and pan designations are not usually marked except in aircraft grades.

Allen-head cap screws are unmarked, but they are usually grade 8 or better. Unfortunately, frequent use tends to round off the corners of the wrench or to strip out the head. If working space permits, you should change over to hex-headed cap screws. The strongest cap

screws are made for aircraft, but they are also the most expensive, unless you can find them in a surplus store.

Thread patterns, noted by the bolt size and a single number which means the number of threads per inch (4-40, 10-32, ¼-20, etc.) for machine screws, nuts and bolts, are important especially when the fastener is used in a threaded hole. All

1. Fifty bucks worth of hand tools should cover what the backyard mechanic needs to effect 90% of the repairs that would shape up the old clunker. A set of wrenches, a couple hammers, screwdrivers, pliers, bench tools and the "Basic Auto Repair Manual" can save the do-it-yourself hundreds of dollars in bills. A screwdriver is all that's needed to replace this choke vacuum actuator.

2. Multi-piece toolboxes usually find a home among the professionals. But many serious amateurs also tie up hundreds, even thousands of dollars in sets like these shown. Most packages include ¼, ⅜ and ½-in. drives, a full complement of ratchets, extensions, breaker bars, torque wrenches, sockets, speed handles, end wrenches, hammers, pliers, punches, drills and mikes.

3. Cap screws or bolts are available in varying head designs, all tailored to do a specific job. Some must be tightened by screwdrivers, others by various types of wrenches.

4. We call them bolts, nuts, washers, etc., but the trade refers to them as fasteners. Obviously they come in varying grades depending upon their use and/or need. High-stress areas— like the clutch or crank—require employment of a strong type of cap screw material. Low-stress areas— manifolds or carburetors—can use a lesser strength material.

5. Cap screws too have their design terminologies and characteristics. The better a mechanic understands the whys and wherefores of fasteners, the easier it will be for him to select the right grade and the right torque.

3. Cap Screw Head Designs

ROUND — FLAT — TRUSS — PAN (BINDING) — OVAL — FILLISTER — HEXAGON — CARRIAGE — SQUARE

GRADE MARKINGS					
DEFINITION	No lines unmarked Indeterminate quality SAE Grades 0-1-2	3 Lines—common commercial quality Automotive & AN Bolts SAE Grade 5	4 Lines—Medium commercial quality Automotive & AN Bolts SAE Grade 6	5 Lines—rarely used SAE Grade 7	6 Lines—Best commercial quality N.A.S. & Aircraft Screws SAE Grade 8
MATERIAL	Low Carbon Steel	Med. Carbon Steel Tempered	Med. Carbon Steel Quenched & tempered	Med. Carbon Alloy Steel	Med. Carbon Alloy Steel Quenched & tempered
TENSILE STRENGTH	65,000 p.s.i.	120,000 p.s.i.	140,000 p.s.i.	140,000 p.s.i.	150,000 p.s.i.

GRADE MARKINGS					
DEFINITION	Supertanium	A-354-BD. A490	Socket Head Cap Screw Also N.A.S. Aircraft Std.	N.A.S. 144 Aircraft Std. MS 20000 Mil. Std.	N.A.S. 624 National Aircraft Standard Steel	Aircraft No Number Assigned Steel
MATERIAL	Special Alloy Steel Quenched & tempered	Med. Carbon Alloy Quenched & tempered	High Carbon Alloy Quenched & tempered	High Carbon Alloy Quenched & tempered	High Carbon Alloy Quenched & tempered	High Carbon Alloy Quenched & tempered
TENSILE STRENGTH	160,000 p.s.i. minimum	150,000 p.s.i.	160,000 p.s.i.	160,000 p.s.i.	180,000 p.s.i.	220,000 p.s.i.

4. Fastener Grade Marking Chart

FULL DIAMETER SHANK
EQUAL TO MAJOR DIAMETER OF THREAD. PRODUCED BY CUT THREAD ON EXTRUDED BLANK. CHARACTERISTIC OF MACHINE BOLTS AND CAP SCREWS.

UNDERSIZE SHANK
EQUAL APPROXIMATELY TO PITCH DIAMETER OF THREAD. PRODUCED BY ROLL THREADING A NON-EXTRUDED BLANK. CHARACTERISTIC OF MACHINE SCREWS.

PITCH
THE DISTANCE FROM A POINT ON THE SCREW THREAD TO A CORRESPONDING POINT ON THE NEXT THREAD MEASURED PARALLEL TO AXIS.

MAJOR DIAMETER
THE LARGEST DIAMETER OF A SCREW THREAD.

PITCH DIAMETER
THE SIMPLE, EFFECTIVE DIAMETER OF SCREW THREAD. APPROXIMATELY HALF WAY BETWEEN THE MAJOR AND MINOR DIAMETERS.

MINOR DIAMETER
THE SMALLEST DIAMETER OF A SCREW THREAD.

5. Cap Screw Design

Right Tools for the Job

of the commonly used machine screws or bolts are made in two thread series, coarse and fine, and it is important that even though the bolt diameter is correct for the hole, the threads match those in the hole.

Internal threads and those on the bolt should always be clean and free of damaged or flattened sections before you attempt to assemble any part using threaded holes. Greater care must be taken if aluminum is involved. This applies to everything from installing spark plugs to assembling aluminum transmission cases. Even the poorest grade of steel bolt will cut its own thread in aluminum or soft steel if it has the wrong thread per inch pattern or if it is started into the hole improperly.

A good practice for any assembly is to first try all of the bolts *by finger effort only* into the threaded holes to check for both length and thread. Any doubt about the force required to thread the fasteners by finger pressure should be followed by an examination of both male and female thread condition. Slightly damaged threads on a bolt can be dressed up by filing with a slim 3-cornered file or a thread file, a handy tool in any mechanic's kit. These have eight different thread pattern filing sides and are reasonably priced, but worth a fortune when really needed.

Dressing up inside threads, if only slightly damaged, is best done by running the proper tap into the hole. While not absolutely necessary as part of the basic tool kit, a few taps in the most common sizes will come in handy especially when you are working on older cars that may have been badly repaired by the previous owner. Before getting into the total repair of damaged inside threads, it is best to consider the tools in common use for standard nuts and bolts.

END WRENCHES

Anyone looking at a set of standard open-end, box-end or combination wrenches will immediately notice how the total length increases with the size of the opening. This in itself is a sort of primitive built-in protection against overtightening as it limits the leverage and consequently the foot-pounds of torque that one can apply. It does not consider the strength of the individual, which can often mean a twisted-off bolt. Wrench sizes for American standard nuts and bolts are given in fractions of an inch and note the distance measured across the parallel flat sides of hexagon (6-sided) nuts and bolts.

Metric nuts and bolts are measured across the same dimension with the corresponding wrench size given in millimeters. British cars used to use the British standard system which is measured at the bolt shank diameter. A wrench marked 1/4 W (Whitworth) is made to fit a 1/4-in. bolt, even though the head dimension is 7/16-in. British cars now use American sizes.

Open-end wrenches exert their force against a pair of the parallel sides, and it is important that the proper size wrench

be used. Naturally, one too small will not even fit, but too large an open end will result in insufficient contact area to exert the proper force. It will burr the corners enough to impair the use of a wrench of the proper size, and make it impossible to fit a box-end or socket on the bolt head or nut.

Box-end wrenches and sockets apply their force on a small area on either side of the bolt or nut corners, but unlike the open-end tool, the force is applied to all six corners at once. These are the common 12-point type used on box-end and socket wrenches and are recommended for all general use. A set of combination open- and box-end wrenches is a good investment and will handle most general repair projects.

The adjustable-end wrench or "Crescent" is made by most tool manufacturers, including Crescent Tool Co., and is a very handy tool for the occasional mechanic for those jobs beyond the capacity of the average wrench set. A 10- or 12-in. adjustable will handle sizes slightly over 1 in., saving the need for an investment in an open/box-end set of the larger sizes. Adjustables also come in small editions with a maximum opening of ½-in., and there are click-stop models that hold the jaws firmly at preset positions. One of these, along with a good screwdriver and a pair of pliers, is nice to carry in the glove compartment just for on-the-road emergencies.

SOCKET WRENCHES

Socket wrenches are desirable for their adaptability to a variety of hard-to-reach places. Their speed when used with ratchet handles is a great aid in any mechanical work and no professional mechanic is without a full set of sizes, lengths, and adapters. Screwdriver and Allen screw bits increase the versatility of a socket/handle set and are ideally suited to applying great force in cramped spaces with the right-angle action of such a combination. In addition to these special ends, sockets for nuts and bolts are available in 4, 6, 8 and 12 points. The 4- and 8-point sockets are for square-headed fasteners, while the 6-pointers are mainly for power impact tool use on hex-nuts and bolts.

A common term used in connection with sockets, and the handles for them, is "drive." The connection between socket wrench and handle is by a square projection on the handle fitting into a similar hole in the drive end of the socket. The size of this connection is ¼-in., ⅜-in., etc., up to 1 in. in the standard and most commonly used tools. The size

1. Determining Thread Pattern

2. Socket Configurations

3. Types of End Wrenches

4. Types of Nuts and Washers

1. Thread size and pattern is either coarse or fine and is best confirmed by the use of this simple thread gauge. In any automotive application, one must use the correct pattern and cap screw diameter. If not, you'll strip the threads or break the bolts.

2. Sockets encompass 4, 6, 8 and 12-point configurations. The 4- and 8-pointers are used when fasteners with square heads are encountered. The 6-point types must be employed with impact wrenches or in high torque situations so as not to round off the edge of the bolt head. However, most general repair work features the use of 12-point sockets.

3. The simple end wrench can be purchased as either a box-end (left), open-end (right) or a combination of the two (middle). Box-ends come in handy as a breaker or final tightener. The speedier open ends are better for hard-to-get-at places.

4. What applies to cap screws also applies to nuts and washers. They come in an infinite variety of shapes, sizes and grades. In top row (from left) are a standard, castellated, SPS Flex-lok, jamb, Cone-lock, L&S Stover lock and a nylon insert locknut. Below (from left) are a lock, external tooth and flat washer. To prevent galling, flat washers must be made of the same material as the nut, and the nut must be identical in grade to that of the cap screw.

5. A ratchet box-end wrench is handy in tight places as well as for general use. It speeds up the loosening/tightening process and seldom slips off the bolt head, saving you a lot of knuckle skin in the long run.

6. Every backyard Bignotti should have a couple of crescent wrenches—especially if he owns one of the new, foreign-built subcompacts with their metric bolts and nuts. Crescents will also save you the cost of buying large sockets and/or end wrenches.

7. Most socket sets (breaker bars, U-drives, extensions, ratchets, etc.) come in ¼, ⅜, and ½-in. drives. Small (¼-in.) drives are useful for electrical and body fastener work, the ⅜-in. drive comes in handy when working on the outside of the engine, and the larger ½-in. drive is usually employed in general engine overhaul work or suspension repairs.

8. When the effective length of a torque wrench is changed by the addition of a horizontal adapter, the torque applied to the bolt is not the same as that shown on the wrench. A corrected reading (A) can be made using a formula: $TW = \frac{TA \times L}{L + A}$ where TW is torque value shown on wrench, TA is actual torque to bolt, L is torque wrench length and A is adapter length. If TA=25 ft.-lbs. (300 in.-lbs.), L=10 ins., A=4 ins., then $TW = \frac{300 \times 10}{10 + 4}$ or 214 in.-lbs. Therefore, wrench shows 214 in.-lbs.—but 300 in.-lbs. are actually being applied to bolt. If adapter shortens wrench length (B), use $TW = \frac{TA \times L}{L - A}$. Vertical extensions don't change wrench length, therefore they don't affect torque readings.

5. Ratchet Type Box Wrench

6. Crescent Wrenches

7. Socket Set

8. Torque Wrenches With Adapters

Right Tools for the Job

of the drive is in proportion to the socket size, giving the strength needed for handle length and bolt size. Handles for socket drives come in a variety of models as to length, ratchet, swivel, screwdriver, speed and flexibility, with universal and step-down adapters for using sockets of a different drive size than the handle. There are also open and "crowfoot" wrenches, Allen or Phillips drive bits and ratchet spinner attachments for socket sets, making them a most versatile tool.

A good set of sockets is a must for precision work; it will save a lot of busted knuckles and damaged nut and bolt heads. Just about every part on an automobile held together by bolting has a specific degree of tightness or torque specifications for it. This torque setting is specified for both the tensile strength of the fastener and the required degree of fit or tension between the mating parts.

TORQUE AND TORQUE WRENCHES

Every type and grade of metal has a limit to which it can be safely stretched or stressed. There is an engineering phrase that says, "An over-torqued bolt is already half broken"—which is a good indication of just what degree of stretch fasteners of this type can take. Designers consider many things in selecting the proper size and material for a fastener. As engines, transmissions and suspension components become more complex, their efficiency becomes more and more dependent on just how the various parts are held together. Applying just the right amount of torque or stretch to the fasteners imparts the correct amount of pressure needed to hold the parts together without distortion.

In the case of aluminum and other soft metals, their ultimate strength governs the amount of torque rather than that of the steel bolt. Allowance for heat expansion or soft joints sealed by gaskets also

must be considered when applying torque, as too much pressure could damage or distort the two mating parts.

Tension is not to be confused with torque. Tension is the stretching force along the length of the bolt, or its degree of stretch. Torque is the force required on the bolt or nut to produce the desired degree of stretch in the fastener; it is measured in foot-pounds (ft.-lbs.) or inch-pounds (in.-lbs.). Torque is measured on the basis of a fundamental law of physics regarding leverage: Force times distance equals twist force or torque around a pivot point. If 1 lb. of force is exerted around the bolt or nut center at 1 ft. from that center, the torque is 1 ft.-lb. If the distance is measured in inches, then the torque is read as 12 in.-lbs.

Torque wrenches for applying the proper amount of torque to fasteners are available in four basic forms: The *dial type* incorporates a calibrated dial that indicates by pointer when the desired torque is being applied. The *clutch type* has settings calibrated on the handle with a knurled sleeve for setting to the desired torque (drive is disengaged or slips when proper torque is reached). *Direct reading pointer types* employ a calibrated scale with pointer rod attached to the handle head that indicates torque in direct readings on scale. The *click type* unit produces an audible sound when preset torque force is reached. Some models are available with reversible ratchet, allowing the same handle to be used for general assembly without the need for switching tools.

Sometimes adapters of various shapes must be used with a torque wrench to get around obstructions. If the adapter is in effect only an extension bar, with the drive and hex parts in line with each other, then the torque readings will not be affected. However, if the adapter is similar to an end wrench, in effect making the torque wrench longer, then the torque readings will have to be corrected, depending on how long the adapter is. As torque wrenches do have limits, they are made in a variety of sizes to accommodate all of the limits. Tiny ones

1. Dial indicator on Milbar torque wrench is shown hovering around the 120-in.-lbs. or 10-ft.-lbs. level. This sensitive tool is used in critical areas where precise tightening is mandatory.

2. The offset design of a distributor wrench is a big help in reaching those buried mounting bolts in today's overloaded engine compartments.

3. Restoring stripped threads (like blind spark plug holes) calls for drilling, tapping, then inserting Heli-Coil-type threads to restore the hole to its original size.

4. Breaking a cap screw off in a block or cylinder head always ends in a sweat. First try to remove the residual piece by tapping it with a chisel or a punch. It should unscrew from the hole. If that doesn't work, you can use an extractor or drill out the old bolt and re-thread the hole.

5. As basic to the toolbox as the screwdriver, pliers come in all shapes and sizes. For instance, we've shown (top row, from left) bent needle nose, and diagonal wire cutters; (bottom row, from left) lineman, a pair of double-jointed types and a needle nose.

6. Continental American's standard screwdriver set is ideal for most automotive work. It features both standard and Phillips head tips, various lengths and blade widths.

7. Spark plug-type tire pump fits into spark plug well and pumps up to 105 psi of clean air. A 16-ft. hose, connectors and pressure gauge make this an outstanding replacement for older hand pump.

8. No matter what you think, every mechanic needs his hammers. Claw type will pound 'n' pry; round end of the ball peen makes an excellent gasket shaper, and you can always use a soft-faced rubber or plastic headed hammer to tap in parts without marring their machined surfaces.

9. This 8-piece hex key set by Craftsman has just about every size from 2 to 10mm that you'll need for automotive work.

1. Torquing Bolts to Specs

2. Distributor Offset Wrench

3. Heli-Coils

4. Using Screw Extractor

5. Plier Package

6. Screwdriver Set

7. Spark Plug Tire Pump

8. Types of Hammers

9. Hex Head Wrench Set

for setting fuel injectors have a limit of 150 in.-lbs., while larger handles with higher capacities are required for the 80-150 ft.-lbs. specified for main bearing caps, heads, etc. Heavy-duty ones used on industrial equipment go up to 6000 ft.-lbs. As a rough guide to selection of torque wrench range, here are a few general ratings and applicable common usages:

1) 0-80 ft.-lbs.—⅜- or ½-in. drive.

Spark plugs, intake and exhaust manifold, rocker arm brackets and covers, connecting rod cap bolts, transmission oil pan.

2) 10-150 ft.-lbs.—½-in. drive.

Main bearing caps, cylinder head bolts, main bearings, vibration dampener, transmission pump bolts, connecting rod bearings, power steering pump.

3) 100-500 ft.-lbs.—¾-in. drive.

Main bearing cap bolts, cylinder-head bolts, flywheel, pulley bolts and other jobs on big industrial and commercial equipment.

THREAD SAVERS

Breaking a bolt inside a threaded hole, or stripping the internal threads, are two major problems with fasteners that are sure to plague the amateur mechanic—

they occur quite often even to the trained professional. Stripping threads, especially in aluminum and quite often in the spark plug hole, does not mean the piece must be scrapped, thanks to several handy repair methods.

The two most popular devices for repairing damaged threads in blind holes, spark plug holes, or straight-through ones are the Heli-Coil, made by Heli-Coil Corp., Danbury, Conn., and the Slimsert by Proto Tool Co.

Both require the damaged hole to be drilled out, tapped properly, and then completed by the installation of the new thread assembly. Both are sold in complete kits to handle a variety of sizes and thread patterns, and have the advantage of restoring damaged holes to their original bolt and thread per inch size.

Broken bolts are another serious problem as they almost always break well inside the hole, eliminating the possibility of getting a hold on them with anything. With a little time and effort, and the proper screw extractors, they can be removed without damage to the part other than the cross threading or bottoming that caused the breakage in the first place.

Screw extractors are usually sold in sets, sized to remove anything from ¼-in.

1. Pop Rivet Gun

2. Hand Impact Driver

Right Tools for the Job

to 1-in. bolts or studs. They are fluted and tapered tools of high-grade steel, sometimes with spiral fluting in a left-hand pattern.

To remove a broken bolt, it is necessary to drill a hole into the broken piece as near the center as possible. The extractor is then driven or screwed into the hole and unscrewed while being held with a tap wrench. Penetrating oil on the broken part will often ease removal, and the internal threads should be examined and repaired before you proceed with any further assembly of the component.

Screw extractors are scorned by many automotive machinists because they can break off, leaving a problem twice as bad as a simple broken bolt or stud. Broken extractors cannot be drilled out because they are so hard. Many broken bolts can be removed simply by tapping them with a sharp-pointed chisel so that they unscrew from the hole. If the bolt or stud has been in the hole a long time, as in an old engine block, the best and safest way to get it out is to drill a hole exactly in the middle of the bolt, a hole slightly smaller than the inside diameter of the threads in the block. For example, if the bolt or stud that broke off was of ½-in. diameter (measured across the major diameter of the screw threads), then use a 15/32-in. drill. This will leave just a very thin shell in the threaded part of the block, a shell which you can pick out with a chisel.

SCREWDRIVERS

The screwdriver is such a basic tool that it hardly seems worth mentioning, but so many repair jobs have been butchered by the improper use of this tool that a few tips are in order. First, the slot in any screw has definite dimensions—length, width and depth. Like a bolthead or nut, the screw slot must be driven by a tool that uses all of the available bearing surface and does not slip.

A close look at the blade of a new screwdriver will reveal that the sides near the end are parallel, just like those in the screw slot. When repairing or re-grinding screwdriver blades, remember this: Tapered sides will just wedge the blade out of the slot, reducing the available force and damaging the slot itself. Don't use a big, wide blade on a small

3. Bench Tools

screw, and don't try to turn a large screw slot with a tiny, narrow blade. Screws with Phillips heads, Allen heads or hollow hexagonal heads should always be driven with the proper tool. Any attempts made with a single-bladed screwdriver can damage these screw openings to a point where removal is impossible even with the proper tool for the job.

PLIERS

Pliers are about as basic as screwdrivers, and few homes are without a pair, but the sizes and shapes available require some selectivity on the part of anyone starting to assemble a professional set of tools. One tool maker alone lists 29 different types of pliers in his catalog, with subselections under certain categories. No one mechanic has or needs all of them; a few carefully selected pieces will cover many jobs.

A good pair of double-jointed, straight-jaw pliers are always handy, and some long-nosed ones for reaching into hard-to-get-at places will find ready use on many jobs. Be sure to include a set of diagonal wire cutters, because they are indispensable when doing electrical wiring or setting cotter keys. There are also special pliers for brake springs, hose clamps, retaining rings and the

1. A hand pop rivet gun is a definite must if you plan to do any sheetmetal fabrication or panel reshaping.

2. If you strike this hand impact driver with a hammer, then up to 200 ft.-lbs. of pressure turn the bit as much as 20°. It's also reversible for loosening frozen nuts, screws or bolts.

3. No mechanic's hand tool collection is complete unless it encompasses a selection of bench goodies. Hacksaws, tapes, an electric drill motor, tin snips, brass hammer and chisels are a few of the things needed to make the job go that much easier and better.

small nuts on distributors and voltage regulators. These can be purchased as needed. Two very handy tools are the Vise-Grip (a set of adjustable, locking pliers that stay on when locked and are capable of a very firm grip) and parallel-jaw, adjustable pliers with angled jaws that stay parallel at any degree of opening. The latter are known as Channel-lock or water pump pliers. They are very handy for grabbing both round and square shapes firmly.

Specialty items that are nice to have but not really necessary are battery terminal and spark plug terminal pliers. The spark plug pliers are heavily insulated and allow the plug terminals to be removed while the engine is running without danger of shocking the user with high voltage.

HAMMERS

Often used with little discretion, hammers are a very important part of the mechanic's tool kit. There is a story that German mechanics forbid their apprentices to even have one in their kit, forcing the student to "fit it, don't bang it." A good ball-peen hammer of medium size, plus a soft-faced one for tapping parts into place without damaging them, are really necessary in most of today's automotive repair work. In addition, special hammers for bodywork are a must if any type of sheetmetal repair is attempted, and the handless hammer or bucking dolly in various shapes should be included in the body repair tool kit to make the job easier.

With the multitude of service stations, each with a tire changing jig, it is rare that anyone peels tires off the rims or remounts them by hand anymore. But, just in case the need occurs, a heavy rubber mallet is a must for pounding tire beads back into the rim recess. A rubber mallet also comes in mighty handy when replacing wheel covers; it can assure a tight fit with little danger of denting the covers.

SAWS—FILES—BENCH TOOLS

For any kind of automotive repair work, where parts are removed from the car and refurbished at home, a good bench vise is indispensable. Naturally, it should be well mounted on a suitable work table or bench—not necessarily large, but well anchored and capable of handling the usual pounding without giving way. The bench vise should be securely mounted and have at least 4-in. jaws with soft interchangeable inserts for holding parts that may scratch or be indented by sharp hard jaw faces.

A good hacksaw frame, one that will hold its shape and is adjustable for blades up to 12 ins. long, is needed in every tool kit. While they cost a bit more, the high-speed blades are a good investment as they last a long time. For general work one should have a selection of fine-toothed blades, 32 teeth per inch, for cutting harder steels, and some coarser ones in the 18-to-24-teeth-per-inch size for soft materials. One never knows when a bolt must be shortened or a bit of metal cut for a bracket.

Just about every saw cut must be finished off and a good file, in lieu of a

4. Adjustable Body File Holder

5. Various Types of Files

6. Filing Breaker Plate

4. *If you plan on doing any metal work, this body file holder will come in handy. One like this Craftsman adjusts for concave, convex or straight filing; just turn the center post.*

5. *Files should be selected as to tooth—either fine or coarse. Small, fine files are used for delicate work, the large rasps for body repairs. Illustrated here is the basic rattail, flat, half-round and vixen . . . all well used.*

6. *Rattail file and a good bench vise will almost take the place of a juice-powered bench grinder.*

7. *Specialized tools, like these various types of valve spring compressors and a gasket scraper, aren't that expensive and are virtually indispensable should you plan to replace a blown head gasket or do your own valve job.*

7. Specialized Tools

Right Tools for the Job

bench grinder, is the only answer. Files should be selected the same way as saw blades—some fine toothed, others on the coarse side for softer metals. Included in the file set should be a thin flat-point file for dressing up distributor contacts, plus some slim tapered 3-cornered ones and a round rat tail for cleaning out slots or enlarging and deburring drilled holes.

Any sheetmetal or body shop will require the need for metal shears or "tin snips," and the most versatile are a set of aviation-type shears sometimes called "dutchmen." A full set includes a straight cutter, and a left- and right-hand one since cutting curves is eased by using the one for the direction of the cut—*i.e.*, left or right direction. These are also great for trimming exhaust tubing in the final fitting stages when making custom headers or exhaust systems to suit special needs.

If bodywork is your project, several additional special files should be added to the kit. These come in flat and half-rounded cross sections, have curved teeth more like a series of blades, and are used in a holder that curves them to suit conditions. Indispensable for smoothing or skinning sheetmetal or leaded portions of repaired sections, they are a valuable tool for any kind of bodywork, amateur or professional.

SPECIAL TOOLS

Many automotive assemblies and components require special tools to adjust or repair. One of the most specialized in this area is probably automatic transmission band adjustment. Universal sets for doing this type of work are available in complete form and include the necessary gauges, short-handled end wrenches, a band-adjusting T-handled tool, and complete torque setting chart for all types of automatics. A short-handled torque wrench is needed with a ¼-in. drive and a 0-150 ft.-lbs. range, but if such a tool is already a part of the kit, the additional pieces for doing such work can be purchased as needed.

Front suspension repair, especially wheel alignment work, will require special tools for certain cars due to the dif-

1. *The machined surfaces between the cylinder head and intake manifold must be free of old gasket material and cinching compound if the new gasket is to seal properly. You can always use a large screwdriver or a putty knife for this cleaning operation, but a scraper is better.*

2. *Fully adjustable pullers are "the only way" to force the gear off the end of the crank. If you try it with a hammer, punch or chisel, you'll raise heck with the main bearings.*

3. *While water pump pliers will suffice, hose clamp pliers with specially milled jaws make pulling the rings off the hoses a snap.*

4. *If you plan to work under your car, you'll need a set of axle stands. Too many people have been killed or badly hurt trying to make a bumper jack take the place of stands or a hoist. Stands aren't expensive.*

5. *Drill motors, hones, wire brushes, stones, drills, etc., become an outfit a mechanic cannot afford to be without. Most quality ¼-in. drives will cost around $25-$30.*

1. Scraping Cylinder Head

2. Pulling Crank Gear

3. Depressing Hose Clamp

4. Jack Stands

5. Power Tools

ficulty in getting standard wrenches into some of the tight spots. Most tool makers have such special tools designed for cars with these special requirements.

Similar special handle shapes are available for reaching hard-to-get-at hold-down bolts on both front- and rear-mounted distributors. While not absolutely necessary, they certainly can speed up access to these fasteners through the maze of ignition wires and other under-the-hood plumbing.

The correct bleeding and adjusting tools will make these repair and maintenance jobs a lot simpler, allowing better concentration on the work itself without knuckle busting. Valve adjusting for mechanical overhead systems is best done with a combo-tool that uses a ½-in. drive socket for loosening the lock nuts and a knurled knob that actuates a screwdriver down through the socket for turning the adjusting screw.

Anyone doing brake or fuel line work will need a tubing cutter and a double flaring tool. These will cut and flare properly all types of steel and copper tubing for hydraulic, fuel and oil lines and are the only things for a first-class job of cutting to size without distorting the tubing, and flaring properly for leakproof and permanent joints.

Many a job has been bungled and expensive parts damaged because they were dismantled by pounding rather than by the use of a proper puller. There are a variety of these, both the screw-actuat-

ed type and the impact type. Timing gears, wheel hubs, harmonic balancers, axle shafts, bearings, steering wheels, blind pilot bearings, and even battery terminals often require the use of a special puller to separate them from their related shafts or mountings. In this classification are also stud removers, and while not employing exactly the same principles as a 2- or 3-jaw screw or impact puller, they operate by securely grasping the stud in a wedging manner, allowing it to be backed out in one piece by either socket handle drive or impact wrench.

In addition to the appropriate set of wrenches, sockets, etc., any engine overhauling—even a simple ring and valve job—will require a piston ring compressor of the adjustable type for inserting the newly ringed pistons without breaking the rings. Also included in this tool selection should be a valve guide cleaner, gasket and carbon scrapers, a valve lifter clamp for depressing the springs for removal of keepers, and a grinding tool for lapping the valves to the seats for a leakproof seal.

Glaze-breaking hones, ring groove cleaners, and small cylinder hones for brake overhauls will be necessary for the do-it-yourself mechanic as he expands his efforts into more complicated repair operations.

One can save a lot of money by checking first the tools needed for the job on a particular car and then shop-

ping the parts supply houses for just the minimum required. Tool makers supply tools in kit form for various special parts of the car such as front end, transmissions, distributors, brake service, as well as bushing, seal installers, etc. Check these to see if the present tools will do the job before investing in tools that may only duplicate what is already in your kit.

POWER TOOLS

About the only power tool the home mechanic will find unlimited use for is a ¼- or ⅜-in. drill. These are available in a variety of qualities and prices, and those offered for the home mechanic are adequate for the average user for both drilling and honing. Industrial grades, made for the hard use of the professional, naturally cost more, but in recent years, many of the top power tool makers have designed power tools of all sorts well within the budget of the home craftsman. Try these before investing in extra heavy-duty industrial tools built to last several lifetimes of occasional use.

A good set of bits for the power drill will be a necessity, and the high-speed type is the best investment. There is not much point in buying a set larger than the chuck will accommodate, so govern the size of the set by this standard. Drills come in two basic sizes: number drills and fractional drills. The number drills go in sizes up to No. 1, the largest (.2280-in.), to the smallest, No. 80

Right Tools for the Job

(.0135-in.). There is a limit as to how small a drill can be safely used in a hand-held power drill, so this should be considered when selecting the set. There are also fractional drill sizes ranging from 1/16-in. to 1/2-in., in increments of 1/64th of an inch. The number drill series include letter sizes, A-B-C, etc., commonly used for tap drill holes larger than the No. 1. Whatever drill system is selected, purchase those that come in a metal case as this will aid in keeping the set complete and avoid loss—somewhere in the toolbox—of just the one you need.

If one has the budget and the need, he will find many uses for a bench grinder in the home shop. Sharpening tools, buffing, and wire brushing, to name a few, are easy jobs with a grinder.

Impact wrenches, mentioned earlier, come in both electric and air drive. For the latter, one needs a compressor and air storage tank, and if the shop is so equipped, say for spray painting, etc., then an air drive is a good investment. The smaller heavy-duty models are capable of tightening up to 200 ft.-lbs. of torque, while the equivalent electric drives impart up to 130 ft.-lbs. While standard ½-in. drive sockets can be used for lighter work, it is recommended that the special heavy-duty wrenches and adapters be used for impact wrenches because of the rather sharp blows imparted to the tools.

Body repair work or any kind of sheet-metal modifications will require a heavy-duty disc sander. These are used by professional body workers for everything from rough metal removal to final polishing of the painted and waxed surface. In addition, a vibrating-type sander for fine metal finishing and preparing bare or primed surfaces for painting is a must unless one is ready to spend needless hours doing these chores by hand.

TEST INSTRUMENTS AND MEASURING TOOLS

Every mechanic's toolbox should contain a set of flat steel feeler gauges, plus the round wire type for checking plug gaps. There are regular plug gap gauges that have all of the most common dimensions in addition to a device for bending the outside electrode. The flat feeler gauges are needed for point adjustment and valve rocker settings. For extensive repair and rebuilding of master and wheel hydraulic cylinders, an inside measuring kit is available consisting of a handle and a set of go, and no-go, gauges for determining the exact inside bore diameter of these cylinders.

Micrometers—inside, outside and depth —are needed for just about any major engine overhaul to accurately check bore, bearing diameters, and deck clearances. These will have to be purchased in sets, as no one tool will give the range of measurements needed for automotive work. Outside micrometers have only about 1 in. of range without special adapters, but some are available in sets that will handle everything from 1 to 4

1. Spark plug gapping tools should always feature an adjustment hook, round wire gauges and a fine tooth file. Forget tapping the side wire on the cement. Flat feeler gauges won't get an accurate reading.

2. Drill is perfect for chamfering oil holes or for removing flashing from the inside of a cylinder block.

3. Drill motors can power anything from bits to brushes. If you don't need 'em to cut some holes to mount a bracket, they'll come in handy for buffing out a lacquer paint job.

4. Impact wrenches are expensive, but are quick and efficient. Most amateurs rely upon electric models rather than the compressed air type. Sockets are 6-point types.

5. For anyone attempting to overhaul an engine, precision measuring devices such as inside, outside, and depth mikes are a must. Included in the precision toolbox should be a dial indicator, steel scale, and a vernier slide caliper.

6. The simple compression gauge or tester is used to measure how much chamber pressure engine can build. Pressure differential (from cylinder to cylinder), not total amount, is what's important . . . and so is how you hold the tester to the plug hole. The seal must be good or you'll receive a misleading reading.

7. No backyard tune-ups or engine timing should be attempted unless you have a strobe timing light.

1. Gapping Spark Plugs

2. Chamfering Oil Holes

3. Drilling Holes

4. Removing Lug Nuts

5. Using Inside/Outside Mike

6. Testing Compression

ins. The same is true of inside micrometers and ones used for depth measurement. Learning how to read micrometers takes a bit of study so it is a good idea to become familiar in dealing with the .001-in. measurements before doing any serious work with them. Some micrometers have a built-in vernier so they can measure to tenths of thousandths. For quick measurements to thousandths, or even to tenths, a vernier caliper is handy to have.

Another measuring device is the brake drum and shoe gauge, which is used to detect both drum wear and diameter and to set up shoes on the backing plate. While this gauge is available from tool supply houses, most new car and brake repair shops will have it as a shop tool, not necessarily in the individual mechanic's kit. This is a modest cost tool that one should have for doing serious brake repair or overhaul.

There is a gauge or instrument for testing just about every component of an automobile. The list is long and mostly expensive: Automatic transmission oil pressure, vacuum, engine oil pressure, headlight candlepower, engine coolant temperature, fuel pressure, battery specific gravity, electrical resistance, voltage, current, engine speed, and on and on—an endless number of devices not including wheel alignment and balancing, that are available for automotive measuring, testing and repair work.

For serious engine tune-up and ignition work, the home mechanic's kit should include some kind of continuity tester for tracing out broken circuits, a voltmeter, and a power timing light. Simple volt/ohm ammeter and continuity testers can be purchased at radio supply houses, and many suppliers of automotive ignition testing equipment stock everything from simple meters to very sophisticated multiple units for checking everything electrical.

Continuity lights in the form of plastic-housed glow tubes with a probe and wire clip are modestly priced units that are worth the investment. One can make a simple test light by soldering a pair of wires to the proper contacts of a tail or parking light socket, terminating the loose ends to alligator clips or probes, and using a 12-volt bulb in the socket. This is an excellent light for setting ini-

7. Using Timing Light

tial spark timing by the "points-just-opening" method with the engine dead.

A strobe timing light is used for final ignition timing according to timing marks on the flywheel or vibration damper. They employ a flash or strobe tube that gets its trigger from the ignition high-voltage side. As the light flashes only on the high-voltage impulse, the timing marks apparently stand still while the engine is running, allowing an accurate visual setting of the distributor to the proper timing. One of these should be in every mechanic's tool kit for keeping the ignition in proper adjustment and diagnosing problems.

One of the handiest instruments for checking engine condition is the compression gauge. This comes in various forms, from the simplest one that is held in the spark plug hole while direct readings are noted on the scale, to the more expensive ones with flexible hose, screw-in spark plug fitting, and tell-tale needle that stays at the highest reading

until released. Both do a good job of reading the combustion chamber pressures; choice will depend on the size of your pocketbook.

Car clubs often find that pooling of funds allows the purchase of the more expensive instruments, justified by more use than the individual home mechanic would ever find practical unless he had unlimited funds. Some of the electrical analyzers are great time savers and allow more accurate adjustment of everything from dwell to fuel pump pressure.

One of the best ways to keep and protect a set of tools is to store them in a locked steel toolbox. Tools have a way of disappearing when left around loose, and a lock-type box of adequate size is a good investment. The choice is unlimited and goes all the way from a small kit to a large roll-away. Whatever the choice, anticipate that more tools will be added from time to time, so buy one larger than is needed at the moment and grow into it rather than out of it. ⚒

Specifications—What They Mean

A specification can be anything from a description of the material used in upholstery fabrics to the amount of air pressure that goes into a tire. How you use specifications will depend to a great extent on the amount of training you have had in doing mechanical work, and also on your personality. If you feel that the men who designed and built the automobile in the first place were a bunch of stumblebums who didn't know what they were doing, then you probably will have very little respect for their specifications. A mechanic with that attitude is bound to have a lot of trouble with the cars he repairs. At the other extreme is the car repairman who feels that the Detroit engineers have set up the specifications as strict laws that cannot be violated, to even the slightest degree. Strangely enough, the mechanic who has that attitude will also find repairing cars to be rather difficult.

The specifications were not laid down as the law of the automobile, but rather as guides to show the mechanic how the car was set up when it was brand new. A mechanic working in a new-car dealer service department will follow the factory specifications as closely as possible, but when a car is 2 years old or 5 years old or 10 years old, it is not the same automobile that rolled off the end of the assembly line. The result is that a mechanic has to realize that a slight departure from the original factory specifications, based on his own personal experience, may result in a better running automobile. Before you reach that point in experience, however, you must know how to read and understand factory spec.

There are many types of specifications, and you'll find them published in a variety of formats. Probably the most general and yet the most familiar to the majority of car owners are those found in the owner's handbook. You may not have regarded such commonplace figures as tire inflation pressures and crankcase and cooling system capacities as factory specifications, but they are. So if the mere mention of the word

"specifications" conjures up visions of incomprehensible data, set your mind at ease and follow along as we explore the world of specifications—where to find them and what to do once you've actually got them.

If you've done any work at all under the hood and your car is a recent model, you've probably noticed a label, sticker, or decal marked "Vehicle Emission Control Information." While you might not have thought of it as such, this is really a basic spec chart complete with instructions on how to interpret and apply the information it contains. With nothing more than this chart and a few simple tools, you can keep your engine tuned to factory settings. But many specs are a good deal more exotic; they require a knowledge of exactly where they can be located, as well as a deeper understanding of what makes your car tick.

SOURCES FOR SPECS

There are many sources for factory specifications. Independent companies

1. Feeler Gauge

2. Checking Side Clearance

3. Measuring Valve Spring Height

4. Inside Micrometer

5. Using Inside Mike

1. Clearances can be very important on stock engine setups; on high-perf machinery they're critical. Here the rocker arm adjustment is checked for valve lash with a feeler gauge.

2. Rod side clearance is checked on assembly in block. If it's too close, the rods should be switched about or replaced, or the sides must be ground sufficiently to fall within the recommended factory spec range.

3. Checking installed valve springs for equal height and pressure is an important step in setting up valve action for high-rpm operation.

4. Assembled inside mike has a 2.5 to 3.5-in. rod and .5-in. sleeve, making starting point 3.0 ins. Numbered lines on hub (1) are tenths; spaces between (2) are each .025-in. Numbers on thimble (3) are in thousandths of an inch (reading shows between .010-.011). The total measurement indicated here is 3.260 ins.

5. Rod bore is measured with inside micrometer. This mike is just an easy way to hold it; it cannot be used to adjust the mike.

produce repair manuals that have specs, and many parts companies give out booklets of specifications so that their parts will be installed correctly. The original specifications for all cars are printed by the car maker in what is called the "shop manual." Every year about the time that the new cars come out, a new shop manual is issued to be used any time that year's car is worked on.

The unfortunate thing about shop manuals is that, in most cases, they are printed before any of the new cars actually hit the street. The result is that there are many changes in specifications and repair procedures during the model year that do not appear in the shop manual. The manufacturer takes care of this—as far his own dealers and repair facilities are concerned—by issuing service bulletins on a regular basis.

Some of the manufacturers do not care who does the repairs on their cars, just so they are done correctly. They will send their service bulletins to any legitimate repair facility. Other manufacturers consider their service bulletins in the same light as top secret war communiques, and will not allow anyone outside of their own organizations to see them. This attitude works a definite hardship on the independent garage or service station which has new car customers. If the service bulletins were distributed to all repair outlets, it would be great for the trade, but what good would it do you as an individual car owner who wants to fix his car on a Saturday afternoon? Unfortunately, there is no way at present for a car owner to obtain service bulletins, either for pay or for free. But you can buy all the service manuals that you want, even back as far as 15 years.

If you are interested in factory service

manuals, the address to write for them is usually in the back of the owner's manual that comes in the glove compartment of your car; or you can get the address from any dealer who sells the make of car you are interested in. Now let's take a look at what some of the specifications actually mean.

Dimensions are directly related to performance because of a compromise necessary in mass production known as "tolerances." If every moving part had to fit its mating surface perfectly, the car makers wouldn't be able to produce 9 million cars a year. Therefore, tolerances are allowed which compensate for the imperfections inherent in both man and machine without seriously affecting the proper function of the car. For example, in a popular current V-8 engine, the maker specifies a tolerable variance of from .0007 to .0027-in. in the clearance between the connecting rod bearings and the crankshaft. In the course of a day's production which is in the thousands of units, and with hundreds of parts involved in each unit, the law of averages sees to it that there will be "tight" fits, "loose" fits and, very occasionally, an "ideal" fit. This is the reason why one man's car will go a few miles faster and get a few more miles per gallon than the identical car belonging to his neighbor. It is also the reason why skilled racing mechanics can extract upwards of 600 hp from a "stock" engine that is rated at maybe 250 hp by the factory. They painstakingly "blueprint" every part, honing it to its precisely ideal tolerance—and the resulting collection of parts sings like no engine ever to leave the factories in Detroit.

SAMPLE ENGINE DATA

To give you an idea of how to interpret specs, we've reprinted part of the engine specification chart from the 1975 Chevy shop manual. It shows the specifications for all Chevrolet light truck and passenger car engines for that year. Where explanations seem necessary, we've placed numbers alongside the lines that are keyed to the text which follows below.

In past years, just underneath the type and displacement lines, there were two lines giving the official horsepower and torque figures. These vanished sometime around the 1974 model year, for several

Specifications

reasons. First of all, the 1972 federal edict that "net," rather than "gross," horsepower figures be used caused a dramatic drop in the advertiseable power. Gross power is recorded on the dynamometer with nary an accessory attached to the engine to rob it of one pony. Even the air cleaner and exhaust manifolds are removed, and cooling water is force-fed by an outside pressure system, rather than by the (power-consuming) pump on the engine. The result of these shenanigans is a horsepower reading considerably higher than what the same engine could actually produce in a car.

The net power readings are taken on the engine with all the accessories in place, and being driven. This is a much more honest figure, but it makes some engines look a bit puny if it is compared to what they were advertised as putting out under the old system. Then add to this the actual reduction in power that comes from cleaning up the emissions, and you have a figure that most makers are somewhat reluctant to release.

SPEC EXPLANATIONS

1) Bore and stroke dimensions govern engine displacement. Usually, you can overbore up to .030-in. without weakening the structure of the block. A common hot rod practice has been to increase stroke by welding and regrinding of the crankshaft. Everything else being equal, the larger the displacement, the greater the power output of the engine—and the greater its thirst for fuel. Sometimes, errors creep into the factory specs, and one has crept unbidden into these. The 350-cu.-in. V-8 with the 2-bbl. carb is listed as having a bore of 3⅞ ins. and a stroke of 3.25 ins. (Why do they use both fraction and decimal dimensions in the same specs?), while the rest of the 350-cu.-in. family of engines is listed with a 4-in. bore and a 3.48-in. stroke. What has happened is that the specs for the older, 307-cu.-in. engine have not been fully removed from the chart through the annual updating, even though that engine was last produced in 1972 and these specs are for '75 models. If a specification looks funny, check it. The factory makes mistakes too.

2) The higher the compression ratio, the higher the pressures in the combustion chamber, and the higher the power output. This is a figure that has been falling these days, with the lowered octane rating of fuels and the requirements for lower emissions. Older engines with compression ratios higher than 8.5:1 usually require premium fuel.

3) Firing order alone doesn't tell you enough to let you run the wires from the distributor cap to the spark plugs correctly. You have to know what the numbers of the cylinders are, and that's not given here. Fours and 6's are numbered from front to rear, consecutively. General Motors V-8's have the evens on the right, the odds on the left. So do Chrys-

ler and American Motors V-8's. Ford products have 1 to 4 on the right, 5 to 8 on the left. Cylinder numbers are sometimes cast or embossed onto the intake manifold just above each cylinder.

4) Bore diameter on these engines varies about .003-in., but piston clearance in the bore is in most cases considerably less than that. (Pistons come in different sizes and are select-fitted to each bore.) Small shops do not have the luxury of an unlimited supply of different size pistons, so when they rebuild an engine they simply buy one set of pistons and bore each one of the cylinders to fit a particular piston.

5) Throughout the chart, specs are listed as either "production" or "service." The "service" dimension is a wear limit. If it is exceeded, the part must be

reconditioned or replaced.

6) Taper in the cylinder bore is extremely hard on the rings; it causes them to flex and wear out as the piston strokes up and down. Measuring taper on the thrust and relief sides of the bore is like splitting hairs. The relief sides of the bore are the front and rear, 90° from the thrust sides where the piston skirt slides. Excessive taper requires a cylinder rebore.

7) If piston clearance exceeds the service wear limit, the engine will have to be overhauled or rebuilt. There are several ways to get the piston clearance within limits: The old pistons can be knurled; new pistons can be fitted; or the cylinders can be bored to fit some new pistons.

8) Piston ring groove clearance is the

SPECIFICATIONS AND CAPACITIES — Owner's Data

Refill Capacities (Approximate)		
COMPONENT	U.S.	IMP.
Cooling System (Including Heater) — Quarts		
2300cc Engine		
Non-A/C	8.5	7.0
A/C	9.1	7.5
2800cc Engine		
Non-A/C	12.3	10.2
A/C	13.2	10.9
302 Engine		
All Models	16.3	13.5
Engine Oil (Excluding Oil Filter) — Quarts		
2300cc 4-Cylinder Engine*	4.0*	3.3*
2800cc V-6 Engine*	4.5*	3.8*
302 CID V-8 Engine*	3.5*	3.0*
Transmission		
4-Speed Manual Transmission — Pints	3.5	2.6
3-Speed Automatic Transmission — Quarts**		
w/2300cc or 2800cc Engine	8.0	6.5
w/302 CID V-8 Engine	9.0	7.5
Standard (non-locking) Differential		
2300 cc 4-Cyl.	3.0	2.5
2800 cc V-6	4.0	3.3
Traction Lok Differential +	4.0	3.3
Manual Steering Gear		
Gear Box — Pints	.44	.40
Power Steering Gear		
Gear Box — Pints	.33	2.7
Hydraulic System — Pints**	2.4	2.0
Fuel Tank (Approximate)		
Std. All Models	13.0	10.8
w/Opt. Extra Capacity Tank	16.5	13.8
Air Conditioning System — Lbs. "R-12" Refrigerant		3¼ Lbs.

*Add 1/2 Qt. for filter change.
**Operating level determined by dipstick.
+Special lubricant required for Traction Lok Differential.

Electrical System Specifications		
COMPONENT	STD	HD
Battery		
Volts	12	12
Ampere Hour Rating	41	53
Ground Terminal Polarity	Negative	Negative
Number of Cells	6	6
Number of Plates	54	66
Alternator — Amperes Output	W/O AC	W/AC
Std. Except 302 CID V-8	38	55
Std. w/302 CID V-8	55	61
All w/Rear Window Defroster	61	70

Radiator Cap — PSI	
All Models	13

Owner's manual data for Mustang II includes specifications for service intervals and fluid capacities.

difference between the vertical thickness of the ring and the vertical measurement of the groove. If the rings are too tight in the groove they will not be free to put pressure on the cylinder wall. If they're too loose, combustion pressure or oil will find its way around the back side of the ring, and the result will be lower performance. Ring gap is not critical, as shown by the great tolerance, but gaps too close may allow ring ends to butt, which can ruin the rings. The service wear limit is found by adding the figure shown to the production high limit, which in the case of groove clearance on the 350 top ring would be .0032 plus .001, for a total of .0042-in.

9) "Clearance" refers to clearance between the piston pin and the pin bosses. The interference fit specified in the rod means that the pin is larger than the hole in the rod by the dimension shown, which results in a press fit.

10) Main bearing journals are numbered from front to back. Note that there is about .001-in. tolerance on the journal size. A crank ground to the low end of the specs would have more clearance in the bearings, and would be a freer turning crank. Worn cranks are customarily reground .010, .020, or .030-in. undersize, and used with thicker bearings.

11) Main bearing (and rod bearing) clearance is usually controlled by the diameter of the crank journals, because bearings usually come in one standard size. However, some manufacturers make bearings that vary by tenths of thousandths, allowing clearance to be controlled by select-fitting. Note the re-duced clearance on the front main, and increased clearance on the rear. The front main has to be tighter or it may knock before oil pressure rises when the engine is started up, due to the load of belt-driven accessories on the front pulley. The rear main has increased clearance for greater oil flow, because it is heavily loaded by the power flow and needs extra oil.

12) "Crankpin" means the same as "rod journal." The same methods of obtaining clearance apply here as on main bearings.

(The engine specification chart continues past this point, giving equally detailed specifications on the camshaft, valves and valve springs. However, space considerations prevented the inclusion of the entire chart.)

SCHEDULED MAINTENANCE SERVICES

MAINTENANCE SCHEDULES A AND B

(Schedules A and B have been combined into one chart, follow the schedule which corresponds to your car's code letter)

EMISSION SYSTEMS MAINTENANCE OPERATION	SERVICE INTERVAL — Time in months or mileage in thousands, whichever occurs first.									
	5	10	15	20	25	30	35	40	45	50
Change Engine Oil (1)	AB	AB	AB	AB	AB	AB	AB	AB	AB	AB
Replace Engine Oil Filter (1)	AB		AB		AB		AB		AB	
Torque Intake Manifold Bolts (302)			B	A						
Lubricate and Check Exhaust Control Valve			B	A		B		A	B	
Check Coolant Condition and Protection (2)			B	A					B	
Replace Coolant							B	A		
Check Cooling System Hoses and Clamps (2)						AB				
Check Drive Belt Tension			B	A						
Inspect Drive Belt Condition						B		A	B	
Replace PCV Valve				A		B		A		
Check PCV System, Hoses and Tubes (9)			B	A				A	B	
Clean PCV System, Hoses and Tubes				A		B		A		
Replace Crankcase Filter in Air Cleaner (3)				A		B		A		
Inspect Evaporative Emission Canister (9)				A		B		A		
Inspect Fuel Vapor System (Fuel tank filler cap, hoses and vapor lines)				A		B		A		
Check Thermactor System			B	A		B		A	B	
Check and Adjust Fuel Decel Valve (4 cyl. & V-6 Engines)	AB		B	A		B		A	B	
Check Ignition System with Scope (4)			B	A		B		A	B	
Replace Spark Plugs (1)*			B	A		B		A	B	
Inspect Spark Plug Wires (5)			B	A		B		A	B	
Check Initial Ignition Timing (8)*			B	A		B		A	B	
Inspect Distributor Cap and Rotor (6)			B	A		B		A	B	
Check Spark Control System and Delay Valve			B	A		B		A	B	
Check Idle Fuel Mixture (8)*			B	A		B		A	B	
Check Fast Idle Speed (8)	AB		B	A		B		A	B	
Check Curb Idle Speed (8)*	AB		B	A		B		A	B	
Check Throttle Solenoid "Off" Speed (8)	AB									
Check Choke System (Throttle and Choke Linkage and Air Valve)			B	A		B		A	B	
Check Carburetor Air Cleaner Element (3)			B						B	
Replace Carburetor Air Cleaner Element (3)				A		B		A		
Check Air Cleaner Temperature Control and Delay Valve (9)			B	A		B		A	B	
Replace Fuel System Filter			B	A						
Adjust Engine Valve Clearance (2.8L)			B	A		B		A	B	
Check and Torque all Belt Driven Accessory Mounting Hardware (4 cyl. Engine)			B	A		B		A	B	

OTHER SYSTEMS MAINTENANCE OPERATION	SERVICE INTERVAL — Time in months or mileage in thousands, whichever occurs first.									
	5	10	15	20	25	30	35	40	45	50
Inspect Exhaust System Heat Shields (10)	AB		AB			AB			AB	

WHEEL ALIGNMENT

Next to a good engine tune-up, most cars on the road today could use a front-wheel alignment check. And you'd probably find about 50% of all those over one year old sadly lacking when compared to factory specifications. Front-wheel alignment is really a very simple matter, but the specialized equipment necessary to do the job properly is seldom found outside a repair shop. Yet a knowledge of what's involved can be of help to anyone who takes the time to work on his own car.

The three adjustments involved in wheel alignment are caster, camber, and toe. Caster is the tilt (front or back) of the top of the wheel spindle; positive caster is tilt to the rear, negative caster is tilt to the front. Camber is the amount of tilt at the top of the wheel; outward tilt is positive camber, inward tilt is negative camber. Toe is the difference between the measurement at the extreme front and extreme rear of the front wheels. If the front measurement exceeds that of the rear, it's called toe-out; when the rear exceeds the front, it's known as toe-in. By way of example, we've included the alignment specifications for the 1975 Chrysler products, showing camber, caster and toe-in.

Notice that the specifications are different for cars with and without power steering, and also that the camber is different from left to right. Adherence to these specifications can have a substantial effect on tire life and gas mileage.

GEAR AND AXLE RATIOS

Normally, a customer has no choice in the gear ratios of an automatic transmission unless he has the unit rebuilt and "blueprinted" to his preferred specs by an independent specialist. A choice is sometimes offered in the lower gear ratios of 3- and 4-speed manual transmissions that can alter acceleration potential. If there is a pronounced spread between the lower ratios of a transmission, the unit is known as a "wide ratio," and is probably more suitable for normal driving. Conversely, a lesser spread is known as a "close ratio," and is the one to be preferred for road racing or performance cars. In any case, the final or "high" gear is always a 1:1 ratio except, of course, in the case of an overdrive-equipped transmission.

Specifications

Most car makers do offer a choice of rear-end gears. In past years, the choice could range from as "high" as 2.50:1 to as "low" as 4.50:1. In the interests of fuel economy, the "low" gearing is fast disappearing. The terminology here is confusing, to say the least. The word "high" refers to car speed in relation to engine rpm. A 2.50 gear is an extreme economy ratio, producing about 30 mph per 1000 revolutions of the engine with normal wheels and tires. A 4.50 gear would have the engine turning that same 1000 rpm at only about 12 mph, producing much more acceleration potential, but with a corresponding reduction in economy.

The greater the displacement of the engine, the easier it can pull the high gearing and still give adequate performance. These days, a gear of around 2.73:1 is regarded as "normal" for most standard size cars, with 2.50 gears as a "highway cruising" axle, and 3.0 to 3.30 gears as "high performance" or "trailer towing" gearsets.

Another way to describe gearing is to use the word ratio. A "high" gear such as the 2.5 described above, would be called a "low-ratio" gear. If you had a set of 4.11's in the rear end, they could be called "high-ratio" gears or, if you like the other terminology, "low gears." Admittedly, it can be confusing, but in one case we are talking about the numerical value of the ratio, so the bigger the number, the higher the ratio, as with the 4.11's. But in the other case we are describing the performance of the gears, which have lots of power at low speeds because they let the car get moving easier. So we call the set of 4.11 gears a low gear, and a 2.5 gearset would be a high gear.

METRICS

A new dimension has been sneaking into specifications over the past few years. It's been sneaking into the specs because it's also been sneaking into the cars. The word is metrics. GM has the most conspicuous display, with kilometer scales alongside the miles on all speedometers, beginning with the 1975 model year. Ford has been the most insidious, with several engines in its small cars being built entirely to metric standards. Of course, almost all imported cars use the metric system for their main specs.

What's happening to our familiar inches, feet and pounds? We're the last major country in the world that has not switched over to metrics for all measurements. The present goal for our complete conversion is 1984; however, many areas have already converted. The aerospace industry, for example, switched over several years ago, and the engineers and scientists find it easier to think in metric terms. Your family doctor now operates in the metric system, and all prescriptions are in metrics.

To the automotive technician, a conversion to the metric system will basically mean the purchase of a few new tools and gauges, to conform with the new specification charts he'll be using. He probably has most of the tools now, since the number of mechanics who haven't had to swing a metric wrench at one time or another is getting smaller. A metric torque wrench will be necessary, or perhaps just a new scale mounted on the old one. Finally, a set of metric measuring tools will make it possible to keep the old standards of accuracy with the new system.

What will specifications look like in metrics? As a sample, we've provided herewith a set of descriptive specifications for a 1975-model Chevrolet completely converted to the metric system. The problem, for most people, is the conversion, not the system itself. It's easier to think in the metric system, since everything is in tens and decimals, just like our money. Once everything is in metrics, and you don't have to convert liters to quarts and miles to kilometers, things will be simple. Children in school, starting right out with the metric system, will find that things are a good deal easier than with the present 12 ins. to the foot, 3 ft. to the yard, 5280 ft. to the mile "English" system.

For handy reference, we've also included some commonly used automotive measurements with the factors needed to convert them to the metric system. As you get used to them, you'll find that the conversions aren't really necessary, and that you're thinking in metrics right from the start. ❦

'75 CHRYSLER ALIGNMENT SPECS

Camber	Acceptable Alignment Range	Tolerance for Resetting Alignment
Left Side	0° to +1°	+½° ±¼°
Right Side	−¼° to +¾°	+¼° ±¼°
Caster		
Manual Steering	−1¾° to +½°	−½° ±½°
Power Steering	−½° to +1¾°	+¾° ±½°
Toe-In	1/16-in. to ¼-in.	⅛-in. to 3/16-in.

(Maximum left to right differential should not exceed 1¼° with caster within specifications.)

METRIC CONVERSION FACTORS

You know these	multiply them by	to get these
inches	25.4	millimeters
millimeters	.03937	inches
feet	.3048	meters
meters	3.2808	feet
miles	1.6093	kilometers
kilometers	.6214	miles
cubic inches	16.39	cubic centimeters
cubic centimeters	.061	cubic inches
cubic inches	.01639	liters
liters	61.02	cubic inches
gallons	3.785	liters
liters	.2642	gallons
pounds	.45359	kilograms
kilograms	2.2046	pounds
miles per hour	1.6093	kilometers per hour
kilometers per hour	.6214	miles per hour
horsepower	.7457	kilowatts
kilowatts	1.341	horsepower
pound/feet	.1383	meter/kilograms
meter/kilograms	7.233	pound/feet

SPECIFICATIONS—1975 CHEVROLET CAPRICE SEDAN

	English System	Metric System
Engine type	ohv V-8	ohv V-8
Displacement	400 cu. ins.	6556 cubic centimeters
Bore/stroke	4.125/3.75 ins.	104.8/95.3 centimeters
Compression ratio	8.5:1	8.5:1
Power @ rpm	175 bhp @ 3600	130.5 kilowatts
Torque @ rpm	305 lbs.-ft. @ 2000	42.18 kilogram/meters
Brake swept area	384.1 sq. ins.	2478.2 square centimeters
Turning circle	42.8 ft.	13.05 meters
Wheelbase	121.5 ins.	3086.1 millimeters
Overall length	222.7 ins.	5656.8 millimeters
Overall width	79.5 ins.	2019.3 millimeters
Overall height	53.9 ins.	1369.06 millimeters
Front track	64.1 ins.	1628.14 millimeters
Rear track	64.0 ins.	1625.60 millimeters
Trunk capacity	18.9 cu. ft.	.5352 cubic meters
Curb weight	4730 lbs.	2145.48 kilograms
Power/weight ratio	17.0 lbs./hp	16.44 kilogram/kilowatts

SPECS—1975 CHEVROLET ENGINES

	GENERAL DATA:									
	Type	In Line			V-8					
	Displacement (cu. in.)	250		350				400		454
	CARBURETOR	1BBL.	2BBL.	4BBL.	4BBL.	4BBL.		2BBL.	4BBL.	4BBL.
	EXHAUST	SINGLE		SINGLE		DUAL		SINGLE		DUAL
1	Bore	3 7/8		4				4 1/8		4 1/4
	Stroke	3.53	3.25	3.48				3.75		4
2	Compression Ratio	8.25:1		8.5:1		9.0:1			8.5:1	
3	Firing Order	1-5-3-6-2-4		1-8-4-3-6-5-7-2						

	CYLINDER BORE:					
4	Diameter	3.8745-3.8775	3.9995-4.0025	4.1246-4.1274	4.2495-4.2525	
5	Out of Round	Production	.0005 Max.	.001 Max.		
		Service	.002 Max.			
6	Taper	Production — Thrust Side	.0005 Max.			
		Production — Relief Side	.0005 Max.	.001 Max.		
		Service	.005 Max.			

	PISTON:							
7	Clearance	Production	.0005-.0015	.0005-.0011	.0007-.0013	.0036-.0042	.0014-.0020	.0018-.0028
		Service	.0025 Max.		.0027 Max.	.0061 Max.	.0034 Max.	.0035 Max.

	PISTON RING:								
8	COMPRESSION	Clearance	Production — Top	.0012-.0027	.0012-.0032	.0012-.0032	.0012-.0027	.0017-.0032
			Production — 2nd	.0012-.0032		.0012-.0027	.0012-.0032	
		Groove	Service	Hi Limit Production + .001				
		Gap	Production — Top	.010-.020	.010-.020	.010-.020	010-.020	
			Production — 2nd	.010-.020	.013-.025	.010-.023	.010-.020	
			Service	Hi Limit Production + .01				
	OIL	Groove Clearance	Production	.005 Max.	.002-.007	.005 Max.		.0005-.0065
			Service	Hi Limit Production + .001				
		Gap	Production	.015-.055				
			Service	Hi Limit Production + .01				

	PISTON PIN:						
9	Diameter		.9270-.9273			.9895-.9898	
	Clearance	Production	.00015-.00025	.00045-.00055	.00015-.00025	.00025-.00035	
		Service	.001 Max.				
	Fit in Rod		.0008-.0016 Interference				

	CRANKSHAFT:					
10	Main Journal	Diameter	All 2.2983-2.2993	#1 2.4484-2.4493 / 2-3-4 2.4481-2.4490 / #5 2.4479-2.4488	#1-2-3-4 2.6484-2.6493 / #5 2.6479-2.6488	#1 2.7485-2.7494 / #2-3-4 2.7481-2.7490 / #5 2.7478-2.7488
	Taper	Production	.0002 Max.			
		Service	.001 Max.			
	Out of Round	Production	.0002 Max.			
		Service	.001 Max.			

	Type	In Line	V-8		
	Displacement (cu. in.)	250	350	400	454

	CRANKSHAFT:					
11	Main Bearing Clearance	Production	All .0003-.0029	Auto. #1 .0019-.0031 / #2-3-4 .0013-.0025 / #5 .0023-.0033 Man. #1-2-3-4 .0013-.0025 / #5 .0023-.0033	#1 .0008-.0020 / #2-3-4 .0011-.0023 / #5 .0017-.0033	#1-2-3-4 .0013-.0025 / #5 .0024-.0040
		Service	#1 - .002 Max.; All Others - .0035 Max.			
	Crankshaft End Play		.002-.006			.006-.010
12	Crankpin	Diameter	1.9928-2.000	2.099-2.100		2.199-2.200
		Taper — Production	.0003 Max.			
		Taper — Service	.001 Max.			
		Out of Round — Production	.0002 Max.			
		Out of Round — Service	.001 Max.			
	Rod Bearing Clearance	Production	.0007-.0027	.0013-.0035		.0009-.0025
		Service	.0035 Max.			
	Rod Side Clearance		.007-.016	.008-.014		.015-.021

Where to Get Parts

The buying of parts for an automobile is considerably different now than it was way back when. In the old days, mechanics used to fix things. Wages were very low—perhaps as low as $2 or $3 a day in some cases. From both a time and money standpoint, it was practical to remove a unit from a car, give it to a mechanic and let him spend several hours tearing it apart, replacing the small piece that had broken or worn out, and then reassembling the unit. With the rise in wages, to the point where shop time in some garages now costs as much as $15 an hour, it just isn't practical to pay a mechanic to fix anything. Now, most of the fixing is done on an assembly line in some factory. The repaired or rebuilt units are furnished to repair garages, and all the mechanic does is make a replacement.

In many cases, this replacement philosophy applies to new parts also. Assembly lines are so efficient nowadays that new parts can be built almost as cheaply as the rebuilder can renew an old part. The result is that there is a definite competition between new and rebuilt parts, with new parts frequently coming out the winner, because their cost is very close to that of a rebuilt item.

The replace-instead-of-repair situation can be exasperating to a competent home mechanic. He knows what part is worn out inside the unit he wants to fix, but he can't buy it at the parts house, and is therefore forced to buy the complete unit, spending much more money than he would have spent if he could obtain the individual parts. The replacement philosophy has gone so far that some units are not rebuildable under any circumstances. Most of the late fuel pumps, for example, are sealed. You can't even take them apart. When one goes bad, you throw it away and put on a new one. For that reason, we have not shown in this book how to rebuild certain parts, such as a water pump, because we know that it is extremely difficult to find water pump rebuilding kits nowadays. You are forced to replace the worn-out pump with either a rebuilt or a new one.

We'll get into the advantages and disadvantages of new versus rebuilt parts a little later, but this list of rebuilt items in order of sales popularity will give you an idea of what commercial garages have found practical to replace as an assembly rather than overhaul themselves: generators, starters, brake shoes, fuel pumps, clutch pressure plates, clutch discs, starter drives, water pumps, carburetors, connecting rods, armatures, crankshafts, complete engines, solenoids, voltage regulators, power brake parts, oil pumps, brake cylinders, shock absorbers and transmissions. This order of popularity is an indication of both the frequency of failure and the degree of difficulty in making individual repairs. The latter is not so much a measure of complexity but of the type of assembly required: a generator or alternator has many parts that are soldered or glued together and thus lends itself to production line rebuilding.

The main sources for parts are new-car dealers and automotive parts houses (jobbers). If you go to the dealer you will only be able to buy parts for his make of car, whereas the jobber has parts for all makes. However, there are parts called "dealer items" that have such a narrow application that the jobber doesn't carry them. They are available only from the dealer himself.

Besides dealers and jobbers, there are many other sources for parts. General automotive stores, hardware stores, department stores, wrecking yards and mail order companies are all good sources, but none has the complete selection carried by the dealer or the jobber.

If a week or so's delay in obtaining the needed part won't inconvenience you, a very practical source for quality merchandise is to order it by mail or by phone from the nearest catalog order center operated by Sears, Ward or Spiegel. Sears has a special automotive catalog available free for the asking. Then, J. C. Whitney and Honest Charley have extensive catalogs listing replacement parts as well as hot rod items.

IDENTIFYING THE PART

If you bought your car new, you of course know its specifications in detail or at least they will be listed on your copy of the order form, if you still have it. Detailed information, however, will generally be missing in most used car transactions. You will know the model designation, year, the fact that it's a V-8 or not and whether or not it is equipped with an automatic transmission. Still, this is not enough information upon which to base the purchase of many parts. For example, a 361-in. V-8 was standard in Chrysler Newports of the early '60's, but a 383-in. V-8, identical in outward appearance and dimensions, was optional. Current Mopar twins include the 318- and 340-in. V-8's used in many Plymouth and Dodge models. Similar situations exist in GM divisions, FoMoCo and American Motors. Obviously, many internal parts are not interchangeable on these engines because the bore and stroke differ. These factors, in turn, may or may not dictate differences in fuel, ignition and drivetrain components. Lastly, since auto makers don't like to rely on a single source of supply for a component, they may, like Ford, make some of their own carburetors and buy the rest of their requirements on the outside, in this case Holley. On a given model, these units

1. Buying Specialty Parts

2. Remanufactured Engines

1. Specialty parts dealers can often provide items for specialized applications which may not be readily available from general parts houses, dealerships, mail order firms, etc.

2. New or rebuilt engines can be purchased through new car agencies and garages, and sometimes parts houses. Better companies will usually offer a warranty, something that's lacking in a wrecking yard "as is" deal.

are generally interchangeable as an assembly—but their components are different and cannot be interchanged.

DEFINING YOUR CAR

All auto makers, past and present, have permanently affixed to the vehicle one or more sets of code numbers that together define exactly the specifications and major items of optional equipment that were included when it was built. Changes made by the original or subsequent owners will not be reflected in these codes. Sometimes, decoding information is included in the owner's manual; in all cases it will be found in the first few pages of the applicable shop manual that is available for purchase at prices ranging from $5 to $10 directly from the factory. Information on how to order these manuals (they are available for older cars) is available at the new car dealer, and it's worth noting here that you can make the best use of the book you are now reading by supplementing it with the specific information contained in the shop manual for your vehicle.

The coding systems used vary from make to make, and occasionally within a make from year to year. On recent models, the number has by law been placed on the left corner of the dash panel, or on the left windshield post, where it is visible from the outside, through the windshield. On older cars, you might find it on the left front door post, or on the firewall.

Here are a few numbers you might find on some current cars, with some indications of what the various numbers

mean. The plate on a 1975 Chevrolet Camaro "Type LT," for instance, might read as follows:

1 FS87 T 5 B 100097

Here's what all that means. The first digit, "1," indicates that the vehicle really is a Chevrolet. In the General Motors scheme of things, each division is indicated by a number, and Chevrolet is number one. The code numbers for the other divisions run through Cadillac's 6. The second group of figures indicates the body style and trim level. In this case, it's the GM "F" body, the four place special sports coupe, with the high-line trim. Next comes the engine code; here "T" stands for the dual exhaust version of the 350-cu.-in. V-8, with California emissions modifications. As with most of these number and letter designations, there's no apparent reason for one letter to be used over another to indicate a given product or modification. Perhaps at one time things were neatly alphabetical, but changes in the product line have knocked all that out of whack. The number "5" means that the car is a '75 model. Following the engine and year code is a letter designating the assembly plant where the vehicle was built. Again, there seems to be no real reason, at least so far as someone outside the plant is concerned, for the assignment of the code. The "B" of our sample stands for the Baltimore plant, logically enough, but a "U" would indicate the Lordstown, Ohio plant where Vegas and Monzas are assembled. Point of assembly really isn't important—unless the code indicates that the car was built in a Canadian plant, in which case there may be detail differences in parts from those produced in U.S. plants. Following the assembly plant designation, a six-digit number signifies that our hypothetical Camaro was the 97th unit off the line in regular production. One built this early in production might have detail differences from a later production version.

A Ford sedan might carry the following vehicle identification number:

5 S 56 H 100001

Here, the first digit, "5," indicates that

the vehicle is a 1975 model. (The first digit is the last digit of the model year.) The "S," the second digit, indicates that the car was built in the Allen Park, Mich. pilot plant, and is not in regular production. Here again, the alphabetical list of plants doesn't coincide with the alphabet used to designate them. "A" means Atlanta, but "J" means Los Angeles, and there is no L. The "56" indicates that the car is a Galaxie 500 4-door hardtop. The same number on a Mercury would indicate a Monterey Custom *2-door* hardtop. After the body serial code comes the engine code; in this case, "H" stands for the 351-cu.-in. V-8 with 2-bbl. carb. Finally, a six-digit number indicates the actual number of the unit off the line. In our case, this is a pilot model, and the first one at that. The chances are that a model with this number would never get out of company hands. On Ford cars, a label on the rear of the front door carries other numbers that more closely identify the vehicle and the components used in it. Back to our examples again, we find 57F 1C KA X 2 48. Here, "57F" is also a body indication, once again confirming that we have a Galaxie 500 4-door hardtop. "1C" is a color code, telling us that no matter what color the car is now, the original paint was black. Next comes a trim code, indicating that the low-back bench seat was originally upholstered in black Corinth vinyl. "X" is the transmission code, and means that the FMX automatic transmission has been installed. Next comes the rear axle code, the "2" indicating that the axle is not a limited slip type, and has a 2.75:1 ratio. Finally, "48" is a district office code standing for the district in which the car was originally ordered. This could have some bearing on the equipment installed on the car, as one built for a hot, southern climate might have different equipment from one built for use in northern states; and one built for use on the plains of Texas might carry different equipment from one built for the rarer atmosphere of Denver. On our sample unit, "48" indicates that it was ordered in Detroit.

You might find a Chrysler with a number as follows:

S P 29 K 5 R 100340

What you would have would be a Cordoba—indicated by the "S" in the beginning of the number. The second digit shows the degree of luxury in the vehicle, "P" standing for the premium line. The next two digits give the body style. The Cordoba is a special body, not an adaptation of any other body in the Chrysler range, so the "29" stands for a special 2-door hardtop. The "K" tells us that a 360-cu.-in. V-8 with a 2-bbl. carburetor was installed by the factory. The number "5" reveals that it is indeed a 1975 model; and, finally, the "R" indicates that, like all Cordobas for 1975, it was built at the Windsor, Ontario plant and is actually an imported car. The "340" at the end of the six-digit sequence number shows that it was the 340th vehicle off the line.

As with Ford, a plate mounted elsewhere gives all the data on trim, paint, axle ratios, transmissions and actual date of manufacture on the car. Chrysler mounts the body code plate on the left

Where to Get Parts

front fender side shield, the wheel housing or the left side of the upper radiator support, all under the hood.

American Motors, with fewer car lines and less variation within the lines, also uses a 13-digit number to identify and partially describe each unit off the line. You might find the following number on an AMC car:

A 5 C O 8 7 H 100475

The car described by this number is an AMC Hornet, 1975 model. The "A" at the beginning of all AMC numbers stands for, for a change, AMC. The "5" indicates a 1975 model year vehicle, while "C" indicates that it is equipped with an automatic transmission with a floor shift. The "O" says that the vehicle is a Hornet, and the "8" after that signifies that it is a 4-door wagon—all confirmed by the following "7," indicating that it is a Hornet Sportabout. The "H" means that the 304-cu.-in. V-8 was original equipment, while the six-digit number shows that our specimen was the 475th vehicle off the line at the Kenosha plant.

The vehicle identification number is the one most often used for registration purposes, and is the legal description of your car. When coupled with additional numbers indicating options and trim, your car can be identified accurately for the purpose of buying parts. This assumes, of course, that you can accurately describe the part to the counterman, or, better yet, that you bring the old one with you for positive identification.

PART NOMENCLATURE

The average modern car contains about 15,000 separate parts, and at a given time anywhere from 50% to 75% of these will have application on previous models, depending upon whether it is the policy of that auto maker to make frequent engineering and/or styling changes. Chevrolet, for example, revises its cars in more detail from year to year than does American Motors. There is also a considerable degree of joint usage between makes made by the same parent company.

Internal body parts, transmissions, differentials and suspension components are all widely shared. The parts with a specific application to a single line are usually identification features such as trim, external body panels, instruments and the like.

Ford, Chrysler and American Motors catalog and sell parts on a corporate basis. Thus, any part shared by Ford and Mercury would carry the same number at both dealerships, and the same would be true of Dodge and Chrysler-Plymouth. General Motors, however, is somewhat more complicated. Except for internal body components and in a few isolated instances, engines and transmissions, there is far less sharing between divisions. And when they do share, the part numbers will be different. For example, both Buick and Oldsmobile have offered a Chevrolet-built L-6 engine in their low-line intermediates, but every part in this engine carries a Buick or Oldsmobile part number as well as a Chevrolet number, depending upon the make of car in which it is installed. GM accessory divisions such as United-Delco and Harrison Radiator, on the other hand, employ their own specific part number, regardless of interchangeability.

There once was a day when a certain model Carter carburetor or Bower bearing would fit in a dozen different makes of car. An interchange manual was worth its weight in diamonds, and "The Hollander" was the one to have.

Nowadays such easy interchangeability doesn't exist—but there is still enough similarity between parts that the Hollander manual is a good tool to own. It costs $49.50, covers U.S. cars from '65-'75 and is available from Hollander Publishing Co., 12320 Wayzata Blvd., Minnetonka, Minn. 55343. The Hollander's primary use is in wrecking yards, where a sale might be lost if the counterman didn't know that a certain Chevrolet part will also fit a Pontiac. For car nuts who just want to have a Hollander, the publisher has older editions for a lower price.

You can see now why you just can't go down to the dealer, much less the independent jobber, and ask for a "widget that fits on the whats-it" for your 1967 Chevy. You have to say: "I need an automatic choke temperature sensing unit for the 4-bbl. Rochester on my 1967 SS 396 to replace the old one I have here that's stamped part No. 000001." The counterman will still consult one of his catalogs because he might have to say, "There's a running change on that part. I'll give you part No. 000002 which will fit right in if you use this adapter No. 10000001, and you should have no more trouble." An independent jobber, selling non-official replacements, may or may not know of this change. Be as specific as you can to save both your time and that of the counterman.

WHERE TO BUY PARTS

As we mentioned a bit earlier, the main sources for automotive parts are the car dealer, the independent jobber, the automotive chain store, the mail order house and the wrecking yard. These are not listed in order of preference because there are advantages and disadvantages with each source.

No rule can be made in choosing between the car dealer or a jobber as a parts source. The car dealer is the only source for some parts. Jobbers and other outlets compete with the dealer in the marketplace. You should consider all outlets for parts and buy wherever you find satisfaction.

Of course, if you own a car that is no longer manufactured, like a Studebaker or Kaiser, the jobber and mail order house are your only sources for new parts. Many people think there is a law requiring auto companies to make parts available for a certain number of years after they discontinue a model or go out of business. There is no such law. The leftover parts are bought up by brokers strictly on the basis of how many Kaisers, Edsels, Studebakers or whatever are still on the road; as long as there is a demand, there will be a supply through jobber and mail order channels. Sometimes this demand causes a car to be in a sense, reborn. You can, for example, practically assemble a brand-new Model "T" or "A" Ford from the catalogs of Sears or J. C. Whitney, though it's doubtful that any part would be available for these cars at a Ford dealership.

Chain stores like the Pep Boys, Western Auto, J. C. Penney or the auto departments at Sears and Ward retail stores generally limit their replacement parts stock to fast moving items like plugs, points, fan belts, perhaps a few varieties of voltage regulators and horn

1. Precise identification of specific parts to fit particular system components is often best done by taking the old unit to the parts-buying source for a direct double-check.

2. Damage caused by a minor front-end whack—such as to this radiator due to fan "circling" it—can be rectified in either of two ways: One would be to order a brand-new unit from a car agency. Another would be to locate a same-make, same-model car—whose radiator is still sound— in a wrecking yard.

3. Technology has advanced to where some components, such as water pumps, very seldom wear out or break down. Because of this, rebuild kits or individual parts are unavailable— meaning if your pump goes bad, you'll have to get a complete replacement.

4. For that unusual part needed for a scratch-built model or a restoration job, a swap meet may very well turn up some hard-to-find items.

1. Double-Checking New Parts

2. Replaceable Component

relays, and anything that has a universal fit like sealed-beam headlight units.

Mail order, as we've said, takes a little time but is an entirely satisfactory way of buying parts. The Sears, Ward, Spiegel, J. C. Whitney and Honest Charley catalogs are amazingly complete; all of them stock parts for a wide variety of imported cars. A further advantage is that these firms "guarantee satisfaction or your money back," a protection that may or may not exist when dealing with a car dealer or jobber.

Address requests for automotive catalogs to:

Sears Roebuck and Co.
Local catalog order center

Montgomery Ward and Co.
Local catalog order center

Spiegel Inc.
Chicago, Illinois 60609

J. C. Whitney & Co.
1917 Archer Ave.
Chicago, Illinois 60616

Honest Charley Inc.
108 Honest St.
(P.O. Box 8535)
Chattanooga, Tenn. 37411

NEW VS. REBUILT PARTS

You can get into some heated arguments over which is better—a brand-new part or one that has been rebuilt or reconditioned. The quality of any automotive unit depends upon the inspection procedures that are supposed to eliminate all the faulty parts. There isn't a machine or a man that is perfect. No matter how hard a manufacturer or a rebuilder tries, a certain percentage of the parts he has on hand will be defective. Most of the defective parts will be eliminated by inspection, but some of them will definitely turn up in completely assembled units at the end of his assembly line. The manufacturer and rebuilder know this, so they perform tests on the completed units to weed out the bad apples. The big question is: Do they test every unit, 1 out of 10, or 1 out of 100, or none? There are some manufacturers who don't look at anything after it comes

off the end of the line. They figure that if it's bad enough, the ultimate user—you and I—will bring it back to the store where he bought it, and either get his money back or get another part. Fortunately, there are not many rebuilders or manufacturers with that attitude. The only way you can protect yourself from such fast buck artists is by relying on your own experience and the experience of other people who have purchased parts. If a mechanic tells you that he has had bad luck with a certain brand of either new or rebuilt parts, then by all means stay away from that brand.

You should also listen to a mechanic's recommendation of good parts. Some shops have been using a certain line of new or rebuilt merchandise for many years with a very low comeback rate. Those are the parts that you should use on your car.

If there is no one from whom you can get advice, then the safest way to go is to use what are known as "original equipment" parts. The theory behind using original equipment parts is that if the car maker thought the parts were good enough for him, then they certainly should be good enough for you and me as replacements. Examples of original equipment parts would be Delco-Remy electrical parts and units on General Motors cars, Autolite electrical units on Ford products, and Holley carburetor parts on Holley carburetors. In many cases, it is not necessary to go to the new car dealer to get your original equipment parts. Most of the parts manufacturers who supply the original equipment units to the car maker and his dealers also sell through independent parts stores. For example, all General Motors cars are equipped with AC fuel system parts, but you can buy AC units at almost any auto parts store.

THE ROLE OF THE WRECKING YARD

Members of the National Auto and Truck Wreckers Association (NATWA) don't like to be referred to as operators of "junkyards." Their main function today is to supply the nation's steel mills with the 50% content of scrap steel

needed to blend with the fresh pig iron in each charge of the furnace. In addition, about 70 lbs. of aluminum, 35 lbs. of copper, 30 lbs. of zinc, 20 lbs. of lead and 180 lbs. of rubber are similarly salvaged from each wreck—whether new or old—and ultimately reused.

All yard operators strip some fast-moving or valuable parts from a wreck and stock them for resale. Examples would be undamaged components from an air-conditioning system; batteries, tires and even engines and transmissions from late-model wrecks; and intact sheetmetal parts like hoods, trunk lids, bumpers and grilles. The biggest operators are tied together by a regional teletype system so that if one doesn't have the part, it can be determined in seconds whether anybody has it. In fact, if your needs are put on teletype and no one has the part, odds are that in a few days an accident will happen that will enable your order to be filled. A late-model wreck, totalled from an insurance standpoint, is by no means "junk." It will return at least $500 if properly salvaged. Then, there are still countless rural yards that fill a cow pasture with derelict cars and let you prowl around until you find the part you want. These are self-service stores in the true sense because you do your own dismantling, but it's a fascinating way to spend a Saturday afternoon.

The yards that cater to retail customers will generally be quite obvious because there will be a building to house the binned and inventoried small parts and outdoor display racks for the larger items. You must remember, though, that while the part may *look* serviceable, there is no guarantee that it is, because the yard operator, with the sometime exception of complete engines, doesn't check their function. Therefore, if you want to replace a damaged radiator on your late-model car, go search the yards for a low-mileage identical model that's been totalled from the rear. For older cars, the salvage radiator may be no better than the one you want to replace. The bigger yards know what they can get for an item so there is no sense in haggling. In the do-it-yourself lots, though, start with an offer. ☙

3. Water Pump Cutaway

4. Parts at Swap Meet

Lubrication

Nobody, except perhaps a small boy, finds any particular pleasure in getting dirty. It isn't so bad if only your hands get dirty when working on your car, but when you get grease on your shoulders and in your hair and maybe down the middle of your back from crawling around underneath while doing a grease job, it's no wonder that most lube jobs are done in service stations while the owner just stands and watches. However, paying somebody else to do your oil changes and lubrication can be expensive—not only because you are paying for their labor, but because you are giving them full price or even more for the oil and other parts that they use. A good lever-type grease gun can be purchased from Sears or Montgomery Ward for a few dollars, and almost all discount stores have greases and oils. If you don't mind a distasteful job, you can save quite a bit of money by doing the oil changes and lube jobs yourself.

Lubrication and general maintenance work should be performed on a "mileage" or "time" basis. Either one or both can be utilized, according to driving habits. Simply put, if you don't drive enough miles within a certain time period, say 90 days, the service should still be performed to keep your car in top running condition.

In recent years, all of the automobile manufacturers have extended both time and mileage service intervals with much improved components—filters, corrosion-resistant coatings and permanently lubricated joints. However, due to the differing geographical conditions in the U.S. (cold, heat, dust, moisture), certain components need more frequent servicing than others. Keeping this in mind, you will want to adjust (for some items) the service interval suggested in the lubrication and maintenance chart to suit your car's needs. Trailer towing would also come under this adjustment. It is true that a careful lubrication and maintenance program—one that you stick to—will keep your car looking and running like new for many years.

ENGINE OIL TYPES

Probably the two most important factors in engine life are proper break-in and—from then on—keeping the crankcase full of good, clean oil with an efficient filter. Many people exercise a false economy when it comes to oil changes. They think they are saving money when they stretch the interval between oil and filter changes, but all they are doing is shortening the life of the engine. A good engine is worth a lot more in the long run than a stack of filters and oil cans.

There is a confusing (to some) array of oils and oil types currently available to the consumer. There are 10W's, 20's, 30's, 40's and so on; detergent, synthetic, non-detergent, gear oils, top oils and more. The letter "W" refers to an oil's "weight," which doesn't literally mean how much it weighs, but how *thick* it is; the number preceding the W is the measurement of the oil's thickness, or viscosity. The higher the number the thicker the oil. With so many climatic and vehicle variations, there's no one oil best for every condition. The thicker oils with more viscosity can carry greater loads than thin oils, and can carry more heat without losing their properties. Naturally, the thicker oils tend to make the engine harder to start in cold weather, so you should use a lighter weight oil during the winter. While the best oil to use is usually "the thickest oil you can use and still start the engine," there are some simple guidelines for oil selection: In the summer (all year round in areas with mild winters) you should use a 30W or 40W, and change to a 20W for easier starting in the winter. The SAE (Society of Automotive Engineers) tests oils and assigns the viscosity numbers, so most cans will be labeled SAE 30W. There are also *multi-viscosity* oils. These are special-property oils which combine the easy starting characteristics of thin oil in cold weather, yet under more heat they act

1. Do-It-Yourself Oil Change

2. Magnetic Drain Plug

3. Replacement Oil Filter Element

like higher SAE-weight oils. They range from SAE 5W-20 to SAE 10W-20 and SAE 10W-30 and 20W-40, with the first number representing their cold-starting characteristics (the "W" in this case standing for "winter" as well as "weight") and the second number their hot-operation performance. They are a compromise—although they work well and are recommended by many companies—and they don't last quite as long as the "straight-weight" oils.

Engine oil should be selected to give the best performance under the climatic and driving conditions in the area in which your car is driven. When the crankcase is drained and refilled, the new engine oil should be selected not on the basis of the existing temperature at the time of the oil change, but on the lowest temperature anticipated for the period during which the oil will be used.

There are a great many potentially harmful byproducts of internal combustion gasoline engines—and we're not just talking about the tailpipe pollutants. There are also internal pollutants that

are out to destroy your engine from within. Combustion forms these harmful byproducts that collect in your crankcase: tars, sludge, varnish, acids, bases, abrasives and moisture—all of which are dangerous to rings, bearings, tappets and other engine parts. To combat these engine enemies, the oil manufacturers include additives in their oil to fight the deposits. Two of the basic types of oil are the non-detergent and detergent varieties. The non-detergent oil doesn't have the additives to bear up under attack from the harmful deposits and doesn't carry loads well, even in the heavier weights. It may be fine for your lawnmower engine, but don't use it in your car. It might be used in breaking in a brand new engine (where you want some friction to occur to seat the rings, etc.), but only for a short time and under very light loads.

All modern oils are of the detergent type, with additive packages designed to fight the problems created in hot-running late-model cars in stop-and-go driving. When you see "HD" on the top of the

can, it means the oil is high-detergent (not "heavy-duty," as you might guess), with additives to fight sludge, varnish and the rest. Automobile manufacturers have come up with a rating system for oil performance that you should be familiar with, since all high-detergent oils are definitely not the same.

For many years, oils were graded ML, MM, or MS, for Motor Light, Medium, and Severe. MS was the best oil, because it would stand up under severe service, but it wasn't *the* best MS oil unless it had a statement on the can which verified that it had passed the car makers' sequence tests.

Now, there is a new rating system, with five classifications:

SA oils are non-detergent, with no performance requirements. This classification includes not only high-quality non-detergent oils put out by major companies, but also the dregs from the local tar pit. If you want a good non-detergent oil, you will have to rely on the reputation of the maker.

SB oils have a few additives that pro-

4. Canister-Type Oil Filter

1. Most basic home lubrication work that can be done by any car owner is the oil change. Buy yourself some quality oil at your local department store, and with a drain pan, wrench and oil can spout, you're ready.

2. Magnetic oil pan drain plugs are available at most auto supply stores and, as can be seen in this example, do pick up unwanted metal particles from the pan; these can be disposed of at every oil change.

3. Every other oil change should also include a filter change. Use a filter wrench to remove the old one, clean the mounting surface on the engine, wipe the seal of the new filter with clean oil and install hand-tight or as car-maker suggests.

4. Pre-1968 Chevys used a canister-type oil filter. When changing these, clean the steel can in solvent, then install new element in the can. A new gasket comes with the new filter and should be fitted to the block before installing the can. Kits are also available to convert these Chevys to later spin-on type filters.

5. Our quick-reference guide for periodic lubrication is designed to cover the needs of old and new cars alike, although oil change interval recommendations vary from make to make and year to year. Some of the lube points listed here will not be found on later-model cars, due to the "permanent" lubrication used.

Quick-Reference Maintenance and Lubrication Guide

SERVICE AT INDICATED TIME AND/OR MILEAGE INTERVALS	Months		2		6		12		24	36
	Mileage	Fuel Stop	2000	4000	5000	6000	10,000	12,000	24,000	36,000
Check engine oil level		X								
Check radiator coolant level (remove cap on cold engine only)		X								
Check battery liquid level		X								
Check windshield washer reservoir level		X								
Lubricate generator cup(s)			X							
Lubricate distributor cup			X							
Lubricate water pump(s) if equipped with grease fitting(s)			X							
Change engine oil and filter				X						
Check tire air pressure				X						
Lubricate front suspension on older types				X						
Lubricate exhaust manifold valve				X						
Check brake master cylinder fluid level				X						
Check hydraulic clutch master cylinder fluid level				X						
Check automatic transmission oil level				X						
Check power steering fluid reservoir				X						
Check steering gear lubricant level				X						
Clean and lubricate oil wetted wire mesh air cleaner[1]				X						
Clean and lubricate oil filler cap[1]				X						
Perform minor engine tune-up					X					
Check and clean crankcase ventilation system							X			
Check manual transmission lubricant level (early type)							X			
Check manual transmission lubricant level (full synchromesh type)								X		
Check rear axle lubricant level (early)							X			
Check rear axle lubricant level (late)									X	
Lubricate transmission, clutch and brake linkage							X			
Adust clutch pedal travel							X			
Lubricate universal joints with grease fittings							X			
Lubricate universal joints without grease fittings									X	
Perform brake adjustment[2]							X			
Clean body and door drain holes							X			
Rotate tires							X			
Clean dry-type air cleaner[1]							X			
Replace dry-type air cleaner[1]								X		
Clean polyurethane type air cleaner[1]							X			
Perform body lubrication (hinges, striker plates, etc.)							X			
Inspect brake hoses							X			
Check accessory drive(s) belt tension							X			
Perform major engine tune-up						X				
Clean and refill oil bath type air cleaner[1]						X				
Clean and lubricate accelerator linkage						X				
Clean and repack front wheel bearings								X		
Lubricate dash controls and seat tracks								X		
Major brake adjustment (remove drums, clean dust, lube pivots, etc.)								X		
Check headlight adjustment								X		
Check front-end alignment[2]								X		
Clean battery terminals[2]								X		
Check air-conditioning system (bolts, hose condition, sight gauge)								X		
Replace P.C.V. valves and clean hoses								X		
Inspect cooling system[2]								X		
Lubricate slip yoke (automatic transmission models)								X		
Change automatic transmission fluid									X	
Check shock absorbers and bushings									X	
Replace spring leaf inserts (small pads between leaves)									X	
Check convertible top operation									X	
Lubricate speedometer cable									X	
Lubricate long-life front suspension										X

1 Perform this service more frequently in dusty areas   2 More frequently if necessary

NOTE: The above time and/or mileage servicing intervals are averages based on recommendations from various automotive sources, and are designed to serve primarily as a guide. Wherever possible, it is desirable to refer to specific car manufacturer shop manuals for factory-prescribed servicing intervals and procedures, particularly during warranty coverage periods. Unusual operating conditions—such as extreme heat or cold, extended trailer towing, dusty environment, excessive moisture, etc.—may demand more frequent servicing, which may also be the case with older, higher mileage cars.

5. Periodic Lubrication Chart

Lubrication

tect against scuffing, bearing corrosion, and oil oxidation. These oils give only minimum protection.

SC oils are better. They have additives that protect against high- and low-temperature deposits, as well as rust, wear, and corrosion.

SD oils are the next best. They protect against all the conditions that the other oils do, only more so. If a car maker recommends SC oil, you will be giving your engine greater protection by using SD type oil.

Until late in 1971, SD oil was thought to be the best oil available, but then the strange cases of oil thickening showed up. It seems that increased engine temperatures caused by running lean to control emissions, when coupled with trailer towing or other heavy load operation at high speeds, can heat the oil so that it oxidizes, leaving nothing but a gooey mess that the oil pump can't pick up out of the pan. The result is a thoroughly destroyed crankshaft and bearings, maybe even a seized engine. To combat this, the oil makers have hurriedly come out with SE grade oil. It is now the best oil you can get, at least until some new problem comes up that it can't cope with.

Just in case you see them on the can, let's also go through the oil classifications for diesel use. The old classes were DG, DM, and DS, for Diesel General, Diesel Medium, and Diesel Severe. New diesel classifications are as follows:

CA oils are for light-duty diesel engine service. These oils will give protection from bearing corrosion and high-temperature deposits, but only if high quality diesel fuel is used.

CB oils are for moderate-duty diesel engine service. They are a little bit better than the CA oils.

CC oils are a step better than CB oils. Lightly supercharged diesel engines should use these oils for protection from high-temperature deposits. CC oils are also recommended in some gasoline engines. When used in gasoline engines, CC oils are roughly equivalent to SC classification oils.

CD oils are the best for diesel, but they are definitely not recommended for passenger cars. They are too high in additive content to work well with gasoline engine spark plugs. In diesel engines there are no plugs to worry about.

It will be some time before all the cartons and containers with the old grading system have disappeared. If your car is supposed to use SC or SD oil, but you can't find any, then you should use MS oil that has passed the sequence tests.

Also out on the market now, as if you weren't confused enough already, are the *synthetic* oils. You'll be hearing more and more about these oils, with our resource situation being what it is today, and early tests have shown that they do have some promise. Although they don't have much load-carrying capacity compared to petroleum oils, they do boast of a very long service life, especially in cold weather. In fact, they work so well in cold climates that most of the cars and equipment being used along the

1. Oil Can Contents Explanation

2. Dash-Mounted "Oil Check"

3. Magnetizing Dipstick

4. Strength of Magnetized Dipstick

Alaskan pipeline are using the new synthetic oils.

CHANGING OIL

While motor oil does not lose its "oiliness," it does wear out as its additives are used up in performing their function. That is one particular disadvantage of multi-viscosity oil, which is really more additive than oil. It must be changed regularly. The oil in the crankcase, while performing its many functions to protect the engine from the harmful effects of contamination, becomes more and more loaded with these waste products, not all of which can be trapped by a filter. Oil filters help if properly maintained, but they don't prevent varnish deposits, sludge, or corrosive wear caused by liquid contaminants which will pass through the filter. There is only one sure way to remove contaminated oil from your engine, and that is by changing the oil on a regular basis before the additives are depleted. Adding makeup oil to a crankcase of dirty oil is no substitute for draining and refilling. Today, as always, 3 qts. of dirty oil and 2 qts. of clean oil make 5 qts. of dirty oil.

Automobile manufacturers vary slightly in their recommendations of oil change intervals. And today's new car standards are not retroactive to older model cars. Therefore, engine oil and filter should be changed every 90 days or 3000 miles, whichever occurs first. These figures apply to almost all driving conditions and are well within the manufacturer's recommendations and those of the American Petroleum Institute.

It's advisable to drain the crankcase only after the engine has reached normal operating temperature. The benefit of draining is, to a large extent, lost if the crankcase is drained when the engine is cold, as some of the suspended contaminants will cling to the sides of the engine block and oil pan and will not drain out readily with cold, slow-moving oil. Allow sufficient time for the oil to drain out and replace the plug carefully, starting the threads by hand so as not to strip the oil pan. Oil pan plugs should be torqued 30 to 40 ft.-lbs. After changing the oil and the filter, do not accelerate the engine beyond idle until the oil light goes out or the pressure gauge reads above 20 lbs. of pressure.

Flushing the crankcase with oils or solvent solutions other than a good grade SAE 10W oil is not recommended. If flushing is necessary due to contamination, fill the crankcase with 3 qts. of SAE 10W oil (4 qts. with filter) and idle the engine at 1000 rpm until the oil is hot; then drain the pan and filter immediately after stopping the engine. Install a new filter and the correct grade and quantity of engine oil.

There are some very popular myths about oil changes, especially where older cars are concerned. Some people believe that changing to modern detergent oils in an older engine will "break up the dirt inside and ruin the bearings," but this simply isn't true. An older engine can be flushed out by using good high-detergent oil and changing the oil and filter four times the first month. You can put in the first oil change and in 3 days that clean, new oil will be filthy. The four changes should flush out most of the contaminants and sludge buildup. Then use a good SAE 40W oil and you'll have

5. Checking Steering Gear Grease

6. Power Steering Reservoir Dipstick

7. Refilling Power Steering Reservoir

1. Oil types and viscosity properties are found printed on the back of the can. Weight and classification (10W-40, SD, SE) shows this grade of oil will protect the engine's moving parts in a wide variety of driving conditions. Check factory recommendations for your particular car and the climatic changes it will be subjected to before you replace your oil.

2. The makers of Smiths gauges have come up with a way to check your oil level from the dash, without getting your hands dirty. Called "Oil Check," it's especially practical for vans, where the dipstick is a hassle to get to at every refueling stop.

3. Here's a real shadetree tip for you. You can magnetize your stock dipstick easily, so that it picks up metallic particles you can wipe off when you check your oil. Simply wrap a length of wire around the end and briefly touch the wire ends to your battery terminals.

4. The short surge of current will magnetize the steel dipstick enough so you can even pick up screws.

5. The oil or grease level in the steering gear—normally up to the filler plug—must be checked at the same time you change oil and filter.

6. Like the steering gear, the fluid level in the power steering reservoir must be looked at every 3 months or 3000 miles. Don't overfill reservoir.

7. In most cars, automatic trans fluid is used in the power steering but there are fluids made specifically for power steering, too, like this type for Chrysler Corp. cars.

less blowby, wear and friction.

The engine oil dipstick is marked "full" and "add oil." These notations are marked with broad lines and arrows so that you will know exactly how much oil is in the crankcase and how much you should add if necessary. Never let the oil level go below the lower mark and never overfill the crankcase. Before adding oil, wait until the oil level reading is just below the "add 1 qt." line. Also, if the car has been driven, you will avoid a false reading if you allow a few minutes for the oil to drain back to the crankcase before checking the oil level.

OIL FILTERS

There are two types of oil filter systems: full-flow and bypass. In the full-flow type, the oil filter is in the system between the oil pump and the engine so that all the oil has to go through the filter before it reaches the engine. When flow through the filter is restricted by dirt (which means the filter is doing its job), a valve in the filter (or in the engine block) opens up and allows the oil to go around the filter. Most people don't realize that the valve also opens when the oil is cold, because cold oil is too thick to pass through the filter element. The valve can also open during high-speed operation, because so much oil is being pumped that the filter element can't accept it all.

In the bypass filter system, the filter is on a separate line. Oil goes from the pump to the filter, and then dumps back into the pan. A bypass filter can be removed, and the line plugged, without affecting the operation of the oiling system. On many older cars, the bypass fil-

ter was an accessory added by the dealer if the owner wanted it. Bypass filters are supposedly obsolete, inefficient, and unnecessary. But when you consider how much of the time a full-flow filter is actually bypassing the oil, then the old bypass filter doesn't look so bad. Any filtration is better than none; your engine needs the protection.

Most late model cars use a "can"-type filter that screws onto a special mounting bracket attached to the engine. To change it, you merely unscrew it and throw it away. A complete new element is then screwed on in its place. Before attaching this type of element, wipe the gasket area of the base clean, coat the neoprene gasket with engine oil, and screw the filter can onto its base until the gasket is firmly against the sealing surface. From that point, turn the filter can an additional ½-turn.

Most filter makers consider that anything beyond a ¾-turn will result in the need to use blasting powder to get the filter off when it comes time to change it. But Chevrolet has experienced some leaks when following the ¾-turn rule. They recommend 25 ft.-lbs., which is equivalent to between 1 and 1⅔ turns.

Some throwaway filters have fluted ends that fit a special wrench. Others have a hex so you can use ordinary socket wrenches. Some filters have only a smooth can, so you must use one of those wrenches that looks like a kitchen jar opener and is sold in all the auto supply stores.

Earlier filters are contained in a steel can which also mounts on the engine in either a top or underneath mounting position. The top-mounted filters have a lid that you can remove by unscrewing a bolt; the filter element can then be lifted out. On filters mounted under the engine, the whole can and filter element is removed when the bolt is loosened. In either case, the filter element is thrown out, the container can wiped clean, and a new element fitted.

Remember, the filter holds 1 qt. of oil. Therefore, if you change the filter when you change the oil, you will need to add an extra quart of oil to fill the crankcase.

AUTOMATIC TRANSMISSIONS

Most automobile manufacturers seem to agree that automatic transmission fluids should be changed every 24,000 miles or 24 months, whichever occurs first. The exception is hard service or trailer towing, in which case the oil change should come at 12,000 miles or 12 months, whichever occurs first.

The converter in an automatic transmission holds most of the fluid and it stays there when the transmission is not operating. Draining the pan will only get a few quarts of fluid out of the transmission. If the converter has a drain plug that can be reached from underneath the car, then you can make a complete change of automatic transmission fluid. But in many cases, the converter has no drain plug. So the only thing you can do is change the amount of oil that is in the pan. Even though it is only a partial oil change, it is still a good idea because the new oil that you put in will help to build up the additive content of the transmission fluid.

Lubrication

As mentioned earlier, to check the fluid level in an automatic transmission, the engine must be at normal operating temperature. The check must be made with the engine idling and the selector lever in Park or Neutral. When the fluid is hot, the level should be at the "add 1 pint" mark. *Caution: Do not fill above the "full" mark as this will cause foaming and will result in improper operation.* If it is necessary to check the fluid level when the transmission is cold, fluid level should be at, or slightly below, the "add 1 pint" mark. If it's below this mark, add just enough oil to bring it up to the "add 1 pint" mark. This avoids overfilling.

For many years, the only kind of automatic transmission fluid available was Type A, sometimes called Suffix A. In recent years, Ford has come out with their own fluid called Type F, which is now available from all fluid manufacturers. Type F is the only fluid that should be used in any Ford product automatic transmission. This includes the older transmissions for which Type A was originally recommended. Some of the early Chrysler, DeSoto, Dodge or Plymouth automatic transmissions were of a different design, actually amounting to a manual transmission that was hydraulically shifted. Most of those old units, including the one called Fluid Drive, were filled with engine oil. Before adding any kind of fluid to any transmission, check the factory specifications to be sure you're adding the right fluid.

Most mechanics will tell you that the transmission fluid in modern cars can be as hot as 350°, and to be careful when draining it so as not to get burned. However, at 350° your transmission's life is going to be a lot shorter than if your fluid ran at 200° If you do any towing, or other load-carrying, you'd be very wise to invest in an aftermarket transmission oil cooler. They generally run from $30 to $75 in price and are well worth it. The standard loop-type cooler in the bottom of your radiator relies on already-hot engine water and air to cool the transmission fluid, and just doesn't do a thorough job. Not only will a transmission cooler extend the life of the transmission, but you can safely go longer before changing the fluid. Perhaps a better first investment would be a transmission temperature gauge, so you know exactly how hot yours is running. If it's in that 350° range your fluid won't last the recommended 2 years between changes, and will smell "burned" when hot.

STANDARD TRANSMISSIONS

Most auto manufacturers state that regular transmission oil changes are not necessary on late-model cars whose operation is classified as normal service for passenger cars. This is difficult to go along with and it certainly is not true for the older models. No one is absolutely perfect at shifting, and every time there is a clashing of gears—or even the normal wear of transmission parts—there are bound to be metal particles suspended in the oil. And there is no filter in the transmission to catch these metal particles. Therefore, transmission oil on early model cars should be changed every 6 months or 6000 miles. On newer cars with full synchromesh gears, change the oil every 12 months or 12,000 miles. On some late-model cars there is no drain plug; on others a drain plug is provided at the bottom or low on the side of the transmission for this purpose. If no drain plug is provided, a suction pump must be used to remove the oil.

SAE 90 viscosity grade oil is recommended for year-round use; however, SAE 80 may be used when low temperatures are encountered. Good quality multi-purpose lubricants are defined by the number MIL-L-2105B. Except for checking fluid level at engine oil change intervals and draining the oil, there is no maintenance on the transmission other than lubricating the gearshift mechanism. A 30W engine oil is excellent for this purpose, and you should wipe all the pivot points clean before oiling. Some older cars have a grease fitting on the steering column to lubricate the shift levers and linkage.

Many lubricant manufacturers now make multi-viscosity transmission lubes as well as engine oils. In some cases, it is difficult to find single-viscosity transmission lube such as 80 or 90. The 90-140 that most stations carry now seems to work just as well as the old single-viscosity grades.

STANDARD AND LIMITED-SLIP REAR AXLES

On most late-model cars you will not find a drain plug at the rear axle. Late-model cars may go 2 years or 24,000 miles before the fluid should be changed. Older model cars should have their oil changed every 6 months or 6000 miles, whichever occurs first.

Again, the oil level should be checked with the fluid hot, and it should be up to the bottom of the filler plug. If checked cold, it should be approximately ½-in. below the filler plug.

The standard weight of lubricant for rear axles and transmissions has been 90W (not to be confused with weights of engine oils, since they are measured quite differently from transmission lubes), but more suitable for heavy-duty use would be a straight 140 or the service-station type 90-140. Although you will hear of "special" lubricants for limited-slip rear axles, you can actually use regular lubes—*but* you should add some limited-slip additive to avoid chattering noises in the friction clutch plates. It's available at your local Chevrolet dealer under the name of "Posi-Traction additive" (part #1050428). It gives a higher load-bearing ability to the lube—and at a price of around a buck, you can't beat it with a stick.

If the rear axle is ever submerged in water, such as on a boat launching ramp where water can enter the axle vent, and contamination is suspected or evident, replace the lubricant immediately to avoid early axle failure.

1. Checking Rear End Fluid Level

2. Transmission Dipstick

CHASSIS

Between 1961 and 1963, American automobile manufacturers introduced what are called "long-life" front-end ball joints that only require lubrication every 3 years or 36,000 miles, whichever occurs first. These semi-permanently lubricated ball joints should be inspected every 6 months—or whenever the car is serviced—for signs of damage to seals, which can result in loss or contamination of lubricant. The special seals at each joint are the key to this extended lubrication period, and if they become damaged in any way they must be replaced and the joint lubricated.

It's easy to tell if your car has the long-life ball joints: the car will not have any grease fittings. Instead you'll find a tiny threaded metal plug. The procedure for lubricating these new type ball joints is to remove the plug and screw in a special grease gun fitting. Stop filling when lubricant begins to flow from the bleed area at the base or at the top of

the seal, or if the seal begins to "balloon." Remove the grease fitting and reinstall the plug.

The only types of lubricant that should be used in these semi-permanently lubricated joints are moly-disulfide greases. They are long lasting and highly waterproof.

Cars without the long-life ball joints should be lubricated every 60 days or 4000 miles. These joints have what are called Zerk fittings installed at each lubrication point, and if you expect to have a trouble-free front end and one that is

safe, you must lubricate these joints regularly. The reason is that these Zerk fittings, even though they have a ball-check valve that doesn't let grease leak out, do let in a small amount of dirt and water. Also a certain amount of dirt and moisture works its way in at the joint. To get rid of this dirty grease, it's necessary to flush it out with new grease periodically before it does any damage. All Zerk fittings must be wiped clean before injecting any new lubricant.

While it's possible that you may want to lubricate your own car with a hand-

3. Auxiliary Gauges

1. Checking the rear-axle lubricant level is easy. Remove the plug on the differential cover and insert your finger. The fluid should be up to the plug hole. Draining late rear ends to change the lube usually takes a while, as the rear cover must be removed to drain the differential.

2. Fluid level and smell are both important when you eyeball the trans dipstick. Too much or too little fluid can drastically affect the performance of the unit. And so can overheating. If fluid is acrid or extremely pungent, it has been subjected to severe heat and must be changed.

3. You don't need all the gauges a race car would, but if you do any heavy-duty driving or towing, it's a good idea to have a transmission temperature gauge to tell you whether your transmission is in need of an aftermarket fluid cooler.

4. Accessory transmission coolers come in many sizes and are available at most auto supply stores. They're a wise investment to protect against fluid overheating and breakdown.

5. Installation of most accessory coolers can be accomplished in about 2 hours. They can be mounted in a number of locations, but the premium spot is between the grille and the radiator, where the cooler will get plenty of fresh air routed over it.

4. Accessory Transmission Coolers

5. Ideal Trans Cooler Location

Lubrication

operated grease gun, it's easier and faster in a service station with a high-pressure grease gun. Also, a service station or car dealer will have a complete lubrication chart (number of fittings, location, types of lubricant and refill quantities) on every car so that you can be sure of a thorough job. There are exceptions to this if you have replaced any factory parts that did not have a lubrication fitting with one that does. An example might be universal joints or idler arm, in which case you must make the attendant aware of the change, so that he does not miss properly lubricating it.

Other chassis pivot points, such as rubber shock absorber bushings, spring leaf bushings and leaf liners or pads, and anti-sway bars, do not require lubrication. They are made to run dry; if they wear out, they should be replaced. However, after many years and miles of use they sometimes get squeaky; then, and only then, should they be lubricated with a special rubber lubricant spray. Be sure to mention this to your dealer too, as they sometimes make it a point to spray only older cars.

Clutch, brake and parking brake linkages should also be lubricated about every 6 months. Wipe all the pivot points clean and lube with 30W engine oil. Lubricate the pivot points inside the car sparingly so as not to cause dripping which will stain upholstery.

On some older cars (especially Ford products '32-'48) it is necessary to lubricate the clutch throwout bearing shaft, and a Zerk fitting is provided for this purpose. Use only a small amount of lubricant, as excessive grease may work its way onto the clutch and cause it to slip when engaged.

UNIVERSAL JOINTS

Most cars, except some of the late models, will have lubrication fittings at the driveshaft universal joints. They should be lubricated every 4 months or 6000 miles—but sparingly and very carefully so as not to pump out the seals. On cars with torque tube drive there is only one fitting, and that is where the driveshaft meets the transmission output shaft at the ball joint. This joint must also be lubricated carefully so as not to damage the rear transmission oil seal.

On some late-model cars without lubrication fittings on the universal joints, the manufacturers say that lubrication is not necessary for the life of the joint and that only periodic inspection is necessary to check for leaking seals, in which case either the seal may be replaced or the complete universal joint.

Because auto manufacturers vary so widely on universal joint lubrication, it's best to consult your owner's manual to see if lubrication is advisable for your make, year and model. If there is no universal joint grease fitting and lubrication is advisable, it should be done every 2 years or 24,000 miles. To lubricate this type of joint it is necessary to remove the driveshaft and disassemble the U-joints as if you were going to renew the bearings. (That operation is described in the chapter on driveshafts.)

STEERING GEAR

The lubrication installed in the steering gear at time of assembly is a high-quality product, and regular or seasonal changes are not normally required.

Steering gear oil level should be checked at every engine oil change interval; its normal level is up to the filler plug. Some steering boxes use grease instead of oil. Your owner's manual or local lubrication expert will tell you which should be used.

POWER STEERING

Check the power steering reservoir level at every engine oil change. The reservoir will either have a dipstick for measurement, a "full" mark on the housing or a notation on the cap to fill to ¼-in. below top.

Most power steering units use automatic transmission fluid, but special power steering fluid is available, and the units seem to work a little bit better on it. Both special steering fluid and the auto trans fluid will mix compatibly, so there is no necessity for emptying the system when adding fluid. Do not overfill any power steering unit. Overfilling can cause pressure to build up that can blow the seals in the pump.

1. Chassis Lube Diagram

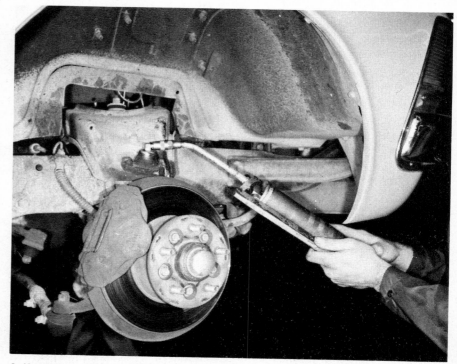

2. Hand-Operated Grease Gun

1. *Chassis lubrication diagrams—such as for this '72 Chevy—can be found in any dealer's service manual. It allows the car's owner to see where the lubrication points are, the location of the oil and fluid reservoirs, and when they should be checked, refilled and/or replaced.*

2. *Low-cost, hand-operated grease guns, although not as fast, will do every bit as good a job as the air-operated ones found in gas stations or dealer's repair shops. Many outfits come complete with swivel heads for difficult-to-reach fittings.*

3. *All Zerk fittings must be wiped free of old grease or road scum build-up before fresh grease is added. The accumulation will contaminate the fresh grease if this isn't done.*

4. *Late-model cars are equipped with plugs instead of grease fittings and these must be removed for lubing.*

5. *Clean the area around the plug, remove the plug and insert a grease fitting. After lubrication, replace the threaded steel plug.*

6. *U-joints on late-model cars have no grease fittings either; to lube them they have to be disassembled—but most replacement U-joints such as these will have the lube fittings.*

WHEEL BEARINGS

Front wheel bearings are one of the most important lubrication points on a car and yet one of the most neglected. It is highly imperative that they be cleaned, repacked and the seals inspected every 12 months or 12,000 miles. This includes all cars, both old and late models, regardless of make.

To lubricate the front wheel bearings, it's necessary to remove the wheel and hub assembly.

The condition of ball and roller type bearings that have been in service cannot be judged until they are thoroughly cleaned. There is always enough dirt present to affect the "feel" of the bearing and give the impression that they are just a bit rough.

Bearings with seals or shields on both ends should not be washed in solvent since there is no way to replenish the grease supply. This type is merely wiped clean and checked for a rough or noisy "feeling."

Unsealed bearings should be washed thoroughly in clean solvent which has not been used for other parts. Slosh the bearings up and down rapidly in the solvent to flush out all dirt and metal particles. It may be necessary to soak hardened dirt and lubricant from bearings; however, do not let them touch the bottom of the pan and pick up any dirt that may have settled there.

After washing, blow out the bearings with clean, dry air, directing the air stream squarely into the open side. Hold the inner race and turn the outer race slowly by hand. *Never spin the bearings with air pressure.* It's not only hard on the bearing, but dangerous. That bearing will spin at several thousand rpm, enough to make it disintegrate like a fragmentation grenade, and you know what damage they can do.

Most dealers with service stations have a pressure packing tool that forces the lubricant throughout the bearing. This is the best way; however, it may be done by hand by carefully pushing the grease down in between the balls or rollers. It takes time to do this, and you must work the grease in from all open sides.

Rear wheel bearings get their lubrication by "splash" from the rear axle gears, although some very old cars have a lubrication fitting at the ends of the axle housing. Check this out. Also, they only require one quick shot of lubricant so as not to damage the seals or force lubricant into the braking surface areas.

AIR CLEANERS

There are four main types of carbure-

3. Wiping Off Zerk Fitting

4. Removable Plug in Grease Fitting Hole

5. Inserting Grease Fitting

6. Replacement "Lube-able" U-Joints

Lubrication

tor air cleaners in use today: the dry replaceable paper element, the oil-wetted wire mesh, the oil-wetted polyurethane, and the oil bath.

The dry replaceable paper type should be cleaned every 6000 miles and replaced every 12,000 miles or 12 months. To clean this type of filter, drop it repeatedly and squarely on a clean, flat surface until all loose dust has been removed. Turn the element over and repeat the process. (Air blast cleaning is okay if done very carefully.) Now visually inspect the element for any breaks or holes in the fiber and replace it if any dust leaks are found. Before installing the element, wipe all dust from the interior of the air cleaner and install the element by turning it 180° from removal position. When element and cover are in place, tighten the wing nut securely by hand to ensure a good seal.

Oil-wetted wire mesh cleaners must be cleaned every 4000 miles. This type is washed in clean solvent by sloshing up and down and then setting aside to drain dry. Oil the element liberally with 30W engine oil, allow the excess to drain off, then reinstall your element.

The polyurethane type filter is washed in clean solvent and squeezed dry. Soak the element in 30W engine oil before replacing it. This type may be cleaned every 6000 miles in most areas.

Oil bath air cleaners are serviced by emptying the oil reservoir and washing the entire unit in clean solvent every 10,000 miles. The reservoir is then refilled with 30W engine oil to the level indicated on the unit. Some oil baths also have a wire mesh filter which is serviced as outlined for this particular type.

Never dunk an entire air cleaner in solvent. You may think you are going to get it really clean, but all you will do is get solvent inside the air chamber, and it will take you about 2 weeks of rich running on your car before all the stuff evaporates.

Oil filler caps with mesh breathers should be washed every 4000 miles with solvent. Slosh the cap up and down in the solvent rapidly and tap squarely on a flat surface until all dirt is removed. Allow cap to drain until dry and lubricate with 30W engine oil.

On late-model emissions-control cars, the breather mesh that used to be in the oil filler cap is now in the air cleaner at the end of a hose running from the sealed filler cap. The reason for the breather mesh inside the air cleaner is not to protect the engine, but to keep oil fumes off the air cleaner element. Clean the breather mesh in solvent, but leave it dry when you replace it.

GENERATORS AND ALTERNATORS

Most generators have oil cups at one or both ends of the housing. These cups should get two or three drops of 30W oil every 2000 miles or at engine oil change intervals.

Alternators are equipped with sealed bearings and lubrication is not possible. If a bearing goes bad (usually from water, so cover vent holes when washing or steam cleaning your engine), it must be replaced. No other maintenance is necessary except wiping dust from vents.

DISTRIBUTOR

Most distributors—except on late-model cars—have an oil cup outside the housing. This should be filled every 2000 miles—or at engine oil change intervals—with 30W oil. Many distributors have a felt wick underneath the rotor. A few drops of oil on the wick will keep it moist so that the breaker cam will move freely on the shaft. However, the wick does not lubricate the advance weights. They should be checked whenever the points are going to be replaced.

WATER PUMP

Almost all water pumps have sealed bearings which never need service for the life of the pump. When the bearing goes bad the pump is replaced. How-

ever, preventive maintenance means adding a can of Rust Inhibitor and Water Pump Lubricant to your radiator every 6 months, unless you are running antifreeze. In that case, the antifreeze is all you need. Adding rust inhibitor to the antifreeze might prolong the life of the water pump, but in our experience it lowers the boiling point of the coolant enough to cause boiling over and coolant loss.

Some older cars have a grease fitting on the water pump, and this type should be lubricated every 2000 miles, or at engine oil changes, with special water pump grease. It's waterproof.

EXHAUST MANIFOLD VALVE

The exhaust manifold valve should be lubricated at every engine oil change to keep it operating properly. If this valve sticks, engine efficiency will be impaired. Lubricate both sides of the shaft with a mixture of graphite and kerosene, or you can purchase special exhaust manifold valve lubricant at a parts store.

ACCELERATOR LINKAGE

All the pivot points in the accelerator linkage should be lubricated at the 10,000-mile mark when the engine tune-up is performed. It's not difficult to understand that smooth operation of the accelerator linkage is important to safety and control of your car. Use 30W engine oil on all pivots and grease on all sliding arms. Some car makers suggest keeping linkage dry, so it won't pick up dirt and wear faster.

SPEEDOMETER CABLE

To service a noisy speedometer cable, disconnect the cable at the speedometer head and remove the shaft. Clean the shaft thoroughly and then lubricate. Insert the shaft back in the cable, being careful not to let it touch the ground and pick up any dirt. Wipe the excess lubricant from the end of the cable and reconnect to the speedometer head.

1. Applying Rubber Lube

2. Lubing Throttle Linkage

1. *Rubber-mounted pivot points on shocks, springs, torsion bars, etc., are lubricated with a silicone-based rubber lube applied with a squirt can— but only if they are squeaking. Otherwise they should be left dry so they won't slip and wear out.*

2. *If it moves, don't salute it, lube it! All pivot points in the throttle linkage require the oil treatment every 10,000 miles.*

3. *Older distributors had an oil tube on the side. A few drops of oil here at each oil change interval will keep the distributor shaft alive.*

4. *The moving parts attached to the car's body require periodic servicing. Work your way back from the front, catching the hood latch, release cable, safety catch, etc., then on to the door latches, hinges, striker plates, trunk lid catch, key lock and trunk hinges.*

5. *If your engine leaks oil from somewhere, you'll never find the source until the engine is cleaned up so you can spot leaks. Scrape off any heavy accumulations of dirt with a putty knife. The rest can be cleaned at the do-it-yourself car wash with spray-can solvents. Have the engine warmed up beforehand and cover the carb and distributor with plastic bags. Spray the solvents and let them soak, then hose off dirt.*

CONTROLS AND SEATS

Once a year do a little "spring lubing" inside the car. Dash control knobs that you push and pull should be wiped clean (remove any rust spots with crocus cloth) and lightly lubed with grease. Push the knob in and out to work in the lubricant. Also lubricate the open cable ends where they attach to the heater, the air conditioner, windshield wiper, fresh air intakes, etc. And don't forget the seat tracks. It's always annoying and difficult to try to adjust a seat that won't slide smoothly. Lubricating power seats is especially important.

BODY LUBRICATION

Don't forget that there are literally hundreds of body parts that need regular lubrication too, and they should be serviced every 6 months to keep your car in top condition.

All rotating parts and hinge pins are to be lubricated with 30W engine oil. All sliding and rubbing contact parts are lubed with grease. The only exceptions to this are the door and tailgate striker plates and bolts, the ends of the sunshade rods—which both require non-staining stick-type lube—and the door key locks, which use powdered graphite.

Accumulated dirt, dust and old lubricant should always be wiped off before applying new lubrication. Then operate the mechanism to work it in, wiping off any excess. All rubber moldings should be lubed with a special rubber lubricant to keep them from weather cracking and to prolong their life. Rubber lubricant soaks into rubber and soon disappears. We have been experimenting with silicone (either spray or grease) and find that it does an excellent job of protecting rubber parts from deterioration.

Start at the front and work your way back. Lubricate the hood latch, release cable and safety mechanism and the hood hinges. The doors are next—striker plates, door locks, striker rotor, hinges and hold-open mechanism and/or torque rods, the latching mechanism and key lock. If you have a station wagon or pickup, don't forget the tailgate hinges, lock and support rods. And way out back, put a little lubrication on the gas cap cover door hinges. If you have a convertible, you'll want to do the folding top mechanism, but apply it sparingly (have a rag handy) so as not to get any lubricant on top of upholstery. Oil frequently seeps out onto the paint a few days after lubing door hinges and other body parts, so use just as little oil as possible, unless you want to be a traveling advertisement for 3-in-1.

We'll leave the window regulators up to you. Normally, they will probably never need care unless you have an older car, or trouble develops inside the door panel. But if it's difficult to turn the window crank, remove the upholstery panel and determine the cause. It may just need aligning and lubrication. By servicing it now, before it breaks entirely, you'll save some money.

To remind you of your regular lubrication and maintenance program, the accompanying chart will tell you at a glance the items that need service on a "mileage" and "time interval" basis. As previously mentioned, some of the items will need adjustment according to your driving habits and geographical location. Stick to it and your car will always be in top condition and serve you reliably. ♣

3. Oiling Distributor Shaft

4. Lubing Latch

5. Cleaning Engine

Tuning Your Engine

Ever since somebody coined the word "tune-up" it has been used and abused so much that nobody really knows what it means anymore. Probably the main reason is that nobody knew what the guy meant when he conceived the term in the first place. If we ever meet him, we will certainly ask.

Because a tune-up varies so much, depending upon what garage or what mechanic is doing the work, we can only tell you what we feel a tune-up should include. We have known garages that included a check of the brake fluid and a windshield cleaning in their regular tune-up procedure. There's certainly nothing wrong with that, but what we will deal with here are just the bare necessities in what we consider a basic tune-up.

AIR CLEANER

Much of a tune-up involves using your naked eye to look for parts that are out of adjustment, worn out, or just plain dirty. For instance, the first thing that is usually done in any tune-up is to remove the air cleaner. We do this for a couple of reasons. The most obvious is to get the cleaner out of the way so we can work on the engine. The other is to examine the filters that are inside it to see if they are in need of replacement.

If your car has the type of filter that traps dirt because it is moistened with oil, then all you have to do is wash it out in solvent, put some clean oil on it, and it's ready to go back on the car. Incidentally, if you should be washing any of the old-fashioned air cleaners that have a large silencing chamber, do not submerge them in a bucket of solvent, because the solvent will run inside the silencing chamber where you can't pour it out. It will take about two weeks to evaporate out of there, and all during that time your car will be running rich because of the solvent fumes.

Many cars today use the dry type of air cleaner element made out of folded paper. You don't need any fancy testing rigs to determine if it is good. Just hold the element up to a naked light bulb and you can see if it's clean or not. On late-model cars, there is another filter inside the air cleaner can that stops oil fumes coming from the hose that connects to one of the rocker covers. That filter should be washed out and reinstalled.

GUM AND VARNISH SOLVENT

Removing the air cleaner exposes the top of the carburetor. So this is an excellent time, before you touch anything else on the engine, to feed some tune-up solvent through the carburetor with the engine running at a fast idle. This is a step that is seldom done in commercial garages because it smokes up the neighborhood and it takes a lot of time. However, it is probably one of the most vital parts of the whole tune-up. It must be done before the tune-up is started, not afterwards. The tune-up solvent does a good job of loosening up carbon accumulations in the cylinders. The carbon starts flying around and one of the first places it lands is on the spark plug. Sometimes the loosened carbon will foul the plugs so badly that they can't be cleaned and reused. So the only time to do it is when you know you are going to change the old plugs anyway.

When feeding the tune-up solvent through the carburetor the basic idea is to feed it as fast as you can without killing the engine. This amounts to a delicate balance between one hand holding the throttle and the other tipping the can. When you get down to the last part of the solvent, let it all run in so that the engine is flooded and dies. Then let the car sit a while so that the solvent will have a chance to work on the combustion chamber deposits. The final step is the blowout. Drive the car slowly and accelerate from zero to 30 at wide-open throttle a few times. Continue until all the smoke is gone and you can see out the rear window once again.

CRANKING VOLTAGE

Cranking voltage at the battery termi-

1. Tune-Up Parts

nal of the ignition coil should also be checked before you proceed any further with the tune-up. If, while making the cranking voltage test, you use a tachometer or your good ear to tell if the engine is being cranked at a normally fast cranking speed, then you have checked the battery, the generator, the starter, the ignition switch and the wiring in just a few seconds.

If that doesn't sound right to you, let's analyze it. When the cranking speed of the engine is normal, you know that the starter and the battery are good. If the coil is receiving at least 9 volts, you know that the wiring from the battery through the ignition switch to the coil must be good. How about the generator? Well, if the battery cranks the engine normally and supplies normal voltage to

the coil, it must be adequately charged. And if it is charged, it follows that the generator has to be okay.

The cranking voltage test is done with a remote starter button which is connected to a terminal on the starter solenoid so that you can operate the starter directly from the battery. On some cars, you can't reach the solenoid, so the way to do it is to locate the wire that runs from the solenoid to a plug on the firewall and puncture its insulation with an ice pick. When the ice pick touches the wiring within, electrical contact is made and the remote starter wire can be connected to the pick. The procedure varies with the make of car. If you have trouble and can't seem to get the starter to work with a remote starter button, the easy way to do it is to just sit in the car and

use the normal ignition switch. Position your voltmeter so that you can see it through the windshield during cranking, and the job's done. Remember that the voltmeter goes to the battery terminal of the coil, not to the distributor side. To keep the car from starting so that the engine will crank long enough to get a good reading on the voltmeter, you should pull the wire out of the center tower of the distributor cap and use a short jumper lead to ground it to the engine. Another way of keeping the engine from starting is to either disconnect or ground the wire to the points. Be very careful you don't ground the wrong wire, or you will burn up the ignition switch, and maybe the car, too.

The battery only puts out a little over 9 volts during cranking because of a phe-

1. Parts used in most basic tune-ups include air and fuel filters, spark plugs, point set and condenser, and battery terminal protectors.

2. Cleaning battery posts is a breeze with this dual-purpose tool by Snap-On. Leading edge on heavy gauge snap ring does the trick nicely.

3. With its six metal blades embedded in plastic, Snap-On battery tool has wide edge on older wire brush terminal cleaner; this one really does the job quickly and cleanly.

4. California has always required different smog equipment from the rest of the country—consequently, tuning specs are also different. To prevent any confusion and improper tuning, Detroit has posted a tune-up decal in every engine compartment. The practice began with most '68 models and has continued since.

5. A dirty air cleaner element can cut your gas mileage considerably. You can check the condition of one by shining a droplight through the back. If light won't go through, then you should replace the element.

6. If you have access to an air hose you can blow (from the inside) some of the loose dirt out of an air cleaner and recheck with droplight.

2. Cleaning Battery Posts

3. Cleaning Cable Ends

4. Emission Control Plate

5. Checking Paper Air Cleaner

6. Cleaning Dry-Type Element

Tuning Your Engine

nomenon known as voltage fall-off. Were you ever in an old house where the lights used to dim every time the refrigerator went on? A similar thing happens when the battery is operating the starter. A tremendous amount of current is flowing out of the battery, which causes the battery voltage to drop. We expect a certain amount of voltage fall-off, so long as it's not too much. If the voltage falls off too much, we know that the battery is weak or worn out, or there's a bad cable connection, etc. We check the voltage at the battery terminal of the coil because that is the most important point. If you don't have sufficient voltage there, you don't get any spark.

If you don't get at least 9 volts at the coil during cranking, the first thing to check is the battery. A 12-volt battery should put out approximately 12.6 volts when it's not running anything. If it only puts out an even 12 volts, it is low. If you don't have a voltmeter, you can't very well check cranking voltage, but you can listen to the cranking speed, and that will tell you quite a bit in itself.

TUNE-UP EQUIPMENT

On most cars, a tune-up is only necessary once a year or every 12,000 miles. However, beginning with the 1975 models, some changes were made. All domestic cars were equipped with high-energy, pointless ignitions, and smaller filler tubes permit the use of only unleaded gas. Lead deposits foul and erode spark plugs; without the lead, plugs are good for 22,500 miles. Eliminating the breaker points and condenser has reduced the ignition tune-up to merely a plug change and a timing check. So it's hard to justify purchase of a voltmeter or other tune-up equipment if you are only going to use it once a year. However, with the cost of labor skyrocketing these days, you will find that buying a tune-up in a garage will cost you more than buying all your own tune-up equipment and parts and doing the job yourself.

Only a few pieces of equipment are necessary in order to do a tune-up. It would be nice if you had a timing light, a tachometer, a dwell meter, a remote start button and a compression gauge; however, the only one that you really need is the timing light. Sure, it is possible to set timing statically, but on a modern engine there is too much chance for error, and the recommended way is to use a light while the engine is running. The tachometer you can do without, because you can pay a garage man a couple of dollars to set the idle speed for you. The dwell meter is not necessary if you have a specification book which will tell you what the point gap should be, and you can set that with a feeler gauge. The remote start button, as we have already pointed out, can be eliminated by utilizing the ignition key switch on the instrument panel.

1. Pulling PCV Valve

2. Checking PCV Valve

3. Checking Compression

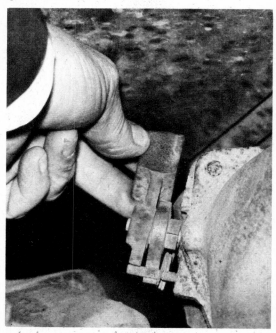

4. Heat Riser Valve

You may feel that it is absolutely necessary to take a compression check, but it isn't. A garage man takes a compression check only because he has to guarantee his work. He knows that tuning a car with poor compression is not done because the car should first have a ring and valve job. But even the worst old clunker will run better if it has the timing set, points gapped correctly, and the spark plugs either cleaned or replaced.

When you do the tune-up yourself, you don't have to guarantee it to anyone. You just want your car to run better and it will not matter what the compression is. Taking a compression check on your own car will, in many cases, just make you feel bad, because you'll find out some disappointing news that you didn't know before. However, if you are buying a car or checking out somebody else's car, then by all means make a compression check because it will tell you the condition of the engine.

TIMING LIGHT TESTS

If you do have a certain amount of equipment, you should use it to take measurements before you start doing the tune-up so that you will have some basis for making adjustments afterwards. It is entirely possible that the ignition timing or the idle speed is not set to stock specifications. Maybe the idle speed is set a little faster so the engine won't die. Or maybe the timing is retarded a little to take care of cheaper gas, or

1. The PCV valve in your rocker cover or carburetor needs to be removed and checked once or twice each year for clogging.

2. By shaking the smog valve, you can hear if the inner element is free. If it rattles, it's okay; if it doesn't, it's clogged and should be replaced with a new one.

3. Before doing a tune-up, it may be a good idea to make a compression check. It will tell you if there are any major engine problems such as worn rings or valves.

4. If your car has a heat riser between the exhaust manifold and the exhaust pipe, check to see if it's operating freely and not frozen with carbon or rust. If frozen, spray it with some solvent or choke cleaner until it's working again.

5. There's usually a fuel filter in the gas line or carburetor that should be replaced periodically. Those located within the carburetor are either paper—like this one—or solid; but both types are backed by a spring so remove the nut slowly. When replacing the bronze filter, make sure the small section of the cone is facing out.

6. If you get a lot of black smoke from your tailpipe in the morning, maybe your choke is sticking. Spray lubricant for freeing chokes is available in spray or squirt cans.

7. Pouring a little cleaner into the carburetor while the engine is running helps to clean out the motor by dissolving carbon and deposits.

5. Fuel Line Filter

6. Freeing Choke

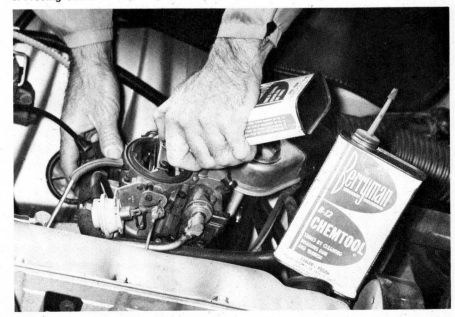

7. Blowing Out Carbon Deposits

Tuning Your Engine

advanced a little to give more acceleration. If you don't check timing and idle speed before you start fiddling with the distributor, there is no way—after you get the engine running again—that you can get it back to where it was.

Suppose you check an engine that has the ignition timing set 4° advanced from where it is supposed to be. If it runs well, and it doesn't ping, you'd better leave it there because the last guy who set it probably knew what he was doing. Any time you touch the points you automatically change the ignition timing. So if you dive right in to replace them without checking the timing first, you may find that you are experimenting for three weeks afterwards trying to get the timing set so that it gives the performance you had before you changed the points.

With a timing light, you can also check the vacuum and centrifugal advance curves in the distributor very easily. With everything hooked up normally, all you have to do is run the engine up slowly to about 2000 rpm and watch the timing marks move on the front pulley as you shine the timing light on them. As you open the throttle to run the speed up, the vacuum advance will change the position of the marks, and you can see what's happening right on the front pulley. Pull the vacuum advance line off the distributor and then you can check the centrifugal advance. Of course, you are not accurately measuring the advance when you are doing this, but at least you can get an indication that both vacuum and centrifugal advance are working to some degree.

There are timing lights on the market that have an adjustable electronic delay. With them you can actually measure the amount of advance you are getting on the front pulley, because turning the little knob on the light will bring the marks back in line with each other. It's a slick unit but it's very expensive and not too practical for home use. Your best bet is to check it as we have suggested and if you see the marks jump around, or if it appears that you're not getting enough advance, pull the distributor out and take it down to a garage so that they can set it on the distributor machine.

TUNE-UP PROCEDURE—REMOVING AND READING PLUGS

(Tune-up specifications for the last few model years are given in the back of this book. For older cars, consult your owner's manual, a factory shop manual, or, beginning with most '68 cars, there is a tune-up decal located somewhere in the engine compartment—Editor.)

To begin the tune-up, remove the PCV valve and shake it next to your ear; if it rattles, then it's okay; if not, replace it. If you want to take a compression test, then remove all of the spark plugs—but mark the wires first as to cylinder location to ensure proper replacement later. If you choose to skip the compression test, move on to the plug change. To prevent misplacement of wires, remove and replace only one plug at a time. As you remove them one by one, take a close look at each one and arrange the old plugs on the fender so that you can remember from which cylinder each originally came. By inspecting ("reading") the color and condition of each

plug, you can diagnose problems that may be occurring within the cylinder.

Reading plugs is not too difficult after you've looked at a few. If the plug's ceramic insulator and electrodes are covered with soft, wet, oily deposits, then the plug will probably misfire and the engine will perform poorly. This is caused by excessive oil reaching the combustion

1. Light tan or gray-colored ash deposits and some electrode wear are typical of a normal plug. If the porcelain is extremely white, the engine may be running too lean.

2. If the deposits are black and heavy, the trouble is probably that of excessive oil in the cylinders. However, it could also be caused by flooding of the carburetor.

3. Here's the best reason we know for blowing out an engine before you tune it up. That way, the splash fouling will occur on the old plugs.

4. You will see a broken insulator like this every once in a while. It is caused by severe detonation—or it could be caused by pressure on the center electrode when gapping plug.

5. These dry, fluffy black deposits may be caused by a rich mixture, which may in turn be caused by a clogged air cleaner or sticky choke. If only one plug is fouled, suspect the electrical circuit to that plug, the plug itself, or that cylinder.

6. Plugs do wear out. If there is a lot of wear on the electrodes and the insulator looks pitted, it's time to replace the plug.

1. Normal Plug

3. Splash Fouling

4. Chipped Insulator

2. Oil-Fouled Plug

5. Carbon-Fouled Plug

6. Worn-out Plug

chamber due to worn piston rings, worn valve guides, too much oil in the oil pan or a clogged crankcase vent. The cause should be determined and the problem corrected—but, in the meantime, a plug that's one step hotter will fire through some of the deposits. If the firing end is covered with dry, fluffy black carbon deposits, then: the plug is too cold; the

7. Flaky, white or yellow deposit is caused by scavenger additives in the gasoline. These deposits will come off easily in a plug cleaner.

8. A plug has to get pretty hot to melt the electrodes like this. It could be caused by lean mixture, advanced timing or even crossfire from another spark plug wire.

9. These electrodes have been hot, but not enough to melt. The plug could be the wrong heat range—or the trouble could be caused by overly advanced timing or low-octane fuel.

10. Everything's slightly bent out of shape here because of a nut or washer bouncing around in the cylinder. Changing the plug will not solve the problem until the foreign matter is removed from the engine.

11. Some plier-type gapping tools will bend the side electrode like this, which doesn't necessarily ruin the plug, but the same tools also put pressure on the center electrode. This pressure may push the center electrode right out of the plug.

12. Most spark plug gap gauges have an electrode bender as part of the tool, to adjust the gap to specs by bending the side electrode.

choke hasn't been opening completely; the carburetor mixture is overly rich; the plugs aren't getting enough voltage to fire the mixture; the condenser in the distributor is weak; or the valves are sticking.

In some cases, raw fuel can be seen and smelled on the plug—a situation caused by a clogged needle valve in the carburetor or a sticking or improperly adjusted float level. If the electrodes are burned away or the insulator tip is blistered or deformed, then you've got a dangerous situation. These are signs of initial pre-ignition and if corrected at that point, then engine damage may be avoided. It's caused by excessive spark advance, a plug that's hotter than specified, or using fuel that's inferior or too low in octane for the compression ratio of your engine. High-compression engines need high-octane gas; thus, any engine having 10.0:1 compression or more is likely to ping on today's low-octane gas. For this reason, a high-compression engine should be protected from pre-ignition by retarding the ignition timing a few degrees under the original specification.

A kind of dull white to light brown on the plug porcelain is fine—but this depends a lot on the year of the car. Late-model cars run so lean that their spark plugs will be just about pure white almost any time you look at them. Modern combustion chambers can run the plugs that white because the plug position in the cylinder is such that the incoming fuel keeps it from burning up. Unless you have a problem with plug fouling, you should use the same heat range plug that came in the engine, or its equivalent in another maker's line.

We might mention here about the "rebuilt" spark plugs that you see in grocery stores, drug stores and just about every place except where they sell auto parts. Most of those plugs say "rebuilt" on the package. We don't know what their definition of rebuilt is, but we do know that the rebuilding we have observed consisted only of sandblasting the plugs to clean them. The sandblaster that they use is extremely powerful, much more so than you would find in any service station or auto repair shop. We have used the rebuilt plugs and found in our own experience that they foul much quicker than new or normally sandblasted plugs. Apparently, sandblasters create microscopic craters in the porcelain and, naturally, these craters will collect the fouling deposits that the smooth surface of a new plug won't.

One reason that the rebuilt plugs have prospered is the difficulty of getting anybody to clean spark plugs these days. Most service stations and garages have a plug cleaner somewhere off in the corner that is either broken or hasn't been used for 15 years. There is nothing wrong with cleaning plugs in a normal sandblast cleaner. If they will come clean, the center electrode should be filed to a sharp edge, the gap reset, and they can then be used over again. If the porcelains will not come clean because of splash fouling or other deposits that won't come off, the plugs should be thrown away.

INSTALLING PLUGS

As you install the new plugs, set the electrode gap with the proper tool and make sure the electrodes are aligned; if not, carefully bend the side electrode

7. Scavenger Deposits

8. Pre-Ignition Damage

9. Burned Electrodes

10. Mechanical Damage

11. Bent Side Electrode

12. Bending Side Electrode

Tuning Your Engine

until they are. Never bend the electrode by tapping or hitting it. That procedure just might crack the porcelain and ruin a good plug. Once the gaps are set to specifications (usually .035-in. with conventional ignitions and .060-in. on some breakerless), put a drop of engine oil on the threads of each plug before threading them home. If you ignored our earlier suggestion and removed all the plugs at once, then you've got a small problem—the wires are all messed up and you have no idea which one goes where. If you can find the firing order of your engine, the solution is quite simple. The firing order—the sequence in which the cylinders receive spark—is usually cast on the intake manifold or available from your local repair shop. You can usually find at least one plug wire that you know is on the right plug. Trace that wire back to the cap and then follow the firing order around the cap in the direction that the rotor revolves. This will tell you to which spark plug each wire should go. On most distributor caps, No. 1 is marked so that you have a starting point for your firing order.

Once the plug wires are in place, inspect them for condition. Heat and grease can deteriorate the insulation and make it brittle, causing it to crack and break. Pulling on the wire rather than its boot will remove it from the plug quickly but it can also break the wire internally, enlarge existing cracks and greatly increase resistance. Increased resistance lowers voltage to the plugs; the result is incomplete combustion, misfire, and a generally poor-running, gas-guzzling engine. If the wires still feel flexible and aren't visibly cracked, clean them of any grease (this should be done periodically). If they're obviously cracked or broken, replace them with a quality, brand-name silicone suppression wire.

INSTALLING POINTS

Now it's time to remove the old breaker points and install new ones. However, if your car is a domestic and a 1975 model or newer, then it has no points or condenser because it's equipped with a transistorized breakerless ignition. Since there are no points to wear, timing should not change—although it's a good idea to check it from time to time anyway. This higher voltage ignition—and especially the use of unleaded fuel—has extended plug life to 22,500 miles; therefore, ignition tune-ups on these cars involve nothing more than a plug change, inspection and maintenance of advance units, a timing check and an inspection of the distributor cap and rotor for cracks or burning. Unlike conventional ignitions, there is no provision for dwell adjustment. In fact, merely connecting a tach/dwell meter to a breakerless distributor may damage the meter.

For those cars having points, we recommend that you put the points in without removing the distributor from the car. You may have to crawl over the fender and lean on top of the sharp points of the engine in a very uncomfortable position, but installing points in the car will get you into a lot less trouble

than pulling the distributor and then trying to get the thing properly timed when you put it back in. In a commercial garage it's a different proposition. They want to check the vacuum and centrifugal advance curves, so they may pull the unit and test-run it on their machine.

You can tell a lot about the vacuum and centrifugal advance difficulties you may be having just by looking at the distributor parts. If you have a Delco distributor with the weights up on top where they are easily seen, check to see if the weights move freely back and forth and that the springs are not rusty or broken. You can check the vacuum advance with a Mity-Vac suction pump while watching to see if the breaker plate moves back and forth. If it doesn't, there's a hole somewhere and you'd better get a new vacuum advance unit.

New points are usually lined up fairly well, and there are thousands of mechanics all over the country who don't even look at them before they put them in. But it's a good idea to check the points' alignment because they will last a lot longer if you do. The idea is to have the point faces meet squarely so that, in the case of conventional points, the only contact is exactly in the center. If you have the points with the hole in the middle, then the contact is a full circle rath-

1. When cleaning and gapping old plugs, you should pull back the side electrode so you can get a thin file in to file the center electrode flat.

2. A flat feeler gauge may throw your gapping off, so the best gapper for plugs is the round wire type.

3. When reinstalling plugs in the engine, a short piece of rubber hose can be used to hold the plug while you start it into the threads. It's safer than starting them with wrench.

4. If the spark plug ends of your secondary ignition wires are loose on the plugs, you can get a better connection by tightening the ends with needle-nose pliers.

5. A small wire brush like this K-D #103 is useful in a tune-up for cleaning the ends of your spark plug cables and the terminals in your distributor cap.

6. Some tuners may possibly miss the corrosion buildup inside distributor cap terminals. This tool has wire brush on end for cleaning these hard-to-get-at places.

7. The inside of your distributor cap should be checked carefully for corrosion on the terminals or any carbon "tracks" around cracks.

1. Filing Center Electrode

2. Round Wire Plug Gapper

3. Hose for Starting Plugs

er than a single point. Point alignment can be checked by looking through the points parallel to their surfaces with a white card held behind them. You can easily see if they are twisted at all. To line them up, bend only the stationary point until the contact faces meet squarely.

The design of the points will determine whether you do point alignment before the points are put in the distributor or afterwards. On a General Motors V-8, the point assembly is made in one piece so you can do the alignment while you're holding the points in your hand. Some other cars have the points in two pieces with the pivot post mounted on the distributor breaker plate. To align those points you have to have them mounted on the breaker plate in their normal position before attempting to bend the stationary point. You can use ordinary pliers to bend the stationary point, but you might slip and ruin something. A special tool with a hook end is much easier to use.

Handling the points may get grease on the contact surfaces, or they may be coated with a factory preservative. To ensure a clean surface, wipe the contacts with carbon tet or a grease-removing solvent before installing them.

If you haven't put points in a distributor before, move very slowly when removing the old points. You want to get the new ones back in exactly the same position with all the screws in the same place and all the leads positioned exactly where they were before. There's a lot of movement that goes on underneath the distributor cap. If everything isn't in the right place, things can get all tangled up, and then it's no spark.

What you do with the points after they are installed will depend upon your make of car. In a Delco distributor with an Allen head set screw you don't do anything because the point gap will be set after the engine is running. Most other cars require that you use a feeler gauge to set the actual point gap in thousandths of an inch. When you check the gap, turn the ignition key until the rubbing block of the points contacts the high spot on one of the cam lobes. When it does, the points will open. If you feel like checking things out, measure the point gap on several cam lobes. You'll find that it varies a couple of thousandths. Nothing's perfect these days.

To get the cam lobe exactly under the point rubbing block, you can "bump" the engine with a remote starter button or the ignition key. The easiest and most accurate way is to loosen the distributor hold-down bolt and turn the body of the distributor either way until you get what you want. After the gap is set, move the distributor body back where it was, so that the engine will start easily.

DISTRIBUTOR MAINTENANCE

Many distributors have a small felt wick in the upper center of the shaft. To keep the centrifugal advance operating smoothly, lubricate it by adding a few drops of oil to the wick at every tune-up. GM's V-8 distributor has its advance weights above the breaker plate so there is no oil wick. On those distributors, carefully remove the springs—but re-

4. Tightening Plug Cables

5. Cleaning Cable Ends

6. Cleaning Distributor Terminals

7. Inspecting Cap

Tuning Your Engine

member which one went where. Remove the weights, lightly sand the underside, clean them with solvent and oil them lightly before installing. A distributor cam lubricator is also found on most Delco distributors. On 6-cylinders, it is round, on V-8's, rectangular. The pre-lubricated wick should touch the cam lightly, and once every 12,000 miles it should be rotated so that the fresh side can be used. At 24,000 miles it must be replaced. Never lubricate the wick—but on those distributors without them, lightly coat the cam and the breaker point rubbing block with high-temperature ignition grease. These measures protect the cam and the rubbing block from the eroding effects of friction.

Before installing the cap, examine it as well as the rotor for cracks. Very often undetected damage at these points can cause trouble not apparent in circuit test procedures.

HEAT RISER AND BATTERY

With the plugs in, the points set and the wires on, the engine is almost all put together—but you're not ready to start it up yet. A good tune-up involves more than just points and plugs. Somewhere in the exhaust manifold you may find a small flapper valve. It's called the heat riser valve and it's responsible for giving good warm-up when you first start your car. The heat riser valve has a spring to hold it in the closed position. It is forced open by exhaust gas pressure when the engine is running at high rpm. The valve should move easily when you touch it and the spring should return it to the closed position when you let go.

When the heat riser valve is closed, the exhaust gases are blocked and detoured through a passageway underneath the carburetor before they can exit through the exhaust system to the muffler. Some cars (mostly Fords) do not have a heat riser valve. They get heat to the manifold by circulating radiator water through a passageway under the carburetor. Late-model cars using temperature controlled air cleaners do not have the valves either; but they do have a flapper valve in the air cleaner snout that gives the engine hot air off the exhaust manifold or cool air from under the hood, depending on the temperature. A quick check for the flapper valve is to move it with your finger to see if it's free. If you want to check it out thoroughly, you can watch it move as the engine warms up.

Cleaning battery terminals is also part of the basic tune-up. You should remove them from the posts, scrape away any corrosion that you find, lightly grease the

1. Installing Points

2. Point Aligning Tool

3. Lubricating Wick

ROTOR

LOCATOR (ROUND)

LOCATOR (SQUARE)

CENTRIFUGAL ADVANCE MECHANISM

CAM LUBRICATOR

CAM LUBRICATOR REPLACEMENT

RETAINER

WICK

ADJUST SQUARELY AND JUST TOUCHING LOBE OF CAM

CAUTION! NEVER OIL CAM LUBRICATOR— REPLACE WICK WHEN NECESSARY

4. Lubricating Cam

5. Advance Weights

6. Greasing Distributor

1. Everyone can understand a spark plug replacement, but some amateur mechanics are wary of replacing their own points and condenser. Actually, it's really quite simple.

2. Proper alignment of the point arm is vital to a good tune, but you must remember you can only bend the stationary point—with pliers or a tool like this. The GM-type point like this can be adjusted off the car.

3. Six-cylinder Delco distributors (left) use a round lubricating wick to keep the cam greased. Delco's (GM) V-8 distributors (right) often use a rectangular wick. Both types are pre-lubricated at the factory and they should never be lubricated again. The wicks should be rotated to the clean side at 12,000 miles and replaced at 24,000.

4. If your distributor has no lubricating wick, lightly lubricate the cam with high-temperature ignition grease before installing points.

5. For proper operation of the Delco distributor, both the distributor cam and the centrifugal advance weights (the part being held up) should be cleaned of any rust or old grease.

6. Other points that should get the clean 'n' lube treatment include the pivots for the advance weights.

terminals with Vaseline to prevent future corrosion, and then make sure they are good and tight when they go back on. Using a solution of baking soda and water, wash away any acid deposits from the top of the battery. They are very conductive, and if allowed to build they can drain power from the battery.

The fuel filter is another part of the basic tune-up. It should definitely be replaced, whether it happens to be the in-line type or a little insert that goes in the carburetor inlet.

SETTING DWELL AND IGNITION TIMING

Now's the time to fire up the engine, but check your timing light hookup first. It's much less shocking if you hook it up with the engine dead. On Ford and Chrysler products you will already have set your point gap so you don't have to worry about that. But on a Delco-Remy distributor the point gap is set after the engine is running. If you have a dwell meter, set it to 30° and forget about it. But you don't need a dwell meter with a Delco distributor. Use an Allen wrench or one of the special little wrenches with a cable handle that you can buy in most auto parts stores. Lift the window in the side of the distributor cap and turn the Allen screw clockwise until the engine starts to misfire. Sometimes the engine

will just flat die without even giving a hint of misfiring. In either case back off counterclockwise ½-turn and your distributor point dwell will be set perfectly at 30°. Check it with a dwell meter if you want to, but it isn't necessary.

The procedure of backing off ½-turn has been standard for some time, but it has been found that spring tension can cause the screw to move a little later on, if the final turning movement is in a counterclockwise direction. The latest recommendations now call for backing off one turn and then going clockwise ½-turn so that the last movement is against the spring tension rather than backing away from it.

You must remember to adjust the initial timing after you adjust the dwell. Any change in point gap will change timing, so you must make your timing setting last. To check the timing, loosen the clamp bolt at the base of the distributor and turn the whole distributor while the engine is running to get the timing marks to line up under the timing light. The timing light must be hooked to No. 1 cylinder, of course, and the vacuum advance hose should be disconnected and plugged so that there is no chance for the vacuum to affect the initial timing. Remove and plug both hoses on cars with double chamber advance units. Chrysler products with solenoid controlled distributors should have both the vacuum hose and solenoid wire disconnected. Always remove the solenoid wire from the carburetor, not the distributor. This prevents accidental shorts and damaged wiring.

Also, you must have the engine speed at the specified idle, so allow the engine to warm up and the choke to open fully before making any adjustments. If the engine is idling too fast, the centrifugal advance will start to take over and your timing setting will be all out of whack. After the timing is set according to specifications, it's a good idea to make a final check of both centrifugal and vacuum advance by watching the timing marks under the timing light as you rev up the engine. Then the idle mixture and speed settings should be made according to the procedure described in the "Fuel System" chapter in this book. The carburetor should be checked to see if the choke is free. The choke unloader should be working properly. The fast idle

Tuning Your Engine

mechanism should give the right speed, and the anti-stall dashpot—if there is one—should keep the engine from stalling when you let the throttle snap shut. Your basic tune-up is now complete.

TESTING VACUUM

A tune-up can produce an amazing improvement in engine performance—but there are times when a tune-up isn't the complete cure. If the tuning was done correctly but the idle remains rough or the engine continues to misfire, then the problem lies deeper than points and plugs. A vacuum gauge can be a great help in locating the cause. Prior to 1970, a normal vacuum reading was 18-21 ins. of hg. vacuum at idle. Anything less meant that the valves were leaking, the rings were shot, or any of dozens of ailments. The only exceptions were high-performance cars with a lot of overlap in the valve timing. In 1970 and '71, ignition timing was retarded to reduce emissions; this caused vacuum to drop to 15 ins. of hg. on many cars. For '72, valve timing overlap was increased to control

nitrogen oxide emissions, and exhaust gas recirculation (EGR) became popular. As time passed, air/fuel mixtures became even leaner, engines ran hotter, timing was retarded even further and idles grew slower and rougher. The result is vacuum readings so low that you won't believe your gauge. Many '72's and '73's idle at 13 ins. of hg., and the '74's and '75's dropped to 11 and 12 ins. So if you check a late engine for idle vacuum and get a low reading, don't start tearing it down to do an overhaul until you check the vacuum above idle, or even while driving the car. You'll probably find that the vacuum is good at speeds above idle. If it isn't, make a compression test or cylinder leakage test to be sure the problem is really inside the engine before you tear it down.

HAVING A GARAGE TUNE-UP

Other tasks that are sometimes included at extra cost in the tune-up are: an overhaul of the carburetor; a check of alternator output and voltage settings; a battery breakdown test; a starter draw test; an oscilloscope test of the ignition; a check of air/fuel ratio at the tailpipe; an exhaust emissions test; and many

other tests until you end up having everything on the car replaced except the hood ornament. A lot of these tests are good. We personally feel that an oscilloscope is the greatest thing since sliced bread, and a check of air/fuel ratio or emissions is the only way to go. But when you are working on your own car you have to be practical. You can't go out and buy $500 worth of equipment when you only have one car to work on. So what do you do if you want those other tests made? You go to a garage . . . but which one?

The best way to narrow down the selection of garages and service stations is to ask friends and neighbors where they go for tune-ups and repairs and what they think of the work and service. The next step is to look over the work that was performed and see that it was done neatly and that the engine compartment was left clean. If they replaced the points, see if they cleaned the old grease off the distributor cam and then regreased it. It's a little thing, admittedly, but it's important if you want the job to be a lasting one.

In almost every town there is always talk of an "old-timer" who can tell exact-

1. Point Alignment

2. Delco Cap Latches

3. Distributor Testing

Gapping Points

ly what's the matter with your car as you turn into his driveway and before the turn indicator shuts off. In some cases this is true—though maybe not quite that fast. This fellow is the type who grew up with automobiles and never worked at anything else. He's been up against every problem there ever was and knows every part inside out—mainly because in his time he has had to rebuild the parts himself. There was no such thing as inexpensive rebuilt parts, and to buy a new part was costly. And certainly, there was no electronic tune-up equipment. This type of person is fading out of the picture. Age, and the fact that labor is so expensive, make it cheaper to install a rebuilt or new part instead of fixing the old existing one.

The modern garage or repair shop of today is based on its mechanics' ability to tell what is wrong and replace the part. By this replacing of parts they can bring your car up to good running condition as usually defined by the term "factory specifications."

WHAT IS A DIAGNOSTIC CENTER?

A modern diagnostic center is a highly organized method of testing, checking and analyzing every safety and performance factor of a motor vehicle. All tests are conducted with sophisticated electronic and dynamic equipment and instruments with a degree of accuracy never before attained in the servicing of automobiles.

The most important service a diagnostic center provides is to take the guesswork out of locating vehicle malfunctions. In difficult cases it can save you many more times the cost of the diagnosis. Basically, it tests a car through its complete speed and power range while it is hooked up to sensitive electronic gear. The chassis dynamometer can accurately simulate any type of road operating condition—such as acceleration, cruise, high speed and uphill pull. For instance, if you have a complaint of "missing" at 50 mph or poor acceleration, the trouble can be diagnosed accurately and quickly right in the shop and under almost the same conditions you experienced while driving your car on the road. An additional benefit of chassis

1. Getting the right alignment on the points assures that the contact pattern will be centered.

2. When installing the distributor cap, make sure that it is centered. The latches must engage the proper slots, as on this Delco.

3. Garages and tune-up shops use sophisticated gear for checking and adjusting distributors, but you can set points with just hand tools and a clean feeler gauge.

4. A portable instrument very handy for on-the-car testing is a tach and dwell meter, useful for setting idle and checking distributor dwell angle.

5. General Motors V-8 distributors from 1957 up have a "window" (arrow) through which points can be adjusted while the engine is running.

4. Portable Tach/Dwell Meter

5. GM Distributor "Window"

Tuning Your Engine

dynamometer operation is that the complete driveline of the vehicle can be tested without leaving the shop. This includes clutch, transmission (manual or automatic) and differential.

Don't get the idea that a diagnostic center is the same as a dyno tuning shop. Much of the equipment is similar and some of the tests are the same, but the big difference is in the work performed and the end results. The function of a diagnostic center is to work to factory specifications and nothing more. Diagnostic center equipment tests and evaluates the performance of your car's engine and tells the operator what work needs to be done to return your car to a satisfactory operating condition as established by the manufacturer. In other words, plugs (gap and heat range), points (gap and dwell), coil, timing, advance, etc. are all set and checked for proper operation according to factory specifications. Nothing is altered internally, nor is there any deviation from the program of testing. As a rule, when this close-tolerance tune-up work is performed by a diagnostic center, you should notice an improvement in performance, mainly because most cars operate at a minimal level.

Diagnostic operations have been the center of considerable controversy since they started popping up everywhere. Small, independent garage owners will tell you that a diagnostic center is a production line designed to sell parts and services, and that frequently the work done is not really needed at all.

Diagnostic center personnel, in turn, say that a small, independent garage does not have a dynamometer and other equipment necessary to make a complete test of your car.

The new car dealer then gets into the act by claiming that he is the only one who is in close touch with the factory, so he is therefore the only one who knows how your car should run.

All of these factions are correct to a degree. Actually, it really doesn't matter where you take your car for service. What does matter is the honesty, capability and knowledge of the people who work on your car, regardless of what type of establishment they work in. If you find a place that keeps your car in good condition to your satisfaction, then stick with it, whether it happens to be a service station, an independent garage, a new car dealer or a million-dollar diagnostic center.

ELECTRONIC IGNITIONS

Beginning in 1975, all U.S. cars have been equipped with breakerless electronic ignitions. This is a case where the strict federal emissions laws have resulted in some benefit to the consumer other than reduced pollution. The Detroit automakers would probably have come around to such advanced ignition systems eventually, but the emissions standards pushed up their timetable by about 10 years. Chrysler had begun the movement two years earlier, but it was the 1975 requirement that catalytic conver-

1. DISTRIBUTOR CAP
2. ROTOR
3. DUST SHIELD
4. TRIGGER WHEEL
5. FELT PAD
6. SENSOR ASSEMBLY
7. SHAFT ASSEMBLY
8. HOUSING
9. VACUUM CONTROL
10. SHIM
11. DRIVE GEAR
12. PIN

1. American Motors' BID Ignition

ers be installed that forced everyone else to follow suit.

When an engine misfires, raw, unburned fuel goes through the exhaust

1. Breakerless magnetic-pickup systems are now used on all makes of cars. This is an exploded view of the BID system used by American Motors.

2. GM's High-Energy Ignition system looks unlike any other, though it is a magnetic unit also. This '76 Cadillac distributor differs in that the coil is mounted inside the cap. The black box module, shrunk in size by modern electronics, now fits where the condenser used to be located.

3. There are few adjustments that you can make to your new electronic ignition without complicated test equipment. The air gap between the central reluctor and the magnetic pickup can be checked with a brass feeler gauge, but by design, such systems do not require adjustments.

4. A pair of insulated pliers made specifically for pulling plug wires is necessary to handle the vulnerable silicone-insulated wires and boots used on today's electronic ignitions.

system. Since contact with this fuel would be disastrous to the expensive catalytic converter, a way had to be developed to make engines run as independent of maintenance as possible.

Though the factory electronic units go by different names, they are all the same in principle. Your familiar ignition points, controlled by a distributor cam, have been replaced by a triggering device. The triggering unit, either a magnetic type or a photocell type, simply signals the "black box" module when to shut off juice to the coil. This collapses the magnetic field in the coil and sends high-voltage current to the spark plugs. Most of these systems utilize higher secondary voltages and wider spark plug gaps to keep the plugs firing cleaner and longer under the harsh combustion chamber conditions created by today's lean air/fuel mixtures.

Since these triggering devices do not actually touch the high voltage, they do not deteriorate the way points do, and they should require no adjustment. Most of them do have an .008-in. air gap setting, but this should need no adjustment unless the distributor is torn down for a rebuild. Even then, the air gap must be set with a *non-magnetic* (brass) feeler

gauge in order not to disturb the magnetic pickup.

There is little for a home mechanic to adjust on these systems, and even most troubleshooting can only be done with factory electronic testers. Dwell is controlled by the black box and is not adjustable, but you can set your initial timing and check the vacuum advance unit as previously described.

Be aware that these high-energy systems utilize special plug wires, too. Larger 8mm secondary wires are used, along with high-temperature silicone insulation. These are excellent wires, but they require special attention. The silicone insulation can withstand lots of under-hood heat, but it can also stretch completely out of shape when you pull off a wire to change plugs. Grasp these wires only by the silicone boot with an insulated set of plug-wire pliers, and remove them with a twist-and-pull action. Otherwise you may separate the interior connector. When reinstalling a silicone wire, smear a little silicone grease or spray inside the boot to make future removals easier. Except for spark plug changes, the standard tune-up has almost disappeared! When problems do crop up, take the car to your dealer for testing. ♦

2. GM's High-Energy Ignition

Labels: COVER, COIL, #1 TERMINAL, CAP, ROTOR, NOTCH ENGAGES TAB, MODULE, POLE PIECE, PICK-UP COIL

3. Checking Air Gap

Labels: PICK-UP COIL ADJUSTMENT, AIR GAP, NON-MAGNETIC FEELER GAUGE

TWIST & PULL

4. Removing Silicone Secondary Wires

Understanding Emission Control Systems

During the past decade, the automobile has become a political football. It seems that almost everyone who has some kind of axe to grind has taken up the cudgel against the private automobile. Safety experts condemn it, so the government moves with a heavy hand into automotive design. Pollution authorities blame it for the ever-increasing black cloud that hangs ominously over the nation's urban areas, and so the government dictates what the engine can discharge into the atmosphere. Motorists grumble about lack of power, poor operation and the increasing cost of the fuel required to run each new model year's engines.

While the whole world seems to have gone mad, the smog problem also seems to worsen every year despite everything that's being done to control it. Smog first started in Los Angeles, but now there's some eye irritation in all large (and many small) cities in the United States. It affects our breathing and can even cause death. Scientists tell us that the country loses millions of dollars every year from damage to plants and farm animals caused by smog. Whether you agree with their analysis that a photochemical reaction in sunlight between hydrocarbons and oxides of nitrogen that come out of the automobile crankcase and exhaust pipe is the main cause of smog (and many don't), the important thing is that laws have been passed to control such emissions from cars.

The average driver, who never looks under the hood of his/her car, isn't too concerned about the matter, because he/she leaves such problems up to a mechanic. But the hot rodder and those who work on their own cars must study the law, understand it and abide by it. The days when engine modifications could be freely made are gone forever. Today you must know the federal and state laws that apply to you and you must also comply with them. If you make an engine modification that's illegal, you can be fined or denied a renewal of the license plates or tabs for your car.

Since all this smog business began in California, let's examine the situation in that state. If you live outside California, don't make the mistake of thinking that the same thing can't happen in your state. It can and probably will sooner or later, even if you have never shed a smog-caused tear or seen the kind of ugly brown haze that settles across the Los Angeles basin. Smog is now a national problem, and the present tight California emissions levels will soon become Federal standards applicable to all states.

THE CRANKCASE

Most people think that the only thing that blows out of an automobile crankcase breather is oil smoke, but that's not quite true. The hydrocarbons that cause smog are basically unburned gasoline and are emitted from the breather as well as from the car's tailpipe. The breather is a surprisingly big contributor; approximately 25% of the unburned hydrocarbons emitted by an uncontrolled vehicle come from the breather. So let's take a look at crankcase devices to begin with. Then we'll get into exhaust controls proper.

No piston ring ever manufactured provides a positive seal between the piston and the cylinder wall; they all leak, even when brand-new. Prove it to yourself by screwing an ordinary pressure gauge (without the valve) into the spark plug hole. Crank the engine over until the piston is at TDC at the end of the compression stroke and stop. The pressure rises as the piston goes up, reaching a maximum at the top of the stroke. Now watch the pressure gauge after the piston stops and you'll see that it only takes a few seconds for the pressure to leak away. Where does it go? Between the cylinder wall and the rings, that's where. When the engine is running, this leakage takes place fast enough to build up pressure in the crankcase.

It happens because the combustion in the chamber doesn't burn all of the fuel; most of the time, it only burns that which is atomized. The remainder clings to the combustion chamber sides and cylinder walls, and so it doesn't burn. More specifically, the fuel gets into that small space between the top of the piston and the cylinder wall.

When combustion takes place, the force of the burning gases pushes the piston down to make everything work, but that same force also pushes the unburned fuel down past the rings and into the crankcase. A scientific analysis of these blowby gases has found them to

1. Closed-Crankcase System

1. Hose connecting air cleaner to rocker cover identifies this as a closed-crankcase ventilation system.

2. When the spring-loaded PCV valve is in the closed position (top), the engine is either off or in a low-vacuum situation. A high-vacuum situation, such as deceleration, pulls the valve against spring pressure (middle) and permits only limited flow through its orifice. Normal operation (bottom) allows flow both around and through the PCV valve.

be mainly unburned gasoline. Now, if this unburned gas were allowed to build up in the oil pan, it's easy to visualize what would happen. Before long, the oil would contain so much gasoline that it would no longer work as a lubricant. These blowby gases are also responsible for the varnish, sludge and acid that begin to eat at the bearing metal.

Automotive engineers recognized the problem long before the politicians discovered smog. The engineers tried to get the vapors out of the crankcase, but without too much success. To remove the vapors, almost every manufacturer settled on a road draft system. A tube connected to the crankcase extended below it so that the draft of air flowing underneath the car would create a slight suction at the end of the tube, drawing the vapors out of the crankcase. Naturally, there had to be a hole somewhere else on the engine where fresh air could enter. This hole was usually placed in the oil filler cap, along with some kind of an oil-wetted mesh inside the cap to keep dust out of the engine.

As long as the car was traveling fast enough to create a draft on the tube, the system worked pretty well. But at speeds below 25 mph, it didn't work at all, except to let the crankcase vent itself just from pressure of the gases. Delivery trucks and taxicabs might go for days without ever going over 25 mph, but they weren't alone; slow-moving boats had the same problem. So the problem is not really new. Positive crankcase ventilators of various types have been used for many years on vehicles operating under such special conditions.

CRANKCASE DEVICES

There are four types of crankcase devices, usually called PCV (Positive Crankcase Ventilation) systems. In all PCV systems, the road draft tube is either nonexistent or plugged. Type 1 (see illustrations) has a hose running from the crankcase through a valve to the intake manifold. Manifold vacuum sucks the gasoline vapors out of the crankcase and into the intake manifold, from which they are carried into the combustion chamber and burned. Fresh air enters through the oil filler cap.

The vacuum connection to the crankcase does not necessarily have to be directly on the crankcase; it can be practically anywhere on the engine, depending upon how the system was designed. On a V-8, for example, it is convenient to put the oil filler cap on one valve cover and the vacuum line on the other, since the valve covers are internally connected to the crankcase through the pushrod holes and oil drain holes in the block.

This arrangement will not work on an inline engine, however, since both oil filler and vacuum line would be connected to the same valve cover, unless the valve cover had an internal sealing plate which would force the vacuum line to pull vapors up from the crankcase. But regardless of where the vacuum line is located, its purpose is the same.

In a Type 1 system, the PCV valve can have either a fixed orifice or a spring-loaded plunger. Six-cylinder engines usually have the fixed orifice, and V-8's

have the plunger. If the engine has an intake manifold explosion or "backfire," the spring plus the force of the backfire closes the valve to prevent flame from getting into the crankcase and causing an explosion. But when the engine is under high-vacuum conditions such as idle or deceleration, the plunger moves against spring pressure to a minimum flow position. When the engine is under low vacuum or a partial load, the spring moves the plunger to a central position for maximum flow. Under wide-open throttle conditions with zero vacuum, the spring closes the valve, but the blowby gases are still sailing past the rings into the crankcase. The only place they can go under this condition is out through the oil filler cap. The same thing happens with the fixed-orifice system, since there's no vacuum to draw the gases into the intake manifold. So Type 1 is not perfect, because it allows the gases to escape into the air at zero vacuum.

Much the same as Type 1, the Type 2 system uses a special PCV valve and oil filler cap. The valve is a diaphragm type that regulates the amount of flow according to crankcase vacuum. If the crankcase is under pressure most of the time (as it would be on a worn engine), the valve opens up to take care of the blowby gases.

The Type 2 oil filler cap has a calibrated hole, large enough to let in fresh air but small enough to keep the crankcase under vacuum. Type 2 systems can be installed only on engines with a "tight" crankcase, because any leaks that allow air to enter the crankcase make the valve open wide, creating a condition that may lean the fuel mixture to a dangerous level.

Type 3 is the same kind of breather that home mechanics have used for years to cure a bad case of excessive crankcase smoking. It's simply a tube running from the crankcase to the air cleaner that lets fresh air enter the engine via the oil filler cap, pass through the tube into the carburetor and then enter the engine. Since blowby gases are mainly unburned gas, this system tends to richen the mixture, a fact that must be taken into account when designing the carburetor.

2. PCV Valve

Emission Control

Type 4 is a combination of Types 1 and 3. It's sometimes called a CCV (Closed Crankcase Ventilation) system. A sealed oil filler cap prevents crankcase gases from escaping under zero vacuum conditions as they would with Type 1. A tube from the air cleaner goes to the rocker cover, carrying fresh air down into the crankcase. From that point, blowby gases go through the hose into the PCV valve and into the manifold, just as in a Type 1 system.

When the Type 4 system is under zero vacuum, there's no suction on the crankcase (just as in Type 1), but the gases go from the rocker cover through the hose into the air cleaner, where they're drawn into the engine. If an engine has a lot of blowby, some of the gases will pass into the air cleaner at all times. The resulting oil fumes will ruin a dry paper element in a short time. The remedy here is either to fix the engine so that it doesn't have as much blowby or else change to an oil-wetted type of air cleaner element.

That's a brief rundown on the four types of crankcase devices. As you see, they aren't really difficult to understand. It's amazing that something this simple could have caused as great an uproar as it did among car owners and mechanics alike when Type 1 devices were factory-installed on all new cars sold in California in 1961. Problems arose at that time because few people understood just how the things worked, and there were some cases of poor design that aggravated matters. But the manufacturers cleared that up, and smog valves settled down to their job.

The uproar began all over again in 1963-64, when the new cars were equipped with a Type 4 system instead of Type 1, and devices were required by law on some used cars. The used-car situation was really bad, because mechanics and car owners didn't always follow instructions when installing the devices. One source of trouble was the installation of a crankcase device on a worn-out engine. In such a case, the device could cause plug fouling, along with other complications. But the law simply stated that such a device *must* be put on a car, with no provision for the fact that once it was installed, the car might not run properly. With a worn engine, the only solution was either to junk the car or do a ring and valve job, and the work often cost more than the car was worth.

But in all fairness, we must point out that if an engine is worn so badly that it won't accept *any* properly installed crankcase devices, then it must really be in terrible condition. There's no such thing in California as an exemption for worn engines. The car must comply with the law or it can't be operated on public streets. It's that simple. This may seem unfair, but in many states, a cracked windshield, bald tires or a brake pedal that goes down too far also disqualify a car from being driven until it's fixed, and fixing such a car may also cost more than it's worth.

Occasionally, a smog device is installed and the car runs rough, or a smog valve is changed and the car won't idle without shaking you off the seat. This can be due to installation of the wrong valve or system for that particular engine. You can't just make up a smog device from tubing, hose and a few other available parts. The entire device must be designed to fit and be approved for that particular engine by the proper authorities. It must also be installed exactly as the instructions indicate and the tune-up must be performed according to specifications or the engine won't perform, smog device or no smog device.

Do smog devices do any good? Well, they do a better job of crankcase ventilation than any road draft tube ever did, resulting in less oil contamination and a longer-lasting engine. Crankcase systems do cause a slight increase in intake

1. Types 1 & 2 PCV Systems

2. Type 3 PCV System

3. Type 4 PCV System

valve and intake manifold deposits, but the increase is so slight that authorities claim it won't hurt an engine.

Maintenance of the crankcase device is important. If the valve or hoses are allowed to plug up, damage to the engine can result. Some car manufacturers say that the system should be checked at every oil change; others recommend cleaning or replacing the valve once a year or every 12,000 miles. Checking the valve is simple. It should be clean, and the plunger should be free so that it rattles. If it's the fixed-orifice type, the hole should be clear of all obstructions, as should any hoses. Any flashback screens in the hoses should also be clean. The Type 2 valve is never cleaned, but a simple test by mouth suction will tell you if it's all right.

Different systems are found on models of different years. While there are exceptions, you'll usually find the following: California models 1961-63½ have factory-installed Type 1 systems. California models 1963½ and later have factory-installed Type 4 systems. Prior to 1963, cars sold outside California had no crankcase system; 1963-67 cars manufactured for sale outside California have Type 1 systems, and from 1968 on, the Type 4 system has been used on all cars nationwide.

If your car came with a crankcase device, then you must not remove it under penalty of law. If your car did not come equipped with a device, certain situations require that you install one. In most cases it depends upon the year and model of the car and where it's registered. California law states that models from 1955 to 1962 must have a crankcase device if their ownership is transferred to someone who lives in a county that requires the device. This doesn't mean that the new owner can then remove the device once the car has been registered under his name, either. After installation of a crankcase device, you're breaking the law if you take it off.

Some exceptions have been provided in the law for certain types of engines, but these are gradually being closed. Motorcycles are also exempted. We won't go into all of the technical details pertaining to California law here, as the idea is only to give you general knowledge of the California situation and what you might expect in your own state. Now let's examine exhaust controls and find out how they work.

EXHAUST CONTROL SYSTEMS

If hydrocarbons are mostly unburned gasoline, then it follows that when an engine is putting out hydrocarbons, it's running on a rich mixture. If the engine could be made to run on a leaner mixture, it wouldn't create nearly as much pollution as it does with the richer one. The first requirement is to find out whether a particular engine is running rich or lean. This is done with an exhaust gas analyzer, a test instrument manufactured by tune-up equipment makers. These analyzers have been around for many years now, and basically they all work the same way. They measure the thermal conductivity of the exhaust gas, which is directly related to how rich the engine is running.

The analyzer meter gives its reading in terms of an air/fuel ratio, which may range anywhere from 11:1 up to 15:1. If the meter read 12.5:1, it would mean that the engine was running on a mixture with an air/fuel ratio of 12½ lbs. of air to 1 lb. of fuel. A rich mixture is one that contains an excessive amount of fuel, and a lean mixture, of course, is just the reverse. Any reading near the 15:1 end of the scale is lean, and a reading on the 11:1 end of the scale is rich. Theoretically an engine could run as rich as 8:1, but it would carbon up quickly. The leanest mixture the analyzer will measure is 15:1.

Most engines without exhaust emission controls run about 12:1 at idle. At cruising speed, they usually lean out to somewhere around 14:1. The richer mixture at idle is necessary because some exhaust gas remains in the combustion chamber at idle speed. The idle problem is compounded if the engine is cold. A cold engine *really* needs a rich mixture, since gasoline vaporization is poor at low temperatures. Engines also run rich when decelerating, but under most other operating conditions, they run sufficiently lean to avoid the worst of the exhaust gas air pollution.

So the problem really narrows down to elimination of the rich mixture during cold starts, idling and deceleration. The auto manufacturers have devised several systems to do this within an ever-tightening network of laws, and we'll examine each system in turn.

AIR-INJECTION REACTORS

Three major gaseous pollutants in automobile exhaust have been identified as harmful to man: unburned hydrocarbons, carbon monoxide and oxides of nitrogen. A fourth pollutant, sulfur dioxide, is also present, but in extremely small amounts because of the negligible amount of sulfur in refined gasoline. Sulfur is more of a factor in diesel and industrial exhausts, which use fuels having a higher sulfur content.

Of the three pollutants, researchers recognized early that carbon monoxide (CO) was not an important contributor to the formation of smog, but that it must be controlled since it is a deadly poison which unfortunately does not betray its presence by any characteristic odor, color or taste. Of the remaining two pollutants, researchers in the '60's realized that unburned hydrocarbons (HC) contributed to smog and lead-containing vapors (from tetraethyl lead, the commonly used antiknock compound), but did not yet realize the importance of nitrogen oxides in photochemical smog formation. Consequently, after crankcase emissions had been eliminated, regulations then focused on CO and HC from exhausts.

Both of these pollutants are products of incomplete combustion; if all the hydrocarbons in fuel were completely oxidized during combustion, they would form carbon dioxide (CO_2) and water vapor (H_2O), both completely harmless. Therefore, reasoned the automakers, all that is necessary to meet the laws is to make sure that an overabundance of air mixes with the fuel. All this air could not be mixed with the fuel in the combustion chamber, since the mixture would then be too lean to burn properly, but it could

1. Types 1 and 2 crankcase systems (see text) allow air to enter the crankcase through the oil cap. They suck gasoline vapors into the intake manifold. Type 2 differs from Type 1 in having a small opening in the filler cap and in the use of a different PCV valve.

2. A Type 3 crankcase system sucks the vapors into the air cleaner rather than the intake manifold, but the principle is the same.

3. A Type 4 crankcase system is the same as Types 1 and 2 except that the oil cap pulls air from the air cleaner rather than straight from the atmosphere. Its advantage is that under low-vacuum conditions, the carburetor will suck in vapors which would otherwise escape through the filler cap.

4. A sophisticated air-injection system as used on engines in the early '70's employed a diverter valve and a check valve in its pressure line.

VACUUM SENSING LINE FROM INTAKE MANIFOLD

INJECTION PASSAGES TO EXHAUST PORTS

CHECK VALVE

DIVERTER VALVE
• DUMP VALVE
• PRESSURE-RELIEF VALVE

AIR PUMP
• INLET

4. Air-Injection System

Emission Control

be added *after* combustion in the exhaust manifold. Thus was born the air-injection system.

Essentially, this system is little more than an engine-driven pump that transfers air from outside the engine into the exhaust passage close to the exhaust valves. As the unburned fuel comes out of the exhaust valves, it combines with the fresh air provided by the pump and actually burns right in the exhaust passage. This means that the exhaust system gets considerably warmer than it would without the pump system, and it also means that there has to be a lot more ''plumbing'' to handle the increased air movement.

A benefit that theoretically should be derived from the warmer exhaust is longer muffler life, but this does not seem to have been realized in practice. And mechanics who work primarily on the small 4-cylinder engines used in Pintos, Vegas and the import cars will tell you that those with air-injection systems tend to have a much shorter exhaust valve life.

Let's take a look at exactly how an air-injection system works. Mounted at the front of the engine, the air pump is driven by the front pulley via a belt. All pumps draw their air from the engine compartment, but different manufacturers have taken different approaches. Some pumps have a filter on their air intake, while others receive the air from the clean side of the carburetor air cleaner.

The air travels (under pressure of about 1 psi) from the pump to a manifold on each cylinder head. Then it moves into the injection tubes that direct the air to the underside of each exhaust valve. Some engines, such as those on Buicks, use a passageway cast into the cylinder head instead of an external manifold. On Chevrolet V-8's, the injection tubes enter the exhaust manifold, and from there they go up the passageway to the exhaust valve.

All air-injection systems have check valves with a one-way diaphragm to prevent the hot exhaust gas from backing up to the pump in case of high exhaust-system pressure, pump belt failure or air hose rupture. All late models have a diverter valve that prevents excessive pressure in the system from causing a backfire. The diverter valve does this by sensing sudden increases in intake manifold vacuum. These cause the valve to open and vent air from the pump to the outside. A pressure relief valve is contained in the same housing. Early models used a bypass valve which performed the same function as a diverter valve. Pump relief was provided by a second valve in the air pump itself.

The diverter or anti-backfire valve works by sending the air output from the pump directly into the intake manifold instead of into the injector tubes. This leans out the excessively rich mixture that occurs just after you lift your foot off the gas pedal. If this mixture were not leaned out, it would explode in the exhaust system and produce a loud noise in the tailpipe.

Some anti-backfire valves dump atmospheric air into the intake manifold instead of pump air. Other types don't dump air into the manifold but allow the pump air to exhaust into the carburetor air cleaner instead. This effectively cancels any airflow through the injector tubes and silences the sound of the exhausting air. The design of the backfire valve depends upon who's sitting at the drawing board and what he feels is necessary in order to prevent the engine from backfiring.

The backfire valve only operates to eliminate backfire just after the driver removes his foot from the pedal; after that, the air-injection system returns to normal operation whether you put your foot back on the gas or leave it off. These diverter valves can make some strange things happen when the car is started. The valve is controlled by engine vacuum, and it takes a couple of seconds for the vacuum to build up. Until it does, the type of valve that dumps air into the manifold is wide open, allowing outside air to enter. Some engines may shake like Jello until the vacuum builds up sufficiently to close the valve. This doesn't really do any harm to the engine or anything else, but it can certainly make the driver wonder just what's going on under the hood.

If the air-injection system consisted of just the pump and its corresponding plumbing, things would be fine. But it also requires changes in the carburetor, distributor, cooling system and many internal changes in the engine proper. This means that it's impossible to transfer an air-injection system from one engine to another. It might be possible to design a universal system, but the cost would be fantastically high and would probably involve changing everything on

1. Air Pump and Filter

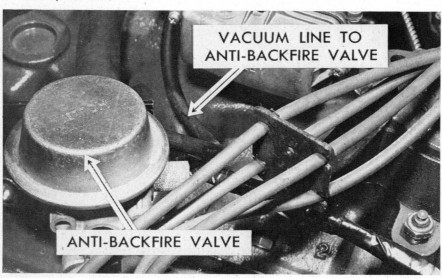

2. Anti-Backfire Valve

1. Some early air pumps used a large external filter to help muffle the noise of air pump operation as well as filter incoming air.

2. Anti-backfire valve is controlled by engine vacuum. When engine is decelerating at high vacuum, anti-backfire valve is actuated and relieves pump pressure so that no air is pumped into exhaust manifold.

3. Late-model air pumps use a diverter valve to prevent excessive system pressure from causing a backfire. Filter is an integral part of pump on this Delco unit (arrow).

the engine except the crank, block and rods. And who could get the Big Three to cooperate on such a project?

Like all other smog controls installed to date, the air-injection system is really an emergency system hung on the car's engine because nothing else that would drop emissions to the level specified by the politicians was available. Air injection will be around for a long time yet, too, because despite those who placed their money on alternative systems, manufacturers are discovering that with many engines, meeting the latest specifications requires a combination of emission control systems.

IGNITION-INDUCTION SYSTEM

The ignition-induction system was pioneered by Chrysler Corp., which installed

its Clean Air Package (CAP) on 2000 of the 1963 Plymouths. As these cars were sold only to fleet accounts in the Los Angeles area, a careful check on how they performed was feasible. This led to approval of the CAP system in November 1964. This exhaust emission system worked so well that similar systems were adopted by the competition (sometimes from sheer desperation), and ignition-induction variations are now used on many new cars.

Sometimes called an engine modification system, an ignition-induction system reduces emissions at idle by using a carburetor that's set lean. On some cars, the idle mixture screws are installed with a pin in the throttle body to prevent anyone from backing them out to obtain a richer mixture. If the screws are backed out with force, they break, and the car-

buretor must be removed from the engine. The pins and screws are then replaced with parts from a special kit. Other cars use idle mixture screws with limiter caps that butt against the carburetor to prevent the screws from being turned beyond a certain point. Still other carburetors don't use limiters because their idle mixture needles were designed so that the mixture cannot be excessively enriched even if screws are backed out.

If setting the carburetor to run extremely lean were all it took to reduce emissions, there would be no problem. But as we have explained, the engine wouldn't run properly on such a lean mixture.

Exhaust dilution of the mixture at idle requires an air/fuel ratio of about 12:1. The mixture is also very thin because it's under a high vacuum. Both of these

3. Diverter Valve

Emission Control

problems can be overcome by opening the throttle wide enough to get a denser mixture, as well as more airflow to scavenge some of the exhaust gases from the cylinder so that the engine will run at 14:1. The result is fewer emissions, but the engine then idles so rapidly that you can't hold it down. If you don't change the idle speed or adjust the air/fuel ratio, then retarding the spark is the only remaining way to get engine speed down to a normal idle.

And that's just what Chrysler did; all CAP engines have an initial spark setting that's retarded as much as 15° from normal. This is accomplished by a ported spark. When the throttle is closed, the spark port is above the throttle plate. Since there's no vacuum on the advance diaphragm, the distributor goes into full retard. But when the throttle plate is opened, the spark port is uncovered and the vacuum diaphragm advances the spark up to a conventional setting.

With this system, the spark is retarded during deceleration, because the throttle plate is closed at that time. The designers discovered, however, that the only way to reduce emissions during deceleration is to *advance* the spark. This is done by placing a little spark valve in the line between the carburetor and the vacuum advance diaphragm, connected to manifold vacuum.

Whenever the driver lifts his foot, this spark valve sends full manifold vacuum to the distributor advance diaphragm, which then advances the spark. The spark valve will hold the distributor in full advance position as long as the deceleration continues, even if the car is going downhill from here to you-know-where. But as soon as manifold vacuum drops below about 21 ins. (the figure is lower on '72-'73 models), the spark valve changes the distributor back to carburetor vacuum and the distributor works normally again.

The CAP system has been modified by other manufacturers so that it operates a bit differently, but it does the same thing. Some designs do not use a spark valve because their carburetors do not go rich during deceleration. Others use the spark valve, but their purpose is to eliminate exhaust popping, not to lower unacceptable emissions.

The Chrysler distributor has one vacuum diaphragm to advance the spark all the way from retard position to full advance. Some Ford engines use a dual diaphragm with two hose connections, while Pontiac uses a single diaphragm with two hose connections. On Fords and Pontiacs, one hose goes to carburetor vacuum and the other to manifold vacuum. The carburetor vacuum hose controls the distributor in the normal way, but the manifold vacuum hose pulls the breaker plate to the retard position during idle and deceleration.

Actually, this dual system is exactly opposite to the CAP system, which goes to full advance during deceleration. Ford and Pontiac were able to get away with this on some of their engines because of changes in combustion chambers, cam timing, stroke length and other internal modifications. But the system didn't work on all engines in their lines, so you'll find some that continue to use the spark advance valve. A similar situation exists on late-model Chrysler Corp. cars. Some engines use a spark advance valve and some don't. As you can see, there's no such thing these days as simply setting the idle speed and letting it go at that; a

1. Chrysler Electric Assist Choke

2. OSAC System Schematic

1. In 1973 Chrysler Corp. brought out an electric assist choke to reduce emissions during starting and warm-up. Heater element is located in choke well and is completely covered with a nonconductive insulation. Time/temperature control unit operates heater. Ford used a similar electric choke.

2. In 1973 Chrysler Corp. introduced Orifice Spark Advance Control (OSAC) as an anti-NOx device. It operates by delaying vacuum advance during acceleration. Delay is accomplished by restricting airflow from distributor advance chamber to carb port.

3. Close-up of OSAC valve mounted on firewall shows vacuum lines running to carb and distributor. Special thermal cutoff device incorporated in the OSAC valve assures satisfactory driveability when the outside temperature drops below 58° F.

tune-up man has to understand the system he's working on and how it affects the engine. And he must be sure that he has the exact specifications for the engine he's tuning.

Some late-model Chrysler product carburetors have an idle speed adjustment screw that seats against a little metal contact on the side of the carb, with a wire running to a solenoid mounted on the side of the distributor. When the throttle is in the idle position, the idle speed screw touches the contact, retarding the spark. If the carburetor also happens to be equipped with an anti-dieseling solenoid, then the contact for the screw is located at the end of the solenoid plunger.

What the solenoid retard does is bring the spark to a retarded position, thus slowing the engine down to idle at a reasonable speed. The solenoid is just a small electromagnet mounted on the distributor vacuum advance chamber. It exerts a small amount of pull on the rod that links the vacuum diaphragm with the breaker plate.

The old system of ported spark and a long throw on the single vacuum diaphragm worked very well for Chrysler, but the distributor solenoid modulator does an even better job, because it allows advanced timing during a cold start. When cold-starting an engine, the fast-idle cam holds the idle speed screw away from the retard solenoid contact. A cold engine needs all the help it can get, and the slight spark advance (about 5.5°) comes in handy for quicker starting. As soon as the engine warms up, the choke opens and the fast-idle cam goes off. Then whenever the throttle is let down to the idle position, the solenoid is energized and retards the spark, thus keeping the idle speed at a reasonable level.

Along with other changes, this system was modified on 1972 models so that it receives its power from the starter relay. Thus the distributor solenoid now works only during engine cranking. It advances the spark 7.5° for better starting. Simplification of the system was made possible by the introduction of Chrysler's electronic ignition system.

Chrysler also added an electrically assisted choke system to its entire engine line in 1973. This system was designed to provide a quicker choke opening at temperatures above 63° F and a slower opening below 63° F. Ford uses a temperature-sensitive bimetallic disc as a switch to control the ceramic heater within the thermostatic spring of the choke on its 4300 4-bbl. carb. This electric choke draws power constantly from a center tap on the alternator, but the disc switch remains open and no current is supplied until under-hood temperatures reach 60° F. Then the switch closes. Current supplied to the ceramic heater makes the thermostatic spring pull the choke plates open within 1.5 minutes.

Chrysler's original CAP system has now been changed to CAS (Cleaner Air System). The changes involved inside the engine were many and subtle. They made a considerable difference in emissions, but called for very little change in servicing. Some strange things were done with the controls on some of the carburetors. There are 4-bbls. with single idle mixture screws, similar to some old Holley designs. Some carburetors have a bypass airflow (nonadjustable) that directs air below the throttle valve to break up raw fuel. But even with the advanced thinking behind CAP and CAS, in 1973 Chrysler found it necessary to resort to an air pump system in addition to the ignition-induction system in order to make certain engines in its line conform to emissions standards.

A temperature-sensitive vacuum control valve is used on many cars. This screws into the water jacket and connects to the distributor, the carburetor and the intake manifold. The source for the distributor vacuum advance unit is the port above the throttle plate, resulting in no spark advance at idle. A retarded spark at idle may make an engine overheat in heavy traffic, so if the control valve senses excessive heat, it changes the vacuum source from the spark port in the carburetor to full intake manifold vacuum, causing the spark to advance and speed up the engine to help conquer the overheating. This thermal switch is not really much different from the old air-conditioning idle speed-up solenoid used on many early air-conditioned engines.

But if you think that Chrysler's solenoid retard is complicated, take a look at Ford's Electronic Spark Control (ESC) system. A speed sensor hooks into the speedometer cable to control the spark advance according to the car's speed. There's no spark advance at all until the car accelerates to about 23 mph, when spark advance works normally. On deceleration, the distributor modulator valve shuts off the vacuum to the advance unit as the vehicle speed drops to approximately 18 mph. Then the spark is allowed to retard.

The electronic module works in conjunction with the usual dual-diaphragm Ford vacuum advance unit. The diaphragm closest to the distributor is for retard and is connected to manifold vacuum; the other connects to the spark port on the carburetor, above the throttle plate. This ESC system is entirely separate from the electronic rpm limiter on some Ford products; the two units have no connection and could be used on the same engine if Ford wanted to install them that way.

GM and Chrysler also have spark control systems. The GM system is called Transmission-Controlled Spark (TCS). A switch in the transmission connects to a solenoid that controls the vacuum applied to the distributor diaphragm, resulting in the elimination of vacuum spark advance in all lower gears. On a 4-speed box, you get vacuum spark advance in 3rd and 4th gears, but only in top gear with all other transmissions.

3. OSAC Valve

Emission Control

COMBINATION EMISSION CONTROL VALVE

Chevrolet eliminated the TCS solenoid in 1971 in favor of a vacuum-electric gadget called a Combination Emission Control (CEC) valve. This device looks very much like an anti-dieseling solenoid, but it doesn't do the same job. Unfortunately, it occupies the same space on the carburetor, so many mechanics have probably used the CEC valve plunger to set curb idle speed. Just for the record, never use a CEC valve plunger to set the idle speed; the normal idle speed adjustment screw on the carburetor is the proper place to go for that setting.

CEC does exactly the same thing as a TCS system with vacuum spark advance, but an additional function opens the throttle on deceleration. If the throttle is allowed to close to the curb idle position during deceleration, a high vacuum results and pulls huge amounts of raw fuel through the carburetor idle system. But keeping the throttle slightly more open reduces the vacuum and creates fewer emissions, because then the mixture is not as rich.

CEC does both jobs at the same time. Whenever there's vacuum spark elimination, there's also a greater throttle opening on deceleration. The CEC valve can do both at once because it has a long plunger, one end of which shuts off vacuum to the distributor while the other end moves away from the throttle linkage. When the transmission shifts into top gear, electricity flows to the solenoid coil in the CEC valve, moving the plunger out. This movement uncovers a hole to allow vacuum into the distributor. At the same time, the end of the plunger moves out to prevent the throttle from closing completely.

Additional controls complicate the CEC valve. A temperature switch cancels the whole operation to allow vacuum advance below 82° F. A time-delay relay cancels the CEC valve for 15 secs. after turning on the ignition switch, providing vacuum advance for easier drive-away and fewer stalling-after-start problems. Curb idle speed on CEC-valve carburetors is set with the idle adjustment screw, as we said earlier. The deceleration idle (considerably higher than curb idle) is set with the CEC valve plunger in the energized position. If the curb idle is set with the CEC valve plunger, the throttle will be held open too far on deceleration, giving you quite a surprise when you take your foot off the gas and the car keeps right on going. The vacuum hose connection on the CEC valve differentiates it from the ordinary anti-dieseling solenoid, which has no hose.

Because the throttle is automatically held open on deceleration, it isn't necessary to idle the 1971-'73 cars as fast as in the past. Idle specs have dropped 50-100 rpm, making anti-dieseling solenoids unnecessary in many cases. Since air conditioning demands faster idling, which leads to dieseling, a solid-state timing device on air-conditioned Chevrolets holds the compressor on for 3 secs. after the engine is turned off. This extra load slows the engine down and keeps it from dieseling.

NOx SYSTEM

In the late Sixties and early Seventies, as researchers delved more deeply into the complex chemical reactions which formed smog, they found that the various oxides of nitrogen played a key part. There are four such oxides: nitrous oxide (N_2O, commonly called laughing gas), nitric oxide (NO), nitrogen dioxide (NO_2) and nitrogen tetroxide (N_2O_4). Since it is very cumbersome to refer to these gases individually, pollution researchers lump them together and refer to them collectively by the generalized chemical formula NOx.

It was found, unfortunately, that high combustion temperatures increased the formation of NOx. Since manufacturers were by then installing air-injection and lean-burn systems (to control HC and CO emissions) which increased combustion temperatures, they were actually *increasing* NOx emissions! Hastily backtracking, legislators quickly set new limits on NOx. The fact that NOx reduction requires engine modifications almost exactly opposite to those required to reduce HC and CO emissions is the principal reason that the latest control systems are so complex.

Installed on all California cars in 1971 (and nationally in 1972), Chrysler's NOx system took the place of the previously mentioned solenoid-controlled spark advance. It used a special camshaft with increased overlap, which produced more exhaust contamination in the cylinder. This reduced peak combustion temperature. Also installed was a 185° thermostat in place of the previous 195° one.

Until the 1973 model year, the heart of Chrysler's NOx system was a solenoid vacuum valve that controlled vacuum spark advance. On manual transmission cars, this valve was connected to a transmission switch to eliminate vacuum advance in all but top gear. In any other gear position, the valve was energized, shutting off vacuum to the distributor. In high gear, the transmission switch broke the electrical circuit to the solenoid, the spring in the valve opened the passageway and vacuum was allowed to advance the spark. The only additional control on manual transmission cars was a thermal switch mounted on the firewall to sense the temperature in the fresh-air

1. How EGR Works

2. Chrysler EGR System

cowl inlet. Below about 70° F, the thermal switch broke the circuit to the solenoid valve, which allowed normal vacuum spark advance; above that temperature, the thermal switch made the connection and allowed the NOx system to operate as described above.

Automatic transmission cars were different—they also had an increased-overlap cam, a 185° F thermostat and a solenoid vacuum valve, but the control mode was different. A control module, vacuum switch, thermal switch and speed switch all worked together in order to signal the solenoid when to turn distributor vacuum on or off.

Chrysler NOx control on the '73 line was handled by a temperature-actuated Orifice Spark Advance Control (OSAC) and Exhaust Gas Recirculation (EGR) system instead of the solenoid vacuum valve. When going from idle to partial throttle, a small opening in the OSAC valve delays the change in ported vacuum to the distributor by about 17 secs. When reversing the sequence (part throttle to idle), the change is instantaneous. Since vacuum is provided by a tap just above the carburetor throttle plates, manifold vacuum is not present under idle conditions. As soon as the throttle plates open slightly, though, the system kicks into operation, provided the temperature is 58° F or higher.

EXHAUST GAS RECIRCULATION

Simply stated, EGR is a system whereby a controlled portion of the exhaust is circulated back to the intake. Since the exhaust contains no free oxygen, it acts as a suppressant upon the combustion process and lowers combustion temperature, thereby lowering NOx emissions. The plumbing necessary to accomplish this varies with the manufacturer. On Chrysler cars it is handled by a ported vacuum control, a venturi vacuum control or a floor jet system, depending upon the particular engine involved.

Ford's approach to EGR ties into the engine coolant temperature as the actuating device, instead of the air temperature as used on GM and Chrysler cars. While the end result is the same as these other systems, Ford's is rather complicated in that the coolant temperature can be 60°, 95° or 125° F, depending upon the engine application involved. Ford also uses three different types of EGR valves: a poppet, a modulating and a tapered-stem, again depending upon application. The temperature-control device that activates the Ford EGR system is a vacuum switch similar to the distributor vacuum control valve used in '72.

To eliminate the add-on piping system used in other EGR designs, exhaust gases are picked up from the exhaust crossover passage in the intake manifold and routed through a thick carburetor

3. Ford EGR System

1. The EGR valve acts as one-way switch, routing exhaust gases to intake manifold except during idle/deceleration condition, when addition of gases to incoming air/fuel mixture would cause rough engine operation.

2. All 1973 cars used an EGR system. One arrangement was Chrysler's Proportional Exhaust Gas Recirculation, which incorporated an EGR valve and sophisticated vacuum sensing to assure proper flow of exhaust gases.

3. Ford's EGR system is considerably more complex than that of other manufacturers. An internally channeled spacer unit fits between intake manifold and carb and has valve mounted at its back. Depending upon engine, the valve may be a poppet, modulating or tapered-stem type.

4. Pinto equipped with 2000cc engine and manual transmission used a Decel valve for 1973. Mounted on intake manifold, the valve metered extra air/fuel during deceleration to permit more complete combustion.

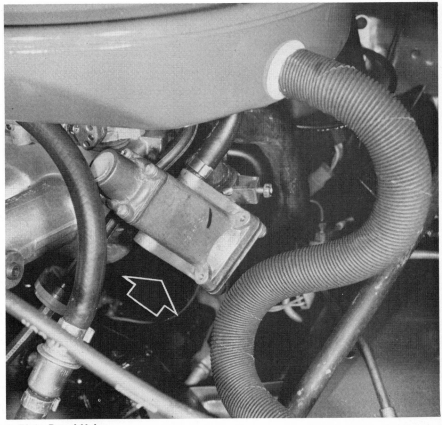

4. Pinto Decel Valve

Emission Control

spacer to the EGR valve, which meters the gases back through another passage in the spacer. This means that the exhaust gases are directed to the primary bores, where they dilute the incoming air/fuel mixture headed for the combustion chambers. Since vacuum for EGR operation comes from the carburetor's primary bore in this system, you'll find two vacuum ports on the carburetor: one for EGR control and one for the distributor spark advance.

Ongoing production changes have modified some Ford carburetors so that they use a single port for both applications. A more complicated version of this system was necessary to produce acceptable engine operation at high-speed cruising conditions. This high-speed modulator subsystem is used on the 351-C, 400, 429 and 460-cu.-in. engines. It is similar in concept, components and operation to the ESC system.

Since EGR is really effective only against NOx emissions, it is almost always used in conjunction with another system effective against HC and CO. Most manufacturers team EGR with air injection, which, as you know by now, makes for a *lot* of plumbing under the hood. (For more on EGR, see the exhaust system chapter which begins on page 204.)

AIR CLEANERS

Not the simple filter container sitting atop the carburetor that it was just a few years back, today's air cleaner unit is directly linked to the emissions control systems. As a result, it contains a variety of exotic devices, such as vacuum temperature sensors, cold weather modulators, vapor canister connectors, crankcase closure connectors with internal PCV filters, catalyst protection sensors, a vacuum-operated motor or diaphragm/butterfly to regulate intake air temperature, etc. And if your engine is to operate correctly, each of these devices (not all air cleaner units use all of the above) must do its job correctly.

First of all, replace both the filter element and the PCV pack at specified intervals. Don't try to stretch that dirty filter a few thousand extra miles. During replacement, use a hand-operated vacuum pump to check the operation of all vacuum-actuated sensors, switches, modulators, etc., to make sure they're working within the manufacturer's specs. Keep the heat control door and linkage in the air cleaner inlet free from grease and dirt build-up, and take care not to pinch connecting vacuum lines when removing or replacing the air cleaner unit.

If your car is equipped with a fresh-air inlet zip tube, watch for cracks in the tube or leaking connectors and patch or replace them as required. And if you develop what seems to be a carburetor problem on cold-morning starts, troubleshoot those air cleaner subsystems before blaming your trusty 2-bbl.

VAPOR CONTROL

Beginning with California cars in 1970

and nationwide in 1971, an additional system entirely separate from the exhaust and crankcase emission controls has been added by manufacturers to reroute any gasoline vapors that might escape from either the fuel tank or the carburetor. Except for a line going to the engine crankcase, the fuel tank is completely sealed. Gasoline vapors move along the line and are stored in the crankcase until the engine is started; then they are sucked into the intake manifold and burned. To keep liquid fuel from getting up to the crankcase, a vapor separator on top of the gas tank sends all liquid fuel back to the tank, where it belongs. Some vapor control systems use a canister filled with activated carbon to trap the vapors instead of letting them enter the crankcase. The carburetor float bowl also connects to the crankcase or the carbon canister (whichever is used), so that vapors from the float bowl will not escape into the atmosphere. AMC has introduced a fuel filter with a return line on '75 models to prevent excessive build-up when the car is at rest.

CATALYTIC CONVERTERS

Beginning with the 1975 model year, virtually all new cars sold in California and the great majority of 49-state vehicles were equipped with a catalytic converter system to lower hydrocarbon and carbon monoxide emissions. Two types of converters are presently in use: the GM/AMC unit containing pellets coated with platinum and palladium, and the Ford/Chrysler unit containing a ceramic "honeycomb" core coated with the same catalytic agents.

Regardless of type, all converter systems operate in the same way. Exhaust gases are passed through the converter, where the catalytic material converts HC and CO gases to harmless water and carbon dioxide by promoting further burning or oxidation of the pollutants. To provide sufficient fresh air for this process to take place, many engines also require the use of an air pump system. The combustion-type reaction also raises the exhaust system's heat level by several hundred degrees, necessitating special heat-absorbing shields.

1. Vapor Control System

2. Ford Improved EGR Control

Leaded gasoline contaminates and destroys the catalytic agent. Thus all catalyst-equipped cars are fitted with a special fuel tank filler tube which accepts only the smaller fuel nozzles used to pump unleaded fuel. But excessive richness in the air/fuel mixture will also ruin the converter. High-speed deceleration increases the amount of unburned HC in the exhaust, so the converter is then momentarily overloaded. The heat resulting from the reaction can melt the converter. Ford and Chrysler applications are equipped with a catalyst protection system to prevent this, while GM and AMC applications do not require such a system.

Far from foolproof, the catalytic converter can be rendered useless in several ways. Any engine condition—such as misfiring—which leads to an excessively rich exhaust will harm the catalyst. Running out of gas can also destroy the converter, especially if you pump the pedal and try to nurse the car along as far as possible before stopping. If you should happen to run out of gas, shift the car into neutral as soon as you're aware of the problem and coast over to the shoulder to stop. This will prevent damage to the converter while leaving sufficient gas in the fuel system so that you won't have to prime it when you've filled up the tank and are ready to start again. Pumping the pedal or priming the carburetor to restart the engine should be avoided at all costs. Despite what you may have heard, regular tune-ups and servicing of a converter-equipped car are even more important than they were in the past.

In 1975 Congress relented and allowed the '76 emissions levels to remain the same as in '75, instead of being much tighter on NOx as previously planned. With this breather, manufacturers concentrated on economy for 1976. Catalytic converters became standard everywhere, while Ford came up with an improved EGR system to supplement the converter. Called Proportional EGR, it used exhaust back-pressure instead of manifold vacuum to regulate the amount of exhaust flow routed to the intake. Mileage was improved with all manufacturers, since heavier reliance on the converter to clean up HC and CO emissions

allowed them to bring back economy-producing spark advance systems.

What of the future? Emission controls for 1977 were about the same as in '76, but GM showed the way to better economy by downsizing and lightening its full-size cars. Vehicle weight is the single most important factor in fuel economy, so we can expect to see smaller and lighter cars in all lines from all manufacturers. This is especially true since Congress has mandated mileage requirements, which the automakers must meet by the mid-1980's.

Congress also holds the key to future emission systems. If allowable emissions levels don't get much stricter than they are now, the control systems we now have will probably stay pretty much as

they are, at least for a while. And we have now achieved, after all, a 90% reduction in pollutants compared to an uncontrolled automobile. But if emission laws keep tightening, we'll probably see more electronic fuel injection (standard on the Cadillac Seville and several foreign cars), stratified-charge engines (like the Honda CVCC) and diesel engines. An interesting recent development that has gone into production in Sweden is a "closed-loop" engine, which continuously scans its own exhaust electronically and makes instantaneous modifications to keep itself clean. Take heart. The longer the automakers live with pollution laws, the more effective the control systems they come up with will be. The end result—clean air—is worth it. ♛

3. GM Catalytic Converter

4. Chrysler Catalytic Converter

1. Late-model vapor control systems use a charcoal canister that traps fuel vapor which would otherwise escape from fuel tank or carb bowl. A vacuum-operated valve on top of canister channels vapor flow to engine.

2. For 1976 Ford introduced an improved EGR system which used exhaust back-pressure to modulate the EGR valve, instead of depending solely upon intake manifold vacuum. Ford claimed better economy and driveability with this revised control system.

3. Every car now uses a catalytic converter, the magic chamber full of expensive catalysts which completes the oxidation of CO and HC. GM's version rather resembles a pancake.

4. Chrysler's converter has a heat shield attached and its internal construction differs from the flat GM version, but the function is the same.

Starting System

It happens all the time. Somebody calls up a garage and says, "My car won't start." The garage man immediately comes back with, "Will it turn over?" And the owner answers, "Yeah, if I drive it off a cliff, but what's that got to do with it not starting?"

Right there is the basis for a beautiful argument, all because the car owner does not understand the difference between a car that won't start and one that won't turn over, or crank. The starting system might be in beautiful shape with a battery powerful enough to light up New York City. When the key is twisted to the start position, the engine spins faster than it does when you're driving down the road. But it doesn't start.

Then there's the situation where the battery and starter give a few weak gasps and then everything is as quiet as a calm day in the desert. In this case we say that the engine will not turn over or won't crank. We don't know if it won't start because we can't crank it to find out.

Most of the problems with the starting system are caused by the battery. Not that the battery is a weak point. It's just that it only lasts so long—and that usually isn't long enough. Suppose your car won't crank some morning. Is there any way that you can tell what is the matter? You bet there is. You can pinpoint the problem by turning on the headlights. If they are normally bright, it's likely that the battery is OK. But if they're dimmer than a candle flame in a high wind, the trouble is almost certainly in the battery or its connections.

Let's assume that your car's headlights are very dim. The next step is to determine the condition of the car's battery. If the charging system is doing its job and the battery still tests weaker than an old dry cell, you'd better start shopping for a replacement. Don't wait for a complete battery failure.

BATTERY TESTS

Several tests can be made to find out if your starting system is doing its job. The easiest and most practical is to check starting voltage at the battery terminal of the coil while the engine is cranking. You should get at least 4½ volts on a 6-volt system, or 9 volts on a 12-volt system. You should check cranking speed of the engine at the same time, either with a tachometer or a well trained ear. If the cranking voltage and speed are above the minimum specifications (published in factory shop manuals), then there is likely nothing wrong with the starting system.

If all is not well with the cranking test, the next step is a check of battery voltage while the battery is not doing anything. It's called an open circuit voltage test, because all the circuits connected to the battery are disconnected, or turned off. Anything above 12.5 volts is considered OK. A 6-volter is OK at about 6.2 volts.

Suppose some of the above tests are marginal. Then the thing to do is make a high-rate discharge test with a battery-starter tester. However, you should not make this test if the battery is undercharged. Charge it up first, until the open circuit voltage is above 12.5 volts. If it won't charge up to that level, you know you have a defective battery. The high rate discharge test is made by drawing three times the ampere-hour rating out of the battery while observing the voltage. For example, a 60 ampere-hour battery (20-hr. rating) should be tested at 180 amps. If the voltage on a 6-volt battery stays above 4.8 and on a 12-volt battery above 9.6, then all is wonderful in batteryland. If it won't, get rid of the battery: you're flirting with a no-start situation.

Suppose the battery checks OK, but you know the car won't start because you had to take the bus to work yesterday. In that situation it might be a good idea to buy a monthly pass for the bus. But the situation is not that desperate. You know the battery is OK, so the trouble must be in the starter. If you want to check it, a battery-starter tester will measure the amount of current the starter is drawing. If it's drawing in excess of specifications, that's proof that the time has

1. **Portable Battery Charger**

2. Non-Fill Battery

1. A portable battery charger can return its cost in a short time. This Sears unit can be used as a 50-amp booster or 10-amp charger that automatically reduces its power flow to 5 amps as battery nears full charge.

2. The new Delco Freedom battery, like the older Energizer unit, is liquefied then sealed at the factory. Owners of these batteries won't have to worry about filling the cells. Vaporized electrolyte is trapped in a baffled tank above the cells where it condenses then returns to battery fluid.

come to put on your old clothes and take the starter off the engine.

Battery testing used to be a lot easier when the cell connectors were exposed on the top of the battery. Then you could test each cell with a voltmeter or a load tester.

The internal cell connectors that are now an almost universal feature of automotive battery construction do not permit access to the poles of the individual cells. *(No attempt should ever be made to jab voltmeter prongs through the cases of such hardtop batteries.)*

High-discharge tests provide useful information only after the battery has been charged, and are therefore of little value in troubleshooting. In fact, if the battery does not have at least a 50% charge, such tests can seriously damage the battery.

Hydrometer testing is a better means of checking cell condition—particularly for the backyard mechanic. Battery-testing hydrometers can be purchased for as little as 50 cents, and really excellent instruments sell for under $3 in many automotive supply stores.

In using the hydrometer, all the filler caps are first removed from the battery top and the tube on the tip of the tester inserted in turn into each cell. By squeezing the rubber bulb and releasing it, a quantity of the battery's water-and-acid mixture is drawn up into the glass barrel of the instrument. Inside the hydrometer barrel is a weighted float with

numbers on it. The numbers on the scale read from 1.300 to about 1.100 and indicate the comparative weight or density of the solution. The reading is taken at the surface of the liquid in the tube.

A fully charged cell will test between 1.275 and 1.280, while a cell in good condition may be anywhere between 1.280 and 1.250. A cell in only "fair" condition will produce a reading between 1.250 and 1.225. Any reading below 1.225 indicates a poor charge and, if a cell is found to be below 1.150, the battery is for all practical purposes dead.

If the cells test in the "poor" range the battery must be given a recharge. This can be done at a service station or with one of the popular little "trickle" battery chargers that have become popular for home use. By testing the cells during charging it is possible to tell when the process is complete. As stated above, a fully charged cell will test at 1.275 to 1.280 (or even 1.300). A half-charged cell will read from 1.200 to 1.225 and isn't ideal.

If any cell is lower than the others by .050 or more, that cell is shorted and the battery's days are numbered. Also, if charging can no longer bring the cells of the battery up to at least a 50% charge (about 1.200), the battery is really shot and should be replaced immediately.

Hydrometer testing should also be a part of the routine servicing that you give your car. By testing the battery every 2 or 3 weeks, most battery trouble can be headed off before it has had time to become serious.

To get the most accurate picture of the battery's health, the hydrometer tests should be made under proper conditions. Never take readings after adding water to the cells or after a long, high-speed trip. The best readings are obtained 2 or 3 days after water has been added and the car has been driven in normal service. To make the test, the car should have been left standing for several hours or overnight. The engine is then started, switched off, and the battery giv-

en about 5 mins. to "recover." The cells are then tested with the hydrometer. Readings taken at this time will give the truest picture of the battery's actual condition.

It should be noted that temperature has a definite effect on the readings you will get with your hydrometer, due to the fact that the density (specific gravity) of the battery electrolyte changes with the temperature. When the battery is hot (in summer), the hydrometer readings will be lower; when the battery is cold (in winter), the hydrometer readings will be higher.

Readings are considered to be correct when the temperature of the battery liquid is 80° F. For every 10° above 80° you must add .004 to the original reading; for every 10° below 80° you must subtract .004. Thus, a cell that produces a reading of 1.225 might appear to be in fair condition, but if the temperature of the fluid is only 40°, the correct measurement would be equal to only 1.209—a poor figure. For accurate readings, you can measure the temperature of the battery acid before testing it. In fact, a few of the more expensive hydrometers have a thermometer built-in for this purpose.

Besides making tests, there is another way to keep an eye on the condition of your car's battery. Most present-day cars have the so-called "idiot lights" to indicate a lack of battery charging rather than the more accurate—and, of course, expensive—ammeter. The trouble with the idiot light system is that it does not tell the driver if his battery is being overcharged.

Overcharging can be very harmful to an automobile battery. The best way to detect it—short of installing an ammeter—is to make a frequent check of the water level in the battery's cells. Normally, an automotive battery requires water only four or five times per year (hot climates excepted), but if yours seems thirstier than a sun-dried sponge, it's time to check the voltage regulator before trouble develops.

Starting System

Low battery electrolyte is caused by a high charging rate because the excessive charging heats up the battery, thus evaporating the water. High charging rate comes directly from a voltage regulator that is set too high, not from the current regulator. Six-volt regulators should keep the voltage below approximately 7.2, and the 12-volt systems below 14.2. Higher voltages are permitted if they are necessary to keep the battery charged.

BATTERY CABLES AND CONNECTIONS

Of course your "headlight test" might have turned out differently. Let's suppose that the lights were quite bright and that a hydrometer test proved the battery to be in top shape—yet, when you try to crank the engine, the lights go completely out. If this is the case, the trouble is probably a bad battery cable connection.

The battery terminals are the first thing to check. As pointed out earlier, these are often subject to looseness and acid corrosion. In an emergency, you can often get started by having someone press the tip of a screwdriver into the joint between the cable terminal and the battery post. The permanent cure is to get the

BATTERY EFFICIENCY AT VARIOUS TEMPERATURES

Temperature	Efficiency of a Fully Charged Battery
80°F.	100%
50°F.	82%
30°F.	64%
20°F.	58%
10°F.	50%
0°F.	40%
—10°F.	33%

UNDERSTANDING THE NEW BATTERY RATINGS

PHYSICAL SIZE — Battery size does not necessarily indicate quality, but it's important for replacement fit. The best battery in the world won't do any good if it doesn't fit into the battery box in your car.

AMPERE-HOURS — A measurement of the amount of amperes the battery will put out for 20 hrs., ending up with 1.75 volts per cell. For example, a battery that will put out 5 amps for 20 hrs. (5×20) is a 100-amp-hr. battery. This 20-hr. rating is being discontinued in favor of the "reserve capacity" rating.

RESERVE CAPACITY — This new rating gives the number of minutes that the battery will sustain a 25-amp discharge at 80° F. and still remain above 10.5 volts. This standard gives you a rough idea of how long you could run everything in the car (about a 25-amp load on most cars) if the charging system went dead. The higher the rating, the better the battery.

0° CRANKING POWER — Given in voltage and minutes. A 150 or 300-amp load (depending on the capacity of the battery) is applied to the battery in 0° air temperature, and the voltage is measured after 5 secs. The number of minutes in the ratings is how long it takes the battery to fall to about 5 volts (specifications vary) with the same load. In both cases, the higher the reading, the better the battery. This 0° cranking power rating is being discontinued in favor of the "cold cranking power" rating.

COLD CRANKING POWER — A new rating giving the amount, in amperes, that a battery can put out at 0° F. for 30 secs. In making the test, the load on the battery is adjusted until the battery voltage drops to 7.2 (12-volt battery) and then the ampere flow is measured over the 30-sec. period. The higher the rating, the better the battery.

NUMBER OF PLATES — More plates mean more active material for producing power. However, if the plates are extremely small, a battery might have a high number of plates, and still have comparatively low power. Plates are made by applying lead to a grid, so they're sometimes called grids.

MONTHS OF GUARANTEE — Can be used to figure the cost-per-month of owning the battery. This month-guarantee figure can be misleading. A battery might be guaranteed for several years, but in the last year of its guarantee it might not have the power to light a dome lamp. Therefore, it is wrong to suppose that just because a battery is guaranteed for several years, you won't have to buy another battery until that time is up. Life of a battery depends on how hard you work it, how well you keep it charged and full of water, and how it was originally constructed. Generally, the higher capacity (and higher priced) batteries will last longer.

1. Using Battery Tester

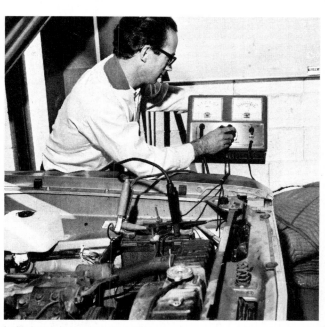

2. Measuring Battery Condition

cables into good electrical contact with the battery.

The boltless clamps used to attach cables to the battery posts on many late-model American cars are easily damaged by corrosion. Many starting problems originate right here. If the cast-in spring on these terminals has been eaten away by corrosion, the clamp must be replaced. Bolt-on types sometimes become so corroded that the bolt must be cut with a hacksaw in order to free the terminal clamp from the battery post. New bolts for these are available separately, which can save you the trouble and expense of installing a complete new cable terminal.

If the cable connections are corroded solidly onto the battery posts, a battery terminal puller should be used to remove them. These inexpensive tools work by pulling the cables straight off the post. Trying to remove frozen clamps by twisting or hammering on the terminals can cause serious damage by breaking the post's internal connection with the battery plates. Even cars that have shown no particular starting system weakness can often have their starting ability improved by removing the cable connections, brightening the terminals with emery cloth, and reinstalling them tightly. This is an especially good precaution before winter arrives.

The cables that connect the battery to the starter and to the chassis of the car are much heavier than any other wiring in the automobile. This is because the amount of current they must carry is much greater. The heavy flow of electricity necessary to start an engine would burn up ordinary wires as quickly as a burning fuse. Should some of the strands of wire forming these cables be broken, a greater load is thrown onto those that remain. Such breaks usually occur near the terminals and, quite often, spilled battery acid is to blame for the damage. If this appears to be a possible cause for insufficient current reaching the starter, or if terminals themselves

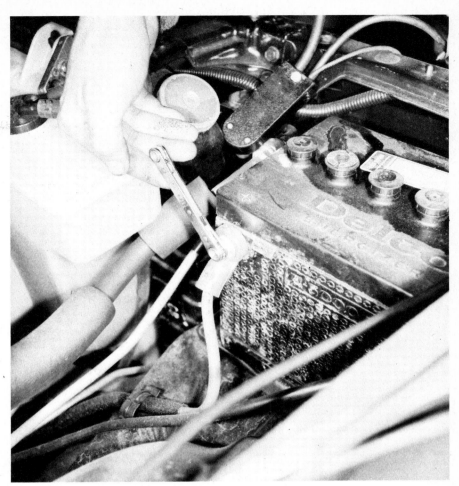

3. Removing Side-Mounted Terminals

1. Thexton Hydro-mite battery tester is temperature-corrected to give accurate readings of battery condition. Each floating ball indicates 25% of charge; if all four float, the battery is fully charged.

2. A battery's condition can be evaluated in many ways. Most pros have testers like this Allen Battery-Starter unit. Testers like this allow the mechanic to measure the voltage level when 3 times the rated ampere-hour of the battery is drawn out. If the battery "lives" up to its rating, then a no-start problem could lie in such diverse areas as bad terminal connections, ignition or starting switches, solenoid or starter motor, or breaks in the wire.

3. Standard Delco Energizer has vent caps and must be filled periodically like any other battery. Treat its terminals with care; a 5/16-in. wrench fits cable connector and should be used to avoid rounding its corners. Tighten at 15 to 20-in.-lbs. only; if connector is tightened too much, it'll break the internal seal and cause battery failure.

are in poor condition, the terminals can be removed from the cable, the damaged portion can be cut off, and the terminal—or its replacement—installed.

Usually, the terminals supplied by the car maker are either soldered or crimped onto the cable. Soldered terminals can be removed by heating them with a propane torch or over a gas burner. A damp cloth should be wrapped around the cable's insulation to keep it from accidentally being barbecued. Crimped-on terminals must be cut off, discarded, and new terminals installed in their place. Replacement terminals are available which require no soldering to attach them to the cable. A portion of the insulation is simply stripped from the cable and the terminal secured in the correct place by tightening two small screws or bolts.

On some cars the ground cable connects the battery directly to the engine block. On others, the battery is grounded to the car's body and another ground strap—often located between the engine and the firewall or between the transmission and the frame—connects the engine block with the chassis. Any of these connections can provide a source of potential trouble. If there is poor electrical contact at these points due to paint, corrosion, dirt or loose connections, starting problems are as certain as a cold winter in Minnesota. A reconditioned used car that has had the engine steam-cleaned and repainted sometimes will have paint on the engine block under the ground

cable terminal. This can also happen on new cars. All such ground connections should be removed from the engine or body, the mating surfaces brightened with emery cloth, and the connections re-bolted tightly together. *Poor ground contact has often been the cause of hard-to-trace car troubles.*

The battery's "hot" cable may pass through one or two switches or solenoids before reaching the starter. Follow this cable all the way to the starter and see that all connections are clean and tight. Insulation may also be worn from the cable in spots—particularly on long cables that may pass under the car. This can allow a short circuit to take place should the bare wire come into contact with the car's frame or any other grounded part. Not only would this lead to more fireworks than a flame in a gunpowder factory, it could discharge the battery to a big, fat, permanent zero. Repairing the insulation temporarily involves nothing more than wrapping the worn spot with a few inches of plastic electrical tape. This repair can later be made more durable by applying a coat of liquid rubber compound over the tape.

SOLENOID AND STARTING SWITCH

If the car doesn't crank, but the lights remain bright, or if they dim only slightly when the starter is switched on during the "headlight test," look for trouble in the magnetic starter switch or solenoid.

Starting System

In fact, if the trouble is in the solenoid, the starter may not run at all, or may run without turning the engine.

Two types of starters are used on late-model automobiles. American Motors cars, Plymouths from the late 1950's and early 1960's, Studebakers, and many Ford products have *Bendix drive* starters. GM cars, Chrysler products including late Plymouths, VW's, and many of the later FoMoCo models employ *overrunning-clutch* types. The latter have a solenoid mounted directly on top of the starter which pushes the starter pinion gear into mesh with the engine's flywheel ring gear during the starting operation. Bendix drive starters have a pinion gear that is mounted on the starter shaft in such a way that it is thrust into engagement with the flywheel ring gear by the starter motor's rapid speed buildup. But Ford's positive-engagement starter uses the magnetic force of the starter itself to engage the starter drive and needs no separate solenoid to assist it in its function.

In cars with Bendix drive starters the solenoid is actually only a magnetic switch that connects the starter to the battery. Since it has only an electrical function, it need not be mounted on the starter, although sometimes it is. The solenoids of overrunning-clutch starters must, however, be mounted on the starter because in addition to connecting the battery to the starter, they must move the starter pinion gear into engagement with the engine's flywheel.

When the ignition is turned to the "start" position, or when the starter button is pushed, current is not sent directly to the starter. Instead, it energizes the solenoid (in Ford or GM products), which in turn connects the heavy "hot" cable of the battery to the starting motor windings. Chrysler products are slightly different. They use an additional gadget called a starter relay, mounted on the firewall in the engine compartment. In the Chrysler system, the ignition switch energizes the relay, then the relay energizes the solenoid, and finally, the solenoid makes the connection between the battery and the starter.

Solenoids can be tested without removing the unit from the car.

Using the following simple jumper cable test you can quickly condemn or exonerate the solenoid as the source of the trouble.

1) Carefully (sparks may fly and a lot of heat can be generated) connect the two large terminals of the solenoid with a heavy jumper cable. The starter should turn the engine normally. If it does not, the trouble is not in the solenoid.

2) By attaching the jumper cable between the "hot" terminal of the battery and the correct small terminal of the solenoid, it should be possible to make the starter operate normally. On some early Chrysler products, touching a hot lead to the wrong small terminal will burn up the neutral safety switch. The terminal to avoid is the one with a wire running down to the transmission. If in doubt, disconnect both small leads from the solenoid, then connect a hot lead to

one small post and ground the other. If the starter operates, the trouble is *not* in the solenoid, but in the ignition switch, starter button, automatic transmission "neutral" switch, or it could be in the wires connecting these controls with the solenoid.

The magnetic switch (often called a solenoid) on Ford cars with all types of starters usually has two small terminals. The "hot" jumper should be connected to the one closest to the large terminal whose cables go to the battery.

3) If connecting the "hot" side of the battery to the solenoid's small terminal causes the starter to run, but does not turn the engine, the trouble is in the starter drive mechanism.

4) Assuming that the battery tests OK, and none of these tests gets a reaction from the starter, try connecting a heavy jumper cable directly between the battery's "hot" side and the solenoid terminal that leads to the starter or to the terminal on the starter itself. If this does not cause the starter motor to run, the trouble is in the starter—not the solenoid.

When making the above tests it is neither desirable nor necessary to have the ignition turned on. However, when using jumper cables there is always a chance for accidental contact with other electrical connections. For this reason, it is *always* advisable to disconnect transistor ignition systems and alternators before making jumper cable tests, since accidental shorts can destroy these units instantly.

You must also be extremely careful about making any sparks near a battery.

Whenever a battery is being charged, hydrogen gas is created in the cells above the electrolyte. This gas can stay there a long time, even when the car is not being operated. All it takes is one spark to set it off, and you have an exploded battery, with everything nearby drenched with sulphuric acid. When connecting jumper cables, make the connection to the hot battery post first, then connect the ground jumper to someplace away from the battery, such as the engine block. If any sparks fly when you connect the ground, they will be far enough away from the battery to keep from blowing it up.

If the tests do prove the trouble to be

1. Any do-it-yourselfer can easily afford an inexpensive "trickle" charger to augment his lack of taking long, battery-charging trips. These units, however, cannot rectify the problem of a "used up" battery or a malfunctioning voltage regulator.

2. S-K battery pliers, with their thin jaws set at a 30° angle, will go a long way to end the threat of rounding off the flats on the nut of a battery terminal. Never pound or violently twist the terminal to free it from the post. Chances are you'll damage or break internal connection.

3. Some motorists have experienced hard starting problems which were ultimately traced to poorly grounded battery and/or starter motor. Always make sure the battery and starter ground strap is securely attached to your car's frame.

1. Trickle Charger

2. Battery Pliers

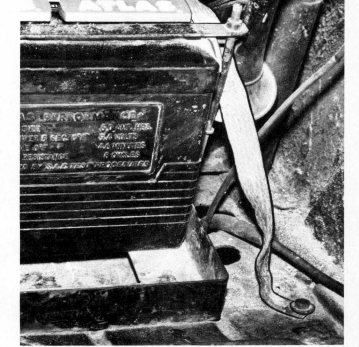

3. Battery Ground Strap

in the starter solenoid or magnetic switch, the only repair practical in some cases is to replace the entire unit since they may be sealed assemblies. However many units, such as the Delco solenoids on GM cars and many Ford trucks—as well as some of the magnetic switches used by Plymouth—*can* be disassembled. In these, the internal contacts can be examined and repaired. If the contacts are in good condition and the plunger works freely, the solenoid *should* work. If it does not—sorry, the windings are probably burned out.The exact condition of the windings can be checked with an ohmmeter or with a battery-powered tester.

To repair the starter solenoid on a 4- or a 6-cylinder inline engine it is not always necessary to remove the unit from the car, but on most V-8's the solenoid is otherwise inaccessible. In some cases it's necessary to remove the starter before you can get at the solenoid at all.

SOLENOID REPAIR

Firewall-mounted solenoids must be replaced, but the type that is mounted on the starting motor can be repaired.

If the solenoid is coated with grease and road dirt, it should be thoroughly cleaned before removing the cover from the contact points. Otherwise, dirt may get onto the contacts to cause trouble later. Except to remove the battery cable and the small wire from the dashboard starter control, it is not necessary to take any of the other nuts and washers off the terminals. In most cases there is just one small screw that holds the dust cover in place. After removing it, the cover can be lifted off the solenoid's contact assembly. Some late Delco solenoids

have two screws holding the cover in place. The cover on these also contains the stationary contacts, so remove it very carefully.

If they are not attached to the cover itself, the contacts can be dismounted from the body of the solenoid by undoing two small screws. Once these are out, the stationary contact assembly can be lifted and pushed to one side while still connected to the wires that enter the body of the solenoid. The assembly can be further dismantled by taking off the nuts holding the contacts, but this is only necessary if you have purchased a rebuild kit that contains new contacts.

The contact disc—a large brass washer that moves against the stationary contacts—can become quite pitted and worn, as can the stationary contact to which the battery cable is attached. If the battery contact and the contact disc are not badly burned, but only coated with dirt and deposits, they can be sanded or filed smooth. However, if the contacts are causing starting troubles, it is likely that they are worn quite badly. In most of these solenoids it is not necessary to file the contact surfaces flat nor to replace the parts. By simply removing a snap retainer, the contact disc can be taken from its shaft and turned over. This puts the "new" side of the disc toward the contacts. Similarly, the battery contact retaining nut can be loosened about 3/16-in. and the contact rotated 180° to put its "good" side under the contact disc. The other contact cannot be turned since one of the wires leading to the solenoid windings is welded onto it. However, this contact seldom wears as badly as the other, and it can quite easily be restored to like-new condition by a few strokes with a file. Complete

contact assemblies and solenoid rebuild kits are also available at very moderate cost at auto parts dealers.

If your jumper cable tests seem to indicate that there is a burned-out winding in a starter-mounted solenoid, always remove the dust cover and check the wires connecting the windings to the contacts. In a few cases what have appeared to be burned-out solenoids were able to be returned to service after a simple wire repair. It's always best to check this before tossing the unit into the trash can.

When reassembling the solenoid, make certain that the contact shaft and the plunger work smoothly. A binding contact can produce a no-start just as quickly as a flat battery. If the plunger has been left attached to the starter drive, don't tighten the bolts that hold the solenoid until it has been aligned to allow the plunger to move effortlessly.

After cleaning and reassembling the solenoid, ground the case and connect the small terminal to the "hot" side of the battery. There should be a click as the solenoid coil moves the plunger into "contact" position and another click when the connection is broken and the spring causes the plunger to retract. If there is no click, the windings are defective, which means a new solenoid must be installed.

STARTING SWITCH TROUBLES

If the car's solenoid checks out all right, but trouble is indicated in the circuit that connects the dash control to the solenoid's small terminal, there are a number of possible malfunctions to be considered. The most likely trouble spot is the ignition switch itself in cars

Starting System

equipped with "key" starter controls. This switch is used at least twice every time you drive your car. Consequently, considerable wear can take place—especially if the lock and cylinder are never 'lubricated. Key-starter switches are sealed units which must be replaced in their entirety.

If you suspect that the reason for a no-crank condition is the key switch, disconnect the plug at the back of the switch and connect a jumper between the hot terminal and the terminal that operates the starter. If your no-crank condition disappears with the starter suddenly springing to life, you know that the problem was in the key switch. A wiring diagram will help you find the right terminals and wires without having to trace the wires from one end to the other.

To remove the ignition switch from the dashboard, any individual wires should be carefully disconnected from the back of the switch and labeled to facilitate their installation on the new unit. If there is a plug, free the locking tangs and unplug it. The ground cable should be disconnected from the battery to prevent shorts during the switch-changing job. After the wires have been disconnected the switch can be removed from the dash. This is done by unscrewing the retaining ring that surrounds the lock cylinder. A special wrench will fit the slots in the ring, or pliers may work. Care should be exercised to avoid marring the dash or the ring. It isn't necessary to change the key and tumbler portion of the switch. It can be inserted into the new switch. But in some designs you have to remove the tumbler barrel before you can unscrew the retaining ring from the instrument panel. The clue is a small hole in the front face of the switch near the keyhole. Shove the end of a paper clip into the hole while you turn the key, and the whole key and locking mechanism will come out into your hand. Then you can unscrew the retaining ring and remove the body of the switch.

Installing the new switch is simply a reversal of the removal operation. If the terminals on the wires are corroded, they should be brightened with abrasive cloth before reconnecting them.

Battery current is supplied to the starter button or ignition switch by a wire that first passes through the ammeter, or perhaps a circuit breaker, relay, or junction block. Locate the "hot" wire behind the ignition or starter button and trace it to determine if it comes from the ammeter or any other electrical unit. By attaching your jumper to both terminals of each component you can bypass them temporarily. If the key or starter button operates the starter normally with the jumper in place, but not with it disconnected, then the trouble is an open circuit in the electrical unit being bypassed.

If one of these units is the source of your trouble it will probably have to be replaced. The jumper wire can be temporarily left connected across the terminals so that the car can be driven until a replacement part is located and then installed.

Late-model cars have the ignition "switch" in the steering column. If you suspect a bad switch, the column-mounted cars can either be a blessing or a chamber of horrors. To find out if your particular car is a blessing, look on the steering column between the instrument panel and the floorboards. If you're lucky, you will find your ignition switch mounted on the column with two bolts, and connected by a rod to the key lock up near the steering wheel. Removing the switch is easy, because the wiring unplugs and the two bolts are all that holds the switch in place. The switch mounting holes are slotted so you can get the switch slide in the same position as the lock.

Chevys are a special case. Their ignition switch is on the lower part of the column, but not low enough to remove it without dropping the column. That's right, you have to take off the two nuts that hold the column to the dash and lower the column until the steering wheel rests on a block that you have placed on the seat. Without the block, the column might come down far enough to break off the little string that runs up to the shift indicator. Once you get the column down, it's obvious how the switch comes off.

If you don't have the switch on the lower part of the steering column, then your personal chamber of horrors is that complicated area under the steering wheel. The wheel must be removed, and sometimes part of the top end of the column, in order to get the switch out. It's not an impossible job, but we suggest you have the shop manual for your car before you tackle it.

Another potential trouble spot is the "neutral safety" switch found on cars with automatic transmissions. The purpose of this switch is to make it impossible to start the car unless the selector is in the "N" or "P" position. Needless to say, this switch also receives a great deal of wear. Also, since it is frequently located at the lower end of the steering column or under the car, road splashes can eventually take their toll. Many cars have the neutral safety switch conveniently mounted on the steering column

1. The best way to break 'em free from each other is to first loosen one nut, then use a cable puller to lift offending terminal off the post.

2. Some no-start situations can be attributed to terminal looseness or acid corrosion. Baking soda and water will clean off most of the buildup, but you'll need a stiff wire terminal cleaning brush to finish the job.

3. Spreader pliers should be used to increase the inside diameter of a terminal so it will fit over post.

1. Cable Puller

2. Cleaning Corroded Terminal

3. Spreading Terminal

just below the instrument panel. The switch holes are slotted so you can get it in the right position to allow the car to start in park or neutral only. On some automatic transmissions—such as on Chrysler Corp. cars—the neutral safety switch is located on the transmission itself and can be reached only from under the car. After bypassing the switch with a jumper (making sure the transmission selector is in neutral or park position), it should be possible to start the engine normally if the trouble is in the neutral switch.

Although it is the most likely suspect, the neutral switch itself may not be the actual culprit. An incorrectly adjusted shift linkage can produce the same symptoms. Neutral switches that work off the end of the selector shaft can be checked for improper action of the transmission linkage. However, about all you can do with the "plug" type switches on Chrysler Corp. cars is replace them—since that's where the trouble usually is. Then if the new switch doesn't work, but the jump wire will, you'll have to get the shift linkage adjusted at a transmission shop.

Neutral safety switches that screw directly into the transmission are made with a hex that allows them to be removed with a thinwall socket. Those that mount at the end of the steering column or are actuated by the linkage arms on the transmission are detached by the removal of two or three screws.

STARTER DRIVE DIAGNOSIS

If the starter motor runs normally when the dashboard control is actuated but

fails to turn the engine, the trouble lies in the starter drive assembly. There are several other symptoms of drive trouble in addition to this, however. Horrible grinding noises accompanying starter operation are reason for immediate attention. Continuing to use the car will only lead to further damage to the starter drive and to the teeth of the flywheel ring gear. If there is a grinding sound, but the engine does not turn, it could mean that the engine or transmission will have to be pulled and the flywheel gear replaced, but the trouble could also be merely a broken overrunning clutch, in which case you could make the repair.

Sometimes the starter drive pinion gear will jam in the engaged position. If the car's engine is running you'll probably be able to hear an unusual noise which is the starter or starter gear being driven by the engine. If the drive jams during starting, the engine probably will not turn but a groaning or humming sound will be heard from the starter as though it was trying to turn the engine but lacks the power. Bendix drive starters are far more likely to jam than positive-engagement types. A jammed drive can be freed by putting the transmission into high gear and rocking the car forward and backward. This is not possible with an automatic transmission of course, and the starter must be removed to free the drive.

STARTER REMOVAL

If the drive assembly is not functioning properly, it will be necessary to remove the starter from the car on all but a very few engines. Even then it is usually far

easier to make repairs with the starter out and on the work bench.

Start by disconnecting the battery, then the cables and wires from the starter or solenoid terminals. Locate the bolts that mount the starter on the flywheel housing (*not* the long bolts holding the starter together) and remove them. Undo the bolts under the starter first and those holding the top of the starter last. When the last bolt is almost out, the starter should be supported in some way to keep it from falling. It may be necessary to tilt the starter slightly to clear the starter drive around the flywheel.

On some V-8's it is necessary to remove the exhaust pipe or jack up the frame slightly so that the starter will clear the upper front suspension arm as the starter is withdrawn. After the starter is out, look into the opening in the flywheel housing and inspect the condition of the ring gear. The flywheel may be turned by prying with a large screwdriver. If it is stripped or broken the car will have to go to a garage for repairs.

STARTER DRIVE REMOVAL

Starters with Bendix drive need not be further disassembled when you work on the drive assembly unless there is a separate housing surrounding the drive and pinion as on some Ford-Autolite models. Delco, and other positive engagement starters, must have the long bolts that pass through the starter taken loose and the housing surrounding the drive assembly removed. It is also mandatory that the starting drive actuating lever be unbolted to allow the drive assembly to slide off the starter shaft. The solenoid

Starting System

need not be dismounted from the starter for removal.

The Bendix drive assembly found on American-made starters is held in position on the armature shaft by a locking screw and two keys. Using a large screwdriver, compress the starter drive spring slightly at the end toward the starter motor. It is then possible to get at the locking screw and remove it. Some very early Ford starter drives can also be taken apart and individual parts can be replaced.

STARTER DRIVE INSPECTION

Whether the drive is an overrunning-clutch or Bendix type, the first thing to look for is broken or cracked springs. The overrunning clutch should be checked for proper action. It should be possible to turn the pinion gear clockwise (counterclockwise on VW's), but not in the opposite direction. Inspect the bushings inside the drive assembly. If they are badly worn the drive may bind or slip out of engagement.

All Bendix drives should be checked to see that the pinion gear turns smoothly as it slides in and out on its spiral-cut "worm." By looking inside, you may be able to locate small broken pieces that indicate an internal failure. It is extremely important that the drive assembly operates without the slightest binding.

Inspect the pinion gear for burrs and worn or chipped teeth. Also, look for bent tangs on the drive spring.

In many cases, starter drive trouble is due only to dirt and old grease preventing proper operation. However, overrunning clutches on U.S. and VW cars should never be cleaned with solvent, since they are packed with a special long-life grease at the factory. Solvent cleaning would remove this.

Bendix drives should be cleaned in kerosene but no additional lubrication applied, since oil on the "worm" could attract dirt and grit which would interfere with its smooth operation. If the worm is cleaned in solvent, then a light oil mist should be applied to the worm.

Unfortunately, all recent American starter drives—both Bendix and overrunning-clutch types—are serviced only as complete units. Any broken, worn, or damaged parts mean replacement of the entire assembly.

When a new overrunning-clutch drive assembly is installed, make certain that the starter shaft is clean and free of rust and corrosion. This will contribute to smooth action and a longer life for the new part. Rust spots can be polished away with fine steel wool and crocus cloth.

After the drive assembly and the starter have been put back together, check to see that the parts work correctly and effortlessly before reinstalling the starter on the engine.

It should be noted that the Bendix-type "Folo-Thru" starter drives on Ford cars have an internal lock pin that keeps the pinion from moving on the worm once it reaches full-engaged position. This pin will not disengage unless the starter is

mounted on the engine and the engine speed reaches 310-390 rpm. Occasionally, a person who is not aware of this thinks that the drive unit is faulty because the pinion does not retract by hand, but it is perfectly normal.

STARTER MOTOR

Until now we have only talked about those parts of the starting system that *control* the starting operation. Now it's time to take a look at the part that does the actual work—the starter motor. Starter motors are normally a very dependable part, and most of the common troubles that interfere with their operation are elsewhere in the system. The types of troubles that strike the motor itself are likely to be simply the result of normal wear. Most such problems are capable of being coped with by the backyard mechanic. However, starters that have operated under some abnormal conditions can have certain internal electrical defects that call for the attention of a trained service man. You can usually save money in such cases by simply turning the starter in on a rebuilt one. Still, you should know how to check out the starter if for no other reason than to know if it should be scrapped.

There are three or four tests you can make of starter efficiency, with the starter off the car. We assume you have already checked cranking voltage, cranking speed, and starter current draw, and found something wrong. Or maybe you suspect something is wrong, but you don't have the equipment to check it out. In either case, let's get the starter off the car and take a look at it.

The first test is to rotate the armature by hand and feel for any dragging. Many starters fail because the bushings or bearings wear and allow the armature to drag on the fields. If the armature does not spin freely, then you've found the problem.

The second "test" is to check for worn bearings. Wiggle the shaft from side to side. If there seems to be a considerable looseness, try rotating the shaft while at the same time exerting heavy side pressure. If there is extreme binding

or mechanical interference, the bearings will need attention.

On some starters, the bushings that support the starter shaft cannot be replaced and an entire new end plate must be obtained. However, in most cases the bushings are removable. The bushing at the flywheel end of the starter can be quite easily driven out with a piece of round steel somewhat larger than the starter shaft or with a regular bushing driving tool. A new bushing can then be installed in its place. Lubricate the outside of the new bushing so that it will go into place with a minimum of binding. A

1. Troubleshooting your starting system (like on this Ford) isn't hard, if you know what you're looking for and where to place a heavy-duty jumper cable. (1) Your solenoid is OK if, when you "jump" the two large terminals on the starter switch, the starter works normally. (2) When you connect the hot side of the battery (+ post) to the small terminal (S) of the solenoid and your starter works, you have problems in the ignition switch, starter button, neutral safety switch, or wiring. (3) If when you attach the jumper cable from the hot side of the battery to the starter side of the ignition switch and the starter motor turns, you've got problems in the ignition switch area. (4) If a jumper placed here allows the ignition switch to start the car normally, you've got troubles in the wire to the switch. By the way, if your starter motor clicks as if the battery is dead (but you know it's fully charged) yet finally makes contact and lights your engine off, either your solenoid or switch is going away and should be replaced soon.

2. These are the two basic external types of solenoids or starting switches. At bottom is GM unit, attached to the top of the Delco-Remy starter. The one at the top is a Ford starter switch, usually placed somewhere on the firewall.

3. Many Ford ignition switches look like this. When plugging in the connector, make sure the locking tabs are fully engaged.

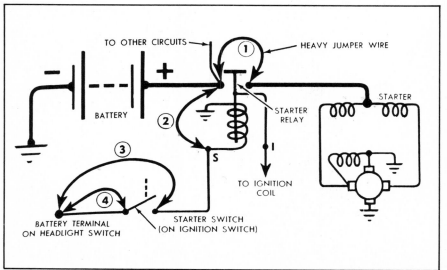

1. Troubleshooting Ford System

block of wood should be held against the end of the bushing (if a bushing driver is not available) and tapped *lightly* with a hammer until the new bushing is seated. The bushing in the other end of the starter presents more problems since the bearing end is capped and the bushing cannot be driven out. Some starters have a removable bearing cap that must be replaced along with the bushing, but in most starters the bushing must be cut out with a hammer and a small sharp cold chisel before the new one can be put in. There are tools available that thread themselves into these bushings so

that they can be pulled out, but at $10 you'd spend more on the tool than you'd save by not buying an entire end plate which has a new bushing in it. Always have the new bushings on hand before taking out the old ones. Replacements may not be available for your particular starter.

Finally, a starter "no-load" test should be performed before disassembling the starter—providing all seems normal when turning the armature shaft by hand. The no-load test is a bench test only and cannot be made with the starter mounted on the car. It also requires an amme-

ter which will register up to 200 amps for Bendix drive starters and up to 500 amps for Ford positive-engagement overrunning-clutch types. The positive engagement Ford starter has an initial high current demand because the drive is being actuated by the starter's windings.

With the starter running, the ammeter should indicate approximately 0-80 amperes, according to the car maker's specifications. This should be the *maximum* for a 12-volt system. Higher readings indicate such faults as shorted windings, a rubbing armature, tight bushings or a bent armature shaft. If the starter fails to run and the ammeter registers zero, the trouble is likely open windings or worn-out brushes.

You can perform the same test *without* an ammeter by simply using two jumper cables. Connect the positive cable to the starter terminal and the negative cable to the starter frame. This should be reversed if the starter is from a car with positive ground. Of course, you will not be able to check for shorted windings as you would with an ammeter, but you will find out if the starter runs at all. Also, if it seems to turn slowly, a bent shaft, tight bushings, or rubbing armature can usually be detected. If these conditions are not present, the slow running just *might* be the tip-off that there's an armature short.

In the days of manual transmission cars, it was easy to perform a starter lock test by putting the car in gear, applying the brake, and operating the starter. A certain amount of current would flow through the starter, and it could be measured with an ammeter, then compared with specifications. In these days of automatic transmissions, the lock test can only be done on a starter test bench, and they are scarcer than males at a Women's Lib meeting.

STARTER MOTOR DISASSEMBLY

The same long through-bolts that release the drive housing also allow the starter to be opened up once they are loosened and taken out.

After the through-bolts are out, you will be able to remove both ends from the starter motor. The drive assembly must also be removed as described earlier. The other end plate contains the brush holders, and therefore the brushes must be lifted out before the end plate can be taken off. This is also a necessary operation prior to replacing the bushings in the end plate. The two ground brushes can have their wires unscrewed from the starter frame and the brushes left on the end plate if desired. The brushes on Delco starters are attached to the brush holders with screws. After the end plate is off, the brush holders and springs should be removed from it and the mating surfaces cleaned thoroughly before the new brushes are put in. A word of caution: *do not* clean inside of case with solvent as it will damage armature and field coil insulation. Merely wipe off with a clean cloth.

If the commutator was not checked earlier, it must be supported on "vee" blocks and rotated against a dial indica-

2. Solenoid and Starter Relay Switch

3. Ford Ignition Switch

Starting System

tor or a reference block that can have the clearance checked with a feeler gauge. If the commutator is found to be eccentric, the armature must be chucked in a lathe and *very light* cuts made across the face of the commutator until it is once again round and concentric with the shaft in its center. After turning the commutator on Delco starters, the mica strips separating the brass segments of the commutator should be under 1/32-in. using a section of hacksaw blade. The undercutting should also be about .002 wider than the insulation strips. On Autolite starters, the commutator is polished with #00 or #000 sandpaper to remove all burrs left by the turning operation. Autolite also recommends not undercutting the mica, but make certain that no brass particles are left on the insulation strips between the segments. If you do not have a lathe available, the armature can be taken to an automotive machine shop to have the work done. There are also some special tools made for turning commutators and undercutting mica. They take the place of a lathe and do an excellent job if used correctly.

STARTER BRUSH REPLACEMENT

Brushes should be replaced if they are not making good contact with the commutator or whenever they have worn down to a length of 5/16-in. Always install a complete set at one time to equalize wear.

After removing the brushes from their holders and the end plate from the starter, the armature can be taken out. The old brushes may then be removed. This calls for some work with a soldering iron, since the four new brushes must be soldered to the field and ground wires in place of the old ones. On Autolite starters, the two ground brushes sometimes do not require unsoldering since the new brushes come with the wire already attached. These can simply be screwed onto the terminal. All carbon, grease and dirt should be cleaned from the end plate, and if the insulation barrier between the field brush holders and the end plate is cracked or broken, the entire end plate should be replaced.

The new brushes may now be soldered onto the correct wires. Any flux that remains from the soldering job should be cleaned off with baking soda and water.

How to insert the brushes into the starter will be obvious after you have made a couple of false starts. In general, starters without slots in the frame must have the brushes in place before the armature is inserted. When the starter has slots, then the end plate and armature are installed, and the brushes put into their holders through the slots. The brushes must pivot freely or slide freely, whichever method is used, so that they will have good, firm contact with the commutator.

The ground wires should be reconnected in their original places before the end plate is completely in place. Be

careful not to pinch the brush leads between the end plate and the frame. Also, if there is not a dowel or notch to locate the correct position of the plate on the frame, mark the plate and frame when taking the starter apart so that they can be reassembled in their proper relationship. Once the starter ends are in place, the two through-bolts can be inserted and tightened.

If electrical trouble exists within the windings of the armature or field coils, the repair is definitely not one to be attempted at home. In fact, having the starter rewound by an automotive electrician would be more expensive than simply replacing the starter with a rebuilt one. New armatures and field coils are available from new car dealers' parts departments, but the cost is sometimes equal to that of a rebuilt starter at an independent parts store. Therefore, the main value of the following tests to home mechanics is (1) to determine if the starter really needs replacement, (2) to pinpoint the trouble so that you can replace the starter's armature or frame with a used part, and (3) to test used components to make sure that they are serviceable.

Tests for grounded circuits in field windings and armatures can be made with a voltmeter and the car's battery, a self-powered ohmmeter, or a simple battery-operated test light. By connecting one test lead to the shaft and touching the other to the commutator, you can quickly detect grounded circuits in an armature. If any current passes through to the shaft, as indicated by a voltmeter reading or by the test lamp lighting, the armature is probably defective. The trouble was probably caused by failure of the winding insulation. The only practical repair is to replace the armature—if this is economically possible. Otherwise install a

rebuilt starter. A device known as a "growler" is sometimes used to test armatures for shorted windings.

An open circuit in the armature can often be detected by examining the commutator for signs of burning. The burned place is caused by an electrical arc that is formed each time the commutator segment connected to the open-circuit winding passes under a brush rubbing surface.

The field coils can also be tested for grounded circuits using a voltmeter or test light. The same hookup is used as in testing the armature. The field brushes *must not* be in contact with the starter frame during the test. One lead from the battery is connected to the starter terminal, and the lead from the voltmeter or test lamp is touched to the starter frame. If the voltmeter shows a reading or if the test light comes on, it is an indication that the field windings are grounded.

Open circuits can be tested by attaching the battery lead to the starter terminal, and the voltmeter or test lamp lead to each of the field brushes in turn. Do not test the ground brush. If one or all of the brushes fails to light the test lamp or produce a full voltmeter reading, the field coils have an open circuit. If an open circuit is located, the wire leading from the brush to the coil should be checked for breaks. If the open spot is in the windings themselves, you will either have to get the field coils replaced by an automotive electrician or turn the starter in on a replacement.

Summing it up, let's remember that internal starter troubles are generally as rare as free samples at a U.S. mint. However, some makes do have starting motor problems because their starters are too small for the job they have to do. The trouble usually shows up as a drag-

KEY AND LOCK CYLINDER ASSEMBLY

LOCKING MECHANISM ACTUATED BY IGNITION SWITCH KEY AND LOCK CYLINDER

ACTUATOR

IGNITION SWITCH ACTUATOR ROD

IGNITION SWITCH PLUNGER

NUT AND WASHER ASSEMBLY

HOLE FOR LOCKING PIN

IGNITION SWITCH AND WIRING ASSEMBLY

NUT AND WASHER

GEARSHIFT LEVER

CONNECTOR PLUG TO 14401 WIRING HARNESS

STEERING COLUMN

1. Ford Ignition Switch

2. Chevrolet Ignition Switch

1. Many late-model cars with locking steering columns have their ignition switch low on the steering column, as on this Ford.

2. A Chevrolet ignition switch, which is typical of GM cars. The steering must be lowered to get the switch off the column.

3. Major pieces shown in this view of a disassembled Ford starter (late model) are, top: commutator and starter drive and long bolts; center: pole shoe cover, shifter forks, and starter drive housing; bottom row, from left: starter cover band and end plate assembly.

3. Late Ford Starter

ging armature from worn bearings or bushings. Open-circuited or shorted armatures can result, too.

Many short trips cause a starter to be used more than normally. On long trips a starter might be used only once a day. The type of driving has a lot to do with how long the starting system will be trouble-free, just like everything else on a car.

Before you perform any exploratory surgery on the starter motor itself, be very certain that the other parts of the starting system have been thoroughly tested and inspected. Furthermore, many starter troubles have been licked just by taking the starter apart and cleaning it. This is something to remember when installing a used starter. Clean it before you hang it on the engine and you're much more likely to be satisfied with your "bargain" replacement.

HARD-STARTING CAUSES

Sometimes the starting system gets blamed for trouble that isn't really its fault. More than one amateur mechanic has ended up with a dismantled starter in his lap while the real trouble lurked in the engine room. While these things are not, strictly speaking, starting system troubles, we'll list them here so that you'll at least be warned and on the lookout should your starter fail to turn the engine over some bright and sunny day.

1) Hydrostatic lock occurs when a cylinder becomes filled with water. (Or, in rare instances, gasoline or oil.) Liquids will not compress—that's what makes hydraulic brakes possible—and if there is a greater volume of water in a cylinder on its compression stroke than the combustion chamber can hold, the engine will not turn. The usual cause is a leaking head gasket or a cracked cylinder head.

2) Oil rundown is a condition that usually strikes the turnpike traveler. After bombing along at 75 or 80 mph for 3 or 4 hrs., the oil in an engine can get pretty thin and watery—especially if it is some kind of 30¢-per-quart "cheapie," or hasn't been changed since the election of '68. The trouble starts when you pull into a service station for gas. After your tank has been filled and the windshield scrubbed you prepare to continue on your happy way, but the starter will hardly turn the engine! It sounds as though the battery has run down—a highly improbable condition on a long high-speed trip. The real trouble is that your hot, thin oil has run right off the cylinder walls, leaving them as dry and unlubricated as scorched sandpaper.

Don't let some "sharpie" sell you a battery—save your dough for an oil change. To get started, just take off the air cleaner and pour some SAE 10 engine oil into the carb intake while someone else runs the starter. The cranking speed will soon increase and the engine should fire right up.

3) Heavy oil can place a tremendous load on the starter in cold weather. If you still have SAE 30 in the engine when the first cold blast of winter arrives, don't blame your misery on the starting system. With the temperature at 10° or 15° below the freezing point, even the best starting system probably won't budge an engine that's been sitting out all night with a crankcase full of summer-grade oil.

4) Carbon buildup in the combustion chambers can both increase the effective compression ratio of an engine and, when heated to incandescence by a high-speed run, convert your engine into a "diesel." Carbon particles may remain glowing coals for many minutes after the engine is switched off. When you try to restart the engine, the increased compression and the glowing carbon cause the fuel to ignite before the spark plugs

fire. Since ignition is taking place long before the pistons near the top of their stroke, the engine tries to run backward, fighting the starter. Lots of people have spent money on their starting system trying to cure this before finally pulling off the heads to get rid of all that carbon.

Excessive initial spark advance or a defective distributor can cause symptoms similar to those produced by carbon buildup; however, this will also cause trouble when the engine is cold.

5) Mechanical interference is another possible source of starting trouble. It's usually the result of improperly done tune-up or repair work—such as installing the camshaft 180° from its correct position.

If you have been working on the car, and it then refuses to start, check on your own work before condemning the starter.

6) Antifreeze lockup will call a halt to engine cranking just as quickly as a mechanical lockup. Antifreeze is not a lubricant. When it seeps through a head gasket and gets on the cylinder walls, the pistons and cylinders like each other so well that they are inseparable. This problem usually shows up on the first attempt to start in the morning, after the antifreeze has had all night to do its seeping. The test is to drain the cooling system and fill it with water only. Usually, the cranking problem will go away. You should then put a good sealer in the cooling system and then just refill it with antifreeze.

In some cases the antifreeze contaminates the engine so badly that merely draining the cooling system will not help. In that unhappy situation you have to use a compound known as Butyl Cellosolve in the oil. It will pick up the antifreeze from the engine, if you follow directions on the package.

7) Piston seizure, similar to oil rundown, can also cause a no-crank condition. If the cooling system is partially

Starting System

clogged around the cylinders, local hot spots develop which expand the cylinders unevenly. If magnified, the cylinder surface might look like a plowed field. The hillocks grab hold of the piston and won't let it move in the cylinder. It will happen every time the engine gets up to operating temperature. Let it cool, and the engine will start normally. A thorough cooling system cleaning will get rid of this problem. We have seen some people cure it by putting in high-powered starters and heavy-duty batteries, but that's like putting a cork in your tailpipe to stop exhaust smoke. It may cover up the problem temporarily, but it won't cure it.

MORE STARTING POWER

The stock starting systems on most cars were designed to do their job on stock engines. Some of the last 6-volt systems were hardly up to their work even then! As soon as you start boosting compression ratios and fiddling with ignition and valve timing, you're making the starting system's life a little more fraught with drudgery.

There are no "hopped-up" starter motors marketed at the local speed shop, but there is something almost as good waiting at the nearest parts store or wrecking yard; namely a truck starter. Most of the standard blocks used in passenger cars also get punched out and draped with different accessories for use in trucks. In most cases the heavy-duty "commercial" starters will bolt right onto them. You can usually find out "what'll fit what" by checking the exploded view drawings in the dealer's parts catalog.

Commercial starters have a greater current demand than those found on standard cars and, therefore, depend on a more powerful battery. This is something that should be considered anyway when planning a starting system for your "rod."

Cars that were originally built with a 6-volt electrical system can have their starter changed to a more powerful 12-volt number without completely rewiring the car and throwing out all 6-volt instruments and accessories. The answer is a "6-12" starter-electrical system. The heart of the system is an automatic voltage converter switch such as the Orpin unit. All you do is add a second 6-volt battery and wire the batteries and starter into the switch according to the directions. This system will automatically shoot 12 volts to the starter for cranking the engine without increasing the voltage to the rest of the electrical system.

There are also several conversion kits that permit using entire 12-volt engines in 6-volt cars and 6-volt engines in 12-volt cars. The 6-volt starters can be fitted to engines that originally had 12-volt jobs, but converting a 6-volt system to 12 volts will get you much more reliable starts than a 12-to-6 starter swap.

This should give you a good idea of just what takes place in a modern-day automotive starting system. Starting systems have come a long way since the day of the crank, but they still aren't so overly complicated that the home mechanic can't service them. This is especially true in preventive maintenance, which includes battery terminal cleaning and checkups, tightening connections and inspection of wiring. This is all part of good-car-care that will result in dependable transportation for you—from the very start. 🐝

1. Delco-Remy starters have changed very little over the years. Recent models have had two distinguishing features added to them: non-reversible solenoid contacts and a fully enclosed drive housing.

2. Worn brushes can cause a no-start problem. Pin retains entire assembly, which, when removed, allows brushes to be replaced.

3. Brushes are attached to holders with small screws. No solder needed. Disassemble one pair of brushes at a time. Use other pair as an example.

1. Cutaway of Delco-Remy Starter

2. Worn Brushes

3. Brush Holders

1. Solenoid disconnect is done from under hood. On some late-model cars, plumbing is heavy, so you'd do better to work from underneath.

2. Once solenoid is disconnected, removal of two bolts will allow starter to be pulled. Bolt location differs from year to year and car to car.

3. Starting motor removal from majority of GM cars is best accomplished from underneath. There's another bolt on the side opposite from the one marked.

4. Dual exhaust on same GM car as in photo #3 shows how access to starting motor can vary, depending upon the particular car and how it's equipped.

5. FoMoCo starting motor is mounted to flywheel housing with two horizontal bolts. Access on '73 Ford LTD is exceptionally easy compared to many cars.

6. Here's a late-model T-Bird starter mounted exactly as in LTD, but note how access is obscured by crossarms and suspension linkage.

7. Getting at this '73 Valiant starter is no picnic. Steering linkage and dual exhaust pipes hamper removal of the lower bolt, making removal tedious.

8. Lower bolt on this '72 Le Baron is difficult to get to. Upper bolt on Chrysler Corp. V-8's is reached from under hood, with equal difficulty.

9. Easiest starter to remove is that on a Chrysler Corp. Slant-6. As on this '72 Duster, the starter comes out easily from under the hood.

HOW-TO: Ford Starter Teardown

1. *Ford starters can best be removed by disconnecting starter cable at relay (drop steering idler arm on Montego), take off mounting bolts.*

2. *To disassemble this Ford starter, loosen and remove the brush cover band, starter drive plunger lever cover and the cork gasket under it.*

3. *Next insert needle nose pliers and a hook made from a large cotter key, and lift out the brushes so the end plate can be taken off.*

4. *With the brushes now out of the way, you can fully remove through-bolts and pull off the starter end plate with the brush springs on it.*

5. *Extract pivot pin which retains lever. Now is a good time to look at the contacts at the other end of the lever to be sure they are OK.*

6. *Starter gear plunger lever can now be lifted out. Remove armature. Use brush or air to clean field, coils, armature shaft, brush end plate, etc.*

7. *Inspect pole shoes to see if the armature has been rubbing them. If it has, the armature bearings have gone away, and shaft has sagged out.*

8. *If starter drive gear assembly is to be reused, remove stop ring retainer and the stop ring from the end of armature shaft; remove drive.*

9. *Place the drive gear assembly on the new armature with new stop ring. Install the fiber thrust washer on commutator end of armature shaft.*

1. To disassemble, check Delco-Remy starter, remove through-bolts off commutator end frame, then pull motor connector strap terminal screw.

2. Slide field housing away from lever and nose housing. If solenoid is OK, and you're just checking armature, leave solenoid alone.

3. Once armature is out of field housing, check commutator. If it's grooved, rough, or out-of-round, it must be turned down smooth.

4. If armature touched or rubbed against field coils, chances are bushings in commutator end frame are gone and should be changed.

5. Worn brushes can cause a no-start problem. A pin retains entire assembly, which, when removed, allows brushes to be replaced.

6. Brushes are attached to holders with small screws. No solder needed. Disassemble one pair of brushes at a time, use other pair as example.

7. Drive is kept on armature shaft by three pieces. First take thrust collar off end of shaft. Note flange goes toward body of armature.

8. Next, retainer must be driven back along armature shaft. Use a deep socket and plastic-head hammer; don't punch it off with a ball peen.

9. Once snap ring is exposed, remove it with two screwdrivers. Drive assembly can be slid off armature shaft and replaced, if necessary.

HOW-TO: Chrysler Starter Teardown

1. Begin removing MoPar starter by disconnecting battery ground strap, hot cable from starter, and solenoid lead wires at solenoid terminals.

2. Remove stud nut (bolt holding starter to bellhousing); slide trans oil cooler tube bracket off stud prior to removing starter, end head.

3. With long bolts removed, you can pull frame off to expose terminal screw, wrapped wire connection of shunt field at brush terminal.

4. Armature can now be pulled up and out of gear housing, starter frame and field assembly. Then remove the steel and fiber thrust washers.

5. Extract brush holder plate screw before taking off steel insulation washers from solenoid. Remove brush hold plate (with brushes) as unit.

6. Now, solenoid/brush assembly can be pulled from gear housing well, the nut, steel washer and sealing washer from battery terminal.

7. After nut on solenoid terminal is off, solenoid lead wire to brush terminal post must be unsoldered so solenoid assembly can be removed.

8. Brass washer contact disc that makes the electrical connection between the battery and starter, is subjected to pitting and/or burning.

9. The contact disc can be removed, replaced or reversed by releasing it from contact stud, plunger. Pop off snap retainer holding it on plunger.

10. After removing the contact disc, turn it over and return it to the plunger. This new, fresh side saves you from buying a new contact disc.

11. In order to get at the starter drive, all you have to do is grab one of your trusty screwdrivers and pry off the dust cover.

12. Release U-shaped retainer that positions driven gear on pinion shaft. Be careful; retainer is under pressure and can spring away.

13. Retainer ring on front of pinion shaft can now be released. Don't use a spreader any larger than shaft's O.D. or ring can be damaged.

14. Tap pinion shaft toward rear of housing. Extract retaining ring, thrust washer, clutch, pinion (shifter forks, nylon actuators) as unit.

15. With pinion shaft removed from rear of the starter housing, check it carefully for any burrs, cracks or other signs of wear or damage.

16. Large friction washer on driven gear is subjected to wear because it absorbs shock of large gear being driven to rear of the housing.

17. Clutch assembly can be removed as well as the clutch shifting fork assembly. Do not soak in solvent; wipe all pieces with a clean cloth.

18. Check the wiring on inside of field for breaks or signs of burning. Make sure screws that hold pole shoes in are good and snug.

Ignition System

The ignition system of the internal combustion engine has very probably had more development work done on it than any other part of the automobile. Even so, it is still a long way from being perfect. Just in the past few years we have seen transistor ignitions appear that weren't much good and capacitor discharge ignitions come on the scene that were a lot better. The ignition has a very difficult job to do.

As the entire purpose of the ignition is to fire the fuel/air mixture compressed in the engine combustion chamber, with only a storage battery as a power source, the system's basic functions are quite clear: 1) Convert the relatively low voltage of the storage battery to the high voltage needed to fire the plugs, and 2) control the timing of the firing to suit varying engine speeds and loads.

The ignition system has two electrical circuits. The primary circuit operates on battery current controlled by the ignition switch and the breaker points—or in the case of the breakerless systems, by the transistor. The secondary circuit carries high voltage current induced in the coil and consists of a high tension cable between the coil and distributor, the distributor rotor and cap, the spark plug cables and the spark plugs.

When the ignition switch is turned on, the current flows from the battery through the switch to the coil primary windings, then to the distributor points which are connected to ground. Any time that the distributor points are closed there is a continuous flow of current from the battery through the ignition switch through the coil primary and through the points. This flow of current through the coil primary creates a magnetic field which stays there as long as current is flowing and the points are closed. As the engine rotates, the distributor cam pushes the points apart, which breaks the primary circuit and stops the flow of current. When the current flow ceases, the magnetic field in the coil collapses; instantly, induction pulls the current from the primary to the secondary windings. Since there are so many more turns of wire in the secondary, the voltage from the primary is multiplied many times—to as much as 25,000 or 30,000 volts. The secondary windings are connected to the spark plugs so that the high voltage can jump the spark plug gap, thus firing the mixture and making the engine run. The distributor cam is timed to the engine so that it opens the points at exactly the right moment, when the combustion chamber is full with the fresh charge of fuel/air mixture.

A condenser is connected between the coil primary and the points. The condenser's purpose is to assist in the quick collapse of the magnetic field in the coil. Many textbooks state that the condenser is in the circuit to keep the points from pitting. If that were all the condenser did, you could remove it and the car would still run. We have never found an engine with conventional (non-transistor) ignition that would run without a condenser. So this proves, at least to us, that the condenser does much more than just keep the points from pitting. Now that we have a general idea of how the ignition system works, let's look at the various components.

THE COIL

An automotive coil is an induction transformer not much different from the little transformers that are used to run

1. Basic Ignition Circuit

A   When the distributor contacts are closed the magnetic field builds up in the ignition coil

B   When the distributor contacts open the magnetic field collapses and a spark is produced at the spark plug

2. How Spark is Induced

toy trains. A train transformer takes 110 volts out of the wall outlet and converts it to a safe low voltage so that your hair doesn't stand on end every time you touch the tracks. The ignition coil works the other way around. It takes the 12 volts that is available at the battery and changes it to 10,000 or 20,000 or even 30,000 volts—whatever is needed to jump the particular gap at the spark plug.

Every modern coil has three terminals—two small threaded posts for the primary wire and a large center tower which is the connection for the secondary. Inside the coil is an iron core with the primary and secondary windings wound around it. The ratio of turns between the primary and secondary windings determines how big the step-up in voltage is between the battery voltage and secondary voltage. Because the step-up is from comparatively low battery voltage to very high spark plug voltage, the primary has relatively few turns and the secondary has many.

Current flow in the secondary is created in the coil and flows out along the secondary lead to the distributor and then to the spark plugs. If you study electrical circuitry, you will be told that all current must return to its source in order to make a complete circuit. If the circuit is broken anywhere the current will not flow. The theory works fine with low voltage but it is a source of embarrassment to many automotive instructors when they attempt to explain the path of ignition system secondary voltage. One end of the secondary winding goes out to the spark plug. The other end may be grounded to the coil can, or in most cases is grounded to the primary windings. The standard explanation of the secondary current flow is that it goes out through the spark plug wire, jumps the gap at the plug and then returns through a ground path into the battery and back through the primary windings. It may be very convenient to explain secondary current flow in this manner but the theory just doesn't hold water when you actually analyze it.

The next time somebody tells you the secondary current has to have a return path through the coil winding, ask him to reach over and touch a bare spark plug wire tip while the engine is running. He probably will refuse because he knows that the secondary current will go into his body, which can in no way be a return path to the coil windings. If you want to experiment even further, get a long spark plug wire and plug it into one distributor tower with the engine running. Walk around with the wire in your hand and touch it to various objects. You will find that the spark will jump to just about anything. In fact it will jump to any mass of electrons big enough to attract it.

When removing or installing primary wiring connections to the coil, be sure to observe proper polarity. These connec- tions are marked either positive (+) and negative (-), or "batt." (battery) and "dist." (distributor). Most cars are currently using 12-volt ignition systems with negative gound, but earlier Fords to 1956 with 6-volt systems used positive ground. When replacing coils it is important to use only those that match the rating and polarity of the system. Reversing polarity or using the improper voltage-rated coil will result in poor voltage output to the plugs.

CONDENSER

The condenser is attached across the breaker points of the distributor. Some distributors have the condenser installed inside the distributor housing, others are externally mounted. In either case it has only one lead wire, the other connection being the outer case or mounting bracket which is grounded. The wire lead is connected to the coil primary, usually at the same place as the wire from the coil to the distributor points. The condenser is a very important part of the point switching system and is in the circuit to speed up collapse of the magnetic field in the coil. It is, in effect, a small storage tank with capacity that is balanced to the circuit.

Condensers develop internal leaks that disturb this balance, the effects of which show up in the form of metal transfer on the points themselves. Even a new condenser in perfect condition will cause this metal transfer if it is not of the proper capacity. Condensers are rated in microfarads (mfds.), which can be measured with a condenser tester.

Condenser capacity usually runs from .21 to .25 mfds. If you have a problem of rapid point pitting on a particular car, it

3. Cutaway Distributor

4. Coil Construction

5. Unitary Points/Condenser

1. Simplified ignition circuit shows basic components in primary and secondary circuits.

2. When the magnetic field collapses, induction pulls the voltage from the primary windings into the secondary windings. Since there are so many more turns of wire in the secondary winding, the low voltage in the primary is multiplied many times—to as much as 25,000 or 30,000 volts.

3. High voltage exits from the coil's tower and then travels through the short secondary wire to the center tower of the distributor cap. The voltage enters the interior of the cap, makes contact with the rotor, then travels down to its pointer end where it jumps the gap to one of the cap's terminals. The spark goes up the terminal, through the spark plug wire to the plug. It jumps the plug gap and fires the mixture in the combustion chamber; and it does all that in just a fraction of a second!

4. Cutaway of typical coil shows primary and secondary windings with insulation. Iron core is necessary to create magnetic field.

5. Delco first introduced its unitary points and condenser in '72, but the government challenged its higher replacement price. Delco withdrew the unit from the market—but in '74 it was released again and accepted by all concerned.

Ignition System

is possible to reduce the pitting by selecting the proper capacity condenser. Condenser selection according to capacity is rarely done nowadays because of the amount of time it takes.

Examination of the points will indicate over- or under-capacity of the condenser by applying the "minus-minus-minus" rule: *If the minus (negative) point is minus metal (pitted), then the condenser is minus capacity.* Increasing condenser capacity would correct the condition. Conversely, if the pit were on the positive point, then the condenser would have too much capacity, and another condenser with less capacity would be the solution. This applies to both 6- and 12-volt systems, with either negative or positive ground.

Few mechanics bother to test condensers—it's easier to put in a new one. However, many apparent cases of low-capacity condenser damage result from poor ground contact between the condenser case and the distributor. A new condenser won't help unless the mounting area is kept clean and bright.

Delco introduced a new unitary points/condenser unit for use on some '72 GM cars. Mounted on the points, the condenser is connected to the insulated point arm by two thin ribbons of metal that flex each time the points open and close. With no wire lead connecting the points and condenser, there's much less radio interference and therefore no need to use a metal shield over the points. But as this design is somewhat more complex to make than the older separate points/condenser, the manufacturer believed he was justified in asking a higher price for replacement units.

When the price commission took exception to the replacement unit price and insisted that it be reduced, Delco simply removed it from the market; so what started out as an improvement in the ignition system turned into just one

more small example of govermental interference in automotive design, with the customer coming out on the short end, as usual.

Unfortunately, those distributors designed for the unitary points had no mounting hole for a separate condenser. Consequently, to install separate points and condenser, it became necessary to drill the proper holes or install a GM conversion kit. However, the kit and its installation added another $15-$20 to the price of a tune-up. Those people were trapped; reluctantly, they paid their $20—just in time to see the government permit the return of Delco's UNI-SET. The unit returned in late '74 and it appears to be identical to the original product. Designed for GM's V-8 distributor, the UNI-SET is approximately $1.75 more than the individual condenser and point set, but installation is faster, and, as before, those annoying distributor shields can be discarded.

SECONDARY WIRING

The secondary or high-voltage wiring—those connections from coil tower to center of distributor and the individual ones from distributor to spark plugs—differs a great deal in construction and capacity from that used to carry the current from battery to coil (primary wiring).

Unlike the primary wire, cable used in the secondary circuit must be heavily insulated to contain the high voltage current it carries. Most cars have cables sheathed with Hypalon insulation. This has good resistance to oil damage and it withstands the higher underhood temperatures of today's cars better than the neoprene insulation which was used in the past. If you replace the spark cables, stay away from glossy, plastic-insulated wires with "poly" or "vin" in their trade names. Some of these are transparent and look good on show cars, but their polyvinyl chloride insulation melts easily near a hot exhaust manifold. A silicone rubber insulation is used on cables designed for maximum heat resistance.

Belden 7770, Autolite 7SH, and cables sold under the generic name "7SH" in speed shops are examples. They will usually operate continously at 450° F. without failure.

All cars now use resistance type high-tension cable, but some of it isn't very resistant to internal breaks and burnouts. The conductor is usually a nylon or glass fiber string impregnated with carbon—at least on production cars.

For '75 all domestic cars use breaker-less ignitions, and to handle the increased voltage and heat, larger wires with silicone insulation are standard.

If you're careful to pull on the plug connector and not the wire when removing the cables from the spark plugs, the factory installed resistance cable can last a long time. However, many resistance cables have a soft "fluffy" conductor which fails to provide good contact for the terminals. The result is often a tiny spark which arcs between the carbon impregnated yarn and the terminal. The heat eventually burns away the conductor and produces an ignition failure.

Because of burnouts, and breaks caused by careless handling, resistance cable has gotten a bad name with many car owners. It should not be replaced with metallic conductor cable, however—for the sake of your spark plugs and the neighbors' TV. Instead, replace the factory cable with one of the reliable brands of resistance cable.

All wires, whether metallic or resistance types, should be checked with an ohmmeter. If the resistance of any one wire is above 40,000 ohms, suspect a bad wire. But before you condemn it, measure a new wire of the same type for comparison. Resistance specifications for wire vary several thousand ohms, depending on the manufacturer. While checking with the ohmmeter, flex the wire to see if there are any breaks in it. If the ohmmeter jumps to infinity, there is definitely a break. Don't worry about an increase of a few thousand ohms. That's normal with carbon-string wires.

1. Anti-Static Shields

RESULT OF UNDER-CAPACITY CONDENSER

RESULT OF OVER-CAPACITY CONDENSER

2. Results of Wrong Condenser

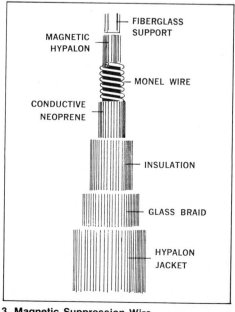

FIBERGLASS SUPPORT

MAGNETIC HYPALON

MONEL WIRE

CONDUCTIVE NEOPRENE

INSULATION

GLASS BRAID

HYPALON JACKET

3. Magnetic Suppression Wire

4. "Regular" Ignition Wire

6. Belden Conductor

5. Resistance Spark Plug Wire

7. Coated Metallic Wire

1. Since there is no condenser wire, radio interference is greatly reduced by the installation of Delco's UNI-SET, making these anti-static shields unnecessary. However, if you want to keep the shields and stick with the less expensive conventional point set, then be sure to buy the points with the slip-fit wire bracket rather than the screw type. If the screw (arrow) is used with the shield, it will probably make contact with the shield and result in a short circuit.

2. Rapid point pitting may be caused by a faulty condenser. It may be of the wrong capacity for your car. A quick check of the points will tell you. Using the "minus-minus-minus" rule you can determine if the condenser is over or under capacity. If the minus (negative) point is minus metal, then the condenser is under capacity. If the pit is on the positive point, then it's the result of over-capacity.

3. Magnetic suppression wire has a complicated construction.

4. Here's the wire that practically every mechanic is familiar with—good ol' metallic core with rubber insulation, neoprene outer covering.

5. This "whisk broom" is really the inner core of one brand of resistance spark plug wire. The filaments are impregnated with carbon and encased in a nylon sheath.

6. Belden IRS has a 1-piece tubular conductor with a strengthening nylon cord through its center and rubber insulation with a neoprene sheath.

7. This is really old stuff— metallic wire, with rubber for insulation, is further coated with a mixture of cotton and lacquer.

You may wonder why the new-car makers continue to use carbon string wire when all the aftermarket companies are promoting other types of resistance wire. The main reason is that carbon string wire is the only type that provides maximum suppression. The other wire designs have good suppression, but they don't quite keep the interference level down to that of carbon string wire.

SPARK PLUGS

Often termed the barometer of engine condition, the spark plugs have one main function: to fire properly under all normal engine operating conditions.

The art of "reading" a plug to determine engine operating efficiency is also covered in the tune-up chapter, but as part of the ignition system alone, there are certain telltale points that are important to "lighting the fire."

First, you'll need the correct plug for your engine. This is usually just a matter of walking into the parts store and telling them what kind of car you drive. They'll check a chart prepared by the spark plug company and give you the right plug—hopefully. Mistakes are occasionally made, so it's important to know a bit about spark plug design to protect yourself from accidents.

It's impossible to put an 18mm (thread diameter) plug into a 14mm hole, but a plug with the wrong *reach* could be installed. Reach refers to the length of the threaded portion of the plug shell. Always check the reach of the new plugs against that of the old. Installing a plug with a ¾-in. reach in an engine made for ⅜-in. reach spark plugs could bend the valves or knock holes in the pistons. Installing a short reach plug in a deep hole won't cause mechanical damage,

but it'll mean a definite power loss and very quick fouling or burning of the spark plugs.

It is also imperative that a spark plug of the proper heat range be used. If a plug is too "cold" for your engine, it will not retain enough combustion chamber heat to burn fouling deposits off its firing end. If the plug is too "hot," it will retain excessive combustion chamber heat. This can be extremely dangerous. Not only do overheated plugs wear out quicker, but they may become incandescent and ignite the fuel/air mixture in the cylinders before the spark actually fires. This is called preignition and, if sustained, can destroy pistons or even an engine. The destruction occurs when the mixture is ignited prematurely and the resulting burn and expansion pushes down on a piston that is trying to rise. Consequently, something has to give.

You can tell whether a plug is of the proper heat range by comparing its number to those recommended for your car. Looking at the length of the insulator nose will tell you comparatively little regarding heat range these days due to the many other variables in spark plug design. To avoid problems, use only the plug specified for your particular car, or its equivalent number in another brand. For instance, an AC44 has the same heat range as Champion's J-12Y, thus they're interchangeable.

A final factor to be considered when changing plugs is gap style. There are two popular types used in cars today. The first, called *standard gap* is the traditional plug design with its ceramic insulator nose wholly contained within the plug shell. The second type, called *projected nose,* is actually in wider use among car makers than standard gap plugs. Its insulator nose extends beyond the end of the threaded portion of the plug shell.

Both standard gap and projected nose plugs may be listed as alternatives for your car in the spark plug manufacturer's chart. If so, pick the projected nose type even if it costs a few cents more. They'll give better fouling resistance and increased power in most engines—although, in some cases, the spark may have to be retarded a few degrees to eliminate excessive "ping." Don't use projected nose plugs in engines for which they are not recommended—especially in flathead powerplants or those with highly domed pistons. There's a chance that the valves or piston crown will strike the plug nose. Plugs with platinum or other fine wire electrodes and surface gap plugs having no side electrode should not be used unless specified by the car manufacturer.

Used plugs that have been operating at the proper heat range, and whose electrodes are not badly eroded or burned, can be filed and regapped after cleaning and will give added satisfactory mileage. The spark will jump from a sharp edge on the center electrode more easily than from a rounded, worn electrode. Put the spark plug shell in a vise, then bend the ground electrode out of the way and file the center electrode flat and sharp with a small file. Blow all the filings out and set the gap with a round

Ignition System

wire gauge. If the insulator was previously sandblasted clean, you will now have new-plug performance from your old plugs. Always do the sandblasting before you file the electrode, because the sand will take away the sharp edge. Also, sandblasting or cleaning solvent are the only ways to clean plugs. Wire buffing wheels on a bench grinder are definitely out, because the wire wheel leaves metallic tracks on the porcelain that cause misfiring. Never adjust plug points by applying pressure to the center electrode, as damage to the insulator tip will result. Bend only the side or ground electrode when setting gap—and do so only with the proper tool. Never bend the electrode by hitting it against something—this sort of thing can crack the porcelain and ruin the plug.

When installing new spark plugs, do not take their gap settings for granted. Sometimes the same plug will be used on different engines with different gap settings. So you must check the gaps to see if they are set for the engine you are working on.

Care should be taken when installing plugs, new or used. Be sure that the cylinder-head plug holes are cleaned and free of dirt or carbon particles both at the gasket seat and inside the threads. Plug threads should also be clean, undamaged, and lubricated.

Screw plugs in finger-tight against the gasket, then go an additional ¼ to ⅜-turn with a plug wrench. A ⅜-turn is quite sifficient on those plugs with gaskets, but for tapered plugs (those without gaskets), 1/16-turn is the suggested limit. Any more and you might have to blast them out later.

On Chrysler's big Hemi-head engines, the plugs are mounted in long tubes and no plug gasket is used. The tube should be checked for burred edges and cracks in the plug mounting area. If the engine has an aluminum head, always inspect the plug threads with a jeweler's magnifying glass for any plug thread irregularities, and reject those with burred threads. A bad thread can quickly destroy the threads in an aluminum head and require that a Heli-Coil insert be installed to save expensive repairs or actual replacement.

RESISTOR PLUGS

Originally designed for the old flathead-6 Chryslers to allow wider gaps, which then gave a better idle, resistor plugs are now available for almost any car. If your engine has non-resistance metallic wires (recommended for racing only), resistor plugs will help quite a bit in reducing gap growth.

Resistor plugs of 5000 ohms are standard equipment on late GM cars, which also use resistor wires. Before both resistor wires and plugs were used together, the resistance value of the plugs was 10,000 ohms. Champion makes both values: the 10,000-ohm with an R prefix, and the 5000-ohm with an X prefix. Theoretically, you should use the 5000-ohm plug with resistor wires, and the 10,000-ohm plug with metallic wires. But you can pair them up the opposite way, and it won't have any effect on engine operation. Other plug makers appear to have dropped their 10,000-ohm plug and are presently making only the 5000-ohm model.

SERIES GAP PLUGS

Series gap plugs, which have an internal air gap that the spark must jump before reaching the electrodes, are gaining wide acceptance among car owners. They have the ability to clean themselves quickly of fouling deposits accumulated in low-speed, stop-and-go driving when ''opened up'' on the freeway. It takes time for spark voltage to rise to the level required to jump a plug gap. If the plug

1. Plug boots that cover the plug can sometimes be the catalyst producing flashover. Plug insulator was ruined by carbon track. Both plug and boot must be replaced.

2. All ignition wiring, resistance type or otherwise, can be checked with an ohmmeter. Extremely high reading reveals defective wires.

3. No matter how careful you are, you just can't gap plugs with a flat feeler gauge. You must use a round wire gauge.

4. If the spark plug gauge will pass through the gap with a slight amount of friction, then you can be sure that the gap is correct.

5. Five types of electrode design, from left to right: First two are racing plugs with thick metal shells and heavy-duty electrodes. Plug on left is projected-nose type with special clearance gap, while second one is a retracted-gap for use with high-compression heads and/or superchargers. The third is an aircraft plug with three side electrodes. Fourth is heavy-duty truck plug with thicker electrodes for cooler operation. Last plug is standard-gap projected-nose type for use in passenger cars.

6. The plug on the left is a standard-gap plug because its ceramic insulator nose is contained within the plug shell. Plug on right is a projected-nose plug because the nose extends beyond the end of the shell. The projected-nose protrudes further into the combustion chamber so that it's right in the path of the cool, incoming air/fuel mixture. At high speeds, it's colder than a standard plug; however, at low speeds the long insulator makes it hotter, which reduces fouling deposits.

7. Champion gap tool is handy, since individual gap gauges are retractable. Gapper is less likely to make a mistake with this setup.

1. Bad Plug Insulator and Boot

2. Checking Wire with Ohmmeter

is fouled, conductive deposits may drain off enough voltage before its peak is reached to cause a misfire. By forcing the spark current to jump an internal gap first, it is certain to be at full voltage before ever arriving at the electrodes.

TESTING SPARK PLUGS

The best advice we can give you here is to forget it. There is no way to test spark plugs outside an engine, unless you own a million-dollar laboratory. The air pressure "plug tester" used in many garages is merely a way to pacify car owners who ask for a plug test. We like the plug tester, not for "testing" plugs, but for showing the action of the spark on a fouled plug, and for demonstrating spark action between the electrodes. Plug testers don't really test plugs because they are at room temperature, and the combustion chamber in the engine is at several thousand degrees. A visual inspection of plugs will tell you more than any tester. The inner porcelain should be clean, and the center electrode should

be square and sharp, with the proper gap in evidence.

DISTRIBUTOR TYPES

There are three basic distributor systems in use on late-model American passenger cars: the conventional coil-condenser-contact point, the point-controlled transistor, and the pulse-controlled transistor. All are a combination of engine-driven rotor and electrical or mechanical switching, whose function is to deliver a usable spark.

CONVENTIONAL DISTRIBUTOR

Distributors, whether conventional or transistorized, are driven by a gear on the engine camshaft. The distributor shaft drives the breaker point cam and the rotor. Because the gearing of the distributor shaft is in time with the engine, care must be taken when replacing it to see that it is in the correct position. The simplest way to do this—after disconnecting all wires, removing the distributor cap, and loosening the mounting

clamp—is to mark the outside of the case for reference to a similar mark on the engine block, then slowly withdraw the distributor without turning it. As it is pulled out, the rotor will turn slightly as the helical (spiral) gears disengage from the cam gear.

When it is completely disengaged, mark the rotor in reference to a similar mark inside the distributor housing. Aligning these reference marks before reassembling will put the timing close enough that you should be able to fire up the engine, provided the engine crankshaft has not been turned while the assembly was out of the engine block.

The timing of the spark to the stroke of the pistons must be varied in relation to speed and load conditions. Timing is adjusted automatically by the distributor's internal spark advance system. Most distributors employ two forms of spark advance—a centrifugal mechanism that advances or retards the distributor cam in relation to the distributor drive shaft, and a vacuum diaphragm which advances or retards the position of the breaker point assembly relative to the distributor cam. Most Volkswagens and certain other economy cars use only the vacuum controlled automatic advance mechanism.

Most cars being built today have dual chamber vacuum advance units to reduce exhaust emissions at low speeds. These can be identified by the two vacuum lines leading to the diaphragm chamber on the distributor. An important exception is to be seen on recent big-engined Chrysler products. This distributor uses an electrical solenoid to retard the spark at idle or during certain types of low-speed driving. It can be identified by the plastic "box" located on the side of the distributor which houses the retarding solenoid.

Ignition points are made of very hard, tough tungsten alloys but are nevertheless subject to wear and spark erosion, and thus require periodic replacement. They control both the low-voltage saturation of the coil when closed, and the release of the high voltage when they open. It is important that they are erosion free and mate as perfectly as possi-

3. Plug Gapping

4. Checking Plug Gap

5. Different Plug Electrodes

6. Plug Types

7. Gapping Tool

Ignition System

ble to ensure total contact. The time the points are closed (measured in degrees) is called dwell or cam angle and will vary according to point gap.

Wide point gaps open slowly, causing excessive arcing and burning; and the wider the gap the shorter the dwell, which causes insufficient coil saturation and a missed spark (or maybe a whole bunch of missed sparks and an engine that won't run). If too close, the points are snapped open, and have a tendency to bounce. A close gap gives more dwell, but the points don't separate enough to give a clean collapse of the primary, and we have a misfire.

The distributors used on some cars have two sets of points (dual points) connected so that the primary current flows when either set is closed. The points are staggered so that one set opens before the other, with the spark occurring when the second set opens. Because of the staggered position, the first set closes before the other, increasing the dwell for more spark intensity at high rpm.

Another wear point is the rubbing block, a phenolic or plastic block that wears very well if there is a slight amount of lubricant in the form of light oil or a sparing smear of grease on the cam whenever points are checked or replaced. Many GM distributors have an oil-saturated wick for lubricating the rubbing block, and this should be changed, not re-oiled, when replacing points.

You can buy a "point file" in almost any auto parts house, but you would do yourself a favor by using it to file spark plugs, not points. If the points need filing, they should be replaced. Line up the point surfaces as we indicate in the tune-up chapter, and then set the gap either with a feeler gauge or a dwell meter. Don't ever attempt to gap worn or pitted points with a feeler gauge. A feeler gauge will not be accurate on a rough surface. Worn points must be set with a dial indicator or a dwell meter.

With new points, some mechanics recommend a setting that is about .003-in.

wider than specified to compensate for the initial rubbing block wear. This is usually not necessary if the rubbing block lines up with the cam.

Make sure the rubbing block is resting exactly on the tip of the breaker point cam when you set point gap with a feeler gauge.

Tampering with the centrifugal or vacuum advance mechanisms without the proper test equipment may result in permanent damage to the engine from incorrect spark advance. There are specified advance curves for both of these functions for each make of car, and they are available to mechanics with test bench facilities for checking out and adjusting to manufacturers' specs.

Rebuilding for such things as bearing or shaft replacement also requires expert techniques and special tools; it is impractical for the occasional home mechanic to attempt.

POINT-CONTROLLED TRANSISTOR DISTRIBUTOR

Transistors—those mysterious "things" that have revolutionized electronics, miniaturized our radios and television sets, and are now used in automotive ignition systems—are accepted as a rather commonplace component, yet few people really know what they are and what they actually do in a circuit.

Transistors are a combination of man-made crystalline materials which can be

1. Plug Core Bridging

2. Chamber Deposits

3. Foreign Particles

4. Glazed Plug

5. Cutaway of Dirty Insulator

6. Plugs Ruined by Detonation

7. Dirty Insulator

8. Hot and Cold Plugs

9. Tip Temperature Extremes

10. Testing Coil Polarity

likened in operation to a relay with no moving parts or a current-operated switch. They act as an insulator or non-conductor until such time as small amounts of current are applied to the proper segment, then they become highly conductive and capable of carrying large amounts of current.

They are used as a master switch (in-

1. Core bridging—buildup of combustion chamber deposits between insulator and shell—is caused by poor oil or bad oil control.

2. Combustion chamber deposits can also lodge between the electrodes, thus shorting out the plug. Cleaning and regapping are the answer.

3. This is what can happen when dirt, dust, and sand enter with the fuel/air mixture. Ineffective air cleaner and bad intake gasket or loose bolts are usually the cause.

4. Fast acceleration after prolonged low-speed driving can produce a hard, glassy brown coating on the insulator tip and electrode. Glaze is conductive and can ruin plugs.

5. If you were to cut away the outer shell of the plug, this is what a dirty insulator would look like. Sandblaster will remove this.

6. Detonation can not only ruin pistons, but also spark plugs. The ground electrode was snapped off clean by the force of detonation.

7. A dirty insulator top can cause flashover, and a dead cylinder. Clean upper insulator with a rag and solvent only, never by sandblasting.

8. The plug with the longer nose will run hotter because the heat cannot get to the cooling water as easily. The hot plug will stay clean longer, but it may burn up too.

9. Fouled plug at bottom is too "cold." Plug at top shows signs of overheating, with the possibility of preignition damage. Condition of plug in the middle shows proper heat range choice for particular use.

10. To test for reversed coil polarity, remove one plug wire, hold wire and pencil with clothespins and start the engine. Insert point between wire and plug. Spark flaring between pencil and plug means correct coil polarity.

stead of the points) to trigger the coil saturation and collapse; the points are used to control the very low voltage necessary to make the transistor act as a higher voltage switch. As a result, the points are handling much smaller amounts of current than with a conventional system. Arcing, and the need for a condenser to reduce it are eliminated, increasing point life considerably.

Because of the very rapid flow of current, there is no appreciable time lag, and timing procedures and advance adjustments are the same as with conventional systems. Transistors are sensitive to heat and other electronic breakdowns and should be checked for shorting if the ignition fails to fire.

Heat sensitivity is partially controlled by mounting the transistors in a finned case or heat sink. However, this alone is not enough protection if the unit is placed where severe engine heat can reach it. On stock, factory-installed transistor systems, never change the location of the heat sink. When installing an optional transistor system, mount it in the coolest part of the engine compartment you can find.

Points do have to be checked but only to compensate for rubbing block wear, which, after the initial break-in, should stay stable for about 20,000 miles. However, as with all point systems, the rubbing block and distributor cam should be lightly lubricated with ignition grease to reduce wear. As the rubbing block wears, the point gap decreases, thus altering ignition timing; lubrication reduces these changes—but timing must still be checked periodically.

Be very careful not to use an oily feeler gauge, since even the lightest film on the points can cause trouble with the low voltage carried by the contacts in a transistor system. Coils for transistorized ignition systems are slightly different in their primary windings from standard ones. It is recommended that only coils made for these systems be used, since adding only the transistorized switching unit with the standard coil could shorten the life of both parts, in addition to reducing the efficiency of the transistor.

PULSE-CONTROLLED TRANSISTOR DISTRIBUTOR

The magnetic-pulse distributor goes back to the '60's when it was introduced as an option on the Corvette Sting Ray. The system was expensive and few were

built, but it was continued into '71. That same year, GM used Pontiac as a guinea pig for its new Unitized ignition. The distributor in this system is basically the same as the Corvette magnetic-pulse type but the amplifier was replaced with an electronic module. The module does the same job as the amplifier, except that it's much smaller; also, instead of being mounted on the firewall or fender, it is screwed directly into the distributor housing. The distributor cap is larger than a conventional cap because a small ignition coil attaches to its top. As the name implies, the Unitized ignition combines the coil and the module into one unit. The system continued as an option into '73 but only on 455, 4-bbl. engines. It proved to be efficient and dependable so GM made a few minor changes and released it to the public as standard equipment on all of their 1975 cars. It is now called "HEI" or High Energy Ignition. On V-8's the coil is integral; on the other engines it's externally mounted.

GM was the first to have magnetic-pulse ignition, but Chrysler Corp. was the first to standardize it. The Chrysler distributor with separate amplifier was optional on some '72 models; for '73, though, it was the only distributor available. Ford installed its Solid State Ignition on some '74 models but, as with Chrysler and GM, it became standard equipment for '75. AMC joined the others in '75 with its Prestolite-manufactured Breakerless Inductive Discharge (BID) system. Each of these units differs somewhat in design; however, each is a highly sophisticated version of the point-controlled transistorized ignition in that all switching is done electronically. There is no rubbing block wear and no point gap to maintain, ensuring long and uniform operation. Both vacuum and centrifugal advance mechanisms are used to compensate for varying engine speeds and loads in much the same manner as with conventional point-type distributors.

The pulse amplifier unit has no moving parts, and exclusive of the permanent lubricated bearings in the distributor, there are no rubbing or contacting parts that require adjusting to compensate for wear. A periodic check of both primary- and high-voltage wiring and both advance mechanisms should be all the maintenance required for the pulse-controlled transistor ignition system.

The internal construction of the

Ignition System

magnetic-pulse distributor consists of a rotating pole piece in place of the breaker point cam. This has the same number of equally spaced lobes as the number of engine cylinders. It rotates inside a magnetic pickup assembly which takes the place of the breaker plate/contact point assembly. This magnetic pickup is composed of a permanent magnet made of ceramic material, a pole piece and a pickup coil. The stationary pole piece, like the rotating pole piece, has equally spaced internal lobes or teeth, one for each cylinder of the engine. This magnetic pickup, located in the lower section of the distributor housing, is moved by the vacuum diaphragm to control vacuum advance. The rotating pole piece is coupled to the centrifugal advance mechanism, providing spark control compensation for engine speed. A rotor tops the whole internal assembly and acts as the high-voltage distributor to the individual spark plugs.

As the distributor's internal components rotate, the teeth in the rotating pole piece line up with the internal projections on the permanent magnet pole piece, causing an induced current in the pickup coil. This current is sufficient to trigger the transistors in the ignition pulse amplifier circuit, resulting in coil saturation, release of coil high voltage to the distributor, and proper distribution to the spark plugs. Because of the rather complicated circuitry in the pulse amplifier system, it is recommended that it be tested only with the proper equipment and by qualified ignition experts. A mistake in polarity, or high voltage reaching low-voltage segments of the circuits, can result in permanent damage to the transistorized circuit.

TROUBLESHOOTING THE CHRYSLER ELECTRONIC IGNITION

With the Chrysler electronic ignition system, a bad coil causing a stumble seems to be the number one problem you'll encounter. Chrysler uses an oil-filled coil, and as primary buildup time is considerable, the coil tends to consistently overheat and eventually burns out. Chrysler originally used the same switching module for all applications, but in an effort to correct the coil burnout problem, the switching module transistor was changed to three different ones, identified by the sticker color on the module—gold, green and silver.

Because the switching module controls engine firing, you must be careful not to replace a defective module with one of the incorrect rating. If you install a 6-cylinder module on an 8-cylinder engine, it will fire too slowly and the result is a sluggish running car. But operating a 6-cylinder engine when incorrectly equipped with an 8-cylinder module will cause too rapid a rate of firing; at high engine speeds, the rpm will build up and the engine will blow. Incidentally, the switching module has a tendency to vibrate loose from its firewall mounting, so it should be tightened periodically.

If your Chrysler electronic ignition quits dead on the road, check the pickup coil tooth. The Chrysler distributor continues to use the single-pivot connection on the breaker plate, which is characteristic of the conventional Chrysler distributor. With sufficient wear, the

1. Wobbling the plug while cleaning, is important. It allows sand to get into all parts of plug and remove carbon particles.

2. Before removing the distributor, observe the direction of the rotor's pointer and align it with a spot on the engine. Make a reference mark in chalk on the engine so that the distributor can be returned to the same location.

3. Typical Autolite-Ford dual-advance distributor, combining a single-diaphragm advance unit with centrifugal advance weights located below breaker plate.

4. Many distributors have a lubricating wick in the top of their shafts. Periodically, soak it with a few drops of oil. This will keep the centrifugal advance working smoothly. GM's V-8 distributors have the advance weights on top, so there is no need for an oil wick.

5. To actually remove the distributor, simply disconnect the vacuum advance line, take off the primary wire and distributor cap, and loosen the hold-down bolt. On most cars, the distributor can be lifted out after the bolt is removed.

6. You can adjust the point gap on this Delco-Remy "window" distributor while the engine is running, either with or without a dwell meter.

7. GM's 6-cylinder distributor has no point-gap window. The gap must be adjusted with the cap removed like any non-GM distributor. Unlike the V-8 distributor, this Delco model has the centrifugal advance below the breaker plate.

1. Cleaning a Plug

2. Distributor Removal

4. Distributor Lubing

3. Dual-Advance Distributor

5. Distributor Hold-Down Bolt

breaker plate loosens; then, when the vacuum advance kicks in, it pulls the pickup coil down. This causes the breaker plate to lean or tilt and eventually brings the coil's tooth into contact with the revolving reluctor teeth, breaking off the coil tooth and stopping the car. By the way, those reluctor teeth are very sharp—and would you believe that some people (including mechanics) think those teeth should actually be filed to get rid of the sharp edges? Don't do it!

A third potential problem area lies in the secondary circuitry—Chrysler didn't change it one bit, so all the secondary problems you'd encounter with a conventional ignition and distributor are still quite apparent.

TROUBLESHOOTING GM'S HIGH ENERGY IGNITION

Since the High Energy Ignition puts out about 10,000 volts more than a conventional GM system, a larger distributor cap and rotor are required to keep the high voltage from leaking; but as the new distributor cap is no thicker than the conventional one, it's prone to trouble. Why the extra voltage? Well, when GM engines were set very lean at idle back in 1971 to help meet the emissions specifications, a phenomenon referred to

as "acceleration glazing" (caused by excessive start/stop driving) reduced spark plug life by about 50% on the '71-'73 models. This occurred because there was insufficient voltage available to fire the glazed plugs. So, to extend plug life back to its original 10,000-12,000 miles, GM increased the system voltage and we're right back where we started.

The High Energy Ignition is really too new to allow us to locate all of the gremlins that can and will pop up, but you should be aware that each application uses a different cap-mounted coil. They all *look* alike and *hook up* alike, but system specifications and coil windings differ, not only from GM division to GM division, but from engine to engine within a division. Don't substitute a coil that does not carry the same part number as the one it replaces, or you'll blow it. You'll also destroy it if you hook up a dwell-tach test unit to the coil terminal marked "tach," if that unit lacks the circuit capability required to test a transistorized ignition.

You may also have problems with the GM pickup coil. Occasionally, one will overheat and exceed the stated ohm value. The engine will not start again until the pickup coil cools to under that stated value. This is a tough one to test for, as the pickup coil is down in the distributor;

by the time you clear a path to it, it's likely to have cooled sufficiently to test out okay—then what do you do? If you suspect pickup coil malfunction, heat it up and cool it down quickly for test purposes using a ladies' hair drier and a can of refrigerant.

TROUBLESHOOTING FORD'S SOLID STATE IGNITION

The '74 Ford system experienced considerable trouble in the form of poor signal transmission, caused by loose connections between the distributor and the electronic module. Packed in the ends of the connector plugs, to keep moisture out, is what GM refers to as "DEC" grease, for "Distributor Electronic Control." Whenever you disconnect these plugs, replace the DEC grease in sufficient quantity to cause it to ooze out when the plugs are reinstalled.

Ford changed the harness wire pin connectors and the wire colors for '75, which is of no interest unless you find it necessary to test the pin connectors to troubleshoot the circuitry. And if you do, like most of us, you'd expect that the '74 and '75 systems are the same. So if you get a series of weird readings, let that jog your memory—you're testing the wrong circuits for the wrong thing.

6. Delco-Remy "Window" Distributor

1. Breaker Plate Attaching Screws
2. Condenser Attaching Screws
3. Condenser
4. Breaker Plate Assembly
4a. Cam Lubricator
5. Vacuum Control Assembly
6. Vacuum Control Attaching Screws
7. Housing
8. Cap
9. Rotor
10. Contact Point Attaching Screw
11. Contact Point Assembly
12. Weight Cover Attaching Screws
13. Weight Cover
14. Weight Springs
15. Advance Weights
16. Cam Assembly
17. Main Shaft Assembly
18. Roll Pin
19. Drive Gear

7. Six-Cylinder GM Distributor

Ignition System

TROUBLESHOOTING THE AMC BID SYSTEM

The major malfunction to date with the AMC BID system is a tendency toward sensor failure—and when the sensor fails, the engine quits, as in the case of a Chrysler electronic ignition with a broken pickup coil. It's a good idea to carry a replacement sensor unit with you, along with a copy of Petersen's *How To Tune Your Car,* 4th edition, which contains a step-by-step installation procedure. A few minutes spent with a screwdriver and pliers can save you a hefty tow bill.

DISTRIBUTOR INSTALLATION

When installing a distributor that has been removed from the engine without being marked, it is important to establish an initial timing setting. For this operation it is necessary to line up the timing marks on the flywheel or vibration damper in relation to the compression stroke of No. 1 cylinder.

Since modern auto engines are not equipped with provisions for handcranking, a remote starter switch or someone blipping the starter switch in the car will be necessary to get the timing marks coordinated with the compression stroke.

Remove the spark plug from No. 1 cylinder. For deeply recessed plug access on some Chrysler Corp. engines, a compression gauge is almost a necessity. Hold your thumb over the plug hole or observe the gauge while blipping the starter switch, noting a pressure buildup, which will indicate that the piston is coming up on its compression stroke. Watch for the timing mark which indicates the proper number of degrees before top dead center for ignition timing. Some vibration dampers have calibrations on either side of top dead center, so be sure the engine is stopped on the factory recommended timing mark.

Install the distributor so that the rotor lines up with the No. 1 cylinder spark plug lead on the cap. Ease the assembly down into the block mounting hole and engage the lower gear with the one on the camshaft. As these gears are helical, the distributor shaft will turn as the teeth are meshed, naturally causing the rotor to turn also. Be sure to allow for this and set the rotor off just enough before inserting the assembly into the block hole so that when it is fully seated, the rotor is in the No. 1 cylinder position.

Install the distributor mounting bolt and clamp, but leave it loose enough so that the distributor body can be turned. Turn the distributor body slowly, opposite to the direction that the cam rotates. Stop turning the distributor the instant the points open, then tighten the holddown bolt and your engine will be timed close enough to allow it to run. You should only have to turn the distributor a very small amount. If, before you start turning it, the rubbing block is on the wrong side of a cam lobe (closing side instead of opening side), then when you turn the distributor to the point opening

1. **Prestolite Dual-Point Distributor**

2. Solenoid Controlled Distributor

3. Tach Drive

4. Rotor Alignment

5. Transistor Circuit

6. Breakerless Distributor

1. Chrysler has used the Prestolite dual-point distributor on some of its high-performance models. This unit differs from the Ford dual-point unit in that it has both vacuum and centrifugal advance.

2. Chrysler products with solenoid controlled distributors should have both the vacuum hose and solenoid wire disconnected when setting the ignition timing.

3. Dual-point Prestolite unit was used on Chrysler high-performance models. Housing is cast iron instead of aluminum. Some models of the dual-pointer came with tach drive, but fit only Chrysler engines.

4. The rotor may turn as the distributor is withdrawn from the engine. Note its final position. When reinstalling the distributor, place the cam in this same position and it should turn back to its original position as the cam and distributor gears engage.

5. The Ford contact-controlled transistor circuit—used in the '60's—is nothing more than a conventional ignition system with a transistorized switching device inserted between the points and the primary circuit. Points only tell the transistor when to turn the current on and off.

6. Delco Remy's breakerless distributor was an option on some GM cars—particularly the Corvette. It was the forerunner of GM's present High Energy Ignition. HEI's control module is very small and usually mounted within the distributor. The module on this earlier unit was much larger and usually mounted on a fender or nearby on the firewall.

position, the rotor will no longer be under No. 1 segment in the cap. If this happens, you are probably one tooth off. Remove the hold-down clamp, lift the distributor until the gears demesh, and move the shaft one tooth in whichever direction you need to go. Then move the distributor body to the position where the points are just opening. The important part of this procedure is determining exactly when the points open. You can do it with a piece of tissue or cigarette paper between the points. The paper will come loose just as the points separate. A better way is to use a test light connected to the distributor primary terminal and ground. If your test light does not have a battery in it, turn the ignition switch on and the test light will be off while the points are closed. When the test light comes on, you will know the points have opened. If you have a battery-powered test light, then disconnect the primary wire from the distributor and connect the test light to the distributor primary terminal and ground. The light will be on when the points are closed and will go off the instant they separate. Remember that you turn the distributor body opposite to the direction that the cam rotates.

After tightening the hold-down clamp, check to be sure the points are just opening, and that the rotor tip is under the No. 1 segment in the cap. If, no matter what you do, the rotor and point timing won't check out, then you may have one of those rare cases of a distributor that is assembled wrong. There have been some cases where a cam that is pressed onto the shaft has slipped, making it impossible to set the point and rotor timing correctly. The engine may run, but not very well because the rotor is

between two segments and the spark sometimes goes to the proper cylinder and sometimes to the wrong one. Your chances of encountering this problem are extremely rare.

Static timing should always be followed by a timing light check with the engine running. When using a timing light, the vacuum hose must be taken off the distributor and plugged. Remove and plug both hoses on cars with double chamber advance units. Chrysler products with solenoid-controlled distributors should have both the vacuum hose and solenoid wire disconnected. Always remove the solenoid wire from the carburetor, not the distributor. This prevents accidental shorts and damaged wiring.

Before replacing the cap, examine it as well as the rotor for cracks. Very often undetected damage at these points can cause trouble not apparent in circuit test procedures.

CAPACITOR-DISCHARGE IGNITION

Transistor ignitions came on the marketplace with a big splash. It seemed as if everybody was making one. It also seemed as if every garage had one lying in the corner somewhere that they had taken off because it didn't work right.

Ignition System

Transistor ignitions were largely a failure, because the transistors were so delicate. All you had to do to blow one of them was to pull the wire out of the coil and crank the engine. The tremendous build-up of voltage would back up and blow one or more of the transistors.

Capacitor-discharge ignitions are admittedly a type of transistor design, but they are considerably better and a great deal tougher. A transistor ignition employs the same old method of collapsing the coil field to create the secondary spark. The capacitor-discharge or CD ignition uses an entirely different method. It charges up a capacitor, which then is triggered by either points or a pulse-control distributor so that the capacitor fires a charge through the coil primary. Because the capacitor kicks about 250 volts into the coil's primary windings instead of the 6 or 12 volts of a conventional ignition, the result is a powerful spark that does the job a lot better than either transistor or conventional ignition systems.

A capacitor-discharge ignition will fire spark plugs that a conventional ignition could never hope to fire, because the capacitor-discharge ignition does not rely on a slow build-up of voltage. It zaps the coil and the coil zaps the spark plug—immediately, so that there is no chance for any leak of voltage that could cause a misfire (with the exception of some bad wiring). For more information on CD and transistor ignitions, see Petersen's *Basic Ignition and Electrical Systems No. 5.*

IGNITION BYPASS

It may seem strange, but the ignition coil does not receive full battery voltage during normal running of the engine. A primary resistor is inserted in the circuitry between the ignition switch and the battery terminal on the coil. Current from the battery flows through the ignition switch, through the resistor, then into the coil primary and on to the distributor points. The resistor cuts down on the amount of current flow in the circuit so that the spark is not as strong as it would be if the resistor were not there.

Cutting down on the spark output may seem foolish, but the system is designed that way for a particular purpose. It would be easy to design an ignition coil that would work on full battery voltage. But then the coil would only be able to put out a spark of the same strength no matter what the conditions were. We need an excessively strong spark during cranking to get the engine started, but once it's running, we don't need as much spark. What the engineers have done is to design a coil that works with a resistor to give a normal spark during running, but when the engine is being cranked, a special circuit bypasses the resistor so that the coil receives more voltage.

The coil was not actually designed to work under full battery voltage. When it is operated on full battery voltage, it puts out a spark that will knock you right out of the engine compartment. However, it would be impossible to operate the coil on full battery voltage very long. It would burn up. So the coil receives full battery voltage only during engine cranking, via the bypass circuit.

The resistance itself may be in either of two forms: a wire wound around a ceramic insulator (a ballast resistor) and mounted on the firewall or near the coil; or in the case of Delco systems, a resistance wire between the ignition switch and the coil. If the car starts but stalls as soon as the key is turned from the "start" to "run" position, it may be that this wire is burned out. Connect a jumper wire from the hot side of the battery to the small coil terminal that's not connected to the distributor. If the engine keeps running, you'll know that the resistance wire is shot.

SPECIAL IGNITION ACCESSORIES

By and large, steer clear of "something for nothing" thingamajigs that are guaranteed to intensify your ignition miraculously. These gimmicks are usually just resistance-increasing bits of metal, air gaps or coils that will produce a hotter spark, but they are terribly overpriced. Series-gap or resistor spark plugs perform the same function for only pennies more than standard plugs.

1. Chrysler Corp. went over to the electronic (transistor) ignition system with its 1973 models. Also available on some 1972 models, Chrysler's EIS includes a no-points distributor for minimum maintenance requirements.

2. HEI (High-Energy Ignition) is used by GM on all of the company's 1975 cars. It's the only Detroit ignition that mounts the control module inside the distributor. When making repairs to the HEI, use only the parts intended for that car. Buick, Olds and Pontiac use a pickup and coil with polarity opposite to that of Chevy; interchanging them will cause hard starting and backfiring during engine cranking.

3. Exploded view of Ford's breakerless distributor shows that it is not too different from the conventional type. Eight-tooth armature and magnetic pickup replace the movable and fixed points respectively. Wiring harness connects with electronic amplifier and signals it when to break the primary circuit to make a spark.

4. Chrysler V-8 and 6-cylinder distributors are very similar except for the cap and reluctor. Basically, the only difference is in the number of cylinders used.

5. Inside AMC's BID distributor, a star-shaped armature, called a trigger wheel, has replaced the movable point. A magnetic sensor has replaced the fixed point and the condenser.

6. Accel, a long-established, well-known company in racing circles, has expanded into manufacturing ignitions for family car replacements. Many other aftermarket ignitions are also available.

7. Jacobs' computer ignition is a CD system capable of being used with either breaker or breakerless distributors. It will beep when in service and has a 3-way switch: on, anti-theft (grounded coil) and off. In the off position, the system reverts to stock.

1. Chrysler's Breakerless Distributor

PERMANENT MAGNET · POLE PIECE · PICK-UP COIL · IGNITION COIL · SWITCHING TRANSISTOR · DISTRIBUTOR · RELUCTOR · BALLAST RESISTOR · CONTROL UNIT

2. GM's HEI System

VACUUM UNIT ATTACHING SCREWS · THIN "C" WASHER · PICKUP COIL LEADS · ATTACHING SCREW · MODULE · GROUND SCREW · MODULE CONNECTOR · CAPACITOR

Spark plug cables with silicone rubber insulation should be used wherever unavoidable proximity to the exhaust headers requires extra heat protection. Solderless plug connectors (such as the Rajah brand of terminal ends) have been and still are the mark of well-maintained ignition systems.

Spark plugs are no exception to the something-for-nothing pitch in exaggerated advertising claims. Plugs from reliable manufacturers are the result of extensive, costly research and development, but none can compensate for a poor ignition system or a worn-out engine. Special racing plugs are available in a wide variety of reach lengths and thread diameters. Because of their wire-type electrodes, they require special tools for changing the gap. When buying such plugs, make sure that the proper gapping tools are included as part of your purchase.

ELECTRONIC IGNITIONS

All American automakers have converted to some form of breakerless ignition in the past few years. In addition, a veritable plethora of aftermarket electronic ignitions fill the shelves of auto parts stores from coast to coast. Little has been changed in the ignitions of Chrysler, Ford, GM or AMC cars, but buyer pressure has pretty well forced all the poorly made replacement units off the shelves.

If your present car is not equipped with an electronic ignition, consider these reasons for converting to one soon. Basically, Detroit converted for two reasons: increased gas mileage and less trouble in meeting emission standards. Emission controls must, by law, be guar-

anteed for 50,000 miles; while breaker point distributors will not perform adequately for that length of time, electronic ignitions will. Mileage is improved, in most cases, because the hotter spark burns the air/fuel mixture more thoroughly. Virtually no maintenance is needed on an electronic distributor for over 50,000 miles, and usually only one spark plug change is needed during the same period.

3. Ford's Breakerless Distributor

4. Chrysler V-8 Distributor

1. DISTRIBUTOR CAP
2. ROTOR
3. DUST SHIELD
4. TRIGGER WHEEL
5. FELT PAD
6. SENSOR ASSEMBLY
7. SHAFT ASSEMBLY
8. HOUSING
9. VACUUM CONTROL
10. SHIM
11. DRIVE GEAR
12. PIN

5. AMC's BID Distributor

6. Accel's Conversion System

7. Jacobs' Computer Ignition

Charging System

Would you believe that you could generate electricity just by moving a coil of wire or even a single wire between the ends of a horseshoe magnet? We don't know why it happens, but really there's no need to. As long as we accept the fact that magnetism plus movement will create electricity, then all we have to do is learn how to use it. If moving the wire between the ends of the horseshoe magnet will create electricity in the wire, it seems logical that we might get more electricity if we use two wires. An automotive generator actually uses a lot of wires and gets a lot of electricity, enough to charge the battery and run the car's complete electrical system.

There's another peculiarity about this magnetism and electricity business. Granted: magnetism and movement will create electricity. But it also works the other way around; electricity will create magnetism.

GENERATOR SYSTEMS

Here's the way it works in an automotive generator. The frame of the generator has some coils attached to it called the field coils. In the middle of each field coil is a hunk of iron called the pole shoe. The pole shoes are a kind of weak magnet, probably not even as strong as the little magnets that you use on a magnetic bulletin board. But the magnetism that is in the pole shoes is enough to create electricity in any wire that moves through the magnetic field. The wire in which the electricity is created is in the armature. Of course, the armature has a lot of wires because we want a lot of electricity.

When the engine starts, the generator is turned by the fan belt and electricity is created in the armature because it is rotating in a magnetic field. If the weak magnetic field around the pole shoes was all we had, then we wouldn't get much electricity out of our generator. But a generator feeds itself. The electricity that is created from the armature is fed back into the field coils. This additional electricity strengthens the magnetic field around the pole shoes and causes a greater strength of electricity to be created in the armature.

Now that we have the thing going, electricity in the armature is available to charge the battery, run the lights, blow the horn, or anything else. The problem is getting the electricity out of the armature while it is moving. This is where the commutator and the brushes come in. One brush running on the armature picks up the electrical current and connects to a wire that runs the current out of the generator so that it can be used

to operate the car's electrical system. From the light bulb, radio, ignition system or whatever unit is being operated, the electricity returns along a ground path to the frame of the generator and then through the other brush back into the armature. In most cases the electricity must return to its source in a complete circle route. In fact, the word circuit means "circle."

A generator alone can be hooked up to the electrical system of the car and it will put out both current and voltage enough to do the job. But you will have no control over it. The faster the engine goes, the more the generator puts out until it reaches a point where it blows itself right out of the car from trying to put out more than it can stand. An uncontrolled generator will put out 30, 40 or 50 volts, even higher. The car's system is made to run in the area of 12 volts, so we must do something to control the output of the generator if we don't want to burn out all the light bulbs and blow up the radio.

Remember we said that a generator starts putting out electricity because of residual magnetism in the pole shoes. But any electricity above that very small amount depends upon a feedback of current from the armature into the field windings. If the current were not fed back into the field windings, generator voltage would never rise. It just wouldn't charge. To control the generator then, all we have to do is regulate the amount of current that flows through the field windings, and that is the function of the regulator.

Regulation in all modern generators is done with a vibrating regulator. The regulator is set up so that field current runs through a pair of points. Underneath the points there is an electromagnet operated by electricity from the generator. There are two of these electromagnetic regulating units in the regulator, each with its own pair of points. One of them keeps the voltage from going too high, and the other limits the current. If either voltage or

current rises above a safe value, the strength of the magnet increases so that the points are pulled apart. The instant the points separate, the generator goes dead because there is no field current. When the generator goes dead, this kills off the electricity it is feeding the electromagnet, and so the magnetism dies and a spring pulls the points back together. The instant that the points come together, the generator is back in business, and then the same thing happens all over again, separating the points.

Any time either current or voltage rises to the preset value, the voltage or current regulator points will start vibrating. Adjustment is by setting the tension on the spring that pulls the points closed. It amounts to a balancing of the two forces—the spring versus the magnetism that tries to pull the points apart. This, combined with the vibrating of the points, results in a system that can be set to current or voltage limits as close as 1/10th of a volt.

A third unit in all modern regulators is the cutout. If the generator is to charge

1. Look carefully at the electrical plug (arrow) on this 1972 Delco alternator. Contacts are arranged edge-to-edge, which indicates this is an integral charging system, with regulator inside alternator.

2. Standard Delco alternator (with regulator on firewall) looks pretty much the same, but contacts placed side-to-side are the tipoff. Service on this model is similar to that on older Delco alternators.

3. Inside integral Delco alternator, held by three Phillips-head screws, is the regulator. Diode arrangement is different, too, much easier to change than on older models.

4. These are typical generator mountings on late-model car, showing retaining brackets and belt adjustment provisions.

1. Delco Integral Charging System

2. Delco Standard Alternator

the battery, it must be electrically connected to the battery. If the engine is stopped and the generator is still connected to the battery, current can flow from the battery into the generator in an attempt to turn the generator into a motor. All that the cutout does is disconnect the generator from the electrical system whenever the generator is either not working or is operating at so slow a speed that current would flow from the battery to the generator. When the engine is at rest, the cutout points must be open. Any time the engine is running above idle and the charging system is operating correctly, the cutout points must be closed. If you are lucky enough to have a car with an ammeter that is sensitive to small fluctuations in current flow, you will notice that as you allow the engine to come down to a normal curb idle, the ammeter will go slightly to the discharge side of zero and then it will spring back to the zero position. What has happened is that the generator is turning too slowly to charge the battery, so the battery starts to feed current back into the generator. The minus reading that you see on the ammeter is that current flow back through the generator. But it doesn't show on the ammeter very long because that reverse current forces the cutout to open and then the ammeter returns to the zero position. If your car only has a red discharge light instead of an ammeter, then you can't watch all these fancy goings-on.

Normal and abnormal charging is far more easily spotted if the car has a dash-mounted ammeter. Usually, the ammeter will show a charge rate of about 7 to 10 amps at normal driving speeds soon after the engine is started. This may be as high as 20 amps following a very long, hard cranking session in cold weather. After the car has been driven for a short distance at highway speeds, the reading should drop to about 2 to 5 amps—depending on how many lights and accessories are in operation. At an idle, the ammeter should indicate no more than a 3-amp discharge, although this may fall to as much as a 15-amp discharge if several accessories are in use. Cars equipped with alternators should seldom show any discharge.

The ammeter needle should never follow engine speed from one extreme of the dial to the other. If it does, the headlights probably also grow very dim proportional to rpm. This condition—or a constant discharge reading, exceptionally high amperage at highway speeds, and conspicuous deviations from the "norms" outlined above—are all signs that the charging system needs work.

DIAGNOSIS AND CORRECTION

Low charging or *no charging* is undoubtedly the most common type of trouble. If the generator light has come on—and stays on—or the ammeter shows a constant and steady discharge, there is no charging taking place at all. If this is accompanied by rising cooling system temperatures, it is probably a broken fan belt, but if the belt is properly tensioned and in one piece, the charging system is the culprit.

A glowing generator light, or an ammeter reading slightly below zero when

3. Delco Integral Regulator

driving at highway speeds, means a low generator output. Once again, this may be only a sign that the fan belt is loose, but if it's not, the trouble is electrical.

Perhaps you're driving along and the ammeter dips suddenly into the discharge zone and then bounces back a few moments later to a point well up in the charge zone. This shows that the charging system is functioning only part of the time. An "idiot light" that winks on and off as you cruise, indicates the same type of trouble exists. If the light has a slight glow, look for a high-resistance connection at the starter solenoid or the ignition switch.

In some cars, the light will glow at cruising speed even though the entire charging system is in excellent condition. Why does this happen? Well, here's a simple explanation. In the first place, we know that the light is connected between the generator output and the battery, and when the generator is dead or at low rpm its voltage is less than the battery's, so current flows from the battery through the light to the generator. We also know that when the generator is charging, it raises the voltage throughout the electrical system of the car. And since the voltage on both sides of the light is the same, no current flows through it and the light stays off. However, in some cars—and here's our problem—the wire from the battery to the light is too long, and this results in more voltage on the generator side of the light. Because of the unequal voltage, current flows through the light and makes it glow.

You can eliminate the bothersome glow by running a wire directly from the battery terminal of the regulator to the battery side of the ignition switch. This will equalize the voltage and keep the light out. But if you are going to go to all that trouble (and if you're *that* sensitive about your generator), why not install an ammeter so you will really know what's going on? Instructions come with every new ammeter, and they're not hard to install if you follow directions carefully.

Anyway, with a light or a meter, you can still have charging system troubles; with the following series of steps you can diagnose and correct the problem.

Step 1—Examine the Battery. Test it with a hydrometer. If it is fully charged, discharge it by running the starter for a few moments. Then start the engine. If the ammeter shows a normal charge rate it may be that all is well, but probably

4. Generator Mountings

the low-charge, no-charge condition will still be present if the original indication of trouble was a discharge reading and not merely a zero reading. If hydrometer testing shows all of the battery cells to be uniformly discharged, there is a definite charging system problem.

Step 2—Clean the Connections. There is very little use in trying to test the charging system unless you're sure that all connections are making good electrical contact. Sometimes a bad connection can be located with the engine running by having someone watch the ammeter while you wiggle the various wires and terminals that are part of the charging circuit. The connections involved are those on *both* ends of the battery cables (if these are at fault the engine probably won't start anyway), the two terminals on the generator, all voltage regulator connections, and those on the back of the ammeter and ignition switch—as well as the primary (small) wires on the coil and distributor.

Battery cable terminals should be removed and cleaned with sandpaper or a wire brush. Corrosion should be washed away with a solution of baking soda, detergent, and water. Shims can be placed on the battery posts if the cables no longer fit tightly, and new cable terminals installed if necessary. After clamping the terminals in place, they should be lightly coated with vaseline to ward off renewed corrosion. Make absolutely certain that the ground connections are good electrically and, if there is a separate ground strap between the engine and frame, this must also be checked.

Other connections can simply be removed, both surfaces brightened with sandpaper or emery cloth, and the parts rejoined tightly.

Step 3—Eliminating the Regulator. When the battery and connections look good but the charging system still won't put out, the next step is to find out whether the trouble is in the generator or in the regulator. First, disconnect the field wire at the generator itself. You can usually tell which of the two wires connected to the generator goes to the field because it will be slightly smaller than the armature wire. The field terminal may have an "F" stamped next to it, or it may even have a paper ring around it underneath the wire warning that it is the field terminal. This warning, incidentally, is to keep you from connecting any radio condensers to the field terminal. They will really raise heck with the regu-

Charging System

lator. After disconnecting the field terminal at the generator, fold a piece of tape around it so that it won't ground out and ruin the regulator.

There are two types of circuits that supply the current to the generator fields. One is called the "A" circuit and the other the "B" circuit. Most General Motors cars are "A" circuit, and Fords are usually "B" circuits. In an "A" circuit, ground the field terminal. If it's a "B" circuit, connect a jumper wire from the armature terminal to the field terminal. If you can't remember which circuit your generator has, try grounding the field terminal first and then try it with the jumper between armature and field. With the correct field connector, run the engine to see if the generator will put out. Because you have an uncontrolled generator, you must not run the engine too fast or the generator will put out excessive current.

During the test, all accessories such as windshield wipers or radios should be off so that they won't be damaged. But it's a good idea to turn the headlights on because that tends to draw enough current from the generator so that the voltage will be down a little. You should have a voltmeter to make the test but you can do it by watching the brightness of the headlights if your battery is a little bit weak. On a voltmeter, an uncontrolled generator will show at least 15 volts and as high as 20 or 30 if you're crazy enough to run the engine that fast. If you are going to do it by watching the headlights, watch to see if they get brighter when you rev up the engine. If the generator puts out, and you are still having trouble, it's in the regulator.

Step 4—Generator Removal. Let's assume that electrifying the fields did nothing, and the generator's output remained lower than the hobnails on a coal miner's boot. This means that you must re-

move the generator from the car for bench testing.

The first step in taking out a generator is to detach the wires from it. Label the wires in some way—perhaps wrapping one with a bit of tape—so that you'll be able to put them back in the same position they were originally.

The generator is supported on the engine by three bolts. You'll have to use a wrench on both ends—on the nut as well as on the bolt—to undo these, but fortunately, the car makers have used different hex sizes for the nuts than they have for the bolts, so you won't need two wrenches of the same size to do the job. Usually the bolts are 1/2-in. and the nuts 9/16-in.—common tool sizes.

Loosen the bolt that fastens the generator to the slotted belt-adjusting bracket first. This will allow you to slip the belt off and swing the generator to a position that makes removing the other two bolts easier. After you've taken the nuts and lock washers off the two mounting bolts, remove the belt-adjusting bolt completely and support the generator with one hand while taking out the mounting bolts with the other. The generator can then be lifted away from the engine.

Step 5—Generator Examination. Once the generator is out of the car, undo the two bolts that hold the brush end plate onto the generator body. These are at the end opposite the fan belt pulley. If the generator has an inspection band,

1. Generator Disassembly

1. Generators will reveal a lot about their condition if you just take them apart and look. In many cases, all that is needed is new brushes.

2. When you get the pulley off the armature, this is what the whole mess looks like. Don't try to slide the front bearing and plate off the armature shaft until you have removed the pulley and the Woodruff key.

3. Put too much oil in the cup next to the pulley and the only damage will be oil flying out all over the engine, but if you over-oil the rear cup, the excess may flood the commutator and knock out the generator.

4. Generator armature and field terminal points are usually marked, but not prominently. If you can't find any well defined marking, the one with the large-diameter wire should be the armature terminal.

5. After this little plate is removed, the bearing will fall right out into your hand.

2. Pulling Pulley from Armature

3. Generator Oil Cups

4. Terminal Markings

5. Removing Bearing Retainer

this may be removed instead. You should then be able to see the brushes and commutator end of the armature.

The brushes are two graphite-carbon blocks that are mounted in spring-loaded holders. They are pressed by the spring against the commutator—a shiny brass part on the end of the armature shaft.

Check the condition of the commutator while turning the generator shaft by hand. If any of the brass segments are pitted or burned, the armature probably has shorted or grounded circuits and should be removed for testing.

If the commutator is fairly clean, smooth and bright, lift out the brushes and examine them. Brushes that are worn down to a length of 5/16-in. or less are definitely in need of replacement. On the other hand, the brushes may appear to be in good condition. In this case check to see that they slide smoothly in their holders and that the springs are not broken or out of place.

If you've left the generator on the car and are making the examination through the inspection ports in the generator frame, it is often possible to pinpoint brush trouble by pressing down on the brushes with the tip of a screwdriver while the engine is running. If the generator begins charging, the brushes are not making good contact.

Step 6—Servicing Brushes. If the brushes are sticking in the holders, are worn down to minimum length, or the commutator and brushes are coated with grease or a brownish-green glaze, you've probably found your trouble— especially if the ammeter (or "idiot light") indicated a no-charge or only intermittent charging periods.

Greasy or glazed commutators and brushes can be serviced with the generator in the car—providing it has an inspection band. The commutator can be cleaned by inserting a strip of #00 or #000 sandpaper or crocus cloth between it and one of the brushes and rotating the generator by hand until the

brass segments are bright and shiny. The sandpaper is then turned over and pulled between the brush and the commutator to make a clean and properly contoured surface on the brush end contacting the commutator.

If the brushes are worn out, new ones must be installed—although an *emergency* on-the-road repair can sometimes be affected by placing a wadded piece of paper between the spring arm and the brush to increase the pressure. Clean the commutator and look closely at the spaces between the segments. If the insulating strips between the segments are flush with the surface of the commutator (or are projecting above it), the armature should be removed and taken to an automotive machine shop for servicing before new brushes are installed. At this time the armature will be checked to see if the commutator is round and concentric with the shaft. If it is not, it will be placed in a lathe and light cuts made across the face of the commutator until the wear is corrected. The insulating strips will then be undercut to a depth of about 1/32-in. using a special tool. You can do this commutator work yourself if a lathe is available and then carefully undercut the insulating strips using a section of hacksaw blade.

The brushes on all modern generators have wires attached to them. It's an easy job to unscrew the old wires from their terminals and fasten the new ones in their place. Give the holders a check to see that the brushes move freely and sand the new brushes to shape by drawing a strip of fine sandpaper under them after they are in position against the commutator. When you put the brush end plate back onto the generator body, be careful not to pinch any wires between it and the generator frame. One of the brushes is grounded to the end plate. The other one, the insulated brush, connects to the armature terminal on the generator. A pinched or grounded wire on the insulated brush or any of its

connections will keep the generator from charging and may cause permanent damage. The end plate on a generator usually has a rivet or other projection that fits in a notch on the field frame so that you can get the end plate back in the right position.

If brushes were causing your trouble, you should have it licked now—so put the generator back on the engine, tension the fan belt, and hook up the wires. You're all ready to go!

Step 7—Armature Bench Tests. Back in Step 5 we talked about inspecting the commutator for burned or pitted segments. Actually this is one of two or three possible indications of a shorted, grounded, or open-circuited armature. Loose or broken wires are sometimes visible, and in rare instances the armature may become so overheated that solder will melt from the commutator connections and be thrown onto the inspection band. If severe, either of these last two forms of damage should be cause for installing a new or rebuilt generator. If only one or two wires are loose, they can be resoldered, the commutator turned, and the armature tested for other damage. If none shows, the armature is fit for further use. However, it should be remembered that the damage is probably not due to trouble in the generator, but to a faulty voltage regulator. The regulator should therefore be tested and adjusted or replaced before putting in the generator or its replacement. Otherwise, another generator burnout will probably result. In all probability the original cause of the generator failure was overcharging. The no-charge condition occurred only after the windings had burned out.

If the armature is in really bad shape, there may also be trouble in the field coils. But, in the case of burned and pitted commutator segments, the damage is likely limited to the armature alone. The extent of the damage can be determined with accuracy only by testing both the

Charging System

armature and the field assembly. Should the trouble be restricted to the armature —or for that matter, to the frame—it may be possible to save a few dollars by replacing only the part needed. However, if the price in your locality turns out to be over half that of an entire rebuilt generator, it's probably best to settle for a complete replacement. When a used part or a used (not rebuilt) generator is to be installed, it should always be tested before being put into the car.

It may be desirable to "farm out" all charging system test work. The majority of automotive machine and supply shops have complete test facilities on hand for this. If you suspect internal generator or alternator defects, the unit can be taken to them for testing and, if it's repairable, you can buy the parts and put them in yourself. If not, they'll be more than happy to sell you another generator or voltage regulator for a reasonable price.

In checking the armature for open, grounded or short circuits, there are several tests that can be conducted:

1) *Open circuits* in the armature are the usual cause of burned segments on the commutator. The burning is produced by an electrical spark that arcs each time the segment connected to the open circuit passes under a brush. Further testing requires specialized equipment not normally available to the home mechanic. Burning is also occasionally caused by oil or grease on the commutator, in which case the generator will begin charging after the commutator has been lathe-turned, undercut, and the brushes sanded to fit.

2) *Grounded cirucits* can be detected with a voltmeter or a battery-powered test light. You can make your own tester using some dry cells, two wires, and a flashlight bulb. Grounded armature circuits are found by touching one test wire to the armature core and the other to the commutator. If the lamp lights, the armature is grounded and must be replaced before further tests.

3) *Shorted circuits* in the armature require a test device called a "growler" to locate them—and a bit of experience in its use. If you have this test made, and a short *is* found, you'll have to replace the armature or obtain a rebuilt generator.

In most cases, it's not necessary to take the fan belt pulley and front end plate off the armature while making the above tests. However, if a new armature is to be installed they must be taken off. To do this it is only necessary to undo the large nut at the center of the pulley. It may be impossible to get this nut loose without clamping the armature in a vise. If you do, use soft jaws or two pieces of wood to protect the armature core from damage. You should not attempt to remove the pulley nut by holding the pulley. If you do, the result will probably be a bent or mangled pulley. The only correct way to remove a one-piece pulley is to disassemble the generator so you can put the armature in a vise. The exception to this is the impact wrench method, used mainly by generator rebuilders. Because the armature is heavy, an impact wrench can spin the pulley nut off or on with the generator fully assembled.

There is a Woodruff key located in a slot between the pulley hub and the generator shaft which you must be careful not to lose as the pulley is slipped off the shaft.

Step 8—Field Coil Bench Tests. Field coils rarely give any trouble. Maybe that's the reason why a lot of mechanics don't know how to test them properly. The field coil, being responsible for creating the full strength magnetic field in the generator, must not have any shorts, grounds or opens. Let's see now what effect each one of these conditions would have on generator output.

1) *Short Circuits.* Field coils are designed with a certain length of wire wrapped around the pole shoes. This particular length of wire has limited resistance, and therefore it determines how much current will flow through the field coils. If somewhere in the field coil there is a bare wire touching another bare wire, then the distance that the electricity travels will be shortened and we have what is known as a short circuit. A short circuit eliminates some of the wire that the electricity travels through and therefore cuts down on

1. Brush Insulation

2. Comparing Commutators

3. Cleaning Commutator

STRIP WILL VIBRATE WHEN SHORTED COIL IS DIRECTLY UNDER IT — Steel Strip

GENERATOR ARMATURE

"Growler"

4. Growler Test

some of the resistance in the circuit. Less resistance means that more current will flow in the field coils, which burns up the regulator. This situation is rare, but it is one instance where our field electrification test made earlier will get you in trouble. A generator will put out fine with shorted field coils, but the regulator has great difficulty controlling it and eventually burns up.

Shorted field coils cannot be checked with a test light or any other simple instrument. A field current draw test is required and to do it you must have an ammeter that will read accurately to a fraction of an amp. Field current draw on most 12-volt generators is only about 1½ amps. If you can find an automotive electrician who will make the field current draw test for you while you have the generator apart, it's a good idea. However, you must select your automotive electrician carefully. Most mechanics will think you're some kind of a nut if you ask them to make the test. The specifi-

1. Recognizing the insulated brush is easy. Just look for the strip of insulating material between the brush holder and the field frame.

2. The upper commutator has a normal amount of streaking from the brushes, but the lower one is black from excessive accumulation of carbon, which must be removed by sanding with sandpaper.

3. Many generators will not charge simply because the commutator has an excessive accumulation of carbon from the brushes. A little sandpaper will clean it up nicely.

4. The growler test will find many shorts in armatures, but not all of them. Some will only show up when the generator is running.

cations on field current draw are in the shop manual for your car.

We feel we should warn you about a common mistake made by generator rebuilders, especially with 12-volt Ford generators. It seems that there are a lot of parts floating around a generator rebuilding shop, whether it's big or small. If they aren't careful, they can easily get 6-volt field coils in a 12-volt generator. When you put it on your car, it will do all kinds of crazy things, like charging at idle, or making a buzzer out of the cutout above idle, with the red light flashing on and off. No adjustment of the regulator will cure the problem, but since the regulator is the part that is acting up, you will probably be sure there is something wrong with it. The problem is that the 6-volt fields are allowing twice as much current to go through the regulator control circuit. Get a generator with the right fields and you won't have any more trouble. You can also get some wild regulator gyrations if the wire that connects the two fields in a Ford generator is grounded out against the through-bolt. In either case, a check of generator field current on the assembled generator would locate the trouble.

2) *Open-Circuited Fields.* This is another rare one, but it's easy to check. All you have to do is trace the wiring in the fields until you find each end. One end will be connected to the field terminal on the generator frame and the other will either be connected to the insulated brush or to a ground somewhere in the generator. To check it, just use a battery-powered test light connected to each end of the field coils. If the light lights, you're in business. If it doesn't, you have a broken wire somewhere and a generator that will not charge.

3) *Grounded Fields.* This is another easy one to check. If the field circuit is grounded in the generator (a "B" cir-

cuit), then you will have to disconnect the grounded end in order to make the test. If the field is not grounded in the generator (an "A" circuit), then you don't have to disconnect anything, but be sure that the field lead is not touching the case. To make the test, just put one probe of your battery-powered test light on the field terminal and the other probe on the generator case. If the light lights, something is getting through where it shouldn't, so you'd better find the ground or get yourself another generator. The ground in the field circuit could produce either over- or undercharge, depending upon the design of the system and where the ground was. You can see that checking out the fields correctly is important unless you have so much money that anytime something goes wrong you can throw away the old regulator, generator, and wiring in favor of a complete new system. Admittedly, that is much faster than intelligent diagnosis, but it certainly is expensive.

VOLTAGE REGULATOR

Voltage regulators can be a pretty complicated business for the backyard mechanic to handle. In fact, the majority of automotive service garages do very little actual work on them. The faulty unit is simply exchanged for a new replacement regulator.

It would be more expensive for the average customer to have his old regulator tested and repaired than to simply have a new unit installed.

There are a number of safe and simple repairs and adjustments that you can make yourself, and in about 90% of the repairable kinds of regulator trouble, these uncomplicated fixes will cut the ice. If the regulator is so ancient that wear and old age have destroyed the last vestige of its original factory adjustments, the contacts are probably so burned that even the most professional test and repair work couldn't save it. If somebody else hasn't tinkered with them, most regulators will retain their adjustments quite accurately. If something has caused them to go out of balance electrically—such as burned-out resistances—they probably would need replacement, anyhow.

Although commonly called "voltage" regulators, regulating voltage is only one part of their function. After taking out the screws and removing the cover, you will

Charging System

see that there are actually two or three coil-like units inside—although some alternator-equipped cars have just one relay.

A closer inspection will reveal that each relay has at least one pair of electrical contacts. Many regulator problems are nothing more than dirt, corrosion, and burned faces on these points. It's not uncommon for moisture to find its way inside the cover and contribute to the formation of a white, powdery corrosion residue that eventually finds it way onto the contacts. In such cases all that needs to be done is a little "house cleaning."

After all foreign matter has been removed from the regulator, the points can be cleaned with a strip of crocus cloth. However, the wires leading to the voltage regulator should be disconnected before you attempt this or other point-polishing operations. If the contacts are conspicuously burned or pitted, you may have to do some smoothing with a point file or fine emery cloth before applying the final polish with crocus cloth. The more mirror-like you leave these surfaces, the less likely future burning is to occur. Following the "sandpaper treatment," the contacts should be cleaned with alcohol to remove any grease or dust that might initiate fresh erosion.

After resurfacing the contacts, the air-gap between them must be set to the correct width. A specification book or shop manual for your particular car will list this under "voltage regulator specifications." Most public libraries have shop manuals on their shelves that tell how to fix particular makes, and one of these may be borrowed to find the regulator specs for your own make and model.

The gap is adjusted with the movable contact held at its widest point. The stationary contact arm is then bent until a feeler gauge of the correct thickness will just slip into the opening. Care must also be taken to align the contact points so that they will meet squarely when closed.

If the contacts have only been cleaned, or polished lightly with crocus cloth, no further adjustment will probably be needed. If more than .002-in. or .003-in. was removed, the spring tension may require some adjustment, but even then only very slight deviations from the original specs are usually found.

Three or four means of effecting voltage regulator spring-tension adjustments are in current use. The most common form consists of a flat leaf spring on top of each unit which presses against an angled metal strip projecting from the frame of the relay assembly. Spring tension is adjusted by bending this piece of metal so that it produces more or less of a deflection in the leaf spring. Another frequently seen type of adjustment utilizes screws that are threaded into the relay frame. These can be turned in and out to change the degree to which the spring is flexed. The last common domestic type employs small coil springs to pull the contacts together. These are adjusted by bending the lower spring hook to increase or decrease the tension on the spring.

Before adjusting the regulator you should know the function of each relay. One of these units—which all generator system regulators have in common—is the circuit breaker or "cutout." You can spot the cutout by its heavy windings, larger (or dual) contacts, and by the fact that it is located at one end of a 3-unit regulator adjacent to the "BAT" (battery) terminal. It is also the only relay whose contact points are held *open* by spring pressure rather than closed. This relay prevents battery current from flowing "backward" into the regulator and generator when the engine is idling or the ignition is turned off.

The centermost relay is usually the current regulator. It too has a heavy winding, but less of it. The purpose of

this unit is to limit the maximum flow of electricity out of the generator.

Also, there is the voltage regulator itself. Its windings consist of many turns of fine wire. The voltage regulator relay is a limiter, which protects the electrical system of the car by keeping the voltage below a set limit.

REGULATOR ADJUSTMENTS

One fault with voltage regulators is that they are too easy to get to. If the car makers would seal the voltage regulator in a fireproof, theftproof box so that nobody could fuss with the darn thing, there would be a lot less trouble with charging systems than there is today. Because the regulator is so easily fiddled

1. Checking Armature for Ground

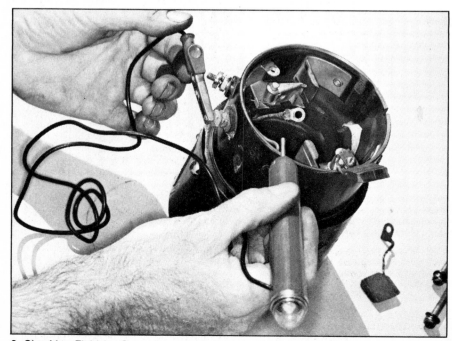

2. Checking Field for Ground

3. Checking Field Continuity

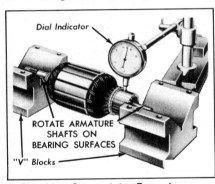

Dial Indicator

ROTATE ARMATURE
SHAFTS ON
BEARING SURFACES

"V" Blocks

4. Checking Commutator Runout

*1. Checking the armature for ground.
If the light comes on, then we
know the armature is bad.*

*2. Checking the field windings for
ground. Note that the field lead is
disconnected from the insulated
brush holder. If a ground shows up,
we know that the holder itself is
not causing the problem. The stud
through the steel frame could also
be disconnected to eliminate it as
a possible source of a ground.*

*3. Checking the fields for
continuity. The light should come
on unless the field windings
have a break somewhere.*

*4. Whenever brushes are changed, the
commutator should be checked for
runout and smoothness. Turn true in
a lathe if necessary. In many cases,
mica insulation must be undercut.*

*5. When new generator brushes have
been installed, they should be
sanded as shown to assure good initial
contact and proper wear pattern.*

USE *Sandpaper* ONLY
CUT STRIP SLIGHTLY
WIDER THAN BRUSH

HOLD END PLATE
FROM TURNING

Soft Jaws
in Vise

PULL IN DIRECTION OF ARMATURE ROTATION

5. Seating Brushes

with, everybody who has a charging system malfunction immediately takes the cover off and starts playing with the thing.

In nine cases out of ten, it's the generator that wears out. Either the bearings go bad, the brushes wear out, the armature flies apart, or maybe even the belt is loose. But in spite of that, everybody goes directly to the regulator and starts playing with it. We want you to know how to make regulator adjustments, but you'll be a lot happier and better off if you will concentrate your efforts on the generator and be positively sure that it is OK before you start working on the regulator. Adjusting a regulator is not difficult, but you have to have a delicate touch—and an accurate voltmeter and ammeter. Let's take a look at the three units in the regulator, one at a time.

1) *Voltage Regulator.* The voltage unit is a limiting device. It doesn't do a thing until the voltage gets up to the point where it might damage the electrical system. Then the voltage regulator cuts in

and keeps the generator from burning out all of the light bulbs.

A generator does not put out full voltage all the time. One of the characteristics of an automotive generator is that it cannot put out maximum voltage and maximum amperage at the same time. When it is putting out maximum current or amperage, the voltage falls to a comparatively low level. When the generator is putting out maximum voltage, there is practically no current flow at all.

A generator is somewhat like a city water system. It supplies current and voltage to all of the electrical units in the car in the same way that the big water pump down at the city water works supplies water and pressure to all the homes in town. If everybody turns on the faucet at the same time, the pressure will drop but the flow of water will increase so that everybody gets an adequate amount. If only a few people have the faucet turned on, then the pressure builds up while the flow of water is considerably less.

The automotive generator works the same way. When you have a lot of accessories on—headlights, radio, air conditioner—then the voltage falls because the generator is supplying a lot of current. When you turn everything off except the ignition, then the generator voltage rises and charges the battery until the battery gets up to a full charge, at which time the generator voltage tries to rise above the fully charged battery but is prevented from doing so by the voltage regulator. This is the only time that the voltage regulator actually works—when the generator is operating at high voltage, as it would against a fully charged battery.

In order to test the voltage regulator, we either have to have a fully charged battery in the car or we have to fool the generator into thinking that there is a fully charged battery in the car. This fooling process is done simply by inserting a ¼-ohm resistor in the line between the generator and the battery. Some of the tune-up equipment companies make ¼-ohm resistors, and sell them for use with an ordinary voltmeter, but most of the generator testing in garages is done with a volt-amp tester, which has the resistance built into the unit. The resistor limits current flow the same way a fully charged battery would, and the generator voltage rises to the point where it is controlled by the voltage regulator. With a ¼-ohm resistor in the line and the engine operating at about 2000 rpm, all you do is take your voltage reading off the armature terminal either at the generator or at the regulator, whichever is most convenient. The reading you get will be the voltage as limited by the voltage regulator.

Some regulators have double contacts in the voltage relay. One pair of contacts is called the series set, and the other the shorting set. In Delco-Remy regulators, the series set is the lower one, and the shorting set is the upper one. In Chrysler and Ford regulators, the position of the two sets is reversed. When the regulator is limiting the voltage at low speed, and the generator output is low, the regulator vibrates against the series contacts. At

Charging System

high speed, and close to zero output, the regulator vibrates against the shorting contacts which results in about 1/10- to 1/2-volt less than when the series contacts are used. A 1/4-ohm resistor used with a double contact regulator will check the shorting contacts. To check the series contacts, about 10 to 15 amps must be allowed to flow which means you must remove the 1/4-ohm resistor and put a light load on the system. The process is admittedly tricky, but modern volt/amp testers will do it with just a few twists of a knob. However, the difference between operation on the series and shorting contacts is so small, that a quick check of the system voltages with the battery operating against a 1/4-ohm resistor (or a fully charged battery) is usually sufficient. The purpose of the double contacts is to ensure more precise control of voltage, and longer contact life. Changing the voltage setting is the same on either single or double contact units.

To increase the setting, you merely increase the spring tension that holds the points together on the voltage unit. If the voltage is too high, a little less spring tension will lower it. It takes a delicate touch because a very slight change in spring tension will give a big change to the voltage. It also takes certain precautions to keep from burning everything up. You should shut the engine off and disconnect the battery ground cable before you take the cover off the regulator, because if you accidentally move the cover sideways while you are taking it off you can easily ground out something and burn up the regulator.

After making each adjustment, the cover must be in place on the regulator because it holds in the heat and also has an effect on the magnetic field. When you fire up the engine, you can see on your voltmeter the change that you have made, but it's a good idea to allow the engine to go back down to idle so that the cutout opens. Then bring it up again and check to see if the reading is in the same place. Allowing the cutoff points to open like this is called "cycling the regulator," which gives it a little exercise and helps stabilize the reading you get.

2) *Current Regulator.* To check the current regulator we must have maximum current flow out of the generator to find out if the current regulator will limit the flow to a safe value. We don't want the 1/4-ohm resistor in this case, but we do have to disconnect the battery wire at the regulator anyway in order to insert leads from the ammeter. A test ammeter is always connected so that all of the electricity flows through the ammeter or the shunt that is part of the ammeter. With the ammeter connected and the engine running, we turn on as many accessories as we can in order to get maximum current flow. If you don't have enough accessories to get a large current flow, then you can crank the engine a few times in order to run down the battery a little.

If you get enough load on the generator, the current flow will rise high

enough that the current regulator unit will regulate it. Current regulation is necessary for only one reason—to keep from burning up the generator. The generator is peculiar in that the faster you turn it the more it will put out. It can easily burn itself up if it doesn't have the current regulator in the system to protect it. If your car does not have a lot of accessories and you always keep your battery in good condition, it's possible to drive for several years without ever needing your current regulator. The current regulator is adjusted the same way that the voltage regulator is—simply by increasing or decreasing the spring tension on the points.

3) *Cutout.* If we didn't have some way to disconnect the generator from the battery when the engine was idling or

1. Belt Adjustment

2. Tightening Belt

not running, the battery would discharge back through the generator and be dead in a few hours. Any time the engine is idling or not running, the cutout points are open, disconnecting the generator from the battery and the rest of the car. A generator is a self-generating device, so the minute it starts turning it puts out current and voltage. The current goes up through the wire to the voltage regulator, but it can't get any further because the cutout points are open. However, some of the current is taken from the wire through the cutout coil and directly to ground. The cutout coil thus acts as an electromagnet to close the cutout points. The electromagnet overcomes the spring that holds the cutout points open. We can adjust the spring tension so that the cutout will close at any voltage we de-

3. Three-unit Regulator

4. Regulator Wiring

sire. Cutouts are usually set about 1 volt above normal battery voltage. Thus, a 12-volt system with normal battery voltage of 12.6 would have its cutout set at approximately 13.5 volts. As long as the generator is operating at a normal or high speed, the cutout points will remain closed because current flows at all times through the cutout coil. However, when the generator speed falls down to a slow idle or the engine is shut off, current immediately runs from the battery to the generator in a reverse direction through the cutout coil. Because the current is now running in a reverse direction through the coil, it reverses the magnetism in the cutout and forces the points open. The current that forces the points open is called the reverse current, and it can be measured with your ammeter in the circuit. Reverse current usually runs less than 5 amps. If it takes any more than that, the cutout points are probably sticking.

There is very little that can go wrong in any of the three units in a regulator. They are adjusted accurately at the factory, and ordinarily they will stay in adjustment through many years of use. The only weak element in a regulator is the points themselves. They pit and the point surfaces get so bad that they won't conduct electricity any more. If you get in there with a riffler file and really clean out the points well, you can reset the regulator and probably get another 5 years of service out of it. If you do file away a lot of metal to get the points

1. You may have to adjust the belt tension two or three times until you get it to where it's exactly what you want. New belts will stretch, so check them again after about a half hour of running time.

2. If generator must be pried against to adjust fan belt tension, use a piece of soft wood. Make sure belt has correct degree of side play as specified in owner's manual.

3. Typical 3-unit regulator, with voltage, current, and cutout relays. Point spring tension on this model is changed with screws.

4. Wire going to base of regulator is merely a ground to insure that the regulator points will work correctly. It's a good idea.

clean, it will be necessary to set the point gap and also the air gap between the armature and coil.

You can see that the adjustments on a regulator are somewhat complicated, and this is the reason that very few adjustments are ever made in commercial garages. It's much easier to throw the old regulator away and put on a new one. New regulators that are made by major companies are usually adjusted perfectly at the factory and do not require any checking or adjusting when they are installed. If you buy a rebuilt regulator, or one that is not a major brand, you had better check it carefully to see if it's in adjustment.

ALTERNATOR SYSTEMS

In order to be precise both generators and alternators produce alternating current, and therefore might properly be called alternators. Yet, their electrical circuitry and construction features make them as different as boys and girls. The brushes of a generator are arranged so that the current reaching the armature is always of the same polarity. This is really quite inefficient, since only a small part of the generator's armature windings are producing useful energy at any one time. The rest are just waiting their turn and placing a drag on the engine's horsepower. Having a relatively low output for its size, the generator is often unable to supply the current demands of modern cars equipped with many electrically operated accessories. This shows up especially in city driving where you'd best not try to use the heater, lights, wipers, and radio all at the same time, or you might not start up next morning.

Alternators will produce usable electricity from *all* of their windings *all* of the time. Thus, they can be smaller and lighter, yet still put out almost full voltage even with the engine at an idle. Alternators do this by using some ingenious little devices known as rectifiers. A rectifier is a small disc formed from a substance that has the highly unique property of allowing electricity to flow through it freely in *one* direction, but not in the other.

The rectifiers—there are six of them —are divided up into two groups of three each. One group allows a steady flow of positive-polarity electricity to pass

through while rejecting negative current. The other group permits the passage of negative current while rejecting the positive current.

The diodes—another name for the rectifiers used in alternators—can be burned out almost instantly if current of the wrong polarity is accidentally routed into them. One of the most common causes of "sudden death" among diodes is the incorrect use of jumper cables to start balky cars in winter time. Some cars have the positive pole of the battery grounded while others have a negative ground system. Frequently, someone will unthinkingly connect a booster cable from the positive side of his battery to the negative pole of the other car. Zap! —no more diodes.

A *no-charge* condition is, of course, the most frequently encountered charging system trouble. Your first action should always be to check for the obvious. Has the fan belt broken? Is it loose and slipping? A quick glance at the water temperature indicator may give you the answer. If a no-charge is shown by the glowing indicator light, but the battery is fully charged, there is probably just a bad connection in the indicator light circuit. A careful inspection under the hood, giving special attention to the battery cables, wiring and drive belts, should eliminate many of the possible causes of the failure. But if all proves to be in order, there are still other easily-checked items that can solve your problem—or at least point to the correct solution.

ELIMINATING THE REGULATOR

If the alternator system isn't working properly, the first thing to check is the battery. Be sure it's right before you go any further. When you are sure that the trouble stems from undercharging, overcharging, or no charge at all, it's time to determine whether the regulator or the alternator is at fault.

A generator creates its own field current, but an alternator receives its field current from the battery. There are several different circuits, but in most of them current flows from the battery, through the ignition switch, through the regulator, and into the alternator field. The regulator controls the alternator by

1. Always mark across housings before splitting halves. Assembly will be easier if the housings are put back together the same way they came apart.

2. Never clamp pulley in a vise. Use an Allen wrench in the end of the shaft, and the pulley nut can be removed with hardly a grunt or groan.

3. Spacer ring is important. It keeps pulley fan from scraping on housing. Rebuilt alternators may come without pulley or spacer, so save old ones.

4. Surprise! There's another spacer inside. Three capscrews hold felt dust shield and keep bearing in housing. Bearing taps out of housing easily.

5. Take out four through-bolts, remove drive-end housing with rotor, and this is what you see. To remove stator, take off three nuts (arrows).

6. With the stator out of the way you can see the diodes, and with their leads disconnected, you can now easily test them with a battery test light.

7. Positive diodes are pressed into the plate, and negative are pressed into the housing. Pressing diodes in or out requires special tools. Don't hammer!

8. To reassemble, brushes must be held down in holder with drill bit pushed in from outside housing. Do it carefully so you don't damage brushes.

9. Line up housing marks, put bolts back in, then pull drill bit out and brushes will go against rotor slip rings. Your alternator job is finished.

1. Three bolts hold the Ford-Autolite alternator together. Be sure you mark the housings before disassembly. Rotor comes off with drive-end housing.

2. Stator and diode plate are removed as a unit, but first you have to collect an endless number of nuts, steel washers, and insulating washers.

3. Arrows indicate the four posts that attach the diode plate to the housing. All posts and washers must be assembled exactly as removed, or it's no charge.

4. Little box is really a condenser. Arrow points to three stator leads that are soldered to diode plate. If any diodes are bad, entire plate is changed.

5. Removing diode plate reveals an extra lead. It is the Y connection between the three stator phases. It should be tucked away, insulated from ground.

6. Testing rotor for continuity. Test bulb should light when probes are put on both slip rings. If no light, the rotor must be changed.

7. Testing rotor for ground, with the probes on shaft and one slip ring. If bulb lights, rotor is grounded, and must be changed.

8. To reassemble, load brushes into the holder with springs underneath, then slip drill bit in from outside housing. Work carefully, don't damage brushes.

9. After assembly, bit is pulled out to allow brushes to ride on slip rings. Note the five posts (arrows). Some are insulated, some not. Don't mix 'em.

Charging System

cutting down on the amount of current that goes to the field. Transistor regulators are different, and we suggest that you leave them to the experts, because it is very easy to blow a transistor if you hook testing leads in the wrong places.

To eliminate a mechanical regulator from the charging circuit, all you have to do is disconnect the field lead at the alternator and attach a hot lead directly from the battery. You will then have full field current. Make sure all the accessories in the car are off, then start the engine and take a reading of the voltage at the alternator output terminal with the engine idling. If the battery is fully charged, you will get 14 volts or more at idle. If the battery is low, you may have to increase the engine speed slightly above idle. Either way, if you get 14 or 15 volts out of the alternator, you can be pretty sure that it is OK, which means the trouble must be in the regulator. Revving the engine to produce more than 15 volts is unnecessary, and may blow some part of the electrical system. Never run an alternator with the output wire disconnected. They will put out 200, or even 300 volts, which is enough to fry the alternator and maybe a few other units as well. If the alternator does not put out 15 volts in this test, then there is something rotten inside it. The regulator may also be bad, but you can't check it out until you know the alternator is doing its job.

ALTERNATOR BRUSHES

Yes, Virginia, alternators *do* have brushes—and one of the nicest things *about* alternators is that many of them can have the brushes quickly removed and checked without taking the unit apart or removing it from the car. This is true of all Chrysler alternators, as well as the larger GM and Ford units. Sticking or worn-out brushes are a common source of trouble.

There are two brushes in an alternator. They are located in the alternator housing on the end opposite the V-belt pulley. On Chrysler Corporation units, one brush is mounted in an insulated plastic holder that has the alternator's field terminal attached to it. The ground brush is mounted separately in a metal holder that is screwed onto the alternator end housing. Taking off the field wire and removing the Phillips-head screws from the holders will get the brushes out and into your hands quicker than you could spend $10 on a spree in Tijuana.

GM's Delcotron alternators employ two systems of brush mounting. On the larger types, the brush holder—complete with the two brushes, the alternator terminals and a capacitor—can be taken out simply by removing all the wires and undoing two regular screws. The small 5½-in. Delcotron must have its four through-bolts removed and the end housing taken off before you can get at the brushes. The alternator should be removed from the car to do it, but some mechanics have found out that they can remove the end housing with the alterna-

tor still mounted on the engine. They don't even remove the belt. It's a neat trick if you're in a hurry.

The larger Ford alternators have two separate brush holder assemblies that are threaded so that they may be screwed directly into the alternator's end housing. These are easily removed using a wrench on the large hex at their outer ends. Like the small GM units, Ford's little ones must have the end housing taken off before you can work on the brushes.

On the Chrysler units it is sometimes possible to locate brush trouble by loosening the holders slightly and wiggling them while the engine is running. If the ammeter needle jerks up into the charge range, or the "idiot light" winks while you are doing this, you are on the right track. But remember one thing when working on the alternator or generator with the engine running. Those fan blades going around between the engine and the radiator may be invisible, but they're still plenty solid! Don't become so interested in what you're doing that you accidentally saw off a finger.

ROTOR TESTING

If you have a testing ammeter avail-

able, you can make a further check before disassembling the alternator that will show up trouble in the brushes and slip rings, or perhaps point to burned-out rotor windings. You can take the alternator out of the car for this test if you want to.

Disconnect both wires from the alternator's terminals. Connect the ammeter's positive lead to the battery's positive terminal. The battery must be fully charged. Attach the other ammeter lead to the alternator's field terminal. As mentioned earlier, this is on the insulated brush holder of Chrysler products. On most alternators it is marked "F" or "FLD." Connect a jumper wire from the battery's negative pole to the frame of the generator—although this is not necessary if the alternator has been left mounted on the engine. Turn the alternator shaft slowly by hand. The ammeter should indicate a field coil draw of between about 2.3 and 3.0 amps at 12 volts—depending on the make and model car. A lower reading indicates a high resistance in the circuit, which means poor electrical contact between the brushes and the slip rings, or maybe even a faulty field winding. Higher-than normal readings indicate that there's a possible ground or short in the rotor coil.

1. Generator and Regulator Wiring

2. Alternator and Regulator Wiring

3. Screw-type Adjustments

4. Testing Cutout

Most ammeters are not accurate enough to read to 1/10th of a volt. So it isn't practical to measure field current draw unless you have an accurate ammeter. If you do get an ammeter that will measure in tenths of a volt, be very careful when hooking it up. An accidental ground can burn out a low reading ammeter very quickly. It's a good idea to hook up your ammeter in series with an adjustable rheostat just in case current draw might be excessive.

If you haven't guessed it by now, the difference between a generator and an alternator is the location of the magnetic field and the wires in which the current is generated. In a generator we have a wire rotating in a magnetic field. An alternator is just the opposite, with a magnetic field which rotates inside of a coil of wire. When we measure field current in an alternator, we are measuring the amount of current that flows through the rotor coil which rotates in the center of the alternator. Brushes last a lot longer in an alternator because all they are required to carry is the small amount of field current, whereas in a generator they must carry all the current a generator produces.

Current in the alternator is produced in the stator, a heavy coil of wire that encircles the rotor. Because the stator has so many more loops in it than there are in a generator armature, the alternator will put out current at a much lower rpm than the generator. Alternators will charge at a normal curb idle. Some of them—the heavy-duty ones used on police cars—will even put out 100 amps at idle. And the alternator has another advantage in that it does not need a current regulator because it is self-limiting. You can spin it as fast as you want to and it will only put out so much current, so there's no danger of burning it up.

Alternators are a lot easier to work on than generators, once you get the hang of installing the brushes. Some alternators require that a small pin or drill be inserted to hold the brushes in place while the alternator end-frame is being put in position. Many alternators are designed to work with only a single unit regulator which controls voltage. A cur-

1. This diagram shows the relationship of the generator to the voltage regulator and battery in a Ford system, which has the field grounded at the generator, known as a "B" circuit.

2. General Motors has several wiring setups, all using the same alternator. This schematic is for an indicator lamp (idiot light) with field relay.

3. Cutout at right has normally open points. The others are normally closed. Note lock nuts on adjusting screws.

4. A shorted cutout can be found by testing between the "BAT" and "GEN" terminals. If an ohmmeter reading is obtained, the unit is faulty.

5. Field relay in Ford regulator rarely needs adjusting. A special bending tool is recommended, but pliers will work when adjusting regulators with bendable posts.

5. Regulator Adjustments

Charging System

rent regulator is not needed because the alternator is self-limiting in its current output. A cutout is not needed because the diodes themselves prevent any reverse current flow from the battery. There is a certain amount of drain through diodes because they are not perfect, but normally it would take several months before the diodes would discharge the battery completely, so the current drain is not enough to worry about. Besides the voltage units, some regulators have a relay which may be used to feed current to the field, to turn out the light on the dash, or to do both these functions.

REMOVING THE ALTERNATOR

On most cars, the alternator is an easy component to remove. It is often mounted high up on the engine and, unless buried under a maze of power accessories, even the low-mounted ones are easy to pull. After disconnecting all wires from the alternator and labeling them for future replacement, the bolt holding the alternator to the slotted belt-tensioning bracket can be readily loosened. Two wrenches—one for the nut and one for the bolt—must be used. Once the bolt is loose, swing the alternator into the position that makes reaching the other two bolts easiest. When the nuts and lock washers are off these, the adjustment bolt can be taken out and the alternator supported by hand while the remaining bolts are taken from mounting brackets.

ALTERNATOR TESTS AND REPAIRS

When disassembling the alternator, it is necessary to first remove the brushes and holders on those units which do not require dismantling to do so. The bolts or screws holding the end shields can then be removed and the housing pried apart gently with a screwdriver. You will then have complete access to the rotor, stator and diodes. With the help of a battery-powered ohmmeter or test light the following tests can easily be conducted:

1) *A grounded rotor* may be detected by touching one test lead to the rotor shaft and the other to each of the slip rings. If the ohmmeter reads low, or the lamp lights, the windings are obviously grounded and a new rotor is required.

2) *Open circuits* in the rotor are found by touching one test light lead to each slip ring. If it does not light, the windings are open and the rotor unit must be replaced.

3) *A shorted rotor* can be checked with an ohmmeter or a low reading ammeter. As most rotor specifications are given in current draw, the usual way of checking for a short is with the ammeter. The same technique and cautions apply as when checking field current draw on a generator, covered earlier in this chapter.

4) *Grounded stators* are tested for with the help of a 110-volt test lamp, or an ohmmeter. Connect the test leads to the frame and to any of the stator leads. If

1. Transistorized Regulator

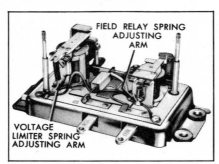

2. Regulator Adjustment Points

the lamp lights, or a low ohmmeter reading is shown, the stator windings are grounded.

5) *Open stator windings* will not light the test lamp when its leads are connected to successive parts of stator leads.

6) *Shorts* in the stator are very difficult to pinpoint—even with special equipment. However, if the rotor, stator, brushes, and diodes are all OK when tested for *other* flaws, and the alternator output *still* remains low, shorted windings are the probable cause.

DIODE TESTS AND REPLACEMENT

The diode can be tested either with a 3-volt battery-operated test light, or an ohmmeter powered by a 1.5-volt battery *and no more*. The test lead probes are first touched to the wire and to the case of each diode in one direction, and then reversed to test it in the opposite direction. A good diode will light the lamp or produce a high ohm reading in one direction, but not in the other. If both readings are about equally high or low, or if the light will or will not light in both

1. Terminals on most GM transistorized regulators are identical to those on conventional regulators and the various types are often used interchangeably on the same model.

2. Regulator relays with coil tension springs are sometimes adjusted by bending the hook—or spring adjusting arm—that holds the lower end of the spring in place.

3. Check diodes in transistorized regulators by unsoldering their lead wires and testing with an ohmmeter. A high resistance must be recorded in one direction, and a low resistance in the other.

4. Regulator that goes inside Delco alternator may be colored black or white, but pay attention only to the part number, not the color. Regulator at bottom has been cut away to show miniature circuitry.

5. Delcotron has not changed much over the years. Diodes are still pressed in. Note internal fan on alternator at right.

directions, the diode is considered to be bad.

For many years diodes were replaced by unbolting or unsoldering their leads and then using a special C-clamp tool to press them out of the alternator housings. Today, diodes cannot be replaced individually on many alternators. They are mounted in a circular plate that contains all six diodes. If one diode tests bad, you simply unbolt the plate and throw the whole thing away. In some cases, no soldering is required. If you do replace a diode or diode plate that requires soldering, there are certain precautions that you must take.

When soldering the diode's leads, a heat dam (a small metal clamp that drains off excess heat) should be attached to the wire between the solder joint and the diode itself during the soldering operation. Otherwise, you'll barbecue the diode. Delcotron positive diodes have red markings, the negative diodes are black.

REGULATOR CHECK AND REPAIRS

One of the first things to look for are burned-out fuse wires in Chrysler-built regulators. Two fusible wires are commonly soldered into these units to protect the system from damage due to shorts, excessive charging, and other electrical system overloads. The wires act as fuses, and whenever too much voltage passes through them, they simply overheat and melt. They are then no longer usable.

The fusible wires can be seen after removing the cover of the regulator unit. If they *have* burned out, a complete test of the regulator's operation should be made before soldering in new fusible wires and placing the regulator back in service.

To replace the fusible wires, it is first necessary to *cut* the remains of the old ones from their terminals. You should not try to unsolder these since by doing so you may damage the fine wire coming from the relay coil. Tin the end of the new fuse wires using rosin-core solder *only*. The tinned end of the wire is then inserted into the hollow rivet at the base of the regulator so that it is against the old piece of fuse wire that was left after cutting. Apply solder to the tip of the iron until a drop falls onto the joint being formed. When both wires are soldered at their lower ends, the opposite end may

3. Testing Diodes

4. Delco Integral Regulator

5. Delcotron Alternator

Charging System

be wrapped around the upper terminals and soldered—even though the original wires may only have been twisted into place.

The regulators used by Chrysler Corp. cars have just one relay unit. GM regulators have two relays and Ford even goes as high as three. Two GM-Delco types are in common use. One is a conventional load limit cutout and voltage regulating combination, and the other employs two transistors plus load and voltage relays.

The first thing to look for is dirt, corrosion residue, and burned areas on the contacts. The contacts can be cleaned with crocus cloth or a fine file. GM recommends filing with a riffler file only. Once the contacts are assured good condition, the point gaps and air gaps (the space between the relay coils and the movable point arm) should be checked and adjusted to the manufacturer's specifications.

Delco regulators have an adjusting screw to control the air gap on some units. This is a little 6-lobed knob on top of the voltage control relay. The point gaps are adjusted by bending the stationary contact mounts. On the transistorized unit the two screws holding the contact bracket are loosened and then the entire bracket moved until the correct point adjustment is attained. Single unit regulators such as those on Plymouths and other Chrysler products have their air gaps adjusted with the stationary contact bracket attaching screw fully tightened. The factory tolerance for regulator adjustments is usually around ±.002-in., which should give you a little leeway for point cleanups. Readjustment will therefore not usually be necessary unless considerable metal is removed. If the points are so badly burned that more than .004-in. must be filed from them, there's a good chance that the unit should be replaced, anyway. When you perform point cleaning and adjustment jobs with the regulator in the car, the wires connecting it to the battery should always be taken off and insulated.

1. You will rarely have to take an alternator apart this far, unless you buy a junked model for rebuilding, which may save some money.

2. Polarizing is necessary whenever you change a generator or regulator. Momentarily touch a jumper from the regulator BATT terminal to armature.

3. Wire connections on this Ford alternator look complicated, but they are easy to get back on right if you mark the wires.

4. On most alternators, the output terminal is directly connected to the battery, which means it's hot all the time. If you accidentally place a pair of pliers or a wrench so there is a connection between the output terminal and ground, you may burn up the wiring to the alternator. So be careful when working near the output terminal.

REGULATOR ADJUSTMENTS

There is no cutout or current regulator in most alternator regulators, so all you have to make adjustments on is the voltage unit. It is adjusted in much the same way as a generator voltage unit, covered earlier in this chapter. But there is one big difference. If you use a ¼-ohm resistor to simulate a fully charged battery, you must be careful to keep the engine speed down. Run the engine only fast enough to make the alternator work against the regulator. You can easily see it on your voltmeter. When the regulator starts controlling the voltage, the meter needle will hold steady somewhere between 13 and 15 volts. If you run the engine too fast, the alternator will barbecue the ¼-ohm resistor. It will even do it on a piece of test equipment. We recommend that you check alternator voltage settings against a fully charged battery, so that you don't have to worry about burning up test equipment.

POLARITY

Whether the charging system in your car has an alternator or a generator, correct polarity is a very important consideration. Alternator systems can be seriously damaged by even momentary reversals of polarity, and the voltage regularity in any system is also highly vulnerable. The following precautions should always be observed when working on the charging system:

1) When putting in a battery, *always* make absolutely sure that the ground polarity of the battery, regulator, and generator or alternator is the same. Do not install regulators from negative ground systems in cars having positive ground.

2) If you have occasion to use a booster battery and jumper cables, be sure that you hook the positive pole of the booster to the positive pole of the battery in the car, and the negative pole to the negative side of the battery in the car.

3) When connecting a charger to the battery, the positive lead from the charger must be connected to the positive battery pole and the negative lead to the negative pole.

4) Never continue to drive a car when

1. Ford Alternator

2. Polarizing Generator System

STA

BAT

WHITE-BLACK STRIPE STA.

WHITE FLD.

GRD.

BLACK-YELLOW STRIPE BAT

BLACK-RED STRIPE

3. Ford Wiring Harness

4. Output Terminal

Charging System

charging system trouble is evident. In the event of a loose connection that produces an open charging circuit, unregulated current of the wrong polarity may be allowed to enter the battery or alternator diodes.

5) Do not short across or ground any of the terminals on the regulator or the alternator *on alternator systems.*

When a new regulator or generator is installed, or when the old one is reinstalled after testing, the generator *must be polarized.* If this is not done, the generator—or regulator—will probably be burned out in a very short time. This is especially true on cars that have "idiot lights." An ammeter will show a no-charge more reliably following installation of an unpolarized unit. Polarizing the generator and regulator is a step that is often overlooked when making engine swaps. If you're the hot rodder type, don't bypass this vital step before "firing 'er up" for the first time, or you'll have part of the rod-building job to do over again—plus the cost of a new generator and regulator, or both.

Polarizing the generator is necessary to restore the residual magnetism to the pole shoes. A generator that sits around on the bench for a long time, or one that has been dropped during handling, may lose its residual magnetism. The momentary surge of current through the field coils that you give when you polarize the generator is enough to restore the residual magnetism. Polarization amounts to electrifying the fields with a battery. But it must be done in the right direction. The generator and all wiring should be installed and ready to operate. With the engine dead and the ignition off, connect a jumper lead to the battery terminal of the regulator and touch the other end of the lead to the regulator armature terminal for just a fraction of a second. It

1. Wiring diagram with Ford alternator and transistorized regulator. Modern charging circuits like this require very little maintenance.

2. MoPar alternator is of same basic design as Ford alternator, except that until 1972 the rectifiers (diodes) mounted directly into the stator rather than a separate subframe, and could be replaced individually. From 1972 on, rectifiers are mounted in negative and positive heat sink units and entire assembly must be changed if one or more rectifiers are bad.

3. Ohmmeter hook-ups used to test diodes and field current. Test A: This is a check of the positive diodes. Note reading and reverse test leads. The meter should record a high reading in one direction and a low reading in the other. Test B: Perform same test as A. Similar readings in both directions mean faulty negative diodes. Test C: Meter should read a maximum of 7-10 ohms. Low reading means bad brushes.

4. The insulated brush can be removed separately from Chrysler Corp. alternators. Notice also the three diodes in their external heat sink adjacent to the terminal in the rear.

only takes just a touch and the job is done.

Polarization is not necessary on an alternator because it does not have a cut-out. The alternator gets field current whenever the ignition switch is on, so there is no need to polarize it or make any jumper connections when installing a new alternator.

BEARINGS

Generator and alternator bearings have a particular notoriety for "going out" at the worst possible times. Even if they don't seize up half-way between service areas on the New York Thruway, they can still start making more noise than a worn-out cement mixer filled with empty beer cans—usually when you've just driven off on your first date with the prettiest girl in the whole world.

Most generators have one or two oil holes that are meant to be given a tall drink of engine oil when the car is greased. Unfortunately, these are frequently overlooked by filling station attendants, since some cars have them and others do not. The generator must be lubed according to schedule.

Most alternators, and an increasing number of generators, have "oil-less" bearings—which is to say, they have been prelubricated at the factory or are only packed upon installation. On the majority of alternators, the bearings must be replaced if they have lost their lubrication. Delcotron 6-in. and 6.2-in. units can have their bearings removed and relubricated with Delco No. 1948791 grease or its equivalent. The 5.5-in. Delcotron has ball bearings only at the drive end so that is the only end that can be repacked.

If bearings have gone bad in an alternator or generator you will, of course, need to replace them.

The bearings can be driven out of the end plates using short sections of pipe that have approximately the same diameter as the inner and outer ball bearing races. On most units, the brush-end bearing has a stamped metal grease retaining cap over its outer end. The bearing is driven from the "inside" so that this cap is forced out by the old bearing. A new cap is sometimes a part of the replacement kit. Check before destroying old one.

The drive-end bearing can be removed only after the V-belt pulley has been tak-

1. Alternator and Transistorized Regulator

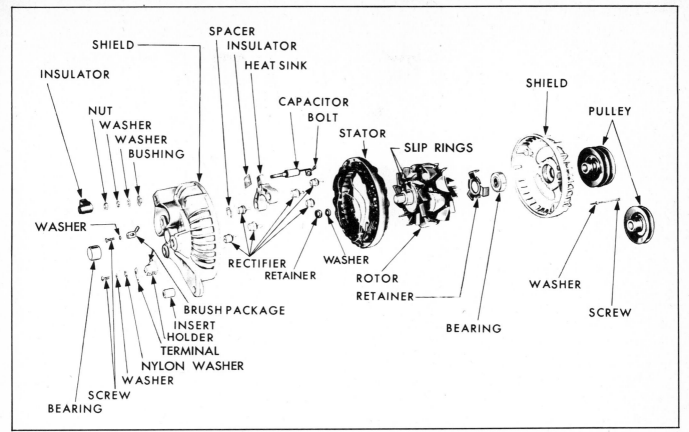

2. MoPar Alternator

INSULATOR
SHIELD
SPACER
INSULATOR
HEAT SINK
NUT
WASHER
WASHER
BUSHING
CAPACITOR
BOLT
STATOR
SLIP RINGS
SHIELD
PULLEY
WASHER
RECTIFIER
RETAINER
WASHER
ROTOR
RETAINER
WASHER
SCREW
BRUSH PACKAGE
INSERT
HOLDER
TERMINAL
NYLON WASHER
WASHER
SCREW
BEARING
BEARING

3. Delcotron Diode and Field Test

INSULATED BRUSH
ASSEMBLY

4. Insulated Brush Removal

en off the shaft. On Chrysler alternators this requires some special tools, since the pulley is an interference fit with the rotor shaft. In view of the fact that the tools cost more than having the bearing replaced in a shop, it's probably best to farm out the entire job. On other generators and alternators a nut is removed from the center of the pulley and the pulley slipped off the shaft. On Ford alternators a gear puller can be used without damaging the pulley. Delcotron alternators have a particularly nice feature for pulley removal. The end of the rotor shaft has a recess that will accept a 5/16-in. Allen wrench. The Allen wrench allows you to keep the rotor shaft from turning while undoing the 15/16-in. nut

with a box wrench. When reinstalling the pulley nuts, a torque of approximately 50 ft.-lbs. is adequate.

Pulleys themselves frequently go bad—especially on generators that have stamped metal pulleys made up of two spot-welded halves. The reason for their failure is not that the pulleys are of inferior quality, but that fan belts are often overtightened. A fan belt that does not have the correct degree of deflection, as it is specified in the car owner's manual, puts an extremely heavy strain on the generator pulley as well as on the generator and water pump bearings. The pulley, being weakest, is usually the first part to fail, but if the car's owner has been careless about oiling the generator

bearings, they are also quite likely to burn out.

When tensioning the fan belt, use only a soft piece of wood to exert pressure against the side of the generator. On V-8's with high-mounted alternators or generators it is usually possible to tension the belt correctly with only hand pressure. Incidentally, *never* pry against the side of an anti-smog pump to adjust belt tension. The housings are very thin and can be easily bent, which will interfere with the action of the air pump's rotor.

Once the pulley is off the shaft, the bearing can be driven out along with the rotor or armature by suitably supporting the end plate and tapping on a short

Charging System

length of pipe set against the *outer* bearing race. In some cases a bearing retainer must first be removed. Assuming that the bearing is no good, it can be clamped in a vise and the shaft driven out by placing a block of hard wood against it and striking it with a hammer. If you are trying to "save" the bearing, a special puller is needed in order to prevent damage.

The new bearing can be driven into the end housing using the same piece of pipe that was used to remove the old one. The bearing and end plate are then driven onto the shaft using a smaller diameter piece of pipe (⅞-in. or 1 in. works for most bearings) to drive against the *inner* race. Amply detailed instruction sheets often come with rebuild kits.

The brush-end bearing is frequently a simple bushing that can be removed and replaced with the use of a regular bushing driver tool or a piece of pipe or steel rod somewhat larger in diameter than the armature shaft. When driving in bushings and bearings, always lubricate the outside to help them slide into place more easily. Also, be very careful that they are started straight to avoid damage. Alloy end frames can be very easily deformed if excessive force is used in removing and installing bearings. Always support the bearing area as closely to the edges of the bearing assembly as possible to prevent this. Chrysler alternators should have the pulley pressed onto the shaft before the brush-end housing is installed on the alternator so that the force can be directed against the rotor shaft itself.

In conclusion, let it be said that charging systems, like many of the electro-mechanical components found on modern automobiles, *do* have some rather complicated aspects. But they also have some extremely simple qualities as well. At first you may feel yourself incapable of handling some of the electrical diagnosis and adjustment, and may wish to leave this to an "expert" while limiting your own part of the repair work to removing and installing the related components.

However, if your repairs include changing a regulator or an armature, keep the old part. Practice making your own tests, and take it apart if you wish to find out what makes it "tick." The next step is to conduct the tests used in making adjustments on the regulator in your car—without actually making the adjustments. Eventually, the electrical parts of the charging system will lose much of their mystery, and the first time your checkup actually finds something wrong, nine times out of ten you'll have lost your reluctance to make the necessary repairs and adjustments yourself. It may be only changing the generator brushes, or setting the regulator cutout, but it's a step in the right direction.

It has been said that familiarity breeds contempt. The old graybeard who authored that famous cliche neglected to mention that it is only fools who become contemptuous—on the other hand, the wise develop confidence. 🏛

1. Chrysler Alternator

2. Motorola Alternator

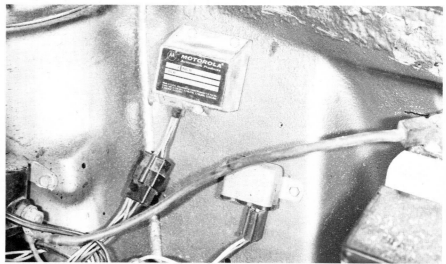

3. Solid-State Regulator

1. This is a Chrysler alternator separated into the two pieces by removing the through-bolts.

2. Low-mounted alternators like this Motorola are difficult to reach for belt tightening. When you remove this unit, take it out from the bottom.

3. Motorola solid-state regulator is a nonadjustable plug-in unit on the fenderwell—if it malfunctions, you have to replace it with a new one.

4. This is the solid-state diode rectified voltage regulator unit incorporated as an integral part of all 1973 Delcotron alternators. It's a replace-only unit if it goes bad.

5. Voltage regulator adjustment is made with screw (1). Incorrect adjustment on this unit caused the lower points (2) to arc continuously, burn out, and ruin regulator assembly.

4. Delcotron Regulator

5. Voltage Regulator Adjustment

1. Disconnect plug at regulator (1) and at terminals (2,3). Run hot wire to (2). Engine at 2000 rpm should give 15 volts at output terminal (4).

2. To remove and replace the brushes, the first thing that you have to do is remove the two screws that hold the terminal plate in position.

3. The plate with ground terminal attached lifts right off once screws are removed, but you may have to jiggle plate a bit first time around.

4. Underneath the terminal plate, you'll find an insulator. This is a very important piece; don't forget to replace it and don't lose it.

5. Nothing further is required to get to the brushes. Assembly lifts out with ease and replacement brushes are a relatively simple slip-in.

6. Removal of four through-bolts is necessary to split the housing. As with any alternator, mark position of housings for correct assembly.

7. Disconnect terminals that come through the housing to remove diode plate. Lay out variety of washers in the order of removal to avoid mistakes.

8. Unless you want to unsolder diode leads, this is as far as you can go. If diodes or stator have to be changed, you'll have to unsolder leads.

9. American Motors uses a Motorola charging system. ID plate on side contains alternator rating and information needed for replacement parts.

Lights, Gauges, Wiring

This chapter is the do-it-yourselfer's paradise. Since the first automobiles came out, car owners have been carrying spare fuses, spare light bulbs, and maybe even doing a little bit of their own wiring when they want to add an accessory. If you're a little bit timid about working on some of the more complicated units of the car—such as the starter, the generator or engine parts—the lighting system is a good place to get started and build up your confidence. It's also a good place to practice ahead of time so that when a headlight or even a fuse burns out in the middle of the night you have a pretty good idea of what you have to do to fix it. The wise driver will keep a roll of electrical tape, extra fuses, a spare sealed beam headlight unit, and some simple tools in the car at all times to cope with any highway emergencies that may come up.

FUSES AND CIRCUIT BREAKERS

A fuse is nothing more than a glass or ceramic insulator with metal contacts at the ends which are connected to one another electrically by fine wires or thin metal strips. The latter will melt like a chorus girl's heart at a millionaires' convention if a precise electrical current load is exceeded. Short circuits that might otherwise transform your car's wiring into a Fourth-of-July display of flaming spaghetti are quickly "switched off" when the fusible wire burns apart.

Lately, car makers have been eliminating many fuses in favor of circuit breakers. The circuit breaker is basically an electro-mechanical device that functions as a fuse does, but has the added advantage of being able to restore the flow of electricity automatically once the

trouble is past. Headlights, wipers and other safety accessories are often controlled by circuit breakers to prevent their complete failure in the event of an intermittent short. After all, no one wants to have his lights go out while crossing the Nevada desert at 90 per—just because something went haywire with the cigarette lighter!

Circuit breakers are sealed assemblies and should one go bad (which seldom ever happens) the whole unit must be replaced. Just make certain that you install a new one of the identical type and amperage as the original. In many cases the circuit breaker is an integral part of the headlight switch, in which case that part must be replaced in its entirety. Late GM cars have a release button on the switch behind the dash which, when pushed, allows the light control knob and shaft to be pulled completely out of the dashboard before removing the re-

1. Pacer Dashlamp Access

2. Bulb Corrosion

3. Twin-Filament Bulb

1. Once in a while, car manufacturers make things easier to work on rather than harder. The dash cover on this '75 AMC Pacer snaps off to expose the instruments and warning lights.

2. Most bulbs ground through socket. If the bulb doesn't work, check the filament first and if it's all right then clean any corrosion from socket.

3. Note the two terminals on this typical twin-filament bulb. Sockets for these will have two wires; one may be for stoplight filament, the other for turn signal or taillight.

4. The fuse panel has been hard to reach on many cars for years, so some manufacturers are trying to make it easier to service—such as on this '75 Dodge truck where the fuse block is exposed at the center of the dash when the large glovebox door is open.

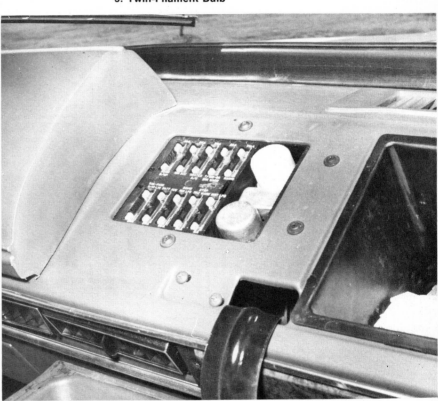

4. Dodge Pickup Fuse Panel

tainer ring that mounts the switch on the automobile.

The majority of American cars have their fuse panel located under the forward edge of the dashboard. On some models the fuse panel is located on the firewall just above the driver's feet. Most fuse panels have each fuse marked according to its function (radio, heater, etc.) and its amperage. Check the ampere rating for the fuses in your car and buy a few extras to slip into the glove compartment. This simple act could save you lots of trouble.

On many fuse blocks there isn't enough room to label all of the circuits that the fuse protects. Only the most prominent item, such as the radio or the wipers, will be printed on the fuse block. If some electric unit on your car stops dead, but you can't find a label for that unit on the fuse block, check the wiring diagram in the factory shop manual. In some cases, the owner's manual will give a more complete description of the circuits protected by each fuse. There may also be fuses in some other location, nowhere near the main fuse block.

A fuse that blows—or a circuit breaker that cuts out—may indicate either a shorted circuit or one that is being overloaded. If the fuse blows again after it replaces the original, or if the circuit

breaker cuts out repeatedly, it's time to plop on your Sherlock Holmes cap and start looking for the source of the trouble. However, if the second fuse doesn't blow, the first incident was possibly only the result of a momentary overload. This may occur on those rare occasions when several accessories sharing a common fuse are in operation simultaneously. Should one accessory begin drawing abnormally high current—as a windshield wiper may when pushing aside heavy snow—the fuse may be momentarily overloaded. A circuit breaker will simply cut the current for an instant and then things should return to their normal conditions.

FUSIBLE LINKS

A few years ago it wasn't unusual to hear of a car that had burned up from a

short in the wiring. All it took was a bare wire against the frame or body and the battery would pour out enough current to heat up the wire, set the insulation on fire and turn your pride and joy into smoldering ashes. It is now extremely unlikely that car fires will ever occur from shorts or grounds in wiring. Every car today has one or more fusible links, that will burn in two if they are forced to carry any overload of current.

The fusible link is a piece of wire about 6 ins. long that is spliced into another wire. The link can be in many different locations in the engine compartment or behind the instrument panel. In some cases it is identified by a special color or a lettered tab. It may be looped so it stands out from other wiring, or it may blend in so you don't even know it's there. Some links can burn in

Lights, Gauges, Wiring

two without any change in appearance, but the better links have a special insulation that bubbles and swells when the wire burns up. New links are available at parts stores and dealers. The old link should be cut out and the new link spliced and soldered into position. If the new link comes as a piece of bulk wire, take care to see that it ends up the same length as the old link after being spliced in.

WIRES—SHORTS AND GROUNDS

Shorted wires are the usual cause of blown fuses. Whenever a "hot" (as opposed to a grounded) wire starts to suffer from worn or frayed insulation, there is danger of a short. Occasionally some Grade A boulderbrain decides that it's too much trouble to keep replacing fuses, so he deftly inserts part of a 10-penny nail into the fuse holders. It would be better simply to trace down the short, but never mind, that's even harder than changing fuses. Precisely this kind of bonehead play burned up a car in New Jersey just a few years ago. Unfortunately, it was parked in the garage under the owner's new split-level house at the time. If you want to start fresh with a new house and car, plus all your belongings, that's one way to do it—but it can be a bit expensive.

The first places to check for worn or broken insulation are at metal clips or other wire supports. On some cars, wires may pass *under* the automobile. Here, exposed to weather and road splash, the wire's normal life expectancy is considerably reduced.

In one case, a car owner's lighting-system fuse kept blowing. After replacing the fuse several times, repeated taping and inspection of the wires and much soul-rousing profanity, he finally noticed that the fuses only blew when the brakes had been applied for a few seconds. The trouble? Worn insulation on the one wire he didn't check: the brake light switch wire. It was located under the car and its insulation had practically rotted away. When the brake pedal was depressed, the arm on the brake light switch barely touched the wire, but it was enough to produce a shorted circuit. Three inches of plastic tape around the wire got him home, and a new wire provided a final solution to the problem.

Other wire trouble is frequently encountered at the terminals. Corrosion and vibration can eventually produce poor contact. A regular check for terminal tightness and a cleaning with abrasive cloth when trouble strikes will usually prevent or cure most bad contacts. Broken wires can be repaired in one of three ways. First—and best, if the insulation is in generally poor condition—is to replace the wire in its entirety. Second, wires can be spliced by simply twisting the ends together, soldering the joint if possible and covering the area with electrical tape. A coating of liquid rubber over the taped joint will make a very permanent and weatherproof joint. Third, in some cases it is possible to install a

1. Lamp Retaining Tabs

2. Adjustment Screws

3. Square Sealed Beams

crimped-on splicing tube. These splicing tubes, however, require a special tool to compress them.

A great variety of specialized wire terminals are available from automotive supply stores. These also must be crimped into place with a special tool. Such wire terminals require no soldering, and they always ensure a flawless electrical connection.

HEADLIGHTS

Replacing a burned-out sealed-beam unit is perhaps the simplest of automotive repairs, next to changing fuses. Still, more first-time home mechanics have botched this job than would ever care to admit it, even to themselves.

Dual headlight installations employ two different types of sealed-beam units. The high-beam lamps which "go out" when the headlights are dimmed have only two terminals on the back, and their lens is marked with a number 1. The other kind of unit operates on both high and low beam, and like the sealed-beam lamps found on cars with single headlights, it has three terminals on the back. The lens of these is marked with a number 2. Before buying a new one, be sure you know whether you're replacing the high/low number 2 lamp or the high-beam number 1 lamp only. On cars with the dual lights arranged side by side, the outermost lamps are the 3-terminal high/low combination. On Pontiacs, Plymouths and other cars that have one light mounted above the other, the upper unit is the high/low number 2 lamp.

The first step in making the actual replacement is to take off the decorative

1. Arrows indicate typical sealed beam retaining tabs. Loosen screws just enough to rotate the retainer so it can be pulled off over the screw heads. The other screws are for beam adjustment; leave them alone.

2. On some cars, the beam adjustment screws are exposed to allow access without having to remove the trim ring.

3. GM broke the square-headlight ice on some '75 models, and now the style is widespread throughout the industry.

4. Adjustment of square lights is about the same as for round ones, but bulb replacement may mean complete removal instead of just loosening of retaining screws (arrows).

5. Taillights on many cars are now accessible from inside the trunk, eliminating the need to remove lenses from outside. This is the inside rear body panel on a Buick Regal.

6. If you can't locate taillight bulbs from inside the trunk, then the outer lens has to come off. You'll usually find two or more Phillips-head screws.

7. Some switches are quite difficult to get to. Here the radio had to be pulled to allow enough room for access to the light switch. A special tool for removing the collar on the front side of this switch is shown in shop manuals, but often a large screwdriver with a wide blade will do.

8. Flashers for most late-model cars are simple plug-in types. They come in many different electrical values, according to the number of bulbs on the car in the flashing circuit. The best ones are the heavy-duty types.

4. Square Bulb Adjustment

7. Light Switch Removal

5. Taillight Access

6. Taillight Lens Removal

8. Turn Signal Flasher

Lights, Gauges, Wiring

trim surrounding the headlight. On most cars with dual lights there are three or four screws used to do the job. Cars with single lights usually have only one screw directly at the bottom of the chrome ring. Once the trim is off, there will be several screws visible around the circumference of the headlight. Three of these will be removed to change the sealed beam unit. The other two must not be tampered with since they are for aiming the lights. These aiming screws are larger than the retaining screws and are therefore pretty easy to spot.

Once the retaining ring surrounding the light is off, the sealed beam unit can be pulled out and the plug withdrawn from its terminals. Putting in the new lamp is simply a reversal of the removal process—but be sure to position the lens so that the word "TOP" is at the top where it is supposed to be.

HEADLIGHT AIMING

Twenty years ago the highways were peppered with immature squirrels who deliberately aimed their car's headlights in a way calculated to blind other drivers. Quite a few even mounted spotlights for this very purpose. If your lights were brighter than the other guys, you were a bigger man. Or at least brighter.

Well, the police finally got tired of hauling dozens of these rabbit-brained anthropoids off to the cop shop every night, and state legislators passed laws in many locales that required car owners to either obtain a certificate to the effect that their headlight aiming had been carried out by a "professional," or to have the headlight aim checked annually by state-licensed inspectors.

If you live in one of these areas where the government is trying to save the populace from its own folly, there's not much you can do about aiming your own headlights unless only a state inspection is required. However, if there are no such legal requirements in your particular state, you can do your own headlight aiming with relative ease.

You'll need to find a place where your car will sit level, such as a paved driveway or parking lot. Or you can drive your car to such a place and lay a carpenter's spirit level on the front bumper and on one of the door sills (with the door open). Even on a level surface, the car may not sit absolutely level, or the bumper may be mounted in a slightly tilted position in relation to the car, so mark the location of the bubble in the level with a grease pencil. Rock the car from side to side and allow it to assume its normal attitude before making the tests with the spirit level.

The car can then be driven home to your own un-level driveway and a jack or two used to adjust the level of the car slightly to duplicate the bubble positon obtained with the car on level ground.

The car should be positioned 25 ft. from a garage wall or an aiming screen improvised from a large piece of cardboard. The aiming screen should have one horizontal line and three vertical lines drawn upon it. The horizontal line

can be laid out with the help of the carpenter's level and should be at the identical height above the ground as the center vertical line should be at the car's exact centerline. This can first be drawn at right angles to the horizontal line, if desired, and the aiming screen shifted from side to side until it is lined up with the center of the car's hood. You can "sight" through the rear window to do this. If there is no distinct centerline in the hood, the center can be located with a tape measure, a small suction cup placed there for a "front sight" and a yardstick held straight up from the trunk lock for a "rear sight."

Two other vertical lines are then drawn which are the same distance apart as the centers of the car's headlights. These should be located equidistant from the centerline, which will place them directly in front of the car's lights.

The adjustment on all Type-2 units is made with the headlights on low beam only. This will assure adequate illumination with the lights dimmed, and the built-in angle between the high and low beams will take care of the aiming for the "brights." Type-2 units, whether used on two- or four-headlight systems, have a "2" molded into the lens for identification. If the car has dual headlights, the high-beam-only #1 lights are adjusted separately. Three other prerequisites must be observed if you wish to do a good job: (1) Have the tires inflated to the correct pressures. (2) Have the car filled to capacity with gas, water, and oil—but no cargo or passengers. (3) Make sure all grille, fender, and headlight assembly bolts are tight.

AIMING TYPE-2 UNITS

On most cars you will have to remove the headlight trim ring to gain access to the adjusting screws. Some late-model cars, though, have access holes in the trim rings that allow you to stick a

1. New Sealed-Beam Lamps

2. Non-Powered Testing Light

screwdriver through for adjustments.

Switch the lights to low beam. Cover the right headlight with your jacket, an old blanket, your mother-in-law, or anything else that's handy. Adjust the left light vertically until the top edge of its high-intensity zone is exactly on the horizontal line. The vertical adjustment screw is at the top of the sealed beam unit on most cars. When adjusting the aiming screws, move them first counterclockwise until the lights are definitely *out* of adjustment, and then gradually clockwise to bring them in. Otherwise the spring may not expand properly and will later allow the lamps to change aim.

After positioning the light vertically,

1. Everybody's coming out with new sealed-beam units. The two curved sealed-beams—from GE—are their "Plus 25" offerings, which give 25 ft. more visibility. The flat-faced lamp is the GE "Blazer Beam," which is an auxiliary driving light.

2. The reliable, non-powered testing light is still invaluable in tracing wiring problems. The light bulb in the handle is easily changed when it burns out. To use one, simply ground the clip and touch the sharp probe to the wire in question. If it's hot the test-light bulb will light up.

3. In addition to the normal wiring diagrams, some new shop manuals, like this one for a '75 Dodge, have easy troubleshooting charts for various electrical subsystems on the car.

use the same procedure to move the beam horizontally until the left edge of the high-intensity zone is 3 ins. (2 ins. in some states) to the right of the vertical line in front of that headlight. The light's horizontal adjusting screw is located to one side of the sealed beam mounting. By moving the covering from the right headlight to the left, it will be possible to make the same adjustments to the right side. This is the end of the job for cars with single lights. Dual headlight units must still have their #1 lamps aimed.

AIMING TYPE-1 UNITS

The actual work is done exactly as it was in aiming the #2 lamps, but the beam is positioned differently on the screen. Cover the three lights not being adjusted. Aim the exposed high beam until the center of its "hot spot" is 2 ins. lower than the intersection of the horizontal line and the vertical line in front of that light. On station wagons and softly sprung sedans the hot spot should be centered further below the horizontal line to compensate for vehicle loading differences. This measurement depends on your state's particular motor vehicle requirements.

If you have a car with single headlights that is equipped with the old 5000 series sealed beam unit (without the #2 on the lens), then they should be adjusted while on high beam only, according to the instructions given above for aiming #1 units (those with a single-filament high beam).

SOME OTHER LIGHTS

Burned-out taillights, instrument panel bulbs, and what have you, are usually fairly quick and easy to change. The average car has about 15 or 20 small lamps—not all of them the same size. When a small bulb stops functioning, you should take it out and check to see that the lamp itself is really to blame. Quite often, parking light and turn signal units will suffer the ravages of weather, water and roadside mud until the wires or sockets themselves finally succumb to corrosion and rot. If the bulb turns out to be OK, insert the probes of a test light into the socket (with the switch controlling the light turned on) and see if current is actually reaching the lamp. If it is, the trouble is probably nothing more than a coating of crud on the socket or bulb contacts. Scraping the terminal contacts on both the bulb and socket should do the trick. Poor ground contact could also be a factor, so don't forget to polish up the lug pins on the lamp base, and also the slots in the socket that they fit into. Check the ground between the socket and its holder, between the holder and the fender, and between the fender and the body. The electricity has to get back to the ground terminal of the battery. It can be stopped at any one of those points. We have fixed many an old car that was hopelessly rusted up by running a ground wire from the bulb sockets to the frame of the car. It's a lot easier than trying to get a ground through all that rusty sheetmetal.

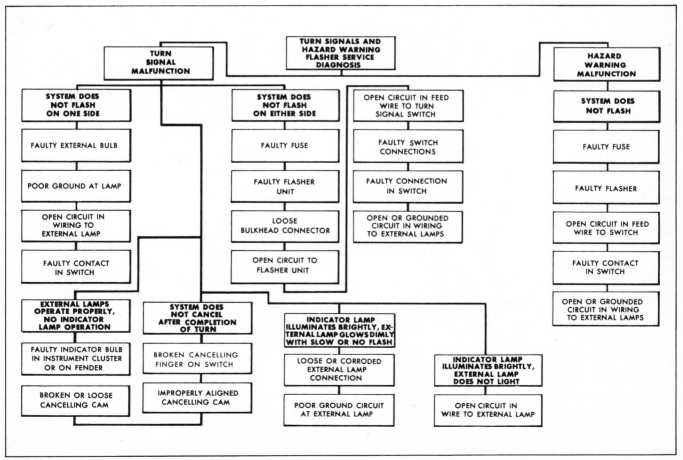

3. Troubleshooting Diagram

Lights, Gauges, Wiring

If no current is reaching the socket, a broken or shorted wire—or possibly a faulty switch—is at the bottom of it all. However, most switches operate more than one bulb, or at least something else besides the bulb. If the other components in the circuit are functioning properly, the trouble is not likely to be in the switch itself.

Every bulb has a number printed on its base, and when buying a replacement you should try to find a lamp having the identical number. Often, the parts store will have a chart or booklet listing the bulbs used for particular applications in various makes and models of cars. Tell them what kind of car you drive, and which lamp has burned out, and they'll probably be able to fix you up.

The lights on the outside of the car's body are pretty easy to work on, but some of those located behind the dashboard seem to have been put there by Houdini's ghost. Trying to get your hand up through the maze of wires and controls sometimes requires the agility of a serpent and the patience of a saint. These small instrument panel lamps are usually retained in sockets that can be taken out of the back of the instrument panel by turning them about ¼-turn counterclockwise and pulling them out. The sockets on a few cars simply press into holes in the back of the panel. Once the socket is out it can be pulled from under the dash, the old bulb exchanged for a new one, and the socket reinstalled behind the instrument panel.

Taillights, backup lights, parking lights, and turn signals are generally serviced by removing the lens and trim ring. Most cars have from one to four screws holding the trim ring in place and, once these are taken out, the ring, lens, and gasket will come off to give access to the bulb. Actually, on most late-model cars—including nearly all Chevrolets—it is possible to replace the bulbs in the tail-, stop-, and backup lights from inside the trunk. These lights have sockets that can be pulled out in a way very similar to the bulb holders used on the back of the instrument panel—making the whole job easier.

Many of the bulbs used in rear-end lighting are "combination" types that have two filaments and serve as both a taillight and turn signal, or as a stoplight and taillight. For this reason it is imperative that the same type of bulb be used. Also, only by installing bulbs of the right specifications can you be sure of getting the precise degree of brightness required by the motor vehicle laws.

SWITCHES

If the bulbs are all OK, but your stoplights or backup lights *still* won't work, or dimming your headlights for an upcoming car sometimes makes them go *completely out,* you've got switch troubles. Usually, the only cure is to put in a new switch.

In the case of light, heater, and windshield wiper switches that are mounted *through* the dash, it's necessary to take off the control knob before the faulty unit can be removed. In the majority of cases, a small set screw—often the "Allen" variety—must be taken from the underside of the knob before it will come off the shaft. Some controls may have knobs that are threaded onto the shaft and can simply be unscrewed, while others employ spring retainers that are freed by inserting a small wire into a hole in the bottom of the knob. As mentioned earlier, the knob and control shaft on some cars is taken out as a unit by pulling the control to the "ON" position and depressing an under-dash button located on the switch body to free it.

1. A voltmeter can be very useful for detection of any shorts or open circuits in wiring. Test probes here are inserted in a separated inline connector—not to measure current, but just to tell if it is on or off.

2. Late-model dimmer switches are one-piece units with plug-on terminals for wiring. They normally can't be disassembled for owner-servicing.

3. Most gauges can't be taken apart for repairs, but this fuel gauge can be adjusted with a small screwdriver.

4. It isn't easy to get your hands up there to do instrument or wiring work. One trick is to remove the radio and work through the opening. Removing the ashtray can help, too.

1. Searching For a Short

2. Dimmer Switch

3. Adjusting Fuel Gauge

4. Under-Dash Work

The ferrule nut that holds the switch in the dash often takes some pretty exotic shapes. A few are easy to grip with fingers or with common tools, but others are intended to be taken off with a special tool. It's usually better to improvise such a tool from wood or wire than to try "brute force" (such as a pair of pliers), which will only lead to unsightly scratches on the ferrule nut and dashboard. Once the switch is out of the dash, the wires can be disconnected and a new switch installed.

Whenever you change a switch, it's a good idea to label all wires so that they can be reinstalled in the correct positions. However, most late-model cars have plug-in connectors that preclude any possibility that the wires may be-

come confused. These plugs also make the job much quicker and easier. As a further precaution, the battery ground cable should always be disconnected during the switch-changing operation to prevent accidental shorts that could blow fuses, start fires or drain the battery.

While nearly all switches are serviced as complete units only, there are a few which may be returned to useful service by simply tightening, adjusting or lubricating the switch or its linkage. Stoplight switches that are operated mechanically off the brake pedal can cause two kinds of easily fixed trouble. Those found on older cars with brake pedals that pass through the floorboards are located *under* the car, and are therefore frequent victims of dirt and corrosion.

These switches have a lever on them which contacts the brake pedal. The lever is spring loaded so that it will swing around in an arc as the brakes are applied and the pedal arm moves away from it. The switch lever is connected internally to a pair of electrical contacts which trigger the stoplights when they come together. If the switch lever's shaft becomes rusted or coated with dirt, it will no longer turn properly to follow the movement of the brake pedal arm. Result: no stoplights. In most cases a few drops of "Liquid Wrench," or a similar rust-dissolving oil, will free the frozen shaft. In bad cases the switch can be removed and washed in kerosene. After the Liquid Wrench or the kerosene bath, work the lever back and forth a few times and it should start to move freely once again. If it does not, the spring is probably broken and a new switch will be required.

The stoplight switch used on late-model cars with "hanging" brake pedals is usually mounted under the dashboard just below the steering column on the brake pedal stop. Any trouble caused by these switches is more likely to result from vibration than corrosion. Should the retaining nut become loosened, it may allow the switch to move away from the pedal and the stoplights will remain permanently on. The switch must be re-mounted tightly in such a position that electrical contact is made when the brake pedal is depressed ⅜- to ⅝-in. from the fully released position, when the brake is "off."

Some stoplight switches are a friction fit in their bracket. To adjust them, push the switch toward the brake pedal with the pedal depressed. When the pedal is released, it will bottom the switch and push it back in the bracket to the right operating position.

The backup light switches fitted to most of the automatic and column-shift transmissions seldom cause trouble since most are mounted on the steering column inside the car and out of the

Lights, Gauges, Wiring

weather. If one goes bad, simply put the selector switch in neutral, disconnect the wires from the switch, unscrew the unit from the car, and install a new one. However, many cars with floor shifters have the backup light switch mounted on the side of the transmission *under* the car. These switches and their connections can take quite a beating from the weather, and may eventually cause trouble. Also, the small rod connecting the switch to the reverse gear bellcrank may become loose or rusty and fail to function at all.

To replace such a switch, the wiring is disconnected at an inline plug some distance from the switch itself. The cotter or wire clip is then removed at the point where the reverse lever rod is connected to the switch's control arm. Then you can remove the switch and its splash shield by taking out two screws. The bracket remains mounted on the transmission and should not be disturbed. After the new switch is in place, test its action by shifting the transmission in and out of reverse. The mounting holes on the switch are elongated, making it possible to adjust the switch's position for proper operation.

Like a well mannered rattlesnake, dimmer switches usually give some warning before they slip you the needle. You'd be well advised to investigate the cause of any malfunction at the first sign of trouble. Otherwise, you might suddenly find yourself driving 60 mph on a winding, tree-lined road without any headlights to show you the way.

Sometimes dimmer switch trouble is nothing more than a sticking plunger. Dirt and snow from your shoes may work its way into the switch and cause it to jam. Remove the switch and blow out any debris that's under the pedal cap and inject a few drops of penetrating oil into it. If the switch now works normally, you're back in business.

If the headlights refuse to go on and you suspect trouble in the dimmer switch, you can check the circuit with a jumper wire. By connecting the center wire leading to the switch to one of the other two wires, you should be able to make the lights operate on either bright or dim. If the jumper wire gets results, the trouble is probably in the switch. But, before condemning the dimmer switch itself, be sure that the trouble isn't poor contact between the wires and the switch terminal connections.

Most dimmer switches can be removed by folding back the upper left corner of the front floor mat and removing the wires and mounting screws from the switch assembly. Most late-model cars have a multi-wire plug connector which is simply pulled from the terminals. Place the multi-plug connector on the terminals of the new switch and check the headlight operation. If everything works OK, bolt in the new switch, replace the floor mat, and the job's done.

If the neutral safety switch found on cars with automatic transmissions goes bad it can stop you deader than Sitting Bull stopped Custer or, if it permits the engine to be started with the gear selec-

tor in the "drive" or "reverse" range, it might even convert your car into a lethal battering ram. As part of the circuit controlling the starting system, its failure will be more than a slight inconvenience.

One type of neutral safety switch is screwed directly into the transmission, and the other mounts with two or three screws somewhere on the transmission selector linkage. It is commonly inside the console on cars with floor-mounted gear selectors, and somewhere on the steering column of others. Once the ac-

tual location is determined, the removal and replacement operation should be fairly obvious. In some cases the trouble is nothing more than dirty, burned, or grease-coated contacts. A little judicious cleaning will usually be all that's needed. But if there is obvious breakage, or signs of wear, get a new switch.

Many of the less elaborate instrument layouts can be serviced without taking the panel out of the car. However, most of the cars that have "extra" instruments installed as "options" must have the

1. Speedometer Disconnect

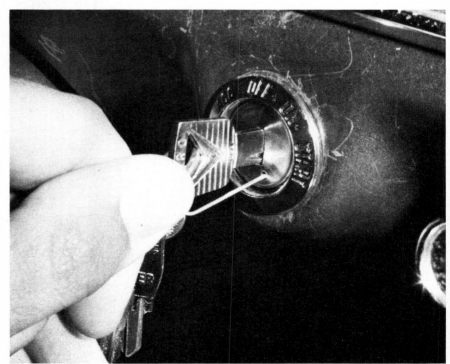

2. Ignition Switch Removal

1. *Many late-model speedometers have a thumb-latch to disconnect the cable, instead of a threaded-ferrule connection.*

2. *If your ignition-switch lock has a small hole in front, it's made for easy removal of the lock cylinder. Insert a paper clip in the hole, turn the key all the way, and the paper clip depresses and releases a spring so the cylinder can be removed.*

3. *Accessory gauges are commonly installed in a trio panel under the dash, to replace the "idiot lights." This car owner has added extra gauges in console as well as dash.*

4. *This close-up shows how some gauges are marked. Ground post is by itself; ignition wire runs to the accessory post of ignition switch; the other goes to gauge's sender.*

5. *A tachometer has been one of the most popular accessory gauges for years. Some are made only for one type of engine, but this Dixco can be used with 8's, 6's, and 4's, simply by changing the resistors.*

3. Accessory Gauges

4. Gauge Terminals

5. Back of Tachometer

panel removed before you can get at the gauges. To avoid electrical damage, the battery ground cable must always be disconnected when the instrument cluster is being taken out. On most cars it is also necessary to remove the steering column housing, or in some instances to "drop" the column assembly from its dash mounts. Since in many cases the instrument cluster will slide along the steering column jacket as it is removed, the jacket should be wrapped with masking tape to protect it from scratches.

Before loosening the cluster from the dashboard, the retaining collar holding the speedometer cable must be unscrewed and the cable slipped out of its socket in the speedometer head. If there is an oil pressure line (as on many GM "sports" models), this must also be taken off. The screws holding the instrument cluster in place may then be removed. There are generally from four to six of these located around the cluster, Phillips-type screws being commonly used to retain it.

Once the retaining screws are out, the cluster can be pulled out of the dashboard. When there is adequate working space between the cluster and the dash, the remaining wires can be unplugged or disconnected if it is desired that the instrument cluster be removed completely from the car. However, if the car has console-mounted instruments, it may be necessary to dismount the main instrument cluster before the front of the console can be lifted off.

Since many instrument panels are now being made of plastic, there may also be one or more ground straps to provide ground polarity to the instruments. When replacing the panel, be very sure to reinstall these properly to secure the best possible electrical contact and assure a good ground.

FUEL GAUGE AND VOLTAGE LIMITER

All modern fuel gauges are electrically operated and are actually nothing more than simple devices capable of measuring the amount of voltage transmitted from a sending unit located in the car's fuel tank. There is also a voltage-limiting relay in the circuit to prevent inaccurate readings due to voltage changes initiated outside the gas gauge's own wiring sys-

tem. On some automobiles the voltage limiter is an integral part of the fuel gauge itself, but it may also be a separate behind-the-dash unit. In most cars equipped with electric oil pressure and water temperature gauges, these units are connected to the same voltage limiter as the fuel gauge. In rare cases, each gauge may come fitted with its own built-in limiting device.

A fuel gauge that shows a "full" tank whenever the ignition is switched on is probably not "stuck" as it may seem to be. There are three other far more likely electrical causes for this malfunction. The most common is an improperly grounded gauge or instrument cluster. If the cluster is not grounded, all other electrical gauges will also be against the peg at the high end of their scale. The ammeter, however, will not be affected, and an electric tachometer that is not properly grounded will read a constant "zero." The only necessary repair in such cases is to restore good ground contact to the instruments or to the panel. In the case of a plastic panel, there is often only one ground connection or ground strap for all instruments. The in-

Lights, Gauges, Wiring

dividual units are then grounded to one another. This is why all gauges may be affected by a poor ground potential. If the car has a metal panel, however, the problem may affect only the fuel gauge.

You can test for faulty ground connections simply by connecting a jumper wire to some grounded point on the car and touching its opposite end to the back of the high-reading instrument (or zero-reading instrument in the case of the tachometer). If it then reads normally, you've found the trouble.

A faulty voltage limiter can also cause the gauge(s) to read high or low—either at one peg or the other, or at any "odd" place in between. If the needles occasionally make sudden "surges" to higher-than-normal readings, this is also the result of a faulty voltage limiter.

A quick check of the instrument voltage limiter can be made by connecting one lead of a test light to the temperature-sending unit on the engine and the other lead to ground. Leave the instrument wire attached to the sending unit also and have the ignition switch turned on. A flashing lamp indicates that the limiter is working. A voltmeter can also be used to make this test. The reading should fluctuate between 0 and 7

volts on a vehicle with a 12-volt electrical system.

If the car has only a fuel gauge, the limiter can still be tested, but it will probably require that the instrument cluster be removed from the dashboard. The limiter is tested by connecting a jumper wire from the "hot" post of the car's battery to the input (battery) terminal on the limiter (or fuel gauge, if the limiter is an integral part of it). Another jumper is connected from the grounded battery post to the case of the limiter or gauge. A test light—or the correct polarity lead of a voltmeter—should also be connected to the battery's grounded pole, and the remaining voltmeter or test light lead touched to the limiter's input terminal. A full 12-volt reading should be shown or, in the case of a test light, the bulb should burn brightly. The test lead must then be moved from the input terminal to the terminal that leads to the gauges. There should be a fluctuating reading of from 0 to 7 volts, or a flashing test light. If not, the limiter (or gauge-limiter combination) is defective. If such is the case, it should be replaced.

Another possible cause of a constant "full" reading is a short in the wire coming from the tank. If the wire proves to be OK, the gauge well grounded, and the voltage limiter operating properly, any trouble that exists must be in either

the gauge mechanism itself or in the tank's sending unit.

The next item to check is the proper grounding of the sending unit. Clean away a small area on the fuel tank and another on the top of the sender. (Its location on the fuel tank can be determined by inspecting the tank to find the gauge wire's connecting point.) Attach a jumper wire to a good ground on the car's body and touch the other end to the clean spot on the fuel tank. If the gauge reads normally, the trouble is a poorly grounded tank. If the gauge still does not read accurately, touch the jumper to the clean spot on the sending unit. A normal reading here indicates poor ground contact between the tank and the sending unit. Should the reading still be "off," the trouble is either in the gauge or in the sending unit mechanism.

The best way to make further tests is with the help of an extra sending unit. By doing this, you can avoid going to the trouble of needlessly removing the car's sending unit from the gas tank. The extra sending unit can be a junkyard cheapie and does not even have to be from the same model car as yours. It must, however, be in good working condition. Once you've obtained the extra sending unit you can wire it to the car's gauge by grounding it to the vehicle's body with a jumper wire and attaching the

1. Wire Splicing

2. Insulating Shrink Tubing

gauge's lead wire to the test unit's terminal rather than to the terminal on the sender in the car. Turn the ignition switch to "on" and move the float of the sending unit up and down. The needle on the instrument panel should traverse the full range from "empty" to "full." There should be no sticking or jerkiness in its movement. If the gauge does not work properly, it will have to be replaced. If it *does* work properly, it means you'll have to work on the sending unit in your car.

It may be necessary to take the tank out of the car on some makes, but it's usually possible to remove the sending unit with the tank still in the car. However, be sure you disconnect the battery cables first. One little spark is all it would take to turn you and your car into a king-size torch.

Clean all undercoating, dirt and corrosion from the area around the sending unit and take out the cap screws or locking ring holding it in place. Locking

1. When making wiring repairs, good splices are vital to trouble-free service. First skin the wires and intersperse the strands; then twist the strands, heat the joint and apply solder for a positive connection.

2. Shrink-tubing is available at most electrical supply houses, and is better than tape for splices. The heat of a match is enough to shrink the tubing tightly over a connection.

3. If you don't have access to a soldering gun or electrical outlet, then neat/simple solderless terminals like these are for you. They come in sizes for every gauge wire and type of connection you could need.

4. Special pliers are used to crimp solderless terminals onto the wires.

rings are designed to be removed with a special wrench, but we have found that a large screwdriver laid across the ring will get enough bite to remove it. Remove the sending unit from the tank and clean away all dirt and corrosion from its electrical connections and components. Working a safe distance from the open gas tank, connect the sending unit to the gauge wire and to ground as you did with the test sender. Use a couple of long jumper wires for this. If the sending unit now operates the gauge normally, your cleanup did the trick. If not, you'll need a new unit. Before putting the unit back, you should get a new gasket from your car dealer. Sealer or gasket cement is unnecessary. Just put it on dry.

TEMPERATURE AND OIL PRESSURE GAUGES

If your car should be equipped with electrically operated temperature and oil pressure gauges, the tests used on the fuel gauge should work on these as well. If their needles move to the maximum reading when the ignition is switched on, the trouble is poor ground contact, a faulty voltage limiter, or a shorted lead wire. A "zero" reading means broken or dirty electrical connections, a faulty voltage limiter, or a defective sending unit or gauge. If the gauge can be made to go from "zero" to "maximum" by disconnecting the wire from the sending unit and grounding it, the trouble is in the sending unit, which must therefore be inspected and cleaned or replaced as an assembly.

Electric gauges commonly used in modern cars work on the thermal principle. That is, voltage differences produce temperature changes in the gauge's mechanism which in turn move the needle. If the instrument panel loses its ground contact, the needles on the fuel,

temperature, and oil pressure gauges may be forced far above their normal maximum dial readings. This may result in the permanent destruction of their accuracy. When a good ground is restored, the gauges will operate normally once again but at somewhat higher levels. If it's possible to "get inside" the individual gauges, you can usually restore their accuracy with a little judicious bending or—in the case of most imported cars—some careful fiddling with the calibration adjustments. If the gauges are "sealed units," then they'll have to be replaced.

Water temperature gauges that are connected by a long copper tube to a fitting in the engine's cylinder head are thermo-mechanical rather than electrical in operation. When the copper tube is broken, the gas or liquid it contains is lost and a new gauge—complete with tube and sensor—must be obtained. So long as its tube is not bent, dented or broken, these instruments are quite accurate and free of service problems.

Oil pressure gauges that actually have an oil line leading to them can eventually be rendered inoperative if the tube becomes plugged with sludge. It is usually possible to unplug these by simply disconnecting both ends of the line and blowing it out with compressed air.

AMMETERS

Ammeters are always made as sealed assemblies and cannot be repaired. Trouble—though seldom encountered on ammeters—is always shown by a constant zero reading. An operating ammeter will always show a discharge when the headlights are switched on and the engine is not running. Since ammeter failures are so rare, it is always advisable to check the wiring thoroughly before condemning or replacing the instrument itself.

3. Solderless Terminals

4. Crimping Terminal

Lights, Gauges, Wiring

SPEEDOMETER SERVICING

The speedometer head should be serviced only by an authorized agent. If you try to save a few bucks by working on it yourself, you'll probably end up paying twice the amount in fines for speeding. However, you can reduce the labor costs somewhat by removing and installing the unit yourself.

On some cars—including practically every import—the speedometer can be removed from the back of the dash. This is done by unscrewing the speedometer cable, disconnecting the illuminating light(s) and taking out the two screws holding the speedometer onto the rear of the panel. Most late-model American cars must have the instrument cluster taken out of the dash as described earlier, and the speedometer subsequently dismounted from the removed cluster.

With all the furor about the difficulty of repairing cars, many of the car makers are now designing speedometers and other instruments that come out the front of the dash, after a small piece of trim is removed. Look for these easy removal jobs before you start crawling under the instrument panel with a flashlight.

If the speedometer makes weird noises—particularly in winter—or if the needle jerks back and forth instead of producing a steady reading, the trouble is probably that the speedometer cable needs lubrication. A broken cable will prevent the speedometer (and odometer) from registering at all.

To remove the speedometer cable for lubrication or replacement, it is first disconnected from the back of the speedometer as outlined earlier. Once the retaining ring is unscrewed or unlatched from the speedometer it should be possible to pull the cable's flexible conduit from behind the instrument so that the cable itself may be withdrawn from it. If the cable is broken it may be necessary to remove the retaining ring that holds the conduit to the transmission housing and take the lower half of the cable out from that end. On some Oldsmobiles the speedometer is driven off the left front wheel. By removing the hub cap, the cable can be withdrawn from the center of the wheel spindle.

Use only an approved speedometer cable lubricant. Ordinary grease will become stiff in cold weather and liquify in summer. Apply the lubricant to only the first three-fourths of the cable as you reinsert it into the conduit. Enough grease will rub off in the first part of the conduit to lubricate the remainder of the cable. When the cable reaches the transmission, it is often necessary to rotate it several times before it engages the recess in the transmission's speedometer drive gear. Once the cable is in place the conduit should be reattached to the speedometer head and the car road tested to check its operation.

INDICATOR LIGHTS

When the ignition is switched to the "on" position, the oil, temperature, and generator lights should come on. If one fails to do so, the bulb and its connections should be checked to locate the trouble. If the generator light stays on after the engine is started, the charging system and the indicator light circuit should be checked.

A temperature indicator that continues to report a "cold" engine even after the car has been driven for several miles, or indicates a "hot" engine immediately after starting, probably has either a defective sending unit or a shorted wire between the sending unit and the indicator light.

Oil pressure indicators that come on and stay on while the engine is running should always be ample reason for turning off the engine and leaving it off until the trouble is pinpointed. Start by checking the oil level. If it's OK, the trouble may be only a dirty sending unit—or more serious, a defective lubrication system. Take the sending unit out and examine it. If the opening in the end is clogged with sludge, clean it and reinstall the unit on the engine. Start the engine briefly. If the light goes out, fine. If not, try a new sending unit. If it does not work, start checking the lubrication system.

Faulty sending units that fail to switch on the indicator light when the ignition is turned on can be spotted by taking the wire from their terminal and grounding it. If the lamp lights, try cleaning the sending unit. If it still does not function properly, replace it.

TACHOMETERS

Cable-driven tachometers are not used on American cars except Corvette and some Chevys that use Corvette distributors. In actual practice their cables are serviced and lubricated exactly as speedometer cables are, and again, as in the case of the speedometer, actual repair of the instrument itself should be trusted only to authorized service agencies. The "factory-option" tachometers commonly installed on U.S. cars are serviced only as complete units—which means if yours goes bad you'll have to buy a new one. However, those sold as add-on accessories—providing they are a well known and reputable brand—can usually be repaired by the maker. Their addresses can often be found by checking the ads in the better-known motoring magazines.

Probably the most common tachometer failures are those traceable to poor connections. In some cases the tachometer's only ground contact is provided by a wire serving the instrument's dial-illuminating light. If its socket does not fit

1. Assorted Connectors

tightly, there may not be adequate contact. Poor ground potential is always the first thing to check for when an electric tachometer fails to operate. The actual test is made by touching a grounded jumper wire to the tachometer housing while the engine is running. If the tachometer proves to be properly grounded, its connections with the ignition switch, coil or distributor (depending on the car) should then be inspected for poor contact and repaired if found to be the problem.

CUSTOM GAUGES

Most custom gauge installations consist of an oil pressure and ammeter duo to replace the idiot lights. The oil pressure gauge is easy to hook up, with its plastic tube and brass fittings. The usual place for attaching the tube is at the sending unit for the idiot light. A surprising number of the ammeters in dual installations are never hooked up, because the wiring is difficult to figure out. The ammeter should be spliced or connected into the wire that conducts charging current to the battery. If the ammeter is going to read correctly, the electrical load of the car (everything electrical except

1. Here are some typical connections and methods of installing terminals. Butt connector used in #1 permanently connects two wires. Shrink tube will cover joint and insulate it. More than one wire can be joined, such as in lighting circuits as shown in #2. Bullets are crimped and insulated before insertion into the connector. Another possible joint would be with common "eyelet" terminals as in #3.

2. These are some of the symbols used in wiring diagrams and what they stand for. Note the six cells in the battery, indicating it is a 12-volt. A 6-volt would have three cells.

the starter) must be connected to the same side of the ammeter that the generator connects. On a generator car, the connection can usually be made at the starter solenoid. Alternators may require some extra wires to make the ammeter work right. Before buying an accessory ammeter, take the instructions out of the box and make sure you can understand the hookup. If the instructions are poorly written (as many are), then you'd better find a good automotive electrician.

Some of the more elaborate hot rod and custom car dashboards will sport such extras as a voltmeter, differential temperature, transmission temperature, head temperature and inside-outside air temperature gauges, an accelerometer and perhaps an altimeter. These should be installed and serviced according to the instructions and recommendations given by the instrument manufacturers.

TURN SIGNALS

The heart of any turn-signal system is the flasher with its regular beat. But it's a strange heart, because it stops working whenever a bulb burns out. Replace the bulb and the flasher will work again. The system is designed that way on purpose, so the driver will know he has a bulb burned out. The flasher depends on a certain amount of current flow to heat up a wire and cause the flasher points to separate. When the points separate, the circuit is broken, so the wire cools off and lets the points go together again. If a bulb is burned out, there will not be enough current flow to heat up the wire, so all the other bulbs on that side of the car will burn steadily, with no flasher action at all.

This type of flasher is designed with a specific load. It is made in different current-carrying capacities, according to the number of bulbs that need to be flashed on one side of the car. In the

Tung-Sol brand, the first digit of the part number indicates the number of bulbs the flasher will operate on one side of the car (223 for two bulbs, or 322 for three bulbs). Signal-Stat doesn't have such an easy numbering system, but their specific-load flashers must still be selected for the number of bulbs on one side of the car.

Specific-load flashers can burn out easily, or their flashing rate will change if the wrong bulbs are installed in the turn signals. If you are having problems, check the flasher for the right part number, and look up the wattage of the bulbs you are using. Heavy-duty bulbs have a different current draw than standard bulbs, and that can goof up the flasher action, also. Heavy-duty, specific-load flashers are better made, but they still must be selected according to the number of bulbs.

Variable-load flashers, sometimes called heavy-duty, are wired differently so they will flash anywhere from one to six bulbs at the same flashing rate. Hazard warning flashers are the variable-load type and can be used on any car as long as the total number of bulbs on both sides of the car does not exceed the design capacity (usually six). Of course, you could put a hazard warning flasher in your turn signal circuit and it would work fine. But then you would never know when a bulb burned out, because the flasher would keep right on working away.

Because the hazard warning system is a second source of electricity feeding the same bulbs, some strange feedback situations can occur, but they are nothing to worry about. In some cars you can have a lot of fun with your technically minded friends by leaving the ignition switch off, turning on the radio and the hazard warning switch, then stepping on the brake pedal and listening to the radio play a song about Ralph Nader.

2. Wiring Diagram Symbols

Lights, Gauges, Wiring

Another peculiarity is that the hazard flashers won't work if you step on the brake. This also means that they won't work if the stoplight switch is maladjusted, so it is on all the time.

In the regular turn-signal system, the stoplights are tied in so that the stoplight on the side being flashed is disconnected by the turn-signal switch. The stoplight has to be turned off because the turn signal uses the same bulb. If it wasn't turned off, stepping on the brake would cancel the turn signal on the flashing side.

Older cars with a single turn-signal indicator light on the instrument panel use a 3-prong flasher. The third prong is connected to the indicator. Inside the flasher, a special relay feeds current to the indicator, flashing it just like the signal lights. The special relay has to be there to prevent a feedback that would flash all the lights instead of just those on one side, because the indicator light is grounded directly to the body of the car. The "P" terminal on 3-prong flashers goes to the indicator light.

Later cars with a single indicator light use a 2-prong flasher. They get away with it because the indicator light is grounded through the front turn-signal light on the opposite side from the one that is flashing. This produces the strange situation wherein you notice that the indicator light doesn't work when you signal to one side, and the signals don't flash at all when you signal to the other side, but the indicator light burns steadily. The problem is a burned out front bulb on the side that doesn't flash.

If your car has two indicator lights, both right and left systems are separate, which eliminates all the strange symptoms mentioned above.

Many cars have the flasher on the fuse block. If you can't find it, turn the signals on and then start hunting for the noise. If your hand touches the flasher, you can feel the vibration of the relay. Luckily, most late-model cars have plug-in flashers, so you can unplug and replace the flasher behind the instrument panel strictly by feel, without ever seeing where it plugs in. Be sure to take your wristwatch off when you grope behind the instrument panel. A metal watch can cause a bad short, and you could even get a burned wrist for your trouble.

REWIRING

When building a hot rod, or when doing extensive rewiring on any car, all electrical components should be in place before you start stringing wire. This will allow you to cut all wires accurately to length and bind them into neat bundles with electrical tape.

The ends of all wires should be fitted with appropriate terminals and connectors. Merely wrapping the bare wire around the terminal screw is neither a neat nor a professional way to build a car. Furthermore, such haphazard connections will almost always produce trouble later on. A wide variety of automotive terminals and connectors are readily available from parts stores.

With the proper tools, materials and information, anyone can do automotive wiring or rewiring, even if they've never attempted it before. More detailed information on accessory wiring and wiring a car completely from scratch can be

1. Custom Wiring Harness

2. New Type of Wiring Diagram

3. Fusible Link

1. If only Detroit could do their wiring harnesses this simply! Here's a perfect example of well-executed rewiring done at home by the owner of this street rod. Note the neat bundling of wires, color-coding and extensive use of solderless terminals.

2. New type of wiring diagram used in '72 Chevrolet factory manuals has no lines between connections. Each connection can be identified with a number and letter. Take the horn, for instance (arrow). It is in circuit 29, which is the horn circuit. The number on its right shows: 12, the gauge of the wire; DG, dark green; and 16B, the location of the other end of the wire. Simple! This new system is designed to make it easier to read wiring diagrams.

3. Fusible link repairs are easily made. Strip insulation back, splice wires with a splice clip and solder. Insulate with tape or shrink-tube.

found in Petersen's *Basic Ignition and Electrical Systems No. 4.*

WIRING DIAGRAMS

It is almost impossible to do an intelligent job of tracing electrical malfunctions without a wiring diagram for the particular make and model car you are working on. In the past, wiring diagrams were often difficult even for most mechanics to read, since they included many symbols which—although meaningful to engineers and trained electricians—were practically incomprehensible to the average person who read them. Nowadays, automotive wiring plans consist of more-or-less accurate pictures of the actual electrical components with lines drawn between them to indicate the interconnecting wires and circuits.

Chevrolet began a new system in their '72 shop manuals that does not have the lines drawn between units. Instead, each connection has a code number, with a corresponding number where it is connected to another unit. Doing the wiring diagram this way eliminates the laborious process of drawing the lines (and also eliminates the foulups when the lines are drawn incorrectly). Maybe other manufacturers will eventually adopt this system, and the traditional wiring diagram with the squiggly lines will disappear.

Each line or connection in most diagrams is labeled with a letter or number (or both) that indicates the color of the actual wire's insulation. If, for example, you wish to know which wire on the back of the ignition switch is connected to the ignition coil, you can quickly learn its color by checking on the diagram. If

it indicates a *yellow* wire between these two units, you should be able to find it easily at the coil and on the ignition switch itself. Wires that are thought to have shorts or grounds can thus be located, disconnected at each end, and tested with a battery-operated test light or voltmeter to determine if trouble really does exist.

Wiring diagrams also make it possible to determine what electrical components share common circuits. This makes it much easier to isolate trouble that is located in one component but is affecting other units as well. Wiring diagrams for your individual car can be obtained either from a factory shop manual or from one of the independently published books that deals with the repair of specific makes.

The best wiring diagrams we know of are put out by National Automotive Service, Dept. SP, P.O. Box 10465, San Diego, Calif. 92110. They take the factory diagrams and redo them, correcting mistakes and rearranging the elements so that all units are in the same relative place in each diagram. They don't sell single diagrams, but they put out a repair manual each year that has all the diagrams for that year's cars, plus a lot of other info. Both Chilton and Motor also publish repair manuals, available at your local bookstore, but their wiring diagrams are in a separate book.

With the diagram's help—plus a few tools and some of the practical knowhow gained from this book—you should be able to keep your car's lights lit, horns tooting, and instruments registering accurately. What more could one ask for when all's said and done?

Passenger Restraint Systems

From the first seat belts in the 1907 Thomas Flyer of racing fame to today's lap and shoulder belts, this simple yet highly effective safety device has come down a long trail littered with legislation on one side and public apathy on the other. Lap belts have been offered as options on cars since 1950, but the 1958 Corvette was the first to make them a standard feature. They became standard on all cars in 1964, after several states passed legislation requiring them on all new cars.

Despite the fantastic safety record of lives saved due to their use, seat belts have always been neglected by the public. Washington, ever prepared to save the public from itself, has issued a steady stream of legislation over the years to get more people to use their seat belts.

Effective Jan. 1, 1968, Federal law required belts for each occupant and also shoulder belts (an extra $22) for driver and outboard passenger. What a mess!

Five buckles and one belt tongue on each front bench seat; it took five minutes just to figure out who got which seat belt.

In time everyone learned to live with the restraints, but still very few used them. In October of '68, only 35% of those owning seat belts used them, and less than 5% used their shoulder belts.

Ford's 1970 models ended the confusion with a new 3-point system that eliminated the buckles for the shoulder straps. The strap tongue (the end opposite the buckle) hooked onto the outboard lap belt tongue before or after the lap belt was buckled. New seat belt retractors eliminated the need to adjust the belt for different wearers. The retractors locked the webbing at the desired length, in a manner similar to the mechanism in a window shade. Fewer buckles and new smaller buckles relieved the cluttered look of 1968 and '69.

In 1973 Federal law required Detroit to include a seat belt reminder in each new

car to encourage greater use of the unpopular restraints. A seat sensor in the front passenger's seat and a switch in each of the two lap belt retractors determined whether or not the belts were buckled. If left unbuckled, a flashing light ("fasten belts") and a buzzer went off and continued to operate until the belts were fastened. Most drivers soon learned to defeat the system by tying knots in the belts or by tucking the belt end under the carpet. Shoulder belts remained unused due to the absence of retractors, but '74 brought a change.

IGNITION INTERLOCK

In hopes of delaying the air bag, Detroit reached 'way up its sleeve and pulled out the interlock trick. They had no alternative—the law said that all 1974 U.S. cars must have it. Most of the '73 components were retained, but in addition to the buzzer, the engine wouldn't crank until all front-seat occupants had

1. Air Bags After Deployment

1. *There may be air bags in your future new car whether you want them or not. Impact, deployment and deflation all take place in an instant. This wrecked Mercury shows the bags for driver and passenger deflated.*

2. *If you've got troubles with the warning system on your '73 GM car, here's the diagram to follow. The A, B, C and D styles refer to all body types except Camaro and Firebird (F), Nova, Ventura and Omega (X) and Toronado, Riviera and Eldorado (E). The H body type is represented by the Vega.*

3. *This is the schematic for Mopar's interlock. The neutral start switch (also called neutral safety switch) indicates that this is the automatic trans model. The standard trans cars' interlock is hooked into the parking brake.*

buckled their respective shoulder/lap belt combinations.

Interlock could be a real nuisance, but Detroit compensated by giving us some great new shoulder belts. The old design ('68 through '73) was much too confining, and without retractors the belts had to be folded to be put away. They required readjustment for each new wearer, and once in place, allowed very little movement of the upper torso. Stretching for the glovebox meant unfastening the shoulder belt.

These drawbacks were annoying, but evidently not as annoying to most drivers as the ignition interlock proved to be. The '74 and later shoulder belts featured retractors, and both lap and shoulder belts were connected to each other, so that buckling was a one-handed opera-

tion. The inertia-reel retractors were good news, though, and have remained on all cars right up to the present.

The belt reels permitted the user to move about, but under rapid deceleration they locked up and restrained. All makes but Chrysler used the "vehicle-sensitive" type of reel. A pendulum or similar device within the mechanism sensed any panic stops and locked the harness snugly around the user. Chrysler used the "belt-sensitive" type, which locked whenever there was a sudden pull on the belt. A quick movement by the wearer could lock it up, which could prove quite a drag for girl-watchers. By their comfort and convenience alone, the new restraints could increase seat belt use, but the interlock was there just to guarantee it.

'75 DISCONNECTS

The ignition interlock system proved to be complex and troublesome in use. So complex, in fact, that some manufacturers had to produce complicated pieces of test equipment just to trace the troubles in the system. And so troublesome that even when the system was working perfectly, it was more unpopular among drivers than any other federally mandated device yet installed on a car. In fact, it probably generated more dislike than any other device ever installed on a car for whatever reason.

In the face of this public outcry, something had to go, and the mandate for the interlock was what went. As a placebo for the safety bloc, which was beginning to see the glimmerings of a lowered auto accident death and injury rate because of the increasing use of the belts required by the interlock, the law was amended to require a warning signal and a light. The law stipulated that the signal device could cut off after a few seconds, though, leaving only the light to annoy those who refused to buckle up.

As a result of the changes in the law, troubles with the interlock systems can now be repaired much more easily. No longer do the expensive electronic devices have to be used. If the ignition interlock on a 1974 or early '75 car or the warning system on an earlier model gives you trouble, just disconnect it. There are two catches, though. Catch number one comes from us, and really should come from you: Promise yourself that you'll still use the belts. That's the cheapest insurance you can buy, and the rest of your family will thank you for the thought.

Catch 22 comes from the government: The law is worded in such a way that if you want to completely disconnect the system, that's fine...provided you do it yourself. A dealer or an independent mechanic can do the job, but not the cheap and complete way. They are required to do it the partial, expensive way, leaving the buzzer and warning light hooked up. The system is complex enough for this operation to cost you at least $25.

Here's how to do it the cheap way. The whole system is built around seat sensors that inform the logic module that someone is sitting in the seat. It stands to reason, then, that if the sensors are disconnected, the logic module will never know when a seat is occupied, and

2. GM Warning System

NOTE:
SCHEMATIC IS SHOWN WITH IGNITION
SWITCH OFF AS IN POSITION 1. RUN IS
POSITION 2. START IS POSITION 3.

3. Mopar Interlock Schematic

Restraint Systems

the car can be started and driven just as in pre-interlock or warning days.

First, look under the seats. In some cars this may require standing on your head or using a mirror. A wire with a connector on it can be seen leading into the upholstery under every seating position. This is the wire to the sensor. Disconnecting it usually requires a screwdriver in order to pry apart the lock on the connector. Then pull the connector apart. If your car has power seats, be sure that the connector you disconnect is the one for the sensor, not for the seat actuator. If, after you pull the plug, you get into the driver's seat and find that not only will the car still not start but the seat will not move, you undid the wrong plug. Reconnect that one, uncouple the other one and you'll be right where you want to be. The car should then start on demand with no complaints from under the dashboard.

BEYOND SEAT BELTS?

As long as the bulk of the driving public refuses to wear their safety belts, the government will continue to require Detroit automakers to install devices for our protection in spite of ourselves. When even the bureaucrats decided that the interlock was in the end a bad choice, they had to think of something else, badgered as they were by insurance companies and safety critics like Ralph Nader. They began to feel that the final answer was "passive restraint," which protected the driver and passengers even when they didn't want it. The critics and insurance companies clamored for something new, the *air bag.*

A truly passive restraint, the air bag sits under the dash. In case of an impact, an explosive charge inflates the air bag instantly, cushioning and almost surrounding the motorist. While the principle of the air bag is sound and many have been built for insurance company fleets, there are some drawbacks.

The explosive device that fills up the bag so quickly—within a fraction of a second if it is to be effective—can be damaging to your hearing. In a Department of Transportation test of an experimental safety vehicle equipped with air bags which was hit by another vehicle at 60 mph, the four electronically-monitored dummies were said to have survived the crash, but the air bags blew out all the car's windows. Photos showed flying glass as high as 12 ft. above the car.

In addition, even though the bags do a good job of protection in frontal crashes, they are much less effective in side impacts or rollovers. Since DOT Safety Standard No. 208 says that protection must be afforded for rollover incidents, all of the air bag systems so far proposed must include a lap belt, which would seem to make them less than completely passive after all.

1. General Motors' interlock. For '74, GM used two types of logic modules: an electromechanical (relay) type or an electronic type. The belt switches on the relay type are normally closed, but they are normally opened on electronic models. If you have to replace a faulty module, be sure to use the same type; otherwise the system will work backwards. If you use the wrong one, car will start only if buckles are fastened before you sit on seat and then unbuckled before turning key to start.

2. Ford owners, especially Mustang and Pinto, beware! Reports show that your cars have been having interlock troubles, so this schematic is for you.

3. American Motors' seat belt warning system (1973). On automatic transmission cars, the system is wired into the neutral safety switch located on the transmission. Cars with standard transmissions are activated by the parking brake pedal. With that one exception, the schematic is the same for all AMC models.

1. Basic GM Interlock System

2. Ford Interlock Schematic

3. AMC Seat Belt Warning System

Most studies have shown that wearing a lap and shoulder belt set is the best protection yet devised for all conditions. A 1974 DOT study, however, showed that belt usage was only at a 50% level at best, so the air bag subject has refused to die.

The automakers claim that a mandatory air bag would cost the car buyer an extra $225 to $300 (as opposed to the $90 or so extra that the lap and shoulder belts cost at first), yet proponents of the device claim it would be comparable to belt costs if the bags were installed on all cars.

At the time this was being written, the DOT had cancelled an agreement with the automakers to install some 440,000 air bags on 1977 cars, and Secretary of Transportation Brock Adams was preparing to hold public hearings to decide what should be done about making people wear their seat belts. It may be some time before we see viable alternatives to present non-interlocked belts, although Volkswagen has been experimenting with a passive set of belts that automatically enclose you when you get in the car. Puerto Rico and Australia have taken the problem out of the car makers' hands and put the responsibility squarely on the motorists' shoulders by enacting laws that *require* the wearing of seat belts.

Some U.S. insurance companies have talked of voiding people's insurance if the insured is not wearing his seat belts at the time of an accident. There was even a major court case in which the settlement was reduced substantially because the judge ruled that not wearing seat belts constituted "contributory negligence." If the plaintiff had been wearing his belts, he would have sustained much less injury. Therefore his compensation was reduced, even though the accident was not his fault. The only certainty about the air bag controversy is that it won't be settled immediately, since the automakers will probably go to court if the lawmakers reinstate requirements for passive systems.

TROUBLESHOOTING A RESTRAINT SYSTEM

If your warning system fails to operate,

check the fuse box for a bad fuse. If you find a bad one, replace it. If it blows again, check for a short (a grounded wire) or a loose connection under the dash. Either the buzzer or the warning light can go bad, but usually both don't fail at the same time. If the system still fails to work after you've checked the fuses and eliminated shorts or bad connections, check for loose connectors (especially at the relay) or an open circuit (use a continuity tester) in either the body wiring harness or the instrument panel harness. If an open circuit (pierced or broken wire) is found, repair or replace the harness.

Check the relay for proper ground, using a test lead to ground out the relay. The relay provides the ground for the buzzer and light. Normally its contact points are closed, permitting current to flow through to complete the circuit. If the buzzer works with the test lead, you know that the relay is bad or improperly grounded.

If the car will start in forward or reverse, then the neutral safety switch on the transmission is faulty, and this affects the warning system. On stick-shift cars, check for a bad parking brake warning switch. If the parking brake warning light doesn't work or stays on when the brake is released, then that switch is bad or a wire is shorting out on the frame. Failure of the parking brake light stops current to the seat belt buzzer and light.

If all of the above prove to be good, then the problem probably lies in the retractor switch—either improper grounding of the switch or a bad switch. Check the ground. If it's okay, check continuity at the switch terminals. If the circuit is open with the belt fully retracted, replace the retractor and switch assembly. (Remember, this includes both belt halves.)

If the light and buzzer don't come on when the passenger is seated, check the passenger's retractor switch. Switch contacts should be closed when the belt is fully retracted. If not, replace the retractor assembly. Place weight on the seat cushion and check the seat sensor terminals to ensure that the contacts are closed. If they are open, replace the sensor as described below.

BUZZER WON'T SHUT OFF

Now, here's a problem. What if your buzzer won't shut off? Check first for any shorts at the seat belt retractors. Check the retractor switch terminals with a continuity tester. If the contacts are open with the belt fully extended, the switch is all right; if they are closed, replace the retractor and switch assembly.

The problem can also be a short in the seat sensor. Disconnect the seat switch connector and check to see if the switch terminals are shorting to ground when weight on the cushion puts pressure on the switch. If a short is discovered, replace the switch. Unfortunately, this requires that the seat be detached from its adjusters or from the floor and tilted backward. Find the switch and remove it. Install a new one, making sure to put it in exactly the same place.

GM bench seats and swivel buckets require loosening the right side trim cover from the seat cushion just enough to provide access to the switch. The switch is cemented to foam padding, so you must break that bond. The new switch has adhesive on the bottom. American Motors seats must also be detached, and AMC bucket seats are like GM bench seats in that the sensor is cemented to the foam. This necessitates partial removal of upholstery.

A super-sensitive seat sensor (say it ten times quickly) can make the buzzer sound with an empty seat. In most cars, this would mean replacing the switch, but the American Motors design permits sensor adjustment without removing the switch. Switch sensitivity can be set by bending the switch's contact strips. With each adjustment, kneel on the seat until the cushion bottoms out. When the weight of a 50-lb. object sounds the buzzer, then the adjustment is correct.

Even though we have told you how to disconnect your early interlock system, please remember our "catch number one": Always wear your seat and shoulder belts even when the electronics aren't there to remind you. If not for your own sake, do it for your family. Someday we may all have to pay extra for a passive restraint device we don't want, simply because some of us now forget to buckle up for safety.

Fuel System

It's unfortunate that the carburetor is up on top of the engine, because in that position it's too easy for everybody to fiddle with. Most so-called carburetion problems are caused by ignition timing, spark plugs, loss of compression, inadequate fuel delivery to the carburetor, or maybe even a clogged air cleaner element. The carburetor itself rarely gives much trouble in normal operation.

Spark plugs, coil, distributor, engine compression, engine vacuum, and fuel delivery should all be checked before you tear into that carburetor. Not that carburetors can't cause trouble. It's just that carburetor trouble usually comes on slowly from an accumulation of dirt. Breakdowns and other malfunctions that occur suddenly like a thunderstorm in the middle of a big blue sky are not usually caused by the carburetor itself.

Carburetors have so few moving parts that there really isn't much in them that can wear out. The throttle shaft or the accelerating pump are probably the biggest offenders in the wear department. The throttle shaft wears from the pressure of the throttle return spring and lets air into the engine where it shouldn't be, or at least not very much of it. The accelerating pump plunger wears out and

doesn't squirt as much as it should, causing a flat spot when the driver steps on the gas.

The rest of the carburetor doesn't have any significant wear points, but it has about a jillion points where it can get dirty. If you have trouble with your carburetor, the chances are about a hundred to one that it's caused by foreign matter reaching the carburetor through the air or through the fuel, or by gummy fuel deposits.

Did you ever drive a car that stalled at every signal? Maybe you've known of a car that lost power when it got up to cruising speed, or maybe you know somebody whose car billows black smoke out of the tailpipe as he drives down the street. Those things can be caused by dirt trapped in the carburetor.

The dirt or foreign matter may be rust particles that slough off the sides of the gas tank, or dust in the air that is inside the tank. When the dirt is carried up to the carburetor by the fuel, it means trouble. Airborne dirt gets lodged in the air bleeds and passages, upsetting the balance between air and fuel that the carburetor is made to control.

And even if you had a perfectly clean atmosphere for your engine to operate

in, with hygienically clean gasoline and a scrubbed fuel system, you would still have a dirty carburetor in time because of the way gasoline evaporates. Not all the substances that make up gasoline will readily pass into the air and turn into smog. The heavier fractions of gasoline turn to a kind of gooey mess which eventually hardens about the same as a good brand of household glue.

So dirt is the primary enemy of the carburetor. A good tune-up man's carburetor work consists mostly of disassembly, cleaning, and reassembly, without making any adjustments at all. This is true even when he replaces parts, such as accelerating pumps and needle seats. The old and the new parts go back into the same positions, so that all he has to do is make careful checks of specifications.

However, there is one other cause of trouble in carburetors that has plagued good tune-up men since the first carburetor popped and sputtered into life. That cause is the inept workman. Call him backyard mechanic, peppertree mechanic, garage mechanic, tune-up expert, or just plain car owner. It doesn't matter what his title is or where he works. If the man working on the carburetor has

DISTRIBUTOR
- Electronic Ignition
- Reduced Tolerances
- Permanently Lubricated

CARBURETOR
- Improved Distribution
- Leaner Mixture
- Faster Acting Choke, Electric Assist
- External Idle Mixture Limiter
- Solenoid Throttle Stop
- Gasoline Vapor Control
- Idle Enrichment
- Altitude Compensation (California 4 bbl)

INTAKE MANIFOLD
- Improved Hot Spot

OVERFILL LIMITING VALVE

COOLANT CONTROL IDLE ENRICHMENT VALVE

CHARCOAL CANISTER

ORIFICE SPARK ADVANCE CONTROL VALVE (OSAC)

PRESSURE-VACUUM RELIEF FILLER CAP

LEADED-FUEL RESTICTOR

DOMED FUEL TANK

CCEGR TEMPERATURE VALVE

INCREASED CAM OVERLAP

AIR PUMP

MODIFIED COMBUSTION CHAMBER AND REDUCED COMPRESSION RATIO

HEATED INTAKE AIR

EXHAUST PORT AIR INJECTION

CLOSED CRANKCASE VENTILATION

OXIDATION CATALYTIC CONVERTER

VAPOR-LIQUID SEPARATOR

EXHAUST GAS RECIRCULATION
- EGR Control Valve
- EGR Vacuum Amplifier
- EGR Time Delay

1. Chrysler Emission Controls

not taken the time to learn a little bit about how it operates, then he is going to cause trouble not only for himself, but for every mechanic thereafter who tries to undo his fumbling fingers.

Trying to correct malfunctions can take an awful lot of time if you don't know what you're doing. You could spend days taking a carburetor apart, putting it back together, running the car and then going back through the same procedure all over again, simply because when you get the carburetor apart you don't know what to look for.

Other malfunctions cannot be seen, but once you know how a carburetor works all you have to do is stop, look, and listen, because the carburetor is trying to tell you something if you have the knowledge to understand it.

Now let's take a look at what makes the carburetor the smoothly operating mechanism that it is, with quick descriptions of the six basic systems.

1. Emissions controls for '75 include catalytic converter, temperature and throttle position controls. All parts of the system are interrelated. This is the Chrysler system.

2. This little beauty is mounted on intake manifold of '72-'73 Buicks. It lets exhaust gas recirculate into manifold at throttle openings above idle.

3. Six-cylinder GM engines have two electric gadgets for '72-'73. Upper one is familiar CEC valve. Its stem (1) is for CEC valve setting. Solenoid body (2) is turned to set curb idle.

4. There's no normal throttle-cracking screw on '72-'73 GM 6-cylinders. "Solenoid off" idle speed is set with an Allen wrench in end of solenoid.

5. Pushing on the needle for any reason is verboten. The rubber tip of the needle can easily be compressed out of shape.

6. Fuel flows into the bowl past the needle whenever the float drops enough to let the needle come off the seat.

2. Buick Exhaust Gas Recirculator

3. Rochester 6-Cyl. Carburetor

4. Low Speed Idle Adjustment

TIP COMPRESSED

5. Don't Do This

6. Float System With Needle Open

Fuel System

FLOAT SYSTEM

Fuel enters the carburetor through the inlet seat and fills the float bowl. The fuel rises in the bowl, lifting the float, which pushes the needle into the seat and regulates the flow of gasoline.

The object is to keep the fuel in the bowl at just the right level. Too much, and the engine will run rich. Too little fuel in the bowl and the engine will run lean, maybe even coughing back through the carburetor. Sometimes the coughing back results in a flame that's about 3 ft. long shooting from the air horn. You only have to see that once to have a lot of respect for a carburetor that's being run without an air cleaner. At the very least you will make sure it's not pointed in your direction.

To adjust the fuel lever, you bend an arm on the float or bend a little tab that is attached to the arm and pushes on the needle. The "float level" specification is a measurement from some part of the carburetor casting to the float, when the float is resting on a closed needle. If the float is attached to the bowl cover then the measurement is taken between the float and cover, with the cover inverted so that the weight of the float closes the needle.

If the float is attached to the bowl itself then the measurement is taken from the top of the float to the top edge of the bowl, with the float and needle in the closed position, of course. To get the needle and float into the closed position on this type of float system, you might

1. Float system with a horizontal needle. A vertical needle works better. The tube at upper left is an internal bowl vent which raises pressure above the fuel when the engine is running at speed.

2. Float level is the only internal adjustment on a Holley. The measurement is made at the location shown, but it differs with other models of carburetors, so you should check your shop manual for correct specifications.

3. Float adjustment on a Holley 4-bbl. is made with a screwdriver. The entire seat assembly is threaded, and can be screwed up or down to change position of the float.

4. On some carbs you can actually check the wet fuel level, as on this Holley 1-bbl. Economizer diaphragm is removed to provide a hole for scale.

5. Main metering system has several functions. Note that end of main nozzle is in middle of narrowest part of venturi, where the suction is greatest. This is single-venturi carb.

6. Main nozzle is sometimes called main discharge tube. Holes in tube bleed air into fuel to help atomize it.

7. Suction in the venturi pulls fuel out of the nozzle. Actually, it's the pressure on the fuel in the bowl that pushes the fuel out of the nozzle.

1. Float System With Needle Closed

2. Checking Float Level

3. Adjusting Holley Float Level

push the float and needle closed with your finger—but don't

That was OK in the old days when we had steel needles, but now there are teflon-tipped needles, neoprene-tipped needles, and teflon or neoprene inlet seats. These needles and seats will last a long time with only the pressure of the float against them, but the pressure of your finger pushing on the needle may be too much, and you will end up with a groove in the neoprene. The neoprene will slowly come back to shape, eliminating the groove so that a few hours later the float level has changed from where you set it. If the neoprene or teflon does not come back to shape, the groove may cause flooding because it provides a place for particles of dirt to lodge.

To get the float and needle into the closed position on a carburetor with the float attached to the bowl, invert the carburetor and take the measurement. With the carburetor on the car, the easiest way to do it is to pour some gasoline into the bowl until the float rises to its maximum height, then take the measurement. There is usually a tolerance on float adjustments and a good mechanic will adjust to one end or the other of the tolerance because he knows a particular carburetor will run best with that setting.

It's important that you don't confuse fuel level and float level. Float level is a measurement from the float to some part of the carburetor bowl or the cover. Fuel level is an actual wet measurement of how far the fuel is from the top of the bowl. If the float needle and seat are attached to the bowl, then the actual fuel level can be measured with a scale. If the float needle and seat are attached to the bowl cover, then the fuel level cannot be measured in most cases unless the carburetor manufacturer has provided sight holes in the end of the bowl. The fuel level specification, if given, is really nothing more than a double check to be sure you have set the float level correctly and accurately.

When the engine uses fuel and the float drops, it is possible on some carburetors that the needle could fall out of the seat. If this happened the carburetor would receive just a little more gas than it needs. The engine would be flooded, not only on the inside but probably on the outside.

To keep all of that from happening there is a little tab on the back side of the float that limits the drop. The float drop measurement is taken with the bowl cover off the carburetor. Hold the cover in the normal position and measure from the underside of the bowl cover to the float.

If the float is attached to the bowl itself, there usually is no float drop measurement. The float in that case may be designed so that at maximum drop it rests on the bottom of the bowl.

If by some chance the little tab that limits float drop has become bent, then the float may not drop enough. In this case the needle will not pull away from the seat far enough, and you might have fuel starvation at wide open throttle.

Dirt, as mentioned, is a big enemy of the float system. If it weren't for dirt there probably wouldn't be any need for all the fancy filters that we have on cars nowadays. The needle and seat are so sensitive to dirt that the smallest particle can cause flooding. This is the reason for using teflon or neoprene seats and needles. The theory is that teflon or neoprene has enough give to it that it will conform to the shape of the speck of dirt and seat around it. Sometimes it does, sometimes it doesn't.

If a particle of foreign matter should cause the needle valve to leak, then enough fuel can be pumped into the engine to kill it, and make restarting almost impossible until the excess fuel evaporates. If you ever see a carburetor that is all beat up around the needle and seat area, it's a good bet that the driver was standing there beating on the carburetor trying to jar a piece of dirt out of the seat so the flooding would stop.

You can see that keeping the fuel at the right level is very important. We'll find out why when we go into the main metering system.

MAIN METERING SYSTEM

Now that we have the float bowl full of gasoline, the next step is to get this gas mixed with air and feed it into the engine. The base of every carburetor is really nothing more than an air valve with throttle plates hung on a shaft controlled by your foot. Wide open throttle means just that. When you step on the gas you are opening the throttle valve so that the

4. **Checking Wet Fuel Level**

5. **Venturi Operation**

6. **Main Nozzle**

7. **Main Metering System**

Fuel System

maximum amount of air can enter the engine. But in order for the engine to run, this air has to have gasoline mixed with it in the right proportion. This is done by running a tube from the float bowl ending in the middle of the air stream where it goes through the carburetor. The end of the tube, called the main nozzle, is positioned so that it is in the center of the venturi, a narrow section of the air passage through the carburetor. Because this section is narrow, it causes reduced pressure at the end of the tube, and this reduced pressure or suction draws fuel from the float bowl where it mixes with the air, then goes past the throttle valve and on to the combustion chamber. The tube begins in a well at the bottom of the float bowl called the main well. Fuel enters the main well through a calibrated hole called the main jet, which is located at the bottom of the float bowl so that during all types of engine operation it will always be submerged and able to draw fuel.

The main metering system has had many refinements since the first simple carburetor was made. There may be air bleeds or little baffles in the main nozzle and there may be vacuum or mechanically operated metering rods in the main jet. The object of all the refinements is to be sure that the engine receives more fuel when it needs it and less fuel when it doesn't.

Metering rods are designed so that they stay in the main jet when the engine is running at low power. But when the engine is running at maximum power, the rods will lift out of the jet so that the engine gets the fuel that it needs. At any point between closed throttle and maximum power, the rods will be partially in or partially out of the jet, according to how much fuel the engine needs at the time.

Mechanically operated rods are lifted by a lever hooked to the throttle. Vacuum-operated rods are pushed out of the jet by a spring and pulled down into the jet by engine vacuum acting on a piston hooked to the top of the rod. A passageway from the intake manifold

runs up through the carburetor so the engine vacuum can act on the piston.

Without engine vacuum the carburetor wouldn't work. This vacuum exists below the throttle valves when the engine is running, and at idle on a good engine is about 18-21 ins. As the throttle is opened, engine vacuum drops off until there is zero vacuum at wide open.

It's rare to have a main metering system plug up completely unless it was done deliberately for a test of mechanics, such as the Plymouth Trouble-Shooting Contest. If the main nozzle was plugged, but the main jet still open, the carburetor would idle perfectly, but gasp and die completely the second the throttle was opened. However, if the driver got his foot out of it quick enough, the idle system would take over again and the car would come down to idle perfectly.

We have to have an idle system, because at idle the throttle valves are almost completely closed and there is not enough flow of air through the venturi to draw fuel out of the main nozzle. Now let's see how the idle system does its job.

THE IDLE SYSTEM

At idle the engine is drawing air around the throttle plate, which is just barely open, but this air has no fuel in it. The fuel is coming through the idle port hole in the throttle body below the throttle plate. An idle mixture needle screws into the outside of the throttle body and is used to regulate the amount of fuel flowing through the port and into the engine.

Fuel enters the idle system through a tube which is mounted in the carburetor,

1. Idle Air Bypass

2. Metering Rod System

3. Adjustable Idle Air Bypass

usually between the float bowl and the carburetor throat. The end of the tube is a calibrated hole, called the idle jet. Fuel comes up through this tube, makes a U-turn, picks up some air through air bleed holes, then goes through a long passage to exit underneath the throttle plate. Some idle tubes can be changed merely by unscrewing them, but others are part of the metering cluster and the whole cluster must be changed in that case.

As the throttle is opened, the high vacuum beneath the throttle plates starts to fall off and fuel flow lessens through the idle port. To keep the engine from faltering at this crucial moment, another hole called the idle transfer is uncovered which feeds more fuel to keep the engine going. By this time enough air is coming through the venturi that the main metering system will start to take over. However, in most carburetors the idle system will continue to feed even up to as high as 70 mph.

It's important to keep clear in your mind that the engine idles on air from two sources and fuel from one. Air goes into the engine around the partially opened throttle plate, and a fuel and air mixture enters through the idle port, controlled by an idle mixture screw. The screw is spring-loaded, and you control the idle mixture by setting the screw.

Engine idle speed is something else. You control that with a spring-loaded screw on the throttle shaft. When the

4. Idle System

1. In 1968, Oldsmobile used a Quadrajet that cracked the throttle plate for idle air. In 1969, they allowed the throttle plate to close completely, and idle air came through an adjustable bypass.

2. Metering rod is hooked to a piston and spring, with engine vacuum acting on the piston. Any fuel that flows out the main nozzle has to go through the main jet first.

3. If idle air is supplied through a bypass, the throttle plates can be allowed to close almost completely at idle. This helps to prevent carbon formation in the throttle bores, which causes erratic idling.

4. Note how the idle tube picks up fuel from within the main well. Some late-model carburetors designed for emission control have the idle tube outside the main well.

5. In this type of spring-operated accelerating pump, it doesn't matter how fast you step on the gas—the spring itself is what pushes the pump plunger down.

6. The "duration spring" is actually an override spring that prevents everything from bending if the driver shoves his foot down too fast. The discharge check ball usually has a spring or a weight to help prevent fuel from being drawn into the venturi at high speed.

7. Little lever opens the bowl vent whenever the throttle linkage is at the idle position. Bowl vent is really not part of idle system, but it prevents rich running at idle (and hard starting) by venting fumes.

5. Accelerating Pump Duration Spring

6. Accelerating Pump System

7. Bowl Vent Lever

Fuel System

driver takes his foot off the gas, the throttle will close down to the setting you have made with the idle speed screw. If you have made the wrong setting and the throttle closes too much, the engine will die. If the screw holds the throttle open too far, then the driver is going to have to put both feet on the brake to keep the car from driving down the street at a 40-mph idle speed.

So far, we have a carburetor that will cruise and idle, but what happens when we really step on the gas? It will fall flat on its face. To cure the problem we need an accelerating pump.

ACCELERATING PUMP SYSTEM

If we open the throttle suddenly on an engine, the air reacts instantly and rushes past the throttle blades, but the

1. Accelerating pump on the AFB is adjusted for more or less stroke by bending the pump link.

2. Only one screw holds the Holley accelerating pump cam, but it can be put in two different positions to control the length of the stroke. Cam is hidden behind throttle lever.

3. Holley accelerating pump outlet check is under the pump nozzle. Many carbs have a removable nozzle with a needle or ball check under it.

4. When manifold vacuum is high and during closed or partly closed throttle, the power valve piston is held up off the valve.

5. As the throttle is opened, vacuum drops and the spring opens the power valve to allow extra fuel into the main well.

6. Here the power valve and power piston are separate. In the power valve the top hole that the plunger sticks through is merely the entrance for the fuel. The calibrated holes are the ones on the side just above the threads.

fuel coming out of the main nozzle takes a little while before it catches up. During this period the engine will run lean and stumble. The problem is solved by using an accelerating pump. It's nothing more than a piston hooked to the throttle linkage and operating in a cylinder so that every time we step on the gas a squirt of fuel goes into each throat on the carburetor. The pump only squirts when the throttle is moved. At all other times it does not feed any gas but just sits there

waiting until the time when you put your foot down.

The pump system includes an inlet check valve and an outlet check valve so that it can suck fuel into its cylinder from the bowl on the upstroke and then squirt this fuel into the carburetor throat on the downstroke.

Some pumps are not directly operated by the throttle linkage but *allowed* to operate by the linkage. They have a duration spring that actually pushes the

1. Pump Arm Adjustment

2. Holley Pump Cam Adjustment

3. Holley Pump Check Valve

4. Power Valve Closed

5. Power Valve Open

pump down. This is done so that the length of time that the pump is operating is always the same, no matter how fast the driver opens the throttle.

The well known "flat spot" on acceleration is usually caused by something wrong in the accelerating pump. Most of the time it is a pump piston that doesn't fit well in its cylinder, either because the piston is worn out or because it is made of leather and the lip of the leather curled up when the piston was installed. Or it could be maladjusted linkage, so that the pump stroke is too long or too short.

The jet that controls the amount of squirt on an accelerating pump is usually built into the pump nozzle, mounted above the venturi. In an extreme case, that defies the best efforts to correct the trouble, it is possible to drill out the pump jet for a little more squirt, so you won't have that sickening feeling of nothing happening when you mash your foot down to the floor.

With the system so far described, our carburetor will work fine, until we get up to wide open throttle. Then the engine needs more fuel than is admitted by the main jet. To let this fuel in we must have what is called the power system.

POWER SYSTEM

Main metering jets with or without metering rods work fine above idle at almost any cruising speed but when the engine is really called to put out, with the throttle wide open, the main jet just doesn't let enough fuel in. In order to admit more fuel, there is another passage into the main well and up into the main nozzle. This passage is closed at all times except when the throttle is opened enough to allow engine vacuum to fall below about 10 ins. At that point a spring opens the power valve and additional fuel is allowed to enter the main well, go through the main nozzle and into the venturi.

Power valves can be vacuum or mechanically controlled. Some Stromberg carburetors have the power valve at the bottom of the accelerating pump cylinder so that when the throttle is open wide and the accelerating pump bottoms, it tips a little plunger opening the power

6. Power System

valve. Other power valves operate off engine vacuum opposed by a spring, and they can be either a piston operating in a cylinder or a diaphragm.

The unfortunate thing about a power valve is that you may not know if it is bad until it is too late. If a power valve should fail in the closed position, the engine would not get the fuel it needs at wide-open throttle, and it might even run lean enough to burn a hole in a piston, depending on how long you ran the engine wide open.

Luckily, vacuum-operated power valves are held closed by engine vacuum, and opened by a spring. So if they fail, they usually fail open, allowing a lot of fuel to go into the engine at all speeds above idle, and in some designs even allowing fuel to dribble out onto the top of the engine, which is good if the driver pays attention to the smell of gasoline. Of course it's not so good if somebody starts lighting matches in your engine compartment.

HIGH SPEED PULLOVER

Main jets must be lean on late models to cut down on emissions. Unfortunately, the main system is so lean that there isn't enough fuel supplied under a high-rpm, part-throttle condition. At part throttle, the metering rod hasn't lifted to the high speed step because engine vacuum hasn't dropped low enough. But the engine needs more fuel because of the high rpm. Rochester carburetors provide this extra fuel with a pullover system, which consists of a passageway from the float bowl up to the air horn, exiting above the choke valve. There is usually one hole for each carburetor throat. Because of their position, these holes are sensitive to air velocity. Any time there is high air velocity through the carburetor, as at high rpm, the pullover holes feed additional fuel into the airstream. Pullover starts at about 50 mph on part throttle. Pullover is also called High Speed Fuel Feed, or Auxiliary Fuel Feed.

Fuel System

Now with all of the systems we have described so far we have a carburetor that will really run. There is only one thing wrong, it won't start. For this we have to have a choke system.

CHOKE SYSTEM

If an engine could be heated up to operating temperature before you started it, you would never need a choke. This is one reason why people who live in California with its warm climate can in many cases take the choke off their carburetors and never have any trouble. But if they had to live in the Midwest or in the East through one winter, they would find out just what a choke is for.

A cold engine is just that. It is so cold that the fuel condenses out of the mixture onto the intake manifold passageways and the walls of the combustion chamber.

Fuel alone will not burn. It has to be mixed with air. The only way we can get a mixture on a cold engine is to feed more fuel into the engine than we need to make up for the fuel that condenses. The choke is an air valve placed above the main nozzle, so that it can shut off all the air going to the engine. This allows the full force of engine suction to operate on the main nozzle so the engine gets the fuel it needs.

The problem with chokes is not in making them work but in getting them to shut off (open) at the right time. The choke is closed by a thermostatic spring and opened by this same spring when heat from the exhaust manifold allows it to relax. However, the spring control alone is not enough. To get a more positive control there is a vacuum piston that opposes the strength of the spring, and the choke valve itself is offset so that the air entering the carburetor tends to push it open. When it all works right we have what is called an automatic choke, instead of the old fashioned manual choke that the driver had to remember to open himself. When it doesn't work we have a big problem, and the engine will lope and blow black smoke out the tailpipe.

Sticking chokes have been so much of a problem that now some carburetor manufacturers are coating their choke shafts with teflon. It seems to work, although the adjustment of a choke will probably continue to be a touchy problem for some time.

UNLOADER

Nobody should ever go to wide open throttle on an engine while it is cold, but some drivers will. Other drivers will very absentmindedly pump the throttle when trying to start the engine, thus flooding it. Both of these conditions are taken care of by the choke unloader. It's a little tang that opens the choke enough to clean out the engine when the throttle is pushed to wide open position.

1. High-speed pullover holes in '72 Rochester 2-bbl. are shown with carb top inverted, but they can easily be seen on car by removing air cleaner.

2. Rochester 2-bbl. carbs used on Vega in '71 and later had a different power valve: gravity operated; no springs, just a weighted needle. Early models had metering passage built into carb.

3. Late Vega 2-bbls. use power valve with metering at inlet orifice. Shake valve and you can hear weight rattle.

4. The choke system is a balancing of forces. The offset choke valve, the vacuum piston, and the heat from the stove all tend to open the choke, while the thermostatic coil spring is attempting to close it.

5. Well-type chokes do have an adjustment, but it is usually only a setting made at the factory.

6. Exposed spring on Rochester carbs is choke closing assist spring. It ensures full closing of the choke.

7. Choke springs are getting extremely sophisticated. Hidden under this cap (arrow) is a bucking spring (2-bbl. GM models) that works against choke coil spring for precise choke opening.

1. High-Speed Pullover Holes

2. Gravity Power Valve.

3. Power Valve Metering Hole

4. Choke System

5. Well-Type Choke

FAST IDLE

While the choke is operating, the engine can't use the extremely rich mixture unless it is run at a faster than normal idle. To accomplish this we have a fast idle cam and linkage that works in conjunction with the choke to raise the idle speed any time the choke is operating.

MULTIPLE BARREL CARBS

All of the systems described so far have pertained to a carburetor in its simplest form, but we haven't said anything about the number of barrels or throats on the carburetor.

Most engines from one cylinder up to six cylinders have a carburetor with only one throat. In that case there is only one of each carburetor system. Some 6-cylinder and some V-8 engines come with a 2-throat carburetor. In that case, the main metering system and the idle system are duplicated for the second throat.

The float system does not have to be duplicated because the bowl has enough fuel capacity to serve two main jets with ease. The same reasoning applies in the accelerating pump system. One pump is used, but it has two nozzles, one for each throat.

The power system also stays basically the same as in a 1-bbl. carb, except that it feeds two main metering systems instead of one. In the choke department there isn't much change either; they just make the choke valve big enough to cover both carburetor throats.

When we go beyond two barrels, however, there are some real differences. In a 4-bbl. carburetor the two barrels that the engine runs on normally are called the primaries. The extra two barrels only operate at high engine speed, when most needed.

As mentioned before, the carburetor is really nothing more than an air valve. At idle the air valve or throttle is closed because the engine doesn't need much air. As the engine goes faster it needs more air, or we might say that if the engine gets more air it will go faster.

At low speeds around town only a small throttle opening is needed to make

6. Rochester Choke Assist Spring

7. Rochester Bucking Spring

Fuel System

the engine do its job. When we get out on the highway we open the throttle and we go faster, up to the point of wide open throttle. But the engine won't go as fast as it is capable of running because it isn't getting enough air.

It's like the nozzle on the end of a garden hose. You open it up all the way, but you still don't get enough water. The only solution is to get a bigger nozzle.

To solve this problem the 4-bbl. carburetor was invented. The engine runs around town at low speeds on the primary barrels, but when we get out on the highway and really want to go, all we have to do is step on the gas and the secondary barrels open up. Then we have all the air the engine needs and away we go.

Admittedly, the job could have been done with a larger carburetor, eliminating all the complicated vacuum and mechanical controls that operate secondaries, but in that case there is a problem with driver education. An engine needs just the right amount of air to do its job. With a large carburetor the driver has to have an educated foot, and open the throttle just the right amount so that the engine doesn't get so much air that it gasps and wheezes. A 4-bbl. with primaries and secondaries is the only an-

swer, because it gives the driver more positive control of his car.

There is no general rule about what systems feed the secondary barrels. Of course there is a main metering system, but there may be a power system or even an idle system. It all depends on what problems faced the designer and how he went about solving them.

Secondaries can be either vacuum or mechanically controlled, with maybe a velocity valve to boot. Mechanically controlled secondaries start to open when the primaries reach about ¾ throttle. The secondaries open at a faster rate, so that all four barrels reach wide open at the same time.

It is possible, on mechanically controlled secondaries, for the driver to open the throttle wide at a low speed when the engine doesn't need all that air. To correct this mistake, there is usually an air valve or velocity valve in the secondary barrels above the throttle

valve. The air valve does not open until there is a sufficient rush of air past it to raise a weight or compress a spring. Of course the only time we have sufficient airflow is when the engine is going fast, which is the only time we need the secondaries anyway.

Vacuum-controlled secondaries do not have this problem. They are controlled by either manifold vacuum or venturi vacuum, so they open only when the engine needs the extra air, regardless of what the driver does or what he wants the car to do.

Now we have a carburetor that will work under just about any engine condition but there are other features that have been added to make it work a little bit better.

CARBURETOR HEAT

If you do a lot of driving around town, you need a heated intake manifold to im-

1. With the engine at normal operating temperature and curb idle, the cam is placed in this position to set the fast idle speed to the specified rpm. Specifications and adjusting techniques vary on every carburetor, so be sure you work from the right instruction sheet.

2. Holley 4-bbl. fast idle is adjusted by bending this little arm that rests on the fast idle cam.

3. Screw at arrow on the 4300 is for fast idle adjustment only.

4. On this Rochester BV, as on some other carburetors, there is no separate fast idle screw. If the idle speed screw is set correctly, then the fast idle cam will determine the fast idle speed, providing the choke rod has been set to specifications. The choke rod is shortened or legthened by bending.

5. The famous (or infamous) link and slot on the Holley 4-barrel. It's a safety feature, designed to positively close the vacuum-operated secondaries if they should stick open. Accessory manufacturers have made all kinds of gadgets to link the primaries and secondaries together, using this slot and removing the vacuum diaphragm (or creating a leak so it doesn't work). Some of the gadgets don't work very well.

6. Holley 4150 has a thick metering block between the bowl and the main body on each side of the carb. This model has fully mechanical secondaries, with a separate accelerating pump for both primary and secondary.

7. This slotted machine screw goes in this position only, when replacing the bowl cover on the 4300.

1. AFB Fast Idle Adjustment

2. Holley Fast Idle Adjustment

3. Autolite Fast Idle Screw

4. Rochester BV Fast Idle

5. Holley Secondary Link

6. Holley 4150

7. Autolite Special Bowl Screw

prove the low-end response. At a low speed the fuel mixture is moving slowly through the intake passages, and droplets of fuel have a tendency to fall out of the airstream. A heated manifold helps to keep the fuel vaporized. Heat comes from the exhaust gases which are usually channeled in some way so that they go up under the base of the carburetor to heat the intake passages. However, we do not want the fuel in the carburetor bowl to become heated, just the intake passages themselves. So you may find carburetors that are installed on their manifolds with a large insulating block or extra thick gasket.

ANTI-STALL DASHPOT

If you step on the throttle hard to go across an intersection, and all of a sudden you decide, because of the sudden appearance of a large object such as an 18-wheel truck, that it would be a good idea to stop, your engine may die when you take your foot off the throttle, unless it has an anti-stall dashpot, also known as a slow-closing throttle dashpot. The engine dies because you have already started a big load of fuel on the way to the cylinders but when you take your foot off the throttle, you shut off the air supply. The large load of fuel then floods the cylinders and kills the engine. An anti-stall dashpot stops this by holding the throttle open for a few seconds and allowing it to come down to idle slowly, which gives enough time for the engine to burn off the rich mixture.

By now you should have a pretty good idea of how the carburetor works. So let's go into a little troubleshooting and some of the repair procedures that you may have to perform.

IDLE MIXTURE ADJUSTMENT

One of the oldest tests in the world for finding out if a carburetor is operating correctly, is to make an attempt to adjust the idle mixture needles. If possible, mixture needles should always be adjusted with the fingers. If it is necessary to use a screwdriver because you can't get to the needles with your fingers, be very careful that you do not screw the needles in so far that you force them into the idle port hole. If you do this you will either put a ridge on the needle or may even break off the end of it.

Idle mixture is adjusted by screwing the needles in for a leaner mixture or out for a richer mixture. The usual setting at which almost any pre-smog engine will idle is 1½ to 2 turns unscrewed from the completely closed position. Late-model emission control carburetors

Fuel System

may require 3 turns before they will keep running. When you adjust idle mixture, the engine must be at operating temperature. The choke must be off and the fast idle cam must not be holding the throttle open.

Many other things must be checked before you actually set the idle. In some cars the headlights must be on so that the alternator puts a load on the engine. Some cars are adjusted in drive, some in neutral. Get the correct specifications for the car you are working on and be sure that you follow them to the letter. When the engine conditions are the way they should be, then it's OK to go ahead with the actual idle speed and mixture adjustment.

Screw one idle needle in slowly and you should notice a point where the mixture becomes so lean that the engine starts to falter. This is called the lean roll point or sometimes the lean fall-off point.

Unscrew the needle and you should notice a point where the mixture becomes so rich that the engine starts to roll; this is called the rich fall-off point.

Late models run so lean that these points can be very hard to detect. On pre-smog carburetors, the usual setting for an idle needle is midway between the two points, or a little bit toward the lean side for better mileage. On emission control carbs we deliberately adjust for a poor idle, screwing the needles in (leaner) until the rpm drops by a specified amount. This is the only way that a late-model car will pass the idle emission test. However, if done exactly according to your factory shop manual, the idle will not be bad enough to bother you, and the air will be a heck of a lot cleaner. An exception to the rpm-drop method is

1. Business End of Holley 4500

2. Holley Secondary Metering Plate

3. Rochester 4MV Idle Screw

IDLE AIR ADJUSTING SCREW

4. Old Holley Idle Adjustment

5. Air Valve Piston

those engines with air injection pumps (smog pumps). These engines must have a richer exhaust to burn up the hydro-carbons, so the mixture needles are usually adjusted ¼-turn out (richer) from the lean roll point.

AIR/FUEL RATIO

Air/fuel ratio is a fancy term that you won't hear much. What you will hear is talk about a carburetor running rich or running lean. Running rich means that the engine is getting too much fuel; running lean means just the opposite. Sometimes running rich provides an obvious symptom such as black smoke coming out of the tailpipe, but most of the time if the mixture is off it will show up either as poor gas mileage or a lack of power.

If you want power, it takes gasoline to produce it, so you can usually assume that the engine is running too lean if it doesn't seem to have much push. If the gas mileage is so poor that you can't even make a short trip without stopping at three gas stations, then you can be pretty sure that the mixture is too rich.

Carburetor men measure the air/fuel ratio with an exhaust gas analyzer. The analyzer takes a sample of the gas from the tailpipe, and a meter gives the ratio of air to fuel by weight. An engine will run from about 11-to-1 up through 15-to-1. Carburetor men have always felt that mixtures leaner than 16-to-1 wouldn't even run an engine, but with refinements in emission controls, the carburetor makers are now talking about mixtures in the area of 20-to-1. The ordi-

nary exhaust gas analyzer is useless with such lean mixtures. The needle will reverse, going off scale to the rich side. So most shops are now getting hydro-carbon meters, which are expensive.

Some carburetor men don't use an exhaust gas analyzer. But the ones who do have found that the small amount of time it takes to hook the analyzer up will save them a lot of trouble in the long run because it gives them an immediate check on how well the carburetor is running, both before and after they have worked on it.

It is not necessary for you to go out and buy an exhaust gas analyzer. A good one is expensive, a bad one is worse than none at all. And there are some bad ones on the market. The point is that when working on a carburetor you are mainly concerned with mixture control. Power, performance, and smoothness are all dependent upon having the right amount of gasoline in the

air to match the needs of the engine.

Of course the greatest enemy of mixture control is dirt. If the idle mixture needles will not adjust or you keep having problems with rough idle and stalling, just look at the outside of the carburetor. If it's all encrusted with fuel residue and dirt, you can be pretty sure it's almost as dirty on the inside. So the first thing you have to do is get it clean.

CARBURETOR CLEANING

Removing a carburetor is more or less an obvious procedure. It is held on at the base by studs and nuts. Remove the nuts, the throttle linkage, the hot air tube to the choke housing (if there is one), and any wires to such things as the transmission kick-down switches or air-conditioning idle speed-up switches. Remove the carburetor and take it to the bench for disassembly procedure.

Exploded views of carburetors usually show the parts as if they were disinte-

1. Secondary linkage on Holley 4500 is concealed in a cavity between the throats. Linkage is rugged.

2. On the Holley 4160, the secondary metering block is a thin plate with no replaceable jets.

3. Secondary linkage on Rochester 4-bbl. is a rod that can be adjusted by bending. Screw (arrow) is for curb idle adjustment.

4. The idle air screw is a means of supplying air to run the engine when the design of the carb allows the throttle plates to close completely at idle. You'll never find this one if you don't know it's there, because the air cleaner stud screws in on top of it. A disadvantage is that idle adjustments must be made with air cleaner off.

5. Air valve piston on the 4300 has small spring underneath that returns the air valve to the closed position.

6. Power piston stem on 4300 is just visible between halves of float. It opens the power valve, which is in the bottom of the bowl.

7. When the Rochester 4-bbl. choke is on, this little tab prevents the secondary air valve from opening. That's so you can't get on it when the engine is cold.

8. Carter AFB primary main jets are in the little niches (arrows). Secondary main jets are in the end of the bowl.

6. Power Piston

7. Rochester Choke Lock-Out Tang

8. AFB Main Jets

Fuel System

grated by a bomb. Never under any circumstances take a carburetor apart this far for cleaning. A good rule to follow is that anything with a gasket should be removed so that the gasket can be renewed. Also any jet that is screwed in should be removed so that the cleaning fluid can get up into the passages behind the jet. Choke vacuum pistons should be removed if they are of the type that is built into the carburetor.

Never under any circumstances should throttle shafts or choke shafts be removed for ordinary cleaning. If you do you'll just be making a lot of extra work and you won't be accomplishing anything because the cleaning solution easily finds its way alongside the throttle and choke shafts without their being removed. If power valves are the screw-in type, they can be removed. If they are pressed or staked in, they should be left alone.

After the carburetor is disassembled, the large parts should be put in a basket and the small parts in a closed screened container which will allow cleaning solution to enter but keep the small parts from being lost. A good holder for small parts is a tea ball, ordinarily used for making tea, available at any store with a housewares counter.

The basket for the large parts comes with either a 3- or 5-gal. bucket of commercial carburetor cleaner. However, if you are only doing one or two carburetors a year, you can buy the carburetor cleaner in pint cans to do the cleaning. Use a coat hanger to fish the parts out. The cleaner is a very powerful chemical—you should never put your fingers in it and be very careful not to splash it in your eyes.

Some cleaners will clean a carburetor in 20 mins. Others won't do a very good job. You will have to find out by experimenting with what is available in your area. Any cleaner will ruin rubber or neoprene parts, so if there are any parts like this in your carburetor be absolutely certain they are removed before the carburetor is dunked.

After the carburetor has remained in the cleaning solution long enough, the whole basket should be removed and allowed to drain. Then all the parts can be submerged in cleaning solvent or kerosene. If the carburetor cleaner did its job right, the solvent is only to wash out the cleaner, but in some cases you may have to use a brush with the solvent in order to loosen and remove some of the more stubborn deposits.

Swish the carburetor around in the solvent so that all the cleaner is washed out of it. Then remove the carburetor piece by piece and blow all the passages with compressed air. If you don't have an air compressor then blow the passages out with a tire pump. At least be sure that you blow the carburetor with something so that you will remove any remaining pieces of dirt.

After the carburetor is clean, it's simply a matter of reassembling it with new gaskets and new parts where necessary and checking the various adjustments on the fuel carburetor. You should never put a

1. Inside The Float Bowl

2. AFB Air Valve

3. Heat Riser Valve

carburetor back together with the old gaskets unless it's an emergency. At least buy a gasket set or have one on hand before you start the job.

The next step up from a gasket set is a zip kit or pep kit. This includes gaskets plus a few of the parts that wear out, such as needle and seat and accelerating pump. If the carburetor is really in bad shape, then you will need an overhaul kit which includes just about every part on the carburetor that could wear out except the shafts. If even an overhaul kit won't restore the carb, then your only recourse is to buy the parts that you need. However, it is usually cheaper to buy a new carburetor than it is to go that far.

While assembling the carburetor you will set the float leve, but that is ordinarily the only internal adjustment. After the carburetor is assembled there are all kinds of external adjustments that make it operate correctly.

When you buy a repair kit for your carburetor there will usually be a sheet included that will show all the adjustments and specifications. If not, there are auto repair manuals available at bookstores that will give you this information. Also the factory shop manual put out by the manufacturer of your car has all this data.

If after you get the carburetor back on your car, it still doesn't run right, you may have to change the jets. This is usually not necessary. In fact, in some cases it will increase exhaust emissions and is therefore illegal. But changing jets is a procedure that you must know to make a carburetor work correctly.

IDLE JET

After the fuel enters the idle jet it picks up air as it moves through the idle passage in the carburetor. When it reaches the idle port below the throttle

4. Anti-Icing System

5. Anti-Stall Dashpot

6. Rochester 4MV

7. Mixture Screw Retaining Pin

1. Lift the Rochester 4-bbl. bowl cover off and this is the sight that will greet you. We have also removed the float, needle and baffle.

2. Remove the secondary clusters on an AFB and then the secondary air valve will come out.

3. This may not look like part of carburetion, but it is. If the heat control valve is stuck shut, forcing too much heat up under the carburetor, it can cause uneven running.

4. Some cars have trouble with throttle plate icing, which causes the engine to die or results in extremely rough running. This system on a Chrysler Slant-6 channels heated air to underside of throttle plate and prevents icing.

5. Anti-stall dashpot on autolite 4300 is not connected to engine vacuum. It works on a bleed-down principle.

6. Ever hear of a Chevy burning up? Sometimes this plug falls out, which gives the engine a gasoline bath.

7. To prevent over-rich adjustments, the idle needles on some carbs are limited with a pin in the body of the carburetor.

8. Go easy when using a screwdriver on idle mixture needles. They can easily be ruined if they are screwed in tight against the throttle bore.

8. Adjusting Mixture Screws

Fuel System

plate, it is in reality a mixture of fuel and air, and it is the amount of this mixture that you control with the idle mixture screw. However, the idle mixture screw does not control the fuel that comes from the idle transfer port. That fuel mixture is controlled by the size of the idle jet and the idle air bleeds.

If the idle jets are screwed in it's a simple matter to change them. However, if they are pressed into a metering cluster, the only way to change idle jet size is by drilling or buying a different cluster, if one is available—and it usually isn't.

MAIN JET

Main jets are usually screwed in and easily changed. However, main jets for the secondary side of a 4-bbl. carburetor may be just orifices which are not removable. When removing main jets be sure to use a screwdriver that fits the slot in the jet. If you don't, it's very easy for the screwdriver to slip part way out of the jet and chew up the soft brass. On a carburetor that uses metering rods, the usual procedure is to change the rods.

POWER JET

If you want a richer mixture at wide open throttle, but wish to retain the mix-ture you already have at cruising speed, then the power jet is the one to change. A lot of ingenuity has been used in the design and placement of power jets and sometimes you have to use almost an equal amount of ingenuity to find them. Some of them cannot be changed because they are nothing but a restriction in a passageway. Others can be changed or drilled in order to enrich or lean the wide-open throttle mixture. In most carburetion tuning on stock automobiles, the power jet is seldom changed. The best reason for this is because the only way you can check the mixture to find what you have is to put the engine on a dynamometer—and there aren't many dynamometers that are readily available.

ACCELERATING PUMP JET

Accelerating pump jets can also be a restriction in a passageway that is impossible to change or even drill. Sometimes the restriction is in a removable pump nozzle that is screwed into the carburetor throat. If so, the nozzle sometimes has a number stamped on it which indicates the size of the accelerating pump restriction.

Drilling or changing of accelerating pump jets is usually done to eliminate a flat spot on acceleration that cannot be cured by lengthening the stroke of the pump.

It is possible to have 99 identical carburetors that will run well, but on the 100th one the accelerating pump might be just a trifle lean, causing a flat spot when you step on the gas. In that case a larger pump jet or pump restriction does wonders to cure the problem. This procedure should only be attempted by a carburetor expert because ordinarily you can set the pump linkage for a longer stroke to overcome any flat spot.

FLOAT LEVEL

It's easy to think of the fuel level as the measurement of how high the gasoline is in the float bowl, but this is not the part that's important. The critical point is the main nozzle and whether the gasoline is right at the tip of it ready to spill into the venturi or way down inside where the venturi suction will have to build up considerably before any gas will come out.

Fuel level can be so high with a maladjusted float that gasoline actually drips out of the nozzle when the engine is shut off, or fuel level can be so low that venturi suction cannot pull the gasoline out of the nozzle and the engine will gasp and wheeze instead of cruising along.

A high fuel level can cause dying on turns or dying on sudden stops, and a low fuel level can cause poor response

1. *Replacement mixture screw caps come in all sizes to fit various carbs. These are Rochester.*

2. *Mixture needle on left has 15 degree taper, providing finer (less sensitive) adjustment on '72 Buick 2-bbl. Needle at right is old style, with sharp taper.*

3. *Idle mixture screws have limiter caps, to prevent over-rich adjustment by tuners.*

4. *Electrical connection on this Carter AVS is for the solenoid retard on the distributor. It retards the spark at closed throttle. Idle speed screw is above terminal*

1. Mixture Screw Limiter Caps

2. Idle Needle Taper

3. Idle Mixture Screw Caps

4. AVS 4-Barrel

when the main metering system attempts to take over from the idle system. With experience you will be able to recognize high fuel level or low fuel level because of the way the engine acts.

Suppose you have a car that runs very good at high speed but extremely rich at idle so that the engine rolls. You adjust the idle mixture screws but it doesn't help, so the logical thing to suspect is the fuel level. There are many problems that are obvious if you just give them a little thought and analysis.

CRANKCASE VENTILATION VALVES

The so-called smog valve can cause mixture problems too because it is allowing crankcase vapors to enter the engine. These crankcase vapors are mostly

5. Many cars use anti-dieseling solenoids. Normal curb idle is controlled by the adjustment screw in the solenoid itself. If the solenoid has a wire only going to it, then it is a true anti-dieseling solenoid. But if there is also a vacuum line to the solenoid, then it is a CEC valve, which is never used to set curb idle.

6. Rochester 4-bbl. with anti-dieseling solenoid. Curb idle is set with the solenoid adjustment.

7. The Combination Emission Control Valve (CEC) is used mostly on Chevy cars, but also appears on some other GM makes. Curb idle is set with the normal throttle cracking screw, not the CEC plunger screw. There is a specification in rpm for the plunger screw, but setting it is not necessary unless you disturb the original setting. CEC valve rpm setting varies as much as 300 rpm above normal curb idle. If you set curb idle with the CEC valve plunger by mistake, engine braking on deceleration will be greatly reduced, which can be dangerous.

unburned gasoline or just air, on an engine in good shape. On an engine in bad shape there is a lot of oil smoke mixed in with them.

The only thing you can do with smog valves is to make sure that the hoses connecting them do not have any leaks and that the valve itself is clean. If the valve is an orifice type, a visual inspection is good enough. If the valve is a plunger type you should use both a visual inspection and shake the valve to be sure that the plunger is completely free inside.

Smog valves can be cleaned in carburetor cleaner, although many car makers recommend replacement instead of cleaning. Since the smog valve is allowing unburned gasoline or air to enter the engine, if you pinch the hose or if you put your finger over the end of the valve, the engine will actually idle slower because you are taking some of the air and gas away from the idle mixture. If the engine does not idle slower then you can be pretty sure that the valve is plugged or restricted.

AIR CLEANERS

Nothing will make an engine run rich

quicker than a clogged or restricted air cleaner. If the element in your cleaner is made of foam or steel mesh, it should be cleaned in solvent or kerosene, shaken or squeezed dry and lightly re-oiled. Foam-type elements must be handled with care because they are fragile and frequently split at the seam where they are glued. If you have this trouble, instead of repairing them or getting another foam element, there are paper elements available that will take the place of the foam.

If you have a paper element, you can gently tap it or blow it to clean it. But the best idea is to throw it away and put on a new one. The best test ever devised for a paper element is to hold it over a bare light bulb. A new element will look bright and clean while a dirty one is obviously plugged up.

When cleaning air cleaners of any kind, the housing should be cleaned with solvent, but do not submerge it in a solvent tank. There are inner chambers that can become full of solvent and it's impossible to pour it out. Also be very careful not to cut your fingers when you are wiping out the inside of an air cleaner. The cleaner is made of sheetmetal,

5. Anti-Dieseling Solenoid

6. Anti-Dieseling Solenoid on Rochester

7. Chevrolet CEC Valve

Fuel System

and there are sharp edges that can really cut.

FUEL DELIVERY TESTING

If possible, you should not think in terms of testing a fuel pump no matter how much you read elsewhere about testing procedures. If you will think only of testing fuel delivery at the carburetor, you will be a long way toward solving whatever the problem is.

To test fuel delivery take the line loose at the carburetor, slip a tight fitting rubber hose over this line and let the hose dangle over the fender into a bucket. Then start the engine and let it idle just on the fuel that is in the carburetor bowl. You will get a series of squirts into the bucket as the fuel pump operates. An experienced mechanic can just look at the size and length of the squirts and tell if the pump is in good condition or not, but you should actually measure the amount of fuel that you get in half a minute. Ordinarily this would be about a pint if the pump is in good condition.

We had a peculiar experience with a new fuel pump that illustrates the fuel delivery problem. The car would starve for fuel on full throttle acceleration, especially on long, uphill, freeway on-ramps. The original fuel pump on the car was a Carter, but instead of buying another Carter we bought a brand new pump made by another company. With the new pump installed, the fuel starvation was still there, even though the new pump put out a pint of fuel in less than 30 secs. Everybody we talked to said there couldn't be anything wrong with a fuel pump that would put out like that. But we stuck to our guns, hunted up a Carter dealer, and bought an original equipment Carter pump. After installing it, the car ran beautifully, without a trace of fuel starvation. Then, to satisfy our curiosity, we tested the new Carter pump, and found out it would put out a pint in 18 secs. That's a heck of a lot of fuel, but evidently the engine needed it, and Carter's original equipment pump was designed to put it out. The other manufacturer's new pump was evidently a universal design that would fit anything, but it wasn't good enough for our engine.

If you have good fuel delivery then you are pretty sure there is nothing wrong from that point all the way back to the tank, but you still haven't tested the passageway from the carburetor inlet fitting into the float bowl. This passageway frequently contains a bronze filter. The easiest way to test it is to dip it into a bucket of gas and see if it will hold the gasoline. If it does, throw it away and put on a new one, because that means that the pores in the bronze are filled with dirt.

	GEAR						
Transmission	Park	Neutral	Reverse	1st.	2nd.	3rd.	4th.
3 Speed	-	-	-	-	-	Vac.	
4 Speed	-	-	-	-	-	Vac.	Vac.
Torque Drive	-	-	-	-	Vac.	-	-
Powerglide	-	-	-	-	Vac.	-	-
Turbo Hydra-Matic 350	-	-	Vac.,	-	-	Vac.	-
Turbo Hydra-Matic 400	-	-	Vac.	-	-	Vac.	-

CEC Valve Adjustment

CEC (Combustion Emission Control) valve is a complicated arrangement because it does so many different things. Using a combination of electricity and engine vacuum, the valve controls spark advance and throttle opening. The valve is normally closed, which shuts off vacuum to the distributor and eliminates all spark advance. When the transmission is in a position labeled "Vac" on the chart, the transmission switch opens, which operates the reversing relay to energize the valve. This opens the vacuum line to the distributor, giving normal vacuum advance, and also extends the plunger to the high gear deceleration position which gives a larger throttle opening on deceleration for fewer emissions. The water temp switch is in the circuit so that the CEC valve is energized below 82°. The time delay relay energizes the valve for 15 seconds after the ignition switch is turned on, to improve cold running. But we're not through yet. An additional solid state device turns on the air conditioner for three seconds after the ignition switch is turned off, to stop the engine and prevent dieseling. This is '71 model. The '72's have slightly different hookup, to keep you on your toes.

1. Hot Idle Compensator

2. Compensator Cover

3. Idle Jets

4. Main Jet Location

5. Chrysler Retard Solenoid Contact

6. Removing Main Jet

7. Carburetor Cleaning

1. Remove the cover on this carb and there is a hot idle compensator. Note gasket, important to prevent leaks.

2. Under this cover on a Rochester may be a hot idle compensator or nothing at all.

3. Idle tube is another name for the idle jet. The calibrated restriction is at the lower end of the tube where it appears pinched together.

4. Autolite 1101 upper body. You might also hear this called the air horn or the bowl cover.

5. Terminal on Chrysler product Carter retards spark at idle. If contact is not made, idle will be too fast, since spark will remain advanced.

6. Main jet on this Ford-Autolite 2100 carb is on the floor of the bowl.

7. Carburetors should be disassembled thoroughly for cleaning, but only by removing screws or clips. It isn't necessary to remove any rivets or lead plugs that are pressed in.

If you don't have good fuel delivery at the carburetor, then start checking each component all the way back to the tank. This may include a fuel filter mounted on the engine, a fuel filter on the tank side of the fuel pump, a filter in the line between the pump and the tank and maybe even a filter on the pickup tube inside the tank.

Any of those filters could be restricted because of dirt or water. If they are, change the element or if it's a throwaway filter, change the whole filter. If you find nothing wrong with the filter, then it's time to start checking for a kinked line. This can happen because somebody jacked up the car where a line runs outside the frame. Or it could have been caused by a mild collision that kinked a hose. Take nothing for granted when you work on a fuel system. Just because a rubber hose looks good on the outside doesn't mean that the inside isn't all swelled up so that it won't pass any fuel.

A complete fuel delivery test also involves testing the pressure at the carburetor. Do this by inserting a T in the

line and checking fuel pressure with the engine idling, or pressure can be checked statically. Disconnect the line from the carburetor and hook it directly to a pressure gauge, then idle the engine and check the pressure.

Correct pressure can be anywhere from 1½ lbs. to 6 lbs. at idle. On older cars, part of the pressure test was to shut the engine off and see if the pressure would hold, or at least only fall very slowly. This test is not valid on late-model cars, because they have a bleed-back feature in the pumps or in the fuel filter that allows fuel pressure to drop to zero whenever the engine is shut off.

Did you ever park a car in the hot sun on a day when the mercury was up at the top of the thermometer? Fuel pressure can go high enough to override the float and fill the bowl to over-flowing so that fuel runs into the engine. Then when you come back to your car you have several minutes cranking ahead of you before you finally get your flooded engine cleaned out. The bleed-back feature on late-model cars eliminates this problem. When the engine is shut off,

Fuel System

fuel pressure drops immediately to zero and, therefore, prevents flooding.

FUEL PUMPS

Finding the fuel pump is not too difficult, but removing it can really be a job because in many cases it is in the most inaccessible part of the engine compartment. Fuel pumps usually operate off an eccentric on the camshaft with an arm and some linkage to move the diaphragm up and down. An inlet and outlet valve work with the diaphragm, creating suction on the line from the tank and pressure to push the fuel up to the carburetor.

Fuel pumps are very dependable. Usually their malfunctions consist of a cracked or broken diaphragm which allows fuel to leak out onto the ground. They can have problems too with worn linkage which reduces the stroke on the diaphragm so that the pump can't put out the way it should.

Older pumps were put together with screws and could be disassembled. The diaphragms and valves were replaceable and it was possible to rebuild the pump like new. But rebuilt exchange pumps were inexpensive so it really didn't pay to put in a new diaphragm and valves yourself. The result was that most parts stores quit handling replacement parts for pumps and only sold rebuilt exchanges or new pumps. In a few years there won't be any more rebuilt pumps, because the late-model cars all use a pump with a crimped edge instead of screws. Those pumps cannot be taken apart. They must be thrown away when they go bad. The most practical thing to do in any case when a fuel pump is bad is to throw it away and put on either a good rebuilt or a new one.

FUEL PUMP REMOVAL

To remove the pump, simply disconnect the lines, take off the two capscrews holding the pump on the engine block and remove the pump. There are usually two fittings where a line enters a pump. If you put a wrench on the outer fitting and start turning it to take the line

loose, the chances are good that you're going to ruin something, because the inner fitting will turn also. Whenever you take a line loose, always use two wrenches, one to hold the inner fitting and the other wrench to turn the outer fitting. Ideally you should use tubing wrenches to keep from rounding off those brass fittings.

After the lines are disconnected and the pump is removed, there will be some fittings still screwed into the pump. These must be transferred to the new pump. If they are directional be sure they are installed in the new pump, pointing in the same direction they were on the old pump. That will make it a lot easier when you put the new pump on the car.

Before you install the new pump compare it with the old pump from every angle. The mounting flange and the arm must be exactly the same configuration as on the old pump. There is nothing more sickening than the sound of hearing your camshaft break in half the second you turn your engine over because the pump arm was jammed between the cam and the block. Many pumps have the same body and flange, the only difference being in the arm. So be very careful.

If there is a pushrod that operates the pump, be sure the pushrod is not worn. If in doubt, replace it. A worn pushrod will not give full stroke.

Some pumps are dual, with one half pumping fuel and the other half creating

vacuum to act as a booster for the windshield wipers. Of course you only find those pumps on a car with vacuum wipers, and most cars nowadays use electric wipers. But if you do have a car with a double pump that's giving trouble, it's a good idea to check the camshaft eccentric. Those double pumps put an awful lot of pressure on the cam eccentric and can wear it down to where it's just a little bit of a nub. In case the eccentric is worn, the easiest way to fix it is to put on an electric pump. Otherwise, you'll have to tear the engine down and put in a new cam.

ELECTRIC FUEL PUMP

Foreign cars have used electric fuel pumps for years but they have never caught on for domestic vehicles. Probably the reason is that electric fuel pumps can cause operating difficulties if the driver is not aware he has an electric pump. The electric pump is operating any time the ignition is on. If a piece of dirt gets under the needle valve in the carburetor and the engine floods and dies, the driver may leave the ignition switch on. Of course the electric pump is still operating, so it'll pump the complete contents of the gas tank into the carburetor and out over the top of the engine and onto the ground, which is a bit inconvenient.

There are ways around that by installing an oil pressure switch so that the electric pump will not operate until the

1. Holley Secondary Main Jet

2. Economizer Valve

3. Main And Power Jets

MAIN METERING JET

4. Adjusting Float Level

BEND ARM TO ADJUST

BEND TANG TO ADJUST

5. Checking Float Drop

6. Float Level Gauge

1. With the Holley secondary metering body removed, you can see the little holes on the bottom of it that are the secondary main jets. They are not removable.

2. Holley calls this little screw-in part an economizer valve, but it's really a power valve, or power jet.

3. Rochester model B 1-bbl. has power jet under cap next to main metering jet. Check power jet to be sure spring is not broken. Broken spring makes engine run rich all the time.

4. Float level adjustment is usually achieved through bending a float arm or tang. This 4-bbl. carburetor features both methods. On the left is the bending point for setting the level, and on the right is the adjustment for float drop.

5. Float drop is not as precise a measurement as float level. In many cases there is no precise point on the float from which float drop is measured.

6. This single-barrel Holley carburetor is representative of many 2- and 4-bbl. units in that float adjustment is done by bending the float tab rather than the float arm.

7. On Holley 4500, accelerating pump discharge check is under the pump nozzle on top of the carb. Holes in nozzle meter the fuel.

8. Here, when the float is adjusted correctly, gasoline should just wet the bottom of the threads in the sight plug hole. Note the float-adjusting nut and lockscrew atop the bowl of this 4-bbl. Holley. If you have already set the float with a gauge and the fuel level doesn't reach the bottom of the sight plug hole, you should reset the float with the lockscrew and nut until the wet fuel level is correct. Best results are achieved with the adjustment being made while the engine is running at a normal idling speed on level ground.

9. Four long screws hold the Holley 4-bbl. bowl in place. This is center-pivot float bowl, for racing.

7. Holley 4500 Accelerating Pump

8. Holley Sight Plug

9. Removing Holley Bowl

Fuel System

oil pressure comes up. But then you have the problem of getting fuel to the bowl after the car has been sitting awhile. This means that the driver must hold down a push-button bypass when starting. It can also be done the other way around with a switch to turn the pump off in case of carburetor flooding so that the engine can be cranked to clean it out without getting fuel. Some installations on new cars use an oil pressure switch in conjunction with a starting motor bypass. The pump operates only when there is oil pressure, or when the starter is operating. So don't be surprised if you turn the ignition switch on with the engine dead and the pump doesn't work. It's not supposed to.

There are many types of electric pumps around. They are designed mainly as pusher pumps, so they must be mounted as close to the gas tank as possible and as low as possible so that they don't have to suck the gas uphill from the tank.

If you do decide to install an electric pump on your car, check the specifications of the pump carefully. Some of them do not have enough capacity and

you will find your engine running out of fuel when it needs it the most. When installing an electric pump, it is best to bypass the mechanical pump that is on your car. If you don't bypass it you'll have to worry about two pumps, because even though the mechanical pump is not doing any pumping, it still has a diaphragm that can rupture and leak gasoline. After installing an electric pump always test the pressure and volume compared to the old pump to be sure it is adequate.

FUEL FILTERS

Fuel filters or screens can be in some surprising places on an automobile. As long as they work right you don't care where they are, but when they plug up and your car can only run a block without stuttering and stumbling, you have to find those filters in a hurry to clean them out. Regular cleaning and maintenance of filters will eliminate the trouble.

Some filters have an element that can be cleaned, such as a ceramic or metal screen, and others use a paper or fiberglass element that must be replaced. With a little experience you can tell by looking at an element whether it should be cleaned or replaced. If in doubt,

check the specifications for your car in the factory shop manual.

Many carburetors have a filter made out of bronze at the fuel inlet. You would think that this filter could be cleaned, but for some reason or other when the dirt settles in the pores of the bronze it stays there, and there really isn't much you can do except change it. How do you know when to change it? Well, the hard way to find out is to be going up a long hill at wide open throttle with a heavy load on your car and momentarily run out of gas. The easy way is to take the filter out, dip it in a bucket of solvent or gasoline and see if the solvent runs through it. If the solvent stays in the filter just like you had a cup of coffee in your hand, then you'd better throw it away and get a new one.

The next place you may find a filter is on the engine a few inches from the carburetor. If it's a glass bowl type, it will probably have a replacement element in it. The element, however, could be made out of ceramic material. In that case, all you have to do is clean it and put it back in. The inline or can-type filter will also be found mounted on the engine between the carburetor and the fuel pump. This filter may be made of metal or plastic (so that you can look into it to

1. Heated Air Entry

2. Bronze Carburetor Filter

3. Vega Fuel Pump

4. Air-Conditioning/Fuel Filter

see if it's dirty). The best way to change these (whether they are transparent or not) is on a strict mileage basis, again, referring to the factory shop manual.

Some of the can-type filters are made specially for air-conditioned cars, with a bleed hole that bleeds fuel back to the tank. This is done to help prevent vapor lock, which is caused by fuel vaporizing in the fuel lines before it reaches the carburetor. Vaporizing fuel, of course, will go right out through the bowl vent, thus leaving the engine with no fuel to run on. The fuel is actually boiling in the line, vaporizing at a rate faster than the fuel pump can pump it. So the carburetor is receiving nothing at all except vapors—and it's kind of hard to run an engine that way.

This usually happens on a hot day in the middle of summer, on a long hill in heavy traffic. The only thing to do is to get some kind of liquid on the fuel pump and on the fuel lines—even if you have to pour Coca-Cola on them. The liquid will cool the lines and the pump so that they will work again.

Fuel filters can also be found on the pump itself, either on the pressure side

1. Typical heated air entry used on all late-model cars. System usually takes place of heat riser valve that was formerly found in exhaust.

2. A bronze filter—at the carb's inlet side—is usually a spring-loaded device that seats the W-shaped filter against a small gasket. When plugged, it can cause agony.

3. Vegas use an electric fuel pump, combined with tank pickup unit and gauge. Note fiberglass screen (arrow). It's necessary to protect the pump, but it can be a source of fuel starvation if it gets clogged.

4. Typical vapor-diverter filter used on General Motors cars.

5. Inlet fitting on '72 Rochester carbs is different; you have to look closely to see it. Old fittings seated on a shoulder, but new one seats at inner end to keep threads dry and clean.

6. Modern fuel tank package houses a combination fuel pickup, filter, and gas gauge sending unit.

or the vacuum side. If they are part of the pump, they usually take the form of a glass bowl with a changeable element; however, in some cases there may be no element. With no element, the glass bowl merely acts as a sediment trap.

In the line from the fuel pump back to the tank there may also be a filter mounted somewhere on the frame-rail; and in the tank itself, on the end of the pickup tube, there is a filter made of fiberglass on every late-model car. These fiberglass filters on the pickup tube are designed to plug up in case any water gets in the tank, and they really do a good filtering job.

If you've ever seen a carburetor with water in it you won't forget it. A white residue forms created by a reaction between the water and the metal of the carburetor. It plugs up everything, and there's just nothing you can do except throw the carburetor away if the reaction has gone on for very long.

Filters are really important because of all the foreign matter that gets into the gas tank and comes from the tank itself. It's impossible to keep a gas tank full at all times. When it isn't full, water vapor can condense out of the air onto the sides of the tank causing rust. These rust particles will come through the fuel line and cause all kinds of trouble in the carburetor.

If you do get water in the fuel tank, you will have to remove the tank to clean it out. So, next, let's take a look at how that's done.

FUEL TANKS

If you take fuel out of the tank, you have to let air in—so there has to be a vent somewhere on the tank, usually in the cap. If all caps were vented there wouldn't be any problem, but some tanks have a separate vent with a sealed cap. Put a sealed cap on a tank that is supposed to have a vented cap and you're going to have trouble. Your fuel pump might be strong enough to suck so hard that the walls of the tank actually collapse. But probably long before that happened the engine would run out of gas from fuel starvation. About that time somebody will take the cap off the tank to see if there's any gas and of course that let's the air in. Then the fuel pump will pump until it reaches the point where there is a vacuum in the tank once again.

If you are in doubt about the kind of cap your tank is supposed to have, crawl under the car and see if there is an actual vent coming off the tank somewhere. If you see a vent tube then you can be pretty sure that the tank is supposed to have a sealed cap. Also, if you ever take a cap off a tank and hear a rush of air into the tank, you can be pretty sure it has a sealed cap on it but it should have a vented cap.

If you have been unlucky enough to get water in the gas tank, it will plug up the fiberglass filter that is used on the end of the pickup tube on late-model cars. Ordinarily this means removing the tank because there is no tank drain on most cars manufactured nowadays.

Always siphon a tank completely dry before attempting to remove it, then remove all lines, wires and filler neck braces, and put some blocks up under the tank to hold it while you remove the two long straps that hold it against the car. Then remove the blocks and lower the tank.

You can clean the tank out by pouring solvent in through the filler neck opening and through the opening for the tank gauge unit. Tank gauge units usually use a locking ring which takes a special wrench, but with a little ingenuity and some careful prying you can usually get the gauge unit out. Don't pry on the pickup tube under any circumstances because it's very fragile. Tank gauge units should always be handled with extreme care so as not to bend the gauge arm or break any of the soldering loose.

LINES AND FITTINGS

It used to be customary to have a steel line running from the tank up to a point on the frame near the fuel pump, then a flexible hose went across to the pump and another steel line went from the pump to the carburetor. Some later cars made the steel line jump off the frame and go through a long arc and attach directly to the fuel pump so that the flexible line was unnecessary. Still later models use a combination of neoprene rubber and steel lines. Copper line should never be used in a fuel system because it sometimes can have a reaction with the gasoline.

Any flexible fuel line should be inspected from time to time to be sure it is not cracking; other than that, there is no maintenance required on fuel lines.

5. Rochester Fitting

6. Fuel Tank Gauge Unit

Fuel System

Whenever you replace a line be sure that the fitting is matched. Just because two fittings will screw together does not mean that they are going to make a good seal. Several different types of brass fittings are in common use on automobiles today. If you have to replace a fitting be sure that the new one is exactly the same, both inside and out.

FUEL INJECTION

Beginning with the midyear 1975 models, Cadillac has offered an electronically controlled fuel injection system as an option on the large cars and as standard equipment on the 350-cu.-in. engine. While this system looks complex, it does the same basic job as a carburetor, and provides a fuel/air mixture in the proper ratio for complete combustion under all conditions of engine operation. In addition, fuel injection can provide more accurate metering of the mixture to the engine under all operational conditions than can a carburetor—and it allows a considerably quicker response to the driver's demands.

Basically, the system involves electronically actuated fuel metering valves which spray a carefully controlled amount of fuel into the engine. The valves are mounted in the intake manifold with their tips close to the heads of the intake valves. This is known as port injection. Injector valves are timed so that the fuel charge is ready for the intake stroke of each cylinder.

Fuel pumped from the tank is supplied to each injector from a pipe known as a fuel rail. This is connected to a return line, so that fuel not used by the engine is allowed to flow back to the tank. Pressure in the line is maintained by an electric pump mounted just forward of the fuel tank, and an additional booster pump is mounted inside the tank itself, to prevent any chance of vapor lock on the suction side of the system.

In some fuel injection systems, the injectors all operate continuously. This type of system is found on several imported cars. On other systems, the injectors operate in sequence, as the respective cylinders require their charges. The system used on the Cadillac is a compromise; it divides the eight cylinders into two groups, which are operated alternately, all the injectors in each group being opened at the same time.

An electronic control unit, looking something like a transistor radio, monitors and controls the whole operation. This is mounted under the dash, and is actually a carefully programmed analog computer. The control unit takes into account such variables as manifold pressure, throttle position, water temperature, underhood air temperature and engine speed. It translates these inputs into opening and closing times for the injector groups, and is thus able to provide accurately metered fuel to the engine. As with a carbureted setup, the fuel injection system can be broken down into subsystems. There are four major subsystems used in the Cadillac setup.

FUEL DELIVERY SUBSYSTEM

This system consists of tank, fuel pumps, filter, pressure regulator and injector valves. The pumps are activated when the ignition switch is turned on and the engine is cranking or running. If the engine stalls, or the starter does not engage, the pumps shut off after about one second. Fuel is pumped from the tank through the filter, the supply line and the pressure regulator to the fuel rail and the injectors.

In the tank, a reservoir directly below the intake of the in-tank pump makes sure that there will always be a sufficient supply of fuel to the pump, no matter what the attitude of the car. In addition, the return line from the pressure regulator ends in the reservoir, which assures that there will always be an adequate supply of fuel under the pump.

The in-tank booster pump is part of the fuel guage sending unit, and assures a supply of fuel to the chassis-mounted pump; it also precludes any chance of vapor lock occurring on the suction side of the system.

The chassis-mounted pump is of the constant-displacement type and is driven by a 12-volt motor. It has a flow rate of 33 gals. per hour under normal operating conditions, and supplies fuel at 39 psi to the injectors. An internal relief valve opens if pressure rises above 55 psi, thus protecting the rest of the system. The pump is mounted under the car on all models, just forward of the left rear wheel.

The fuel filter has a disposable paper element which is designed to be replaced every 22,500 miles. On the large models, the filter is in the engine compartment; on the Seville it is mounted on the frame, near the left rear wheel.

In the fuel pressure regulator is a valve, controlled by spring pressure and vacuum from the intake manifold. As the manifold pressure changes with the needs of the engine, the pressure regulator responds by sending fuel back to the tank in order to maintain a constant 39 psi across the injectors.

The injectors are solenoid-operated valves that meter fuel to each cylinder. Pulses from the electronic control unit open the valve for the time required to inject the proper amount of fuel into the cylinder. The valve sprays the fuel as a mist of fine droplets. These valves require special handling because of the delicacy of the metering tips.

AIR INDUCTION SUBSYSTEM

This system consists of the intake manifold, the throttle body and the fast idle valve. Air enters through the throttle body and is distributed through the manifold. Airflow is controlled by the butterfly valves in the throttle body, and additional air for cold starts and warm-up is provided through an electrically controlled fast idle valve.

The dual-plane manifold differs from a carburetor type unit in that: only air is delivered through the runners, there is a port above each cylinder for injector installation, and no exhaust heat passage is used. Provision is made for EGR within the manifold.

The throttle body looks somewhat like a carburetor, in that it has two throttle bores and butterfly valves. It is only an air valve, however. An adjustable idle bypass is incorporated into the body, and the throttle position switch is on an extension of the butterfly-valve shaft.

The fast idle valve incorporates an electric heater and a spring and plunger,

1. Cadillac Fuel Injection

2. Cadillac Injectors

3. Pressure Regulator

4. Throttle Body Sensors

1. With the air cleaner removed, the fuel injection system on the small Cadillac is revealed in all its glory. Throttle body (1), fuel rail (2), injectors (3) and fuel pressure regulator (4) are clearly visible.

2. Injectors fit into manifold just above intake valves. Fuel from fuel rail is squirted into cylinders when the electrically operated valves are opened.

3. Fuel pressure regulator—almost completely lost in maze of plumbing—maintains a constant 39 psi in the line across the injectors.

4. Electrical gadgetry attached to side of throttle body consists of throttle position switch (1), which signals computer about acceleration, and fast idle switch (2), which opens the throttle butterflys when the engine is cold.

5. Diagram of system shows relation of components to each other. Some version of this system will probably show up on other makes in the future.

5. Cadillac System Schematic

and is connected to a heat-sensitive element. When the engine is first started, the valve opens to allow extra air to enter. As the element warms up, the valve gradually closes, allowing the idle speed to slow. The valve closes completely when the element reaches 140°. The higher the ambient temperature, the faster the valve will close.

ENGINE SENSOR SUBSYSTEM

Sensors are connected to the electronic control unit, providing it with separate signals which it analyzes to specify the proper fuel delivery. The Manifold Absolute Pressure sensor monitors the changes in intake manifold pressure that result from engine load, speed and barometric pressure (altitude). The sensor is mounted inside the electronic control unit and is connected to the throttle body by a vacuum line. The throttle-position switch transmits position and movements of the throttle and the accelerator pedal to the electronic control unit. The switch is mounted on the side of throttle body. Two temperature sensors monitor air temperature in the intake manifold and coolant temperature in the engine. They send their signals directly

to the electronic control unit. The speed sensor is incorporated within the distributor; it consists of a magnetic rotor and two reed switches. Two types of information come from the speed sensor: that relating to synchronization of the electronic control unit with the intake valve timing, and engine rpm for scheduling of the fuel delivery pulses.

ELECTRONIC CONTROL UNIT

The electronic control unit receives information from the sensors, encompassing engine coolant temperature, intake manifold air temperature, intake manifold absolute pressure, engine speed and firing position, and throttle position and change of position. The control unit processes this information then sends out command signals that affect electric fuel pump activation, fast idle valve activation, injection valve activation and EGR solenoid activation. Air/fuel ratios for all driving conditions are programmed into the control unit, which then sends out the signals to the injectors.

In servicing the electronic fuel injection system, it is best to first compare its parts with those of a conventional carbureted system—then the location of possible sources of trouble is easier. However, the comparison is not a direct interchange. The following list indicates equivalent parts in the two systems:

CARBURETOR SYSTEM	INJECTION SYSTEM
Accelerator pump	= Throttle position switch
Fast idle cam	= Electric fast idle valve
Float	= Fuel pressure regulator
Power valve/ metering rods	= Manifold absolute pressure sensor
Metering jets and idle fuel system	= Injection valves, electronic control unit

Fuel in this system is under pressure most of the time, and starting to dismantle the system without relieving that pressure could result in a faceful of gasoline, or worse. For that reason, a pressure relief valve—the standard Schraeder type of tire valve—has been installed in the system near the fuel pressure regulator. Some fuel will come out with the opening of the valve, but it can be mopped up with a shop towel before it gets anywhere it shouldn't.

The only other precaution to take in working on the injection system is to be sure to install the special conical gaskets in the fittings between the fuel rails and the injectors and pressure regulator. These gaskets are not installed in production, but must be used any time the system is taken apart. They cannot be reused, but must be replaced with new ones each time a fitting is disassembled for any reason.

Fuel System

FORD'S VARIABLE-VENTURI CARBURETOR

The Ford Motor Co. is convinced that this is the carburetor of the future. In fact, they plan to supply it on the full Ford line by 1980. The VV2700 (Variable-Venturi) carb made its debut in California on the 1978 Pinto, Bobcat, Mustang, Comet and Capri lines of cars. The 1977½ model Ford Versailles was also introduced throughout the country with the VV2700 carburetor as standard equipment.

Ford has spent $3,000,000 and seven years to perfect an idea that has been around for some time. Those of you who have owned English cars or motorcycles will be quite familiar with the SU, Solex and Amal carburetors, in which the air-flow is controlled by engine demand via a vacuum-actuated piston assembly.

When the throttle butterflies open, the engine vacuum lifts a piston to open the carburetor intake sufficiently to meet engine demand. A tapered needle attached to the piston is withdrawn from a calibrated jet to allow just the proper amount of fuel to enter the airstream at any given opening. This ensures achievement of the correct air/fuel ratio over the entire engine range from idle to wide-open throttle.

This system works quite well, but it has one inherent drawback: The venturi size remains constant regardless of air-flow. The venturi is a slight constriction of the carburetor throat that momentarily restricts the airflow, thus increasing its velocity through the venturi and creating a small vacuum as the air expands after passing through the venturi. The increased velocity and vacuum jointly serve to draw fuel through the jet and mix it with the incoming air. At medium and full throttle, this works well, but at partial throttle the airflow is too slow to

draw and mix the fuel properly. Another problem is sluggish throttle response at the low end because the slow-moving air needs a short period of time to increase its velocity in response to the throttle opening, producing a slight lag or flat spot in the acceleration curve.

Ford has cleverly overcome these problems by varying the venturi size to suit the air demand. High air velocity at the venturi at low speed is achieved by reducing the size of the venturi. As the engine's demand for air increases, the vacuum-controlled venturi opens to match the need, thus sustaining a high-velocity airflow through the venturi at all throttle settings. An old fixed-venturi carburetor (Model 2150) produces 30 ft./secs. of air velocity at just off idle, while the VV2700 has a 218-ft./sec. air velocity at the same setting. That's quite a difference! Fuel flow is controlled by the proven tapered needle and jet system. This high-velocity single fuel metering system results in a more precise control

1. Ford VV2700 Carburetor

2. VV Components

of the air/fuel mixture throughout the engine's range of operation. Another benefit is improved driveability while meeting the stringent California emissions standards. To help start the engine, there is also a special cold enrichment system. 👑

1. On cold start, bimetallic choke coil lifts CER, metering more fuel to the enrichment system. The CES opens when key is in crank mode, as bimetallic valve adds more fuel while cranking. The CER holds the venturi slightly open to stop flooding and gives a slighty rich mixture for cold drive-away.

2. You can't tinker with this carb. The CER and VCR controls must be set to within .005-in. with a dial indicator. The VCD senses the amount of vacuum between the venturi air valves and throttle butterflies and controls the venturi air valves. The idle solenoid closes the throttle butterflies completely when ignition is off.

3. Venturi air valves withdraw the tapered fuel-metering needles from calibrated jets on left side of venturi. Controlling the size of the venturi opening maintains high air velocity at all throttle settings. Rollers seal cover.

4. Underside of carb cover reveals floats and venturi air valve pivots. Air valves must move freely. As air valve moves, changing the size of the venturi opening, incoming air is accelerated as it squeezes past the restriction. Fuel from the jets is mixed with high-velocity air. The air/fuel ratio is controlled by the position of the tapered needles in the calibrated jets.

5. This is the secret. Venturi air valves have curved leading edges on left. The air is squeezed between carburetor throat wall and edge of venturi valve. Free-floating tapered needles meter exact air/fuel ratio for any air valve position. The needles pass through calibrated jets in carb body.

6. Cover off carb bowl reveals the square carb throats. The control vacuum is drawn from between throttle butterflies (bottom of throats) and the venturi air valves in carb cover. CES opens as engine is cranked, while EMV opening is controlled by fuel temperature. The colder the start, the greater the amount of fuel admitted to the starting enrichment system.

5. Venturi Air Valve

3. Throttle Setting Components

4. Underside of Carburetor Cover

6. Carburetor Bowl Interior

Overhauling Your Engine

Overhauling an engine is not simply a matter of taking it apart and throwing it back together. A man who rebuilds engines can truthfully be called an automotive machinist. He has to be able to work accurately to tolerances of less than a thousandth of an inch. It is true that he does not have to have as delicate a touch as someone who works on carburetors or distributors, but his sensitivity with a micrometer equals that of anyone who sets the gap on a pair of distributor points to the thickness of a feeler gauge.

A properly done engine overhaul will result in the same amount of life that was obtained from the original engine. Done incorrectly, an engine overhaul will result in burned valves, high oil consumption, knocking bearings and a car owner who firmly believes that engine rebuilders are bungling thieves and that the only way to go is with a new car. Actually, an engine can be rebuilt literally as good as new if proper techniques are followed.

DISASSEMBLY

Repair of a specific portion of the engine, such as a valve or piston, may be performed in most cases with the engine still in the chassis, but an extensive overhaul necessitates that the engine be removed from the car. This is one place the amateur can create many problems for himself. All the engine wiring must be disconnected, the exhaust pipe and fuel line must be removed, the throttle linkage must be detached and the radiator hoses must be loosened.

Unless the mechanic has worked on a specific car several times, he usually finds it helpful to tag each electrical wire with a piece of masking tape, making a note on the tag as to exactly where the wire connects (generator field, coil, oil pressure, etc.). The fuel line is loosened at the fuel pump and plugged (otherwise the gas may siphon out and create a fire hazard), then the line is tucked out of the way. An exhaust headpipe is often difficult to remove due to rusted nuts. A generous application of rust penetrant will cure this problem quickly. Before the bolts that hold the transmission and engine together are removed, the engine weight must be supported by either a hoist or a jack beneath the oil pan. The front motor mounts can usually be loosened at any time. While all the various accessories can be removed while the engine is still in the car, it is simpler to leave them in place for the time being. However, always remove the carburetor before lifting the engine from the chassis or you stand a good chance of breaking the alloy casting. If the distributor is adjacent to the hoist chain, remove it too.

Once the entire engine package is removed from the vehicle, direct disassembly can begin. At this time it must be pointed out that whatever comes off the engine first will usually be the last for reassembly.

As each major component or group of parts is taken from the engine, those caked with grease or oil should be set in a bucket of solvent and cleaned. Always work with a group of parts, such as connecting rods and pistons, to avoid misplaced pieces. The order of disassembly is not terribly important, but as a matter of convenience, the heads are usually removed first. What is found beneath the valve covers will be a direct indication of engine condition—thick sludge is normally a sure sign of a heavily worn engine.

The intake manifold must be removed, followed by the valley cover. Next, all head bolts can be removed, and in the case of an overhead valve engine, the rocker arm shaft assembly can be taken off as a unit. Heads on any engine are usually quite heavy, so remove with caution. OHV heads are no problem, but flathead engines often use studs rather than capscrews to position the heads. If this is the case, the head may seem firmly rooted in place. While there are special cutters that slip over the stud and simplify removal, the more common method is to gently tap around the head circumference with a mallet. Once the head is loosened slightly, screwdrivers can be inserted at each end. Then pry lightly and tap until the head is off.

In the absence of a good engine stand, the engine can be set vertically on the bellhousing and the water pump/timing chain housing removed. The oil pan follows, with the oil residue at the pan sump bottom telling more of the engine condition story. Any kind of bearing wear or excessive metallic wear will be apparent as a thick or thin coating on the sump floor. Sludge buildup on the oil pump pickup screen is common if the engine has not been cared for, and it means excessive wear at all lubricated surfaces. Remove the oil pump and set it aside. Do not disassemble the major components at this time. It is easier to take them apart when you're ready to work on them, and this cuts down on the

1. Following the steps taken by a professional engine rebuilder will give you an idea of how a pro gives a worn-out engine a new lease on life. A thorough steam cleaning is done after disassembly to the bare block.

2. All cylinders are rebored, two at a time, with this Rottler Boring Bar. Once the machine is set to specs for the type of engine on the line, the rest is automatic.

3. This is the proper crosshatch pattern in a cylinder bore. If angle is too shallow, rings will not seat during early stages; oil consumption and compression will also be poor.

4. After reboring, cylinders are finish-honed. This produces the desired 45° crosshatch pattern on each cylinder wall, ensuring maximum ring life and minimum oil consumption.

1. Steam Cleaning

number of small pieces lying about the work area.

Use a center punch or number stamp to mark the connecting rod caps; then remove them. Very gently tap the loosened piston assembly out the top of the cylinder. Use the handle of a hammer for this job, not an object likely to damage the rod bolt threads or the crankshaft bearing surface.

It is especially critical to be careful of the crank journals. The rod bolts can scratch a journal easily, and the condition of a journal may not require repair unless it is damaged in disassembly. Before the piston assembly is removed, however, it is necessary to check the top of the cylinder bore for an excessive ridge. Run your fingernail up the shiny part of the bore. If the dull, discolored ridge at the top of the bore is more than a few thousandths smaller than the bore, your fingernail will hang up solidly on the ledge. In this case, the lip may have to be removed with a ridge reamer before the pistons are knocked out of the block. Otherwise it is possible to break the rings and while new rings would probably be needed anyway, the piston

2. Boring the Cylinder Block

3. Crosshatch Patterns

(which might be reusable) could be severely damaged by the broken ring and have to be discarded.

One of the greatest mistakes the mechanic can make is to reassemble the engine with mismatched connecting rods and rod caps. To preclude this, most engines have the rods marked on one side near the bolt to match the caps. There might be a number, dots or lines. If there are no matching ID's, make your own before removing the assembly. After the rods are removed, replace the cap in the proper manner.

The main bearing caps are held in place by large-diameter bolts which usually need a little extra effort to be broken loose. In addition, some engine designs have the main caps recessed slightly in the block web to ensure maximum strength. A slight tap will unseat these caps. The crank is then free for removal.

While it's best to replace camshaft bearings, they may be retained as a last-ditch economy measure. Although this is not recommended, the bearings can escape injury during disassembly if the camshaft is very, very carefully removed through the front of the block. However, before a camshaft can be removed, each valve lifter must be taken out. Observe the location of each lifter carefully. Oversize lifters, especially hydraulic types, are not uncommon.

CLEANING

While it may seem like extra work, no part can be thoroughly inspected while dirty or oily. Obvious broken parts don't require cleaning to verify the need for discarding, but failures are generally small and hard to see. The initial cleansing may be nothing more than wiping an oily part dry, but it is important.

There are a number of different cleaning compounds, but under no circumstances should a highly volatile fluid, such as gasoline or benzene, be used. Kerosene or a commercial cleaning compound available at parts stores is the best, yet inexpensive. Stiff bristle brushes from the dime store are usually sufficient for most cleaning needs, while

4. Honing the Cylinders

small-diameter, round steel brushes are a necessity.

Initial cleaning may be limited to a group of parts. That is, the connecting rod and piston can be cleaned while still assembled, as can the head, distributor, etc. This is merely the first phase of cleanup. Although a thorough cleaning of the cylinder block may be deferred for a while, the crankshaft must receive an intensive cleaning at this time. With the small round wire brush, clean the oil passages in the crank, and use the solvent liberally.

While most mechanics agree that "boiling out" the block and cylinder heads is a good initial cleaning process, many racing engine builders prefer to merely steam clean the block. Their reasoning is that the chemicals used for the hot boiling bath tend to enter the iron casting pores and remain there until the engine is again heated during actual operation. Then the compounds enter the oil. This is of minor concern for a general overhaul, however, and we mention it merely to point out that steam cleaning can be effective.

INSPECTING THE PARTS

It is not difficult to recognize an unusually worn engine part, particularly those parts that generally fail, such as bearings, rings and valves. Obviously, a broken connecting rod is easy to spot. Virtually impossible to see, however, is the rod almost ready to break. Continual work loads imposed upon any mechanical assembly will eventually lead to a failure of some degree. Finding that potential failure early is the key to successful engine rebuilding, and it's the main reason that professional mechanics subject suspected bad parts and vital components to magnaflux inspection.

This type of inspection has become widespread and is now available even in the smallest communities, through either auto parts stores or heavy-duty and farming equipment dealers. Any engine rebuild should include a magnaflux of the crankshaft, connecting rods and rod caps, connecting rod bolts and main bearing bolts. If the engine has been run for a long time, it is also wise to include the rocker arms and rocker arm shafts. Often such an inspection will reveal the smallest trace of a fatigue crack starting at some critical point, such as the radius of a crankshaft rod journal. If caught soon enough, such a potential danger spot can be repaired inexpensively by a machine shop. If a connecting rod bolt is ready to break but appears normal to the eye, the rebuild is likely to be short-lived!

Suspect wear anyplace there is metal-to-metal contact. True, preventing such wear is the job of lubrication, but wear is bound to occur to some degree in any mechanical apparatus. Look at the oil pump as a prime example. Here is a unit continually soaked in oil, but the pump end plate will wear nevertheless, due to the constant contact of the pump gears. Slight wear of any such area will appear as a polished surface. If the surface has not been receiving enough lubrication, the area will turn blue from excessive heat. Grooves worn

Overhauling Engine

in the surface are an immediate indication that the part should be replaced. As a general guide, replace a worn part if there is the slightest doubt of its condition. Take that oil pump end plate, for instance. It could be resurfaced, of course, but the cost of this repair would be more than a new part.

There are three basic types of measuring tools a mechanic uses: inside and outside micrometers, the feeler (thickness) gauge and the dial indicator.

A micrometer or "mike" is designed for linear measurement with accuracy of .001-in. or better. This is well within the range that concerns most mechanics. The inside mike is used for measuring the distance between two parallel surfaces, and is commonly used for the cylinder bore (taper, size, etc.) connecting rod big end and block main bearing bore. The outside mike is used to measure the outside diameter of cylindrical forms and material thickness.

When using an outside mike, always measure several different points on the cylindrical object. For instance, a crankshaft journal may be flat in one spot only, and sloppy mike use would not show that spot. Even if you can't read a mike, you can use it as a comparison instrument and rapidly find any problem areas.

The inside micrometer is a bit harder to use, because the instrument must be absolutely perpendicular to the surfaces measured. As can be seen, if the outside diameter of a crankshaft rod journal is measured, and if a similar measurement is taken of the inside diameter of a coupled connecting rod big end, the difference in measurements should be the exact clearance involved (taking into account the bearing thickness, if the bearing is not included).

A measuring device of sorts is Plastigage, a soft, threadlike, pliable material. Plastigage comes in specified diameters, and when flattened out to predetermined widths will equal some specified clearance. The most common use of this material is to check clearance between crankshaft and main/rod bearings. A short length of Plastigage is laid crossways in the bearing. Then the main/rod caps are torqued to the correct reading. The crankshaft must not be rotated. The caps are then removed and the flattened piece of Plastigage measured to determine clearance.

Feeler gauges are an absolute necessity in any mechanic's toolbox. They range through a variety of sizes and shapes. For engine overhaul, the feeler gauge will come into play often, measuring piston ring end clearance, valve lash, ignition point spacing, spark plug gap, rod side-play, crankshaft thrust play and other critical clearances.

REPAIRING CRACKS AND THREADS

The first thing to check for is warpage of the head(s) or block. Because cylinder blocks are relatively strong structures to begin with, any warping of a cast iron block will usually be minimal.

1. Checking Crankshaft Straightness

2. Miking a Crank Journal

Alloy blocks (aluminum) distort considerably, so they must be checked especially well. The critical areas of block warpage are head and crankshaft mating surfaces. The former may be corrected by grinding or milling if it is not too severe (seldom), and the crankshaft bore can be line-bored (common). The head(s) can be milled or ground true, but only if distortion is minimal (check with the machine shop for this minimum measurement; it varies with engine and operating condition).

To check for distortion, lay a perfectly straight edge of some sort across the surface and then try to slide a feeler gauge between the surfaces. Do this lengthwise, crosswise and diagonally. As a guide, anything more than .020-in. is excessive warpage and requires machine shop correction.

Although corrosion is not a crack, it can cause irreparable damage and must be expected if the engine is very old or of alloy construction. This problem crops up principally in water circulation passages. It will be pronounced around the mating surface openings like those between head and block or water pump and block. If dissimilar metals are used

—such as an alloy block with steel cylinder liners, or alloy heads or alloy water pump housing—an electrolytic action can occur. Clean the affected area thoroughly, grinding away any pieces that could become dislodged and work into the water system. Definitely determine if the sealing surface has been adversely affected. To counteract corrosion, always mix a soluble oil or antifreeze with the coolant.

A cracked cylinder block will show up right away if the crack is external, and it can be welded by an expert professional. Under no circumstance should the amateur try crack repairs without qualified instruction. However, repairs are common when new replacement parts are difficult to find or expensive, such as in the case of an antique engine. External cracks are usually the result of water freezing in the block. The problem cracks are those *inside* the engine.

Overhead valve engines are not prone to internally cracked cylinder blocks, but flathead (valve in block) engines are. The cracks usually occur between the valve seat and the cylinder bore, aggravated by poor water circulation and engine overheating.

3. Polishing the Camshaft

4. Sandblasting Cylinder Heads

1. Quality control inspector then checks crank with dial indicator to make sure that it's straight.

2. He also checks the size of the crank journals with a micrometer.

3. After journals are given the final polishing, all exposed camshaft surfaces will be wrapped with tape to prevent damage while awaiting installation.

4. Heads are sandblasted as the first step in their rebuild. A circular stage carries the heads through the process and returns them to operator.

Cracks between valve ports can be repaired by peening the fracture carefully (small cracks), or by welding. Large cracks that extend well into the cylinder bore make the block unusable.

Sometimes cracks in blocks or heads are repaired by drilling holes at either end of the crack and inserting threaded studs. These studs are cut off at the surface and another hole drilled adjacent to the first, half in the cracked surface and half in the stud insert. This is continued until the crack is filled. But as you can see, crack repair of any kind is tedious, time-consuming and necessarily expensive. Replacement of the part is usually cheaper.

Threaded holes in the block and head(s) can easily become damaged, especially on older engines. The solution is to run the proper size tap into all threaded holes, cleaning away rust and metal or dirt refuse in the process. If the threads have been damaged beyond any return to normal size, the simplest method of repair is to drill the hole oversize and use a thread insert such as Heli-Coil. Use of such thread inserts is especially advisable in alloy blocks or heads.

Slight distortion is a standard part of fastening two metal surfaces together, and it is engineered into both the bolt and the pieces being bolted together. However, in the case of threaded holes in the block or head, this distortion can often be too much, causing the threads to "slip." The resulting lip around the threaded hole will then make subsequent mating less than ideal. The cure is to countersink each threaded hole very slightly.

REPAIRING THE CYLINDER BLOCK

Wear in an engine is usually greatest in the cylinder bore, followed by the crankshaft bearing areas, the valve guides, valve seats, etc. Thus, much attention to basic cylinder block reconditioning is necessary in practically any engine overhaul.

During disassembly, any ridge at the top of the cylinders was removed. This was, in itself, a definite indication of cylinder bore wear. However, a cylinder does not wear the same at top and bottom; rather, the top will wear more than the bottom. The result is a taper to the bore, and this is the culprit that causes most overbore requirements. When bore taper, or the difference in size between top and bottom, exceeds .010- to .012-in., the block needs boring. A very slight taper can be cleaned up by a hone, as can minor scratches on the cylinder wall, but such easily corrected conditions are unlikely to exist in any engine with 50,000 or more miles on it.

While pistons can sometimes be resized if the cylinders are only slightly enlarged by honing, typical rebuild requires a reasonable overbore and new oversize pistons. These pistons should always be bought before the block is bored; then the block is matched to the pistons. Sometimes the piston manufacturer will include the operating clearance in the piston size, sometimes not, so make sure what size you're working with and you won't have trouble.

Increasing the displacement via an impressive overbore used to be a direct route to greater power. However, this was possible only on engines made before the thinwall casting process came into wide-spread use in the late 1950's. This process was designed to reduce engine block weight drastically. Therefore, old engines can usually take up to .125-in. overbore, while thinwall engines can seldom take more than .030-in. This means that a modern engine can seldom take more than one rebuild where boring is required.

If the piston pin has slipped in the piston, it can cause extensive damage to a cylinder wall, sometimes beyond repair with an overbore. In such a case, the cylinder can be bored to accept a sleeve, but the cost is high. If the cylinder has been scored due to broken rings or seizing pistons, an overbore will probably also be necessary. However, if aluminum pistons have only deposited excess alloy material on the cylinder wall, a minor honing will usually solve the problem.

Using a boring bar is not difficult, but such equipment is not likely to be in the amateur's toolbox. Instead, work such as this is best farmed out to a machine shop specializing in such things. Cost is $4 or more per cylinder. Nevertheless, it behooves the mechanic to understand how the boring bar is used.

Boring bars may locate off either the head surface or the crankshaft bore, but in either case the idea is to get a bore that is exactly perpendicular to the crankshaft centerline. Therefore the block must be securely mounted to the cutting equipment. Seldom is the entire cut made at one time; the bar usually needs a few passes through the hole to get the preliminary sizing. Most bars are automatic in that they will shut off when a predetermined depth has been reached, but all of them must be attached to the block carefully to ensure accurate boring for each cylinder.

After boring, each cylinder must be carefully honed, a procedure usually included to give the final sizing. The correct surface for a cylinder wall is not glass-smooth. New rings will not seat when the walls are perfectly smooth, and oil control or compression blowby is sure to be a problem. At the same time a too-smooth cylinder may score from lack of lubrication.

While the honing operation is usually included with any bore job, the mechanic may sometimes be required to do the job himself. The honing scratches are so tiny they can be measured only in microinches—that's one millionth of an

Overhauling Engine

inch! However, he will force the revolving hone down the cylinder at a smooth pace, then pull it back up so that a crosshatch pattern is formed on the cylinder walls. This crosshatch will have lines intersecting from 45° to 60°.

The amount of clearance involved in piston-to-cylinder wall fit varies considerably, due to engine operation. However, since most modern replacement pistons take into account the wide operational requirements of automotive engines, it can be assumed that .001-in. per inch of piston diameter is a safe guide. This means a 4-in. piston needs .0035- to .004-in. wall clearance. In all cases, the piston manufacturer will recommend a clearance, and this should be followed explicitly. It may be as little as .0005-in. Of course, engines that will be operated at rpm higher than stock, such as racing engines, will definitely require greater piston clearances.

After the reboring job, the top lip of the bores can be slightly chamfered to make it easier to get the rings into the bore. The block should be line-bored if necessary. Again, this is a job normally left to a machine shop, because they have the equipment. What is involved is a safety check of the crankshaft bore, since it can distort out of alignment. For line-boring, the main bearing caps are torqued in place; then the bore is trued. The camshaft bore may also be line-bored, but this is not common.

The lifter bores should always be checked, and if the clearance is greater than .005-in., new lifters will be required (oversize). In this instance, the lifter bores are also honed out.

After all the block machine work has been done, remove the soft plugs (freeze plugs) and replace with new ones. These plugs often corrode on the inside, and although they look all right, they may soon fail.

The final block cleaning is now at hand. The block can be given the hot or cold tank cleaning treatment (soaked), or it can again be steam cleaned. In either case, after this cleaning, the newly machined surfaces should be thoroughly washed with ordinary soap and warm water. All oil passages in the block should be cleaned out with the small wire brush and blown clear with compressed air. This operation is vital, since any small particles of metal or dirt trapped in an oil gallery can cause immediate engine failure. After this cleaning, coat all machined surfaces with a light oil to inhibit rusting.

THE CRANKSHAFT

A brand-new crankshaft is seldom necessary to an engine overhaul, unless a journal has been severely damaged. However, it is not common to grind a crankshaft more than .030-in. undersize.

Wear of a crankshaft can come from several different causes. Forces on a rotating crankshaft are much heavier at some points of the journal than at others. As an example, the explosion force, which is much stronger than the compression stroke force, will tend to cause

a flat spot on the journal at that point. A bent or misaligned connecting rod will rotate in a cocked fashion on the crankpin journal, and this will cause the bearing surface to wear in a taper. The engine block may twist during operation, and in the case of engines with only three or four main bearing journals, the crankshaft can distort during rotation. All this tends to wear the main journals in either a tapered or warped fashion, so regrinding is necessary.

Individual bearing journals will not have the same amount of wear because of varying oil supply to specific journals, abrasives entering the oil, misaligned rods, etc. Therefore, some crankshaft reconditioning should be expected.

Very carefully inspect the crankshaft journals, both main and connecting rod, because tiny cracks can develop here long before a failure occurs. If these cracks are visible to the eye, replacement of the crankshaft is a necessity. At the same time, a magnaflux inspection will reveal unseen cracks. Repair of a crankshaft may include regrinding the journals to an undersize or welding and regrinding. If the journal must be repaired in any way, it is advisable to have the edges of each journal radiused slightly. A sharp junction between journal and check encourages stress concentration and metal fracture.

To determine the condition of the crankshaft, measure with an outside micrometer, checking both sides of the journal. Two measurements should be taken at each point 90° to each other (top/bottom and sideways). Because operating pressures create a flat spot on the top of the crank, this measurement is normally slightly smaller than the sideways measurement. However, if this reading shows a difference of more than .002-in., it means that the crankshaft must be reconditioned.

Bearings come in a number of undersizes (the bearing is really oversize, to

compensate for the worn crankpin), from .001-in. on up to above .030-in. If the crankshaft is in good shape except for a minor undersize, a replacement bearing may be all that's necessary. If the shaft needs regrinding, it may be taken down .010, .020 or .030-in. When a shaft is reground, it is usually taken down to a standard undersize to make bearing selection easy.

It is not unusual for a crankshaft to be bent; that is, warped through the centerline. When a machine shop repairs a crankshaft, they always check for this warped condition by using a dial indicator along each main bearing journal. Only minor hydraulic pressure or taps with a sledge are required to straighten the shaft. Even if the shaft proves reusable without journal regrinding, it should be checked for straightness anyway.

Never install a reconditioned crankshaft as it comes from the machine shop! It may not be clean. Anytime a crankshaft is removed from the engine, thoroughly clean each and every oil delivery gallery with a wire brush (preferably stainless steel wire). Wash the crank with both clean solvent and warm soap and water, then blow it dry with compressed air. The tiniest bit of carbon or foreign material in the oil passages can

1. Magnafluxing Cylinder Head

2. Resurfacing Cylinder Head

lead to the sudden demise of an engine.

After the crankshaft is clean, coat the machined surfaces with a light oil and prepare to install the crank in the block.

3. Installing New Valve Guides

4. Grinding Valve Seats

1. Each head is then magnafluxed before further work is carried out. Rejection rate at this stage can run as high as one out of four.

2. Head is resurfaced where necessary to assure a uniform fit when it is replaced on the block. Automatic machine moves the head back and forth under a steady stream of oil.

3. Where heads lack integral valve guides, old ones are machined out, replaced with new ones and honed. This ensures that the valves will all work in a straight line.

4. Cutting a valve seat increases the width of the seat. Final grinding stone used has a 60° angle to face the seat and return it to correct width.

5. Each valve is then checked for straightness and refaced.

5. Facing a Valve

BEARINGS

Rod and main bearings are the most abused parts of an internal combustion engine. They must operate under the most difficult conditions, yet perform faithfully for thousands of miles. And even when they do fail, they are not expected to cause excessive damage to their closest ally, the crankshaft. Because of such high requirements, bearing design and construction have received special attention for as long as automobiles have run.

There is no single bearing metal that can meet the requirements of an engine, at least in the pure state. Such a material would have to have a melting point consistent with manufacturing processes, the proper malleability (softness), low coefficient of friction, high fatigue resistance, resistance to high engine temperatures, resistance to corrosion, ability to adhere to steel or bronze backs (shells) and ready availability at reasonable cost. Since no specific material fits all these conflicting requirements, engine bearings are made of alloys.

These alloys include tin-base babbitt, lead-base babbitt, copper, aluminum and multi-layer copper and aluminum. Most bearings in use today are of the thin-shell type, which consists of a thin layer of bearing alloy supported by a steel backing. For heavy-duty service, such as racing engines encounter, the multi-layer bearing is more reliable.

Unless the engine is being rebuilt with heavy-duty operation in mind, it is best to follow the original manufacturer's recommendation as to bearing type. If the original bearing had a certain type of oil hole and no grooves, then the replacement bearing should be similar (unless otherwise specified). Under all circumstances, the oil hole in the bearing must align with the delivery hole in the block or connecting rod.

Most modern engines keep the bearing inserts in place by a locating lug stamped in the bearing shell and a corresponding slot in the housing to prevent rotation.

Bearing manufacturers also make each bearing half slightly larger than 180°. This allows a little bit of bearing to stick up beyond the intended housing. When the other half of the bearing assembly is installed and torqued into place, this "crush" area makes the bearing seat positively in the housing. Never file the edges of a bearing because it seems too big, and make sure there is no foreign material between the mating edges of bearing halves. In either case, the proper crush would be disturbed.

CONNECTING RODS

Although the engine may have been running reasonably well before disassembly, with no apparent connecting rod trouble, every rod should nevertheless be checked and reconditioned if necessary. Such service is simple: recondition the big and little bores and straighten if needed.

However, reconditioning of the rod is a recent requirement, necessary because of the changes in both rod and bearing design. When engines seldom produced more than 200 hp and internal loads were much less than with modern engines, rods could—and did—seemingly last forever. While the primary function of the rod is to transmit combustion forces to the crankshaft, it has the secondary responsibility of lubricating other parts of the engine. The condition of the rod big end (saddle bore) must therefore be as nearly perfect as possible. If the rod bearing fit is improper, it can cause scored cylinder walls, pistons and rings or excessive oil pumping.

While insert bearings have undergone major design improvements during recent years, connecting rod design has kept pace. Heavy-duty and high-performance requirements have created a full line of top-quality rods for practically any engine. If an engine is going to be subjected to greater than normal loads, better rods should be installed. As an example, a Chevrolet V-8 engine (283-cu.-in. small-block version) can have as much as 5 tons of explosive pressure exerted on the piston. In addition to this tremendous force, at 4500 rpm the rod reverses direction 150 times per second. That's hauling, and the rod is doing a tremendous job under strenuous conditions.

New rods are expensive, so rebuilt rods are commonly used. In this case,

Overhauling Engine

the normal approach is to remove a slight amount of metal from the mating surfaces of the cap. This reduces the internal diameter of the rod, thus allowing the saddle bore to be honed to original size. This kind of rework must be done with the greatest possible accuracy, therefore it is a machine shop operation and should be left to professionals with proper tools.

Should the rod be bent, it can be straightened in a press. If the rod is bent edgewise, such as might occur from seizure, or if bent sideways, the alignment will be improper and cause wear at the bearing. After the rod is straightened, the rod center-to-center length must be accurately measured, and the rod may be checked against a flat surface to make sure all bends or twists are removed.

The small end of the rod must likewise receive attention. If the piston pin bushings are only slightly worn, they may be honed and oversized pins can be installed.

However, if new pistons are to be installed—and this is likely if the block has been bored—the new piston pins will probably be standard. Therefore new bushings will be required for the rod small end. Installing new bushings is easy, and it may be done with an ordinary vise. Care must be exercised so that the bushings enter straight and are not cocked. At the same time, any oil holes must be aligned. Thin-wall bronze bushings must be pressed tightly into the small end rod bore, and then honed to fit the piston pin.

There are two different ways that the piston pin bushing may be clearanced: by expanding hones, or diamond boring. A diamond boring machine is useful when a large amount of material has to be removed, but the best pin fitting is done with a honing machine. It can provide exact pin fits as close as .0001-in.

If a reamer is used, the bushing surface will not be smooth; therefore the pin must do the final fitting during initial operation. Because of this rough surface, a reamer pin fit is called either thumb or palm, meaning the amount of pressure required. A thumb fit requires less pressure than the palm, etc. Far better is the honed or bored bushing, where the fit is determined by clearances in ten-thousandths of an inch. As a rule, a pin will fall through a dry bushing of its own weight when the hole diameter is just right, but will drag somewhat when lubricated. If manufacturer clearances are not available, a rule of thumb is to use .0004-.0006-in. per inch of pin diameter. These clearances may vary according to type of pin action (full-floating, bushed, setscrew, etc.), so checking the engine manufacturer's charts is vital.

The full-floating piston pin design is finding great favor in modern engines, but the pin fit must be very close to perfect. As a rule, a bushed pin hole may use a slip fit of .0002-in. cold. Under normal engine operating conditions this clearance will increase to .0004-in., which is still acceptable for normal engine life.

PISTONS

If the cylinder bores are not worn

1. Using a Spring Compressor

2. Grinding Rocker Arm Face

3. Pressing Out Rocker Arm Bushing

excessively, it is possible to reuse the same pistons with new rings. There is a limit to this economical repair, however, and if the engine has many thousands of miles on it, don't consider this.

There are times, however, when nothing more than minor piston work is necessary. Sometimes, inferior rings are used in an engine, causing the rings to wear out too soon, and in this case a replacement is all that's needed. However, the wear of the rings in the piston grooves may require special piston reconditioning. Because the ring is trying to drag on the cylinder wall, it will work up and down in the piston groove until this groove is opened up, or widened. Excessive widening is normally restricted to the top groove, but if the lower two or three grooves open up, the piston must be replaced. If the top groove is wid-

ened, the opening will taper toward the outside. By cutting the groove with a special grooving tool this edge can be straightened out, and special spacers installed above the top ring. This is to keep the compression ring from traveling a fraction of an inch too high in the cylinder bore and striking any ring ledge.

If cylinder rebore is not necessary, but new rings must be installed, it may be necessary to also expand the piston skirts.

The most common method of expanding a worn skirt is by knurling. With this process, the skirt of the piston is given a waffle-groove effect. A tool forced against the skirt causes some material to displace, or squirt outward, effectively increasing the skirt diameter. Such a process can increase diameter as much as .008-in., often just enough to keep the

piston from rocking in the bore and wearing the rings oval-shape.

There will be a difference in various piston designs. Some will be perfectly round and others will be cam ground; that is, there may be a difference in measurement across the thrust face of the piston versus the piston pin face.

Such a feature will keep the piston quieter when cold, and allow expansion room when the piston reaches operating temperature. The amateur will seldom be faced with this as a basic rebuilding problem, inasmuch as the machine shop or original supplier will grind the pistons to size if necessary.

Whether the pistons are new or used, they should be carefully inspected for cracks, especially around the pin bore and the ring lands. Used pistons should

4. Pressing New Bushing Into Rocker Arm

5. Reassembly of Rocker Arm Shaft

1. An air-operated C-type valve spring compressor is used to hold the spring and seat down while locks are installed. For the tool fancier, this one's elegant.

2. Rocker arm radiused tip is just lightly touched to grinding stone. This trues up the face that operates on the valve stem.

3. New bushings are then pressed into rocker arms for a precision fit.

4. New rocker arm bushing is reamed to factory specifications and then installed on new rocker arm shaft.

5. Reassembly of the rocker and shaft assembly is done with new shafts, springs, etc. as these parts are usually too worn to be trusted. Quality control at Tomadur keeps rejection/return rate to a minimum.

6. A slight amount of metal is removed from the mating surfaces of the connecting rod cap, reducing the internal diameter of the rod and allowing the bore to be honed to its original size.

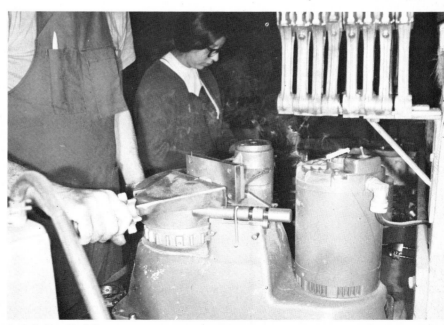

6. Grinding Rod Cap

Overhauling Engine

have the grooves cleaned and all oil holes unplugged.

Assembly of the rod and piston is a precision affair only in that care must be taken to get them together in proper relationship. Individual shop manuals must be consulted in this respect, since different manufacturers use different types of identification. However, if there is a necessity, the piston is identified in some way as to which is the front side and which should be toward the rear of the block. This is another reason disassembly should be thoughtful and careful. In general, the front top edge of the piston will be marked by a notch.

If the piston pin is retained by some sort of lock, make absolutely certain this lock is in place. Small nicks or burrs in the lock groove may cause it to seat improperly and cause serious damage later. When inserting the lock, squeeze it together only enough to slide into the pin hole. If it is compressed too much, it may take a set and not spring outward in the groove sufficiently. Always use new lock rings.

How well the engine performs after the rebuild will depend on how good a ring job the mechanic does. The modern automobile engine works under such severe conditions that every vital part must do its job correctly, and nothing is more vital than proper ring action. To achieve this with a rebuild, the correct replacement rings are mandatory. A brand-new engine works under considerably different conditions than a rebuilt engine. Rust and scale have built up on the coolant side of the bores until a different type of temperature range is occasioned; distortion will change with a rebore, etc. Therefore, it has been found that modern high-speed engines need something different in the way of rings than factory originals. As an example, any rebuild will generally include expander-type oil rings to control the oil under these different-than-new conditions.

Rings are of three basic types: compression, scraper, and oil control. Another division separates the iron rings from spring-type expander designs, in that the expander rings are placed behind regular rings to force the latter more firmly against the cylinder wall and thereby aid sealing.

The compression ring has the prime responsibility of keeping the burning combustion chamber gases from reaching the lubricated part of the cylinder wall (this is called leaking down, or blow-by). The modern engine uses a tapered-face compression ring which will tend to slide over the oiled cylinder wall on the upstroke (thereby not pumping much oil into the combustion chamber), but will scrape excess oil off the wall on the downstroke. Such rings always have the top so marked, and this side must always be positioned up.

The second ring, or scraper, is used to help the compression ring. It scrapes oil on the downstroke and is a secondary seal against blow-by. There are several different designs of scraper rings, and in all cases the manufacturer's recommendations must be followed explicitly. The

1. Honing Rod Ends

2. Press-Fitting Pins

3. Installing Floating Pin

1. Honing restores bore to stock specs. Small end of rod is then bored, bushed, and honed to retain the stock center-to-center measurement.

2. Connecting rods in many stock engines are fitted with pressed-in wrist pins. Pin is a press-fit in rod but a slip fit in the piston.

3. Floating wrist pins are tapped in place with a mallet.

4. Lock rings or pin retaining clips are inserted at ends of wrist pin.

5. Actual block assembly begins with the installation of oil galley plugs.

6. Freeze plugs are seated by gently tapping in place as shown.

4. Installing Pin Retaining Clip

5. Installing Oil Gallery Plugs

6. Installing Freeze Plugs

oil control ring is designed to keep oil from entering the combustion chamber and varies in design depending upon the amount of oil control necessary. These rings are vented so excess oil can be sloughed through the piston and back to the supply point.

Installation of piston rings is a careful, methodical procedure, where sloppy work cannot be tolerated. Never assume that any new part is "just right" for the engine—always measure to make sure. With the piston, the ring groove should always be measured and compared with the requirements of the replacement rings as set forth by the ring manufacturer. Rings are produced to fit factory pistons perfectly, but replacement pistons may vary. Gauges for checking ring groove depth and width are available wherever rings are sold, and should be used. If the piston does have deeper than normal grooves, special expanders are available for the rings in a variety of sizes to counteract the difference. If the grooves are too shallow, it is best to re-groove them more deeply.

Side clearance of the ring is absolutely imperative, and each ring should be checked along with each ring groove. On old pistons the ring groove will usually have worn until excessive clearance is the norm. New pistons, though, can have insufficient ring groove side clearance, which should be .002-in. for the top or compression ring, and .0015-in. for the remaining rings. To check this, slide a feeler gauge alongside the ring to the full depth of the groove. If the rings are slightly large, they can be reduced in thickness by rubbing them against a perfectly flat piece of emery cloth, then polishing with crocus cloth. Sand the top of the compression and scraper rings and the bottom of the oil ring.

Perhaps the most overlooked part of amateur engine overhauls is piston ring end-gap. This should always be checked, and each individual ring must be inserted in the cylinder bore during the procedure. Ring end-gap is normally .004-in. per inch of cylinder diameter for the compression ring, and .013-in. for the remaining rings. For a 4-in. bore, this would mean a .016-in. gap for the top ring, and .052-in. for the remaining rings.

This is a minimum clearance, and having too much is not a problem. Too little will allow the ring gap to squeeze closed, and broken rings and/or lands are the result. If the cylinders have not been rebored, always check this gap at the smallest portion of the bore, or the bottom of the piston travel. If the engine block has been rebored, the fit will be identical everywhere.

To check a ring, insert it about 1 in. down the bore and square it with the wall by tapping lightly with a piston. Measure the gap with a feeler gauge. If it is too little, remove the ring and run an end across a file. Be careful of the tiny parts, as the ends may break. As the rings are gapped, leave them in the cylinder bore until time to assemble to a piston, and mark that piston correspondingly. This will ensure the right rings per bore.

Placing the rings on the piston is a simple operation, but the novice may

Overhauling Engine

break one or two in the process. Slide one lip down at a time if a regular ring expansion plier is not available, and work slowly. Installed, the ring gaps should be rotated 90° or more from one another, otherwise a straight-through gap is left for combustion gases. Multi-piece oil rings must also be treated specially during installation. Place the steel expander gap over a piston pin hole; place one steel segment with its gap 90° off, followed by the spacer or cast iron center section with a gap over the opposite pin hole; then place the final steel segment 180° to the first.

SHORT BLOCK ASSEMBLY

With the piston/rod assembly completed, the basic short block may now be assembled. There are various assembly lubricants on the market, and all work well. Remember that for the first few minutes a rebuilt engine is running, lubrication is super critical. Even when the oil pump has been prerun, oil will take a moment to reach the proper parts. An assembly lube will counteract this early starvation problem and should be used.

With the block upside down on a stand or dolly, wipe the main bearing saddles clean. A tiny piece of dirt behind the bearing will cause all kinds of bearing problems. Install the correct bearing half-shell in both the block and main cap, then install the proper cap to each block web. Lubricate the main bearing bolts with a good anti-seize compound, then torque each cap to the prescribed setting. Do not put assembly lube on the bearings at this time.

With an inside micrometer, check the inside diameter of each and every bearing bore, measuring both up and down and sideways. If everything has been correct up to this point, the measurement obtained should be the diameter of the crankshaft journal plus the prescribed oil clearance. This clearance will vary according to the individual engine, but the manufacturer's specifications should always be followed. In the case of main bearings, the clearance will be somewhere between .0015 and .0025-in. For rod bearings it will be from .002 to .003-in. If the engine will be used in high-performance or heavy-duty applications, oil clearance should be increased slightly, or run at the upper limit. Always consult a qualified mechanic or authoritative publication, such as *Hot Rod*

magazine, for performance specifications.

The connecting rods should be assembled and checked in the same way. However, as mentioned previously, Plastigage may be used to check clearance, and if the mechanic is not sure of his mike-reading ability, this "actual condition" type measurement is recommended for best results.

After main bearing clearance has been checked, the caps are removed and the bearing faces coated with assembly lube. The crankshaft is carefully laid in the block and the caps reassembled and again torqued to specifications.

The crankshaft should spin freely in the bore, without the slightest uneven drag. If it doesn't, something is wrong and work should not proceed until the trouble is found and corrected. Here is one place where the bent crankshaft and/or distorted block will show up immediately. Finally, check the crankshaft end-play, or the amount the crank can slide back and forth in the bearings.

End-play is checked between the crankshaft journal thrust collar and the main bearing thrust flange, using a feeler gauge to measure the distance. Pry the crankshaft away from the bearing surface. High-performance engines will

1. Use camshaft bushing installer to install bushings properly. Tool fits all the way inside cam bushing.

2. Bushings are installed from rear to front. Oil passage holes must line up with feed hole in the block or bearings will seize from lack of oil when engine is operated.

3. Once cam bearings are installed, new welch plug is fitted to back of cam bore. Plug's O.D. is coated with nonhardening sealer before fitting.

4. After removing the protective tape from the cam surfaces, it's carefully installed by hand to avoid marring the bearing surfaces.

5. Cam is seated completely by tapping into place. Note use of bolt screwed into cam face. This centers force of impact, as an off-center blow could mar the bearing surfaces as cam moves backward. Bolt is removed when cam is seated.

6. Camshaft retaining plate is secured in place and tightened with an impact air wrench.

1. Cam Bushing Installation Tool

2. Installing Cam Bushings

3. Installing Cam Plug

4. Installing the Camshaft

5. Seating Camshaft

6. Installing Cam Retaining Plate

have more clearance than stock engines, but as a guide, crankshaft journals from 2 to 3 ins. need .005-in. Journals of 3 to 3½ ins. need .008-in., and journals over 3½ ins. need .010-in.

Assembly of the pistons comes next. The pistons should be liberally coated with assembly lube, or dipped in oil, then a ring squeezer tightened to compress the rings. With the piston in proper position to the block, the piston crown is gently tapped with a hammer handle to force the assembly into the bore. It is vital that the rings be fully compressed into their grooves, or they will hang up on the entrance to the bore and may be broken. Revolve the crankshaft until the respective journal is at the bottom of its travel for each piston insertion, thus gaining working room for the connecting rod. After the last ring has cleared the ring compressor, the piston may be tapped through the bore until the connecting rod seats on the proper crankshaft journal.

For protection to the crankshaft, slip small pieces of rubber tubing over the rod bolts, and carefully guide each rod onto the journal. Once in place, the tubing is removed and the proper cap is installed. After all rods are in place, the caps are torqued to the correct specifications and individual journal side play is checked. This will not have changed normally, but if different rods or crankshaft from the original are involved, this should be checked during crankshaft preparation. This end-play is important to lubrication, and may be checked by inserting a feeler gauge between one rod side and the crankshaft cheek. If it is between .004 and .010-in., this is sufficient for stock engines. High-performance engines will need additional clearance.

Often overlooked by novice mechanics is the fact that oil on a bearing acts as a coolant as well as a lubricant. Oil enters the bearing through a delivery hole, is forced across the entire bearing surface, and exits through the clearance at each bearing side. As engine temperatures increase, the metal will expand. If the side clearance has been insufficient to begin with, the oil flow across the bearing is impaired until heat buildup is increased, failure is near. Too much side clearance is just as bad as not enough, since oil squirting out the side of rod bearings is used to oil cylinder walls, camshaft, and other components.

With the pistons assembled in the block, the crankshaft should still rotate without an uneven drag, although it will take more effort.

THE CAMSHAFT

The camshaft can be a real pain for the novice mechanic. It is one of those parts that wear in a most uneven manner, and unless carefully inspected will contribute to much head-scratching later on. A camshaft may have only one lobe slightly worn, and this will be enough to make the engine run slightly bad. The mechanic may suspect any number of causes before finding the culprit. The cam can twist, which will change the valve timing between front and rear cylinders. It is, therefore, to be suspect from the start of any engine overhaul.

Reconditioned camshafts are available through larger engine rebuilding shops, since they will never return an old cam to an engine. These cams are reground, and often rehardened if necessary, much as a crankshaft is repaired. Whether a new or reconditioned cam is used, the mechanic must be satisfied with spending a few dollars. This is one place it doesn't pay to be skimpy; simply reusing the old camshaft is merely asking for subsequent trouble from the entire valve train.

The camshaft rotates at half total engine speed, yet the very high loads imposed by the lifters make cam lobe wear a foregone conclusion. If an engine is

Overhauling Engine

running rough for no apparent reason, the ultimate cause may be traced to a single camshaft lobe that has worn round, thereby letting one valve loaf on the job. This is not at all uncommon on engines with many miles, and is particularly true of medium-to-high-performance engines.

The selection of the proper camshaft has a direct effect upon how the finished engine will perform. If the engine is to remain stock, then a stock replacement should be utilized. However, it is possible to install a camshaft with different valve timing (the relationship of valve opening/closing to piston location in the cylinder). This does not automatically mean installing a high-lift racing camshaft. There are several different factory-type camshaft patterns available for the small-block Chevrolet engine, for instance (265 through 350-cu.-in. design), and each can actually be called a normal design. However, one will give better low-end torque, while another is better for higher speed operation.

Another example is the pre-1964 Oldsmobile V-8. The 1964 camshaft is an excellent all-around pattern, having been developed for a reasonably large displacement engine that must have both low-end torque and good cruising rpm. This cam can be fitted to any of the earlier Olds V-8's (lifters must also be used), and is superior to any of the earlier cam designs. It costs no more than any of the previous camshafts. As a guide, pick an engine of the same type as that being rebuilt, then investigate the factory parts manual for camshaft specifications. If a 283 Chevrolet V-8 is being overhauled, it is entirely possible to use a camshaft from one of the milder performing Corvettes, and in one simple operation to update the older engine performance.

When the engine block was being cleaned, the camshaft bearings were removed, either by a drift punch or a special puller. If the engine was placed in a caustic immersion bath, the bearings would have been eaten away and useless anyway.

New bearings can be put in at any time, but care must be taken to get the bearings installed properly. Coat the outside of the bearing with engine oil to help installation, and make sure the oil supply holes in the bearing are aligned with those in the block. And make certain the right bearings are being used! Most mechanics install cam bearings with drift punches, firmly tapping each one into place, but the tapping is done on a steel plug that fits inside the bearing, with a shoulder that pushes on the bearing shell. The edge of the bearing must not extend beyond the bearing bore, or it may come into contact with a rotating cam lobe.

After the bearings are in place, coat the inside diameter with assembly lubricant, and very, very carefully slide the new camshaft into position. There are from three to six bearing journals on a camshaft. After each one has passed through a bearing, there is nothing but the mechanic to keep the sharp lobe

1. Deburring Main Bearing Seats

2. Installing Main Seal

3. Miking Main Bearing Shell

1. *Crankcase bearing seats are lightly filed to remove any burring that might affect bearing performance.*

2. *Crankshaft bearings are inserted from the rear, beginning with the rear main bearing oil seal.*

3. *All bearing shells are miked before installation. While this should not really be necessary, even the factory occasionally fouls up.*

4. *Plenty of lubricant is in order to protect the bearings and crank surfaces until oil is pumped through block when engine is first fired up.*

5. *The clean crankshaft is lowered into the bearings with care, then turned to make sure that it's free. Little friction should be felt, as crank is not secured.*

4. Lubing Engine Bearings

edges from tearing up the bearing surfaces. Go slow and easy.

A camshaft will try to wind out of the bore—that is, move forward during running; therefore, some kind of thrust retainer will be involved. It may be a plate that bolts to the block, or simply a rub surface on the timing gear cover. Whatever is used, must be used. Camshafts have end-play specifications just as crankshafts, and should be checked in the very same manner.

If the original camshaft timing gear is in good shape, it may be reused, and is held in place by a Woodruff key. Sometimes a bolt is also included. There will be a timing mark on the front of the timing gear, near one of the teeth, and a similar mark on the crankshaft gear. In some cases correct valve timing is achieved by placing these marks directly opposite each other, and in others there are a specified number of teeth between the sprocket marks.

To set the timing in the first type (called timing marks on center), merely rotate both crankshaft and cam until the respective marks are closest to each other and on a direct line. In the second method of timing, turn the crankshaft until two timing marks are toward the left side of the engine; then adjust the timing chain so that the correct number of sprocket links are in the chain between the crankshaft gear mark and the camshaft gear mark. The timing chain cannot be installed if both gears are already in place, therefore the camshaft timing gear (the big one) is positioned to the correct timing location within the chain (the chain already being positioned on the crankshaft gear), then the timing gear is slipped onto the camshaft register and secured.

Timing of an engine has a tremendous effect upon final performance, and being off one or two teeth will be enough to keep the engine from ever running as it should. However, this is one of the basic precepts of hot rodding and is utilized by all the racing engine builders. Do not attempt any timing modifications to a stock engine without consulting an expert!

Whether or not the timing chain cover is installed at this point depends upon how it mates with the oil pan. In some cases the timing cover must be in place before the oil pan is installed, but most

5. Installing Crankshaft

American cars have independent timing covers and oil pans.

OIL PUMP AND PAN

While the camshaft may be correctly termed the heart of an engine's performance, the oil pump and lubrication system may aptly be called the center of mechanical longevity. Just how long an engine will run depends entirely on lubrication, and the oil pump starts the entire cycle. In this respect it is a cast iron heart pumping a petroleum blood stream.

Location of the oil pump may vary from one engine design to another, but the average system has the pump driven by the camshaft, or at half the engine rpm. This is accomplished by placing the actual pump somewhere in the pan cavity (or low on the outside of the cylinder block), and providing the drive through an extension of the distributor driveshaft. The driving gear which meshes with the camshaft may be on either the oil pump or the distributor.

Two types of pumps are in normal passenger car use: the rotor type common to Chrysler products, and the gear type on Fords. Both obviously do the job, and the only real difference is in the operating clearances. Since they are literally bathed in oil most of the time, mechanical wear is less likely than with other engine parts; still the shaft and end plate must be carefully checked and repaired or replaced if needed.

Wear is most common to the end plate, and if this exceeds .001-in. (wear or warp), the plate must be replaced or machined smooth. Anything under .001-in. wear can be dressed out with emery cloth. To check the clearances of a gear-type pump, place a straightedge across the housing and gears, then slide a feeler gauge between both surfaces. If the distance is greater than .003-in. either the gears or housing must be replaced (whichever is worn). The gears should clear the pump body by a maximum of .005-in. Such tight tolerances are imperative if the pump is to operate correctly.

Overhauling Engine

The rotor pump looks much different from the gear type, having a 4-lobed cam working inside a 5-cavity secondary rotor, but the end plate clearance must also be .003-in. or less. One of the primary rotor lobes must be pushed into a secondary rotor cavity as far as it will go, then the clearance of the lobe exactly opposite must not exceed .010-in. as measured between the primary lobe and a high spot on the secondary rotor. The outer, or secondary rotor is perfectly round, but since it also rotates, clearance between it and the stationary housing should be a maximum of .012-in.

There are no special assembly instructions for oil pumps other than those contained in repair kits, which may include special clearance gaskets for the end plate (necessary for proper end float of the gears/rotors). However, there should be between .003 and .009-in. end-play between the drive gear or shaft retainer and the stationary housing neck.

Use a gasket between the pump and the cylinder block; do not use any kind of sealing compound. The pump may be primed with oil before it is attached to the engine, but more on preliminary lubrication later. It is absolutely vital that the oil pump pickup tube and screen be perfectly clean before reassembly. If the tube or screen rotates in any way, it must be free to do so without binding, and there should be no air leaks in the pickup tubing. Incidentally, the size of the pickup tube has been engineered for a particular engine, so any interchange of tubes may be a detriment unless the inside diameter is the same.

Oil pans as supplied on any engine are designed to do a specific job. The only consideration that might be given to a different, or modified, pan would be to increasing the capacity or including additional baffles. Added capacity will be helpful if the engine tends to run hot (remember oil is a coolant), and baffles will keep the oil from sloshing away from the pickup screen on hard acceleration, deceleration, or violent turns. Such modified pans are common to race cars of every type but not necessary on ordinary passenger cars.

Unless the pan has been damaged by rocks, it will bolt back to the block with no trouble. Gaskets must be included along each rail and at each end, usually attached with a good sealing compound. Do not overtorque the pan bolts, as the light sheetmetal will easily distort and won't seal well.

After the pan is installed, the harmonic balancer or the crankshaft pulley, or both, may be bolted to the crank snout. These pulleys are often cracked or bent, so replacement should always be considered if the unit proves to be bad. The oil filter finishes work to the bottom of the engine, which may be turned over now to complete work on the top portion.

HEADS

Overhaul of automotive heads is almost a special repair project unto itself, since heads play such a vital part in an engine's performance characteristics.

1. Seating Crankshaft Seal

2. Torquing Main Caps

3. Installing Woodruff Key

1. The rear crank flange is gently tapped with a rubber mallet to seat the rear seal. If this is not done, the crank may not rotate once the bearings are installed tightly.

2. Bearing inserts are put into main caps and oiled, then caps are fitted in place and torqued down to factory specs.

3. Tapping Woodruff key in at front of crank finishes installation.

4. Pin pressed into camshaft timing sprocket will fit into cam, assuring that sprocket turns with cam.

5. As crankshaft sprocket is seated in position, timing sprocket is fitted to face of cam.

While the cylinder block, crankshaft and piston assemblies are responsible for changing energy of the burning fuel into mechanical advantage, the cylinder heads are directly involved in the creation of that initial energy. Whereas the other parts mentioned (known as the basic block, or lower end) experience mechanical wear for the most part, the heads are subject to tremendous forces associated with combustion: intense heat, high pressure loads, rapid changes in temperature, etc. At the same time, overhead valve head components experience mechanical wear that is difficult to control. It is a significant tribute to the automobile engineer that problems as this have been successfully solved.

Basic head repair is of a distinct mechanical nature, with emphasis given to valve seats, cracks, distortion, and valve guides. Obviously, these are problems attendant to the overhead valve engine only, since the flathead has the valve mechanism in the block.

A cracked cylinder head may be caused by several factors, such as water freezing (expansion), combustion (pressure), distortion (bolt torque), or running without water (expansion again). Of these, combustion and excessive heat (running without water or detonation) are the common villains. For this reason, head cracks are generally confined to the immediate combustion chamber/valve seat area, and are difficult to repair. Although there is a set procedure for such repair, this is one job that should definitely be left to the professional, as he will have both the experienced skill and the tools to do a good job. As long as the crack is within the valve seat area—that is, normally well into the port and partially in the combustion chamber—the repair is not too difficult. However, a severe crack in the top of the combustion chamber caused by excessive pressures or a mechanical malfunction (dropped valve, etc.) will usually mean a new head.

Discounting cracks, the amateur can do as good a head overhaul as the professional, providing he takes time and works thoroughly. After the rocker arm assembly has been removed during initial disassembly, the only moving parts left on a head are the valves and springs. To remove them requires a special compression C-clamp, one end holding the valve head and the other pressing down on the valve spring. In this way, the valve spring may be depressed enough to remove the split keeper retainers. It's simple with the right tools.

As each individual valve/spring retainer assembly is removed, it should be kept together, particularly the valves. Mechanics use a yardstick drilled full of holes as a handy valve organizer. If the valves are in reasonably good shape, and the valve guides in the head are not worn excessively, each valve should return to its original location—all because each valve/guide combination will not have the same amount of wear as the others. Under such a condition, average repair calls only for valve and valve seat refacing.

With the valve assemblies removed and the spark plugs taken out, there is nothing left in the head that can come out, with the exception of the valve seats and possibly the guides. Both will require attention in a general overhaul of an engine with many thousands of miles.

Before work is started on either of these areas, the head should be thoroughly cleaned. This consists of chipping away all carbon deposits in the combustion chambers and ports, either with a sharp instrument (putty knife, screwdriver) or a rotary wire brush. This is a time-consuming job at best, but should not be overlooked. Oil passages should be cleaned with the small wire brush, and blown clear—a procedure that should be duplicated before reassembling the head.

If valve guides are worn, the valve can hardly be expected to do a good job. Wear is caused by the standard rubbing of metal against metal, a factor aggravated by difficult lubrication requirements. The intake valve stem is constantly being washed by the fuel mixture, and the exhaust valve stem is subjected to intense heat. Add to this the fact that a guide is just that—it must guide the valve in a straight line while the force moving the valve is working through an arc. The tip of the valve stem in contact with the rocker arm is being pushed up-and-down as well as back-and-forth, therefore guide wear is likely to occur in a slotted fashion in line with the force exerted by the rocker arm.

Before guides are replaced, the originals should be measured to see how far each protrudes into the intake or exhaust port. These special shaped bushings can be pressed out, or driven out by hammer if a special punch is available. Replacement guides are available in a number of different metals, depending upon the punishment they must take.

Contemporary engine designs are leaning toward the integral head/guide system, wherein the head metal is also the guide. This kind of approach has several advantages, one being reduced valve temperature as heat is whisked from the valve stem more easily, and another is lower production cost. However, when an integral guide wears, it

4. Installing Camshaft Sprocket Pin

5. Installing Crankshaft Sprocket

cannot be replaced. Instead, valve stems are made in oversizes, such as .003, .005, .015, and .030-in. In this way, the worn integral guide is reamed to the next applicable size, allowing for clearance. This takes special tools, however, and is usually left to the machine shop.

Another type of guide repair, or modification, that has been finding favor with high-performance engine builders is guide knurling. Just as knurling the skirt of a piston will effectively increase the diameter of the piston, so will knurling the inside diameter of a guide decrease the I.D. The guide may be reamed to a larger true size, then knurled back to stock clearances. An advantage of this procedure is the creation of hundreds of small oil traps in the guide wall, which will give better stem lubrication. This, too, is a machine shop operation.

Clearance is a very special problem with guides, and the specified measurement for a particular engine should be adhered to exactly. Excessive clearance around an intake valve is a sure way to encourage high oil consumption. A good insurance against oil sucking into the combustion chamber is the valve stem seal, a nylon insert that fits around the valve stem on the rocker side of the head. These are reasonably priced and easy to install.

No engine overhaul should be attempted without at least refacing the valve and valve seat. It may be nothing more than a touch with the grinding stone, but it is essential to a successful job. While some engines seat the valves directly against the head or block metal, most designs call for specially hardened valve seat inserts shrunk into the head.

These inserts must be carefully checked, as they crack, and may be loose in the block/head. A loose insert, or one that is cracked or burned beyond repair must be replaced. They can be punched out from the back side (through the port), or pried out with a curved bar. They are brittle and the small pieces fly in every direction when they break, so place a rag over the pry bar and wear protective goggles.

The insert does not fit a perfect hole in the head. Instead, the machined depression is an interference fit, from .005 to .008-in. smaller than the diameter of the insert. From this it is obvious the head must be perfectly clean or the little insert won't insert so well. On the other hand, a loose insert will allow carbon to build up around the edge. Although this is such a tiny bit of insulation, it is sufficient to keep the exhaust valve from transferring heat to the head rapidly enough. A burned exhaust valve is next on the list.

If the original insert hole in the head is the proper size, a new insert can be set in place "as is." Otherwise, the hole must be machined to the next insert oversize. To make insert installation simple, place the unit in a freezer. This will shrink the metal more than enough and it will drop right in place. When the insert warms to room temperature it will be tightly wedged in the block or head.

Valve seats must be ground by a tap-

1. Aligning Timing Marks

3. Installing Pistons

2. Protecting Rod Bolts

4. Installing Piston Rings

ered stone. It is absolutely essential that the pilot shaft fit the guide snugly. Too loose a fit allows the stone to wander; this is one reason the guides are reconditioned or replaced before the seats are fixed.

It is possible to rent seat grinders, but since accuracy is essential, such a grinder may not be the best. Fortunately, machine shops and professional mechanics are well equipped for valve work. So this job is a snap for them, and if the head or block is disassembled, the cost is quite low.

Valve seat grinders usually come in a case, complete with a full range of stones of varying angles. The most common angle is 45°, with some 30° designs still in existence. It is imperative that the stone be dressed before use, to insure maximum accuracy (seats should not exceed .002-in. off-center, and can be checked by a dial indicator).

A soft touch is required when you're using a seat grinder. Do not press down. In fact, you should support the weight of the driving motor with your hands. To do a good job, raise and lower the grinder

5. Oiling Piston and Rings

6. Using Ring Compressor

1. Timing chain completes crank/cam assembly and block moves to next station for piston installation.

2. Pistons are inserted wrong way in cylinders while rubber "fingers" are fitted over rod bolts. This protects crankshaft when pistons are inserted properly.

3. Pistons are then reversed to proper position in preparation for ring installation.

4. Working from bottom toward top of pistons, rings are positioned on each one. End-gaps are alternated 90° to lessen chances of blowby.

5. Plenty of lubricant is applied before seating the pistons in bore.

6. With the piston set in block and facing the right direction, the compressor is held tight against block and piston tapped lightly. If not held tight, the rings will pop out of the compressor before they are in the cylinders and are likely to break on the block.

about twice every second. This will let the stone revolve at high rpms, and the cut will be made rapidly. It only takes a few seconds to true up a valve seat (Stellite is different—it takes several minutes because it is so hard to cut with a stone).

A coarse stone is used for the initial grinding, then a fine stone to finish the seat. Because any grinding of the seat face will also widen it, a third stone with a greater angle is used to face the inside or outside diameter of the seat and return it to the correct width. This width is

quite important and should not be overlooked. Exhaust valve seats should measure between .090 and .100-in., while intakes are .070 to .090-in. The exhaust valve has more heat and, therefore, it has more contact area to transfer heat better.

Final head work includes grinding away any sharp edges inside the combustion chamber. The threads of the spark plug holes are an example of this, and although not absolutely essential, this just makes a good job better. The head must be checked with a feeler gauge and straightedge for warpage.

VALVES

The automobile engine is a bag of serious compromises, and the engineers have been able to perform seeming miracles over the years in making an internal combustion engine as efficient as it now is. Part of the problem stems from getting the right amount of fuel mixture into the combustion chamber at precisely the correct time, then effectively sealing that chamber for subsequent fuel burning and expansion. It all boils down to some kind of valve in a 4-stroke engine.

Inventors have spent hundreds of thousands of hours trying to develop a better or more efficient valve, with the list including sleeve valves, rotary valves, poppet valves, slide valves—and still the search continues. In the interim, the standard poppet valve as we know it continues to be developed to ever greater degrees as engine performance requirements continue to increase.

Operating conditions for a poppet valve are brutal, to say the least. Unlike

the other parts of the engine, a valve is exposed to intense combustion temperatures with almost no chance to cool off. While the head of a piston is also exposed to these high readings, it can pass off heat through the skirt and the rod, as well as the surrounding watercooled cylinder block—the valve should be so lucky! Instead, it must have a large-diameter head (to give maximum breathing capacity for best performance) and a small stem. Heat can therefore be passed along only through the tiny stem and during the very few moments of each revolution when the valve face is in contact with the valve seat. Considering that explosion temperatures inside a combustion chamber may reach 5000° F. for a split second, the task would seem impossible. Furthermore, the poor old exhaust valve must open at the most inopportune time and pass the hot gases out the exhaust port. This is why valve jobs are so common to an engine that is in otherwise excellent running condition, and why keeping the valves adjusted is so vitally important.

Temperatures of a valve head may reach 1000° F. or more under these conditions, and certainly higher for racing engines (racing engines use exotic valve materials). It is easier to understand just how difficult a job the valve has when you consider how short a time the valve is seated. If the engine is turning 3000 rpm, or the average cruising speed of most cars, it means that one of the several cylinders will have ignition 1500 times per minute, and that means the valves are off the seat the same number of times. Not very much time for a valve to cool off.

While the seating surface area of the

Overhauling Engine

valve head may only reach 1000°, the center will be 200-400° hotter and the stem just below the head slightly below the 1000° F. This is red hot in any language. If the valve does not seat against the insert exactly right, due to a bent stem or a piece of foreign material, the edge will burn immediately. Once decay starts it spreads rapidly. The intake valve does not have these great temperature problems, because it is seated when the heat is being passed out, and the incoming fuel mixture is at or below atmospheric temperature.

Because of the extreme temperatures involved, exhaust valves are normally made of heat-resistant alloy steel. Sometimes the stems are made hollow and filled with mineral salts such as sodium, which is a fast heat conductor. All the exhaust valve's operating problems are further aggravated by operational changes in the engine. The engine may be in perfect condition cold, but when it warms up to running temperatures, some kind of distortion is likely to occur. This in turn may cause localized hot spots near the valve, with attendant heat problems transferred to the valve. The metal may distort enough to slightly misalign the valve between guide and seat, causing an improper heat transfer, and so on. All this just goes to prove that valves are one of the most important areas of engine overhaul, and must be treated with care and precision.

Of course, if the deposits on the upper part of the valve stem (just below the head) could be minimized, this would in turn cut down on the chances of a valve sticking slightly open—and most of the valve problems would be over. One way to reduce the effect of such deposits (caused by the combustion particles sticking to the exhaust valve as they flow out) is to have the valve rotate slightly each time it is lifted. There are two types of rotating valve designs currently popular, one called the free-type wherein the valve rotates at no particular rate, and the other (called a Rotocap system) where the valve rotates an exact number of degrees each time it is opened.

The amateur mechanic is faced with a basic problem when it comes time to do the valves. If they look to be in good shape before disassembly, then it would seem reasonable to reuse them with no refacing. This is just asking for trouble. It's like putting on three new tires, and leaving a fourth one bad. A valve job should be part of any engine overhaul.

Valves may be lapped if precision grinding equipment is not available, but this is not the best procedure. To lap a valve, special grinding compound is placed on the seat and the valve is rapidly rotated back and forth against the seat. The required tool is a rounded handle with a small suction cup that sticks to the valve head in order to turn it.

There are two kinds of compound available: coarse and fine (the fine is preferred). They come in either oil or water mixtures (use water to remove excess of one, solvent for the other). When lapping a valve, use a very small amount

1. Installing Connecting Rod Bearings

3. Rotating Crankshaft

2. Torquing Connecting Rods

4. Checking Rod Bearings

under the valve head, as it can work down around the clean stem and be just as effective at opening up the guide clearance. Inspect the valve face often, and when a small, even, gray ring appears the full circumference of the face (the width of the seat) the job is finished. Of course, there must be no pits or nicks in the mating surfaces.

Lapping is inferior to precision grinding in every circumstance, and never should a precision-ground valve be mated to a lapped seat, and vice versa. As a guide, restrict valve lapping to conditions where precision grinders are not available, or the valves are in nearly perfect condition to start with.

Ordinary passenger car valves have reasonably thick heads, making it possible to reuse burned valves. When the grinding equipment refaces the valve, it also trues the head and usually very little must be taken from the face to remove minor pits and burn traces. If the valve has burned badly, however, it must be replaced. Normally, there will not be more than one or two badly burned valves involved, since the car will run so poorly with just one bad valve.

After the valves have been ground, they must be cleaned of any stem deposits. The heads are also cleaned, and it is time to assemble the valves in the head.

ROCKER ARMS

As with valves, rocker arms also can and do wear rapidly. They should be carefully inspected for wear at three points: where the valve tip touches the face, the shaft bushing, and the pushrod stud. The stud ball tip may be worn away, or the adjusting threads may be bad. Repair to all these areas may be made by the mechanic, but a cracked or bent rocker arm should be replaced.

If the rocker face is pitted, it may be dressed flat. While such a unit could be retained and the valve lash adjusted with a dial indicator, this would not solve a basic wear problem. If the face pitting seems excessive, it is possible the rocker arm material is faulty.

It is not uncommon for the adjusting stud threads to break or gall in the rocker, so these should be run through with a screwdriver several times as a check.

5. Installing Hydraulic Valve Lifter

6. Exploded View of Lifter

In the exploded view: LIFTER BODY, PLUNGER SPRING, BALL CHECK VALVE SPRING, BALL CHECK VALVE RETAINER, BALL CHECK VALVE, ROCKER FEED METERING VALVE, PLUNGER, PUSH ROD SEAT, RETAINER RING

7. Spraying Head Gasket

1. New connecting rod bearings are fitted to caps before installation.

2. Caps are torqued to factory specs. New lock nuts are used here.

3. Crank is turned to work pistons, once piston/rod assemblies are in.

4. Each rod cap is removed and bearing surface checked after crank has been turned several times.

5. New lifter assemblies are installed. While lifters can be disassembled and tested for their leakdown rate, new ones are really inexpensive in a rebuild situation.

6. The plunger spring in hydraulic lifter keeps the plunger and pushrod seat up against the pushrod. When lifter body is raised by cam lobe, oil trapped underneath ball check valve lifts plunger and opens valve.

7. New head gasket set is sprayed with a gasket adhesive sealer just prior to installation.

The slightest bind means some kind of trouble. If the lubrication has been poor, the stud ball end may have become pitted, and in extreme cases will even wear away in the pushrod socket.

Because both the valve spring and the pushrod are always forcing the rocker upward, all wear of the rocker bushing and the rocker shaft will be on the bottom side. Such wear is readily apparent and common to engines with many miles. To inspect for the wear, force the rocker to the side with a bar. If the shaft is worn, it will show as a ridge of metal riding in the bushing oil groove. Worn shafts should always be replaced, and used with new rocker arms.

When reassembling the rocker and shaft assembly, it is often difficult to get the rockers in the correct place, since exhaust and intake rockers may be of different lengths or shapes, or both. To circumvent this, leave one shaft assembled while working on the other. This is a good guide as to how things are supposed to be put together.

Don't overlook the rocker shaft supports, as they often break from excessive bolt torque.

PUSHRODS AND LIFTERS

Cam-in-block overhead valve engines use pushrods to connect the camshaft/lifter assembly and the rocker arm. Overhead cam and flathead engine designs do not have the pushrods. A pushrod should be inspected for wear or warpage and discarded if either is found. Wear will be found where the rod enters the lifter, or at the upper end that contacts the rocker adjustment (some engines do not have an adjustment if the lifters are hydraulic). A slight pit in the lower ball or the upper socket is a sign of trouble, so replacement is suggested.

Lifters come in two versions, solid (mechanical) and hydraulic. The solid lifter is nothing more than a cam lobe follower, but it has been precision engineered for that purpose. The hydraulic lifter is a different breed of horse.

The hydraulic valve lifter is designed to keep a zero-lash clearance—that is, to reduce engine noise there is no clearance between the cam and ultimate valve stem. If this were the case with

solid lifters, the expansion of the metals would cause the valves to remain slightly open during running temperatures. With the hydraulic lifter, any lash in the system is compensated for by hydraulic (oil) action. A hydraulic lifter has three basic parts: the body (housing), plunger, and valve.

Oil from the main oil gallery passes through the lifter check valve, forcing the plunger up from the bottom and into contact with the pushrod, and ultimately the valve stem. This oil is under pressure determined by metering holes in the lifter and the oil gallery.

As the lifter is raised by the camshaft action, there is a further pressure on the trapped oil inside the lifter. This closes the check valve and the lifter then becomes a solid lifter for all practical purposes. A tiny amount of oil is allowed to leak from between the plunger and the housing during this open valve phase so that when the cam rotates to the closed position, the valve will not be kept slightly open by an over-full lifter. This lost oil is replaced again by oil from the gallery. When an engine with hydraulic lifters is first started, a clattering sound from the lifters indicates that one or more have leaked completely dry and will take a while to pump up again.

It is possible to wear out lifters of this type, although the plunger movement is very small during operation. Dirt, varnish, carbon and similar foreign materials can get into the lifter and cause the check valve to stick. Keeping the engine oil clean and free from either physical or chemical contamination will make you and the lifter great friends.

Economics of engine rebuilding being what they are, novice mechanics often try to "get by" with the old tappets when a new cam or complete overhaul is involved. Good luck. Most modern engines have been designed to include revolving lifters, and this means that lifter-to-camshaft lobe contact points must be absolutely correct. Most cam problems stem from incorrect lifter contact (the contact point should be slightly off center to the "high" side of the lobe).

Camshaft lobes taper from one side to the other, usually between .002 and .004-in. The face of the lifter is ground slightly rounded, or about .002-in., and

Overhauling Engine

by placing the lifter bores slightly to the higher side of the cam lobes, each revolution of the camshaft will cause the lifter to rotate a few degrees. If either the cam lobe or the lifter face are not ground correctly, or have flattened during use, this rotation is nullified and rapid wear in one spot will result.

VALVE SPRINGS

Valve springs are especially susceptible to life-span problems. Spring steel being what it is, operating under even ideal conditions, will not ensure perfect spring life. Therefore valve springs can be expected to fail from time to time since they must operate in unfavorable conditions.

Each and every valve spring should be checked for tension on a special reading scale. The spring must be measured for free (unloaded) height. If this is in the limits prescribed for the particular engine (line them all up together and a comparison check will show minute differences in height), then the spring is compressed a certain distance. At this distance the coils should be exerting a certain amount of pressure. If not, shims may be required between spring and head, or spring and retainer, to get the prescribed pressures.

At the same time, the coils of the spring must not bind against each other, or the spring will break during use. If the springs will not come up to proper pressure with minimum shims, they must be replaced.

HEAD ASSEMBLY

Now everything is ready for assembly of the head. The valves are replaced in their respective guides one by one. The oil seal is inserted over each stem, followed by the spring and shims if necessary. With the big C-clamp, the spring is again depressed and the retainer washer and keepers are reinstalled. The head(s) are then ready to be installed on the cylinder block.

FINAL ASSEMBLY

Unless the camshaft has been changed to a high-lift version, or the piston head design is different, there is usually no need to check piston-to-valve clearance. However, if such a change has been made, this check is imperative, for flathead as well as ohv engines.

To check this clearance, lay thin strips of modeling clay atop the piston for ohv engines, and over the valves for flathead engines. Bolt on the head, using the old headgasket, and torque it to the correct specification. All the valve mechanism must be included. Rotate the engine several times, then remove the head(s). If the clay measures less than .060-in. where it has been pressed between valve and piston or valve and head, more clearance will be necessary. In case of the overhead engine, the clearance must be flycut into the piston or the valve set deeper in the seat (which is

not recommended). For the flathead engine, the head chamber above the valves must be flycut the necessary amount.

If the camshaft or piston design has not been modified, there will be no need for this clearance check, provided all stock replacement parts have been used. The head gasket should be installed as marked, with the indicated top and front portion so placed, if necessary. Sealing compound or aluminum paint may be used on both gasket surfaces, and the gasket prescribed for the engine should absolutely be used. In case a thin high-compression replacement gasket is involved, then the valve-to-head or valve-to-piston clearance will need to be checked.

All headbolts should be inspected before reuse, and any slight distortion means the bolt should be replaced. Coat the threads with an anti-seize compound, then torque the bolts to the prescribed pounds and in the torque pattern established by the engine manufacturer. This pattern usually starts in the middle of the head and works toward either end. It is imperative that the proper torque pattern and pound limits be followed to minimize block and head distortion!

The lifters may be placed in the respective bores before the head is installed (remember, they go back to the same hole they came from), and so may the pushrods. However, the pushrods must be in the rocker arm pivots before any of the headbolts are tightened in place.

The valley cover may be replaced now. Since this is separate from the intake manifold on most modern V-8's, it should have sealing compound included on both sides of the gasket. Also, if small rubber seals are involved around the central hold-down bolt(s), new seals should be included. Nothing is more discouraging than to have an oil leak around these bolt seals after the engine is assembled and back in the car.

MANIFOLDS, INTAKE AND EXHAUST

When the head was being checked for a warped condition, one of the surfaces involved was the manifold flat, for both intake and exhaust manifolds. Naturally,

1. Pre-assembled head is bolted in place and torqued to factory specs.

2. Rocker arm shaft assembly and new pushrods are installed, then head bolts are tightened.

3. Clearance in the hydraulic lifter is checked. If clearance is not sufficient, a shorter pushrod is used; if clearance is too much, a longer one is substituted.

4. Engine is positioned on a run-in stand and coupled to an electric motor that turns the engine over at a constant speed.

5. Compression testing of each cylinder and check of oil pressure completes rebuild. Engine is now ready for painting and sealing in plastic prior to delivery.

1. Torquing Cylinder Head

2. Installing Rocker Arms

3. Checking Hydraulic Lifter

this same check must be given the manifolds, and they must be trued up by grinding, if necessary.

There is not much that can go wrong with the manifold, but if it is cracked the break must be repaired. This can be done by welding or brazing, the latter most common, and is acceptable on both intake and exhaust systems. After welding, the manifold should be heated to relieve any stress concentrations, and the mating surfaces machined true.

The manifolds must be cleaned of any carbon buildup, then assembled to the engine with torque specifications observed. A sealing compound may be desirable around the intake gaskets. The spark plugs are then torqued to the heads, and exhaust/intake opening taped shut. This will prevent any loose "goodie" from falling inside and undoing all the hard work you've just completed.

Valve covers may be installed at this time, but no sealing compound will be necessary as they utilize thick, soft gaskets. Make sure all the block plugs and fittings are in place and the assembly should be complete. All that remains is to hang on the accessories, and you may want to do that after the engine is in the car, to prevent damage to them during the installation.

PREVENTING DRY STARTS

An engine can wear more in the first 30 secs. after it is started up than in the next 6 months if it has a prolonged dry start. Special lubes are available for coating the camshaft lobes to prevent galling. Every other part in the engine should have been assembled with liberal amounts of engine oil. It's good practice to pack the oil pump with Vaseline when it is assembled. A pump primed with Vaseline will start circulating oil almost instantly, whereas one that has to start dry may take several seconds before it can suck oil up from the pan and distribute it through the engine oiling system.

Some engine builders prime the oil pump by driving a dummy distributor with a drill motor. The distributor must have the gear removed so that it does not try to turn the camshaft. The drill motor is chucked onto the top of the distributor shaft, and the tang at the bottom end of the shaft will drive the oil pump just as if the distributor were being run in the engine. It only takes a few seconds of drill motor operation to get complete oil pressure even to the point where it starts squirting out of the rocker arms. Drill motors rotate clockwise, so this technique can only be used on those engines with distributors that also rotate clockwise. If you turn the dummy distributor and the oil pump in the wrong direction, you won't hurt anything but you won't be pumping any oil either. You'll just be blowing bubbles down into the oil in the pan.

A reversible drill motor will work on any engine, but all of the problems with figuring out how to do this can be avoided in the first place simply by packing the oil pump with Vaseline. As soon as the engine oil gets warm the Vaseline melts, and then dilutes to the point where it never congeals thereafter.

ENGINE TIMING

Setting valve lash and timing the distributor are where many amateur mechanics fall down. They may have assembled a very good engine, only to have things unravel in either or both of these categories.

To time an engine, rotate the crankshaft until the No. 1 piston is on top dead center (TDC) of the compression stroke. Move the crank back and forth a few degrees either way and watch the No. 1 rocker arms. If they move, the engine is on the exhaust stroke and must be rotated again. With the piston on TDC of the compression stroke, the timing marks on the crankshaft pulley should be aligned with the timing pointer attached to the timing cover.

Now install the distributor with the rotor pointing directly to the No. 1 distributor cap terminal (the secondary, or ignition wires were taped, remember?). Adjust the distributor by turning it in the direction of rotation until the distributor

points just barely begin to open. In this way, a very slight lead is involved and the engine will start. Final distributor adjustment is then made with the use of a timing light.

It is common for amateurs to get the ignition installed to fire on the exhaust stroke, and this leads to all kinds of frustration. If the engine does not start right away, recheck to see that the distributor is not out of phase with the cylinders.

Setting valve lash is not difficult, but is often accomplished in a most rough-shod manner. Hydraulic lifters require no lash adjustment per se, but some engines call for one turn adjustment from zero lash. This places the lifter plunger in the center of the housing travel. To make this kind of adjustment, loosen the rocker adjustment stud until the valve clatters, then tighten it to zero-lash, or when the valve is quiet (this is a close point, so listen carefully). Now tighten the adjustment screw by one additional full turn; make the adjustment ¼-turn at a time to allow the lifter to bleed down. Some engines have different length pushrods for adjustment.

Adjustment of the solid lifter is made with a feeler gauge and requires nothing more special than patience. The lifter must be on the heel of the cam for this adjustment; that is, the valves must be fully closed. Turn the adjusting screw in the rocker until the feeler is a snug but removable fit, and tighten the locknut. Until proficient in adjusting mechanical lifters, the mechanic should recheck the initial cold settings after the engine has warmed up (the settings are different and are called out in the shop manuals).

ENGINE BREAK-IN

How an overhauled engine is broken in will determine how well it runs. As soon as it is started, it should be set at an rpm equivalent to 20-30 mph, or slightly over 1000 rpm. This allows the oil to circulate through the engine galleries well, and throws oil onto the cylinder walls.

As a rule, don't let the engine idle, and don't operate it with cold water running through the block. So that takes care of the idea of letting the engine break-in with a garden hose stuck in the radiator. The engine must reach operating temperature for the rings to seat, and the closer to the boiling point the better, although it shouldn't be allowed to boil.

After the engine has run awhile, drive it around to get everything loosened up. This will be but a few miles. Then retorque the head and manifold bolts and reset the valve adjustment with solid lifters. The ignition timing should be rechecked, and the carburetor adjusted for correct idle speed.

To seat the rings, accelerate the car at full throttle briefly from 30 mph. This will load the rings and cause the slight wear necessary. Hard rings will take slightly longer to seat. Drive the car under 50 mph for the first 250 miles, and at no sustained high speeds for the first 1000 miles. Drain the oil and change the filter at 1000 miles and then observe regular lubrication maintenance.

4. Engine on Run-in Stand

5. Final Test Before Painting

Engine Oiling

Diagnosing an engine oiling problem, such as excessive wear from lack of oil, or excessive oil consumption from too much oil, requires a lot more savvy than just knowing where the dipstick and the oil filler tube are. The engine oiling circuit diagrams that are in the shop manuals and also in the Petersen *Complete Book of Engines* are not there just to satisfy an engineering curiosity. Those diagrams will point out how the oil gets where it is supposed to be and may give you a clue as to why you are getting either too much or not enough oil.

To fully understand the oiling system of an automobile engine, it is first necessary to understand something about oil itself. In an engine, oil is called on to reduce the friction between moving parts. This will reduce the destructive heat caused by excessive friction, conserve power, and reduce wear of contacting metal surfaces. Oil acts as a seal between the piston ring and cylinder to prevent combustion leaking down into the crankcase; it washes away abrasive metals worn from friction surfaces, and by flowing continually over heated surfaces keeps operating temperatures down. It must do all these things even if the weather should be desert hot or arctic cold.

Under ideal conditions, oil will form a thin film between two surfaces so that these surfaces never touch. Therefore, no metal wear would ever occur. Unfortunately, this ideal condition seldom exists. When ambient temperature is low, oil viscosity is such that the oil does not flow well during engine warm-up. When the temperature is hot, or high, the oil may thin too much and the lubricating film is easily broken. To be of maximum effectiveness, the oil must flow well at cold temperatures but maintain body at high temperatures. During this time, it must also keep an unbroken film between the metal parts.

OIL PANS

Automotive engines use either a wet or dry sump oil reservoir. In the first, the oil is maintained at the proper quantity by a sump in the oil pan. In other words, all the oil is carried within the confines of the oil pan, but must be isolated from the revolving crankshaft by a baffled sump. In the dry sump system, which is something of a misnomer, the main oil supply is kept in a tank outside the engine. The engine oil pump draws the oil from the tank, then another pump scavenges it from the flat pan back to the tank. This type of system is common to aircraft, motorcycles, and racing engines. It is more positive and allows extra cooling because of greater oil capacity, but is also more expensive.

While the transmission and rear-end gears splash the oil around and thus lubricate themselves, the engine needs a more sophisticated approach. Every

1. Enlarging Oil Sump

2. Sludge in Oil Pan

3. Ford Lubrication System

1. During high-speed operation, most of the oil normally in a stock pan is "in suspension," therefore little is ever found in the pan. By enlarging the oil sump of the pan, as seen here, more oil can be carried, thereby allowing any given quantity more time to cool before being circulated again, thus protecting the engine.

2. Ever try to lubricate an engine with molasses? In this instance molasses would probably be as effective as the oily sludge found in this pan. Such a condition indicates infrequent oil and filter changes, which will result in a marked decrease in engine life.

3. These illustrations show how oil is picked up in the pan, delivered through the filter, and carried through the galleries of the Ford 429 engine to lubricate the crank, cam, lifters, rockers and timing chain.

4. Oil pickups are covered with a filter screen to prevent the pump from sucking up any large foreign matter that may find its way into the pan sump. This pickup is stationary, whereas some can swing in an arc about the pan, following oil movement and thereby preventing oil starvation.

5. For best oil flow, considering the ambient temperatures, use an oil of recommended viscosity rating.

4. Pickup Filter Screen

OIL VISCOSITY CHART	
Lowest Temperature Expected	SAE Viscosity Number
Above +32°F.	SAE 30 SAE 20W-40 SAE 10W-30
+32°F. to +10°F.	SAE 20W SAE 10W-30
+10°F. to −10°F.	SAE 10W SAE 10W-30 SAE 5W-20
Below −10°F.	SAE 5W-20

5

moving part inside an engine must be oiled, from the crankshaft bearings to the valves. Splash is not the answer now, although it was common to the low performance engines of years past. It would not work today.

There are three basic types of oiling systems in engines: splash, modified splash and full pressure. In the first, the crankshaft splashed oil around inside the engine and gravity caused it to drain back to the pan. The modified splash design had little troughs across the oil pan. When the connecting rod revolved at the bottom of the stroke, oil was scooped up by dippers on the rod cap. An improvement of this was the addition of oil nozzle pipes that shot a stream of oil into the approaching dipper. Neither the splash nor modified splash are ideal. Most modern engines use full pressure lubrication, whereas an oil pump packs

Engine Oiling

the oil into a main delivery gallery and from there to the points of the engine that are in need of lubrication.

OIL PUMPS

These pumps are engine driven and draw oil through a screen on the pickup tube immersed in the pan sump. Depending upon the individual pump design, the oil is under a specific pressure and goes first to the oil filter (usually), then to the main oil gallery (gallery or header). From the main gallery (which is usually drilled in the cylinder block), the oil goes through secondary galleries to the crankshaft main bearings, camshaft bearings, timing drive mechanism, rocker arms, and lifters.

All this initial oiling route is usually within the confines of the cylinder block and in the case of overhead valves, the heads. Since these passages can, and do, get plugged, that is the reason for emphasis on cleaning during overhaul.

The oil pump is detachable from the cylinder block, and may be located in a number of different places. In some designs, such as Chevrolet and flathead Ford, the pump is actually immersed in oil near the sump; in others, the pump may be outside the block with an internal pickup leading to the sump.

Because different parts of the engine need a diffreent amount of oil, some kind of limitation must be placed in the delivery system. This is normally taken care of by the size of secondary delivery passages between the part and the main gallery, but often a further control is included in the bearing and/or bearing clearance. For instance, in some engines the various main bearings may require different amounts of oil, usually discovered during trial-and-error engineering by the factory. Restrictions in the passages take care of these requirements effectively.

However, anytime an engine is modified for higher performance, the oil pump pressure is usually increased to around 80 lbs. to insure maximum pressure at critical bearing points. When this happens, it is possible to give too much pressure to a particular bearing, and a further restriction in the secondary passage may be necessary. This is often taken care of via drilled jets. Because this is a highly specialized practice, the amateur should never do it without expert direction.

At each crankshaft main bearing, the oil enters the bearing through a hole. Sometimes either the bearing surface or the crankshaft journal is grooved, either partially or the full circumference, to aid oil flow. Part of the oil thus delivered to the bearing will flow across the surface and out the sides to drop back into the oil pan. A greater majority will flow into a hole in the crankshaft journal that connects to the rod journals.

At the connecting rod bearings, the oil will flow across the bearing surface and out the sides to fall into the pan. In some engine designs, the connecting rods are drilled from the big end to the piston pin bore. If this is the case, the oil

1. Exploded View of Oil Pump

2. Priming an Oil Pump

3. Pre-oiling an Engine

1. This exploded view of a 1968 Oldsmobile oil pump illustrates the various components that go to make up such an assembly.

2. It's always wise to prime an oil pump when assembling an engine to avoid scouring the cam, lifters, bearings, etc. One method is to remove the oil pump cover plate and prime the cavity as the engine is being assembled.

3. It's a good idea with a rebuilt engine to pre-oil it by turning the oil pump shaft in the engine with a homemade tool that fits the shaft's slot. Turn with electric drill.

4. Block of typical V-8 shows oil passages. Note oil supply to rocker arms goes through gasket surface into head. Passage should be cleaned whenever head is removed.

5. Cutaway of filter element used in full-flow applications. The different material at left end of element is sisal, used to increase flow characteristics. This "sisal doughnut" was developed to allow depth-flow oil filters to pass the amount of oil needed in a full-flow oil system. The other element material is Vac-Cel, a mixture of cotton linters and rice hulls.

6. This is the type of element used on most new cars. Note that the oil is only required to pass through one thickness of the paper. This filter will last longer than the cotton type, but it does not filter as effectively.

4. Engine Oil Passages

5. Full-Flow Filter

6. Paper Filter Element

then continues up the rod and flows across the pin bushing before falling back to the pan.

Clearance of any and all bearings thus has a direct effect on total oil pressure within the full pressure system. If all the connecting rods have .0025-in. clearance, but one of the main bearings is worn and has excessive clearance, oil pressure will force more than normal oil through this bearing. Therefore, other bearings will tend to run at reduced oil flow.

While direct cylinder oiling has been tried by continuing the oil from the piston pin to a hole in the piston, the most common type of bore oiling is direct

splash. When the crankshaft is rotating in the crankcase, it churns up considerable oil spray, which gets on everything in sight, including the cylinder walls. At the same time, as the rod journal goes through the top portion of rotation, oil being squeezed out the bearing surface is thrown on the walls.

At the front of the engine, some kind of oiling for the timing gears and/or chain is necessary. This may be either a direct or remote delivery, but the common system is from the front camshaft bearing. This oil is then thrown on the gears and chain and drains back into the block through a hole at the bottom of the chamber.

Oil to the valve system in overhead valve engines may be via internal or external passages, with the internal passage most common. An oil passage in the block mates with one in the head. The head passage passes the oil directly to a rocker shaft support and then out the shaft to the individual rocker arms. This supply is usually of low volume, but increases in direct consequence of engine rpm. As the oil squeezes out the sides of rocker and support bearings, it splashes onto the valve stem, and thus lubricates the valve guides. Getting the correct amount of oil to the rocker system is a definite problem on some older ohv engines, such as Ford design. In

Engine Oiling

these cases, an extra outside lube line may be installed (kits are available through most parts supply houses).

Many engines now use stud-mounted rocker arms which receive their oil flow through hollow pushrods. The same oil that operates the hydraulic lifter runs up through the pushrod and through a hole in the pushrod seat at the end of the rocker arm. The oil then runs down into the middle of the rocker arm and lubricates the pivot point at the rocker ball. After a few seconds of operation the rocker arms fill with oil, and then the oil spills over the rocker arm lip at the opposite end of the pushrod and runs down on the valve spring and the valve system. Too much oil on the valve system will flood the guide, and the the high vacuum in the combustion chamber will suck the oil into the engine. The amount of oil that is allowed to go through the guide into the engine is controlled by some kind of seal, which can be a simple O-ring underneath the valve keeper, a rubber umbrella that shields the end of the guide, or even a teflon seal that is a positive fit on the guide. At high rpm the oil that comes through the pushrod can squirt out and hit the rocker cover so that it runs down the inside of the cover without ever getting down in the rocker. The result can be burned rocker balls and very quick rocker arm

failure. Many engines now have little tabs welded to the underside of the rocker covers to catch the oil at high rpm and let it drip back into the middle of the rocker for proper lubrication.

Because wear of all the working surfaces is normal, thus increasing bearing clearances and lowering final point oil pressures, most engines are equipped with pumps of large capacity. To control the oil pressure, then, a special bypass valve is installed, normally in the pump housing. When a predetermined oil pressure is reached, this spring-loaded valve is opened and the excess oil is bled back to the pan. As bearing wear increases, requiring slightly more oil pressure at the pump to compensate for a loss of pressure at the bearing, the relief valve is used less and less. It is possible to shim the pressure relief spring, carefully following engine manufacturer instructions, but under no condition should the spring be stretched in an attempt to increase the oil pressure.

OIL FILTERS

Oil filters may be of full or partial flow design, and the included elements may be of cloth, paper, felt, or combinations thereof. In all cases, their prime job is to remove physical contaminants that get into the oil.

The full-flow filter passes all of the engine oil through the filter before it can reach the various bearing surfaces, while

the partial-flow filter cleans only a portion of the circulating oil at any particular period. The advantages of the full-flow system are apparent, in that nothing harmful should reach the bearings. However, the full-flow filter does not filter constantly. Whenever the oil is cold or the filter is plugged with dirt, a bypass valve opens so that the engine can continue to get oil. Some engine designs have this bypass valve built into the engine block. In others it is in the filter can itself.

Some full-flow elements have a valve built into the element itself to prevent drainback into the pan. If the filter emptied every time the engine was shut off for a few hours, every start would be without lubrication. Because of this extra valve that works with the bypass valve in the engine, it is important that the correct filter element be used. Just because the element fits onto the mounting pad doesn't mean it will work correctly. The wrong element can ruin an otherwise good engine.

There are two types of engine oil filters available today: the depth type and the paper type. In the paper type a special paper is used that will stand up under the detergents, high temperature and pressure in an oil system. The paper-type elements are all designed to trap particles only. The better paper filters will trap particles that can be measured in millionths of an inch. The best paper filter we have heard of is the AC, which

1. Six-Cylinder Lubrication System

2. Camshaft Drive Lubrication

3. Filter Adapter

4. Flared Oil Passage

1. In the oil's journey from the pan up to the rockers, it is pumped through a filter. If the filter is plugged with impurities, a bypass system will reroute the oil, as on this Chevy 6-cylinder.

2. A small oil gallery feeds oil directly to distributor gears, while splash takes care of the timing chain and its sprockets on this Buick design.

3. A number of companies have oil filter adapter kits for Chevy V-8 engines, '56 through '67, allowing use of modern disposable filters rather than the cartridges. This one is by AC, of General Motors.

4. It is wise to flare the oil passage on cylinder blocks, like this Ford, where the filter hooks up. Likewise, the same operation can be accomplished on Chevrolets where the pump rides on the rear main cap. All of these "tricks" are designed to improve oiling.

will trap particles as small as 30 microns, a micron being one thousandth of a millimeter.

Engineers who believe in the paper filter design say that it isn't necessary to refine the oil as you filter it. If you remove the solid particles—the grit and the dirt that do the damage to the rubbing surfaces in the engine—then it doesn't make any difference whether the engine oil is as clean as when it was first put in. A good paper filter will stop all of the solid matter but will pass any of the detergent or anything that is actually dissolved in the detergent.

Those who back the depth-type of filter, and this includes Ford Motor Co. because all of their engines are factory equipped with depth-type filters, feel that simple filtration of the solid particles in the oil is not enough. The depth-type filter not only removes solid particles but it attempts to remove water and other liquid contaminants that are actually dissolved in the oil. In a depth-type filter the oil has to pass through several

inches of filtering medium. Oil will stay clear a lot longer with a depth-type filter, but one of the reasons it stays clear is that a certain amount of the detergent in the oil is being removed.

For many years, depth-type filters were not used on full-flow systems, because the extreme thickness of the depth-type filter would not pass cold oil. The result was a filter that only did half a job, because the bypass valve was open during a good part of engine operation.

The Baldwin Manufacturing Co. pioneered the use of a sisal doughnut in one end of the full-flow filter. The doughnut passed oil freely, but with very little filtering effect. The result was a filter with bypass action (filtering only part of the oil) on a full-flow system. A controversy still exists between the various filter companies over which is best for a full-flow oiling system—paper or depth type. Baldwin Manufacturing Co. stays out of the controversy by manufacturing and selling both types, for almost every car. Therefore you can pick whichever you think is the better.

What about toilet paper filters, the accessory gadgets that you buy and change yourself because very few service stations will have anything to do with them? Toilet paper filters are the depth-type but the trouble with them is they are too efficient. They not only remove the contaminants but they have a tendency to remove most of the detergent also. That's why a toilet paper filter will keep the oil as clear as if it had just been put in. Keeping the oil that clear is defeating the purpose of the detergent that we put in it in the first place. Those detergents have to circulate to do their job.

Toilet paper filters, in our opinion, must be changed at the recommended intervals in order to avoid shredding of the paper from the high temperature and pressure of the oil. There is a screen in the toilet paper filter can, but it is about the same mesh as ordinary window screen, and we feel it will not stop small particles of paper that could be shredded if the toilet paper were left in for long periods of time. We have personally disassembled an engine that had the crankshaft passages plugged with shredded toilet paper, but in all fairness to the toilet paper filter makers we feel that the engine had been run with the same roll of toilet paper a heck of a lot longer than the recommended period.

We do not like the look of dirty oil on the dipstick any more than anybody else does, but we must face the fact that oil in today's engines is designed to get dirty. It gets dirty because it's cleaning the engine, and it should be changed whenever it has become so loaded with contaminants that it can't do an effective cleaning job any longer.

If you keep a new car only a few months, it is doubtful that changing the filter or the oil will give you any benefit, other than keeping your warranty in effect. But if you keep your car, new or used, for several years, then filter elements and oil are cheap. The best of each will keep your engine running longer, with less trouble, if they are changed often.

Cooling System

Although we often describe automotive engines as being either air-cooled or liquid-cooled, all are cooled by air in the final analysis. The use of a circulating coolant fluid is nothing more than an added step that transfers excess heat caused by combustion to a point outside the engine where it can be dissipated. So why use this secondary step? Why not just design all auto engines to be air-cooled? Good question—it's true that air-cooled engines are efficient and dependable; they warm up more quickly than the liquid-cooled variety and run at a slightly higher temperature.

But when you consider today's engine requirements, air cooling is impractical for most, and impossible for many. Such a system requires deep cooling fins on the block and head to draw the heat from the combustion chambers, and a fan to force cool air across the finned area. To a large extent, this necessity tends to dictate engine design and so becomes self-restricting. Air-cooled engines currently in use (most notably the VW and Corvair) are referred to as pancake designs, as cylinders are horizontal and semi-independent instead of being grouped in a vertical block.

Enclosing the basic engine in a container or water jacket filled with a fluid (usually water) that will absorb the excess heat is the most common type of automotive engine cooling. This is done by casting passages into the engine block allowing the water to circulate around cylinder walls, valve seats, valve guides, the combustion chamber top and wherever else heat must be removed. As some spots in an engine may run hotter than others, it's common practice to include deflection guides in the passages and distribution tubes or water nozzles to direct water to potential dead or hot spots.

There's a limit to how much heat water can absorb before it begins to boil away, and so it has to be circulated constantly. As the water in the jacket is heated, it must be moved outside the engine to a place where it can cool. In a liquid-cooled system, that place is the radiator and there are two methods of moving the water—natural and forced circulation.

Natural circulation, or thermosiphon, is no longer commonly used—today's engines are too large and run too hot to depend upon water expansion for circulation. Briefly, it works like this: As the water surrounding the cylinders heats up, it expands. Like hot air, hot water is lighter; as it rises, the heavier and cooler water from the bottom of the radiator displaces it. The hot water goes through a hose to the radiator where it becomes heavier again as it cools and sinks to the radiator bottom, exerting pressure on the hot water presently surrounding the cylinders. This action is a continuous cycle and the hotter the engine, the faster the water circulates, maintaining fairly constant cylinder wall temperatures, as long as the engine is a low-output, low-compression design. In a modern engine with increased horsepower output, thermosiphon won't do the job.

Forced circulation, a much more dependable method, uses a belt-driven pump mounted at the front of the cylinder block. The pump is simply a housing with an inlet and outlet for water travel and an impeller, or flat plate with a number of blades or vanes, mounted on the pump shaft. As the pump impeller rotates, it pushes cool water into the cylinder block that forces the hotter water out. The faster the engine runs, the faster the water pump works.

RADIATOR DESIGN

The hot water is pumped into the radiator, a tank-like device used to bring a large amount of hot water in contact with a large amount of cool air to let the heat transfer from water to air. Forced into the radiator's upper tank, the hot water cools as it filters down through tiny copper tubes in the core (copper is an excellent conductor of heat) and into the lower tank where it returns to the engine block. Most radiators are made of copper and brass, but some models of Corvette have an aluminum radiator. While there are five basic types of core construction, tube-fin and ribbon-cellular are most often used today.

Obviously, the greater the distance between the upper and lower tank, the

1. V-8 Coolant Circulation

2. Oldsmobile Fan Shroud

3. Vega Coolant Siphon

Cooling System Capacity in Quarts	"Prestone" Brand Anti-Freeze Coolant Required (in Quarts)											
	2	3	4	5	6	7	8	9	10	11	12	13
5	−12°	−62°										
6	0°	−34°										
7	6°	−17°	−54°									
8	10°	−7°	−34°	−69°								
9		0°	−21°	−50°								
10		4°	−12°	−34°	−62°							
11		8°	−6°	−23°	−47°							
12		10°	0°	−15°	−34°	−57°						
13			3°	−9°	−25°	−45°	−66°					
14			6°	−5°	−17°	−34°	−54°					
15			8°	0°	−12°	−26°	−43°	−62°				
16			10°	2°	−7°	−19°	−34°	−52°				
17				5°	−4°	−14°	−27°	−42°	−58°			
18				7°	0°	−10°	−21°	−34°	−50°	−65°		
19				9°	2°	−7°	−16°	−28°	−42°	−56°		
20				10°	4°	−3°	−12°	−22°	−34°	−48°	−62°	
21					6°	0°	−9°	−17°	−28°	−41°	−54°	−68°
22					8°	2°	−6°	−14°	−23°	−34°	−47°	−59°
23					9°	4°	−3°	−10°	−19°	−29°	−40°	−52°
24					10°	5°	0°	−7°	−15°	−24°	−34°	−46°

4. Coolant Chart

greater the cooling effect that takes place in the core. But the low-silhouette designs of recent years required that the vertical core be redesigned and so today, the crossflow or transverse core is popular. This amounts to tipping the radiator on its side, with the top and bottom tanks becoming side tanks and water flowing horizontally instead of vertically. In many transverse designs, the water pump pumps into the "bottom" tank (the one without the radiator cap). The result is reduced pressure against the cap, allowing the temperature to rise higher before the cap blows. "Blowing the cap" on a vertical tube radiator is common whenever the tubes get clogged with rust or scale. The water can't get down through the tubes, so it goes out through the cap. Changing the cap won't help, because there's nothing wrong with it. The only remedy is to clean out, boil out, or rod out the tubes, depending on how bad they are.

In a transverse core radiator, plugged tubes will slow down the circulation and

1. Coolant circulation is a simple but essential system to proper operation of an engine. Any blockage in the path of the arrows will cause overheating, possible damage.

2. Fan shrouds come and fan shrouds go, but Oldsmobile's Venturi Ring is the most sophisticated yet. The ring only clears the tips of the fan blades by 2/10-in., which makes the fan more efficient. In order to maintain the blade tip clearance, the venturi ring is mounted on the engine, with a flexible rubber seal between the ring and the radiator shroud.

3. In case you hadn't noticed, the Chevy Vegas coming out now do not have any coolant drains. The only way to change the coolant is to siphon it out. Easiest way is with Thexton's new Syphone-Aire, which uses air or mouth pressure to start the siphoning action.

4. Cooling system capacity can be found in your owner's manual, and then with this chart you can add antifreeze to protect to the lowest expected temperature.

5. The same cars often have different fan assemblies. Make sure you replace with fan of your model.

may cause overheating, but they will not cause the cap to blow and lose water because the water pump is exerting pressure on the "bottom" tank. There have even been some vertical designs that pumped into the bottom tank (notably Pontiac), but they aren't common.

FAN DESIGN

To increase the radiator's cooling action, a fan mounted on the water pump shaft and driven by the same belt draws air through the radiator core. There are several types in use: the fixed fan that rotates constantly with the pump shaft; a thermostatic fan that slows down when cooling is not needed; a centrifugal fan that reduces its speed at high engine rpm; a fluid coupling fan that adjusts its speed to driving conditions; a flexible blade fan that reduces pitch at higher speeds for easier turning, etc. As any fan requires engine power to rotate, these latter types reduce drag on the engine and so increase available horsepower. If radiator placement is too far from the fan, a sheetmetal shroud is used to prevent recirculation of the same air, thereby increasing the fan's efficiency. Blade number and arrangement differ depending upon requirements.

CAPS AND PRESSURE

Pressurizing a radiator system improves its cooling efficiency and prevents evaporation and surge losses. The pressure cap increases air pressure in the system by several pounds per square inch, allowing water to be circulated at higher temperatures without boiling. With the greater difference between the water and outside air, heat passes from the water faster. A pressure cap contains a blowoff valve and a vacuum valve and seats tightly over both the filler mouth and its edges. A calibrated spring in the blowoff valve holds the valve closed, producing pressure in the system. If the pressure exceeds the amount for which the system was designed, the valve blows off its seat, relieving the excess. When the engine has been shut off and cools down, a vacuum might form, dropping the inside pressure sufficiently to let outside air pressure collapse it. If a vacuum does start to form, the vacuum

5. Fan Assemblies

valve opens to let air into the system before damage is done.

Many cooling systems now use a coolant recovery system in conjunction with the radiator. This small additional tank provides room for its expansion. It eliminates loss of coolant when the engine is turned off and "boils over." The pressure cap used on a radiator with a recovery system must have a gravity-operated vacuum valve. If the vacuum valve is spring-loaded, it must hang open or it will prevent the flowback of coolant to the radiator.

ANTIFREEZE

Up to this point, we've referred to coolant and water as one and the same, but ordinary water is no longer recommended and seldom used today except in emergencies. Antifreeze solutions with an ethylene glycol base have replaced the use of plain water. When mixed proportionately with water, they provide protection from freezing temperatures and prevent a cracked engine block. They also contain additives to combat corrosion and neutralize rust formed in the engine block before it can plug the radiator core.

For best corrosion resistance and rust prevention, a 50% solution of antifreeze and water should be used. This will raise the boiling point at sea level to 227° F.; 15° higher than plain water. And a 50% solution will lower the freezing point to -34° F. That is much lower than most areas need, but the 50% solution should be maintained even in hot climates because of its corrosion protection.

Glycol is more expensive initially, but it doesn't boil away, and it's a good water pump lubricant. However, if you have a leaking head gasket, a cracked block or cylinder head, the glycol will pass into the oil, and contaminate it very quickly.

Cooling System

If it's not caught in time, this can lead to a locked-up engine, since glycol will congeal when it mixes with oil and in doing so, completely plug oil pump screens, oil filters and oil passages. A white discoloration on the dipstick is the danger signal, and the most convenient check point is the oil filter. If the filter sludge looks like curdled milk and molasses, you've got troubles, but it's worth attempting an oil flush before bracing yourself for a complete engine teardown to clean up the mess.

Hustle down to your local paint supply store or wholesale dealer and purchase a quantity of butyl "Cellosolve." A retardant used to slow the action of solvent, butyl "Cellosolve" is packaged on a regional basis according to frequency of use; in warm climates, it's available in 5-gal. or larger containers, but those who live in colder areas can find it in 1-qt. cans. How much you'll need depends upon your crankcase capacity. Figure adding two parts butyl "Cellosolve" to one part SAE 10 oil.

Drain the engine oil while it's warm. If your engine uses a disposable oil filter, leave it in place; if it has a cartridge filter, remove the filter and replace the empty can. Fill the engine with the mixture then start it up and run at fast idle, watching the oil pressure and operating temperature carefully during this time. The oil pressure should read normal and operating temperature must remain above 150° F.

Stop the engine after approximately 45 mins. to 1 hr. and drain the crankcase. If the contamination was really severe, it may be necessary to repeat the operation more than once to completely dissolve the sludge. After you're satisfied that the sludge is gone, refill the engine with a flushing oil or fresh 10W oil and run at fast idle for another 10-15 mins. Drain the flush oil and then replace the disposable oil filter with a new one, or insert a clean cartridge into the can, and refill the crankcase with the oil you'd normally use. Having saved the engine from total disaster, all you have to do now is find the leak and correct it before driving the car again.

It may be possible to free a "seized" engine by circulating hot water of at least 140° F. through the cooling system. Attach a hose from a hot water source to a nipple installed in a core plug hole, then allow the water to flow through the engine and out through the radiator fill neck. If the engine will turn over on the starter, follow the steps outlined above with butyl "Cellosolve."

If the engine doesn't turn over, remove the spark plugs and pour undiluted butyl "Cellosolve" through each hole until the pistons are covered. Wait about 15 mins., then jump on the starter again. Let it spin until the mixture has been pumped out through the plug holes. Now, replace the plugs and, again, follow the steps indicated above with butyl "Cellosolve."

Anti-leak antifreezes have been on the market since about 1969. Some people

1. Pump Components

2. Vacuum Valve

3. Coolant Reserve System

feel that there is a danger of plugging up the cooling system, that perhaps anti-leak really means anti-flow. Such fears are groundless. In the few cases where plugging has occurred, the cooling system was on its last legs, with rust-clogged passages that probably would have plugged up anyway the first time the car hit a good bump and shifted the sediment around. The cooling system should never be drained and new anti-freeze dumped in unless you flush it out. And it's a good idea to use flushing chemicals, too.

In 1972, Prestone announced a new antifreeze called Prestone II. It has a new formulation for better engine protection and without any anti-leak properties. So those of you who didn't feel quite comfortable with the anti-leak formulas can now head for your nearest Prestone dealer. If you like anti-leak, look for du-Pont or Dow brands.

1. Water pumps should be replaced as a unit, but an understanding of how they are constructed can help when you try to diagnose problems

2. This type of cap is open to the atmosphere until the rush of air or coolant trying to escape closes the vacuum valve. A cap like this is easier on the radiator because the system is only under pressure part of the time. Other types have a spring on the vacuum valve, which does not allow any pressure to escape. Spring-type vacuum valves will not work with a coolant recovery system. Use the open type.

3. Coolant reserve systems, such as this '73 Dodge version, prevent the loss of radiator coolant. Special pressure cap allows coolant to overflow into plastic reserve tank. When engine cools, pressure differences between tank and radiator cause coolant to flow back into radiator.

4. This pressure tester will determine if there are internal leaks in the cooling system.

5. Add an adapter and you can also test the cap. This one's a dud.

6. Three types of intercoolers. Fitted into the radiator's bottom tank, they allow automatic transmission fluid to circulate for cooling, preventing transmission overheating.

7. Service stations usually have a Bloc-Chek kit. This simple test for exhaust gas leakage involves a change of fluid color if gas is present.

RUNNING PURE WATER

In older cars, you could run pure water with a rust inhibitor and not hurt a thing. Don't try this on a late-model car, because your hot indicator warning light will not work with pure water. Here's why. New cars recently came from the factory in most cases with a 33% anti-freeze solution and a 14-lb. pressure cap. With this combination, the coolant will boil at approximately 256° F. Temperatures in the 250° range may seem awfully hot, but they won't hurt the engine as long as the coolant doesn't boil.

4. Pressure Testing

5. Cap Pressure Check

7. Exhaust Gas Check

6. Intercoolers

With no danger present at the lower temperatures, the engineers designed the warning light to come on at about 256° F. If you run pure water, it will boil at 247° with the factory 14-lb. cap. Thus, with pure water your engine could be boiling, sustaining a lot of damage from uneven cooling, and the hot warning light would never come on. For proper warning light operation, you must run at least a 33% antifreeze solution, and 50% is even better. New cars are now coming off the end of the assembly line with 44-55% antifreeze. Your owner's manual will tell you how much you should have. If not, stick with the 50% solution.

COOLANT ADDITIVES

There are many chemical compounds and additives on the market designed to give last-minute hope to the unfortunate soul facing a major radiator repair job. These chemicals range from pellets to be dropped in the radiator to fluids designed to dissolve rust or stop radiator leaks. Use of these products inevitably guarantees that the repair will have to be done anyway, but buying a $3.00 can appeals to the innocent who is otherwise faced with a large repair bill, and he figures it's worth the gamble. Radiator shops will tell you that stop-leak prod-

ucts are really one of their most dependable business builders, followed closely by the anti-rust solutions. However, many new cars come from the factory with some kind of anti-leak chemical in the cooling system. The difference is that the factory knows exactly how much to put in. They don't just dump a lot of goop in that will plug everything up.

If the leak is a minor one, the stop-leak solution may work temporarily, but most drivers then put off the inevitable repair and that's where they make their mistake. Remember, the radiator is made of brass and copper and these metals don't rust—they corrode. Corrosion is a chemical process that is self-accelerating in nature and once it starts, the affected area must be completely cleaned to stop it.

Any rust found in the coolant comes from the engine's water jacket and can settle in the tiny radiator tube passages, blocking coolant flow. So you're actually faced with two different problems that using chemicals to solve will only aggravate. Anti-rust solutions will actually free rust that has accumulated in the water jacket passages and let it circulate into the radiator; stop-leak solutions will plug minor holes that corrosion continues to enlarge.

But if you have one of the 1973 Hornets without air conditioning, it's probably fitted with an aluminum fin radiator; check before you add anything to the cooling system. These are identified by two decals containing warning and repair information. Hot water or steam are the only cleaning agents to use, as anything caustic will eat holes in it faster than moths in a wool factory. Repairs should be done only with Alcoa Flux #64, 30/70 or 40/60 tin-lead solder and a minimum of heat.

So what's the answer? Simple—change the coolant at regular intervals. All major brands of antifreeze contain additives to

Cooling System

prevent radiator corrosion and the formation of rust in the block, but these additives wear out long before the antifreeze itself. Change the coolant once a year and save yourself a lot of headaches. If you're old-fashioned and still insist on running water during the summer months, be sure to use anti-corrosion and rust inhibitor additives with it or you'll defeat everything that antifreeze has done for your cooling system.

The new super cooling additives are another controversy. They are supposed to transfer heat better than any antifreeze, and thereby keep the engine cooler. Prestone engineers tell us that they have never found a chemical on the market that will increase the heat transfer any better than antifreeze. And in some cases the super cooling additives will affect the anti-foaming properties of the antifreeze, thus giving less efficient cooling.

FINDING LEAKS

One source of damaging corrosion comes from exhaust gas leaking into the cooling system. The strong acids in the gas combine with the water in the coolant and eat away at the radiator tubes.

You can also check exhaust gas leakage by using a block check kit. Insert the block check tool into the radiator filler neck and hold just above the coolant level. Squeeze the bulb and fill with air. If the tool fluid changes from its normal blue to a transparent yellow, exhaust gas is present. By running the engine with the spark plugs grounded on one bank at a time, you can determine which head gasket is at fault on a V-8 engine. An equally simple way is to disconnect the upper hose, drain the radiator until the coolant is just above the cylinder head and remove both thermostat and fan belt. Start the engine and accelerate rapidly a few times. If exhaust gas is leaking, the coolant level should rise considerably, and bubbles will appear.

Water leaks in the cooling system will cause a loss of pressure and can lead to serious problems. To check for a water leak, top up the radiator to about ½-in. of the filler neck and run the engine until it's at operating temperature. Then attach a pressure tester in place of the cap and apply 15 psi pressure. If it holds steady, there's no leak, but a pressure drop tells you to check the hose connections, water pump, radiator and engine expansion plugs for an external leak. If the pressure tester needle fluctuates, you've got an exhaust gas leak that should be checked out. Pressure caps can also fail and should be checked with the same tester. If your cap won't hold the rated pressure, replace it with a new one of the proper rating.

Some radiators contain special tubing in the bottom tank that acts as an intercooler or heat exchanger. Automatic transmission fluid flows through this intercooler and prevents the transmission from overheating. An intercooler leak not only affects your cooling system's performance but can spell transmission problems if it's not taken care of.

1. Thermostat Operation

2. Flushing Coolant

THERMOSTATS

Check the thermostat when you change the coolant. This simple temperature-sensitive valve tends to fail gradually, either from corrosion or foreign matter. Thermostat failure (or the use of none at all) means that the engine will not reach its proper operating temperature because the coolant circulates through both it and the radiator at all times. Operation below proper temperatures results in premature engine wear. The heater also works very inefficiently, if at all, a condition easily noticed during cold winter months, but not necessarily in the summer. Unscrewing the cap screws holding its housing lets you reach the thermostat easily. The housing is usually found at the point where the outlet hose is attached to the engine. Avoid a mess by draining the coolant below the housing level before loosening the bolts.

Thermostats are marked with their designated opening point (usually 180° through 205° F.) and you should always use the exact one specified for your engine. To test your old thermostat or even

3. Stuck Thermostat

a new one (brand new is no guarantee that it will work), rig up a simple apparatus and borrow the kitchen stove. You'll need a water container, preferably Pyrex or equivalent so you can see better, a household cooking thermometer that reads up to 250° or so, a wire hook to suspend the thermostat, a feeler gauge and a piece of string. Insert the feeler gauge between the valve and its seat and attach the string to the gauge.

You'll need the temperature figures for both the initial and fully opened positions. These are available from your dealer or wherever you buy the new

4. Bolt-in Core Plugs

6. Thermostat Bleed Hole

1. Replacement is the only cure for a faulty thermostat. Always check the specs for your engine, since the old unit may have failed because it was the wrong one.

2. Prestone recommends this method of flushing the cooling system. Note accessory deflector in radiator neck.

3. This thermostat is stuck open— but instead of causing cold running, it actually caused overheating, because it was stuck half-way open and didn't allow enough coolant to pass through the system.

4. Bolt-in core plugs are a cinch to install, and to remove if necessary. Some types of block heating elements are inserted in these holes.

5. If you suspect that your dash's temp gauge or light isn't honest, you can check the actual, warmed-up temperature of your radiator water with a high-range thermometer. Most radiator shops will have one and should be glad to check it for you.

6. A thermostat must seal tightly if it is going to give a quick engine warm-up. We have found samples of this particular design of thermostat that allowed enough of a gap when they were closed to give the engine an inordinately long warm-up time. All thermostats have bleed holes to enable air trapped in the block to escape (arrow).

7. Sometimes it's a tricky job to remove spring-type radiator hose clamps. These special pliers make clamp removal a simple, easy chore.

5. Checking Radiator Temperature

7. Spring-Type Hose Clamp

thermostat. It must not touch any surface while being heated and the water should be stirred gently to ensure even distribution of the heat. A typical set of specs for a 195° thermostat is that a .003-in. gauge should slip free within + 3° of the rating and the valve should be fully open at 218° F. To replace the thermostat, let it rest in position with the longer or valve end toward the engine, then refasten the housing. You'll need a new housing gasket which can be purchased ready-cut from a dealership or made at home from ordinary cork gasket stock. The mating surfaces should be clean and the gasket coated with cooling system sealant. The hose is reattached using a screw-type attaching clamp.

FLUSHING PROCEDURES

The average car owner's idea of flushing consists of opening the petcock on the radiator bottom and maybe the two on each side of the engine block (the Vega has none and must be siphoned), sticking a garden hose in the radiator and letting the water flow. Unfortunately, this accomplishes very little. Outside faucets are normally connected only to cold water, so sticking the hose into the radiator filler opening and waiting until the water from the drain cock appears to be clear flushes only the radiator. The cold water keeps the thermostat leading to the engine cooling passages closed and even if the engine drains are open in this procedure, there's incomplete circulation, with residue from old dirty coolant remaining in the engine. The following

step-by-step procedure is basic to an effective annual coolant change.

1) Set heater temperature control to "high." If your car is equipped with a vacuum-operated heater valve (check with your dealer—this is found mainly on newer cars with factory air conditioning), run the engine at idle during all flushing procedures described, as a vacuum valve will only stay open with the engine running. Keep a close watch on the engine temperature gauge.

2) Open radiator drain cock and let radiator drain. Do not open engine drain cocks.

3) Remove radiator cap and put a deflection elbow in the filler neck to prevent excessive splash into the engine compartment.

4) Remove hose from heater supply nipple at the engine block. Point this hose downward for drain.

5) Connect water supply to the heater supply nipple at the engine block. This does not have to be a positive connection; an ordinary garden hose will do as long as most of the water can be directed into the engine.

6) Turn on the water, make sure it is cold and flush for 3 to 5 mins. without the engine running, unless you have a vacuum valve. Squeeze the outlet or upper radiator hose during the last minute of flushing to remove any trapped liquid.

7) Turn off water and close radiator petcock. Reconnect heater supply hose to its nipple and remove deflection elbow from radiator. Be sure the system is normally full of coolant.

CORE PLUGS

Every engine has at least seven "freeze" or core plugs—three on each side of the block and one in the back. These are filled with metal, but it's softer and thinner than the block material. If the coolant freezes, the expanding fluid pushes out the plugs, sometimes preventing block damage but not always. Core plugs are subject to corrosion and can develop small leaks. Most are a simple press fit and can be removed if faulty by drilling a hole in the center and prying out with a screwdriver. Drain the block before starting work and take care not to let pieces of the plug fall into the coolant passage. The same press-in replacement type can be used but bolt-in plugs are easier to seat and remove. These use a toggle bolt that slips into the water jacket, with the plug bolting up with a gasket or O-ring between itself and the block.

HOSE REPLACEMENT

You can sometimes tell how good a hose is by its appearance and feel, but many hoses have a spiral wire reinforcement inside, and this can rust and disintegrate without affecting the outside appearance. Squeeze the hose at midpoint and you should be able to feel the wire; if not, replace the hose. Unfasten the hose clamp, then twist as you pull the hose off. Stubborn hoses may have to be cut off with a knife. Apply a dab of sealing compound around the connecting nipple and fit the new hose over it.

Cooling System

Use screw-type clamps for replacement, as spring-type clamps may leak.

FAN BELTS

Fan belt tension should be checked periodically. Low tension means belt slippage, which will wear out the belt, let the battery run down and cause the engine to overheat. Too much tension overloads the water pump and wears it out prematurely. Adjust by loosening the alternator mounting bolt and moving it toward or away from the engine block before retightening. If you don't have access to a belt tension tool, you can set it by this rule of thumb—belt deflection with your thumb pushing on it, should be about ¼ in. at the midpoint of its longest unsupported section. A loose belt wears out fast, but a tight belt wears out the bushing (or bearing) in the water pump. So, if you don't have a tension gauge, keep that belt a little loose. Belts are much cheaper to replace than pumps.

HOT RODDING THE COOLING SYSTEM

Remember, the manufacturer put no more radiator into your car when it was built than was considered adequate to handle the original engine under normal driving conditions. So if you do anything to significantly add horsepower or change to a larger engine, you should change radiators too. If you have a 1960 model or later, it's likely that there's a heavy-duty package available for it. This package will include the automatic transmission cooler, fan, and water pump with the radiator. But if you stuff a Hemi in a Plymouth Belvedere that came factory-equipped with a Slant-6, you'll have to add a radiator which the factory designed for use with the Hemi. Depending upon your car, this may or may not bolt right in, but there should be no great problem in the installation. Just secure it at the four corners, make sure the fan has proper clearance and connect a pair of universal hoses. Be sure to change the thermostat and pressure cap to conform to Hemi specs.

If the old radiator adequately protects against overheating, there's no point in putting in a larger one. And don't think of radiator "bigness" in terms of coolant capacity; the Model A Ford had a radiator twice the capacity of a current Mustang equipped with a 289-cu.-in. V-8. The differences are the improvement in pump efficiency and the pressurized system, not to mention that the fins are in a better cooling arrangement than the A's old cellular structure.

Eliminating the fan should be approached with caution. You can sometimes improve the engine efficiency if your driving doesn't involve much city traffic. In cases of marginal overheating caused by hopping up the engine, the shrouds used with air-conditioned cars will usually clip right into their non-air-conditioned counterparts. For more extreme modifications, where the shape of

1. Auxiliary Flex-O-Kool

2. Belt Deflection

3. Types of Clamps

4. Accessory Oil Coolers

the radiator is important to achieve a desired styling effect, any competent radiator specialty shop can adapt almost any radiator to your needs, but this is expensive.

Take care when you buy a chrome-plated pressure cap; it must be designed to operate at the same pressure as the original. Radiator covers, which can be as simple as a window-shade-like arrangement pulled by a string from the dashboard, help warmup in extremely cold climates. Visual indicators for the coolant level are quite helpful in discouraging the service station attendant from opening the pressure cap. Filters are sold for cooling systems, but if they contain chemicals, they may not be compatible with the brand of antifreeze you use.

Radiators through the years have been made in different basic designs. The cellular is somewhat inefficient because it won't pass the water fast enough. Tubular is better, but the comparatively recent tube-fin design, in which the fins are made in accordion pleats between the tubes, is a tremendous improvement over the plain tubular core. Changing to a tube-fin core might even solve a hot rod

cooling problem for you if you were trying to run a big engine in a small car that won't accommodate a large size radiator.

That's about all there is to a cooling system. Now if you can just stop service station attendants from removing your radiator cap when your engine is hot and allowing all of your antifreeze to burble out on the ground, you've got it made.

1. Easiest oil cooler to install is the Flex-O-Kool. Bend it to desired shape and wire it to radiator. We installed a Flex-O-Kool on a flathead Ford, it reduced temperatures, and decreased oil consumption. It's available from Car Care Parts, 6900 Valjean Ave., Van Nuys, Calif. 91406.

2. Set belt tension by rule of thumb. Quarter-inch deflection at midpoint saves belt as well as bushings.

3. The wire-type clamp on the left is often used by the factory, but does not seal very well when it gets old. Throw it away and use screw-type.

4. Accessory oil coolers come in all shapes and sizes. If placed where fan causes air blast, they will definitely keep temperature down.

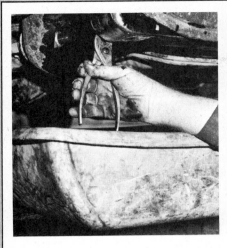

1. Removing a radiator is one of the easiest things you can do in your own backyard. Place a container beneath the drain cock to catch the coolant.

2. Remove the radiator cap so air can displace coolant, then open drain and let fluid out. When radiator is empty, loosen upper connecting hose clamp.

3. Grasp the hose and twist it as you pull it off. It may require twisting back and forth several times to break the hose loose from radiator inlet.

4. The lower hose is usually hard to reach from above. Use an extra long screwdriver to avoid scraped knuckles, or you may have to reach it from below.

5. The automatic transmission cooling lines are best disconnected from below using an open-end wrench. Jacking car up may make access to lines easier.

6. Now, remove the capscrews that hold the radiator shield in place. A box wrench is best to avoid rounding off the heads of the capscrews.

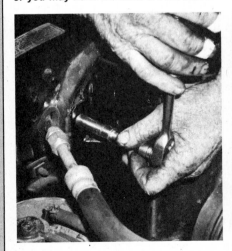

7. A socket wrench will come in handy when you take out the bolts holding the radiator. There are usually four, one in each corner of the frame.

8. Lift the radiator up and out, angling it if necessary. Be careful to not scrape fin surface. On some cars removal of the fan may be necessary.

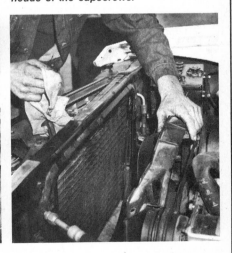

9. Either hang the shield back behind the fan pulley or remove it. Now you are ready for a trip to the radiator shop for repair or cleaning.

HOW-TO: Removing Water Pump

1. Before pulling the water pump, it will be necessary to remove everything blocking access. Here we've unbolted the air-conditioning pump.

2. Once we've got clear access to the water pump, all connecting hoses are detached. Drain radiator to prevent a mess and to save coolant fluid.

3. The fan usually has to come off to provide clearance for pump removal. Be careful not to gouge the radiator fins. Finally, remove the drive belt.

4. After all the pump retaining bolts have been removed, a sharp blow with a mallet will break the pump loose. Some may require only wiggling.

5. Before replacing new water pump, use a dab or spray of adhesive to set the gasket in place. It's no fun to get pump on, then find a gasket leak.

6. Other problems may arise when you dig into the water pump area. Extreme corrosion as shown here means that the radiator hose has to be replaced.

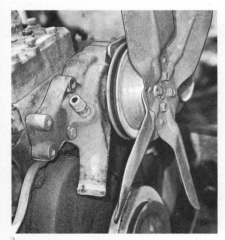

7. In days past, water pumps were relatively simple affairs. It took only the removal of six bolts to remove the pump from a Kaiser-Frazer engine.

8. The pumps used on the 6-cylinder Ramblers were a snap to remove, too. Taking off one V-belt and five bolts put the whole thing right in your hand.

9. But now, the average V-8 engine pump is more complex. You'll have to pull the fan, a pair of belts and three hoses to get this one off a Buick.

10. Other side of the same Buick shows alternator and three hoses which must be removed for pump access. Be sure new hoses are available, just in case.

11. The F-85 uses a shield to protect the distributor in case of water pump failure. It will come off when you remove the water pump unit.

12. Similar to the Galaxie, this Fairlane pump has the alternator bracket attached. It has to be removed before the water pump can be taken off.

13. On the Galaxie 500, the pump has a bracket on either side. Both of them have to come off, making the job just that much more difficult.

14. Other side of the Galaxie looks clean, but that's because the fan and the radiator have been removed. This allows more wrench-swinging space.

15. The Bel Air pump has a bracket and two hoses that have to come off. This will be a greasy, grimy job on older cars with a lot of mileage piled up.

16. Once everything is stripped off, as on this Catalina, there should be no difficulty in getting at the water pump itself. Again, it's a dirty job.

17. Although it may be funny looking when you get right down to it, your Dart or GT won't run very long if the pump fails. This one's easy to pull.

18. Check the thickness and the number of gaskets on the pump. Some pumps may require two gaskets so the impeller doesn't hit block inside pump cavity.

Exhaust System

Many people consider a car's exhaust system in the same light as a sewer pipe. It's necessary, but it isn't something that is very interesting or pleasant to work on. But an exhaust system is not just a bunch of tubes to get rid of waste gases. It can result in your engine running good or bad because of a little gadget in the exhaust called the exhaust manifold heat valve. Many engines have this valve, whether they are 4's, 6's or V-8's. Its purpose is to block the direct exit of the exhaust gases from the manifold and force them along a path that leads through the intake manifold under the carburetor. The exhaust gases heat up the passages in the intake manifold and thereby aid in more complete vaporization of the gasoline. Good vaporization is necessary to prevent a stumble when you step on the throttle. Believe us, the exhaust heat valve really does its job. We have seen engines that could be warmed up until they were just about as hot as you could get them and they would still stumble when you step on the throttle just because the heat valve was frozen in an open position. Free up the valve so that it worked properly and the car would run like it was just off the showroom floor. Cars that do not have the heat valve in their exhaust system usually circulate coolant from the engine block through a passageway in the intake manifold just under the carburetor. Some late model cars have been able to do away with the heat valve because they have a hot air inlet on the air cleaner for the carburetor.

Exhaust heat valves are usually held in the closed position by both a weight and a spring. The spring relaxes as the exhaust heats up because not as much heat is needed under the carburetor when the engine is warm. The weight is offset so that it has a tendency to hold the valve in the closed position, but the valve itself is also offset on a shaft so that any excess rush of exhaust gases will have a tendency to open it. A combination of these factors results in an exhaust heat valve that forces the right amount of exhaust gas through the heating passages in the intake manifold so that the engine operates without any stumble and has sufficient vaporization of the gas to get good gas mileage.

HEAT VALVE PROBLEMS

The valve, regardless of type, can cause a lot of trouble under certain conditions. If the car is driven only short distances at a time and never completely warmed up, the conditions are present in the heavy condensation of moisture while the engine is cold plus the extra carbon caused by the engine running "rich" on a partial choke setting. The moisture and carbon don't need much time to "freeze" the shaft on the butterfly valve in the closed position. Once rust and carbon have a good grip on these exhaust thermostat valves, all the high-speed driving in the world won't free them. All exhaust gases from the cylinders on the side with the "frozen" heat valve must therefore pass through the heat riser passages of the intake manifold. Not only does this make four cylinders practically useless but it also insures an over-supply of heat to the base of the carburetor, making "vapor-lock" a cause of distress in many cases.

If the car is factory equipped with a dual exhaust system, a butterfly-type heat valve will be located between one of the exhaust manifolds and the exhaust headpipe which leads to the muffler. If this valve should become "frozen" due to the above conditions (excessive oil consumption will also help "freeze" the heat valves), the exhaust must still pass through the intake manifold risers and into the opposite exhaust manifold.

If your car uses the obsolete, internal "duck bill" heat valve, the crosspipe between manifolds has to be taken off to make sure that the valve is not choked shut. The other type with an external spring and weight can be checked while

1. Exhaust Manifold Heat Valve

2. Replacing Muffler

3. Cutting Valve Shaft

cool to make sure that the shaft through the collar holding the butterfly valve will move freely. If frozen, it can sometimes be loosened by moving back and forth by hand until the rust is broken loose, then lubricating with special manifold heat valve lubricant. If this doesn't do the job, then a new valve should be installed in its place.

TYPES OF MUFFLERS

Most stock mufflers are designed to lower noise to a minimum and contain a series of baffles and noise-deadening chambers through which the gases must pass. These stock mufflers have a restrictive effect on the exhaust gases but this restriction is not too great at low engine speeds. As the engine speed increases and more gases are crammed through the muffler, the back pressure in the system increases and engine efficiency is lowered. This well known fact has been the big reason for the popularity of dual exhaust systems for many years among the hot rodders, and it is also the reason that most of the higher powered stock cars use dual exhaust systems.

By using a dual system, the automotive manufacturer has cut in half the volume of gases to be muffled by a stock muffler but he has also increased noise. The

1. The exhaust manifold heat valve, at the end of the exhaust manifold, tends to have deposits build up on the baffle shaft, causing the valve to stick and the engine to either vapor lock or stumble on takeoff.

2. Chances of fixing an exhausted exhaust system are next to nil. Most become so corroded by salt or sulphur that the repair job becomes strictly "remove and replace."

3. When carbon and rust "freeze" the exhaust heat valve, best bet is to replace it. Here the valve shaft is cut with a torch; you can use a hacksaw to do the same thing.

4. New shaft and weight assembly is inserted through butterfly heat valve in exhaust headpipe.

5. Spring is fitted on shaft with end of spring against headpipe stud.

6. Retaining spring fits over end of heat valve shaft and headpipe stud. Spring and weight hold valve in closed position.

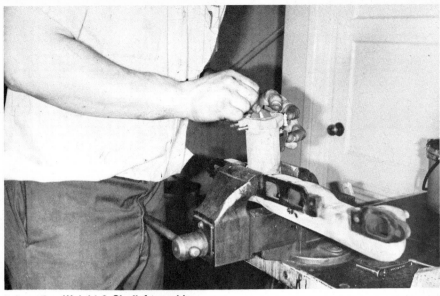

4. Inserting Weight & Shaft Assembly

5. Fitting Spring on Shaft

6. Retaining Spring

Exhaust System

fewer cylinders per muffler, the more the noise. In other words, a stock muffler for each 4-cylinder bank of a V-8 engine will produce more noise than if one of the same mufflers is used for all eight cylinders. To keep this noise down, the number of baffles and chambers has been increased, with the end effect that the newly found horsepower due to the dual system is lost, especially at high engine speeds, due to the increased restriction and back pressure in the muffler.

Straight-through type mufflers are, as the name implies, straight-through with no restrictive baffles or chambers. The center pipe can either be slotted, drilled, louvered, saw cut or even a large twisted spring type. The area between the center pipes and the muffler shell is then packed with steel shavings or fiberglass to absorb the exhaust noise that passes through the openings in the center pipe. While very efficient in exhausting the burned gases, the straight-through type does not always lower the exhaust noise to the desirable minimum. If the noise level is too high after the installation of the straight-through mufflers, a resonator muffler can be added.

The resonator muffler is actually in most cases just a short-length, straight-through muffler, either glass or steel packed, that is installed in the exhaust system to provide extra sound muffling to the exhaust. These resonators can sometimes be placed in the tailpipe behind the regular muffler to provide maximum quietness. Exhaust gases cool off as they near the rear of the car, which causes the volume of gas to be lessened. When resonators are installed near the end of the exhaust system, the cooler gases are more easily muffled due to the decrease in their volume.

While the heat valve is, as mentioned, one of the main causes of grief in the exhaust system, the prime enemy of the entire system is the moisture content of the exhaust gases. This moisture is by no means pure water but contains all sorts of corrosives, the main one being sulfuric acid from the sulfur content of the gasoline and oil. In a car that is being operated mainly for short trips, such as going to the store or school, this acid-laden moisture can collect in all sorts of places where it eats away at the thin-metal exhaust pipes and muffler shell until these pieces look as if moths with tungsten carbide teeth have been at them. Particular trouble spots are dips in the tailpipes ahead of the rear axle, the section just behind the axle, the rear end of the headpipe and the bottom of the muffler shell.

Other areas prone to attack are, unfortunately, the joints where the various pipes are attached to each other, which can make things a bit tough to pull apart. However, there is one good thing about it: This is the one area of repair where you can vent your feelings with a hammer and chisel and epithets.

MUFFLER REPLACEMENT

There is no such thing as "repairing" or "fixing" a deteriorated exhaust system; all you can do is replace it. Conse-

1. Welding Valve

2. Cutaway of a Typical Muffler

3. Exhaust Flow Through a Muffler

4. Bracket and Clamp Support

quently, as long as you confine your attentions to the pipework and muffler, you can bang away to your heart's content. If you have access to a torch and know how to use it, you can flame-cut the corroded joints—which is how the professionals do it—but it isn't absolutely necessary. All that is needed is a hammer, a round-nose or diamond point chisel, a hacksaw and a set of open- or box-end wrenches. Exhaust system work is neither the cleanest nor the messiest form of auto repair work but it is pretty much the simplest and, for the home or amateur mechanic, generally the starting point after plug-changing and simple tune-ups to bolster his confidence.

The first step in any exhaust work, unless you're a midget or claim kinship to the worm family, is to get the car up off the ground. If you can gain access to the use of a hoist or greasepit, so much the better but it isn't necessary. What is necessary is a safe method of supporting the car. By "safe" we don't mean a couple of bumper jacks or packing crates. If you can possibly afford it, purchase four adjustable jack stands from any parts house, Sears, Montgomery Ward or one of the automotive chain outfits such as

5. Bent Tailpipe

1. As butterfly valve revolves freely on shaft, the two are welded with the valve in the closed position. Screw seen here was wedged in against valve to hold it correctly for welding and is removed once job is finished.

2. The quiet stock mufflers, with their many pipes, chambers and baffles, tend to corrode faster than the straight-throughs because they trap and retain exhaust condensation, which is loaded with sulphuric acid.

3. The restrictive nature of common mufflers will seriously affect the high-speed operation of an internal combustion engine. More efficient dual exhaust systems, featuring either smaller mufflers or straight-throughs, can be purchased and installed for less than $100.

4. U-clamps must be securely fastened with enough clearance for the bracket to stop any rattle problem.

5. This station wagon was backed too closely against a parking lot wall, causing a severe bend in the tailpipe that restricts exhaust passage. As you may not realize this happens, it's a good idea to periodically check the pipe.

6. These are the basic tools the pros use to make the job an easier one. Shown top row, from left: vise grip-type welding clamps, air-operated impact wrench; middle row, from left: hacksaw, pipe cutter; bottom row, from left: sheetmetal shears, ratchet-type box-end wrench, and a tube or pipe expander.

7. Even though the high sulphuric acid content of the exhaust gas condensation causes rapid deterioration of the muffler, some tightwads try to extend the life of their noise suppressors by covering the rust holes with pieces of sheetmetal.

6. Exhaust System Tools

7. Rusted Out Mufflers

Exhaust System

Pep Boys or Western Auto. If you can't see your way to such a purchase, borrow the stands. At the very least, go down to the lumberyard and get enough solid 4x8 blocks to hold the car securely once it has been jacked up. Never trust a jack to hold the car while you're working on it, except perhaps to change a tire. Bumper jacks can slip, and even hydraulic jacks can be inadvertently bumped and lose pressure in an instant.

Once you have the car up and blocked, get under it and look at the exhaust system. If the tailpipe shows signs of rot or corrosion, the muffler is almost sure to be the same way inside, even though it doesn't show on the outside. In virtually every case, you'll find that if the muffler needs replacing, so does the tailpipe, and vice versa. This is not necessarily true in the case of the headpipe, the pipe that leads from the manifold to the muffler. It's made of sterner stuff than the rest of the system, and since it's subjected to hotter gases, it tends to stay dry. But if the headpipe is corroded, it's a sure bet that the whole system needs replacing.

When removing exhaust parts, always work from the rear to the front. The tailpipe is removed first, then the muffler and then the exhaust pipe (headpipe). If you can't break the joints loose with Liquid Wrench and you don't have a torch to do it as a muffler man does, then you'll have to cut a slot in the pipe or muffler with a chisel. Of course, that ruins the pipe or muffler, but hopefully that's the part you want to replace anyway. Don't expect to do muffler work with a butane torch or blowtorch. Breaking rusty joints loose requires an oxy-acetylene torch.

Tap the headpipe along its length with a hammer. If it rings true, it's probably in good shape. If it doesn't, it's either cracked or corroded through and should be removed and replaced, which is a simple wrench job. Do the same thing with the crossover pipe in a single system, or if you're changing to duals, remove it entirely to make way for the new left-bank headpipe.

When purchasing new components, be sure you state not only the make and model but also whether the car is equipped with automatic shift or power steering, because these features sometimes require pipe routing that is different from those models not so equipped. With the new equipment in hand, installation is a breeze.

However, a certain amount of care should be taken. Headpipe ends should be thoroughly cleaned with a wire brush and coarse sandpaper if you are retaining the original units. If they are also being replaced, use a wire brush or a knife to scrape the manifold outlet flange surfaces. Make sure that there are no pieces of the original gasket material left, because it can cause a leak when the new gasket and pipe are installed.

Put all the clamps involved near their proper places along the pipe, leaving them loose enough to move freely back and forth. Lift the muffler and slide it on the headpipe, again leaving all clamps loose. Then slide the tailpipe over the rear axle and join it to the muffler. You may have to use a jack on the car frame to raise the frame and body high enough to get sufficient clearance to put the tailpipe in position. If so, put stands or blocks under the frame in case the jack should fail. Loosely bolt all the clamps that attach to the frame to their attachment points. Now the system is in place, but loose enough to move about within limits.

The next step is to align all the components so that none of the piping rubs against the frame, fuel lines or brake lines. In other words, the whole system must be completely isolated from other chassis components except where the various insulated clamps and straps attach to the frame. After a complete recheck, tighten all bolts and clamps so that you have a completely solid system.

There is one thing to remember: You cannot "repair" a faulty exhaust system. Any halfway attempts at plugging holes or making temporary repairs could create a fire hazard or cost you your life, either from carbon monoxide inhalation or from the drowsiness it can cause at the wheel. Replace worn-out components and visually check the system from time to time while the car is being serviced. And watch that heat valve; if you keep it free, your exhaust system will last twice as long—to say nothing of how much better the car will run.

CATALYTIC CONVERTERS

Although the highly touted catalytic converter now used on all cars and most light-duty trucks may not seem to have a proper place in this chapter, it really does. Although it is part of the emissions control systems, which are largely add-

1. Neglected Exhaust System

2. Variety of Mufflers

208/BASIC AUTO REPAIR MANUAL

ons in the vicinity of the induction system, the converter lies downstream in the exhaust system, where it can catch last-minute pollutants that are about to exit from the tailpipe.

Sometime mechanics who are not well-informed about the function of the converter may assume that it is a severe deterrent to the exhaust, which is theoretically supposed to flow from an engine with as little back-pressure as possible (to abet engine breathing). The converter, which looks a little like some sort of muffler or resonator, may appear to be a stumbling block on the road to free-and-easy exhaust. But whatever you do under your car, don't—repeat, *don't*—yank the converter off and expect your car to run any better.

In the first place, a study has shown that the converter does not actually cause harmful build-up of exhaust back-pressure. In the second place, even if your car did run better, you wouldn't know it, because they wouldn't let you bring it to jail with you. That's right, it's a punishable offense to remove a catalytic converter except for the purpose of replacing the core.

Remember, the converter is there for a very specific reason: to help eliminate air pollutants. So let's learn to live with it by understanding precisely what its function on the car is.

Beginning with the 1975 model year, virtually all new cars sold in California and the great majority of 49-state vehicles were equipped with a catalytic converter system to lower hydrocarbon and carbon monoxide emissions. Two types of converters are presently in use: the GM/AMC units containing pellets coated with platinum and palladium, and the Ford/Chrysler units containing a ceramic "honeycomb" core coated with the same catalytic agents.

Regardless of type, all converter systems operate in the same way. Exhaust gases are passed through the converter, where the catalytic material converts HC and CO gases to harmless water and carbon dioxide by promoting further burning or oxidation of the pollutants. To provide sufficient fresh air for this process to take place, many engines also require an air pump system. The combustion-type reaction also raises the exhaust system's heat level by several hundred degrees, necessitating special heat-absorbing shields to protect the car's underbody.

Leaded gasoline contaminates and destroys the catalytic agent; thus all catalyst-equipped cars are fitted with a special fuel tank filler tube which accepts only the smaller fuel nozzles used to pump unleaded fuel.

But excessive richness in the air/fuel mixture will also ruin the converter.

3. Muffler Cutaway

4. Exhaust Pipe Hangers

1. Most mufflers are galvanized or otherwise protected against rust from road salt and water, but the truth is that they rot out from the inside due to corrosive exhaust gases. A bad exhaust system can be a fatal oversight, especially on Eastern cars whose floorpans may be rusted out too.

2. New car agencies stock mufflers and system components for their own brand(s) of cars only, but specialty shops carry a variety of systems to fit most popular makes.

3. Mufflers vary in construction, and there is no way to repair them internally, due to rust-outs, etc. Cutaway shows internal makeup of unit.

4. Replace a clamp if it looks worn or frayed. There are many types to choose from, but pick the style that matches the one you're replacing.

5. Catalytic converters come in many shapes and sizes. They even vary in their location on exhaust systems between different makes. This is a '77 Chrysler with converters shielded to guard against possible grass fires (arrows A and B). First unit in system (A) is used only on California cars; the 49-state versions have converter B only.

5. Catalytic Converters

Exhaust System

Since high-speed deceleration increases the amount of unburned HC in the exhaust, at such times the converter becomes momentarily overloaded. The resulting heat from the reaction can melt the converter. Ford and Chrysler models are equipped with a catalyst protection system to prevent this, while GM and AMC models do not require such a protective system.

Far from foolproof, the catalytic converter can be rendered useless in several ways. Any engine condition—such as misfiring—which leads to an excessively rich exhaust will harm the catalyst. Running out of gas can also destroy the converter, especially if you pump the pedal and try to nurse the car along as far as possible before stopping.

If you should happen to run out of gas, shift the car into neutral as soon as you're aware of the problem, then coast over to the shoulder to stop. This will prevent damage to the converter and also leave sufficient gas in the fuel system so that you won't have to prime it when you've filled up the tank and are ready to start again.

Pumping the pedal or priming the carburetor to restart the engine should be avoided at all costs. Despite what you may have heard, regular servicing and tune-ups of a converter-equipped car are even more important than they were in the past.

EXHAUST GAS RECIRCULATION

In theory, at least, exhaust systems on the later-model cars should have a longer life because of the reduction of nitrogen oxides in the exhaust brought about by the introduction of the Exhaust Gas Recirculation system. EGR, as it's called, first appeared on 1972 Buicks, and variations of the system have been in use on all domestic cars since then. As high combustion temperatures make nitrogen and oxygen combine, nitrogen oxides form and pass through the system into the air as a pollutant. EGR systems simply recirculate exhaust gases through the engine intake manifold and into the cylinders, where they combine with the air/fuel mixture for combustion. Exhaust gases are relatively inert and burn at a considerably lower temperature than the air/fuel mixture in the cylinder at the moment of peak combustion. As a result, they dilute the combustion chamber charge, thus slowing the process of combustion and reducing the combustion temperature to a level where formation of nitrogen oxides is inhibited. EGR complements the AIR system that's been used for several years now to reduce the hydrocarbon and carbon monoxide content of exhaust gases.

A vacuum-operated recirculation-control valve—generally mounted at the rear of the engine manifold and connected to an inline temperature-control valve—is the heart of the EGR system. Vacuum supplied by the carburetor is blocked by the temperature-control valve whenever under-hood temperatures are below 55° F. When the throttle valves are opened beyond the idle position, vacuum is applied against the EGR valve-actuating diaphragm. As the diaphragm moves up against spring pressure, it opens the exhaust gas intake valve, allowing exhaust gases from the manifold exhaust crossover channels to be drawn back into the engine intake. The valve remains closed during idle and deceleration, when the addition of excessive exhaust gases to the air/fuel mixture would cause rough engine idling.

You can't disassemble or service the EGR valve or its companion temperture-control valve, but both can and should be checked periodically for correct operation. This is done by opening the throttle to 1500 rpm. At this point, the valve stem should move downward when the vacuum line is disconnected and upward when it's connected. If it doesn't move at all, replace the unit. While this movement can be felt by putting your hand under the rear of the valve, you're likely to get a bad burn from either the hot valve or the engine manifold. It's much smarter to hold a pocket mirror behind the valve where you can watch its operation as you remove and replace the vacuum line. Check the temperature-control valve when the engine is cold, because this assures that the under-hood temperature will be under 55° F. Start the engine and open the throttle to 1500 rpm. If the EGR valve stem moves as you increase the engine idle to this speed, the control valve should be replaced.

Maintenance of the valve is important, especially as the car gets older. If the valve sticks closed, you won't be able to tell from the engine's performance whether or not the system is functioning properly. And if it sticks in the open position, you'll have a great deal of difficulty starting the car and keeping it going at lower engine rpm. Such is the price of progress.

THE HEAT RISER VALVE GOES VACUUM

The thermostatic, coil-operated heat riser valve has had its ups and downs over the years, earning a rather so-so reputation for reliability on older cars, primarily because most of us forgot that

1. Tightening C-Clamp

2. Tacking Nut to Stud

it was even there. Now, in an attempt to produce better evaporation and a more precise distribution of the air/fuel mixture for '75 models, Ford and General Motors have replaced the thermostatic coil with vacuum operation. (Chrysler is still using the same system as before.)

GM applications of the heat riser (now called an Early Fuel Evaporation System) differ from engine to engine. Some use a vacuum solenoid controlled by a temperature switch, while others have a thermal vacuum switch actuated by coolant temperature. And a few, like Pontiac and its 350X engine series, combine the EFE valve operation with the EGR system, in that the same thermal vacuum switch is used to control both.

Ford chose to mount a vacuum diaphragm on the exhaust manifold, linking it mechanically to the heat riser's shaft. During a start-up period when coolant temperature is low, a ported vacuum switch lets vacuum reach the diaphragm, which pulls the valve closed. But as the engine warms up, the coolant temperature closes the vacuum switch. This blocks vacuum to the diaphragm and opens the heat riser valve.

You'd think that they would have done something to alleviate the old problem of a sticking heat riser valve shaft, like coating it with teflon, but they didn't. So despite the vacuum operation (one more vacuum device to check out), you should continue to periodically lubricate the shaft to prevent it from hanging up. 🦀

3. EGR and Temperature Control

4. Cross-section of EGR

5. AIR Diverter Valve

1. You can use a ½-in. socket and short extension attached to a ratchet to cinch down the nut on the end of the U-clamp. Make sure the nut is securely tightened so it won't work loose and cause a rattle.

2. The pros make sure the nut will never back out by tacking it to the stud. However, it's hacksaw time when an "R 'n R" is necessary.

3. EGR valve (1) is mounted on right rear of '73 Buick engine manifold; exhaust gas intake port connects to intake manifold exhaust crossover channel where it picks up exhaust gases. Valve is operated by vacuum from the carburetor and is controlled by the inline temperature control valve (2).

4. Cross-sectional view of Buick EGR valve shows how the system works. If valve sticks in open position, starting the car becomes a major problem.

5. AIR diverter valve attaches to rear of air pump and opens during sudden deceleration to pass air from pump outside the system. Bolts on this '73 Buick pump are torqued to 120-160 in.-lbs., but vibration causes them to work loose, so tighten bolts every few thousand miles.

6. The venturi vacuum control system used on Chrysler, Dodge and Plymouth cars differs from the ported control system such as Buick's in that an amplifier (1) is necessary to increase carburetor-provided vacuum to operate the EGR valve (2). Temperature control valve is firewall-mounted (3) and connected to amplifier unit. EGR valve is on left side of engine in various locations, depending upon engine size.

6. Venturi Vacuum Control System

Clutch & Flywheel

The clutch is a weak link, not because of any manufacturing oversight or lack of engineering but because it is designed that way. The car makers have tactfully admitted this by refusing to warranty the clutch under any circumstances. They will guarantee that it was manufactured properly and installed correctly, but after that you are on your own. Actually, a clutch is designed to wear out; how fast it wears out depends on you, the driver.

A clutch is nothing more than a rotary coupling device between the engine and transmission that can slip while it's gradually picking up the load of moving a car—and then hook up "solid" when the car gets rolling. Also, the clutch provides a way to disconnect the engine from the rear wheels in order to smoothly shift gears, allowing the car to be stopped without putting the transmission into neutral.

The clutch mechanism is quite simple. There is a friction disc that is splined to the transmission input shaft. This disc is squeezed between the engine flywheel and a heavy pressure plate inside a clutch cover or housing which is bolted to the flywheel.

The pressure plate is pressed forward by some type of spring arrangement, either a series of small coil springs or a circular diaphragm spring.

When the clutch disc is squeezed between the pressure plate and the engine flywheel (engaged position), torque is then transmitted to the rear wheels. To disengage the pressure plate (against the spring pressure), there are several release levers that pivot in the clutch cover. These in turn are moved by a throwout bearing that rides on a collar extending about halfway up the transmission input shaft or clutch driveshaft. The throwout bearing is moved by the clutch release fork that is pivoted on the bellhousing.

The release fork can be actuated in one of two ways: by a fully mechanical linkage between the levers at either end, with the two connected via a rod or a flexible cable; or by what is called a hydraulic clutch. The latter has a master cylinder (similar to that of the brakes) which is connected by linkage to the clutch pedal. The clutch master cylinder operates a slave cylinder connected to the clutch release fork by a short, adjustable rod. When pressure is applied to the slave cylinder, it in turn operates the release fork.

The cable-operated linkage is finding increasing favor among car makers, since it is easier to install and adjust at the time the car is manufactured than a rod-operated or hydraulic linkage. Also, because it eliminates several points of potential wear found in rod-operated sys-

tems, it helps alleviate the mechanic's woes. Its use in modern cars can also be traced to the lack of space in engine compartments, so that a system of rods is almost impossible to install.

ADJUSTING LINKAGE

It should be understood that you must expect to adjust the linkage between the clutch pedal and throwout arm now and then just to compensate for wear of the friction disc facings. Obviously, as the facings wear down and get thinner, the clutch pedal has to move farther and farther to fully engage the clutch. Eventually you reach a point where the linkage is against the outer stop before the clutch is engaged, and then you have definite clutch slip.

The adjustment procedure is so simple that you can figure it out yourself. Get under the car and trace down the linkage from the pedal to the clutch release fork on the engine bellhousing. Your adjustment(s) are generally on threaded rod(s) or at the cable ends going directly to the clutch release fork. Usually there are lock nuts that must be loosened before you turn the rod one way or the other to adjust the pedal free play.

You can determine if the linkage is at fault by checking the amount of play (free pedal travel) at the clutch pedal. Hold a ruler next to the clutch pedal; then depress the pedal with your fingers. It should move inward very easily for only about 1 in. This is designated free play. After that it will seem to strike something and you will have to push much harder to move it. The hard point is where the throwout bearing and the clutch release levers contacted.

A mechanically operated linkage will

have one or possibly two points at which adjustments can be made. The threaded adjustments usually have lock nuts or jam nuts which must be loosened before the rod or cable length can be adjusted. Make two turns on the free travel adjustment, reconnect the clutch rod and check the pedal travel. Repeat this process until you have about 1 in. of pedal travel.

Adjust a hydraulic clutch by the same process. Its adjusting link is between the slave cylinder and the clutch fork. However, before adjusting a hydraulic clutch, check to see if the system is full of fluid and bleed the line to remove any air. Air in the system will prevent the clutch from operating correctly and smoothly.

Bleed a hydraulic clutch the same way

1. Sanding Flywheel

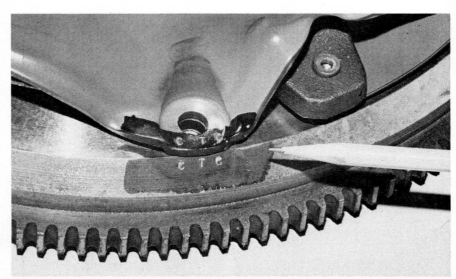

2. Balance Reference Marks

as a brake system. Have someone pump up pressure and hold it while you allow fluid to escape and retighten the fitting. You should do this three or four times, or until all air has been let out of the system. Keep the master cylinder full during bleeding so that new air does not enter the system, and fill to the recommended level when bleeding is complete. Also check fittings for leaks.

REMOVING THE CLUTCH

More serious clutch troubles require taking the clutch assembly out of the car. This is a big job, but not impractical or impossible for the beginner or home mechanic who is willing to work.

Clutch removal by pulling the transmission is the fastest, easiest way for an experienced mechanic, but you'll never believe it if you do it this way yourself because of the many parts that will have to be disconnected.

On a car with an open driveline, start by disconnecting the universal joint(s) on the driveshaft and removing it. Use a plastic sandwich bag to cover the end of the transmission housing, and secure it tightly with a large rubber band. This is to prevent the transmission oil from leaking out as well as to keep dirt from getting in. Disconnect the speedometer cable and transmission shift levers. If the car is equipped with overdrive, disconnect all wires. *Note: Do not attempt to disconnect the overdrive unit from the transmission.* It doesn't come apart this way and must be removed as a complete unit. Disconnect the parking brake cable, remove the rear transmission mounting bolts and support the rear of the engine with a jack or blocks. Now remove the bolts that attach the transmission to the flywheel housing.

At this point you're ready to remove the transmission, but be careful—some transmissions weigh over 100 lbs. It's best to have a friend help you lift it out. The transmission must come straight back until the input shaft clears the clutch splines. With the transmission's high weight leverage, it's easy to let the

1. Crocus cloth or No. 320 or 400 grit sandpaper may be used to remove polish, small marks and/or blue spots from the face of the flywheel.

2. Whenever you have a clutch and flywheel assembly balanced, and it's a good idea to do so, be sure to put reference marks on the pieces so that they can always be reassembled in correct relationship to each other. A good balancing shop will do this for you as part of the job. The pressure plate, disc and flywheel should all be balanced.

3. Clutch work is not as complicated as you might think. Here's an entire assembly laid out for you. The process of getting to the assembly is more than half the battle.

4. Although this is an aftermarket item, it is typical of a clutch. The facing is an organic material. The springs around the center of the disc help absorb the shock of clutch engagement.

5. A slide hammer is a useful tool for removing a pilot bearing.

1. Clutch Drive Shaft
2. Rotating Plate
3. Clutch Drive Shaft Bearing
4. Clutch Drive Shaft Bearing Retainer
5. Clutch Fork Ball Support Bolt
6. Clutch Release Fork Ball
7. Clutch Release Fork
8. Clutch Release Bearing
9. Clutch Cover and Pressure Plate
10. Clutch Driven Plate
11. Flywheel
12. Clutch Drive Shaft Pilot Bearing

3. Disassembled Clutch Components

4. Typical Clutch Disc

5. Removing Pilot Bearing

Clutch & Flywheel

splines bind in the disc, making removal difficult and possibly bending the disc.

On some cars it is possible to remove the bellhousing and completely expose the flywheel and clutch unit; on others the bellhousing may be part of the transmission case. On still others, you will have to be content with the removal of an inspection cover or just the lower half of the bellhousing. The lower-half types make for slower work, because you have to rotate the flywheel to expose each set of clutch mounting bolts. Then when the last bolts are removed, the clutch must be slipped out the bottom. Be careful not to mash your fingers. The clutch is heavy when you only have a small place to hold onto, so don't let it drop on the floor.

Before removing the bellhousing, check to see if there are any brake or clutch linkage brackets that need to be disconnected. If you have a factory shop manual, or better yet, a copy of Petersen's *Big Book of Auto Repair,* it will tell you exactly what needs to be disconnected. At this time disconnect the clutch release fork also. It's held in place only by a spring or snap-spring clip.

With the clutch and flywheel exposed, take a center punch and make a mark at the edge of the pressure plate cover. Make another mark directly opposite on the edge of the flywheel. This is necessary so that the pressure plate and flywheel can be reassembled in exactly the same position, because they may have been balanced as a unit. If you don't do this, you won't know where to remount the pressure plate and your engine might be out of balance. However, if you can see that the pressure plate must be replaced entirely, then marking is not necessary. In that case, the new or rebuilt pressure plate should be a balanced unit, but there isn't any easy way to determine if it has been balanced. In many cases the only thing to do is install the unit and keep your fingers crossed. Luckily, out-of-balance clutches are seldom a problem.

There are two ways to remove a clutch correctly. The first way, and probably the better, is to use a steel bar (jack handle, etc.) to pry down each clutch release finger, one at a time. As you do this, insert a large nut about ¼-in. in height between the release arm and the cover. This releases all the pressure from the pressure plate, and all the cover bolts can be removed quickly and easily in any order.

The second way, which applies to all diaphragm-type clutches as well as the finger type, is to back off each clutch cover bolt in order around the cover, one turn at a time. You must loosen the bolts evenly to keep from warping the pressure plate. At first they'll be hard to turn because of the spring pressure, but when they're about halfway out, the release fingers will contact the cover and relieve the pressure. At this point you can just run the bolts right out.

Once the clutch is out, start inspecting all the components. If the disc is oil-soaked, has cracked or broken friction lining, warped or loose rivets at the hub or is worn down to the rivet heads (bonded lining less than 1/32-in. thick on either side), then the disc must be replaced. Also check for broken springs. Springs that are loose enough to rattle will not cause noise when the car is operating. If the pressure plate is faulty and the clutch disc lining is more than half worn, replacement of the complete unit is recommended in order to get a new, full life span.

Check the pressure plate for scoring, burn marks (blue color spots) or ridges. Generally, pressure plate resurfacing is not recommended. However, really minor burn marks and scratches can be removed with crocus cloth.

Examine the flywheel for scoring, burn marks or deep ridges. If any of these problems exist or if the surface is highly polished, then the flywheel must be resurfaced. Taking a light cut off the face will ensure like-new performance—and it's not that expensive. However, be sure to do this *before* rebalancing.

The clutch release bearing is prelubricated and should *not* be cleaned in solvent. Instead, wipe it clean. Then hold the bearing inner race and rotate the outer race while applying pressure to it. If the bearing rotation is rough or noisy, replace the bearing.

Most release bearing failures are caused by improper clutch pedal adjustments. If the clutch linkage does not have enough free travel, the release bearing will constantly touch the release fingers and will spin whenever the engine is running.

"Riding the clutch," a phrase describing the bad driver's habit of constantly keeping his left foot on the clutch pedal, even lightly, is also a cause for bearing failure. This constant turning heats up the bearing and burns out the lubrication. Shortly thereafter you have a bearing failure. Since this bearing is an inexpensive part, it should be replaced. This goes for the pilot shaft bearing (ball bearing or bushing) too. You should check the pilot shaft bearing for wear or roughness, but it's far easier and safer to replace it and forget it.

If the flywheel is off the engine, it's easy to knock the pilot bearing out. But if the flywheel is still in place on the crankshaft, then the pilot bearing must be removed with a special puller. There are a number of ways to do this, but usually a slide-hammer puller with a hook on the end of it is used. The hook is inserted in the hole in the pilot bearing on one side of the bearing, and the slide hammer is used to knock the bearing out.

Clutch release bearings, sometimes called throwout bearings, are usually pressed onto the bearing hub. The old bearing can easily be knocked off the hub and a new bearing tapped on with a hammer. However, many mechanics do not bother to do this. They buy the bearing and hub already assembled. It's a little more expensive that way, but it saves time and trouble.

Inspect the release bearing hub for burns or scratches. The release bearing should slide freely. If you're in doubt or you feel a scratch, polish it out with crocus cloth. Coat the release bearing hub thinly with oil before reassembling the release bearing and hub assembly.

With your new disc in hand, check it out on the splines of the input shaft. It must slide smoothly. If it doesn't, see what's wrong. Crocus cloth can and should be used to polish the spline to a smooth finish.

If your clutch disc was ruined because of an oil leak, you must determine the cause—engine or transmission—and get the leak repaired before reassembly. If you don't, your new parts will last only a short time.

Now you are about ready for reassembly. Be sure your hands are free of grease for the initial assembly. A greasy fingerprint on the flywheel, pressure

1. This is fairly typical of what you'll find once the transmission and bellhousing have been removed. The clutch assembly usually must be removed from the flywheel before the flywheel is removed from the engine.

2. This artist's cutaway view shows clearly the relationship of the clutch pressure plate, disc and flywheel inside the bellhousing.

1. Clutch Assembly on Flywheel

2. Parts Inside Bellhousing

plate facing or clutch disc can ruin a good clutch job. It can cause chatter. Clean the flywheel and pressure plate faces just before reassembly.

The reassembly process is the reverse of the removal operation. Start by installing the flywheel and putting a thin coat of bearing lubricant inside the pilot bushing or bearing race.

To align the disc, you're going to need some kind of pilot shaft. You can't do it by eye. There are special tools for this, but the most inexpensive way is to cut an input shaft off a junk transmission and use it

Now hold the pressure plate and disc close to where they'll be installed and push the alignment shaft through the disc spline and into the pilot bearing. Line up your center punch marks and start bolting up the pressure plate, using the same procedure you followed during removal.

Note that both the flywheel and the clutch bolts must be torqued to factory specifications. Once the pressure plate is torqued down, remove the spacers and pull out the alignment shaft.

Lubricate the clutch release fork at the pivot points and then complete the reassembly. Remember, you'll need help installing the transmission. Be extra careful not to bend the disc and ruin your clutch job. ✿

CHEVETTE CLUTCH ADJUSTMENT

Normal clutch adjustment on Chevrolet's little Chevette is a little easier than readjusting it after installation of either a new clutch assembly or a new operating cable. To counter normal wear, loosen the lock nut on the ball stud and turn the stud counterclockwise until there is ¾-in. to ⅞-in. of free travel at the pedal. Next, tighten the lock nut to 25 ft.-lbs. of torque, being careful not to change the adjustment.

If you've installed a new clutch or a new cable, proceed as follows: Loosen the lock nut. Then turn the ball stud inward until the release bearing contacts the clutch springs. Next, tighten the lock nut without changing the adjustment. Remove the clutch fork cover and pull on the cable until the pedal rests against the rubber pedal bumper. Push the clutch fork forward until the release bearing touches the clutch spring fingers. Hold it in place. Thread the nut (B) or cable (A) until it bottoms out against the clutch fork. Push the pedal to the floor at least four times to establish cable position at clearance points. Turn nut (B) 4½ times counterclockwise, and then thread the lock nut on cable (A) until it touches nut (B). Tighten the lock nut and attach the return spring. This will produce the desired free play at the pedal.

1971-'74 PINTO CLUTCH ADJUSTMENT

Only one clutch adjustment is required, and it is made where the cable goes through the bellhousing. Early models have a lock nut on the rear face of the housing, as shown in our illustration. Late models have done away with the lock nut, but the adjustment is the same. A quick check on late models can be made by pulling the cable housing toward the front of the car just enough to put the throwout bearing up against the clutch fingers. In that position, the adjustment nut should have ¼-in. clearance from the boss in the bellhousing, as shown. On early models you can't make this check until you loosen the rear lock nut. To adjust the clutch, loosen the lock nut(s) and turn the adjusting nut until the gap is ¼-in., with the cable pulled forward by hand. When tightening the lock nut(s), be sure you don't move the adjusting nut. Ford does not give a pedal free play specification for Pinto. This ¼-in. cable adjustment is the only specification, and it will result in the right amount of pedal free play.

MONZA AND VEGA CLUTCH ADJUSTMENT

Two adjusting points make the Vega clutch adjustment a little tricky. Ordinarily the ball stud does not have to be adjusted unless the clutch is changed, but it's possible that somebody may have turned the stud and gotten everything out of kilter. To adjust the ball stud, you must have a Chevy gauge No. J-23644. It is nothing more than a hook that positions the clutch arm while you adjust the ball stud. You can easily take its measurements at your local dealer and then make your own gauge. In use, the gauge hooks over the front face of the bellhousing and over the clutch fork. While the gauge is holding the clutch arm, the ball stud nut is loosened and the stud screwed in (forward) until the throwout bearing touches the clutch fingers. Tightening the nut locks the stud in position on the bellhousing. Final adjustment for clutch pedal free play is made with the cable pin. Just screw it up against the clutch fork, making sure that the cable is all the way to the rear with the pedal up against the rubber bumper. After the pin hits the clutch fork, screw it in about an additional ¼-turn so that it drops into the groove in the fork. This will give you about 1 in. of free play.

1. First operation involved in pulling a transmission so you can replace the clutch is to remove the driveshaft. Start at rear U-joint.

2. On most cars with floor shifts, you'll have to drop the shifter as a unit, for the simple fact that it is bolted to the side of the transmission.

3. On transmissions with removable pan on bellhousing, pull the pan. This saves you the trouble of having to remove the entire housing.

4. Raise rear of engine slightly with jack to take pressure off crossmember, then remove crossmember. Be sure engine is supported firmly and safely.

5. Once the crossmember is out and speedometer cable and all linkage is disconnected, you can proceed with removing transmission itself.

6. After removal of all linkage, rear crossmember, shifter, etc., it is possible to remove a manual trans by hand. Just don't drop it though.

7. If your starter bolts to your bellhousing instead of the engine, you'll have to remove the starter before you can take off the bellhousing.

8. Next operation involves removing linkage at clutch throwout arm. At this point, clutch and/or housing is ready to be pulled from car.

9. After using a long extension and maybe a flex-socket to get upper bolts at rear of engine, you can remove the bellhousing (heavy!).

10. A special ratcheting tool is used to rotate flywheel around so pressure plate bolts can be pulled. A screwdriver will work here,' too.

11. This clutch assembly came out of a MoPar and was slipping badly at 28,000 miles. Pressure plate face is really worn. All parts replaced.

12. Sandpaper can be used to remove the glaze from the flywheel facing, but if the surface is irregular, you should get the flywheel face ground.

13. Either the front shaft of an old transmission or wooden pilot is used to line up the disc while you start the bolts in around clutch.

14. When all the bolts are started and lightly run down, they should be torqued to keep the pressure even around the circumference of clutch.

15. On cars that permit you to leave the bellhousing in place, install the new throwout bearing in the throwout arm as shown in this photo.

16. When the bellhousing is all one piece you have to remove everything to get at bearing, so it's wise to replace it too when you R 'n' R clutch.

17. Greasing front of splined shaft makes installation of trans easier. You should also grease the surface that the throwout bearing rides on.

18. Once transmission is back in the car, cinch it down and replace shifter and linkage. Be sure to readjust the clutch linkage, too.

Manual Transmission

If Bill Lear had succeeded in producing a steam engine to replace the smog makers we now use, we might have seen the end of all transmissions as we know them today. But Bill Lear didn't quite make it, and it doesn't look like anybody else will, either. So we are stuck with some kind of a transmission to multiply torque so that we can drive our cars.

Obviously, any vehicle with a typical internal combustion engine will need some kind of power-changing device between engine and rear wheels, simply because contemporary engines cannot operate over the very wide rpm range an automobile requires. To start a 3000-lb. car rolling requires more power than is required to keep it rolling. The gasoline engine develops the least amount of torque at low rpm's; consequently the transmission must multiply what force is available at low engine speeds. In this respect all transmissions are alike, both standard and automatic.

The transmission, then, is nothing more than a mechanical torque multiplier. If you want to move that big rock over there, get a longer lever or move the fulcrum closer to the rock. Now consider the teeth of meshing gears as the fulcrum. The gear with the smaller diameter has the advantage of rotational leverage, and since it will turn faster than the big gear, the engine can run at a higher rpm where greater torque is developed.

Gearing, therefore, of both the transmission and final drive assembly becomes directly responsible for vehicle performance. To this end, the truck may have a very high numerical transmission and rear end combination, the better to move heavy loads. The racing car may have lower numerical gear ratios, since the engine is kept running near maximum power range at all times. To clear up a bit of confusion, low numerical numbers (those numbers closer to 1) are generally referred to as being high gearing. High numerical numbers mean low gear ratios. The lower the gear ratio, therefore, the greater the torque multiplication between crankshaft rpm and driveshaft or axle rpm.

A Frenchman named Levassor is credited with inventing the sliding gear transmission, although gear or rotational torque multiplication has been around for many decades. Until the automobile created such a wide-spread demand for special gearboxes, however, the sliding gear-type multiplier was of little necessity. The changes in the very few years since cars became common are readily apparent—the Model A and a modern Ford are proof of that advancement.

Before any kind of detailed work can be accomplished on a manual transmission, it is advantageous to understand just how the pieces function—at least briefly.

There is nothing secret about how a transmission works, and that's why repairs are so easy to handle. However, before tearing into the gearbox, be advised that there are certain tools which are essential to efficient work. First of all, a good set of expander pliers will undoubtedly be needed to remove the several snap rings. Bearing pullers or graduated diameter punches are essential, and even a dial indicator will come in

1. Working on a manual transmission like this Super T-10 is really quite easy; all you have to do is remember the sequence in which you took the parts out, and put them back in same order.

2. Your two basic types of manual transmissions are called selective and progressive. The selective type features neutral in the center or middle of the shift pattern. From neutral, in a selective, you can select any gear you desire. The progressive design, on the other hand, is the type of torque multiplier found on most motorcycles. Neutral is at the bottom of the shift pattern and you must progressively upshift or downshift to reach the particular gear you want.

3. Gear changing on a fully synchronized, constant mesh (including reverse), 3-speed manual transmission is accomplished by shifting forks that have the job of sliding dog clutches over synchros.

4. GM's medium-duty Saginaw 4-speed trans is used on its intermediate cars when a 4-speed is ordered with a 6-cylinder engine. All four gears are fully synchronized. The unit can be distinguished from the Muncie by the fact that the reverse lever is mounted on the side cover rather than in the extension housing.

5. Like the manual 3-speed trannys, modern four-on-the-floors feature a constant mesh principle except when reverse is grabbed. Then a special fork on the linkage meshes the free-wheeling reverse gear to the reverse idler gear on countershaft.

6. Muncie 4-speed transmission is used on most GM high-performance options. The gearbox itself contains the four forward gears, while the tail section houses the reverse gear assembly; trans is quite strong.

1. Super T-10 Transmission

2. Selective and Progressive Transmissions

POWER FLOW

REVERSE

FIRST

SECOND

THIRD

(Arrows indicate engaged synchros.)

3. Fully Synchronized 3-Speed

4. Saginaw Medium-Duty 4-Speed

5. Modern 4-Speed Floorshift

POWER FLOW

FIRST

SECOND

THIRD

FOURTH

REVERSE

TOP VIEW OF REVERSE IDLER GEARS

4-SPEED TRANSMISSION CROSS SECTION

1. Bearing retainer
2. Main drive gear
3. Fourth speed blocking ring
4. Third and fourth speed synchronizing assembly
5. Third speed blocking ring
6. Third speed gear
7. Second speed gear
8. Second speed blocking ring
9. First and second speed synchronizing assembly
10. First speed blocking ring
11. First speed gear
12. First speed gear sleeve
13. Reverse gear
14. Main shaft
15. Reverse idler shaft roll pin
16. Reverse idler gear (rear)
17. Countergear
18. Countershaft bearing roller spacer
18a. Magnet
19. Countershaft needle roller bearing
20. Countershaft
21. Reverse idler gear (front)
22. Reverse idler shaft
23. Speedometer drive gear

6. Muncie 4-Speed

Manual Transmission

1. Shifting Forks

2. Comparison of T-10 and Super T-10

3. Warner T-10 Parts

1. Shifting forks can be worn or bent through hard usage. Inspect both the fork faces and connection pins for excess play if your trans is shifting poorly. Then replace the pins if the slop is excessive.

2. Borg-Warner's T-10 and Super T-10 (bottom) have been the favorite of the performance addicts since the T-10's inception on the '57 'Vette. Its ease of shifting is due to the lightweight gears. The Super T-10 features heavier, stronger gears.

3. The T-10 is basically a Warner T-85 3-speed with reverse gear moved into the extension housing to make room for the 4th gearset. Chrysler, Ford, GM and American Motors have used this first of the four-on-the-floors in many of their muscle cars.

handy. All these may be purchased, of course, or rented.

INSPECTION

Because the transmission gears are literally immersed in lubricant, the early part of the repair will of necessity be dirty. Working in a large drip pan or some kind of shallow tub will confine the oil and make subsequent clean-up much easier. Do not drain the transmission lubricant before initial disassembly, because much may be learned from it.

During initial inspection, remove the top cover plate, if the gearbox is so equipped, or the shifting lever cover. Do not jostle the transmission too much as it is being removed from the vehicle,

since small particles of metal, such as chips from broken gears, will wash around and become lodged in bearings, etc. After the cover plate is removed, feel in the bottom of the case for these pieces of metal. They are not uncommon, and will give some clue as to transmission failure—whether the gear tooth was broken by fatigue or from hard shifting, and so forth. The synchronizer clutches are sure to wear, resulting in fine particles of brass in the case sump.

All the lubricant may then be dumped in the pan, and the gearbox given a cursory cleaning if desired. Disassembly of the component parts comes next, but careful inspection at this point can save much labor. While broken gears are not uncommon within a standard transmis-

sion, excessively worn synchronizers are perhaps the greatest enemy to smooth transmission operation. Because of them, the transmission will not stay in 2nd gear, nor will it shift smoothly without clashing gears, etc. Now is the time to determine just how far disassembly must go to effect a repair.

If gear teeth are involved, very carefully go over each gear. It is possible for several teeth to be broken on the output shaft, but no damage on the counter shaft. If this is true, and none of the counter shaft gear teeth have been gouged or chipped, then nothing more than the output shaft assembly need be repaired. If, however, there is the slightest indication of harm to counter shaft gears, replacement is in order.

Because the synchronizers are constantly being subjected to friction, they should be replaced in practically every repair job.

The hardest part of fixing any transmission is getting it apart and back together. If you can get it apart without having to resort to a hacksaw and a cutting torch, then getting it back together is merely a matter of remembering where all the pieces go. To help your memory along, on the following pages you'll find step-by-step photos covering assembly and disassembly procedures on four popular manual transmissions.

1. Before you drop your trans, find drain plug and remove oil. Then mark chalk across U-joint's face for reassembly in original position.

2. Four nuts, two U-bolts will free assembly from rear yoke. Inspect U-joint for wear at this time; replace or rebuild it if necessary.

3. Remove exhaust system if it is an obstruction to disengaging of shifter linkage or lifting of trans. Now pull linkage cotter keys.

4. Speedometer cable can be disconnected by taking off Phillips cap screw. If location of pipe hampers work, use shorter tool.

5. Disconnect shift linkage at transmission. If linkage is for a floor shifter, you may be able to lift entire assembly from inside car.

6. Middle crossmember, holding tail-shaft, is now unbolted from frame. If handbrake cable is in the way, it too will have to be removed.

7. As arrow indicates, you must support rear of engine when you take off transmission support. If you fail to do so, engine will fall out.

8. You needn't support trans. Main shaft and bearing sleeve on bellhousing will keep gearbox in place as you loosen bolts with a ratchet.

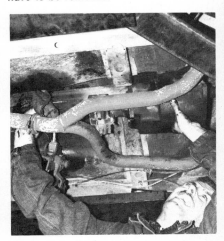

9. "Get all the goodies out of the way!" Exhaust head pipes, linkage and hand brake cables will make a hard job harder if they aren't removed.

HOW-TO: Disassembling a Chevy 3-Speed

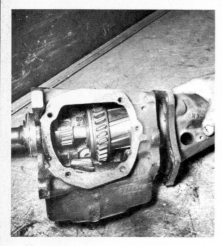

1. Before disassembling/reassembling Chevy's old 3-speed trans, drain lubricant and; remove both side cover assembly, tailshaft housing assembly.

2. Now slide reverse, first gear from clutch sleeve; remove them from case. Remove pilot bearing, retainer screws before tapping out countershaft.

3. Lower countergear to bottom of case before removing clutch gear, bearing. Otherwise bearing will strike countergear. Now pull snap ring.

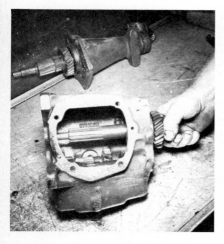

4. Tap end of shaft with a soft mallet to move gear and bearing assembly into front of case. Then total assembly is pulled from rear of case.

5. Now tap out reverse idler gear, thrust washer, thrust bearing and bearing washer after driving out plug located ahead of idler shaft.

6. To take mainshaft off extension, expand bearing snap ring; tap rear of shaft with a soft hammer to free the shaft, speedo drive, and second gear.

7. Place clutch gear in a vise and remove bearing retainer nut and oil slinger with some water pump pliers. Bearings must be pressed off shaft.

8. Replace gears if they show unusual wear; check first, reverse, be sure they slide easily on clutch sleeve. Do same on clutch sleeve-to-mainshaft bit.

9. To remove synchronizer ring from clutch sleeve, turn ring until its ends can be seen through slot. Slide retainer out of groove with snap rings.

10. Cluster is a prime point of hard wear; its bearings should be renewed. Note number of thrust washers on each end of gear; reassemble with same.

11. Before installing assembly, use heavy grease to hold needle bearings in cluster. Fit gear into case; install cluster countershaft.

12. Position reverse idler assembly in case so thrust bearing faces rear. Install idler shaft, make sure flat spot is down so extension will fit.

13. Use cup grease to hold mainshaft pilot roller bearings in clutch gear. Make sure no bearing escapes. Insert clutch gear assembly from inside case.

14. Next insert synchronizers, low/reverse slide gear in case. Install rear housing with main shaft to front of case, finish off with main drive gear.

15. Install clutch gear bearing retainer and make sure oil slot in retainer lines up with the oil slot that's in the front face of the transmission.

16. Now slide reverse/low gear into neutral (center) position on 2nd and 3rd-speed clutch before you bolt side cover plate to trans case.

17. Inspect shifter forks for wear (replace if necessary). Preset forks for neutral. Hump on first, reverse must face toward rear of trans.

18. Use new gasket; coat the capscrews with Permatex No. 2. Cinch up with torque wrench or impact gun. Recommended torque is 15-18 ft.-lbs.

HOW-TO: Assembling a Muncie 4-Speed

1. Drain lube from trans; remove side cover, clutch retainer housing, rear extension housing, countergear, main drive gear units; clean and inspect.

2. Begin assembly by checking bearings for undue wear, then lubricate with light engine oil. Check gears for wear, clutch sleeves for sliding.

3. After inspecting all moving parts, insert rear bearing in rear bearing retainer; release snap ring, position correctly in retainer groove.

4. Once 1st and 2nd gears (with their synchros, clutch sleeves, etc.) have been installed on mainshaft, tap rear bearing retainer onto shaft.

5. Spread snap ring with pliers, then allow ring to align with groove in end of mainshaft to help retain rear bearing. Install reverse, anti-rattle springs.

6. Install 3rd and 4th gears (hub to front of trans), synchronizers and 3rd, 4th gear clutch assemblies with both sleeves to front of trans case.

7. Cluster goes in bottom of case with all bearings held in place by dowel. Then tap main drive gear and bearing into hole in case; work from inside.

8. Position reverse idler gear thrust washer on machined face of ear cast in case of reverse idler shaft. Hold assembly in case with heavy lube coating.

9. Shove reverse idler gear next to thrust washer, with the hub facing to rear of case. Install flat thrust washer on reverse idler gear.

10. Stick cage and its 17 roller bearings into main drive gear; use heavy grease to hold bearings in place. Put oil slinger (concave forward) on gear.

11. Now you can lower mainshaft assembly into case. Be sure notches on 4th gear synchro ring correspond to the keys on the clutch assembly.

12. Align countergear with shaft in rear and hole in front of case, press countershaft in case, push assembly dowel out until shaft is flush with case.

13. Cut on rear of countershaft must be aligned so it will mate to similar cut in rear extension housing to keep shaft from spinning in trans case.

14. Install reverse idler shaft roll pin (pin should be in vertical position), and thrust washer into gear, front boss of case; pick up front-tanged washer.

15. Rear extension housing is turned to reveal shifter fork for reverse gear. Arrow shows slot that reverse idler shaft roll pin aligns with.

16. Pull reverse shifter shaft to left side of extension, rotate shaft to bring reverse shift fork into extension housing (reverse detent position).

17. Start rear extension housing onto trans case, while slowly pushing it on the shifter shaft to engage the shift fork with the reverse shift collar.

18. Pilot reverse idler shaft into extension; slide onto case, attach bolts. Line up shaft with holes in boss and inset lock pin. Install shifter, side cover.

HOW-TO: Disassembling a Warner T-10

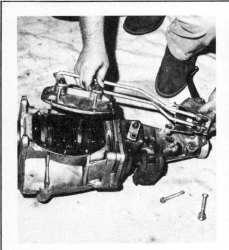

1. Drain out lubricant from Warner T-10 4-speed; shift it into 2nd, remove side cover bolts. Pull cover assembly and gasket off case.

2. Remove front bearing (or clutch gear bearing) retainer bolts from transmission case; slide both retainer and gasket off main drive gear.

3. Take off backup light switch, plunger from trans. Drive lock pin from reverse shifter lever boss, pull shifter out slightly to free fork from reverse.

4. Inspect shifting forks, fork faces, connection pins for abnormal wear or shape. Shifting forks should be replaced to eliminate any excess play.

5. Remove rear extension retaining bolts. Tap housing with soft mallet to loosen it. Slide off housing and gasket. Remove reverse idler from case.

6. Shift transmission into 3rd to keep mainshaft from turning. Slide off snap ring from rear splines on mainshaft; remove speedo, reverse gear.

7. Free self-locking bolt attaching rear bearing retainer to trans case. Remove case-to-retainer pin with channel locks or vise grips.

8. Pull clutch gear snap ring so entire assembly can be removed. You may find it necessary to lightly tap shaft and bearing with a soft-headed mallet.

9. To further inspect mainshaft assembly for wear, remove front snap ring, then slide 3rd, 4th clutch assemblies, synchro rings from shaft.

1. Before reassembling bearings and spacers in countergear, inspect teeth closely for excessive wear, chips or cracks; replace it if worn, damaged.

2. While you're at it, check spacers, countergear roller bearings for wear. Inspect countershaft, reverse idler; replace them if necessary.

3. Use a dowel pin or shaft to retain bearings, spacers; slip solvent-cleaned bearings and washers into countergear. Dip in lube so they'll stay in place.

4. The 40 rollers inside countergear are in 4 rows of 10 each, separated by two narrow spaces, one long spacer. Pin is removed as rollers go in.

5. Liberal application of lube on cluster gear thrust washers helps hold them in place when countergear is inserted into transmission case.

6. Rest transmission on its side, with side cover opening toward assembler. Put countergear thrust washer in place; hold with a coat of heavy grease.

7. Set countergear in place at bottom of case; be sure the tanged thrust washers have not been moved or dowel pin has not slipped away from rollers.

8. Shaft must be removed or it will interfere with assembly of mainshaft and clutch gear. Leave thrust washer in place, countergear at case bottom.

9. Reinstall the 14 roller bearings inside main drive gear; use heavy-duty grease to hold bearings in position while assembly is inserted.

HOW-TO: Assembling a Warner T-10

10. When assembling the front reverse idler gear, make sure the teeth are pointed forward with hub facing to rear of the transmission case.

11. The 1st, 2nd and 3rd gears, with synchro rings, are assembled on mainshaft. Hub of 3rd, notches on synchro ring should always face forward.

12. Install 3rd, 4th gear clutch assembly with taper to front. Be sure keys in hub match notches in 3rd gear synchro ring. Insert main drive gear.

13. Before assembly is put in case, put new selective snap rings (that'll fit in groove) on mainshaft in front of 3rd-, 4th-speed gear clutch unit.

14. Rear bearing retainer can be slid over end of mainshaft. Spread snap ring in pliers so it will drop around rear bearing when aligned with groove.

15. First insert reverse idler shaft into housing, then slide flat thrust washer in place. Tang on thrust washer should face thrust portion of case.

16. Next slip reverse idler gear onto shaft, engaging splines with portion of gear within case. Place new gasket on rear bearing retainer's face.

17. Pull reverse shift shaft partially out of extension; rotate shaft to get reverse shift fork as far forward in rear extension housing as possible.

18. Now, you can start the extension onto the mainshaft while pushing in on shifter shaft to engage shift fork with reverse gear shift collar.

19. When fork engages shift fork, rotate shifter shaft to move reverse gear rearward, permitting extension to mate to transmission case.

20. With pin in shifter lever boss, torque rear extension housing bolts to 40 ft.-lbs.; install rear extension-to-bearing retainer bolts, 25 ft.-lbs. maximum.

21. With hammer and punch, tap clutch bearing in place. Be sure bearing is clean, lubricated, checked for roughness (by turning race in hand).

22. Use snap ring pliers to slide selective fit snap rings, spacer washer, bearing snap ring over maindrive gear and into proper places.

23. Be sure to use a new gasket that's slightly moist with lube, before you bolt bearing retainer to front of T-10 transmission case.

24. New front bearing retainer gasket should be firmly in place and the retainer snug on case. Use good sealer, torque capscrews to 18 ft.-lbs.

25. Shift forks must fit snugly in grooves on 3rd, 4th-speed clutch sliding sleeve and 1st and 2nd-speed clutch sliding sleeve, as shown.

26. Shift trans into 2nd, position side cover, attach new gasket, engage shift forks in collars; install side cover, seal and torque capscrews.

27. After trans is filled and shifter linkage is attached, your just-like-new Warner T-10 transmission is all ready to tackle the streets again.

HOW-TO: Assembling a Ford 4-Speed

1. Assembly is started by putting the cluster and reverse goodies in position, but the cluster is lying on the bottom of the case without any shaft.

2. The reverse shifter shaft is now in and secured. A set screw holds the shifter fork to the rail. Note the holes for two more shifter shafts.

3. Support thrust washer and low gear to prevent them from sliding off end of shaft; then carefully lower output shaft assembly into case.

4. Place front synchronizer into 3rd gear position; install set screw in 3rd and 4th gear shift fork. Move synchronizer to neutral.

5. The mainshaft, with all the gears already on it, goes in through the top of the case. Then the shift forks and the shafts are put into their positions.

6. Tightening the set screw in the shift fork that helps secure it to the rail. All of the steps are described in detail in genuine Ford shop manual.

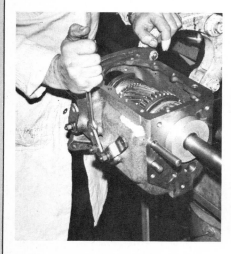

7. The detent on the bottom shift rail screws in from the side of the case. Note dummy aluminum bearing temporarily holding mainshaft in position.

8. Another shift rail is tapped in from the front. Bar across the front of the trans holds the front of mainshaft in position while doing the good work.

9. Not many people have this press, but it's the right way to put the rear bearing into the case—with no beating. Hammer mechanics, please take note.

10. After the bearing is in position, the snap ring slips on easily—if you have snap ring pliers. Another snap ring goes on the shaft against bearing.

11. After the main drive gear and its bearings are slipped into position, the front bearing retainer, with a new seal inside, is bolted on the case.

12. Standing the box on end makes it easier to move the gear cluster into position so the shaft can be inserted. Lower hand is catching dummy shaft.

13. The cluster gear shaft and reverse idler shaft are kept from turning by roll pins that must enter these recesses in the case to be held securely.

14. First a gasket, and then the tailshaft housing is slid into position. A new seal should be installed in the end of the housing, to stop the drip.

15. Extension housing bolts should be torqued to specs, but you'll not see many mechanics who do it. Tightening by feel might turn out inaccurate.

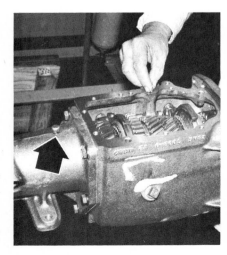

16. Detent for the top shift rail is dropped into the hole, and held in place by the cover. Note breather on top of housing, to relieve pressure.

17. The bolts are well greased so that the torque readings will be consistent, but no sealer is used on the cover gasket. Fluid leaks are not a problem.

18. That's right, even the cover is torqued. If you're going to be superaccurate, why not go all the way? Reminder: Don't forget to put in lube.

1. The '71-'72 Vega (Opel) 4-speed box is a "bottom-loader:" the case cover is at the bottom of the trans instead of side or top. Watch detent plug and spring when pulling cover.

2. Lock nuts, cotter pins and C-clips hold selector lever and shifter shaft arrangement in place and must be removed as a first step before access to trans is possible.

3. Unbolt the extension housing from the trans case. Trans is a German design and requires a good deal of patience during disassembly as working space inside is limited.

4. Loosen and unscrew the backup light switch from the trans case. "Bottom-loader" design makes countergear removal the next step in the disassembly procedure.

5. In order to provide easy access to the countergear shaft for removal, the extension housing must be rotated until its shaft end completely clears this cutout in the housing.

6. Countershaft is removed by driving to the rear with a punch and hammer from the front of the trans case. Watch for a lock ball in rear of countershaft and don't lose it.

7. Countergear can be lifted out easily with all needle bearings intact once the shaft is removed. Be sure and remember to clean and inspect all gear teeth for damage or wear.

8. The countergear thrust washers are removed next. Note the position of the cut edge, as well as the tangs which must fit into the recesses provided in the case when replaced.

9. Now drive out reverse intermediate lever bedding bolt and remove the reverse speed shifter intermediate lever. The rest of Vega box is held together with drift pins.

10. Remove the input shaft and the main drive gear from the front of the trans by pulling straight off. It may be necessary to rock the input shaft back and forth as you pull it forward.

11. Two drift pins hold the selector shaft in place. This one is easy to see and work on, but access to the other pin is gained through hole (A) in case, and punch size used is important.

12. Once the drift pins are removed (use ⅛-in. pin punch), the selector shaft can be pushed out of the trans case and the intermediate levers removed with it. Check levers for wear.

13. Remove the two aluminum gearshift interlock detents from the top of the case (A). Pry out plugs with care to prevent damage to them and remove springs and balls.

14. Knock out drift pin holding 3rd/4th shift fork to shifter shaft. Use care because the shift forks are rather brittle metal and can be easily broken by a misplaced blow.

15. Turn the extension housing until the shifter shaft is exposed, and then tap shaft lightly from the rear of the case until it can be pulled out through the front and removed.

16. With shifter shaft removed, 3rd/4th fork is angled off clutch face and out of case. Rounded notch at shaft hole part of fork must face rearward when replacing fork in case.

17. A special tool is made for driving reverse idler gear shaft rearward and out of the case, but if you don't have this tool, you can do the same with a punch and careful tapping.

18. Shaft uses a lock ball—watch for it when you remove the shaft and reverse idler gear from trans case. Inspect the shaft for burrs and the gear for worn or damaged teeth.

19. The reverse speed shift fork will remain in case unless drift pin (A) and shaft (B) are removed. If the fork is not damaged, there's no reason to remove this one from case.

20. Forks are not interchangeable. The 3rd/4th fork (A) is worn, but legs on 1st/2nd fork (B) are broken. This is more likely to happen during disassembly than during operation.

21. Now withdraw the mainshaft assembly and extension housing from the rear of the trans case. The gear shifter sleeve will be pulled off as you remove the shaft.

22. When you are ready to remove the mainshaft from the extension housing, you'll have to squeeze the mainshaft bearing snap ring together and then draw it forward.

23. After removing the snap ring at front of 3rd/4th clutch assembly, clutch and 3rd gear can be withdrawn from the mainshaft. Do everything you can to keep the clutch intact.

24. Turn mainshaft around and remove the snap ring and washer located behind the speedometer drive worm gear. Pressure clip with lock ball beneath is exposed as gear slides off.

25. Another snap ring is removed to continue disassembly of the gear tower from the rear of the mainshaft. Snap ring pliers are great help when you are doing manual trans work.

26. Washer and spacer are removed from rear of mainshaft inner bearing in that order. Bearing may have to be removed with puller. However, it usually slips right off.

27. The bearing, bearing snap ring and spacer can now be removed from the shaft. Note that the spacer cone faces toward the bearing instead of the 1st gear assembly.

28. When the 1st gear is pulled free from the 1st/2nd gear speed clutch, the clutch will come apart. Remove parts shown, then blocking ring and clutch key spring (A).

29. This 1st speed needle bearing sleeve comes off next and should be inspected carefully for loose, worn, missing or damaged bearings or deformed sleeve.

30. The remainder of synchro-clutch and 2nd gear are removed from the mainshaft, completing disassembly. Be sure and inspect all the gear faces and teeth for damage.

31. Reassembly of the mainshaft begins with the 2nd gear and the 1st/2nd speed synchro-clutch assembly. Set into position against the stop ring on the mainshaft.

32. Replace 1st speed needle bearing, blocking ring and 1st gear. Make sure that the blocking ring cutout engages the synchro-clutch properly and fits into place easily.

33. The mainshaft spacer (cone toward bearing), the bearing retainer snap ring and the inner bearing are replaced next. The bearing should seat easily without need for lubrication.

34. The spacer and washer are then fitted into position behind the bearing. Be sure to inspect the bearing for cracked races, worn balls and other defects before replacing it.

35. Metal spring clip slips under the speedometer drive worm gear. Lock ball is inserted in shaft and gear/clip positioned over it, then the rear snap ring is replaced and secured.

36. The next step is to turn mainshaft around and install 3rd gear and blocking ring, seating against the stop ring on shaft. Gear cone must face toward end of shaft for proper mesh.

HOW-TO: Vega (Opel) 4-speed Overhaul

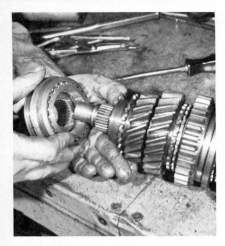

37. The 3rd/4th synchro-clutch assembly is fitted into place, seated and secured with the gear shifter sleeve snap ring, completing reassembly of gear tower on the mainshaft.

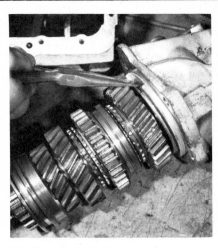

38. Place mainshaft assembly in the extension housing up to its stop, and then secure in place with the mainshaft bearing snap ring. Make sure that the ring engages completely.

39. Reinstall mainshaft in trans case, and then fit the main drive gear and input shaft through front of case to engage mainshaft. Use a twisting motion to fit together.

40. Fit the 1st/2nd gear shifter shaft into the transmission case and through the shift fork; then rotate until the holes line up properly. You are now ready to reinstall the drift pin.

41. Place lock ball into reverse idler gear shaft and push shaft through hole in rear of the transmission case to pass through reverse idler gear with groove end toward front.

42. Reinstall 3rd/4th speed shifter shaft through trans case and shift fork. Use a screwdriver to position the fork while turning the shaft until drift pin holes line up properly.

43. The drift pin holding 3rd/4th shifter fork to shaft is replaced. Be sure and use 3/16-inch or larger punch when reinstalling all drift pins in this particular transmission.

44. Insert new selector shaft oil seals in the appropriate holes on both sides of trans case, then slide the shaft into the case and through the intermediate lever. Install drift pin.

45. The reverse shifter intermediate lever is fitted into place to engage the arm on the 3rd/4th intermediate lever and the bedding bolt (A) is driven into transmission case to secure lever.

46. The countergear uses one set of roller bearings between two spacers at each end. Be sure and coat inside of gear with grease, and then set first washer in position.

47. Place one row of roller bearings in the end of the countergear. Grease makes the use of a dummy shaft unnecessary in reassembling the gear for reinstallation.

48. After the bearings are positioned, you can place the second spacer coated with grease over them. Then repeat this procedure at the other end of the countergear in preparation for replacement.

49. Now you can coat the countergear thrust washers with grease and stick to transmission case. The thrust washer lugs must fit into the slots provided inside the case.

50. The next step is to place the countergear unit carefully in the trans case. This is the only real advantage of "bottom-loader" design as you don't have to struggle here.

51. Place the lock ball in the countershaft recess and slide the shaft through the countergear from the rear of the case. Tap the shaft with a mallet until it's flush with the case.

52. Now rotate the extension housing until the bolt holes line up with the transmission case. You can then replace the bolts and torque each to 21 ft.-lbs. (Coat with a sealing compound).

53. Replace the gearshift interlock detent balls, springs and plugs at the top of the case; then turn transmission case over and insert reverse interlock detent ball, spring and plug.

54. Screw the backup light switch into the rear of the case; then replace the cover and gasket. Tighten all 10 cover screws. You have just completed the Vega 4-speed overhaul.

Automatic Transmission

There is no reason to be afraid to work on an automatic transmission. Once the thing is out of the car and you have a nice big bench or clean floor to work on, it's simply a matter of undoing some bolts and nuts, prying out a few snap rings, and surprising yourself that it comes apart so easily. The hardest part about automatic transmission work is getting the darn thing out of the car. It is so big, clumsy, and heavy that you aren't about to lift it out of there without some help, either in the form of some husky friends or an automatic transmission jack. Dropping the transmission would be a disaster, maybe to your foot but surely to the transmission itself because many of the cases are made of aluminum.

Before tackling your automatic you should get a manual that gives detailed explanations and pictures of the disassembly procedure. The manuals are usually available through your local auto parts store or car dealer. Each one of the manuals will be almost as thick as this book and well worth the several dollars that you will have to pay for it. Without the specialized manual you will be faced with a hit-or-miss proposition, and almost surely your transmission will not go back together the way it should.

Overhaul and repair of any automatic transmission is well within the realm of an amateur mechanic's skill, since it is primarily a remove-and-replace procedure (much the same as manual transmissions). However, the average mechanic faces an automatic transmission repair with some trepidation, simply because he does not fully understand the inner workings of the magic box. Whether the model is an early Hydro, a 2-speed, a Dynaflow, or the modern 3-speed, the same basic design principles are involved.

AUTOMATIC TRANSMISSION DESIGN

In essence, all automatics currently popular include one or more sets of planetary gears, one or more fluid couplings or a torque converter, and control valves to direct hydraulic fluid. The control systems may vary considerably, since an automatic transmission may be controlled manually by the driver (shifting lever), hydraulically by throttle movement, by the engine vacuum, by speed-sensitive governors, or by an electrical device. Additionally, two or three of these types of controls might be included on any one transmission.

The biggest difference between automatics is the type of connection between engine and transmission. The Hydra-Matic of earlier days used a fluid coupling, while the later transmissions rely on the torque converter. The advantage of a torque converter is simple; through ingenious routing of the fluid, considerable torque multiplication can be gained when a car needs it most—at standstill and during the first few moments of movement.

Within either the simple fluid coupling or the torque converter, a pump located near the center of the revolving wheels distributes oil outward through vanes. As the engine rpm drops below a certain point near idle, this hydraulic pressure is not enough to overcome the static weight of the vehicle. However, as engine rpm increases, the hydraulic pressure also goes up. The oil thrown across reaction vanes then begins to turn the transmission smoothly, with a certain amount of slippage. At high engine and hydraulic pump rpm, the driving and driven members of the coupling or converter are operating at a near 1:1 lock-up ratio.

From the driven member of the converter or coupling, power is transferred through a shaft to clutch/drum assemblies inside the transmission housing. These clutches are similar to the single large clutch common to the standard transmission in that they function solely on the principle of friction. Planetary gearsets are connected to the clutch packs, producing the final gear ratios that exit through the transmission output shaft. Of all the workings inside an automatic transmission, the amateur would have most difficulty with the valve control body. For this reason, it is advisable to purchase a new valve body should one be damaged. There is very little choice with the torque converter, as repair of such must be left to the professional shop equipped with specialized tools.

It is virtually impossible to present detailed illustrations on how to assemble and/or repair all automatic transmissions in current use, for this would require the entire length of this book. Rather, we are presenting studies of two popular transmissions that will satisfy a great many readers: the Chevrolet Turbo Hydra-Matic 400 and the Ford C-4 Cruise-O-Matic ⚙

1. Automatic transmissions look scary to the beginner, but there's no reason why any amateur mechanic can't handle the job once he understands the basic principles involved.

2. The illustration shown here is of a 2-speed Ford-O-Matic. Callouts are invaluable because they name all of the components.

1. Removing Auto Trans Cover

2. Ford-O-Matic Cutaway

1. Harold Shafer, R&R man at Steve's Transmission Service, 9012 Sepulveda Blvd., Sepulveda, Calif., installs a C-4 Cruise-O-Matic in a customer's car. Transmission jack is vital.

2. The bellhousing is a separate piece on the C-4, so trans is jacked up under car by itself, then housing is fitted in place. Jack adjustments allow trans movement.

3. Bellhousing is attached to trans with bolts. While it is possible to build your own trans on a bench, a car hoist and jack are necessary for installing the transmission in the car.

4. A new converter is installed in car along with rebuilt trans. If you have pulled or installed an automatic trans on your back, you'll appreciate use of a hoist and jack.

5. After the converter is wiggled into place, Shafer bolts an end wrench along one side of the bellhousing. This holds the converter in place until trans is raised up.

6. Converter is now attached to the starter ring, or flywheel, if you prefer. Four nuts secure ring to the converter which features built-in studs. Unit is rotated.

7. Removable crossmember is attached to the tail housing of the C-4 trans, then member is aligned with bolt attachment holes of chassis. Crossmember is now bolted secure.

8. Remaining operations involve installing oil lines that run to the radiator cooler (to cool the oil) and return, and connecting the speedometer cable and transmission shifting linkage.

9. A liberal amount of trans fluid is doused on forward driveshaft yoke which is then slid into tail of the trans. Rear U-joint is hooked, then trans is filled with fluid.

Automatic Transmission
Ford C-4

Of all the components in a modern automobile, probably none scare the average occasional mechanic more than the thought of tearing into an automatic transmission. Let's face it! Most of us know they shift OK by themselves for maybe 50,000 miles, and the fluid should be changed every 20,000 miles or so, along with the filter, before a teardown is necessary. But few of us really know how they operate, or how they come down and go back together. That's why we rely on shops such as Steve's Transmission Service to rebuild our automatic trans for us on those rare occasions when it is necessary. They are specialists, and know what they're doing. We don't. Right? Well, yes and "know."

They are specialists, and they do know

what's happening. But that's no reason we can't learn to do the same things, like going through a transmission. Take the C-4 Ford Cruise-O-Matic and the Chevy Turbo Hydra-Matic boxes on the following pages. They are commonly used units, found in tens of thousands of cars. Maybe one is in your car, and it needs repairs. You know it does because it slips, or hesitates between gear shifts, etc. Now you're asking us, what next?

OK. By using this manual, and maybe a factory shop manual which will cost you another few bucks, you can easily pull your trans down with a minimum of hand tools. Parts cleaner can be used to wash all of the components, followed by solvent and an air hose to blow the parts and passages clean. New seals, O-rings, gaskets, bands and clutches are available over the counter at your local dealership, parts house, or trans repair service. Perhaps a good buddy will assist you, or at least give moral support. But if you are careful and take your time, there

is little reason you can't rebuild your own automatic trans.

The hardest job comes in pulling and replacing the trans itself. Like the rest of us, you have a few sturdy jack stands that will hold the car a couple of feet off the garage floor, but you don't have a transmission jack handy. It's almost impossible to lift one of these boxes, or lower it, safely without a jack. The answer lies in going to a nearby tool rental agency to rent a small floor-type transmission jack. This is the only way to go to make the job easier and safer.

As we said, take your time, use this manual, and you can do it. ♛

1. Detail drawing of C-4 gear train, showing clutches, band and drum.

2. C-4 intermediate band surrounds reverse-high clutch drum; it is adjusted by an external screw via struts. Low-reverse servo and band action is controlled by applied and released pressure on servo piston.

1. C-4 Gear Train, Clutches and Bands

2. Intermediate and Low-Reverse Servo and Band

1. After thoroughly cleaning all components of the C-4 transmission, apply a little grease to the rear of the No. 9 thrust washer and then insert it in rear of trans case.

2. Following the installation of the thrust washer, insert the spring retainer cage that will support both rollers and springs of the one-way clutch. Inner race will follow.

3. The outer race is already in the aluminum transmission case, so now we can install the inner race as shown; 12 springs and 12 rollers are used in the C-4 one-way clutch.

4. Now the 12 springs and 12 rollers can be installed in the one-way clutch. The two components are alternated between races, as shown, and provide low gear for the Ford C-4 trans.

5. The parking pawl retaining pin is installed in the transmission case, then the pawl and pawl return spring are installed over the pin as demonstrated in this photo.

6. Thrust washer No. 10 is then attached to the parking pawl gear with the aid of a dab of grease. Reason for use of grease is to prevent washers from falling away.

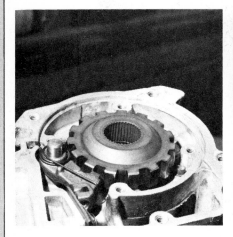

7. The parking pawl gear with thrust washer attached beneath it is now positioned on back face of case. Once transmission is put to use, the grease will mix with trans fluid.

8. The governor distributor sleeve with oil delivery tubes is carefully installed on case. Tap sleeve down snug with a plastic-faced hammer; install bolts with torque wrench.

9. With the secondary governor bolted to the governor distributor, unit (arrow) is slipped over the transmission output shaft. Next, install snap ring to retain governor.

HOW-TO: Assembling a C-4

10. Steve Bustamente, an assembler at Steve's Transmission Service, Sepulveda, Calif., is installing the output shaft with the governor through the rear of the trans case.

11. The rear, or low and reverse, band is installed through the front of the C-4 Cruise-O-Matic case. End of band for the small strut must face toward low-reverse servo.

12. The two band struts (arrows) must be installed as shown, securing the low-reverse band in place in case. Struts lock in tangs on band and ride against aluminum case.

13. After a No. 8 thrust washer has been slipped into low-reverse drum (held firm with grease), the drum (arrow) is slipped through case and into the low-reverse band.

14. Reverse ring gear and the hub are then fitted (arrow) into the low-reverse drum and secured with a snap ring on the output shaft. Snap ring pliers are a must, here.

15. A No. 7 thrust washer is then installed on the rear of the reverse planet carrier (small end), held with grease. No. 6 washer (shown) is applied to front of carrier.

16. Now the reverse planet carrier can be installed in the reverse ring gear. Tabs of the carrier should be engaged with slots in the low-reverse drum, already in case.

17. Lining-covered clutch plates are stacked alternately with steel plates in both clutch packs. These plates wear out, as do the bands, and must be replaced at overhaul.

18. After the outer edge seal is clipped on to the reverse and high clutch cylinder piston, the piston seal is liberally coated with an STP-type of lubricant before installing.

19. An inner seal is installed in clutch cylinder, then reverse and high piston is installed. Now the 10 piston return springs are set in place. They return piston to normal.

20. The spring retainer is held in place with a snap ring, then the clutch is placed in a press, so the springs can be compressed and snap ring installed in proper groove.

21. After the first driven plate is installed in reverse-high clutch, each alternate friction plate is dipped in automatic trans fluid. A clutch pack snap ring holds them.

22. The inner piston seal of the forward clutch cylinder can now be installed. Next, the outer clutch drum seal is installed on the piston and the unit lubed completely.

23. At this juncture, the piston is installed into the forward clutch cylinder, rim outward. One must use caution to make sure that all of the O-ring seals are installed and lubed.

24. The steel ring shown is then installed on top of clutch piston. Make sure clutch piston and cylinder are free of scoring or burrs. Use crocus cloth to remove imperfections.

25. The disc, or diaphragm, spring is now installed in the clutch cylinder, concave side up, followed by installation of the snap ring, which will hold the disc in place.

26. The lower pressure plate is installed first, followed by alternating drive and driven plates, and finally the upper pressure plate and then the snap ring which holds the assembly together.

27. A No. 3 thrust washer is placed atop the forward clutch, then unit is stacked on reverse-high clutch drum, followed by assembly of the forward clutch hub and ring gear.

HOW-TO: Assembling a C-4

28. A No. 4 thrust washer is placed in back of front planet carrier, which is set on clutch assemblies. Now install input shell, shown, with sun gear and No. 5 thrust washer.

29. After installing a new front pump bushing in that unit, drop the front pump drive and driven gears in place. Use caution, and do not scratch or damage the pump gears.

30. Install the four seal rings (arrows) on the stator support, then install stator into front pump. After attaching stator to front pump, check for free gear movement.

31. Install the selective thrust washer (arrow) on rear of stator, followed by installation of smaller selective thrust washer on end of stator shaft, being held by lube.

32. A large O-ring must be installed (arrow), then front pump gasket. A converter anti-ballooning valve is inserted in hole leading to converter. Dab of grease will hold it in place.

33. The complete clutch pack can now be installed through the front of the C-4 transmission case, with the input shell being fed in first. Unit is now nearing completion.

34. This operation is followed by installation of the intermediate band over the reverse-high drum. It would be wise to purchase a shop manual for more detailed instruction.

35. Stator and pump are installed in front case. Pump is held in place temporarily by two bolts until it is put in car. The input shaft is next slipped into the hollow stator.

36. Air hose is held against inlet (large arrow) and trans is tested at 40 psi air pressure to check for any leaks in clutch packs. Intermediate band struts are installed first.

37. Two seals (see arrows) must be installed on the intermediate servo piston, then lubed with STP-type lubricant before installation. These lubing operations are very important.

38. After lubrication, the intermediate servo piston can be inserted into its cover. All brand new seals and gaskets are used at Steve's when any automatic trans is rebuilt.

39. After installing the low-reverse servo piston return spring, lube the cavity with an STP-type lubricant. The piston seal is also lubed before it is installed in the case.

40. After lubing the walls of the servo cavity and installation of the servo piston return spring, install the servo piston and cover, with new gasket. Press cover down and bolt it.

41. The reverse band can now be adjusted. The adjusting screw is then torqued to 10 in.-lbs., then the screw is backed off three full turns to arrive at proper final setting.

42. A new manual arm seal must be installed in the case after it has been disassembled. After this step, the manual arm for selecting reverse and forward gears can be connected.

43. The inner downshift lever can now be installed, followed by tightening of the nut on the manual arm shaft inside case. O-ring seal is installed on the outside portion of the case.

44. After assembling the valve body, the bolts should be torqued to 20-35-in.-lbs. The valve body filter should be torqued to 80-120 in.-lbs. of pressure. Follow these specs.

45. A new rear extension housing bushing should be driven into place, housing installed, followed by valve body installation. The final operation is that of installing the oil pan.

Automatic Transmission
Turbo 400

1. Turbo Hydra-Matic Trans

2. Disassembled Turbo Trans

3. Turbo Drivetrain

Due to the great number of Turbo Hydra-Matic 400 automatic transmissions in service today, it was only appropriate that we should feature a transmission build-up article on this popular unit. The Turbo 400 is found in many of General Motors automobiles, and because many of these vehicles are now approaching 50,000-60,000 miles, the gearboxes are undoubtedly in need of rebuilding.

A visit to Steve's Transmission Service, 9012 Sepulveda Blvd., Sepulveda, California—a large, reputable automatic transmission establishment—permitted us to obtain these step-by-step assembly photos of a 400 going together. Use of this article in conjunction with a factory-prepared manual will permit anyone with a limited number of hand tools to assemble (and disassemble, by reversing the operations) his own Turbo 400 transmission. Scanning through the transmission section of our own shop manual revealed dozens of specialized tools recommended for use in installing seals, etc. Yet, we found during our picture taking session that very few special tools were actually required to complete this transmission.

An inch-pound torque wrench, sockets, a few end wrenches, snap ring pliers and screwdrivers were about all that were really needed, along with a bit of caution and care when it came to installing the seals and O-rings.

Most of us know someone who is a full-time mechanic, and if he isn't a transmission specialist he surely knows someone who is. These people may be able to help you out during assembly when it comes time to install the intermediate clutch piston snap ring, the direct clutch snap ring, or the forward clutch spring retaining snap ring, for example. They may not charge you a cent, thinking you're pretty trick if you have decided to tackle this transmission by yourself. If not, the damage to your wallet won't be that bad.

Too many people are afraid to tackle a job that appears as difficult or challenging as rebuilding an automatic transmission, but if you follow directions carefully, you can't go wrong. So, if you're mechanically inclined at all, and have the time and tools—along with the desire to do it yourself and save some bucks—then just follow the bouncing ball.

1. General Motors Turbo Hydra-Matic transmission is one of the best of the automatics available. A strong unit, it's also adaptable to racing.

2. There are many components in the Turbo 400, but with a little care, the right tools and following the directions, you can assemble one. Across the top we find the tail housing, main case, and valve body. Through the center are the many clutch housings and shafts with the front pump. At bottom are the pan, bands and clutches, converter.

3. Assembled, the Turbo gear train looks like this. The converter is at right. Drive clutches are hidden inside the clutch drums, with the bands outside. Front pump is located directly behind converter.

1. Assembler Steve Bustamente installs rear internal gear to sun gear thrust bearing and two races on rear internal gear mainshaft.

2. After dropping the rear internal gear mainshaft into output carrier, install the output shaft assembly into the output carrier, as shown.

3. The output-shaft-to-carrier snap ring can now be installed. A steel speedometer gear has already been put in place on the output shaft.

4. Before installing the output shaft to the case thrust washer, Steve adds a dab of grease to hold it. Retaining tabs are locked in pockets.

5. A composition ring (arrow) is slipped about output carrier to hold noise down. Another thrust washer is added prior to the reaction carrier.

6. With the sun gear in place, the roller clutch cage and rollers are installed in the reaction carrier, which is then placed on output unit.

7. The intermediate clutch piston inner and outer seals are put in place, then the unit is set into the main center support assembly.

8. The intermediate clutch release springs are installed, then the intermediate clutch spring retainer is installed, held by a snap ring.

9. Center support assembly is turned over, and its thrust washer is then set in place. Clutch piston should be air checked with compressed air.

HOW-TO: Assembling a Turbo 400

10. Grease is dabbed on the needle bearing and thrust washer before it's installed on end of center support. Support to case spacer is now added.

11. The center support assembly is next installed into the roller clutch in the reaction carrier. Be sure to check rotation of center support.

12. Install the rear unit selective washer into slots provided inside rear of trans case. Proper washer was determined by end-play check.

13. Install rear band assembly so that the two lugs index with the two anchor pins. Check to make sure that band is seated on the lugs.

14. Install proper rear selective washer into slots provided inside rear of case, then install complete gear unit assembly into the case.

15. Steve aligns application hole on center support with case application hole. Then he installed a screw for the intermediate clutch apply.

16. Center support to case spacer and snap ring are installed, then intermediate clutches are soaked in ATF before being installed in case.

17. After installation of the three steel and three composition clutch discs, alternated, the intermediate backing plate is installed next.

18. The direct clutch piston outer seal is already installed, and now inner seal is being inserted in the piston. Seals are both lubed.

19. Direct clutch piston is placed into the forward clutch housing, then 16 clutch release springs are set into pockets about the piston.

20. Steve's uses spring compressor to compress the clutch release springs after a retainer plate is installed. Now install a snap ring.

21. The direct clutch backing plate can now be installed in the direct clutch housing, preceded by wavy steel, flat steel and clutch plates.

22. The backing plate snap ring can now be installed in the direct clutch housing. Small screwdriver will assist in getting it in groove.

23. Moving back to the transmission, install the front band with anchor hole placed over band anchor pin and apply lug facing servo hole.

24. The direct clutch drum is now installed in turbo case without the clutch plates (being installed in photos 21, 22); it's easier empty.

25. Steve rotates forward clutch piston as he installs it in the forward clutch housing. A .006-in. feeler gauge helps slide seal down.

26. Sixteen clutch release springs (green) are installed in pockets of forward clutch piston. Always lube seals during assembly; use caution.

27. Place forward clutch assembly in press, install retainer ring and snap ring. Job can be performed without a big spring compressor.

HOW-TO: Assembling a Turbo 400

28. Waved steel plate, then the composition and flat steel plates, alternated, are dipped in fluid then installed in forward clutch housing.

29. Forward clutch hub and thrust washers are installed, followed by direct clutch hub and snap ring. Turbine shaft is on clutch housing.

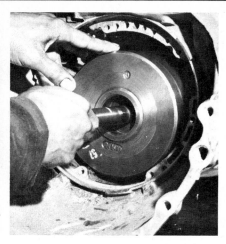

30. Grasp turbine shaft and slide forward clutch drum assembly into direct clutch drum. Direct clutch hub will move right into the drum.

31. Front pump body with driven gear is ready for drive gear. Oil teeth before installing gear. Make sure tangs are installed on the top side.

32. Pump cover can now be installed onto pump body. Hole in bench top accepts shafts of different parts, making work on trans quite easy.

33. A pair of ballpoint pens may be used to index bolt holes; then it's easier to install fasteners. Tighten pump cover bolts to 15 ft.-lbs.

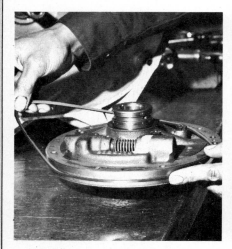

34. Install front pump gasket, then the O-ring seal. Lube seal with STP-type lube; carefully install front pump assembly on trans case.

35. Front pump is secured to case, then end-play is checked with dial indicator. Should be from .003-in. to .024-in. Install new pump seal.

36. At this juncture, the case to center support bolt is installed. Hollow bolt is used as oil passage for intermediate clutch apply.

37. New O-ring is installed on rear servo piston, which is lubed. Then rear accumulator spring is dropped in place, followed by the piston.

38. Metal rear servo gasket is next installed, then rear servo cover is bolted down. Torque all the attaching screws to 15-20 ft.-lbs.

39. The front servo piston can now be installed in case, adjacent to rear servo. Care should be taken to make sure components are clean.

40. Arrows depict six check balls that must be installed in pockets. Now install valve body spacer plate and gasket; gasket next to trans.

41. Valve body can now be installed. Make sure manual valve is properly indexed with pin on manual detent lever and governor pipes are in.

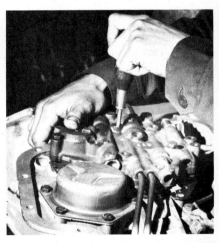

42. Guide pins or screwdriver may be used to align valve body so that screws can be installed. Now install manual detent roller spring assembly.

43. Make sure lead wire clip is installed (except P model), then tighten solenoid, valve body bolts. Install filter intake pipe, O-ring.

44. Use new filter, make sure it's properly installed on intake pipe. Never wash old filter, but replace it. Install new bottom pan gasket.

45. Install bottom pan, torque pan bolts to 15 ft.-lbs. Then, finally, install governor assembly and rear tail housing onto trans case.

Driveshaft & U-Joints

If you've ever wondered why your car has to have a driveshaft, the answer is it doesn't. Most of the motorcycles around use chains to accomplish the same purpose, and their owners wonder why anybody uses a driveshaft.

Chain drive on automobiles went out with button shoes, which must have been an awfully long time ago. Most American passenger cars use a single-piece driveshaft with a U-joint at each end. U-joints allow power to be transmitted through the various angles that the rear end causes as it goes up and down and travels over the road. Working in conjunction with the U-joints is a slip-joint on the back of the transmission, which allows the driveshaft to move in and out. This is necessary because the movement of the rear end actually shortens and lengthens the distance between the rear end and the transmission whenever the rear end goes over a bump.

That's about all there is to a driveline. Ordinarily nothing would ever go wrong here except for possible replacement of the U-joints. Some cars have grease fittings, and you're supposed to lubricate the U-joints when you lube the chassis. In the course of hard driving you occasionally hear of someone breaking a driveshaft or U-joint, but normally U-joints just wear out. You can tell when they're worn and loose by a "clunk" sound when you put the car in gear. Improper rear-end gear lash can also make this type of sound so you'll need to put the car on a lift to check it out.

We have two general types of drive systems on American passenger cars. One is the "torque-tube" drive. Here, the driveshaft is enclosed inside a large tube that bolts solidly to the rear axle. The tube pivots on a large ball joint on the back of the transmission, and there is a

U-joint inside this ball. There is no joint at the back of the driveshaft. The large outside torque tube absorbs torque and drive forces on the rear axle, with radius rods of some kind to keep the axle in line. Cars using torque-tube drive include early Ford products up through 1948, Chevrolets through '54, and Ramblers and big Buicks up to the early 1960's. Torque-tube drive has fallen out of popularity on late cars because the tube telegraphs too much road vibration to the passenger compartment of the car.

All other cars use an open driveshaft with U-joints at each end and a slip joint at the front. The shaft has to transmit only engine power, not take rear axle forces and twisting. These forces are taken either by long leaf springs, as on late Chrysler products, or by trailing suspension arms on late GM and Ford lines that use coil springs.

The principle in coil or leaf spring designs, is really the same. The driveline only has to transmit power, and rear-end drive forces are absorbed either by leaf springs or suspension arms and cross links.

It should be mentioned here that a number of General Motors cars (including Chevrolet) used 2-piece driveshafts with X-type frames in the late 1950's and early 1960's. These had a support bearing near the center of the shaft, in the center of the X-frame, with a short section of driveshaft in front and behind the center bearing. There were three U-joints. Servicing this type of driveline is a little more work, but the operations are essentially the same as for various other designs.

SETTING UP THE DRIVESHAFT

Driveshaft vibration is a chief cause of

roughness and rumble in passenger cars, and companies spend a lot of effort in engineering and testing to get rid of it. They also carefully balance driveshafts on all cars on the assembly line, and adjust U-joint angles and phasing, to control the problem in production, and *you* can mess everything up in a few minutes when you start tearing into a driveshaft and U-joints—if you do not know what you're doing.

In the first place, when removing the driveshaft you should make sure that you will get all elements back in the same position or "phasing" they originally held. U-joint yokes, for instance, should be in the same rotational position on the shaft as they were. This can be easily done by merely marking the shaft and yoke before disassembly. (Usually, there are phasing marks from the factory, but these are sometimes hard to find.) Note that most shafts have their U-joints phased so yokes at the front and rear of the shaft are at 90° to each other. If you should forget to mark, or can't find the factory marks, do it this way as a rule of thumb. But the safest thing is just to remember to mark the shaft and joints when they are removed, and then they can be bolted right back together in that relationship.

Driveshaft or U-joint *angles* are also critical. A little thought will show why. When a U-joint is transmitting power through an angle, the yokes have to flex back and forth at high speed as the shaft turns. The rotational motion they deliver is not an even rotation, but a kind of pulsing motion that speeds up and slows down twice each revolution. The greater the angle through which the power is transmitted, the more uneven this pulsing delivery and the more vibration. The easiest answer is just to see

1. Driveline Types

2. Torque Tube Drive

4. Buick Torque Ball

3. Two-piece Driveshaft

1 The basic driveline types: (A) Torque tube, (B) One-piece open driveshaft, (C) Two-piece open driveshaft, (D) One-piece curved driveshaft without universal joints.

2. Torque tube drive was formerly used on several makes of cars. The tube containing the driveshaft is rigidly attached to the differential housing and absorbs driveline reaction torque.

3. Two-piece driveshafts were used at one time on several U.S. cars, including Chevrolets. Shorter unsupported driveshaft length added complexity, reduced vibration.

4. At the front of a torque tube drive is the "torque ball," an enclosed housing containing the universal joint.

that the driveshaft angles are kept as straight as possible, so the U-joints don't have to flex very much as they turn. The ideal driveline would have zero angles in the U-joints. But, of course, this is impossible with the rear axle bouncing up and down.

Each different car maker has certain recommendations for maximum and minimum U-joint angles. Space won't permit covering all of these, but you can find them in the shop manual for that model at your car dealer. As a rule of thumb, just keep the angles very small with a normal load in the car—like 1° or 2°, and with 3° to 4° as maximum. This is the angle between the axis (centerline) of the driveshaft and the axis of the U-joint yoke at the front and rear end. About the only way you can measure it accurately is with a bubble protractor. This has a long flat flange on one side, to lay against the shaft or yoke housing, with a rotating bubble wheel in the center that will show angles very accurately. One of these instruments is expensive, but a garage may have one.

In most cases, the factory recommendation for setting driveshaft angle involves changing the angle of the rear joint so it exactly matches up with whatever angle the front joint has. When both angles are the same on a 1-piece driveshaft, the U-joints work together instead of fighting each other. When there are

leaf springs supporting the rear axle, the rear U-joint angle—sometimes called the pinion angle—can be easily changed by putting wedge-shaped shims between the spring and its seat on the housing.

On Ford and GM models using coil springs and trailing suspension arms it's usually necessary to shim either at the front pivot of the suspension arm or where the rear axle pivots on the arm. Your shop manual will tell all about it. All you're doing, in effect, is to tip the rear axle nose a little to change the angle between the rear U-joint yoke and the driveshaft.

REMOVING THE DRIVESHAFT

Most cars have a plain open driveshaft with a U-joint at each end and slip joint at the front, either ahead of or behind the front U-joint. Study the design of a typical U-joint and you will see that there are two Y-shaped yokes with a cross-arm piece that connects them, usually with needle bearings where the cross-arm revolves in the yokes. (The cross piece is called the "trunnion.") Most cars use this type of trunnion-type joint.

In this case, the rear U-joint on the driveshaft will be made so the bearing bosses on the rear yoke are split, enabling the joint to be quickly taken apart. The trunnion bearings will be secured to the yoke by simple U-bolts or some kind of little casting with cap screws, or maybe just a strap of steel with clamps or bolts. This design is necessary in order to get the driveshaft out of the car. In other words, you just split the rear yoke bearing retainer (whatever the design), and the U-joint will come right apart and the driveshaft will drop down at the rear. Be careful that you don't drop the trunnion and needle bearings and damage them. The needle bearings should be taped to protect them in storage, until reassembly. Note that the rear half of the split rear yoke is attached directly to the rear axle input shaft. This is called the "companion flange." You won't be doing anything with this in normal U-joint service, unless it's broken.

After the rear U-joint is split and the back of the driveshaft is dropped, the

shaft can be removed by merely pulling it back until the splines in the front slip joint slide apart. This distance might be 2 or 3 ins.

Getting the driveshaft out of a torque-tube car is more of a job. On Fords and Buicks, for instance, you have to loosen the whole rear axle assembly and move it back a little in order to get the ball joint at the front of the torque tube apart. It's simple to unbolt the ball retainer from the rear of the transmission. When taking the ball assembly apart, be careful not to lose the seals and O-rings that retain the lubricant (though these should be replaced with new parts before reassembly). It's much simpler on a pre-'55 Chevrolet with torque-tube drive. Here you just unhook the hand brake brackets and cables from the drive tube, remove the cap screws that hold the ball-retainer collar to the back of the transmission and slide it back on the driveshaft housing (or torque tube). Next remove the cap screws that hold the trunnion bearings to the front yoke. Place a jack under the driveshaft to keep it from dropping, and carefully remove the two front-yoke trunnion bearings. Then the driveshaft torque-tube assembly can be lowered—and the rear yoke of the U-joint will slide right off the shaft splines.

Keep in mind that you rarely have to remove the complete driveshaft from a torque-tube-drive car. Usually, if there's anything wrong, it's the front U-joint or ball joint around it (there isn't any U-joint in the back). So your driveshaft removal job is usually just a matter of removing the front ball-joint retainer from the back of the transmission, and dropping the shaft down to get to the U-joint.

Installing a driveshaft is pretty much the reverse of the above. The toughest part is holding the shaft up while you connect the U-joint. When reinstalling a torque-tube drive, especially where you have replaced the oil seals and O-rings, the ball joint might be too tight in its socket for easy movement of the axle up and down. On pre-'55 Chevrolets this adjustment of the ball tension is made by adding or subtracting shims under the cap screws that hold the ball-retainer to the transmission. With the screws tightened you should be able to move the ball with hand pressure on the tube. If too tight, add shims and check again.

SERVICING U-JOINTS

In late years, the car manufacturers haven't been recommending any regular

Driveshaft & U-Joints

service work on U-joints other than periodic lubrication through a grease fitting. But a few years ago they used to suggest taking them apart, cleaning, and lubricating every 2 years. If you might want to do this on your car, you will need some information on assembly and disassembly.

On a conventional trunnion-type joint, as we mentioned, you have needle bearings on each end of the trunnion where it pivots in the two yokes. It's a bit of a trick to get these bearings out and the joint apart. You will note that the bearing cups are retained in the outer ends of the yokes by C-shaped clip rings in a groove. On many models the clips are on the inside of the yoke, so you will have to tap them out with a punch and hammer. Then there are the designs without any clips at all. The cups are held in place by plastic injected through a hole in the yoke. You can disassemble these joints, because the plastic will shear when you hammer or press the cups out. But you can't use the same cups and trunnion again. You must get a replacement kit that comes with the clips and grooved cups.

After you are sure that there are no clips, or have removed the clips, set the joint up in a vise or on a support of some kind that will be open below the bearing hole in one end of the yoke (there are four of these ends in all). Then take a punch and gently tap the *opposite* bearing cup *inward* with a hammer. This will push the trunnion through the yoke far enough so the bearing cup will drop out of the other end. You have to repeat this the other way, then on the two bearings on the other yoke.

Another approach is to use a punch and tap on the center of the trunnion (at the cross) until the bearings drop out. Just tap easy, not too hard. Be careful not to damage the bearing bores in the yokes or the surface on the trunnion. And it's a good idea to cover the bearing cups with tape to prevent damaging them until reassembly is completed.

Servicing this conventional trunnion-yoke joint is very simple. First clean everything carefully with solvent, including the grooves for seals and rings, then inspect everything. There shouldn't be any excessive wear in the yoke bores or on the bearing surfaces on the ends of the trunnion arms. The needle bearings should look good, with no looseness in their cups and no obvious wear, galling, or broken needles.

After everything is clean and ready for reassembly, put a small amount of chassis grease in the bearing cup. This will be retained by the seal and retainer, and you should have adequate lubrication for at least 2 years; or, as they say, "for the life of the car," on late models.

1. Assembly of bearings to the trunnion. Examine each bearing and bushing carefully, replace if required. Keep it clean!

2. The normal "one-piece" driveshaft, showing two U-joints and slip joint.

Now you're ready to reassemble. This procedure is pretty much the reverse of what you've done. Modern U-joints have seal and retainer rings on the inner ends of the bearing cups, that go between the cup and a shoulder on the trunnion arm. These will have to be assembled before the bearing cup. A standard procedure is just to put the seal and retainer rings on the trunnion, then tap the bearing cups into the yoke bores part way, alternating each end so the trunnion journal can be slipped up inside the bearing. You can readily see the easiest way with your particular joint design. Just be very careful when tapping these bearings into place that nothing gets damaged. It's a ticklish job. Also be sure the little C-shaped clip rings are snug in their grooves. If one of these were to break or slip out you'd have big trouble.

The U-joints in the front end of torque-tube drives are generally of this trunnion-type, with minor variations, so the servicing procedure would be about the same as above.

The unique "ball-and-trunnion" joints used on one or both ends of most Chrysler products of the 1950's (Plymouth, Dodge, etc.) are another deal entirely. These are designed to combine the flexing of a conventional U-joint with the in-and-out motion of the slip joint. There is a round boss on the front end of the driveshaft with a hole in it and a pin pressed through it. Needle bearings and balls are on the outer ends of the pin, and these ride in round slots in a large collar that bolts to the transmission output shaft. In this way we get the necessary flexing and plunging motion by the balls rolling in the slots.

Servicing is quite simple. The drive-

1. Trunnion Assembly

shaft is dropped by splitting the rear conventional U-joint. To withdraw the driveshaft from the front, you have to detach the ring clips that hold the rubber boot, and then the shaft will pull right out of the collar (or body) with the pin and rollers intact. Inspect all parts for wear and clean everything carefully (including the inside of the collar and slots) with solvent. Do not press the pin out of the driveshaft boss unless it is loose. This pin has to be pressed in very accurately, within .006-in. on each side, or you're apt to get driveline vibration. It's rarely necessary to replace a pin. If the rollers, needles or centering buttons are worn they can easily be replaced. When assembling, repack the body or collar with 1¼ oz. of chassis grease, and put the joint back together, following the disassembly procedure in reverse.

A word about servicing the U-joints on Chevrolets of the 1960 era that had the 2-piece driveshaft: To remove the complete driveshaft, you need to remove the bolts that hold the center support bearing to the X-frame, then split the rear U-joint in the usual way to drop the back of the driveshaft. Then the whole shaft assembly can be withdrawn from the front slip joint. The center bearing and support remains on the front shaft.

To remove the center U-joint, take out the large bolt that holds the joint yoke to the front driveshaft; then disassemble the joints in the usual way, as they are of the conventional trunnion-yoke type. It's recommended that you *do not* try to remove the support bearing or bracket. It rarely needs attention, and it's very easy to damage either the bearing or the shaft in pressing it off. Special tools are needed to remove it. Take this job to a Chevrolet garage.

Some cars have constant-velocity joints. They look like a double U-joint with a heavy connecting double yoke. Before disassembly, mark all three yokes with aligned punch marks. They come apart about the same as a regular joint, except that there's a bunch of parts hidden behind the center yoke (a ball and socket arrangement) that keeps the two parts of the joint in line. Watch carefully when you disassemble it so you can get the pieces back together right. During reassembly, line up the punch marks you made before so the joint will keep its original phasing. 🔧

2. One-piece Driveshaft

1. To repack U-joints that do not have grease fittings, unbolt both sides of the U-joint from the companion flange on the differential.

2. Drop the end of the driveshaft from the companion flange. Lower it as shown then pull it rearward until slip yoke comes free of transmission.

3. Clamp the shaft securely in a vise and with a pair of pliers, remove each of the retaining clips. Needle-nose pliers work best on these spring clips.

4. Some types of U-joints have retaining clips on the inside (1). Note the strap (2) that holds cups in place when removing shaft from the car.

5. Use a screwdriver to carefully pry the two free bearing cups before removing the U-joint cross from the shaft. They could fall off and be damaged.

6. There are special tools for this job, but a hammer and a punch will do it just as well. Apply enough force on the flange to free the cross.

7. Once the cross has been worked free, remove the other two bearing cups. Pry them loose with a screwdriver as you did the first pair.

8. Wipe the inside of each cup with a clean cloth. Inspect for signs of wear on needle bearings. Work carefully to avoid disturbing the bearings.

9. Wipe a dab of grease in each bearing cup and replace it. Press the cross back into the shaft, snap in retaining rings, and replace shaft on car.

Rear Axle

With a little luck you could wear out the engines in a half dozen automobiles and never have any trouble with the rear axle. The days are gone when wheel bearings and rear axle gears used to give out with regularity. In fact, it is sometimes a wonder why car makers put so much meat in their axles and rear ends. These units don't really need to be that tough, but we can be thankful they *are*.

A rear axle is basically a simple thing. Its essential purpose is to convert the driveshaft torque into thrust at the two rear wheels by using a form of bevel gear to turn the rotation through 90°. This is the "ring and pinion" gearset in the large center housing. The pinion is the small gear driven directly from the driveshaft, just behind the rear U-joint. This turns a large ring gear that turns the rear wheels. We also need a "differential" here so that one rear wheel can turn faster than the other when going around a corner. This is a small bevel planetary gearset inside the ring gear. The ring gear is bolted to the differential outer housing, and the axle shafts to the two rear wheels are splined into side gears, in turn connected to the ring through bevel pinions. This allows one wheel to overspeed the other and still feed torque to both of them.

There's one serious disadvantage to a conventional differential. It exactly splits the total driveshaft torque between the two rear wheels. This means that if one wheel gets on ice or mud, there's no bite; the other wheel can't transmit any more torque—so the car sits there and spins one wheel while the other is doing nothing, even though it may be on dry ground. You've all seen this effect. This is also a problem on the drag strip, where driveshaft torque reaction tries to lift the right rear wheel and let it spin. Then the other wheel just doesn't do anything.

This is where your "limited-slip" (Posi-Traction, Equa-Lock, etc.) differentials come in. These have special clutches between the side gears and differential case to lock up the assembly when one wheel starts to spin. Some clutches are applied by springs, others have cams that increase clutch pressure as axle torque increases. Either way offers a big advantage on ice or on the drag strip. We suggest ordering a limited-slip differential (about $40 extra) on any high-performance car. Or you can get kits and install them on older cars.

DIAGNOSING AXLE TROUBLES

Most rear axle trouble shows up in the form of some unusual noise from the axle, usually either gear noise in the ring and pinion (seldom the differential) or bearing noise in the outer ends of the axle housing.

Gear noise is a rather high-pitched whine that tends to "cycle"—it gets louder and softer, sometimes higher and lower, in a definite rhythmic pattern. The

1. Standard Rear End and Axles

2. Removing Axle

3. Rear End Parts

noise is much more pronounced at certain car speeds than others. In fact it might also disappear at some speeds. You have to drive the car up and down the speed range on a smooth road to find it, checking under "pull" and "coast" conditions.

Bearing noise is entirely different. It has a lower-pitched whine or growl that remains quite steady, and tends to be louder when accelerating under load than when coasting. Most often the trouble will be in the wheel bearings at the outer ends of the axle (usually just one of them). It usually can be pinpointed by driving the car down the road and suddenly swerving to one side, then the other. This throws additional side load on the wheel bearings—and the growl should get louder. The best way to tell *which* bearing it is with this test (as a bearing can make noise with thrust in either direction or both): have someone ride in the trunk or rear seat to listen on both sides for the noise while you drive.

There's a chance the bad bearing could be one of the differential side bearings or the pinion bearing in the nose of the axle center section. In this case the whine would be higher pitched (because of the higher shaft speed) but would tend to remain steady. Also it would be louder under power, but would not change when you swerve the car on the road. Bearing trouble in the axle center section is much less likely than in the wheel bearings.

There are other possible axle troubles. A broken axle shaft is clear enough. The car won't move with a conventional differential, though it will move slightly under half-power with a limited-slip. A bad grease seal is clear enough—oil all over everything. Main grease seals are at the nose of the center section (just behind the rear U-joint), and at the wheel bearings at the outer ends. Usually it's the wheel bearing seals, as they are subjected to more stress forces under driving loads. Broken gear teeth in the differential are not common, but easy enough to detect. There will be a clunking feel each revolution. And a good fullpower run with teeth out will usually shuck out what's left—so the trouble won't be hidden for long!

MINOR AXLE SERVICE

With a little experience, you can safely tackle some rear axle service, but not too much. It's too easy to mess things up. The simplest job is to pull the axle shafts and wheel bearings—either to replace a broken shaft, wheel bearing or outer grease seal. Even this will take some special tools, and you may have to have the bearing replaced at a garage. But you can pull the shafts, bearings, and seals on most late-model American cars with just a slide-hammer type axle puller and ordinary hand tools, which can be rented, borrowed or bought at a reasonable price.

AXLES WITH RETAINERS AT WHEELS

Jack up the rear end and remove the wheel lug nuts and the wheel. The brake drum is retained by these same nuts, and you can pull this off after the wheel. (It fits on there more snugly, so it will take some yanking—and a gasket may come with it.) When the drum is off, it will expose a broad flange on the end of the axle shaft (forged as part of the axle) that has studs spaced around it for the lug nuts. This is what you pull out of the axle housing; the shaft, bearings, and seals will come with it. But before it will come out you have to go behind the flange and remove the small bolts that hold on the axle bearing retainer plate and brake backing plate (which holds the shoes and cylinders). Remove these bolts and remove the retainer plate. But then put a couple of them back on to hold the brake in place, as this doesn't need to come off when changing axle shafts. Just tighten a couple of them up finger-tight and they will hold the brake.

Now you're ready for the axle-puller. This is a device that has a bracket on one end that attaches to the studs on your axle flange. There's a weight that slides back and forth on a rod attached to the bracket, and you can hammer this against the stop to pull the axle shaft and bearing out of the axle housing. Don't bang it too hard. Take it easy, and work the shaft out slowly so the jarring won't damage the ball bearings. You can buy one of these axle-pullers for your particular car at your car dealer, or universal types are available at any auto parts house. It's a good tool to have.

After the axle shaft and bearing are out, inspect them for wear, corrosion, and cracks. You can tell a bad bearing very easily. It will feel sloppy or rough—

4. Dodge Rear Axle

1. The carrier side bearings are adjusted by means of a threaded ring in this design. Adjustment can only be done properly while the carrier is out of the axle housing.

2. The axle comes out with the bearing, after the bearing retainer has been unbolted from the backing plate.

3. Here are the component parts of a typical differential. While rugged and trouble-free, a differential is a piece of precision machinery that requires expert assembly.

4. Typical modern rear axle unit has inner retainers, straight roller bearings operating directly on the rear axle shafts themselves.

5. This type of differential and rear axle assembly disassembles from the front. It's probably best to let a specialist repair shop handle major rear end jobs.

5. Rear Axle Assembly

Rear Axle

that is, the outer race will be loose on the balls. Sometimes the balls are pitted and galled, and the central ball cage may be loose. Replace the bearing if you have any doubts at all, as they aren't expensive. However it does take a special tool and sometimes a press to remove the bearing and replace it, so you'll probably need to have this done at a shop. And this would also have to be done if you broke an axle shaft.

But if you're just replacing an outer grease seal, this can be done quite easily without removing the bearing from the shaft. There are different types and designs of seals, and sometimes there are two or three on both sides of the inner race of the bearing and a ring around the outside. Usually these rubber seals can be pried off with a screwdriver. This would damage them beyond repair, but you will always be replacing them anyway when you pull an axle shaft. Sometimes seals can be put back without special tools, or with a makeshift drift or collar. Just be careful not to damage the seal surface putting it back on the bearing. And always replace the seal with the open edge or flange facing the lubricant. If you put it on backwards, it won't work.

After everything is cleaned and lightly lubricated with chassis grease, you're ready to put the axle shaft back in. The first thing you have to do here is to run the shaft clear into the housing until you can feel it strike the differential side gear bearing or shaft. This will have splines that must fit the splines on the end of the axle shaft. You just have to feel around with the shaft in there until the end slides into the splines. You can't see anything. Just work it around until it slips in. Nothing to it.

From here you drive the bearing into the outer axle housing with the axle-puller, working in reverse as a drive hammer. (Or you could do it with a heavy hammer on the face of the axle flange.) When the bearing is seated in the axle housing, you just replace the bearing retainer plate (after removing the finger-tight bolts holding on the brake). Tighten these up good and snug. Then back go the brake drum and gasket, and finally the wheel and lug nuts.

AXLES WITH INNER RETAINERS

Chevrolet since 1965, and many other cars, do not have the retainer at the wheel behind the axle flange. After pulling the wheel and the brake drum, you will notice that there are no bolts in the area behind the axle flange that have anything to do with retaining either the axle or the bearing. This type of axle is held in place by a C-washer at the extreme inner end of the axle shaft. To remove the axle, you must remove the rear cover on the rear end housing, which of course lets all the oil run out. Then you have to remove a long screw that holds the differential pinion shaft in position so that the shaft can be pulled out of the differential carrier. Once the shaft is out of the way, the axle shaft

can be pushed inward enough to free the C-washer, which will then fall out into your hand. Once the C-washer is out, you can slide the axle out of the housing. The bearing and seal are pressed into the end of the housing and must be removed with a slide hammer puller that will reach in and pull from behind the bearing.

THE CENTER SECTION

There are two general types of rear axle center-section designs on modern American cars. The most common is where the main axle and differential housing is like a large banjo in the center, with tubes tapering off on each side for the axle shafts and to hold the wheels. The banjo is closed at the back. Then the gears and differential are carried in a cast iron "carrier" that bolts to the front of the banjo. You can get to the gears by merely unbolting the carrier and pulling it out.

In the other layout, the carrier housing is much larger and contains the entire differential. The side axle tube housings

are pressed into this carrier casting, and it's closed at the back by a stamped cover that bolts on. This design is used for the late Chevrolet axle and the small Chrysler models, etc. It has the advantage of keeping all parts in a bit more rigid alignment, but it's harder to work on the gears and seals. In both cases, of course, when removing the carrier, you must disconnect the rear U-joint, drop the driveshaft, and pull out the axle shafts from the outer ends of the axle housing (as outlined earlier).

Obviously any center-section service work will be quite a bit easier on axles with a removable carrier. Here you just unbolt the carrier from the banjo housing and pull it out (after you remove the axles). All gear adjustments can be made right on the carrier assembly. And you can put the assembly up on a bench to work on it. With the "integral"-type axle (late Chevrolets, etc.) you either have to pull the entire axle out of the car to work on it, or put the car up on a hoist and work from underneath.

Rear end gear adjustments are critical for low axle noise, especially with these "stiff" 4.11 and 4.56 ratios. For instance,

1. Unbolting Sway Bar Shackles

2. Removing Differential Cover

3. Removing Pinion Shaft Lock Screw

4. Using Magnetized Rod

5. Removing the C-Lock

1. If your car uses a rear anti-sway bar like this Pontiac Trans-Am, you'll have to unbolt the shackles and swing the bar out of the way.

2. Place a container beneath the differential before removing the cover. This comes under the heading of good housekeeping.

3. After the differential has been drained, wipe exposed parts dry and remove the lock screw holding the pinion shaft in place.

4. You'll have to push each wheel in toward the differential in order to remove the C-lock from button end of axle shaft. A magnetized rod makes removal easy.

5. The C-lock is the key to differential reassembly, so for heaven's sake don't lose it. Pull it out and put it where you can find it again later.

6. Remove the axle shaft from the housing by pulling outward. Be careful not to damage the oil seal in the differential when pulling axle out.

6. Pulling Axle From Housing

gear "lash" (the distance a tooth on the ring or pinion can be moved back and forth before contacting the next tooth) must be held generally between .004 and .008-in. That's pretty tight. Lash is adjusted by shim spacers on the pinion stem and at the differential side bearings. (These adjustments move the pinion gear back and forth and the ring gear from side to side, respectively.) Needless to say, making these adjustments is complicated work. Not only do you need special tools to get at the adjusting shims, but you need a pretty sophisticated dial indicator rig just to *check* lash. So this is best left to pros.

But you can save plenty of money by removing your own replaceable carrier assembly (on 90% of cars) and taking it into the shop for work. Then you won't pay labor for removing this from the axle. You can usually tell whether your gears need adjustment by gear whine on the road—which you can interpret from instructions earlier in this chapter. Also, a quick inspection of the ring and pinion gear teeth can tell a lot about gear lash. If adjustment is right, the wear pattern (where it is shiny and smooth) should be right in the middle of the tooth face. This is both across the tooth and up and down on the tooth. Right in the middle. If there is a wear spot at one end of one tooth and at the other end of the mating

tooth, or if the wear spots are high up on the tooth or low down, or if they are egg-shaped and slightly off center or slightly tilted . . . you can be sure your gear adjustment needs attention.

DETERMINING AXLE RATIO

The ratio of the gears (ring and pinion) in a differential probably has a greater effect on the acceleration and operating economy of a car than any other single factor. Yet it is one of the harder things to deduce—unless you know a little trick or two. Some rear axle assemblies are either color-coded with a blotch of paint—usually covered with grease—or have either the ratio itself or a code number stamped somewhere on the assembly. Unfortunately, the car owner cannot rely on these methods of determining axle ratio—even if he has access to the color blotch or number coding: The factory may have goofed during assembly, or someone, for some reason, may have switched to a higher or lower ratio without bothering to note the change with the proper paint blotch or code number for that particular car. But before we divulge the easy way to determine your car's axle ratio, let's see why it's so important.

The ratio determines how fast the engine turns in relation to rear wheel rotation, or the car speed. With a 3.55:1 ratio, for instance, the driveshaft would turn 3.55 times for each 1 full turn of the rear wheels. (This would be in high gear; but if the transmission is in low or second, the engine would be turning more than 3.55 turns per 1 turn of the wheels.)

In general, the faster the engine turns in relation to car speed, the snappier the acceleration. There have been cases where just changing the axle ratio from 3.55 to 4.11 has improved stoplight getaway much more than the world's best tune-up would have. Conversely, changing the axle ratio from the same 3.55 to, say, 3.10 has produced improved gas economy by from 1 to 2 mpg.

Obviously, it's important for you to know the axle gear ratio that's in your car. In most cases you will have a pretty good idea by the standard ratio that is supposed to be in that model, from the factory catalog. If you bought the car new, there may be a listing of the ratio on the invoice or price sticker. Also, on assembly-line cars there is always a mark of some kind, as noted. Unfortunately, each company uses its own code of numbers or letters to indicate these ratios. There would be no way you could interpret them without consulting the shop manual for your model. Space won't permit any detailed list here, but any car dealer can help you.

Gear ratios do get switched around from time to time—and you may still not be sure of the ratio that's in your car. This will require actually measuring it.

Because gear ratios are always carried out to two decimal places (as 3.55:1) it would seem you'd need some sort of precision measuring device and a sliderule—but, actually, all you need is a jack and one or two jack stands.

Park the car on a level surface, turn the engine off, place the transmission in neutral, leave the parking brake off, and block both front wheels and one rear wheel so the car cannot roll. Jack the car up just enough that the un-blocked rear wheel is free of the ground. For safety's sake, place the jack stand near the jack so the car can't fall on you.

Now, with a grease pencil or other marking device, make a mark on the driveshaft or U-joint just ahead of the differential. Make another mark at the base of the tire (or rotate the tire until the valve stem is at dead bottom). Then, rotate the tire slowly, either forward or backward, meanwhile counting the number of revolutions the driveshaft makes. Go through 10 full turns of the tire until the mark or valve stem is again at bottom center. Naturally, the driveshaft mark will not stop in the same position as when you started. Rather, it will be somewhere in the midst of a revolution and you must determine if it has gone one-fourth of the way around on its final

Rear Axle

turn, half-way, two-thirds, or whatever. Judge the percentage as carefully as you can. Let's say that the driveshaft has rotated 15 times while the tire went 10. Divide the 15 by 10 and you get 1.5. No, this isn't your axle ratio, it's *half* of it. In other words, the way a differential works when one wheel is stopped and the other turned, it goes at twice the rate that both of them would. So what you wind up with is a 3.0 ratio (2 X 1.5). If the driveshaft rotates 15.5 times, then your ratio is 3.10 (15.5 divided by 10, then multiplied by 2).

We could have rotated the wheel just once and counted the driveshaft revolutions, but this would have allowed for a fairly wide margin of error. Doing it 10 times decreases the error—or you could rotate the wheel 100 times and the error would be negligible. But 10 times is close enough. Your answer, you'll find, may not come out exactly on one of the rear-end ratios available for your car for that year (check your owner's manual), but it'll be close enough to one of them that you can determine which it is. If your car had optional ratios of, say, 2.76, 3.10, 3.56 and 3.90, and your math shows it as 3.05, you can bet your bottom dollar you've got the 3.10:1.

If your car is equipped with a limited-slip differential you won't be able to turn one rear wheel while its mate is parked on the ground. The solution is easy: jack up both rear wheels and they'll turn together when you rotate one by hand. If this is the case with your car, *don't* multiply the final ratio by two.

MORE WORDS ON GEARS

As we've pointed out, changing rear-end gears can make a lot of difference in the performance of your car. You can change it to either an accelerating bomb or a gas miser by taking out the ring and pinion and replacing it with one of either a higher or lower ratio. And, fortunately, you can now get a wide range of gear ratios for almost any late-model car, either through a factory parts warehouse or from one of the specialty suppliers. These available ratios run from as low as 2.56 to 6.17 or more. There's something here to fit every need—and the prices are not impossible. They usually run from a low of around $40 for a set of factory gears to $75 to $100 for special-cut gears. Get a catalog and do some shopping around.

Space won't permit a detailed discussion of optimum gear ratios for various requirements. But it's not hard to come up with some suggestions that won't be far off the mark, since the science of

gear selection has become very refined in the last five years—especially as more ratios have become available for various car models. For instance, we know that a ratio somewhere around 3.5 is best for top speed on most cars. This ratio is also a pretty good compromise for the street and highway. (You'll note that many high-performance factory cars have standard ratios in this range.) If you do most of your driving on the open highway, we would suggest a ratio closer to 3.0:1. On the other hand, if you do most of your driving at moderate speeds around town, and want a lot of pep on the street, try gears around 3.9.

In conclusion, a word about installing these special gears. Here again it's a job for a professional. In fact, high ratios seem to take extra precaution on gear lash to get away from whine on the road. Gear noise is definitely more of a problem with high-ratio performance gears. So we would suggest that you just pull out your axle carrier section, take it and the new set of gears to an experienced mechanic, and let him make the change and adjustment. The job requires pulling the pinion stem, the differential case and side bearings—and it requires a lot of special tools. Don't try to do it unless you have the help and advice of somebody with experience—*plus* the proper tools for the job. 🐞

1. Differential Side and Pinion Gears

1. Comparison of two limited-slip differential spiders. Design at left requires four pinion gears between the side gears for high torque capability in small size.

2. Assembly of limited-slip differential. Amount of preload is critical; too little and an unloaded wheel will spin uselessly, too much and differential will act like a locked rear end when negotiating a corner.

3. This type of limited-slip differential uses cone clutches in place of plate clutch packs. Advantages are fewer parts, simpler design, better lubrication and longer life.

2. Chrysler Limited-Slip Differential

3. Cone-Clutch Limited-Slip

1. First step in changing an outer bearing is removing wheel and drum, then undoing the four axle retaining bolts through hole in axle flange.

2. If you're doing the job at home, you can usually get the axle out by putting the wheel back on and hitting the tire outward with a big hammer.

3. Best way to remove axles is with puller like this. Ron Griffin of Griffin Automotive, N. Hollywood, Calif. shows how with this slide-hammer.

4. The inside seal also needs to be replaced, and you can use the end of the axle itself to pry it out once the axle comes loose of differential.

5. On this Olds axle, the bearing is held on by a retainer ring, which must be chiseled off—but be careful not to nick the axle bearing surface.

6. Some people cut old bearings with a torch, but the right way is with a press. Any auto parts machine shop can press off the bearing for you.

7. Before slipping new bearing and inside retainer on axle, be sure the outer retainer (with new gasket) is on axle and facing right direction.

8. Once again, a hydraulic press is the only right way to install the new bearing. It should be pressed on until it seats on axle shoulder.

9. Before installing the axle with its new bearing, you must tap a new seal into the housing with a socket, or other round driver, and hammer.

Brakes-Drum & Disc

Brakes don't ordinarily go bad all at once. It just seems that way. You might drive for many thousands of miles and never have a bit of trouble with your brakes. Then one day you have to make a panic stop and you discover that you would probably get to a halt quicker if you dragged your foot through a hole in the floorboards. The seemingly instant decay of brakes is caused by their over-capacity in most ordinary situations. If you drive like a normal human being, you just don't need much brake. So it's possible to have the brakes worn to a dangerously low level and not know anything about it until it's too late.

The only way to prevent this unfortunate situation is to inspect the brakes regularly. Every 12,000 miles or each year, whichever occurs first, is a good interval for pulling at least one drum and taking a look at what's going on. Pulling all four drums is much better. Whichever you do, you have to know what to look for. So let's start at the beginning and go through the brake system completely.

HYDRAULIC DESIGN

Hydraulics are quite simple and easy to understand, and are based on the simple principle that fluids cannot be compressed like gases. It is therefore possible to move a column of liquid (hydraulic brake fluid) from the actuator or master cylinder, through a pipeline system, to the slave or wheel cylinders, whose movement causes the friction material (brake lining) to come in contact with the wheel driven drum or disc and force it to slow or stop.

The master cylinder is filled with fluid and has a piston at what might be termed bottom dead center, with the connecting rod linked to the brake pedal itself. Hydraulic lines connect this cylinder with the slave units at the wheels. These are best described as a cylinder with a piston at each end. As the pedal is pressed, the master cylinder piston pushes the fluid through the lines to each wheel cylinder, causing the wheel cylinder pistons to push outward, forcing the brake shoes against the drum. Since this pressure is equal to all wheel cylinders, effective braking pressure cannot be applied to any one wheel until all the shoes on the wheels are in contact with their respective drums, providing a self-equalizing effect.

Drum brake systems are designed so that there is always a little pressure in the line when the brakes are not being used. This pressure is maintained by the check valve, sometimes called a residual pressure valve. The large spring in the master cylinder makes it work, and

keeps slight pressure in the lines to hold the wheel cylinder pistons out against the shoe tabs. Without the residual pressure, the pistons might vibrate away from the shoes, which would cause low pedal and lack of brakes. Disc brakes do not use the check valve because their seals fit much tighter, keeping the pistons from vibrating away from the disc. With a disc/drum system, it is necessary to have a check valve in the line to the drum brakes, but not to the disc brakes. In disc/drum systems that have a dual master cylinder, the check valves are in the master cylinder outlet, right where the drum brake line screws on. With a single master cylinder, the check valve has to be further downstream, in the line that feeds the drum brakes.

As we said before, liquids cannot be compressed, but gases such as air can be, so it is very important that such a hydraulic system be free of any bubbles of air. Removal of such extraneous air is done by bleeding, an important part of the servicing procedure. To insure that the system is always air free, cup-like seals of rubber or neoprene are used on all master and wheel cylinders, and a fluid supply reservoir is incorporated into the master cylinder. The fluid itself is compounded especially for automotive hydraulic brake systems and should never be mixed with or contaminated by solvents. It will withstand very low temperatures without freezing and very high tem-

peratures without boiling away; it gets sticky on exposure to air and will ruin paint or brake lining material.

In addition to the self-equalizing feature, and the elimination of mechanical linkage from brake pedal to wheels, hydraulic systems can be used to create multiplication of force or leverage. In mechanical leverage, where the length of the lever determines the increase in force (such as the brake pedal itself), the area of the actuating (master cylinder) piston in relation to that of the slave (wheel cylinder) piston determines the amount of hydraulic leverage. In addition to being used to apply the necessary force of shoes against drums, it is also used to compensate for a change of weight distribution under rapid stopping conditions. Here the front wheels are subjected to as high as 75% of the vehicle's weight and, therefore, must exert more braking force without locking the rear wheels. This is done by making the front wheel cylinders slightly larger in piston diameter than the rear cylinder pistons.

There are tremendous hydraulic pressures involved in the braking system, which is why it's important to be sure that the plumbing and cylinders are free from leaks and bits of dirt or other foreign particles that might disturb the seals, and that the lines themselves are not cracked or fractured in such a way that a sudden surge of pressure will

1. Slider Type Disc Brake

2. GM Proportioning Valve

3. Chrysler Proportioning Valve

4. Ford Proportioning Valve

1. Newest design in disc brakes is Chrysler Corporation's slider type—a single-piston floating caliper that slides on the two machined outer surfaces of the disc during application. A 3rd-generation Chrysler disc design, it offers better performance with simpler construction and is standard equipment on all 1973 V-8 models.

2-4. Combination brake warning switch/ proportioning valves differ in appearance from car to car, but all have same function: (1) Outlet to rear brakes, (2) from "R" outlet of master cylinder, (3) switch assembly, (4) from "F" outlet of master cylinder, and (5) outlet to front brakes.

5. All late model cars now use a tandem master cylinder to prevent 4-wheel brake failures. You'll find a double hydraulic cylinder.

cause them to break. With a pedal force of 100 lbs.—which is not hard to exert under panic stop conditions—hydraulic line pressure will be anywhere from 800 to 1300 psi (pounds per square inch), depending on mechanical pedal linkage and hydraulic leverage between master and wheel pistons. Power-assisted brakes require less foot pressure but exert the same amount of line pressure.

A part of the hydraulic system on late-model cars with dual master cylinders is the brake failure warning light switch, sometimes called the differential pressure switch. The switch consists of a piston inside a bore with one end connected to the front hydraulic line and the other end connected to the rear line. Normally the piston doesn't move, be-

5. Tandem Master Cylinder

Brakes--Drum & Disc

cause hydraulic pressure is equal throughout the system. But if there is a leak in one half of the system, pressure will drop in that half, and the normal pressure in the other half of the system will move the piston in the bore and turn on the light. Some of the switches turn the light on only while your foot is on the brake, while others leave the light on. Late-model switches are made in one piece with the metering valve and proportioning valve. Connecting passages in the one-piece casting eliminate the many lines that looked like a bowl of spaghetti when there were three separate units.

BRAKE DESIGN

All friction-type braking systems are essentially heat systems. Bringing the average-sized car to a maximum effort stop (just short of locking the wheels) from highway cruising speeds generates enough heat in the linings and drums to melt them if it were not dissipated properly. The lining material is very important but it must also be compatible with the drum material, maintaining its coefficient of friction throughout the braking cycle without excessive wear to either lining or drum. Any oil, water, or hydraulic fluid that comes between lining and drum effectively destroys this correct coefficient of friction.

Cooling a conventional drum brake assembly is difficult, and the number of successive high-speed stops is limited to the ability of the brake cooling design to stay ahead of the heat build-up. Cast iron drums, the most commonly used, depend mostly on air passing by them in the rather restricted confines of the wheel recess. Engineers have been improving this airflow by ducting air into the wheel/drum cavity, finning the drums and combining cast iron liners with aluminum drum housings. All for more efficient brakes.

Modern linings also assist in transferring some of the heat, but the necessity of a backing plate makes internal cooling without ducting difficult. In addition

to holding the necessary shoe assemblies, the backing plate is designed to minimize entrance of water and abrasive dirt into the critical space between shoe and drum. While moderately effective in keeping small quantities of dust and water out, large doses get through and are retained by the very same shield. The adverse effect of dust and water (especially the latter) on braking efficiency has been virtually eliminated by the caliper disc systems available on the late model cars.

The efficiency of a braking system, in addition to properly conditioned hydraulics, depends on proper lining material of adequate thickness, internally smooth and round drums, maximum contact between lining area and drum surface, and cooling. In addition to the force exerted on the shoes by the mechanical and hydraulic leverage, additional pressure between shoes and drum is achieved by self-energizing where the actual contact of the shoe with the drum is used to apply additional force to the drum. As the brakes are applied, the friction between lining and drum wants to force the shoes around in the direction of drum rotation. The location of the shoe pivot point determines whether the shoe is forced against the drum (self-energizing) or away from the drum by the rotation of the drum itself. Most designs today get additional power by linking the two shoes together so that not only are both shoes self-energizing, but the primary shoe exerts pressure on the secondary shoe, pushing the secondary shoe into the drums that much harder. This is called "servo" action.

Despite the rather long travel of the brake pedal, the wheel cylinders and brake shoes do not move very far to make contact with the drum, mainly because the mechanical and hydraulic leverage necessary for the pressure requirements.

To compensate for lining and drum wear, an adjustment for setting the shoes closer to the drum is incorporated into the brake assembly. In recent years, a self-adjusting feature has been standardized to eliminate the need for a periodic "setting up the shoes" service procedure. In simple terms, self-adjusting

linkage uses the rotating shoe action in reverse to operate a lever that picks up an extra notch on the star wheel adjuster nut, if wear allows the shoes to move far enough for the lever to engage. Self-adjusters work only when the brakes are applied while the vehicle is moving backwards. They do not compensate for drum expansion caused by heat. If you back up when your brakes are hot, the automatic adjustment can cause the rear shoes to drag when the drums cool off.

ROAD TEST ANALYSIS

Before beginning any type of brake service or overhaul, it is best to determine by actual road test just what might be required. Select a smooth, paved, dry section of street or road free of traffic or other obstacles. At a speed of 20 mph, apply the brakes firmly for as rapid a stop as possible without locking the wheels. If the pedal depresses to within 2 ins. or less of the floorboard, the linings are badly worn, brake fluid level is low, or the shoes need adjusting. A spongy feeling to the pedal indicates air in the system (except on some disc brakes, which are designed that way). With the car at rest, press brake pedal as hard as possible, holding it down firmly to note whether it continues to move slowly downward. Any such movement indicates poor sealing master or wheel cylinders or a leak somewhere in the plumbing system.

Should the car pull to one side or the other, or if one wheel grabs, it is an indication of several possible problems: improper adjustment, grease or hydraulic fluid on the linings, loose backing plate, reversed primary and secondary shoes, brake shoes not properly arced to drum resulting in partial contact, plugged master cylinder relief valve, poor pedal linkage adjustment, or an out-of-round drum. While conducting these rolling brake tests, listen for grinding or rubbing noises with brakes off and applied. Rubbing sounds without brake application indicates improper initial adjustment, faulty or broken return spring, binding wheel cylinder or shoe guides.

Grinding or squeaks when the brakes are applied can mean brake linings worn

1. Leading-Shoe Brake

2. Cracked Brake Rotor

1. *There is no servo-action in a leading-shoe brake, but each brake shoe is self-energizing. Late model cars favor the servo-action design.*

2. *Chalk-marked area has crack in brake disc, rendering it unsafe for use. Discs should be checked for such failures every time pads are changed.*

3. *Velvetouch Metalik brake linings are latest wrinkle for the performance-minded. Since linings were almost as good as new two years after installation, there's something here for the economy-minded also.*

4. *There are pros and cons on arcing new brake shoes before installing them, but many brake specialists wouldn't think of a brake job without this.*

5. *Velvetouch Metalik disc linings should be chamfered at each end before use. As lining material is soft metal, there's a certain amount of residue caused by braking action, and this creates a place for it to go.*

6. *Metalik brake installation is very similar to that of ordinary organic lining, except that starwheel adjuster is not connected to self-adjusting lever. By themselves, there's very little wear; adjustment every 6-9 months will do. Self-adjusters will cause constant drag on linings and wear them down fast. Use heavy-duty shoe return and hold-down springs, too.*

3. Metalik Brake Lining

4. Arcing New Brake Shoes

5. Chamfered Brake Linings

6. Installing Brake Adjuster

to rivets or shoes, dust in rivet holes, improper lining material, oil or grease on linings, or warped backing plates. Faulty front wheel bearings can also affect braking efficiency and cause a lot of unnecessary searching for defect in the brake assembly if they are not checked during the overhaul. Don't get carried away setting up the mechanical linkage for the parking brake, as drag here can ruin a set of rear brake assemblies.

For cars equipped with power assists—either the booster type used on Ford and Chrysler products, or the combined unit featured on GM cars—there is a simple drive test to determine faults in this area that may save unnecessary tearing into the entire system.

With the engine off and the transmission in neutral, press the brake pedal several times which will bleed off the vacuum reserve in the reservoir. Apply a light pressure to the pedal, depressing it just beyond taking up any slack in the linkage, and hold it there lightly while starting the engine. As the engine starts, the pedal will feel like it is dropping away underfoot, requiring less pressure and indicating that the assist system is working. If there is no action, the fault can be assumed to be in the power assist unit.

Again with the engine off, deplete the vacuum reserve as before, then start the engine, run at fast idle for a few moments, then stop engine with throttle closed. Wait for about 2 mins. and try the brake again. There should be enough vacuum reserve in the system for several assisted braking efforts. If there is no such reaction, the cause can be isolated to a faulty vacuum check valve.

RELINING

It is not likely that the home repair enthusiast will have all the equipment necessary for machining drums, relining shoes, or arcing them to conform to the drum diameter. Therefore, the car should be jacked and placed on suitable stands so that all four wheel assemblies can be removed at the same time.

Select a level surface for this jacking operation, preferably a paved one to insure sturdy jack stand foundation and to reduce the possibility of extraneous dirt entering the system. The ideal equipment for this operation is a regular hydraulic floor jack and four jack stands. Remove wheel covers, loosen wheel stud nuts, and with the rear wheels blocked, raise the front end just enough for the tires to clear the ground by jacking in the center of the front crossmember. Place a jack stand under each lower suspension arm as close as possible to the inside of wheel and tire but not interfering with their removal, then lower jack slowly so front end is resting securely on stands. Raise the rear wheels by jacking at the differential, placing jack stands under axle housing carefully so as not to endanger any hydraulic lines that may be strung along this housing.

In lieu of such professional jacking equipment, a bumper jack and a quantity of short pieces of lumber, preferably 2 × 4's about 12 ins. long, can be used very well to raise and hold the car safely off its wheels for brake servicing. With the rear wheels well blocked to prevent rolling, begin by bumper jacking each front wheel separately, just as you would to change a tire. Using the short pieces of lumber, build a stand under the front suspension by placing the wood pieces

log cabin style to the required height. Lower the car and repeat for each wheel. Don't use rotted lumber or skinny pieces on end and expect it to safely support your car. Avoid orange crates or boxes which can collapse and not only injure you, but also damage the car.

A friend with access to a frame-type grease lift in a garage or service station, who is willing to allow it to be tied up long enough to do all of the wheel work in connection with a brake line/drum grind operation, can be a great asset and solve all of the jacking and jack stand problems.

REMOVING WHEELS AND DRUMS

Whatever jacking system is used, the next step is to remove the wheels and then the drums. Begin with the front ones, as in most cases except later model GM cars, the wheel hub is part of the brake drum, and front drum bearings, seals and lubricant. Once the cotter pin is freed of the axle nut, carefully remove nut and washers. The brake shoes may have to be backed off at this point to allow the drum to be wiggled off. The star wheel, similar to a coarse-toothed gear, is located at the bottom of the shoe assembly and is accessible through a slot in the drum.

Some cars like early Lincoln and Mercury have the slot in the backing plate covered by a pop-out plate. If the car has self-adjusting brakes, the adjusting lever must be held out of the way while the star wheel is turned. This means inserting two tools—a thin screwdriver to hold the lever up, and a brake adjusting tool—into the slot at the same time. Follow the same procedure for backing off

Brakes--Drum & Disc

on rear shoes prior to drum removal, if necessary.

It is a good idea to mark the drums and shoes so that each complete assembly can be returned after servicing to the original wheel position. Keeping them in paired sets will save a lot of reassembly time. The marking should include identity for forward and reverse shoes on each wheel. Scratching with a sharp instrument or center punching with a series of coded dots is a good method.

Remove drums, taking care to protect front wheel bearings and seals from dust and dirt. Examine backing plate for presence of wheel cylinder stop plate. Late-model cars have these stops to prevent wheel cylinders from popping out when shoes are removed, as there is always a slight static hydraulic pressure in a well working brake system. If there is no stop plate, a wheel cylinder clamp will be required to hold the cylinders in position while shoes are removed. Under no conditions should the brake pedal be depressed while the drums are removed.

Before proceeding further, study the indicated illustrations to be sure of the identity and functions of the internal brake parts. The brake shoes can now be removed by detaching the shoe hold-down discs, springs and pins, and then the return springs from the anchor pin. In shop practice, this latter operation is done with a special tool but can be accomplished by grasping the long shank of the spring firmly with vise-grip pliers, stretching the spring sufficiently to remove it from the anchor pin. On rear brakes where the parking brake operates on the rear shoe only, disconnect the parking brake cable and remove parking brake strut and lever. Final removal of the shoes front and rear on single anchor brakes, is done by spreading them to clear the wheel cylinder connecting links, whereupon both shoes will come off as a unit, still held together by the adjustment screw and spring.

Total-contact brakes, used on earlier Chrysler products, have a slightly different hold-down and return-spring arrangement, and a special tool is required to prevent damage to the shoes. With guide springs, retainers and return springs removed, further dismantling is the same as with conventional assemblies.

CLEANING AND INSPECTION

Now is the time to clean and inspect the brakes, and while they are removed, the front wheel bearings. If air pressure is available, use it to clean drum dust from all parts, being careful not to blow it into wheel bearing assembly. A stiff brush is a good substitute for compressed air. If very dirty, wash drum, backing plate, and metal part of shoes in clean solvent and dry thoroughly. Be careful to keep the solvent away from cylinder boots and brake lining. Check for pits or dark spots on the bearing races and plan to replace before reassembly if bearing wear is indicated. Check for oil leaks around the rear wheel bearings Dand replace seal if in-

dicated; seepage here can spoil a good brake job very quickly.

Check all wheel cylinders for piston leaks by carefully lifting each boot to note if interior is wet with brake fluid. If so, the wheel cylinders must be overhauled or replaced (this procedure is discussed later in this chapter).

Examine the linings and drums for wear and grooving, to see if braking problems might be caused by other than normal wear. The lining should show evidence of uniform wear both along its contact arc and across it. Thin spots in the center of the shoes are normal with oversize drums, because the shoe radius and drum radius are not the same. Thinner edges side-to-side show that the

shoes have been canted by bent backing plates or anchor pins.

DRUM TURNING

Most drums, after periods of normal use, become out-of-round and almost always grooved from the abrasive action of dust and dirt between linings and drum. Drums can be restored by machining or grinding on special drum lathes, and it is safe to remove as much as .030-in. of material to bring them back to normal roundness and smoothness. This means that the internal drum diameter will be increased by .060-in. and the relined shoes must be altered to conform to the new diameter. This is done by use

1. Lining Wear

2. Hydraulic Schematic

COVER

COVER RETAINING BOLT

COVER GASKET

COVER CLAMP

PISTON RETAINING SET SCREW AND GASKET

PISTON SPRING

CUP RETAINER

PISTON CUP

FRONT PISTON

REAR PISTON ASSEMBLY

PISTON CUP

RETAINER SCREW

RESIDUAL PRESSURE VALVE SPRING

THIN WASHER

"O" RING

PISTON CUP

TUBE SEAT

RESIDUAL PRESSURE VALVE

MASTER CYLINDER BODY

PISTON RETAINER

3. Disassembled Master Cylinder

1. These illustrations show brake linings in different stages of wear. Once the linings get down near the steel brake shoe or pad, it's time to replace the linings. If they aren't changed, then your drums will be ruined, costing you more money, maybe your life if they fail.

2. The proportioning valve limits the pressure to the rear brakes to prevent them from locking up. Also in most disc brake systems, but not shown here, is a metering valve which delays the application of the front brake shoes until the rear brake shoes have had a chance to expand against the drum, thus helping to equalize brake action.

3. If this master cylinder were on a car with disc brakes, the outlet to the disc brakes would not have a check valve, but it would have a tube seat insert.

of oversize lining or shimming standard lining, then arc grinding to conform to the new drum diameter.

LINING MATERIALS

Modern brake lining materials—that used generally for the past 10 to 15 years—is molded, then bonded or riveted to the shoes to insure positive contact and maintenance of constant curve and to prevent shifting or coming off the shoe. Equipment for relining, drum grinding, and shoe-to-drum matching is not only expensive, but requires training for proper use. These factors alone make it impractical for an amateur mechanic to own things as drum grinders, arcing jigs, and a stock of lining material, rivets, and bonding ovens.

Brake lining can be purchased in several ways. Professional brake servicing companies use rolls of material that must be cut to size, drilled and countersunk

for rivets, beveled, and fitted to the shoes. Precut and drilled linings are available to fit specific car models, and replacement shoes, completely lined and ready to install, can be purchased from brake supply houses and new-car service departments. All forms are available in oversize thickness to compensate for drum grinding, as is shim stock for use under standard lining material, although oversize lining is the usual method. Premium lining materials, such as sintered metallic and a wide variety of various degrees of hardness for specific purposes, are available as replacements for standard material. Brake supply houses which handle name-brand items will have specifications for just about any car made, and following their recommendations will provide the right lining for the indicated purpose.

As with riveted linings, bonded materials require special skills and equipment to replace. Old linings must be chiseled or burned off the shoes, which are then carefully sanded in preparation for the liquid cement or special tape adhesive. Cemented shoe assemblies are then clamped in a special jig that applies high, even pressure and heat over the entire contact surface to insure adequate bond. It is obvious that the home brake repairman who purchases relined shoes properly arced to his professionally ground drums is getting a better and lower cost job than he could possibly do himself.

REINSTALLING SHOES AND DRUMS

Installing the relined shoes and matching drums must be done with great care and cleanliness. Avoid touching linings or drums with greasy hands, and allow no hydraulic fluid to come in contact with the lining material. If the shoes and drums have been kept separated in

matching sets as previously suggested, prepare to assemble each to its matching wheel.

While it is readily accessible, the adjusting screw assembly should be dismantled, cleaned in solvent, dried, and lubricated before reassembly. The inboard side of the backing plate should also be cleaned of road grime; this will ease locating the cylinder bleeder valve and anchor pin adjustment, if there is one.

Proper lubrication of all brake friction points is necessary for long trouble-free operation. For this purpose, a special compound brake grease is used. It has properties just for this application that prevent it from running or vaporizing under the heat of severe brake application so that it may be safely used without fear of getting into the drum/lining contact area. However, it should be used sparingly when the adjusting screw mechanism is assembled and at all mechanical contact points between shoes and backing plate. On rear brakes be sure to lubricate the parking brake cable assembly.

If the system has a self-adjusting mechanism, this should be assembled and lubricated prior to the installation of shoes. In any case, the star wheel adjusting nut must be centered over the backing plate slot (if this type of accessibility is provided) or centered to afford proper adjusting movement (if this is done through an opening in the drum itself). As these adjusting assemblies are not interchangeable with the opposite wheels, care must be taken to keep the parts for each wheel exclusively for that wheel.

Place shoes on backing plate, engaging them with the anchor pin and the wheel cylinder connecting links. Be sure the shoes are in proper relative position. Usually the forward has the short lining, but not always. The shoes should be

Brakes--Drum & Disc

marked forward or reverse. If not, and you can't tell by looking at them, ask a professional mechanic who has used that kind of brake lining. Some companies make both forward and reverse linings interchangeable. Others make both linings identical as far as appearance but the composition is different, and the lining will not work properly if shoes are reversed.

Don't feel self-conscious about asking a professional brake man which way the shoes go. It is a problem that has bothered mechanics for years. But be sure the mechanic you ask has had experience with the particular brand of lining or he may not know, either. If the counterman where you buy your parts is really hip, he may be able to help out. But don't necessarily count on it.

If the brakes are of the self-adjusting type, take care when assembling the self-adjuster mechanism. These are not interchangeable from one side of the car to the other and to interchange them will cause the adjuster to retract the shoes rather than advance them when the brakes are applied as the car is rolling backwards. Remember, make sure the parts are not binding on their anchor pin and that both shoe return springs are installed over the adjuster anchor fitting.

Adjusting screws for self-adjusting brakes are assembled with the thread screwed all the way in and then backed off about one turn. The star wheel is positioned toward the rear or secondary shoe, and the self-adjusting actuating lever is spring-linked to the primary shoe and cable- or rod-linked to top anchor pin. Before proceeding further, check operation of self-adjuster by pulling on cable or link toward secondary shoe just

enough to lift lever past a tooth in adjusting screw star wheel. The lever should snap into position behind the next tooth and return to original position when released.

Follow the same greasing procedure when replacing shoes on Chrysler total-contact brakes. Insert the long end of return springs in the shoe web (before placing shoes into position) by sliding them between the support plates and engaging the ends of wheel cylinder pushrods with the toe end of each shoe. Attach short end of return springs to their respective links by prying against them with proper tool. A long-handled Phillips screwdriver is a good substitute. Install guides and retainers making sure that the little lip or guide is positioned in the hole in the support plate.

ADJUSTING ANCHORS

With the exception of the Chrysler total-contact brakes, shoes must be centered in relation to the axle center-line when they are replaced. Professional mechanics use a grinder pivoting on the axle or axle flange for removing small precise amounts of lining material to provide exact and true centering of lining diameters in relation to the drum. Another method is to use a gauge bar pivoting on the axle to determine just how far off center the shoes are and in what direction. Early Chrysler brakes have eccentric anchors at the bottom which allow the shoes to be shifted to the proper position, and the gauge is necessary for this operation. By setting the gauge bar to the drum diameter and the indicated calibrations for proper clearance, the eccentrics are adjusted while checking with the gauge bar.

Early Bendix-type brakes employ two types of anchor pin adjustments for shoe

centering, making it possible to center without grinding or using gauge bars if the refurbished shoes and drums have been properly arced. Some anchor pins have eccentric threaded ends and others are mounted through a slotted hole, allowing them to shift when the nut is loosened. In either case, shoe centering procedures are the same.

Back off adjustment so drums fit easily onto mounting flanges or axles. In the case of front wheels with bearings integral with drum, be sure that bearing assembly is complete and lubricated, and that wheel bearing nut is snug enough to prevent any play in the bearing.

Turn the brake shoe adjusting nut until maximum effort is required to turn the drum with both hands. Mounting the wheel will ease this effort, but two hands should be needed to turn the wheel. Loosen anchor pin nut not over ¾-turn (with eccentric pin type it will be necessary to hold pin with square end tool while loosening nut). Turn eccentric pin to shift shoes. With slotted anchor pin mount, loosen nut and rap backing plate smartly with hammer to ease shifting of pin in slotted hole. Tighten nut and check brake drag by turning drum by hand, noticing any difference in drag from the initial setting. If drag is the same, the shoes are properly centered. If drag decreases, it indicates the anchor pin has shifted. Repeat by again setting brake adjusted nut to hard two-handed drag and effecting further shoe shifting by either turning eccentric or loosening anchor pin nut and then tapping the backing plate with a hammer.

Some cars use a nonadjustable anchor and if the lining and drums are standard it works fine, but when you go into over-sizes there is a problem in getting the shoes centered. Some exchange shoes

1. Wheel Cylinder Boots

2. Wheel Cylinder Cutaway

1. The end components here are press-on boots that cover the ends of wheel cylinders. Next are the metal pistons, which actuate the pushrods, thence the shoes. On the inside, separated by the coil spring, are the piston cups. The hydraulic fluid in the wheel cylinder is in this area, between the cups.

2. This cutaway cylinder reveals the boots on the ends, the pistons and pushrods (held in hand), the piston cups and spring. Fluid enters the cylinder via threaded opening, forcing the cups and pistons out, actuating the brakes.

3. Equal hydraulic pressure does not guarantee equal braking effort on each wheel. If the type of lining or metal in one drum differs from others, brakes may pull to one side.

3. Hydraulic System Schematic

AUTOMATIC BRAKE ADJUSTER

1968   1969

SPRING
ADJUSTER
LEVER
CAGE & SPRING
PIVOT PIN

1. Link   3. Piston   5. Return Spring
2. Boot   4. Rubber Cup   6. Wheel Cylinder

5. Wheel Cylinder Parts

4. Automatic Brake Adjuster

4. The automatic brake adjuster on '69 Dodges reduces possibility of over-adjustment, takes place when backing, with brakes applied.

5. This illustration shows the components of a wheel cylinder.

have the anchor hole relocated so that they fit properly. Otherwise the lining must be arced off center in a special jig that fits on the shoe grinder.

ADJUSTING SHOES

Whether late-model, self-adjusting brakes or older manual models are re-lined, an initial adjustment is required for proper operation. After the shoe center-ing operation on new brakes, or to cor-rect for normal lining wear and to raise effective brake pedal, a minor brake ad-justment is necessary to provide proper clearance between lining and drum. For brakes without self-adjusters, this is best done with all four wheels off the ground. Using a suitable tool through the back-ing plate or drum slot provided, turn ad-justing wheel so there is a slight drag as the wheel is turned. Repeat with each wheel, trying for the same amount of drag. Then, back off an equal number of notches on the adjuster at each wheel—12 to 15 notches are average—making sure that there is no drag. If any is detected, back off an additional one or two notches on that wheel. Apply brake pedal firmly several times and check for drag again.

Bleed the hydraulic system (see details below) and make several slow speed stops to check equal braking. With self-adjusting brakes, centering procedures are the same and setting shoe-to-drum clearance is not as critical. Just be sure that the shoe adjusting screw for each wheel is backed off enough to clear shoes from any detectable drag, then achieve final adjustment by applying brakes while car is moving in reverse which will activate the self-adjuster and bring the shoes to proper clearance.

BLEEDING THE HYDRAULIC SYSTEM

Following any brake reline job, it is just good business to bleed the system, eliminating any air that may have en-tered. The idea behind bleeding is to drive any air out of the master cylinder, lines and wheel cylinders, out through special bleeding valves on each wheel cylinder. These are small fittings that look very much like Zerk grease nipples and are located on the backing plate di-rectly behind the wheel cylinder. Un-screwing them slightly opens their pas-sage into the wheel cylinder; it works like a small faucet with a ball-like end on it. As these bleeder valves are usually covered with road grime, they should be cleaned thoroughly for easy access and operation.

Make sure that the master cylinder reservoir is filled and that a supply of new, clean, hydraulic fluid of the proper specification is available to top this level off as the fluid level drops, depending on the amount of bleeding necessary. Pres-sure bleeding, used by professional brake mechanics, involves the use of a large reservoir of pressurized hydraulic fluid coupled to the system at the master cylinder, and supplying a flow of fluid through all the lines while each wheel cylinder bleeder valve is opened. How-ever, bleeding can be done without this aid by having two people do the job—one to operate the foot pedal, the other to bleed each wheel cylinder.

For bleeding by the two-man method, a bleeding tube and a glass jar or bottle are required. The tube can be procured at any auto supply store and should be long enough to reach from the bleeder ball end to the bottom of the glass jar when it is setting on the ground. Put about 1 in. of clean hydraulic fluid into the jar, slip one end of the bleeder tube onto the bleeder valve, the other into the jar so that it is submerged in the fluid. Open the bleeder valve about ¾-turn and at the same time have the assistant press the brake pedal slowly a full stroke. Close bleeder valve just before brake pedal hits bottom and allow pedal to return slowly to full-out position. Re-peat until expelled fluid flows in a solid stream with no presence of air bubbles. Tighten bleeder valve and remove hose. Be sure to constanly check fluid level in master cylinder and top up with new clean fluid only.

With careful work it is possible for one man to bleed brakes with the bleeder hose method. Just be sure the end of the hose is below the surface of the fluid in the jar. Open the bleeder fitting, then go to the pedal and stroke it easily once or twice using about ¾ of the full stroke. Replenish the fluid in the master cylin-der, then go to the wheel and close the bleeder fitting. Repeat at each wheel. If the lines are empty it may be necessary to run as much as a cupful of fluid through each cylinder to get all the air out. This would require several strokes of the pedal for each cylinder.

The best procedure is to follow a wheel-to-wheel sequence beginning with the one closest to the master cylinder. This applies to caliper disc units and to later model cars with dual master cylin-ders. Begin with the left front, then do the right front, left rear, and right rear. This procedure minimizes the possibility of trapped air entering lines already bled. Under no conditions must the mas-ter cylinder be emptied during the bleed-ing process as this pumps air into the system.

WARNING LIGHT SWITCH BLEEDING PROBLEMS

The warning light switch is designed to turn the light on whenever there is a leak. This includes the "leak" you create when you open a bleeder fitting. If the switch is the type that only turns the light on when your foot is on the brake, then no special procedure is required. But if the light stays on after you take your foot off the brake, it means you have the type of switch that must be centered after bleeding. The design of the switch allows pressure from the non-leaking system to move the piston to-ward the leaking system. If the light is on, you must create a leak by opening a bleeder fitting on the other system. Then you step on the brake pedal gently until the light goes out; close the bleeder fit-ting and you're done. That's the way the book says to do it, and we wish it was that easy. When you step on the pedal, the light will go out, but the piston keeps moving toward the other side, and puts the light on again. Then you have to close the bleeder fitting, open the fitting

Brakes--Drum & Disc

on the other system (front or rear) and try again. After about a dozen trys you will get just the right amount of pressure on the pedal to get the light off. To eliminate all this monkey motion, you can buy a little threaded stud that screws into the switch in place of the electrical connection and holds the piston in the centered position during bleeding.

OVERHAULING THE HYDRAULIC SYSTEM

Hydraulic brake fluid has a distinct, sharp, alcohol-like odor in its fresh fluid state and becomes sticky upon prolonged exposure to air, making it pretty easy to identify should leaks develop in

lines, master or wheel cylinders. Check all lines from master cylinder to each individual wheel, examining any grime-coated wet spots for evidence of hydraulic fluid. Should any lines need replacing, do not attempt to save any of the fluid for re-use as it may become contaminated and cause damage to the system. Use only steel brake line tubing, properly flared for the fittings. The flexible lines from tubing terminus to wheels are armored for maximum protection and should be replaced only with stock replacement parts for optimum service and safety.

WHEEL CYLINDER OVERHAUL

With the drums removed, examine wheel cylinders for leaks by carefully lift-

ing boots from cylinder housing. Evidence of hydraulic fluid under the boot indicates a bad wheel cylinder, and shoes must be removed before attempting to work on that cylinder. Note: Hydraulic fluid will ruin automotive paint finishes and lining material. All parts of the system activated by hydraulic fluid should be cleaned only with alcohol or special fluids compounded for this purpose and available at automotive parts supply houses.

To remove the wheel cylinder, loosen flex line where it connects to cylinder at backing plate. Remove cylinder mounting screws, detach cylinder from backing plate, then finish uncoupling of flex line by rotating cylinder. Some hydraulic fluid can be saved by placing a well-fitting wooden plug into the end of the flex line. This should be tappered slightly but not driven in hard enough to distort line and cause a problem when reassembling is done.

1. Ford/Bendex Dual Servo

2. '68 Chevelle Front Drum

3. Riveted Metallic Linings

1. A servo-action brake is one in which one shoe pushes on the other, giving the greatest braking action to the second shoe.

2. Front brake drums on '68 Chevelle are finned for improved cooling.

3. This NASCAR stocker features a super-size set of brakes. Riveted metallic linings are segmented so they dissipate heat more quickly.

4. Increased use of disc brakes on American-built cars is a boon to safety enthusiasts. Cars with discs stop faster and suffer less fade.

5. This power disc brake system is found on the Marlin, a former AMC car. Four pistons provide plenty of surface area for the linings.

4. Typical Disc Brake

5. Power Disc Brake

Remove boots, springs, pistons and cups from cylinder and place in alcohol or brake parts cleaning fluid. Clean cylinder casting inside and out, but do not let it soak in fluid. Examine bore for scoring and pitting, and cups for swelling. Scored cylinders can be honed to restore the desired mirror finish but no more than .005-in. may be removed. If more is required, the entire cylinder must be replaced. Replacement kits containing all necessary parts for rebuilding wheel cylinders are readily available from parts houses, and all parts should be replaced while the cylinder is apart; a minor attempt at saving here might result in more expensive repairs later.

If the cups are swollen or mushy, it is an indication that the hydraulic fluid has become contaminated with oil, kerosene, or gasoline. Should this condition be evident, the entire system must be flushed and all wheel and master cylinder cups (and in severe cases, the rubber flex lines), must be replaced. Flushing procedures are covered later in this chapter.

Assembly of wheel cylinders must be carried out under clean conditions, free from possible contamination by dirt, oil, water and solvents, or even dirty or greasy hands. With the finger, coat inside of wheel cylinder wall, as well as piston and cups, with clean hydraulic fluid. Assemble carefully in proper sequence for each side, ending with the boots on the ends. Clean end fitting of flex line and screw cylinder onto line by rotating cylinder until snug. Place cylinder in position on backing plate. Secure cylinder to backing plate with mounting screws and complete tightening of flex line. Repeat for each wheel.

MASTER CYLINDER OVERHAUL

Master cylinders fail and require rebuilding for the same reasons as wheel cylinders. Normal wear, contaminated fluid, and dust and dirt entering the system will eventually spoil the sealing and pumping action. Single master cylinders have a piston and sealing cup actuated by the pedal linkage, a boot to protect pedal rod extension, a check valve, a spring and two small holes in the cylinder wall—a compensating port and a breather—connected to the integral fluid reservoir.

When the pedal is pressed, the piston forces hydraulic fluid through the lines, actuating the wheel cylinders. When the pedal is released, it takes a little longer for the fluid to catch up with the piston, creating a pressure differential between piston and primary cup. Fluid from the integral reservoir flows into the cylinder chamber behind the piston and rushes past the primary piston cup to equal the pressure in front of it. As the return stroke is completed, the piston cup, acting as a slide valve, uncovers the compensating port and any excess fluid is returned through it to the reservoir.

A check valve in the output end of the master cylinder maintains 5 to 8 lbs. of static pressure inside the lines, which serves to keep the lips of the wheel cylinder cups tight against the cylinder walls to prevent loss of fluid and entrance of air into the system.

The dual master cylinder, first used in 1962 by Cadillac and American Motors' Rambler and now mandatory on all new cars, has two outlets, two complete piston/cup/spring and check valve assemblies, and two separate reservoirs for fluid supply.

The pistons operate in tandem in a continuous cylinder barrel, and are operated by a single pushrod linked to the brake pedal. One of the outlets is connected to the front wheel cylinders, the other to the rear ones. Failure in one system still gives braking operation to the other. Newest safety version of the dual system is a warning light that indicates failure of either side of the hydraulic system. Failure can also be felt in the pedal itself as the piston of the failing circuit will bottom before the other exerts the required pressure. Pedal travel will therefore be longer.

Replacement parts for either single or double systems, with oversize pistons and cups, are available should cylinder require honing, but the maximum that can be removed is .005-in. Should this honing depth fail to remove scores or pits, the master cylinder will have to be replaced.

When overhauling master cylinders, always use all the parts in the replacement kit to insure long rebuilt life. Use care in reassembly and cleanliness throughout to avoid any grease or dirt entering the system. Clean all parts in alcohol or special cleaning compound for hydraulic systems, and lubricate cups and pistons with hydraulic fluid when assembling.

Dual master cylinders, with their tandem piston assemblies, require a little more care when the cups and pistons are slid into the cylinder barrel, since the outlets are usually at the sides along the cylinder walls. Observe the cups as they are pushed past these holes to see that they do not turn back the edge and destroy their sealing effect. A piece of small-diameter rod, rounded and smooth on the end, can be used through the outlet hole to ease the cups past the openings. Liberal use of hydraulic fluid as a lubricant will help keep the assemblies sliding through the barrel.

Follow carefully the instructions packed with dual master cylinder kits. Some of the kits have an adjustable piston which must be set for your car. If it isn't set correctly, the brakes won't work.

To fill the hydraulic system after rebuilding wheel and master cylinders, fill

Brakes--Drum & Disc

the master reservoirs and proceed as with bleeding the system, only open the bleeder valves fully and keep master reservoir filled as the foot pedal is used to pump fresh fluid into the entire system. Then bleed the system as previously described, after bleeding the master cylinder first.

Some master cylinders are equipped with bleeder valves which operate much like the wheel cylinder bleeders. To operate these, press the brake pedal slowly, and open the bleeder valve near the bottom of the stroke, then close the valve before pedal is released. Repeat, making sure that master reservoir is full, until fluid flows in a steady stream without bubbles. For bleeding without a valve, loosen fitting to brake line and force air and fluid out by pressing brake pedal. Air in system can be heard as it squirts out through fitting. Tighten and proceed with bleeding wheel cylinders. On dual masters, loosen both outlet fittings and proceed as described for single cylinders.

FLUSHING HYDRAULIC SYSTEMS

When preliminary examination of wheel or master cylinder indicates swollen or mushy piston cups, there is evidence that the fluid is contaminated by oil, kerosene, or foreign liquid that de-

stroys the rubber cups. All wheel cylinders and the master should be rebuilt with new parts, but only after the system is flushed. About a quart of brake fluid is required. Follow the same procedure as bleeding but open bleeder valves a full 1½ turns to speed up passage of old fluid being pushed through by the flushing liquid.

After flushing, proceed with wheel and master cylinder overhaul. Upon reassembly, bleed system completely with new hydraulic fluid.

Flushing fluid, an alcohol base solvent available at parts stores, can be used for flushing the brake lines. However, many carmakers warn against its use because of the difficulty in getting it all out of the lines so it won't contaminate the brake fluid. They recommend that any flushing be done with new brake fluid only.

PARKING BRAKES

Parking brakes fall into three types: the cable-operated rear brake shoes, the cable-operated external driveshaft brake, and the cable-operated internal expanding driveshaft type. A need for parking brake cable adjustment is indicated when the parking brake pedal or lever must be activated to the limit of its stroke in order to properly hold the car when parked. A minor brake adjustment on systems without self-adjusters should be performed before adjusting cable-operated, rear-drum-type parking brakes. When this is done, check slack in rear cables to brakes. If more than 2 ins. of slack is apparent, adjust by loosening lock nut on cable usually located in the forward or single cable part of the cable system. Hold cable to prevent it from turning while adjuster is pulled up to the required 2 ins. of slack with parking brake off, then tighten adjusting lock nut. Check for drag by jacking rear wheels

off the ground and turning for any indication that the parking cable is too tight.

The external driveshaft brake used on early Chrysler cars has two adjustments. Before any adjusting is done, jack rear wheels off ground and check for drag. Operate parking brake mechanism while watching external brake to determine if cable has stretched and is not closing band tightly on driveshaft drum. If there is too much slack here, tighten cable tension and check to see if band closes tightly. Should this prove ineffective, the band itself can be set closer to the drum by a band adjusting nut. Under no conditions should the clearance between band lining and drum be less than .015 to .020-in., measured by feeler guage at the band anchor point. Check by turning rear wheels by hand to detect any drag increase after adjustment has been made.

Chrysler cars were also equipped with a driveshaft brake that is just a mechanical version of the ordinary wheel brake. The first check for adjustment should be in the cable. If this does not prove effective, there is a star wheel adjuster for setting out the shoes just as on the wheel brakes. With the rear wheels jacked off the ground, set adjuster nut up until a slight drag is felt, then back off until the drag is eliminated. Do not overadjust either internal- or external-type driveshaft brakes, because sustained friction during driving can cause severe burning of all friction parts in the braking system.

POWER-ASSISTED BRAKES

The power-assisted brake systems generally used on passenger cars do not shorten the stopping distance of the automobile. They are designed to assist in applying pedal pressure to the hydraulic system, thereby reducing the pedal force

1. Cutaway of Worn Drum

2. Brake Tools

LEVEL CYLINDER   TILTED CYLINDER

3. Master Cylinder Reservoirs

1. This drum was so badly worn that it was necessary to completely back off the shoe adjustment in order to remove the drum from the car. Note ridge on the edge of the drum. Each make drum has maximum that it can safely be turned before it must be replaced with a new one. If turned too much, unit will overheat, warp, etc. Then you'll be in deep, deep trouble when your brakes fail at need.

2. Special brake tools make any such job a lot easier and quicker. These are a few of the tools used.

3. This illustration reveals the reservoirs in a pair of master cylinders, both filled to within ¼-in. of the top. Note the one that is tipped, or mounted at an angle, actually holds less brake fluid.

4. If the drums on a car show much wear at all they are probably grooved, therefore should be cut.

5. After being surfaced with a cutting tool, it is wise to have the surface ground with a grinding stone to remove traces of the cutting.

6. Special wrenches, such as brake bleeder wrenches, make this job easy. Angles are such that you can get to the fitting and loosen it.

7. When doing a brake job, make it complete by inspecting lines, too. This flexible line is cracked badly, and may burst under pressure and cause a severe accident.

4. Cutting a Drum

6. Brake Bleeder Tool

5. Grinding Cutting Marks

7. Inspecting Brake Line

normally required in a non-assisted system. Two basic types are used on passenger cars: 1) the Bendix/Moraine composite units composed of a vacuum-actuated power unit combined with a hydraulic master cylinder, and 2) the type used by Ford and Chrysler which uses a vacuum-operated power unit that applies assisting force to the brake pedal linked to the master cylinder. Both systems use engine intake manifold vacuum to operate them, but will operate with increased pedal pressure should the system fail or braking be necessary with the engine not running.

Power units are composed of three basic elements, all of which must function

to achieve assisted braking effort. These are: 1) vacuum chamber which provides the power as long as manifold vacuum is available; 2) the hydraulic master cylinder, necessary to transmit hydraulic force to the wheel cylinders; and 3) the control valve, which is operated by mechanical linkage to the brake pedal and triggers the vacuum force in proportion to the brake pedal pressure and travel distance.

Whether of the composite or isolated type, power units require much the same replacement of parts as do hydraulic systems in that every phase of their operation depends on good sealing and proper operation of the valves.

As outlined in the beginning of this chapter, follow the drive test procedure to determine if braking faults are in the hydraulic system or the power assist unit. Repairs of either the composite Bendix/Moraine or the auxiliary assist units are complicated and require a thorough knowledge of specialized repair procedures. It is best to effect repairs to power assists under the supervision of an expert, or replace the entire unit with a new or rebuilt one. However, before removing for repair, check all vacuum lines from engine manifold to the diaphragm housing, as any breaks or poor connections will hamper proper vacuum to atmospheric pressure balance and the

Brakes--Drum & Disc

unit will not operate as it should.

Pedal adjustment is also critical, especially if the proper ¼ to ⅜-in. freeplay in the pedal action has been reduced and the vacuum valving is not properly releasing. Pedal adjustments are incorporated in the linkage to the power units and are accessible from inside the car on suspended pedal systems. Before adjusting any pedal clearance, make sure the return spring is operating with sufficient force to return the pedal unassisted to its full-out position. If there is no return spring, be sure the pedal is free on its pivot.

CALIPER DISC BRAKES

These have been in growing use on American passenger cars for only the past few years, but race cars and many European passenger vehicles have used them as standard equipment for some time. In general, they are used only on the front wheels of American cars in conjunction with regular drum/shoes in the rear. The Corvette employs discs on all four wheels, and solves the parking brake problem by combining the rear disc with an internal expanding, mechanically operated shoe and drum system.

The operating principle is simple. Imagine a spinning iron disc taking the place of the conventional drum. An assembly known as a caliper, mounted to the wheel spindle and containing a system of hydraulic pistons opposing each other, pushes against the preshaped lining material known as pads or pucks. With the disc in between the opposing pads, stopping is effected much like squeezing the disc between thumb and finger, but with a great deal more pressure and area. Hydraulic pressure at the wheel pistons of caliper disc brakes is almost double that of conventional drum/shoe brakes. When used with drum-type rear brakes, a proportioning valve is installed in the rear hydraulic system to prevent rear wheel lock under braking conditions by allowing more hydraulic pressure on the front, and less on the rear.

Another unit used on disc brake systems is the metering valve. It is in the line to the front brakes. It holds back the hydraulic pressure on the front brakes until the pressure builds up a little, then it trips open and allows the front brakes to come on. The delayed application of the front brakes gives the rear shoes a chance to move out against the drums. The end result is that both front and rear brakes come on at the same time.

Check valves (for maintaining residual pressure in the system) are not used on disc brakes, only on drum brakes. With a disc/drum system, there will be a check valve in the line to the rear brakes (usually in the master cylinder outlet) but no check valve in the line to the front brakes.

Self-adjusting, and with visible indication of lining wear, caliper discs are rela-

tively easy to reline but require care and precision to rebuild. Unaffected by water, dust and dirt—since the close fitting pucks wipe as they are applied and water cannot be trapped on the spinning disc—they are sensitive to oil or hydraulic fluid the same as drum brakes. Passenger car disc systems do have a splash shield to divert dust-laden air and water as much as possible in an effort to reduce disc and lining wear caused by abrasives that might filter in between them.

RELINING DISC BRAKES

Before proceeding with lining replacement, siphon about ⅔ of the fluid from the master cylinder to prevent its overflowing as the caliper pistons are pushed back by the new thicker linings. Early GM 4-piston calipers can have their lining renewed without removing the caliper.

When inserting new linings, note the directional arrow on the steel backing of each one which indicates wheel rotation direction and provides for lining up the grain of the material in proper relation to the disc direction. The caliper pistons will have to be pushed back slightly with a thin smooth tool such as a putty knife to accommodate the new linings.

Budd caliper discs used on earlier Chrysler cars must be removed to replace the linings. This can be done without detaching the hydraulic line by removing the mounting bolts to the wheel spindle. A special tool is required that slides in between lining pads and piston insulator to hold them in position during removal. Then carefully slide the assembly off the disc, invert and remove the shoes one at a time. Replace with new linings, slide the assembly back on the disc, install the retainer and anti-rattle springs, tighten the mounting bolts and remove the special retaining clips. Apply medium pedal pressure while finishing the final tightening of caliper mounting bolts.

The Kelsey-Hayes discs, also used on earlier Chrysler Corp. and Ford Motor Co. cars, can be relined without removing the caliper assembly. They can be identified by an external hydraulic line that connects opposing piston assemblies. The lining material has a metal backing with tabs at each end and two small tell-tale detents. These detents create a scraping metal-to-metal noise against the disc, indicating that the linings need replacing. To replace, the splash shield and anti-rattle spring must be removed and the pistons pressed back into the cylinders by prying against the old lining with a thin smooth tool. It is a good idea to check the level of master cylinder fluid to guard against its overflowing during this operation.

With two pairs of pliers, grasp the tabs at each end of the lining pad and withdraw. Slide new pads into position with lining material facing the disc and the tabs seated firmly on the caliper. Replace splash shield and anti-rattle spring, then pump the pedal hard several times to advance the pistons and properly seat

1. Loose Lug Bolt

2. Stripped Wheel Nuts

3. Disc Brake Wear Sensor

linings. Check the master fluid level and bleed the system if the pedal is spongy.

CHECKING THE DISC

Most late-model cars have a single-piston floating caliper. The caliper can slide back and forth to center itself over the disc, which gives much better braking. In the old fixed caliper brakes, the slightest irregularity in the disc would knock the pistons back in their bores. When you stepped on the brake, you had to pump the pedal to get the pistons back out against the disc. With the floating caliper, it doesn't matter how wobbly the disc is. The caliper rides with the punch and gives a much better brake. All single-piston designs have to be removed from the mounting bracket in order to replace the lining.

The brake disc itself is machined to very precise dimensions and finish. Disc

1. Check the lug bolts in the hubs and axles. Loose bolts or ones with stripped threads can cause trouble by ruining your wheel.

2. Here's an example of how loose lug nuts can destroy a wheel. Latter wobbled badly, grinding away at the nuts. Wheels have come off many times due to loose nuts.

3. Preventing brake wear before it costs a fortune in rotors is easy with new Oldsmobiles. This sensor makes noise when it's time to reline.

4. If your car doesn't have the self-adjusting feature, then you must make future adjustments as the brakes wear, through the drum or through the backing plate.

5. This wheel cylinder broke on a car that was not involved in an accident, and driver narrowly avoiding becoming a statistic himself. Note that anchor pin stud broke first (this pin holds brake shoe springs), later causing wheel cylinder to separate.

6. This Safe Gage set features gages in 1/32-in. increments. They are .005-in. oversize; if any go into a bore of the size they are designed for, this means that bore is oversize by .005-in. or more and is therefore unsafe.

thickness is critical to proper lining clearance and piston travel, and the finish to proper coefficient of friction between pads and disc. Accuracy too, as to run-out or wobble, must be maintained as the calipers are solidly mounted to the spindle and must not be twisted by a warped disc. Run-out can be checked by removing the lining pads and clamping a dial indicator to the caliper. Tighten wheel bearing nut to remove all play from hub. Pick a smooth spot about 1 in. from the outer edge of disc for the indicator ball and turn it slowly. A total run out of .004-in. is maximum, and the disc must be replaced if it exceeds this because machining is not recommended.

Disc wear as to thickness also has limits and this can be checked with a micrometer. Overall wear that reduces the new thickness .035-in. for 1-in. discs, or .010-in. for 1¼-in. Corvette discs, indicates the need for disc replacement. Once a normal wear pattern has developed through use, minor scores in the disc surface have negligible effect on braking efficiency. As most discs are riveted to the hub assembly, replacement involves removing entire hub, drilling out rivets, and installing new disc. They do not have to be reriveted on GM cars as the wheel mounting studs provide necessary alignment. Be sure to secure with the wheel lug nuts when checking new disc for run-out.

CALIPER OVERHAUL

When relining caliper disc brakes, inspect inner cavity with pads removed. Any indication of moisture in the form of hydraulic fluid means that seals, pistons, or both, need replacing. To rebuild caliper piston assemblies, the entire caliper assembly must be removed.

Jack front wheels and secure with stands for safety. Remove and plug each main hydraulic line to save fluid. Remove pads, loosen caliper to spindle mounting nuts and bolts, remove and slide caliper off disc. Note location of any shims used to locate caliper.

Calipers are made in two halves, with the mating surfaces carefully machined for perfect fit. Before proceeding with any further disassembly, wash caliper thoroughly in alcohol or special brake

cleaning fluid prescribed for regular drum-brake wheel-cylinder service. Dry thoroughly and separate caliper halves by removing large cross-bolts. Note that the fluid passages where they cross from one side of caliper to the other are sealed with small O-rings. Remove these carefully and keep with other parts so that they are not forgotten on reassembly. Early Kelsey-Hayes calipers do not use internal crossovers, and the external tube must be removed before separating caliper halves. Do not bend excessively or reassembly will turn out to be quite difficult.

Removal of dust boots and seals is easier if the pistons are pushed back into their caliper half as far as they will go. Carefully pry off boot with thin screwdriver, remove pistons, seals and springs, and clean them all in alcohol or special fluid. Clean out bores and all fluid passages and dry before examining them for scoring or pits. Be careful with any tools when they are used to assist removal of any parts of the piston assembly to avoid puncturing seals and boots, or scratching cylinder walls or piston.

While all rubber parts should be cleaned and examined to determine the specific cause of piston leakage, it is a good idea to replace them all from the standard rebuilding kits available. Pistons and bores should be free of scores and pits. Minor ones can be removed by honing but not more than .020-in. can be removed for cleanup. Beyond that the caliper must be replaced. Bores that show very light scratches or corrosion can be cleaned with crocus cloth, a light abrasive material similar to jeweler's rouge.

With the caliper half clamped in well padded vise jaws to avoid exterior damage, begin assembly of springs, pistons, seals, and boots. Most of the assembly can be done by hand; use hydraulic fluid liberally to lubricate all parts. GM brakes require a special tool to compress piston seal and another for installing boot seal. Use of any other tools for this purpose will result in damage to rubber parts.

Kelsey-Hayes and Budd units, if held securely in a vise, can be hand-assembled with a small smooth screwdriver used carefully to work the lip of the boot into the groove provided around the bore diameter. Use no lubricant other than

4. Brake Adjustment

5. Broken Wheel Cylinder

6. Safe Gage Set

Brakes--Drum & Disc

specification brake fluid as any solvent, grease or oil with a mineral base will damage the rubber parts and void all the work of the overhaul. Make sure that pistons and seals slide easily into cylinder bores, then place O-rings in cavities around fluid crossover passages and fit the caliper halves together. Make sure the mating surfaces are clean and free from nicks before installing cross-bolts and hex nuts. To insure proper pressure between caliper halves, a torque wrench is recommended for tightening assembly nuts. About 55 ft.lbs. for 7/16-in. bolts, and 155 ft.-lbs. for ½-in. will effect mating of caliper halves without damage or distortion. On caliper assemblies with external crossover, check the tube for cleanliness and freedom of fractures before carefully screwing coupling nuts to fittings.

Replace caliper assembly using a putty knife to keep pistons and boots from hanging up in edge of disc. Line up caliper to spindle mounting holes and secure with proper bolts and shims, if any. Check hydraulic line fitting for cleanliness and thread condition. Some systems use a small copper gasket in the male end of this connection which should be replaced to insure a good seal at this critical point. Install lining pads, retaining pins, anti-rattle springs, and splash shield.

Overhauling single-piston floating calipers is a lot easier than overhauling the older multiple piston jobs. To remove the caliper on AMC, Chrysler Corp., or GM cars, disconnect the brake hose, unscrew the two large guide pins, and the caliper will come right off. Ford has a similar construction, except that they use an anchor plate which comes off with the caliper. Don't forget to plug the brake hose after you disconnect it. If you don't, all your fluid will run out on the ground. Also, note the position of various clips, cotter keys, and springs on the caliper so you can get them back in the right places. Once you get the caliper off the car, the shoes will come out easily. The problem is in getting the piston out so you can install a new seal. Air pressure applied to the hole where you removed the brake line will take the piston out fast, so fast that you will probably break your hand if you are holding it in the wrong place. Auto parts stores have a tool made to grip the inside diameter of the piston and remove it, which is much safer than using air pressure. When installing the caliper, follow the instructions in the shop manual for your make and year of car. Some car makers recommend lubricating the bolts with silicone, but others say to have everything clean and use clear water as an assembly fluid. The object is to enable the caliper to slide on the guide pins so it can center itself over the disc. If you lose a mounting bolt or guide pin, get another one from your dealer. The use of ordinary bolts or pins is dangerous. It takes special hardware to withstand the tremendous forces applied to the caliper during braking.

DISC BRAKE BLEEDING

As with conventional drum brakes, the system must be bled if the hydraulic lines are disconnected or the wheel cylinders removed. Most service manuals recommend tightening the caliper to wheel spindle mounting bolts with brakes applied in order to center them properly. Before bleeding, make sure the mounting bolts line up with the holes and then tighten snugly only for bleeding procedure. After final bleeding, apply firm pedal pressure, back off mounting bolt nuts slightly, then torque to final tightness.

Road test at low speed with several good strong brake applications to seat the pads properly before taking the car out for normal driving. Be sure you have brakes before you take the car out.

Keep one thing in mind when working on brakes: They are probably the most important single factor in good vehicle control. Brakes seldom fail, but they can if you don't inspect them periodically for wear or leakage. ⌘

1. Power Brake Cutaway

CHECK VALVE

DIAPHRAGM

M/C PUSH ROD

VALVE HOUSING

VALVE HOUSING SEAL

VALVE RETURN SPRING

SEAL

CENTER PLATE

2. Power Unit Schematic

1. This example of the modern power brake unit is from a 1970 Olds. In cutaway form, revealed are the internal valves and dual cylinders.

2. While the pushrod on a non-power master cylinder can angle as it contacts piston, both pushrods in most power units must remain in straight line. Nut on the end of the master cylinder pushrod is for adjustments.

1. After removing the master cylinder from your car, pop the wire retaining spring loose (or remove fastener) so it can be drained.

2. All brake fluid should be drained out and disposed of. Never reuse any fluid once it has gone through lines or cylinders as it will be dirty.

3. Clamp cylinder in vise and remove retaining clip that holds primary piston and pushrod in place. Pull them and secondary piston out.

4. Note the sludge that had formed in master cylinder and gathered on secondary piston and return spring; this can cause brake failure.

5. If sludge collection has not damaged cylinder bore, it can be honed lightly to remove glaze and a master cylinder rebuild kit used.

6. Rinse cylinder with alcohol and check to make sure all passages are open and alcohol pours through freely, as illustrated in this view.

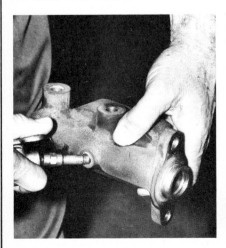

7. Use a high pressure air hose to remove all traces of alcohol from the cylinder and passages, along with any sediment that is still there.

8. Clamp cylinder in vise after pistons are installed. Fill with fluid and pump up by hand to bleed unit. Fluid should pour right out.

9. Now reinstall unit and hook up lines. Vanowen Brake, 11576 Vanowen St., No. Hollywood, Calif., performed operations shown on this page.

HOW-TO: Disc Brake Seal & Boot Replacement

1. After removing cotter pin, then pull retaining pin from the caliper halves. Follow up by removing the brake shoes from the caliper assembly.

2. An air hose placed against the brake line entrance should pop the pistons free. Two came free here. If not, pry them with a screwdriver.

3. Caliper bolts, or retaining bolts, can be removed next. This will allow you to separate the two halves to get at the bores.

4. Clean, denatured alcohol is used to wash brake components. The bores are cleaned up with a super-fine hone within specifications.

5. Pull old seals and boots from the pistons, wash them carefully. Vanowen Brake & Wheel, North Hollywood, Calif., did this job.

6. Assemble boots on pistons, metal side out, seals with wiping edge (side that is cupped or grooved) out. Use plenty of assembly lube.

7. After washing in alcohol, parts are washed in water, then air dried. Bores are lubed, as are the seals and boots, then parts assembled.

8. If you haven't a seal installer, ease the wiping edge of the seals into the bore with a tiny screwdriver, moving it about the edge.

9. A small hammer is used to tap about the metal edge of boot, seating it in the bore. Now install shoes, retaining pin, cotter pin.

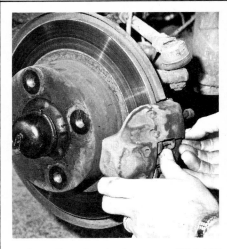

1. To reline disc brakes on a 1500 VW wagon, depress cross spring clip, drive upper pin loose with a punch, then remove same by hand.

2. Pin comes out easily. Note that one end of the pin is split. When reinserting the pins, be sure that the split end faces toward car.

3. Depress the cross spring clip again, then angle the clip up and over the bottom pin and out. The first may be hard, others easy.

4. Now drive the lower pin free with a punch the same as the upper, and remove same. They are tight enough that you can't use a pair of pliers.

5. Make up a pad remover from a coat hanger. Make sure you don't remove the piston shield which has same kind of ends, but the pad itself.

6. The pad on the right has 45,000 miles on it and really shows the wear. For a few bucks and a few minutes, you'll have new brakes.

7. Remove some fluid from master cylinder, then use a piece of aluminum to return self-adjust piston back to original position. Install pads.

8. Once the self-adjust pistons are moved back, insert the new brake pads into the caliper, pushing them all the way into the housing.

9. Angle the new cross spring clip into position, install upper pin. Rotate disc to make sure it's free, then go ahead and install the lower pin.

HOW-TO: Wheel Cylinder Overhaul and Shoe Replacement

1. Remove outer wheel bearing, then replace nut so it can be used to pull seal from drum without damage. This step will work with roller bearings, but will ruin seal with ball bearings.

2. With the brake drum removed, the first operation towards rebuilding the brakes entails removing the secondary (rear) brake shoe return spring with brake tool.

3. Brake spring pliers are used at the bottom to remove brake shoe adjusting spring. Vanowen Brake, 11576 Vanowen St., No. Hollywood, Calif., performed these operations.

4. The primary (front) brake shoe spring and self-adjuster cable are removed, then the secondary shoe hold-down spring. Now the shoes can be removed from backing plate.

5. Remove wheel cylinder hold-down bolts. Bracket shown (arrow) keeps cylinder from coming apart should some part fail during operation. Car being repaired is a late Dodge.

6. Dust boots at each end of the wheel cylinder are removed, along with push rods and pistons. Now the wheel cylinder cups and cup expansion spring can be removed.

7. Physical evidence of sludge accumulation in one wheel cylinder after only 30,000 miles. Each wheel cylinder, the lines, and master cylinder are also contaminated.

8. Denatured alcohol is used with a fine hone in refinishing cylinders. Mike cylinder bores. Maximum overbore allowable is .003-in. After that, new wheel cylinders must be used.

9. The cylinder bore is wiped clean with a lintless cloth after honing and washing with alcohol. Alcohol cuts brake fluid, doesn't leave a residue, and doesn't harm the boots.

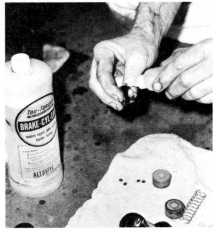

10. All internal cylinder parts are coated with an assembly lube, not brake fluid. Assembly lube will not mix with brake fluid, and will protect parts from any undue wear.

11. Assemble wheel cylinder pieces, then lube brake shoe backing plate platforms and the star adjuster screw with some Lubriplate. This is to reduce wear, help in adjusting.

12. The drum grinder used at Vanowen features both a cutting tool and fine grinding wheel. After removing .008-in. from this drum, note groove and low spot, illustrating drum wear.

13. So, a second pass on the drum lathe was performed, removing all low spots and grooves. A drum gauge is used to mike inside of drum. If it measures too big, it must be replaced.

14. After cutting a groove in these new Bendix linings, to aid in cooling, shoes are arc ground so their radius coincides with that of the brake drum radius that has just been cut.

15. After blowing off all dust, the new rear shoe is slipped behind the wheel cylinder push rod and the shoe hold-down spring and clip are engaged in the brake backing plate.

16. The primary shoe and shoe-to-anchor spring is attached, then the secondary spring, cable guide and star adjusting wheel are replaced. Brake rebuild job is nearly done.

17. Using your special brake spring pliers, install the lever return spring and hook the self-adjusting cable lever up with the secondary brake shoe. These pliers are a must.

18. The brake adjustment gauge is first used to measure the drum I.D., then fit about shoes until they touch the gauge. Star adjuster is backed off three or four notches.

Suspension & Alignment

After so many years of automobile development it seems that by this time the suspension system should have reached a point where one basic design is admittedly the best, and everyone uses it. There is a certain amount of similarity in that most cars use independently suspended front wheels and a solid rear axle, but that's about the only statement you can make that applies to all American suspensions. The little engineering differences that separate one suspension from another are enough to change not only the ride and handling characteristics of the car, but also the way in which alignment is maintained.

Most of us, when considering alignment, think of tire wear, because this is the place where incorrect alignment shows up first. A unicycle doesn't have any problem with wheel alignment or tire wear because one wheel can go anywhere it wants to, but when you get four wheels tied together on an automobile, then they all have to work together. If not, one or more of them is going to be pushed slightly sideways as it rolls down the road, which scuffs rubber off the tread and can make a baldy out of a nobby in a few thousand miles. Alignment also affects the steering and handling of the car. If the wheels are not going down the road in a straight line, it's reasonable to assume that the car is not going to be as responsive as it should be when the driver tries to make it go where he points it.

ALIGNMENT BASICS

Factors involved in front-end alignment (and in some cases, rear-end alignment) are toe-in or toe-out, caster, camber and kingpin angle. Another factor in front-end alignment is known as "Ackermann," from the term Ackermann Principle in which the inside wheel of a car in a turn cuts a sharper angle so that each wheel follows the circumference of a correct circle, the inside wheel scribing a smaller circle than the outside wheel. This is a built-in effect and is a function of the relationship of the steering arms and drag link or the tie-rod and is not normally adjustable on any car.

Toe-in or toe-out describes the relationship of the front wheels to each other when the steering is in a straight-ahead position. In the average car there is a slight toe-in; in other words the front edges of the front wheels are closer together than the rear edges by roughly ⅛-in. It isn't much, but the effect is to keep all the steering linkage in tension, keeping any slop out of it in the straight-ahead driving position where no cornering forces are present to keep things

1. Wheel Alignment and Adjustment

taut. Toe-out is the opposite effect and is found, other than in a faulty system in the straight-ahead position, only in certain front-wheel-drive cars. Naturally, due to Ackermann effect, there is a toe-out in the turn position.

Caster is the effect formed by the inclination of the top of the kingpin or upper ball joint to the rear which imparts an action similar to a furniture caster in keeping the wheels headed in a straight line. You'll see this condition grossly exaggerated in a dragster or Bonneville-type straightaway record car. In the average passenger car this angle is 1° to 3° off a vertical line. On earlier cars with solid axles it is as much as 7°.

Camber, which is referred to as either negative or positive, is the inclination of the wheels inward or outward at the top; in other words, leaning into or away from the car. Earlier cars, meant for use on high-crowned roads, had quite a bit of positive camber (leaning out) to bring the tires perpendicular to the road surface. More recent cars have little or none, and some of the later high-performance cars have from 1° to 2° of negative camber to aid in cornering by offsetting the tendency of a tire to roll under in a turning situation.

Kingpin angle or kingpin inclination is now known as steering axis inclination because modern cars do not have kingpins. The steering axis is an imaginary line that intersects the centers of the ball joints. The angle that this imaginary line makes with the vertical is called the steering axis inclination. If kingpins were used, the steering axis would coincide with the axis of the kingpin itself. A theoretically perfect axis inclination would intersect with the road surface exactly at the center point of the tire's contact with the road. In that theoretically perfect condition the tire would merely

1. Most drivers pay little attention to wheel alignment until their tires are badly worn. Periodic adjustment checks are inexpensive when you compare them to the cost of premature tire wear.

2. Independent front suspensions are responsible for the demise of early drag link steering designs like No. 6. Note that with all the split tie-rod systems, toe adjustments must be made equally on each side to keep the steering wheel centered.

3. Without kingpin inclination, we have the condition on top which will pull the steering wheel right out of the driver's hands when he steps on the brakes. Note that when kingpin inclination line and tire and wheel center do not intersect at the road, the measurement they are apart is called the scrub radius.

4. Positive camber exists when top of tire is tilted away from the car, negative camber when the tire is tilted toward the car. Early-day cars had considerable camber to compensate for the high-crowned roads of the day.

5. The inside wheel has to turn more than the outside. If the wheelbase were longer, you would have to turn the front wheels more to get the same turning radius. The size of wheels and tires and the width of the frame limit how much the wheels can turn.

6. Most modern cars with independent front suspension use A-arms. Shims are used at the A-arm mounts to set front end alignment.

7. Removing the shim from one side of the upper control arm will give more positive caster.

8. Starting out with four shims on each side, we want to change the camber without changing caster.

STEERING CONTROL LINKAGE

1. Haltenberger Linkage (Vertical Socket Type). 2. Center Arm Steer. 3. Parallelogram Linkage (Solid Center Link). 4. Parallelogram Linkage (Center Link Ahead of Axle). 5. Cross Steer. 6. Fore-Aft and Cross Steer. 7. Parallelogram Steer. 8. Long-Short Arm Linkage. 9. Haltenberger Linkage. 10. Haltenberger Linkage (Ahead of Axle).

2. Types of Steering Linkage

3. Scrub Radius

4. Camber

5. Turning Circle

6. A-Arm Front Suspension

7. Positive Caster

8. Changing Camber

Suspension & Alignment

pivot in place when the steering wheel was turned. In most cars the actual steering axis inclination is not that much. The imaginary line may intersect the road surface at the inner edge of the tire, or it may contact the road so far to the inside that it does not coincide with the tire's road contact area at all. If the steering axis were straight up and down, then the steering axis inclination would be zero and the wheel would be forced to rotate slightly every time that the steering wheel was turned. Front ends today are designed as a compromise between the theoretically perfect steering axis inclination and the perfectly vertical steering axis.

The actual measurement between the center of the tire's contact patch and the point where the steering axis hits the road surface is called the "scrub radius." An attempt is made to keep the scrub radius as small as possible when designing front ends so that steering and handling will not be affected too much.

Wheel offset has a big effect on how a car steers and handles because it changes the location of the tire's contact patch. If a wheel is offset to the inside more than stock, it moves the tire's contact patch to the inside so that it coincides with the steering axis. This would probably make it easier to steer the car when parking. If a wheel is installed that has less offset—moving the tire contact patch to the outside of the car for more scrub radius—steering effort would probably be increased. All of these things are figured out very carefully by the manufacturer when he designs the front end. When buying a wheel in a wrecking yard, you should not only look at the bolt circle and the fit on the hub, but also measure the offset. Just because the wheel will bolt onto the hub doesn't mean that it's the right one for the car.

TIRES TELL THE TALE

The first place to check for faulty suspension or alignment is the rubber on the front wheels. Discounting oddball wear that comes from under- or overinflation, check to see if the tires or one tire is worn more on one side than the other; if so, then toe-in of one or both is off. If it is only one that is off, it will show in steering on the road with a definite pull to one side or the other. If both are out of adjustment, tire wear and hard steering in either direction will occur. Tire cupping—an undulating, scalloped wear pattern—can be the result of poor shock absorbers, one wheel out of alignment, a bent spindle, or, what is more likely, a combination of these possibly complicated by loose-tie rod ends which can be caused by misalignment. As a matter of fact, misalignment can, in time, trigger a whole series of ailments and rapid wear. A car that is kept in alignment—with proper tires, good shock absorbers and periodic lubrication—is practically wearproof; but neglect one item and a chain reaction is inevitable.

CHECKING WORN PARTS

Before making any alignment checks or adjustments other than the visual checks and road behavior tests noted above, a preliminary physical inspection must be made. It is absolutely of no use whatever to do any aligning on a system with worn or bent parts or with faulty or unequal-pressure tires.

Jack the front of the car up, one wheel at a time, so that the ball joints are under tension. If at all possible, use a jack stand in conjunction with the jack; even garage-type floor jacks can slip or lose pressure. Grab the upper and lower surfaces of the tire and shake, first vigorously and then gently. The first will give a clue as to whether there is play, and the second will help pinpoint it or show bearing play. A slight movement is all right, but any movement over about a 1/64-in. is too much. Watch or have someone watch to see if there is any

1. Negative Camber

2. Eccentric Bolt

movement and where it is. The trouble may be in the bearing. In this case, remove the wheel and hub and check the bearing—it may be that a simple grease pack and retightening will do the job. If the race is burned or seems gravelly, replace it with a new one, and if you do it to one wheel, do it to both, since the other one will probably be about ready anyway.

Continue the inspection before doing any replacing or adjusting. Now, grasp the wheels and *gently* shake them from side to side to see if there is excessive play in the various linkages and rod ends. Clean and go over each of these as well as all steering linkages.

After you have checked all parts for wear or damage, replace those items that have been found to be functioning improperly.

3. Independent Front Suspension

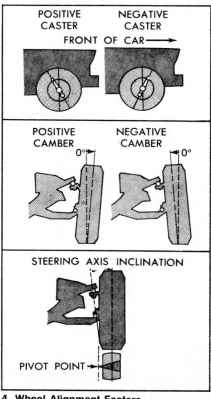

4. Wheel Alignment Factors

BEARINGS

Seldom, if ever, will you find a bearing that will make noise or give any indication that it is bad when you turn the wheel by hand with the car jacked up. A bad bearing will make noise when you're driving the car, but it can be very difficult to tell from which corner of the car the noise is coming. It all boils down to the dirty, time-consuming job of removing the bearings, cleaning them in solvent, and inspecting each ball or roller for pits or roughness. Just one rough roller or ball can sound like a square wheel, so you have to find it, unless you are rich enough to replace all the wheel bearings at once. A clue might be slightly increased play on one front wheel, but don't count on it.

Incidentally, to avoid confusing bearing play with ball joint wear, the car should be jacked up in the opposite way from that for checking the ball joints. In other words, if the spring is above the upper A-arm—as on Ford Motor Co. compacts, intermediates, and Thunderbird, American Motors products, and the Chevy II—the jack should be placed under the lower suspension arm. On those which have the spring *between* the suspension arms, or on cars with torsion bars, the jack should be placed under the crossmember. This keeps the ball joints in tension and allows only the movement at the bearing.

BALL JOINTS

For the next checks, reverse the jacking procedure outlined above; i.e., for cars with springs above the upper arms, jack from the frame or crossmember, and for those with springs between the arms, jack from the lower control arm. In each case use jack stands, since you are going to be doing some vigorous shaking and spending some time underneath the car.

With the car properly jacked for the type of springs involved, two checks are to be made, one for up-and-down play and another for side play. Up and down play, also known as axial or vertical play, should be checked with a long prybar under the wheel and against the ground so you can lift the wheel. Doing the job without a prybar requires a lot of muscle, which most of us don't have. You will find specifications in your factory shop manual for your car. If the specs aren't available, a general rule, suggested by Moog Industries, makers of ball joints and suspension parts, is that any vertical play over .050-in. is too much. However, this is a conservative estimate.

1. With four shims removed, there is a change in camber to the negative.

2. This Ford Maverick lower control arm uses an eccentric to align wheel. Just jack up the car, loosen the nut on the other end of the bolt, attach a socket and breaker bar, and the wheel will move laterally in and out as you turn the eccentric bolt.

3. This is the typical, Detroit-type independent front suspension setup. Two pivoting control arms, of unequal length, support the spindle and use a spring-over-shock between the lower A-arm and the frame rail to help in dampening the vertical travel.

4. You can see from these drawings how the factors in wheel alignment will affect handling and tire wear.

5. Condition of car, especially the springs, has a big effect on wheel alignment. When a car is lowered or raised, it throws alignment off.

6. Control arms are adjusted for front end alignment either by shims or mounting with eccentric bolts.

5. Effect of Spring Condition

BY ADDING OR SUBTRACTING AN EQUAL AMOUNT OF SHIMS FROM "A" AND "B", CAMBER WILL CHANGE WITHOUT AFFECTING CASTER ADJUSTMENT.

TO INCREASE CAMBER: REMOVE SHIMS AT BOTH "A" AND "B".

TO DECREASE CAMBER: ADD SHIMS AT BOTH "A" AND "B".

TO DECREASE POSITIVE CASTER: ADD SHIM AT "A".

TO DECREASE NEGATIVE CASTER: REMOVE SHIM AT "A".

6. Shimming for Alignment

Suspension & Alignment

In some cases a brand new car will have more than the suggested maximum of .050-in.

In all cases, the joint to check is the load-carrying joint. If the spring or torsion bar pushes against the lower arm, then the lower joint is the one that carries the car weight. If the spring is on the upper arm, then the upper joint carries the load. The other joint just follows along and keeps the wheel pointed in the same direction as the car. Follower joints seldom wear out, but it's a good idea to change them whenever the load-carrying joint is changed.

Some manuals give a specification for side play, but it's difficult to check accurately. Side play, with much vigorous shaking, is what the con man shows you when he wants to sell you a set of unneeded ball joints. If your manual gives a side play spec, then by all means check it. Be sure you aren't picking up play in the follower joint or the steering linkage.

Specifics on replacing ball joints on every car are beyond the scope of this book, since the methods both of removal and of attachment vary considerably from car to car, even in a single manufacturer's line. However, certain general remarks are in order. A great number of cars have ball joints that are held to the control arm by a combination of rivets and bolts in varying combinations. When replacement becomes necessary, the bolts are removed in the normal way, and the rivets must be chiseled off. It is easier if the rivets are drilled first but avoid drilling through and enlarging the holes. The replacement unit will have special bolts included to take the place of the rivets and these, not ordinary bolts, must be used. On some Ford products and some GM cars the ball joints are pressed in, and it is inadvisable for these to be replaced anywhere but in a shop equipped with an arbor press to do the job. Some mechanics are real artists with a rivet gun, used as an impact hammer to force the joint into place when the weight of the car is on it. On Chrysler products the joints are threaded into the control arms, and you will need a special ¾-in. drive socket with at least a 3-ft. handle and lots of muscle. On all cars, getting the tapered ball joint stud out of the hole can really be a bear. Smacking the outside of the hole with a hammer may help, but only if you have tension on the stud. Wedges or screw-type pullers are available at some tool stores. If you can look over the shoulder of a local mechanic while he does a ball joint job, you'll be way ahead.

TIE-RODS AND DRAG LINKS

With the ball joints and bearings checked and found within tolerances or replaced, the next place to check is the tie-rods and links and their ends. Checking consists of visual inspection and manual moving of the linkage. It is best to have another person move the steering wheel while you hold a wheel against it, watching the action of the various links and ends. Some play is inevitable

and even desirable, but look for excessive slop that denotes obvious wear. Remember that this play is cumulative; a ¼-in. here and ⅛ there can add up to an impressive total that no amount of aligning will help—in fact aligning is downright futile with a front end that contains more than a minimum amount of excess play. It is also an excellent idea to wash down the linkage with solvent and dry it before trying to make your inspection of grime. It can hide defects and actually give a false "feel" at the various joints. Replace any worn rod ends, checking also for wobble or wear in the tapered holes into which they fit.

ALIGNMENT

Now that everything in the linkage and control departments has been checked and OK'd or repaired, the actual alignment process can be done, with a chance that it will stay that way.

First and foremost, let it be understood that except in dire need, caster and camber settings should not be attempted

1. This wedge-ended tool is called a "pickle fork," and is useful for removing ball joints and tie-rod ends. Sometimes it's difficult with ball joints to get a solid blow because of the rubber boot at top of ball joint.

2. "If it moves, grease it." This might well be your motto, for without proper lubrication at the ball joints and tie-rod ends, these components can wear out long before their time.

3. One of the best methods for the removal of ball joints and tie rod ends is to use a puller such as this tool made by Snap-On.

4. These control arm bushings are made by the JAMCO company and never need lubrication.

5. Some cars still use leaf springs at the rear. Tired springs can often be restored by separating the leaves, sanding them clean and using strips of grease-impregnated cheesecloth between the leaves of the spring. A recent trick is using strips of thin teflon between the leaves.

6. This schematic drawing shows the jack locations, maximum and minimum tolerances recommended by McQuay-Norris for most ball joint front ends.

without a front-end rack. Toe-in settings, on the other hand, are easily done with a minimum of equipment—and that can be homemade.

The first check for misalignment is whether or not the steering wheel is in the straight-ahead position when the car is moving straight ahead. If it is cocked to one side or the other, there is an excellent chance that toe-in is off. Assuming that the wheel has been properly installed in the first place (splined hub only; a keyed hub cannot be installed off-center), the off-center condition will probably be corrected in the alignment process.

By this time, if you have read the foregoing section, you will have noted the construction of the tie-rods and drag links. In most instances the systems will be of two types. In one system, the drag link from the pitman connects with an idler in the center from which relatively long steering links run to the steering arms at the front hub carriers. In the other, the pitman arm attaches to a center link and is matched by an idler arm on

1. Using "Pickle Fork"

2. Front-End Lube Points

3. Snap-On Puller

the opposite (right) side of the same dimensions as the pitman arm. The center link connects these two arms, and from these arms run short links to each front steering arm on the hub carriers. A variation of this has a drag link from the pitman arm to a point on a heavy center link that connects a pair of idler arms, one at each side, each of which connects to the wheels via short links, as in the second system just described.

What is of importance here are the links that run from the steering arms *at the wheels*. It makes little or no difference whether their inboard ends attach to a center idler arm, to the pitman and matching idler, or to a pair of idlers. These links have ends that are threaded right-hand on one end and left-handed on the other so that once the clamps are loosened, they can be turned or twisted. This either lengthens or shortens them depending on which way they are twisted, which in turn increases or decreases the toe-in relative to the centerline of the car at the wheel that is involved.

To find out how much or how little toe-in you have, raise the car and place axle stands under the lower A-arms as close to the wheels as possible. When you let the car down on the axle stands, the suspension must compress to its natural position, as if the wheels were on the ground, or as close to it as you can get. Next, use a piece of chalk to whiten

the center of the tread all around each tire. Then hold a nail firmly against a solid support such as a concrete block, and "scribe" a line in the chalk by spinning the wheel. Now, with the wheels in the straight ahead position, all you have to do is measure how far the lines are apart at the front and rear of the tires. Suppose you got 50 ins. at the front and 50⅛ ins. at the back. You have ⅛-in. toe-in, because the scribed lines are ⅛-in. closer at the front. To be more accurate, the measurements between the lines should be taken halfway between

the top and bottom of the tire. This is no problem in front, but when you move your tape measure in back, the frame gets in the way. What you need is a trammel bar. Get a piece of wood long enough to reach across both front tires, then make short extension pieces with a nail sticking out of each one so that the nail points can be put against each scribed line at the midpoint of the tire. By shifting the trammel bar from front to rear, you can easily see if the scribed lines are closer together at the front by the specified amount of toe-in. If they

4. JAMCO Bushings

5. Leaf Springs

All Ball Joint Suspensions fit into One of these FOUR Categories

Type with Studs Facing Each Other
(Coil Spring Between Control Arms)

Type with Both Studs Pointing Down
(Coil Spring Between Control Arms)

Type with Both Studs Facing Each Other
(Coil Spring Above Upper Control Arm)

Type with Both Studs Facing Each Other
(Torsion Bar Suspension)

6. Ball Joint Suspensions

Suspension & Alignment

aren't, shorten or lengthen the rods until they are.

Now check the position of the steering wheel. If it is centered, you're in business and you can tighten the clamps. If not, lengthen one rod and shorten the other exactly the same amount until the wheel is centered at the straight-ahead position, which is to say the "high spot" in the pitman arm travel.

As mentioned, camber and caster setting are really jobs for shops equipped with front-end racks and the necessary special tools—items that aren't likely to be found in gas stations or neighborhood garages. However, it is worth the time to mention how these values are set into various front ends. Perhaps the most common method is by means of stacks of shims of several standard thicknesses placed in some instances between the cross-shaft of the upper control arm and its frame support.

In other cases, these shims are placed between the pivot bracket of the lower arm and the frame or bracket in the lower underbody. In certain Ford products such as early Fairlanes, '64 and later Fords and Lincolns, the whole upper control arm assembly is moved in or out in slotted holes to which the cross-shaft is bolted. This last requires a special tool and should not be attempted without it. In all recent Chrysler products, the upper arm attaching bolts are equipped with eccentric washers. Turning both equally will adjust camber, and turning one or the other will affect caster. Some late Chevys and early Ramblers have a similar eccentric system applied to the *lower* control arms. Caster adjustments to Corvairs are made by lengthening or shortening the front end tie struts running from the suspension to the frame, changing the tension on the lower end of the spindle.

REAR SUSPENSION

Systems on American cars have pretty well been stabilized in terms of design since the early 1950's. In fact, the basic layout is nearly as old as the automobile in one form. Generally speaking, with only three exceptions, they break down into two types: Longitudinal leaf springs with live ("solid") axle, or coil springs and live axle with appropriate locators.

The exceptions are the Corvette Stingray, '61-'63 Pontiac Tempest, and the Corvair, which have various forms of independent rear suspension systems. The Stingray system uses a transverse leaf spring, a lower control arm with forward locator links, and axle half-shafts with universal joints at each end. Early Corvairs use diagonal control arms with swing axles universally jointed at the inner ends only. Late models use a coil spring modification on the Stingray theme with fully independent axles U-jointed at both inner and outer ends. The third exception, the Pontiac system, is quite similar to that of the early Corvair. It was discontinued primarily due to the inability of the transaxle, which went with it, to take the torque of the various engines with which it came. Due to this transmission frailty, comparatively few of these cars are in current service on the road.

Taking the most common type of rear suspension first—the longitudinal leaf and live axle—prime points of wear, other than inside the axle itself, are few. They are almost all due to neglect, extended hard usage, or impact damage. So simple is the system that, properly assembled, there is very little that can go wrong in terms of alignment. In essence, the basic layout consists of two leaf springs, usually stacks of progressively shorter leaves and a master leaf (occasionally one single broad leaf), solidly anchored toward the front of the car at the frame rail and fastened via a movable shackle at the rear. The shackle allows longitudinal movement of the spring as it bends, but is rigid to sideways movement. The axle housing rests on blocks placed slightly forward of the center of each spring, each end being fastened solidly to, and above, the spring. In case of a multiple spring, the leaves are held together by what is known as a center bolt but which actually runs through directly under the axle housing. Additional clips keep the longer secondary leaves in line.

SHOCK ABSORBERS

On earlier cars, lever action shock absorbers are bolted to the frame rail and attached by a link to the axle housing or its mounting pad. On virtually all modern cars a direct-acting telescope-type shock absorber runs between the mounting pad

and either a bracket on the frame rail or the rear crossmember.

The main points of wear are generally the shock absorbers, the shackles and their bushings and pins, and the front bushing and pin, and finally the leaves themselves on a car that has been neglected or overloaded so as either to bend the spring permanently, wear the ends of the leaves, or break one or more leaves.

Shock absorber wear is easy to detect and easy to fix in case of the tubular type. Press down vigorously on the corner of the car over the particular shock and then release quickly. If the car eases up to just above normal height and then returns gently to normal, the shock is working. If it continues to oscillate you have found a bad one and should replace it. Tubular shock absorbers are not refillable or repairable in service and must be replaced. To replace a shock absorber on the type of suspension under discussion is simply a matter of jacking the car up at the axle and unbolting the shock at the bottom stud or hanger and at the top and then removing it. Replacement is just as simple. Put the new unit in just as the old one was removed, being careful to use the new rubber bushings where noted.

REAR AXLE ALIGNMENT

Misalignment caused by axle displacement is easily detected by running the car over a wet patch of pavement followed by a dry section. The tracks of the rear wheels should be either directly on top or equidistantly inside those of the front wheels. If the track is off to one side or the other, or if a properly aligned front end must be turned slightly to go straight, the rear axle is off to one side or one end of it is misaligned respectively. Jack up the car and look at the lower spring clip plate directly under the axle. Check to see that the spring center bolt (or tie bolt) is in place in the center of the clip plate. If it is not, loosen the U-bolts and, with the spring supported, move the axle until the center bolt centers in the hole in the clip and the spring block. If the clips and bolts are centered, check to see if the axle is displaced sideways. This can be checked any number of ways but the simplest is to measure the distance from the spring to a clearly definable point on the axle housing on each side. If the two mea-

1. Corvette Rear Suspension

2. Ball Joint Wear Indicator

3. Moog Ball Joints

COIL SPRING

ADJUSTABLE UPPER CONTROL ARM

TRACK BAR

SHOCK ABSORBER

CENTER BEARING SUPPORT ASSEMBLY

DIFFERENTIAL CARRIER

CONSTANT-VELOCITY JOINT

LOWER CONTROL ARM

4. Typical Rear Suspension

5. Locking Turntables

6. Steering Wheel Clamp

7. Torquing Wheel Bearings

1. The '63 and later Corvette with independent rear suspension uses a transverse leaf spring reminiscent of the early (pre '49) Fords.

2. Oldsmobile ball joints are designed with a built-in wear indicator for 1973 models. As the joint wears in the housing socket, a rubber pressure ring expands and causes the wear indicator to recede into the housing. Replacement should be made when wear indicator has receded .050-in.

3. Some replacement ball joints, like this Moog unit, are adjustable to compensate for wear. If your old ball joint was held in by rivets, the replacement kit will have special bolts to replace the rivets.

4. Coil-sprung rear suspensions use upper and lower control arms to keep the rear end located and aligned. A track or sway bar is sometimes used.

5. When you pull into a front-end shop for an alignment, the first step the mechanic will take is to lock the turntables in place to protect the swivel bearings while you drive your car onto the rack.

6. The steering wheel (and often the brake pedal) is locked with a clamp like this to keep wheels from moving.

7. One of the first steps in a good alignment job should be adjustment of the front wheel bearings. Use of a torque wrench is not common, but it's the most accurate way to do the job.

surements are not equal, loosen the U-bolts on either end and bump the axle back into place—then tighten up the bolts.

To service shackles, bushing pins, and the spring itself, it is best to remove the spring entirely from the car. It is, strictly speaking, a relatively simple operation but one that requires care. A spring under tension is like a bomb with a lit fuse. If let loose under these conditions it can do a lot of damage, primarily to you.

LEAF SPRING SERVICE

To remove a leaf spring, raise the car and support it with axle stands under the frame, so that the axle hangs free. Then put your jack under the axle and raise it just enough to take the weight off the shackles. If you get the axle positioned just right, you should be able to unbolt the shackle studs and slide the shackles out easily. On some cars the shocks will not extend far enough to let the axle drop to where you want it. In other words, the shocks hold the axle up so that the springs are still under compression. It's easy to disconnect the shocks so you can let the axle down, but be careful of the flexible brake line. With the shocks disconnected you can easily let the axle down far enough to stretch the brake line, pull fittings loose, and generally ruin your brake system. If you have to, disconnect the line, and plan on

bleeding the brakes after you connect it up again.

With the shackles off, it's easy to take the nuts off the U-bolts and drag the spring out from under the car. Leave the axle right where it is, and you will find it a lot easier to get the spring back in.

Using a C-clamp or vise, hold the spring stack together near the center bolt and loosen the bolt, then slowly loosen the clamp or vise until the leaves are loose. Now you can check for broken or cracked leaves, worn anti-squeak inserts, and worn or distorted clips, shackle bolts, and bushings and replace where necessary. To reinstall, simply reverse the above procedure.

While on the subject of leaf springs, it might be wise to bring up the pre-1949 Ford products since there are still a goodly number of these in service either in standard or modified form—i.e., hot rods. In case you hadn't noticed, the pre-1949 Ford is suspended by means of one inverted semi-elliptic transverse spring at either end. The upper part of the spring bears against the front or rear crossmember and the ends ride on shackles at the outer ends of each axle. You don't just jack this one up at the spring and the frame, and lower the jack. If you try that, the doctor will be repairing you, instead of you repairing the car.

The sanitary way to remove a cross-spring is by means of a spring spreader. On these springs, the eyes at the ends

Suspension & Alignment

are rolled downward. A spring spreader is a device that is half thick-walled tube and half threader bar. A large nut rides on the threaded bar which slides into the tube. The ends of each half are beveled like blunt chisels. The nut is run down the bar to the tube, forcing the two halves apart. After inserting the chisel points into the rolled spring eyes, turn the nut which bears on the tube portion and forces the spring ends apart; this relieves the tension on the shackles which can then be removed safely. A less sanitary but effective way is to take a piece of heavy-wall pipe or tubing just a fraction of an inch longer than the distance between the spring eyes, and flatten the ends with the aid of a torch and hammer. By increasing the normal load on the spring as in a bump condition, you can force this bar into the eyes. When the load is removed the bar contains the tension. This is good only if all you want to do is get at the shackle bushings or remove the axle. Once you get out of the car with this system, the spring and bar had best stay together until the load has been replaced.

And don't do the job the way we saw it done by one young man who is alive today only because he's very lucky. He had the spring spreader in position and was trying to hammer the shackles off the end of the shackle studs without any support for the car itself. You must support the car frame firmly on stands. Then jack up the rear end to a point just before the jack starts to lift the frame of the car off the stands. Then you should put the spring spreader into position and put wooden blocks under the tires to support the rear end before removing the shackles. Any work under a car can be dangerous if you don't know what you're doing. When you're not sure, get some confident advice from somebody who has done the job before.

COIL SPRING REAR ENDS

Coil spring rear suspension systems have been used on Buicks literally since the year dot. Variations on this system were adopted by the General Motors compacts in 1961 for the small Buick, Olds, and Pontiac; the latter used an independent system for three years and then fell back into line with the others and used a live axle with locators.

The larger Buicks and the small Buick-Olds-Pontiac compacts differ significantly in detail in terms of the kind of locators used. Where the leaf spring rear suspension is self-locating due to the rigid fore-and-aft, side-to-side mounting action of the springs, coil springs by their very nature can be moved in any direction. Therefore a coil-mounted suspension system must be rigidly held in any direction but that in which it is supposed to move—i.e., up and down.

In the original Buick system, fore-and-aft location was by means of a torque tube, a large-diameter tube that surrounded the driveshaft and was solidly mounted to the differential housing. At the front it was attached by a large, hollow ball joint at the transmission; the ball housed the U-joint at that point. Side-to-side location was by a bar—attached to the axle housing at the right end and running to the frame on the left side—known variously as a track bar, Panhard

rod, and sway bar. This bar is still used on the large Buicks, but the torque tube is no longer with us. In place of the torque tube for longitudinal or fore-and-aft location, two diagonal lower control arms that also carry the springs are used in conjunction with a single upper control arm, adjustable for length and running from just to the right of the differential case to one of the transverse crossmembers.

On the small B-O-P cars (except Tempest '61-'63) the action is somewhat simplified. Two larger control arms are pivoted from the frame ahead of the axle and connect to the lower side of the axle housing at the outer ends. These do the twofold duty of preventing "wrap-up" and locating the axle along the longitudinal line.

The upper control arms provide both lateral and additional longitudinal support, and further control axle-twist. They run from the top of each side of the differential case forward and outward diagonally to the top of the rear crossmember. On both the large Buick and the B-O-P cars sealed, tubular, shock absorbers run from the outside rear of the axle housing diagonally inboard and forward to attaching points on the frame.

In no case do the service manuals give alignment or adjustment instructions on these rear ends. With all the locators properly in place the rear end is in align-

1. Hunter Alignment Arm

2. Loosening Tie Rod Clamp

3. Centering Steering Wheel

4. Making Toe Adjustments

5. Alemite Alignment System

1. There are several types and makes of alignment equipment, but a good job depends mainly on the way it's done rather than the equipment type. In most systems, an alignment arm is attached to the spindle. This is the alignment arm used in Hunter system.

2. Clamps on the tie-rods must be loosened to make toe adjustments. If you live in a very wet climate or if your front end hasn't been aligned in a long time, you may have to soak the tie-rod threads in penetrating oil for a few days and then go back to the shop for alignment.

3. When a car has two tie-rods, you can adjust either one, but this will also change your steering wheel's position. Check this guide for the way to correct placement of wheel.

4. Some alignment systems have wires running from the alignment arms on the wheels to a control panel with a monitor that shows the wheel alignment. This way is quicker and allows mechanic (who is watching monitor) to turn both tie-rods at once so as not to affect steering wheel position.

5. The Stewart-Warner Alemite people have come up with a new alignment system that utilizes line-of-sight, with cross-hair sights in the arms that attach to the car's wheels.

6. Large Ford products present a special problem when making camber changes. These tools make the task a great deal easier.

7. The tools are placed over the upper control arm shaft so that when the bolts that hold shaft in position are loosened, the control arm shaft will not slide around.

8. If it's necessary to change the camber on this Mustang, we go to a cam at the inner end of the lower control arm. Holding one side with a wrench while turning the other will make the camber change.

6. Special Ford Tools

7. Adjusting Ford Front End

8. Setting Camber on Mustang

ment and that's that. If it isn't in alignment, then one or more of these components has been bent or damaged and must be replaced.

On the B-O-P cars, virtually any or all of the various locators can be removed and replaced without removing the axle. All that need be done is to raise the frame to the point where the wheels are off the ground, then raise the axle housing until all strain is off either upper locator, at which point the various fastenings can be undone and the damaged unit removed. The lower locators require that the springs be removed, but here again the job is relatively easy if done with care. Raise and support the chassis so that the wheels are in the air, then raise the axle. Provide slack in the parking brake cable so that it will not be damaged and disconnect the shock absorbers at their lower ends. Remove the bolt and clamp that holds each spring at the lower end and then lower the axle. In replacing the springs, position the springs so that the larger end, which is also ground flat, is at the top of the upper spring seat. Raise the axle and connect the spring to it with the clamp and bolt. If you have found spring sag, there are several remedies: 1) Purchase new springs rated for your model; 2) There are shims available at B-O-P dealers; and 3) If you are looking for stiffer handling or plan on carrying heavy loads, there are special 200- and 500-lb. overload springs available for your car.

A word on coil springs and their removal in general is not out of place at this point. As with any kind of spring under tension, treat them as though they were live grenades. As outlined above, coil spring rear ends do not require any special tools or procedures, just care in assembly and disassembly so that they don't leap out under partial load when you're halfway into the job. Front end springs are a different breed of cat. First, in virtually all instances, the shock absorber rides inside the spring. Removing this leaves access from top to bottom through holes in either end or both, and while some manuals don't specifically recommend using special tools, a simple screw-type coil spring compressor is an especially useful object to have and to use both for simplicity and your own peace of mind. On cars with springs between the control arms it isn't necessary but is handy; on cars with the springs above the upper control arm it is a necessity. Among these are all the Ford products that use the system and certain of the American Motors products.

LATE CORVAIR OR CORVETTE

There are two types of rear end suspensions we haven't touched on as yet— the fully independent units of the '64 and later Corvair, and the Stingray Corvettes. Both are referred to as "4-link" systems using longitudinal torque arms, transverse strut rods and the axle half-shafts themselves. The torque arms also act as hub carriers. The major difference between these two is that the Corvette uses a single transverse leaf spring-stack mounted under the rear of the stationary center section and the Corvair uses

Suspension & Alignment

coils mounted between the frame and the hub carrier ends of the torque arms.

These rear ends are hardly self-aligning, and both have definite camber and toe-in requirements. In no case is this a home garage or backyard type of job. About the only job that should be done on these cars outside of a properly equipped shop, as far as the rear end goes, is shock absorber replacement, which is done as on any other car. Springs also may be removed for renewal where there is a hydraulic floor jack and jack stand available.

In the case of the Corvette, the procedure is as follows: Raise the rear of the car and support it on jack stands placed just forward of the torque arm pivot points. Place the floor jack underneath the outer end of the spring at the link bolt. (Note: the Corvette spring, unlike the early Ford, does *not* have spring eyes. A link bolt through the torque arm holds it.) Raise the jack until the spring is nearly flat. Now wrap a chain of at least 1/4 or 5/16 size around the spring and the suspension crossmember above it, and secure it with a safe grab hook. *Do not use cable, rope or anything else for this purpose.* Cinch down a C-clamp inboard of the chain to keep it from slipping. Now lower the jack and remove the link bolt with the chain holding the spring. Raise the jack again and remove the chain and then slowly let off the jack and allow the spring to release fully. Repeat this process on the other end, and when both are released, remove the four bolts and spring pad under the differential case, then slide the spring out sideways. *Do not take any shortcuts!*

On the Corvair, things are a bit simpler. Raise the rear of the car and place on jack stands as with the Corvette, the stands placed at the pads forward of the torque arms. Place the jack under the torque arm at the hub carrier and raise it up to curb height. Release the rear strut rod at its differential carrier end and release the shock absorber at the bottom end where it attaches to the torque arm. Now slowly lower the jack, allowing the spring to extend to its full length. Remove the spring, spring retainer, and cushion from the frame. To replace it, reverse the above procedure, making sure that the spring is properly indexed into the cushion and seat.

ADJUSTABLE SHOCKS

There are three makes of shocks, or rather types within makes, that can be adjusted, rebuilt, or both. These are all, as far as the American market is concerned, replacement items.

Foremost among these is the justly famous Koni, made in Holland but marketed wordwide. Perhaps its first claim to fame is total, uncompromising quality. Every unit is matched internally to exact tolerances and all the valving and sealing is metallic; there is no plastic, leather or rubber on the piston whatever. Quality aside, what made it really well-known is the fact that it can be infinitely adjusted from just the soft side of firm to nearly rock hard when new. Except for com-

petition, very few are set hard to begin with. Tailored individually for the car involved in terms of control ratio, they are generally installed in their softer setting or just on the firm side and then as time goes on, they can be gradually adjusted to take up for wear or other conditions. Combined with the quality control, this feature makes them good for the lifetime of the car, which more than justifies their initially higher cost. Setting is accomplished on the Koni by disconnecting it

and collapsing the shock all the way, then turning the lower half gently until a slight click is felt. Turning one way hardens it and the other way softens it. The adjustment is done inside by a nut that progressively shuts off orifices in the central valving. Another point with the Koni is that it can be rebuilt and even tailored in action by any of the several distribution centers around the country.

Another of the adjustables is the Armstrong which can be had in both lever

1. Adjusting Strut for Caster

2. Tubular Shock Absorber

MOUNTING EYE
PISTON ROD SEAL
SEAL SPRING
STONE SHIELD
RESERVOIR TUBE
PRESSURE TUBE
PISTON ROD
INTAKE VALVE
PISTON
REBOUND ORIFICE PLATE
REBOUND SPRING
COMPRESSION VALVE ASSEMBLY
MOUNTING EYE

3. Front End Alignment Points

CASTER & CAMBER (Eccentric Bushing)
CAMBER (Shims)
CASTER & CAMBER (Elongated Holes)
CASTER STRUT
CASTER & CAMBER (Shims)
CASTER & CAMBER (Shims)
CAMBER (Cams)
CASTER & CAMBER (Eccentric Washer)
CAMBER (Ball-joint Eccentric or Slots for Ball-joint)
CASTER STRUT
CASTER & CAMBER (Eccentric Washer)
CASTER STRUT
CAMBER (Shims)
CASTER STRUT
CASTER & CAMBER (Shims)
CASTER & CAMBER (Shims)
CASTER STRUT
CAMBER (Eccentric Washer)

4. Positive Caster on Race Car

5. Air Shock

6. Coil/Shock

7. Street Rod Suspension

1. On cars with strut suspension, like this Mustang, the caster can be changed by lengthening or shortening the strut. Loosening one nut and then tightening the other will change the length of the strut.

2. The condition of your shocks has an effect on your handling. There's no sense in spending money for an alignment job if the shocks are shot. Most tubular shocks are of the design shown. Oil, moving through orifices, provides the dampening action.

3. This chart shows the various types of front ends and methods of alignment used on late model cars.

4. Drag racing cars are set up with several times the positive caster of a normal passenger car. By almost "forcing" the front wheels to go in a straight line, this makes the car handle better in straightline racing.

5. Air shocks are popular accessories today for vehicles that carry heavy loads, like campers and trucks. This cutaway shows how pumped-in air fills "bag" around top of shock, to either raise rear of car or provide extra load-carrying capacity.

6. Combination coil springs/shocks are used in many types of racing and street machines. This type features an adjustment (arrow) for changing the amount of spring tension.

7. Very popular with the street rod set are the independent rear ends like the Jaguar and Corvette. Note cam bolt used to set rear wheel alignment.

and tubular form. In the latter form, combined with an integral coil spring, it is used by most of the finest racing cars in the world. Its great advantage is that it can be adjusted from the outside while mounted on the car, a feature also available on a few models of Koni. There are two forms. One adjusts through 10 positions by means of a knob on the side of the shock tube or in the case of a shock meant to ride inside a front spring, by means of a slotted head in the same place that can be turned with a screwdriver. Another form adjusts from the dash through four positions by means of a remote control unit within the car.

A third adjustable is the Gabriel Adjust-O-Matic which is set, like the Koni, by detaching and collapsing the shock to engage a pawl inside the unit. The Gabriel, however, does not have the infinite adjustment of the Dutch shock but has three positions: soft, medium, and hard. Again the prime purpose is to take up for wear and age, but it can be used to make the car suitable for different road surfaces or high speeds. It is much more widely available than the other two and less expensive, which offsets its lesser range of capability.

There is also a so-called adjustable type of shock, the air-filled unit made by Delco for GM cars. This unit is optional as an overload item on most GM cars, especially station wagons and the El Camino pickup. Adjustment is by bleeding air off for softer settings and adding it from a filling station hose for harder settings. However, this is not a true shock

adjustment, but rather a helper spring, since the air does nothing to dampen the action, operating only on bumps.

CHASSIS MODIFICATIONS

The best advice we can give on chassis modifications is that if you don't really know what the modification is for and what it will actually do other than look different—then DON'T.

The chassis setting as it comes from the factory is a compromise meant to give the best ride with the best handling and ease of operation for everyday driving. A little of the ideal is given up in each area to produce a good balance. However, modifications can be and are made to produce a given effect for a given use—but there will always be a sacrifice in one or another area to produce the effect most desired.

A car modified for straight-line acceleration with soft shocks on the front, hard ones on the rear and the suspension raised to provide strong weight transfer to the rear wheels for traction will handle poorly on the street and will be unmanageable in highway cruising.

Conversely, a car set up to handle on a road course for sedan racing with its lowered suspension, stiff shocks front and rear set to a 50-50 or 60-40 ratio, and quick steering, will entail sacrifices in a harsh ride and stiff control at low speeds. Some high-performance factory cars are balanced in this direction for better road handling, however, and if you don't mind a slightly harsher ride they can feel very safe indeed. Low driveways and rutted country roads can be a pain, though.

In other words, don't depart from the factory chassis specs unless you know exactly what you want and can get the advice of an expert on what the effect of any given change will be. This even applies to the widespread practice of switching tires and wheels around either to get the wide look or for more traction. Done right, it's fine, but done without regard to the basic chassis geometry it can result in some funny steering conditions at least and very possibly ruined wheel bearings and even broken spindles. If you want to modify, do it—please do it right. ✦

Manual Steering

hink back, if you can, to your first hot rod, not your first car, but the "soap box" racer you built from scrap wood and some "borrowed" baby carriage wheels. Steering was no problem. Right? You just made the 2 × 4 front axle pivot on a bolt at the front of the "frame" and steering was only a matter of putting your feet on the ends of the axles; or if you wanted to keep your feet in, you shortened your mother's clothesline and used the rope to steer. It seemed logical enough at the time; after all, didn't all those wagons in the cowboy movies steer something like that? Thankfully, steering gear design has progressed steadily since those wagons went out of favor and "the horseless contraption" was invented.

Faster cars required better handling for those poor roads. And when "balloon" tires and front-wheel brakes were introduced, steering became even harder, and led to the development of the steering box. Essentially, the driver steered a wheel at one end of a shaft, at the other end of which was a set of gears that transferred the motion, through arms and rods, to the wheels.

WORM AND SECTOR, WORM AND WHEEL DESIGN

The worm gear was, and still is, almost universal in its use on the steering column shaft. In the worm and wheel design, as the name implies, a toothed wheel meshed with the teeth on the worm, and a shaft connected this wheel with the pitman arm. The worm and sector was simply the same system, but instead of using a wheel, just a piece-of-pie portion of the wheel was used, since within the turning limits of the front wheels most of the wheel-gear could not be utilized.

Friction proved to be the common enemy of all steering designs, and these early types were no exceptions. Most of the loads in the box were concentrated on the gears at their mesh points, and constant lubrication was a necessary drawback. They also required frequent adjustment, and proper alignment became difficult at the mesh point because it was found that the gears wore unevenly. That is, they most often wore out in the straight-ahead position, where they received the most use.

Once the gears were worn, you could adjust them only so much before the gears would bind. The worm and wheel type did at least have the advantage that the wheel could be removed and reinstalled with fresh teeth at the mesh point.

ROSS STEERING

The introduction in 1923 of the Ross cam and lever steering gear was a solid step forward in terms of reduced friction

1. Modern Steering Linkage

2. Worm and Wheel Steering

3. Worm and Sector Steering

4. Saginaw Steering Box

1. For the last 20 years, American cars have used steering gear with split tie-rods rather than the older drag link system because of less lost motion and better geometry.

2. The worm and wheel was one of the first automotive steering designs. It proved to be inefficient, because all the friction was concentrated in the mesh area of the gears.

3. A variation of the worm and wheel was the worm and sector, which was cheaper and could be built as a more compact unit than its predecessor.

4. Here's a Saginaw worm and sector box with the side cover removed to expose the gears. Note the adjusting slot (arrow) for mesh load.

and wear. One long groove (the cam) spiraled around the end of the steering shaft and a lever on the pitman shaft had a peg on it that fit this groove. As the steering wheel was turned, the peg was forced to ride up or down the shaft in the groove, and this action turned the pitman shaft and arm.

The Ross steering was a very good compromise; it was *almost* irreversible. It was difficult for motion to be passed from the wheels back up through the steering wheel, but enough was felt at the wheel to give the driver that important "feel of the road" which gives him confidence in his control.

WORM AND ROLLER

Friction was still a factor to be reckoned with, though, as cars got heavier, tires got bigger and tire pressures became lower for a better ride. It wasn't just that it was becoming harder to steer the car, but friction and wear within the

gearbox was increasing again with these greater loads. So the people over at the Saginaw Steering Division of General Motors started making worm and roller steering in 1926 for the heavy Cadillacs. Basically, the worm on the steering shaft was hourglass-shaped; it was thicker at the ends than in the middle. Instead of a curved sector meshing with it, there was a roller, like a single large gear tooth, which was perpendicular to the steering shaft. It was mounted in roller bearings in a yoke that was part of the pitman arm shaft. These bearings took much of the load and the big roller distributed the wear more evenly. The design was so efficient that it is still used today.

RECIRCULATING-BALL STEERING GEAR

By far the most widely used steering gear today is the recirculating-ball type, introduced on the 1940 Cadillac. Another development by Saginaw, it was basically an improvement of the screw-and-nut design that had been around for many years. A long worm gear was on the bottom of the steering shaft, on which a large, coarse-threaded nut was fitted. The nut was inside a collar or sleeve that could slide back and forth inside the box, and this sleeve had teeth on one side that meshed with a sector gear on the pitman shaft. As the steering shaft was turned, the nut moved up and down the worm gear threads and pushed the sleeve up and down with it, so that the teeth on the sleeve moved the sector and turned the pitman arm.

Actually, it was a lot less complicated than it sounds, and had a number of features that have appealed to later engineers. One of the best features was its irreversibility; only enough road feel

came back through the steering for good control. And it considerably reduced the driver effort involved in steering even such "boat anchors" as the 16-cylinder Cadillacs on which it was used.

That old specter of friction is the area modern engineers have so improved in this basically good design, which is where the recirculating balls come in. The grooves in the worm and inside the nut were machined for ball bearings, so that, in a sense, the balls performed the function of threads and absorbed the steering gear loads and friction. As the car was steered to the right, the balls would circulate in one direction, and in the opposite direction during a left-hand turn. Two tubes connected four holes in the nut/sleeve unit so that the balls could circulate over and over again and distribute the wear evenly among all of them.

Friction was reduced so much that steering was made much easier without having to slow down the gear ratio, which as we have said results in more lock-to-lock turns for the driver. Except for power steering, this represents the furthest advancement of steering gear design thus far, at least on domestic cars.

RACK AND PINION STEERING

Across the Atlantic "river," car manufacturers through the years have utilized some of the same steering systems as we have, though the light weight and smaller size of their cars have permitted the use of generally faster steering ratios. Perhaps the most interesting and different design is the rack and pinion type, seldom found on American cars, but common on most foreign cars and many different kinds of race cars.

In this case the gear on the steering column is similar to the pinion gear in a differential—cut on an angle, and meshed with a steer bar (the rack) toothed on one side. The rack is mounted parallel to the front axle, and as the steering wheel is turned, it operates directly on the steering linkage without the use of a pitman arm or draglink. It's fast, simple to work on, and lightweight because it eliminates some of the usual linkage, which are the reasons it has been such a favorite on race cars and sports cars. Its one drawback is that it has very little inherent reversibility, but in a racing machine the driver isn't worried about comfort or parking ability and is usually interested in more feedback or road feel than the average driver. Rack and pinion steering is thus a natural. Its quick action has made it the standard system on most imported sports cars, which are small and light, and now that Detroit is moving back into the small car business, it's turning to rack and pinion for Pinto-size cars.

For passenger car installations, a compromise is often made by using a shock absorber-type damper on the linkage to reduce the reversibility. Since the damper's action is proportional to the amount of force put on it, small road shocks (desirable road feel) can be felt throughout the steering, but fast, hard, driver-jerking bumps are dampened.

Manual Steering

Currently, however, manual steering gears are made in three basic types. The Gemmer Worm and Roller Gear was used on Chrysler Corp. cars until the end of 1961, and on American Ramblers to date. General Motors passenger cars and Rambler, except American, use the Saginaw Recirculating-Ball type Chrysler Corp. cars, 1962 and up, also have a recirculating-ball type, and so do Ford products. A seldom-used type is the Ross Cam and Lever, used on Jeep and pre-'61 Studebakers.

MAINTENANCE

In most cases, you won't have too many complaints about the steering gear on your car, mainly because modern steering systems are well designed and relatively trouble-free, and besides, you'll probably be spending all of your attention on good stuff like the engine and suspension. Taking care of your steering amounts to no more than checking periodically, keeping it full of grease or 90W oil, and making adjustments when necessary. Rarely will you ever want to *rebuild* a steering box. It would prove to be a pain in the bippy. Most guys are content to visit their friendly/unfriendly neighborhood junkyard for a replacement unit if something goes seriously wrong with it. You could buy a good used steering box and column for what it would cost to replace even one of the gears in your present box with a new factory unit. But, as with anything you buy used or from a wrecking yard, you have to be careful or you'll wind up spending good bucks for an item that later reveals itself to be pure mung.

If you do buy steering in a junkyard, check it over as carefully as you would select a used transmission, even to taking off the box cover and washing it with solvent so you can inspect the teeth on the gears. Inspect the box for defects, cracks, welds, etc., and if it's still in a car, try it out to see if it binds or has any play in it. If you're getting one from another model or year than your own car, see how many turns it is from lock to lock so you can determine if it has the ratio you want.

Before you start thinking about throwing out your steering and replacing it, check into it thoroughly, and even before attacking your steering box, try to determine first if it isn't something else which

1. The recirculating-ball steering mechanism was first used in 1940. It offered extremely low friction and is the most common type of manual box being used today by Detroit.

2. One of the most popular foreign car steering designs is the rack and pinion. Lacking irreversibility, it is often used with a steering damper. This is steering gear from Ford Pinto, one of few U.S. cars using it.

3. Part of the simplicity of the rack and pinion design is that it is connected directly to the tie-rods, so there is no need for idler arms or relay rods. This is Cricket.

1. Recirculating Ball Steering

2. Pinto Rack and Pinion

3. Plymouth Cricket Steering

4. Variable-Ratio Steering gear

may be affecting the handling or steering. Things like poor shocks, unbalanced wheels, a misaligned front end, bad wheel bearings, or improper tire pressure can produce the same symptoms as defective steering gear.

If everything else checks out, then inspect your tie-rod ends and idler arms. As trouble-free and long lasting as these parts are, they wear out long before your steering box. Jack up the front end or put the car on a hoist and push up and down on the idler arm. If it's loose, pull it off and inspect it. Usually there is a bushing in the end that should be replaced. Tie-rod maintenance involves pushing up and down on the end of the tie-rod, checking for play just as with the idler arm. To remove them you may have to borrow a mechanic's "tuning fork" or

"pickle fork," which is a heavy steel bar forked at the end. It's machined at an angle, like a wedge, so that you can put the fork between the tie-rod end and the steering arm. Hitting the end of the bar with a hammer forces the stud of the tie-rod end out of its socket in the steering arm. Above all, the' most important thing to remember when doing any work on the front suspension or steering is to *never* leave out the cotter pins. The life you save definitely will be your own.

GEMMER WORM AND ROLLER

The worm is an integral part of the steering shaft, being hourglass shape, or concave in the middle. It is supported at both ends by tapered roller bearings. The cross-shaft has a triple roller (instead of a sector gear) which fits into the teeth of the worm. An adjustment screw in the cover permits cross-shaft end-play adjustment which determines play between roller and worm. The pitman arm is fastened with a master spline

5. Gemmer Steering Box

4. The Dodge Colt, another mini-car using quick steering, has a variable ratio (15.58-18.18) achieved by a specially contoured worm gear. It uses recirculating balls to attain low friction during operation.

5. This exploded view of Gemmer box shows use of shims to adjust worm gear in the housing. You'll find a box like this on many older cars, but most had only bushings, no needle bearings, on cross-shaft.

6. The Gemmer worm and roller design was used by Chrysler for many years. Cutaway drawing shows construction of box, mast jacket and shift tube.

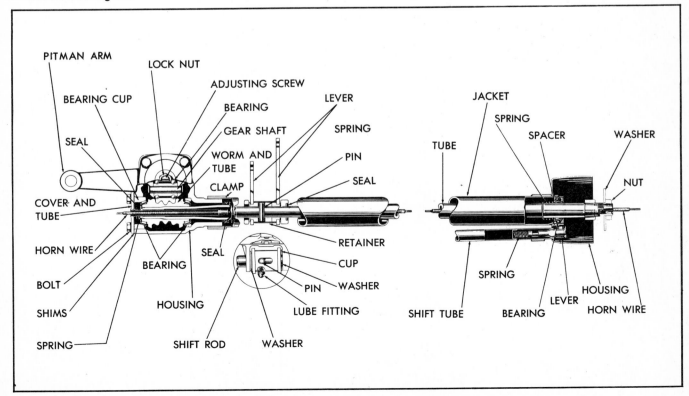

6. Chrysler Worm and Roller

Manual Steering

to the roller shaft by means of a large end nut.

Worm bearing adjustment: If adjustment is necessary, first disconnect the steering linkage from the pitman arm. To eliminate end-play in the steering shaft, loosen the four end cover plate screws, then loosen the cover plate and separate the shims with a knife (be careful not to damage the shims). Remove one shim at a time, retighten the screws, and check for end-play by turning the steering wheel full right and left. Repeat this procedure until there is no end-play and no noticeable tightness in the wheel movement to full right and left. Retighten all four screws. Then check bearing preload with a spring scale on the rim of the steering wheel. If the pull is less than 1½ lbs., remove another shim and repeat operation. If the pull is more than 1½ lbs., add shims to decrease pre-load until satisfactory. Be sure all screws are tight when testing with the spring scale.

Cross-shaft adjustment: Loosen the cross-shaft adjusting screw locknut in the cover. With the steering wheel in center position, tighten the adjustment screw slightly. Check amount of end-play by grasping the pitman arm. When end-play has been removed, use spring scale again on the steering wheel rim; if there is more than a 1-lb. pull above the first scale reading, loosen the adjustment screw slightly. **Caution:** *Do not overtighten.* The steering wheel should turn freely from one extreme to the other without binding or stiffness. When satisfied, tighten lock nut on adjusting screw. Recheck with scale.

Then fill the steering wheel box with proper lubricant. Reconnect the pitman arm to steering linkage, and recheck front wheel toe-in; adjust if necessary.

RECIRCULATING-BALL ADJUSTMENTS

For the late-model crowd, here's the "skinny" on adjusting the recirculating-ball steering. Here you have only two adjustments to make for end-play on each of the shafts. You won't have to worry about worm/nut mesh because the use of the steel balls between the teeth eliminates wear in most cases. Jacking up the car and disconnecting the pitman arm from the linkage is still the first step. Remember, when working on this type of steering system when the linkage is off, don't turn the steering wheel *hard* over to either extreme or you may damage the steel balls. If you suspect that the car may have been in a front-end collision at one time, then loosen the steering column support mount that is under or behind the dashboard to eliminate the possibility of a misaligned shaft during the adjustments. If your car has flexible U-joints in the steering shaft, you don't have to worry about this.

With the steering about one turn from the full left or full right, back off the locknut on the pitman shaft (opposite side of box from pitman arm) and loosen the adjuster a few turns counterclockwise to take the mesh load off the gears.

1. Removing Steering Wheel

2. Using Puller on Pitman Arm

1. The horn button ring can usually be removed by taking a few screws from the backside of the steering wheel. Then a puller like this is used to remove the wheel once the large shaft nut is taken off.

2. A gear puller is required to get Pitman arm off splined shaft of the steering box. The same type of tool is also useful for pulling tie-rod ends from spindle arms with no damage to the tie-rod ends.

3. The typical late-model steering box has a filler plug and only two adjustments, for bearing preload and end-play. Wormshaft bearing nuts may be at the top or bottom of the box, depending on the make of car.

4. On some late-model boxes, there are two different holes for filling and checking the lubricant level. A shop manual will tell you which is which on your car and also what type of lubrication should be used.

5. If you remove the steering box from the frame, make some alignment marks on the box and shaft so they can be reinstalled properly later.

6. You won't have a large enough wrench to loosen the worm bearing adjuster locknut, but a drift pin and a few hammer taps will do it. This job is a lot easier in a vise than on the car in cramped quarters.

FILLER PLUG

CROSS SHAFT ADJUSTMENT SCREW

LOCK NUT

WORMSHAFT BEARING ADJUSTER

LOCK NUT

3. Steering Box Adjustments

Now pull up and down on the steering wheel to check for end-play in the steering shaft. Play can be taken out by another locknut/adjuster combination found at the bottom end of the steering box. The large locknut can be loosened by tapping it with a hammer and punch in the notches provided, if you don't have a wrench that big. Always check for lost motion again after tightening the locknut following an adjustment.

Now you can adjust the end-play in

the pitman shaft and at the same time take care of lash where the sector gear meshes with the teeth on the underside of the ball-nut mechanism. Since the gears are cut at an angle, end-play adjustment of the pitman shaft controls the mesh between them, too. Turning the adjuster *clockwise* will take up the lash, but make sure you don't overtighten it. These adjustments of late-model steering gears will only rarely be needed, but by all rights they should be made with the use of a pounds-pressure gauge on the steering wheel to measure drag or bind. Assuming that you don't have such a gauge, though, you can do it yourself as outlined above, or have it done at your dealer's garage.

Lubrication for the steering box (about SAE 90W) can be purchased at most parts stores or you can have it put in at a garage, since you don't need very much. Some steering boxes use chassis grease. If there is no filler plug on the box, or if it has a grease-gun-type lube fitting, it probably should have chassis grease. Using 90W in a box designed for chassis grease will result in a big mess because the 90W will probably leak out profusely.

STEERING WHEEL REMOVAL

The removal of the horn sounding ring or button can sometimes be more difficult and perplexing than the removal of the steering wheel. One of the cardinal rules of the good mechanic is: *Never use force to remove units or parts, unless*

you know how. Forcing in the wrong place can lead to damage or breakage, and can cost embarrassment, time, and money.

To remove the horn switch or steering wheel, first disconnect the battery to prevent the horn from sounding. *In all cases a wheel puller should be used to remove the steering wheel.* Before removing the wheel, make a scribe mark on the end of the steering wheel shaft and on the wheel hub, so the wheel can be reinstalled correctly. Some cars have a blind spline for this purpose.

REMOVING THE STEERING BOX AND COLUMN

If all of the above adjustments have failed to correct any problems you suspect are coming from the box, then you haven't much choice but to replace the unit. It may look like it's going to be a beast of a job (it really isn't), but keep telling yourself that you need the exercise, or consider it as a challenge. Naturally, you first have to take that steering

wheel off, and for this you're going to need a steering wheel puller or gear puller because it's on there pretty tight. You'll need it to pull the pitman arm from its shaft for the same reason.

Before starting, determine if the gear and column can be removed from the top—by raising it up through the dash over the driver's seat—or by dropping it down through the floor or dash, beside the engine and out from below the car. If necessary to drop it out through the bottom, arrangements must be made to jack up the front end of the car to permit the removal of the gear and also the column assembly.

Once the removal route has been determined, here are the steps you should follow:

1. Place protective cover over the front seat.
2. Disconnect battery cables.
3. Disconnect wires at bottom of the steering column, one at a time and tag each wire carefully.
4. Disconnect steering linkage from pitman arm.
5. Remove jacket tube clamps at steering gear housing (if any).
6. Disengage steering shaft flange from flexible housing. Note: Some late cars have a flex connection between gear shaft and steering wheel shaft. This will make it unnecessary to disturb the steering column and wheel.
7. Remove support clamp at instrument panel.
8. Remove horn and signal wires from steering column below instrument panel.
9. Remove horn ring and steering wheel—a wheel puller is needed.
10. Remove dust shield at firewall.
11. Remove floor opening panel (if any exist).
12. If car has manual shift lever on steering column, disconnect gear shift rods that are at the bottom of the steering column.
13. Disconnect neutral safety switch wire at bottom of column and tag it.
14. Unfasten steering gear from the frame (attached with three or four bolts).
15. If car has automatic transmission, disconnect gear indicator from the dash dial.

After disconnecting the electrical and shift linkage connections from the mast jacket—which is the column or tube covering the steering shaft—you can unbolt the box from the frame, the mast jacket from the dash bracket, and pull the mast jacket into the inside of the car and off. The shift arms on it can be worked through the flexible sealing around the steering column at the firewall. Now the box itself and the steering shaft can be removed from the frame.

Because safety is so important, the collapsible steering column has become a standard item on new cars. Some have a steel mesh section in the middle that folds up in a crash, while later versions utilize two sections held together with plastic pins that shear under impact, telescoping the two sections. When working with such a column, be careful not to collapse it by accident (no pun intended). Don't yank on it too hard, and don't use a hammer on the shaft to loosen steering wheel when removing it. ✦

4. Lubrication Plugs

5. Attaching Box to Frame

6. Loosening Adjuster Locknut

Steering Box Overhaul

Most cars today use recirculating-ball steering, which is generally so trouble-free that all it should ever need is an occasional adjustment. We're presenting this how-to for those of you who *do* have trouble, because sometimes adjusting won't clear up the steering slop.

Once you've determined that it is the box and not some other part of the steering linkage, remove the box from the frame. This procedure will differ with every make of car, so you may want to check in a shop manual. Once on your bench and cleaned up enough to work on, a manual steering box is fairly simple to rebuild. You disassemble it, inspect and clean the old parts, replace the worn parts with new ones, and lube the parts and reassemble. The important thing to remember while you have your steering box apart is to keep all parts spotlessly clean and lubricated with steering gear lube, *not* gear oil. It's a lot of work sometimes to take out and reinstall a steering box, but in the end, rebuilding will "set you straight" for years.

HOW-TO: Over hauling Steering Box

1. This is a Mopar recirculating-ball steering box, but almost all modern boxes are similar. First step is to thoroughly clean box and remove cross-shaft cover screws.

2. Before removing the cross-shaft cover, back off a few turns on the cross-shaft adjuster nut (arrow) to take load off gears, and turn gears to center of travel.

3. With the cross-shaft and cross-shaft bearing and cover assembly removed, use a hammer and punch to get lockring loose on wormshaft bearing adjuster nut.

4. If you don't have the factory spanner wrench to use, the wormshaft adjuster can be loosened by using two screwdrivers and prying against the wormshaft.

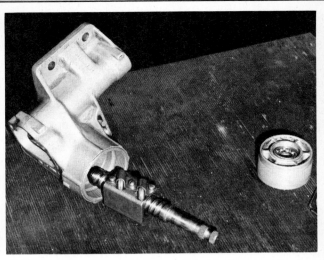

5. The wormshaft adjuster can now be removed after it is threaded all the way out of the housing. Since it is aluminum, take care not to damage the threads.

6. Your steering box probably won't be as clean as this demonstrator unit at Los Angeles' National Technical Schools, but here's the recirculating-ball mechanism.

7. The secret of the recirculating-ball steering is in the ball bearings which take the pressure of the mating gears. Remove cover and ball-return guides from nut.

8. You'll have to run the nut up and down the wormshaft to get the ball bearings to come out, but never run the nut to extreme end of wormshaft with balls in place.

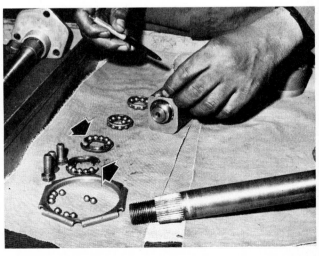

9. With balls out, wormshaft can be removed. After an inspection of nut, wormshaft and balls for any wear or pitting, you can lube and reassemble nut and wormshaft.

10. Eight balls should be greased and kept in the return guides (arrows). The remaining balls should be put in two equal groups and inserted into the wormshaft nut.

11. When an equal loop of balls has been made in each passage through the nut, the ball-return guides and other four balls can be carefully reinstalled.

12. When all the ball bearings are in place, the ball-return guides can be secured with retainer. Check at this point for free operation of wormshaft inside nut.

13. Coat a new thrust bearing (for the wormshaft) with grease, working it in as you would with a wheel bearing. All other parts should be coated with steering lube.

14. After determining that housing is clean and in good shape with no cracks, install the thrust bearing in cup in the lower portion of the steering box.

15. Being careful to keep the ball-nut centered on the wormshaft, slip the assembly carefully into the box, with the end of the wormshaft resting in thrust bearing.

16. Another wormshaft bearing is greased and placed in adjuster. Tape worm splines to protect seal and slide lubed adjuster over wormshaft and thread into housing.

17. *Threads of both housing and adjuster should be lubed, then adjuster should be tightened to 50 ft.-lbs. to seat the wormshaft bearings, then backed off to no load.*

18. *The ball-nut should now be centered in its travel, which means that the central groove should line up with lower cross-shaft cover bolt-hole and cross-shaft hole.*

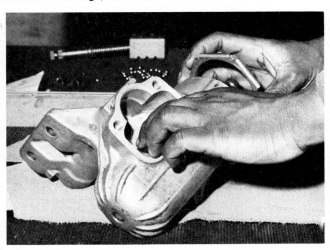

19. *After seating the thrust bearings, tighten the wormshaft adjuster again until the "preload" on the bearings is between 1 and 4½ in.-lbs.; then install locknut.*

20. *The teeth of the sector gear and the wormshaft nut have matching tapers. Cross-shaft adjuster (arrow) puts right amount of mesh-load on the mating gear teeth.*

21. *With locknut loose, cross-shaft can be slid into the centered wormshaft nut and cross-shaft cover can be loosened on shaft and bolted down to the housing.*

22. *Final adjustment of cross-shaft should take 8-11 in.-lbs. to turn wormshaft when wormshaft is ¼-turn off-center. Tighten cross-shaft adjuster nut to 35 ft.-lbs.*

Power Steering

As the modern automobile has grown longer, heavier and more complex, it has also become more and more difficult to maneuver in and out of city traffic. Even high-speed freeway driving can quickly become tiring. To reduce driver fatigue, make parking more manageable, and attract the lady of the house to their particular products, auto manufacturers have increasingly equipped their cars with power steering, either as standard equipment or as an optional (and often advisable) extra.

Power steering includes two basic units: the hydraulic oil pump and the steering unit. Mounted at the front, the hydraulic pump is belt driven by the engine and supplies oil pressure as needed to the steering unit. On some earlier models of the mid-1950 period, and the current Ford-Lincoln-Mercury line, the power steering unit is an "assist" or linkage type and can be replaced without removing the entire steering assembly. On others the unit is coaxial (Chrysler) or otherwise an integral part of the gearbox.

POWER STEERING HYDRAULIC PUMPS

All power steering pumps are constant-displacement type, delivering from 650 to 1300 lbs. pressure, depending upon the type and make of the system and the car. Special power steering fluid or Type "A" automatic transmission fluid is used. This fluid is stored in a reservoir attached to the pump with a filter in the reservoir to prevent foreign matter from entering the system. The pressure relief valve located in the pump prevents the fluid pressure from exceeding the predetermined maximum pressure of the system. Flexible hoses carry the fluid to the control valve of the steering unit. The smallest or high-pressure hose carries the fluid to the control valve of the steering unit. The larger of the two hoses is the return, or low-pressure hose. A flow control valve is combined with the pressure relief valve located inside the pump.

When the fluid circulation reaches about 2 gals. per minute, the flow control valve is forced to open a passage between the inlet and outlet sides of the pump, and all excess oil is sent back to the intake side of the pump and recirculates through the pump. When oil pressure exceeds the fixed pressure limit, the relief valve opens and allows fluid to flow back to the inlet side and recirculate in the pump without raising the pressure in the rest of the system.

There are five types of pumps in use: vane, rotor, roller, sleeve, and slipper. Detailed information for the pump concerned can be found in the shop service manual of the particular car make and model.

Before any major service operations are started, the following items should be checked and corrected.

FLUID LEVEL

Check level at regular intervals. Wipe the cover before opening to prevent dirt getting into the system. If there is no other specific filling instruction indicated, maintain fluid level 1 in. below the top. If fluid is very low, check system for leaks. If only a small amount of fluid is needed, automatic transmission fluid can be used. When using larger amounts or changing fluid it is advisable to use special power steering fluid. Oil should be at operating temperature, wheels in a straight-ahead position, and the engine stopped when you check or add power steering fluid.

BELT TENSION

Belt tension should be maintained to factory specifications with a belt-tension gauge. The specifications vary, so you must check the specs in your manual. A belt that is too loose will result in reduced pump output, while one that is too tight will wear out the bearings in the pump. If you don't have a belt tension gauge, and can't get one, a good rule of thumb is to tighten the belt just to the point where it doesn't slip and squeal when the steering is turned to full lock. Don't ever try this with a worn-out belt, however. Such a belt would probably squeal at full lock no matter how tight it is. Be careful with your pry bar when tightening the belt. It is easy to damage the pump.

Check the belt for evidence of age

2. Ford Linkage Power Steering

1. Eaton Power Steering Pump

3. Integral Power Steering

and wear. Frayed edges, separation of the layers of the fabric (look at the side of the belt), and cracks on the inside of the belt indicate age and brittleness. The application of a good belt dressing will reduce slipping and noise.

POWER STEERING CHECKS

The steering gear, linkage, and front end should be serviced, lubricated, and alignment checked before any major work is attempted on the pump. Check tires for correct air pressure. Steering effort can be checked with a spring scale, with engine idling and front wheels on a smooth floor or driveway. Attach a spring scale to the rim of the steering wheel; as you turn the wheels from one extreme to the other, the pull should not exceed 10 lbs. at any point.

You can check the oil flow and relief valves by turning steering wheel full right or left, with the engine idling. If these valves are working, a slight buzzing noise can be heard. Caution: Do not hold the wheel in this extreme position for more than 2 or 3 secs. If the relief valve is not working, the high pressure might damage the system. If no buzzing noise can be heard, a sticking or malfunctioning valve should be suspected.

POWER STEERING REPAIR

Because the modern power steering unit is a precise piece of engineering, and due to the requirement of a number of special tools, we cannot recommend that the beginning mechanic tackle this job outside of a completely equipped shop with the help of qualified professionals. If any of the faults mentioned above occur and the indicated repair consists of more than linkage replacement, belt tightening, or the use of an additive, take the vehicle to a qualified professional. Do not attempt to do it yourself. On the other hand, if you've got a reasonably well equipped tool kit and some savvy accumulated by working under the hood of your car, there's no reason why you shouldn't be able to disassemble and clean your own pump and steering box, taking care of a leak or two in the process.

We've included a photo story on replacing the O-rings in a Chrysler power steering pump, a job that would be similar on most other make pumps, and one that the average weekend mechanic could tackle. Repairs beyond those on this level are probably best left to a qualified shop that has all the specialized tools and know-how. 🔧

1. Several American Motors cars use an Eaton pump. This is what it looks like with the reservoir, pulley, and brackets removed. It can be purchased in this form for about $65, which is more than a stiff jolt in the wallet.

2. Ford uses linkage-type power steering. The housing indicated by the arrow has several seals inside that are usually the cause of most leaks. The hoses all screw in and can be replaced easily.

3. Most makes (other than Ford) use a power steering unit that is built into the gearbox. The hoses connect directly to the box.

4. Before removing the power steering pump V-belt, detach all connections.

5. You'll need an open-end wrench for this one. When replacing the pump, be sure all fittings are on the snug side.

6. Loosen the pump bracket and slip the V-belt off the pulley. Some mechanics prefer to remove the bracket attached to the pump; others prefer to leave it in place, removing the pump only.

7. Place the pump against a solid object like this vise and break cover seal by tapping with a mallet.

8. With the pump secured in the vise, remove and replace the O-ring seal. If this doesn't stop a pump leak, you'll probably have to buy another unit for best results.

CHRYSLER PUMP O-RING REPLACEMENT

Wheels & Tires

Tires provide a cushion between the wheels and the road to lessen road shock before it reaches a car's suspension. Tires also provide the frictional contact between the wheels and the road necessary to transform the engine's power into motion. Four factors influence the life and service of any tire, regardless of construction:

1. Inflation pressure
2. Tire rotation
3. Tire balance/runout
4. Suspension alignment

If one or more of these factors is neglected, tire wear will be both rapid and uneven, resulting in a premature failure. Proper care of tires and wheels can save you money and possibly your life, not necessarily in that order.

TIRE CARE

The most important as well as the easiest single step in tire care is maintaining proper inflation. Pressures specified by Detroit in owners' manuals, ranging usually from 24 to 28 psi for normal driving, tend to favor comfort and quiet over tire life. A trained, conscientious tire salesman will more likely recommend 30 psi at all four wheels for maximum tire life. A certain amount of air seepage is normal, which is why tire pressures should be checked at least once a month and before any long trip.

These figures are for a "cold" tire. They take into account the normal pressure buildup from the heat generated by the car's motion. A 3-mile drive to the neighborhood service station is enough to raise a cold pressure of 30 psi to a "false" reading of 33 psi. A stop after a long, hot turnpike run can result in normal readings of 36 to 40 psi. Under no circumstances should this seemingly excess pressure be bled off, because pressure readings will slowly return to normal as the tires and the air inside them gradually cool.

Characteristic wear patterns result from incorrect inflation. In the case of underinflation, the center of the tread area bows inward and hardly contacts the road surface, causing the outer tread areas to wear excessively. With overinflation, this pattern is reversed, and the center of the tread wears out first. With proper inflation, there is a certain normal irregularity in the wear between tread ribs, but this occurs early and does not proportionately increase once established. Tread-wear indicators that tell you when a normally worn tire should be replaced are now required in all tires. These indicators, present in all new tires sold in the U.S., are bars cast into the tread at a 90° angle to the direction of the tread. When these "wear bars" appear, they will "cross the T" of the

tread, and it is then time to invest in some new skins. Some states, such as California, have even passed laws *requiring* new tires once the wear bars have become exposed on the old ones.

Belted bias tires develop a characteristic wear pattern in which there is a rapid but even wearing of the second and sixth ribs, counting from the outer shoulder (see chart). This pattern is considered normal wear in relation to the tire's deflection characteristics, and reduced inflation pressures will neither prevent nor compensate for it.

There are recommended rotation patterns for 5- or 4-tire sets. However, tire companies and automakers do not agree as to which, if any, is best. Many even recommend leaving radials alone for their entire life if they are not causing problems. But plain arithmetic shows that if five non-radial tires are rotated every 6000 miles, the car can be driven for a total of 30,000 miles even though each individual tire is in use for only 24,000 miles. It is also likely that an unused spare will tend to deteriorate if it's just sitting in the trunk.

On the other hand, if you have to rebalance all four tires after each rotation, then the cost of this may at least equal the savings obtained from rotation. We'll discuss how to save money on balancing later. Suffice it to say that if it can be accomplished without rebalancing, 5-tire rotation at regular intervals will probably save you money. The problem is that while each tire and wheel may separately be in static and dynamic balance with

its original brake drum (which rotates with them), changing the combinations can upset these happy relationships. But machines now in use across the country balance wheel and tire assemblies off the car, *without* the brake drum, thereby eliminating this problem.

DETECTING TIRE DAMAGE

Tires should be inspected regularly for external evidence of cuts, cracking and separation of the rubber from the carcass. Small tread and sidewall cuts or cracks are of serious concern only when they penetrate far enough to expose the cord material. Assuming the cord is undamaged, exposure is not too much of a problem in a nylon or polyester tire, but a rayon cord will absorb water and may be structurally weakened.

Extra care must be taken on rainy days, because in addition to increased chances of having an accident, chances of cutting your tires also increase. When the tires become wet and soaked, they become more susceptible to surface and cord damage. Dodge those water-filled chuckholes and avoid curbs to extend tire life and save money.

Irreparable damage will occur if the tire is run for any distance in a seriously underinflated or flat condition. This could be just that distance required to get from the fast lane to the emergency repair area of a freeway. Ply and tread separation can also be caused by underinflation, overload, extreme speed or combinations of these conditions. Tread

1. Checking Inflation Pressure

2. Removing Foreign Material

3. Gauging Tread Depth

1. Improper inflation is responsible for more tire troubles than any other single thing, yet it is one of the easiest to check and correct. For most accurate results, use a separate pressure gauge and check tires first thing in the morning, before car is driven more than three miles. For the best ride, use automaker's recommended psi. For best handling and longer life, add 2-6 psi per tire.

2. The next time you've got your car up in the air, check the tires for any foreign material that may be working its way into the surface. Make a chalk mark as a start/finish line, then examine the tire very carefully.

3. Tread-depth indicators are useful for measuring how much rubber is left between the top of the tread and the bottom of the groove. Anything less than 1/16-in. means new tires—by law in many states.

separation usually gives a warning in the form of a loud slapping noise or a lot of vibration. In most cases, depending on the length of time you've owned the tire, the above types of failure will be covered under the tire builder's warranty, which reimburses you for the unused mileage as gauged by remaining tread depth.

TIRE TROUBLESHOOTING

In addition to loss of pressure or chronic over- or underinflation, tire problems can be due to an inherent defect in the tire or improper balancing or suspension alignment, including worn springs and/or shock absorbers. The aforementioned chuckholes and curbs can also cause excessive tire wear by knocking the front wheels out of alignment.

Furthermore, improper caster or camber creates premature wear on one side of each front tire. Caster is the effect formed by the inclination of the top of the kingpin or upper ball joint to the rear. It imparts an action similar to a furniture caster in keeping the wheels headed in a straight line. You'll see this condition grossly exaggerated in a dragster or Bonneville-type straightaway record car. In the average passenger car this angle is 1° to 3° off a vertical line. On earlier cars with solid axles it is as much as 7°.

Camber, which is referred to as either

negative or positive, is the inclination of the wheels inward or outward at the top; in other words, leaning into or away from the car. Earlier cars, meant for use on high-crowned roads, had quite a bit of positive camber (leaning out) to bring the tires perpendicular to the road surface. More recent cars have little or none, and some of the later high-performance cars have from 1° to 2° of negative camber to aid cornering by offsetting the tendency of a tire to roll under in a turning situation.

Toe-in and toe-out define another possible misalignment plane of the front wheels. These terms describe the relationship of the front wheels to each other when the steering wheel is in a straight-ahead position. In the average car there is a slight toe-in; in other words, the front edges of the front wheels are closer together than the rear edges by roughly ⅛-in. It isn't much, but the effect is to keep all the steering linkage in tension. This prevents any slop in the steering in the straight-ahead driving position, where no cornering forces are present to keep things taut. Toe-out is the opposite effect. Other than in a faulty system in the straight-ahead position, toe-out is found only in certain front-wheel-drive cars. Naturally (due to Ackermann effect) there is toe-out when the wheels are turning a corner.

Another form of accelerated tire wear results from driver habits. Rapid front tire wear can be caused by habitual fast cornering. The correction for this, of course, is entirely up to you. If you mend your ways, a tire worn in this manner can be restored to a normal wear pattern simply by moving it to one of the rear wheels.

Jack-rabbit starts or "laying rubber" also wear out the tires quickly, as can be imagined, but also unevenly, for reasons that are not quite so apparent. Maximum acceleration actually bends the rear axle housings temporarily, causing the tires to wear faster on the inner edges—unless, of course, the rear axle is strengthened for racing. An identical wear pattern can also be observed on a car that is habitually operated with a maximum passenger and/or luggage or cargo load.

Heavy braking can also accelerate tire wear. Panic-stricken, lock-up slides

aren't required, just unnecessary brake-pedal jabbing. Sliding the tires with the brakes locked up, though, can cause both short- and long-term problems. The short-term problem is that you're leaving a portion of your tire's life scrubbed off onto the pavement. The long-term problem is the flat spots left on the tread. These cause wheel hop, which also scrubs off tread life.

WHEEL BALANCING

Tire balance and runout are third in importance for extended tire life. Balance can become more and more critical as time goes by. Tires set up a wear pattern almost from the first mile, and this wear pattern, unless corrected, can accelerate wear in certain areas (see charts). If allowed to continue, out-of-balance wear patterns can cut tire life by as much as 50-60%.

Many people are confused about tire balancing. They've heard all their lives that you must balance your tires for longer life. But why? Because tires and the wheels on which they're mounted are manufactured by people, and therefore they are subject not only to the vagaries of nature but also to human failings. During tire manufacture, "hot spots" in the vulcanizing can occur, which in turn cause heavy spots to form at various locations around the circumference of the tire. The various materials used for the tire compound may even form heavy areas because of their basic chemical makeup. These heavy spots can also occur in the wheels. The tire/wheel assembly must be balanced to counteract these uncontrolled weight problems.

Keeping tires in balance in Southern California, or other areas equally blessed with abundant annual sunlight and moderate weather, is very easy. Simply avoid contact with curbs and don't skid the tires by heavy braking or hard cornering. Either of these actions can cause loss of balancing weights or flat spots on the tires' treads.

In other parts of the country, where snow, mud, salt and ice can be a daily occurrence, balancing becomes much more difficult. Slush (compounded of mud, snow and salt) can become packed into rims, both inside and out, and throw

Wheels & Tires

a tire completely out of balance. Heat from high-speed driving may melt and throw off the ice and snow, but the mud and salt can remain indefinitely. Carry a stick in the trunk and clean off the rims once or twice a day during bad weather; it could save dollars in the long run.

Another device, known as Road Huggers (available from Pacer Products, 680 E. Taylor Ave., P.O. Box 9081, Sunnyvale, CA 94088), can automatically, through weight transference, counteract a tire that's out of balance by up to four ounces. Road Huggers are held in place between the rim and brake drum by the tire rim itself, and they can be used on many types of cars with many types of tires.

There are two different types of tire balancing. The simple is called static and the more complex is dynamic. The term "dynamic" encompasses two or three methods of balancing.

Static balancing is a procedure for correcting a tire, wheel or brake drum—or a combination of these—that is "heavy" at a single point. Although this heaviness may amount to only an ounce or so, the effect is greatly magnified by centrifugal force when the wheel assembly is turning at speed. The symptom is a pronounced vibration in the vertical plane at any one or all of the wheels. You can feel it and also see it, because the vibration is transmitted to the body structure nearby, such as the fender. Service stations and garages have machines (and, hopefully, personnel competent to operate them) that tell how heavy a corrective weight should be used and where it should be placed.

Static balancing could probably best be described as a process by which a tire is put in balance so that there is no heavy spot anywhere that will force the tire to rotate when it is hanging free. For example, if we mount a tire and wheel with a heavy spot on a precision spindle so that even the slightest amount of weight will rotate the tire until the weight is at the bottom, then we are checking static balance. The time-honored way of adjusting static balance is with the old-fashioned bubble balancer that enables the mechanic to get the tire in balance without spinning it.

Suppose we had a tire that was 12 ft. wide. We could put a 100-lb. weight on one side of the tire and another 100-lb. weight on the other side of the tire's circumference. As long as the 100-lb. weights were diametrically opposite each other, the tire would be in perfect static balance and it would not have a heavy spot. But when you rotated this monster tire, it would leap clear off the ground, because when one 100-lb. weight was at the top of the tire, the other would be at the bottom. One side of the tire would be trying to leap off the ground while the other side was trying to push itself into the pavement. You can see that the tire, although in static balance, would be so far out of *dynamic* balance as to be practically useless.

Of course, our tires are not 12 ft. wide, but they are 4 or 6 or 8 ins. wide. Within that size it is possible to have a heavy

spot on one side of a tire that, by adding a counterbalancing weight, could be put in perfect balance statically, but not, however, dynamically.

We feel that dynamic balancing should only be done on the type of machine that balances the wheel *off* the car while spinning it on a special arbor. Ordinarily this arbor is made to fit where the wheel bearings go into the drum, so it balances the drum along with the wheel and tire. This is a convenient way of balancing, but it is not necessary to balance the drum; its diameter is too small to have much effect. The wheel and tire are the real culprits.

There are also machines that balance the tire *on* the car while it is spinning under power from an electric motor. Many people claim that such balancing, whether it is done by the operator's feeling for an unbalanced vibration or whether the imbalance is picked up by a stroboscopic light, is dynamic balancing. We feel that this is not the most efficient manner of balancing tires, although it's usually the cheapest because it takes less time than removing the wheels.

If the wheels do not vibrate when spun but the car bounces all over the road when being driven, then there is nothing wrong with the wheel balance, but you probably have a flat spot on a tire or an out-of-round wheel.

Checking tire and wheel radial and lateral runout is another method of determining if a chronic state of imbalance is caused by wheel damage, an improperly mounted tire or a tire with manufacturing defects. To check radial runout of the tire, a dial indicator graduated to a thousandth of an inch is mounted on a convenient fixed surface and zeroed on the center rib of the tire. The assembly is then rotated slowly. The combined runout of the wheel and tire should not exceed .050-in. Lateral runout of the as-

sembly is checked by zeroing the dial indicator on the inside buff (curb protection) rib. It should not exceed .125-in.

To find out whether it is the tire or wheel causing the problem, check the radial runout of the wheel. This should not exceed .035-in. If the wheel is true, the tire is at fault. But before condemning the tire, deflate and rotate the tire a quarter- or half-circumference and check for runout again. This will correct a possible misalignment incurred in mounting.

If both wheel and tire show runout, check to see if all of the lug bolts are properly seated. An improper torquing sequence can cause binding and poor seating of one or more lugs. A tire with excessive radial runout due to a defect in construction should be replaced. Alternatively, the tread may be ground down on a special machine until it is even. This procedure is not used so much for correction (an out-of-round tire is covered by warranty) as it is to obtain a maximum degree of trueness for high-performance purposes. Excessive lateral runout is almost invariably caused by damage to the wheel itself.

A Tire Problem Detector is now being used by some new-car dealers. The de-

1. Tire rotation can extend life. Bias-ply tires can be rotated as in either of the two left-hand plans. Radials must always be kept on the same side of the car, so follow either right-hand plan.

2. Breaking down a tire's bead at home is easy with a bumper jack. Be very careful, however, when refilling. Bring pressure up a few pounds at a time to avoid explosions.

3. These two photos show nearly every product made in the U.S. for your car's wheel and tire care. They're good for everything from increasing longevity to upgrading appearance.

1. Wear and Rotation Patterns

tector works as follows: The car's normal weight pushes the tire against a roller while it is rotated. At the same time a pen draws a "picture" of the tire's circumference on a piece of paper. If there are too many lumps or the tire is out of round, it will show up in the drawing. Of course, this does nothing to fix the tire, but it allows the dealer to point an accusing finger at the tire manufacturer, who then has to give you another tire (you hope).

ROLLER WHEEL BEARINGS

Since the advent of tapered roller bearings for front wheels, car makers now recommend that the bearings and spindle be lubricated only when the brake linings are changed or when the wheel and drum are removed for any reason.

The important points to remember in lubrication and assembly are that the inner bearing races are designed to creep slightly around the spindle. Therefore the latter should be smooth and lightly coated with lubricant to ensure a slip fit. The second point is that the tapered bearings cannot function satisfactorily if any pressure is exerted upon them by the lock

2. Breaking Tire Bead

nut, yet the lock nut must prevent excessive end-play.

Installation with a torque wrench is desirable, but if you don't have access to the tool or to the torque figures specified by each car maker, the following procedure may be safely followed: Tighten the lock nut with an 8- or 10-in. wrench, using enough arm length leverage to ensure that all parts are properly seated while the wheel is spinning. Back off the lock nut until it is finger-loose, then tighten it finger-tight. If the hole in the spindle lines up with a slot in the nut, install the cotter pin. If not, back off to the next slot and install the pin. Finally, clinch the cotter pin and cut off the excess length to ensure that the ends do not interfere with the dust cap or static collector. In some designs a tab-type lock washer is substituted, but a cotter pin is the most common.

For lubrication, use nothing but an extreme pressure (EP), lithium-based grease compound made especially for this purpose. Special packing tools are available for greasing the bearings, but a suitable substitute is to put a quantity of grease in the palm of one hand and work it into the bearing with a rotating motion of the other hand. Prior to lubrication, all parts should be cleaned in kerosene.

If you have access to an air gun, then air pressure may be used to help clean out the old grease, but do not spin the bearing. Never under any circumstances spin a bearing with air pressure or anything else. Not only is that hard on the bearings, it's dangerous, because pieces could fly off the bearing and injure you. On top of that, spinning is completely unnecessary for proper cleaning.

New lubricant should not be added to the old, and whenever these parts are lubricated, a new oil seal should be installed. This seal can be seated by hammering gently on a block of wood placed on the seal.

On cars equipped with drum brakes, it may be necessary to loosen the brake adjustment before the wheel and drum can be removed as a unit. On cars with disc front brakes, the caliper must be removed. The only caution to observe is not to let the caliper assembly dangle on

its hoses. Hang it on the nearest convenient piece of steering linkage. On front-wheel-drive cars such as the Toronado and Eldorado, the rear wheel bearings may be removed, lubricated, and replaced in a manner quite similar to that described above.

BALL WHEEL BEARINGS

Procedures for removal and greasing of ball front wheel bearings are the same as for tapered rollers. However, the installation of the bearings is slightly different. Ball bearings must be installed with a slight preload so that the balls and races are brought into proper contact. All kinds of directions have been devised for adjusting ball front wheel bearings, most of them difficult to understand. Most castellated nuts have only six positions for the cotter key, so even after you get the nut exactly where you want it, you may have to turn it tighter or looser in order to insert the key.

The main thing to remember about ball front wheel bearings is that they must never be adjusted loose. This doesn't mean putting a 3-ft. breaker bar on the nut to tighten it. It does mean that you should have zero play, with a slight amount of preload.

Ball front wheel bearings were a great source of trouble on the cars that used them. Today all cars use tapered rollers, which have eliminated the front wheel bearing problems. No tapered roller will interchange with the old ball bearings, but there is a trick that can be used to prolong the latter's life.

The secret is to use a grease in the wheel bearings that is almost runny. Some chassis lubes are soft and will work fine. If the grease is one of the newer "black" greases with moly in it, so much the better. Never use the old long-fiber wheel bearing greases that were so stiff. The grease has to be loose enough so that it will run back onto the balls after it is thrown off by the rotation of the wheel. Hard greases will fly off the first time the car gets up to speed, and then the bearing will run dry until it is packed again. Invariably, damage will occur to the bearing and possibly to the hub as well.

3. Care Products

Wheels & Tires

SHOCKING NEWS

Suspension components can critically affect safe tire mileage, and they can do it insidiously. In many cases, the driver never becomes aware of the slow deterioration. Suspension components that need periodic repair or replacement are: shock absorbers, ball joints, steering knuckles and A-arms. Except for A-arms (when they go, you know it), these components wear so slowly that the owner is seldom aware of the problem before his car leaves the road, completely out of control. For this reason, it is essential to have front end alignment checked annually. Before your vacation each year is an excellent time. An alignment check will indicate whether everything is all right or if adjustment or replacement of ball joints and/or steering knuckles is in order.

Ride quality tells you if the shock absorbers are no longer absorbing shocks. If your car feels like a boat at sea, wallows over dips and leans excessively on curves, you need shock absorbers. Shocks, as they're more commonly called, are designed to limit spring action. They are made from many patterns and designed for many different applications (heavy-duty trucks, quick-handling sports cars, comfortable sedans, etc.), but the majority have the same basic design: hydraulic.

Hydraulic shocks use a fluid and valves to control spring dampening (different-sized valves for different applications). They force the fluid back and forth, through the valves, to reservoirs on each side of the valves. Forcing the fluid to travel through a restricting valve slows the initial spring hop and then controls spring rebound in the same manner. Just the direction of fluid flow is reversed.

Shock absorption ability diminishes or "goes away" through valve wear, shaft wear and seal hardening. When this occurs, the shock can no longer control its spring, permitting the tire to hop excessively while traveling down the road. A series of events then accelerates tire wear. First the tire hops upward, so that it's no longer contacting the road surface. This makes the tire slow its spinning. Then it contacts the road surface again, which forces the tire to speed up again and scrubs rubber from the tread at the same time. Without an effective shock absorber, this oscillating action is repeated over and over during each mile the car is driven.

The same thing happens on a plane's landing gear. The tires scrub off tread as they speed up to match their rotation to the plane's ground speed upon landing.

Without going into a long discourse on how and why shocks work, we merely wish to point out that when you push your weight down on a fender (front or rear, it doesn't matter) and release it, the car should go up and down only once. If it continues to bounce up and down, replace all four shocks. Not only will your driving be safer, your tires will last longer as well.

Tire care that can be done at home in the driveway is very limited, beyond what we've already discussed. Naturally, treads should be kept clean of damaging objects—rocks, bits of wood, etc. A small screwdriver is a fine tool for this purpose. Using keys could result in damaged keys, and using a pocket-knife could result in a damaged tire or hand if the knife slips. Watch for wear bars appearing in the tread pattern. These are the tread wear indicators molded across the tread direction that appear when wear has exceeded the safe limits of the tire, as mentioned earlier.

If you're driving fewer miles these days, your tires may lose their sidewall resiliency and deteriorate beyond safety limits due to weather checking while they still have excellent tread depth. A splendid product for forestalling this weathering action is Armor All. Through chemical action, Armor All makes surfaces antistatic, able to repel dust and dirt. It also protects tires (and other surfaces as well) against the harmful effects of road salt, sunshine and smog.

TUBELESS TIRE REPAIRS

The advent of the tubeless tire, standard on all U.S. passenger cars since 1955, combined with the so-called "safety rim," has made it difficult for do-it-yourselfers, because expensive special equipment is required to work on tires. This is not just for convenience but to avoid damage to the tire when it is mounted or dismounted. A tubeless tire cannot be changed with the old-fashioned rubber mallet and hand iron without risking permanent damage. A basic tool needed is a tire mounting band. You should really also have an even more expensive item called a bead breaker, to break the bead loose from the rim without damaging either in the process.

When using a tire machine, such as found in a service station, the narrow bead ledge of the rim should be up at all times. This is not necessarily the edge nearest the valve hole. Both the rim edges and tire beads should be lubricated liberally with a thick solution of water and vegetable oil soap (Palmolive or equivalent). Whether mounting or dismounting a tire, the beads should be "inched" into position rather than forced at a single spot.

With tubeless tires, it is good insurance to use a new valve whenever a tire is removed from its rim. Be sure the replacement matches the old one exactly, because valves vary in length and stem diameter. Replacement valves are of the snap-in type and have been prelubricated with silicon for an easy, permanent fit. You'll find an identifying "TR" number molded into the valve base which is common to all brands and is cross-indexed in the catalogs of the individual manufacturers for easy reference.

One caution: Temporary inflation pressures up to 40 psi—but no more—may be used to seat the beads on the rim. Many people have been killed or seriously injured during this step in tire repairs. If the bead is not properly seated, pressures greater than 40 psi may cause it to break with explosive force. As a further safety measure, specialized tire shops use a clamp-on extension chuck on the air line to permit the operator to stand clear of the tire while inflating it.

Repairing small leaks in tubeless tires can be accomplished by any of four basic methods—and two of them do not require removing the tire from the rim or car. The first is to enlarge the puncture slightly if necessary, coat the hole with a suitable rubber cement and insert a rubber repair plug of the proper size. A repair of this nature should be looked upon as temporary.

The second method also calls for a plug that can be applied with the tire on the car, but it is more permanent, because the plug chemically vulcanizes itself to the tire. However, this method requires a kit of special tools as well as compressed air in order to actuate the insertion gun.

Fully permanent repairs involve vulcanization with special dielectric patches applied inside the tire and special tools to supply current and pressure to the patch. This expense is practical only for those engaged in the tire repair business, and of course the tire must be removed from the wheel to do the work.

An adaptation of the chemical vulcanizing procedure is also supposed to be permanent. After a certain amount of preparation, a special patch (Dill Sure-Cure or equivalent) is applied—much like a Band-Aid—to the inside of either a tube-type or tubeless tire. The area around the cut or puncture must be buffed thoroughly with #3 sandpaper, after first treating the area with a buffing solution (Dill B-4 or equivalent). The area is then treated with a self-curing vulcanizing fluid (Dill G-2 or equivalent) and the patch applied. The final step is to "stitch" around the edge of the patch

1. Checking for Loose Bearings

2. Worn Front Wheel Bearings

1. Checking for wheel bearing slop can be done at home in this manner. If tire is elevated it's easier. If tire wobbles slightly in relation to brake, then the bearing is loose and should be tightened.

2. These Ford bearings were just a few miles from destruction when they were removed for a much-needed grease pack. New grease put them right back on the road for many more miles.

3. To repack wheel bearings at home without a professional tool is easy. Just fill your palm with grease (we said easy—not clean) and dig the large end of the tapered bearing into the grease, using the skin of your palm to force fresh grease into all the crevices. Thoroughly clean the bearing in kerosene before repacking it.

4. Alignment, anyone? Improper wheel alignment can cost you money in new tires. Keep away from curbs and chuckholes and your alignment job should last indefinitely.

3. Packing Bearings Yourself

4. Wheel Alignment

with an inexpensive special tool (Dill Part No. 13 or equivalent). This tool looks and functions much like a cookie cutter, except that it doesn't cut; it indents the patch to the surface for better adhesion. The above procedure, too, requires removal of the tire from the rim.

The careless (and expensive to the consumer) practice of "repairing" a tubeless tire by merely installing an inner tube is to be avoided except in an emergency. Tubeless tires are of a different cross-section design than tires designed for tubes, and if a tube is installed in them they will very likely chafe and fail. As we mentioned, tubeless tires have been standard equipment on all U.S. cars and most imports since 1955, and the wheels provided by the car maker are of necessity airtight.

The only exceptions are wire wheels, which had a spurt of popularity as a factory option in the mid-'50's (and are still offered on many of the sportier imports), and certain very early aftermarket dress-up wheels of the so-called "mag" variety. Tubeless tires may lose air if used on some early-model cars, because the rims were not designed to totally resist bead separation during severe cornering. Rare instances of a leak in a modern rim may be repaired by sealants available at specialized tire shops. It is not practical, however, to attempt to seal the large number of spoke sockets in a wire wheel.

INNER TUBE REPAIRS

A permanent repair to an inner tube is best accomplished by vulcanization with dielectric equipment similar to that described above. Even a replacement valve may be installed in this manner. It also should be remembered that if the damage involves the tire as well as the tube, the tire too should be patched. When installing a tube, both it and the tire should be lubricated with a soap solution. A tube-type tire should be inflated slowly while you hold the valve firmly against its hole in the rim. As a final step, deflate completely and reinflate to ensure proper positioning of the tube within the tire.

RADIALS

Radial tires have been standard equipment on most new cars for several years now, and aftermarket equipment for a whole lot longer. They've been touted as having special advantages in the areas of ride, handling, fuel economy and tread life, and most of what you've heard is true. While they're more expensive in first cost than conventional bias-ply tires, or even bias-belted types, they return extra benefits to their owners. But they also have some unique problems.

For example, radial tires cannot be mated to bias-ply tires on the same axle. The difference in handling between the two types makes a combination like this downright dangerous. They must be installed in pairs and mounted on the rear axle first. Again, the difference in handling makes this important. The best thing to do if you're going to go the radial route is to put them on all four wheels at the same time.

Rotation of radials is also different. Radial tires take a "set" in use. A tire fitted to one side of the car cannot be rotated to the other side; it must only be changed from front to rear on the *same side*. If the spare is to be included in the rotation schedule, it must be swapped only with a tire on one side.

The most convenient time of the year to rotate tires, regardless of their type of construction, is during the semiannual snow tire switchover. Radial tire owners should mark on the wheel where it came from: LF, RF, etc. Use a felt-tip pen with indelible ink and write in large letters on the rim's inside surface.

Radials are more susceptible to the effects of out-of-balance wheels and minor manufacturing defects than other types of tires. Bubble-type static balancers just don't work on radials. The "spin-'em-on-the-car" type is only slightly better. For the best results, they should be balanced off the car on a high-speed dynamic balancer that will point up heavy and light spots on both the inside and outside of the rim.

Balance isn't the only problem, although an out-of-balance radial can be extremely annoying. The soft sidewalls of the radials have a much springier effect than the relatively stiff ones on bias tires. As with any other type of spring, the sidewalls have a resonant frequency, which at some speeds harmonizes with and reinforces the resonance of the suspension and chassis, creating a roughness at speed. Trueing up the tires can

reduce or eliminate this condition. It can even happen on cars that were designed from the ground up with "radial-tuned suspension," since it is a tire defect.

Another problem unique to radials, particularly fat ones of low-profile cross-section, is "waddle." This is a side-to-side movement that's apparent at low speeds—below about 20 mph—coupled with a roughness at speeds over 40 mph. It's caused by side-to-side runout in the tire. A bias ply, with its stiff sidewalls, will actually slip its tread a bit on the ground and not pass on the movement. The radial, with its greater contact patch and springy sidewalls, stays put and jiggles the whole car instead. If one of the rear tires has the problem, it feels as if someone is putting his hands on the rear fender and shaking the car. If the problem is in a front tire, you'll be able to see the front-end sheetmetal moving from side to side. In either case, the next drive you take should be to the dealer who sold you the tires or the car, since the only way to cure the problem is to remount or replace the tire, after measuring to determine which one is the culprit. Radial runout should be no more than .035-in. on any wheel, and lateral runout should be no more than .030-in. on a full-size car, .040-in. on an intermediate and .050-in. on small cars. Anything more will shake you up.

MOUNTING WHEELS

When changing a wheel, loosen the lug nuts a little before jacking. The nuts normally rotate to the left to loosen, except on older Chrysler Corp. products, on which the nuts attaching the left wheels require right-hand rotation to loosen. When installing a wheel, first tighten the uppermost nut firmly but not securely and then tighten the one opposite on the bottom. Continue to tighten opposing pairs just enough so that the nuts are firmly seated. When all have been tightened, rotate the wheel and check for an out-of-round condition, which means the nuts haven't seated properly. Then lower the car from the jack and final-tighten the nuts in the same sequence as above. Remember that after 100 or so miles of driving, the nuts should be rechecked for tightness. Car makers specify torque figures (usually 70 ft.-lbs.) for the lug nuts, but the lug wrench provided with the car is of a size that makes it impossible for a person of normal strength to overtighten wheel lug nuts.

Body & Paint

Body and paint is a fascinating subject, with much more science to it than you would think from watching a body man swing his big hammer. Bodywork is fascinating because there aren't any two body men who would repair a car in the same way. It may be termed scientific because the body man who is fast can do the job in an incredibly short time, whereas another body man may take much longer and as a result be making a lot less money.

More than any other types of automotive repair, bodywork and painting should be carefully observed before they are attempted. Most body shops will welcome the amateur who wants to sit quietly by and watch how work is accomplished, and the body men will often pass along pointers as they proceed. The important thing to consider when watching a body man work is how he approaches each and every bent panel.

How a vehicle has been struck—that is, the point of impact—will determine how the repair should be made. This cannot be overemphasized. A really good body repair specialist may sit looking at a wrecked car for an hour before ever touching a panel. He is trying to determine exactly where the initial contact was (usually simple), the angle of the blow, severity, secondary impact points, etc. Once he has figured out exactly where the initial blow was, he may be able to save many hours of needless work.

If a fender has been struck head-on near the headlight, there will be damage far removed from that impact point. Chances are the fender will buckle at one or two places above the wheel opening, a slight buckle may appear in the large area behind the wheel opening, and the panel may have been shoved back against the door. This is where the unskilled workman can get into trouble very quickly.

If some kind of panel-pulling equipment is available, it will be possible to pull much of the damage from the fender without striking a hammer blow. However, if the point of initial contact is hammered out *first,* the remainder of the damage will be exceptionally difficult to remove.

Again referring to the bent fender, if something can be hooked to the headlamp opening area and a pulling pressure exerted, the initial impact force is being reversed. The immediate crumpled area around the front of the fender will distort during this phase, but the force will tend to pull most of the buckles from the rest of the fender. This is imperative, and a part of almost every repair job.

Large body and fender shops will usually have a big pulling rig available. This is nothing more than a large I-beam that runs beneath the car and chains to the undamaged chassis in several points. The pulling apparatus is attached to the front and thus pulls against itself (the body attachments). Finding this kind of equipment for backyard repair is unlikely, so a push may be substituted for a pull. Body shops also have specially designed hydraulic jacks, usually referred to by the trade name of Porto-Power. With the bent fender, such a slim jack may be placed toward the rear of the fender on a strong frame point and the fender pushed back into rough shape. The jack is easier to use, but care must be taken to push the fender back in the same *direction of impact.* If the fender were struck at a front angle, pushing straight forward may do more damage than good. Work a little bit at a time with hydraulic jacks and you'll always come out OK. Of course, an ordinary bumper jack may be utilized where hydraulic jacks are unavailable. Which brings up the question of the tools that may be needed.

TOOLS

Obviously the amateur body man does not need a $1000 tool chest to fix up a dented fender, but there are several tools that are prerequisite. At the same time, many of the specialized body tools will find constant use in all aspects of automotive repair, and should therefore be considered as desirable. Following is a list of tools common to bodywork. An asterisk denotes those tools absolutely essential to the simplest repair job.

Wedge dolly
Combination spoon/dolly
Toe dolly
Anvil dolly (or "railroad" dolly)
*Tear drop dolly
*Scratch awl or ice pick
*File holder (adjustable type)
*Cheese grater (for epoxy fillers)
*Single-blade spoon
Double-blade spoon
Cross-mill shrinking hammer
Double-end flat face hammer
*Pick hammer
*2-lb. sledge hammer
Vise grips (pliers)
Large water pump pliers
*Pry bar
*Hacksaw
*Tin snips
Hydraulic jack
*Electric drill

1. Spray Paint Hood Mask

2. Special Serrated Bolts

3. Ford Shock-Absorbing Bumper

4. Straightening a Deck Lid

1. Newest wrinkle in painting—a hood mask with filter that inflates with air from the air pressure line and dispels toxic fumes from use of new enamel hardener additives.

2. Special bolts attach the Pontiac telescoping box sections to the frame. The bolts "crush" part of the frame and box into each other and have to be torqued to 80-100 ft.-lbs.!

3. Front bumpers on all 1973 cars use an impact-absorbing device to withstand up to 5-mph impact without damage. In the Ford bumper attachment device, an I-beam (1) rides inside a channel (2) and the two are bonded together with a special rubber that returns the I-beam to its original position after impact.

4. Picks in varying lengths, shapes and points are often used in places such as this deck lid where you can't reach the damaged area with a hammer to raise low spots.

5. Major collision repair, such as frame straightening, is best left to a professional with the proper equipment. Here a frame is being heated and pulled into shape on an alignment rack with the use of big chains and "come-along" pullers.

In addition to these tools, you may rent or borrow a welding outfit, disc sander, and paint spraying equipment. Such normally expensive equipment as this is a superb investment, but it is always possible to purchase equipment second-hand and save at least 50%. A good place to start looking for used hand and power equipment is the local body shop.

While the welding outfit is nice to have, you can repair the panel until welding is necessary, and farm the job out, then continue the repair. A disc sander is primarily a time saver, and the apprentice body man invariably finds he will learn the trade better if he concentrates on use of jack, hammer and dolly at first, doing all the finish work with a file. Lots of elbow grease is required with this type finishing, but an excellent job is easier to accomplish.

WELDING

Simple welding is an absolute requirement for any accomplished body repair

5. Frame Straightening

man, although many repairs require little more than simple brazing. Because it is such an integral part of any body job, and actually attendant to most home vehicle repairs, the amateur should spend time becoming proficient with a torch. The best place for the young repairman to learn is high school or college auto shop, but an excellent alternative is the local garage.

Although they may seem rudimentary, there are certain precautions to observe when working with a gas welding outfit. First, always have a small fire extinguisher handy. There are many parts of a car that like to burn, and sparks from panel cutting or welding can get into the strangest places. Small extinguishers are available at low cost, but if nothing better is at hand, keep a water hose nearby. And never forget that a spark can smolder for hours in insulation before breaking out in flames.

Care and use of a welding outfit is explained in booklets available through parts and welding supply stores. They're mighty handy reading. They'll advise always mounting the welding bottles to a cart or chaining them to a work bench. A bottle can tip over and break off the regulator. When that happens either the bottle wants to go into orbit, or acetylene may catch fire. Either way, things get too exciting. Keep the hose connections tight, and turn off the acetylene and oxygen at the bottles after use.

One of the most common mistakes the amateur body man makes when welding is using the wrong torch tip. Because the sheetmetal is usually between 16 and 20 gauge, which means it is thin, a small tip is best (tip size designations vary with manufacturer). A large tip may work, but the heat generated will be transferred to the surrounding metal, causing warpage.

Different pressures are required for welding and cutting different thicknesses of metal. For sheetmetal welding, set the regulators at about 5 psi for acetylene and 10 psi for oxygen. For cutting the same thin sheetmetal, raise oxygen pressure to near 15 psi, and keep the acetylene at or lower than 5 psi. For ordinary work these same pressures will hold, but may have to be raised slightly when cutting frame members or very heavy steel. In no case should the acetylene pressure be above 15 lbs. since acetylene is dissolved in acetone. Too much pressure will cause the acetone to collect in the hoses and create a very dangerous situ-

ation. Normal hoses used for welding should never get more than 30 lbs. of oxygen pressure, and this high setting is used for cutting only.

After the regulator pressures have been set, which determines just how intense or harsh the flame will be, the torch oxygen valve should be opened approximately ⅛-turn and the acetylene valve approximately ½-turn. After the torch is lit, the acetylene valve should be opened until the flame begins to leave the end of the torch tip ("blows" away from the tip). Back the acetylene valve down slightly until the flame just touches the torch tip again. When first lit, the flame is a carbonizing type.

Gradually opening the oxygen valve will make the acetylene "feather" disappear and will produce a neutral flame. For body and fender repair, as well as most general welding, this neutral flame is desirable. To get the neutral flame, the oxygen valve is turned until the feather has been eliminated, and there is just a single small blue flame in the cone. Opening the oxygen valve further will make the flame hotter (known as an oxidizing type).

The intensity or harshness of a flame increases as the gas pressures increase. A flame which is too harsh may agitate the weld puddle violently, making good welding very difficult. A flame that is too soft may not have enough "push" to set the puddle for a good job. After becoming proficient with a welding torch, the body man learns many variations in the use of a single tip.

When welding body sheetmetal, the amateur will do best to tack-weld the separation in several places, making sure each surface is level at the separation. If one surface is lower, the final smoothing process is far more difficult. Keep in mind that metal will tend to "grow" as it is heated. Therefore, if a split in the fender is to be butt-welded, there should be a slight gap between the pieces. If the pieces touch, the welding heat will tend to create a small ridge down the weld, a ridge that must be heated and shrunk out.

When welding sheetmetal it is best to weld forward, ahead of the tip, rather than behind the tip. When welding backward, or moving along with the tip pointing back toward the already welded seam, the heat is increased in the panel, encouraging excessive warpage. When tilting the torch tip at a 45° angle and

Body & Paint

pointing it ahead of the weld, it tends to preheat the metal and make a smooth bead every time. The welding rod is held at 90° to the flame, or 45° from the seam in the leading direction, and the flame is played in a small arc (usually about ¼-in. diameter) as the seam proceeds. A good weld will have consistent ripples throughout.

To weld a break or tear near the edge of a panel (around the flange, etc., which is a common occurrence), first rough out the panel to its approximate shape with a hammer and dolly. If there is considerable stress at that particular point, a jack may be necessary to get reasonable alignment. Clamp the edge of the split panel with flange pliers or vise-grips and tack-weld the break every inch or so. This will keep the edges from creeping during the final welding stage. Start the final weld bead at the apex of the break, working steadily toward the edge.

If a small section, or panel, is to be welded into an existing panel, such as the front section of a straight fender to replace the crumpled part of a fender, the entire cut must be tack-welded as mentioned.

Hammer welding is not common to ordinary bodywork, being more attuned to customizing, but it can save time and effort of leading or epoxy filling. As the weld progresses, working with about ½-in. at a time, the weld is hammered flat with a hammer and dolly while still red. This flattens the entire welded seam and makes working with a pick hammer and file easy. Remember to wear a long glove on the dolly hand, and immerse the dolly in water regularly to remove heat buildup. Since this type of weld requires intermittent use of the torch, it is wise to build some kind of torch holder. In this way the torch will not have to be relit every 3 or 4 mins.

Brazing is simpler to master than welding, and some of the new low-temperature brazing rods are ideal for bodywork. However, the beginner will never know if he is doing a good brazing job or not unless he learns fusion welding also. There are many places where brazing is better than welding, particularly because of the low temperatures involved. At the same time, brass may be filed and ground smooth much as lead, so it is ideal as filler for small holes, etc.

Use of the cutting tip is abused by many amateur welders, simply because they have not considered the problems involved. In bodywork, the majority of cutting will be done on large sheetmetal panels. Because the metal is so thin, a small cutting tip should be selected, and seldom can a gas cut be made without some minor metal warpage immediately adjacent to the cut. For this reason, when a panel is being replaced, always make the initial gas cut 2 ins. from the final cut, then sever the remaining piece with snips or a power shear. Power shears are available that work off ordinary drill motors. As soon as the metal is ready to cut, tilt the cutting tip in the direction of the cut and move briskly. This procedure will cut sheetmetal with a

1. Aligning a Trunk Lid

2. Using Body Filler

3. Transfer Film

4. Hammers and Dollies

5. Pop Riveting

1. Sometimes a small job of panel alignment on hood, doors or trunk lid can be handled simply, without special tools or training.

2. There are two basic ways to fix minor collision damage. The quick and easy route is lots of filler.

3. Simulated wood grain on transfer film is today's counterpart of the wooden-bodied station wagon. Material comes in rolls, is cut to fit desired panel, and is adhesive-backed. Here a door panel is being replaced. Film backing is peeled off, then film is placed over panel wiped with detergent. Heater speeds drying process.

4. The professional must have a variety of hammers and dollies for his work, but you may find objects around your garage to do the job.

5. Blind pop rivet gun is greatest invention since the welding torch, but a heck of a lot less troublesome. Special rivet is inserted in gun chuck, shank inserted in proper diameter hole drilled in pieces to be joined, then handle squeezed. In one operation rivet is flared on back side, excess rivet shank cut off.

6. The best repairs take more time, of course. A good metalman will get the panel as straight as possible first, so that only a thin coat of filler is needed. After preliminary hammering on the dent, grinding the surface shows high and low spots that have to be worked on.

6. Working the Metal

minimum of warpage, but does not work well with heavier steel.

WORKING METAL

As we have pointed out, when straightening a bent panel, the work should start in reverse order from impact. When the pressure that causes subsequent wrinkles and buckled areas down a panel has been released (by pulling or pushing into rough shape), start at the ridge farthest away from the impact point and start working back. In many cases, the minute this last ridge is straightened, most of the other buckles will disappear also.

Take that hypothetical fender again. The front of the fender around the headlight is crushed and wrinkled, but farther aft there is a depression above the wheel opening and a ridge behind that. By placing a spoon on the rear ridge and slapping it with a mallet or hammer,

the ridge will be driven inward and the depression will spring outward to near original contour. Localized stress points have been relieved, leaving only small areas to reshape with hammer and dolly.

The secret to good bodywork is to use the hammer sparingly. If a panel is repeatedly hit with a hammer and there is no support behind the panel, a series of individual valleys is created. On the other hand, if the panel is supported by a dolly and is repeatedly struck, the metal is stretched out of shape. The best procedure is to select a dolly with the same general contour as the original panel line, then slap the panel with medium hammer effort, moving the dolly around beneath all the high spots. When visiting a body shop, note how the accomplished body man strikes a panel with about 60 blows a minute, making a kind of glancing strike on the panel.

To raise a low spot in the metal, place the dolly at the apex of the dimple and

Body & Paint

strike the dimple edges with the hammer. This will raise the section. The kind of hammer used is very important. In the first place, body hammers are relatively light-weight, and they all have specially contoured faces. Using something like a ball-peen hammer to straighten a panel is the quickest route to the junkyard.

Spoons come in various sizes and shapes, but are primarily used on a big expanse of metal where the blow should be distributed over a wide area. They can also be used as backup dollies when space is cramped. Dollies vary in weight, shape and contour, but are nothing more than a hand-held anvil. Watch a professional body man and note how he will often use the dolly to tap up a low spot as he progresses, rather than resort to using a heavy and unwieldy body hammer.

Sometimes there will be small dents that are not easy to remove with a dolly, or perhaps a dolly cannot be squeezed into the area. These dents may be removed with a pick hammer. The pick end of a body hammer may be straight or slightly curved, but in either case the pick tip is rounded, not sharpened. When metal is tapped, the small rounded end will tend to stretch a tiny area, or cause little bubbles to raise. By striking metal from the underside with the pick, and placing a lightweight dolly on the outside panel surface, an area may be raised enough for final working. *Warning:* Never pick up a depression, such as a small dent that has been obviously stretched, and then grind or file the surface without working with a dolly in the normal manner. The little bubbles may be too high and when ground will cause thin spots in the metal, or may even allow the grinder to cut holes.

Obviously, when a severely crunched area is worked, there is lots of hammer and dolly work necessary. Despite the fact that this initial work might make the area seem beyond repair, you'll find that perseverance will prove the metal forgiving. As with that fender again, keep at it with light strokes and move the dolly around to get the proper contours—and soon the right shape will develop.

After the general contours have been reached, run the flattened hand over the surface. Any irregularities will be felt immediately and may be worked up slowly. Finally, file the area with a body file, holding the file flat and making even strokes. Remember that most automotive body panels have at least a simple curve, so do not file in one place long enough to cause a flat spot.

As the body file is shoved across the surface, it will take slight cuts off the high spots and leave the low spots untouched. Raise the low spots with the hammer and dolly, and continue until all the area is being filed with every stroke. A disc sander is faster, but the amateur will find the file gives a better result.

SHRINKING

Any crease type of damage will probably require metal shrinking for repair. As a crease or gouge is worked out with

1. Body Files

2. Using Hammer and Dolly

3. Welding a Patch Panel

4. Using Picking Hammer

5. Block Sanding

1. Files of various grits are used in shaping both metal and filler.

2. A hammer and dolly are the most basic tools in bodywork. You should never hammer on a panel without a dolly to back up the other side.

3. With basic welding knowledge and some sheetmetal, you can easily patch rusted out fenders and rocker panels. After this, the welds are ground down and smoothed into the main panel with filler. This often makes a better repair than just filling rust holes with "bondo."

4. The pointed end of this "picking" hammer is useful for tapping up the backside of small low spots.

5. Block sanding of large, flat areas is best done with shaper that uses replaceable sandpaper strips.

6. Here's the secret of using a disc sander on reverse-crown metal where disc edge would dig in. With disc edge cut this way, it's limber enough to flex with the contour.

6. Modifying a Sanding Disc

a hammer and dolly, the stretched metal involved will not want to flatten out properly, staying as either a slight crater or bump. It may be shrunk out.

Shrinking consists of heating a small spot in the middle of the stretched area where the metal has been made thinner. This will make the metal thicker, and it is easier than you might think. Put a small tip on the welding torch and heat a spot (about the size of a silver dollar directly in the center of the stretched area) to a strong cherry red. Be careful not to burn a hole. Immediately discard the torch and strike a hard blow with a body hammer directly on the heated spot. This will upset the metal and form a crater. Now, while the metal is still hot, hold a dolly against this crater from the back and tap the rim of the crater down with a hammer. Work around the rim in a decreasing diameter as the area cools. Quench about a 6-in. diameter with a water soaked rag to draw the heat expansion from the area, and you should be through. However, if the original stretched spot is large, it may require several shrinkings to straighten the panel. This is one procedure best observed before tried.

LEADING

After welding, and sometimes because of excessive damage, a panel may need leading. This is a process of filling a sunken area to the surrounding metal height. The secret to leading is clean and properly tinned metal. The surface to be filled should be cleaned with a wire brush, extending at least 2 ins. beyond the rim of the indentation or welded area.

There are a number of leading fluxes, both liquid and powder, on the market, but as a general rule use whatever your local body man recommends. To apply the flux, warm the cleaned area and then spread the flux thoroughly. A ball of steel wool clamped in pliers can be used to scrub the surface and get a good tinning job. This is possible because the flux will dissolve the oxide present on any cleaned surface.

When the area has been cleaned and the flux applied, spread a small bit of lead solder to the surface, using a *soft* torch flame as with any kind of soldering. While the lead and metal surfaces are still warm, wipe the solder over the area with a clean rag. This will complete the tinning process, and any place that does not accept the tinning will certainly not accept lead.

Making lead stay on anything but a flat, horizontal panel can be a study in sheer frustration for the beginner. The only solution to this dilemma is practice and patience. Some lead is easier to apply than others, because of the metallic composition, so again let the local body man guide you.

In applying lead, use a soft flame and brush it across the tinned surface now and then to keep the metal warm (not hot!). Hold the lead stick near the tinned area and direct the flame over the stick end until the end begins to sag, much as a heated candle would. Quickly press the stick onto the surface. Keep this up

Body & Paint

until enough lead is on the surface to fill the depression or welded area. As you are depositing the lead, occasionally brush the soft flame back across the deposited lead just to keep the area warm and pliable.

Shaping the lead is done with a wooden paddle frequently dipped in beeswax. The flame is passed across the lead deposit and as the lead becomes plastic (it loses the "sugared" look and gets shiny—be careful, because it is ready to run on the floor!), the paddle is used to push the lead across the surface. Paddle the lead over the entire tinned area and build it up slightly higher than the surrounding surface, scraping excess off onto the floor. Feather the edges smoothly with the paddle to reduce filing effort. While working the lead, if it keeps the sugared brittle look, you're probably working it too cold.

After the leaded area has cooled, it may be worked with the vixen body file. Care should be observed to keep the file flat, as the lead is softer than the surrounding metal and will gouge easily at this stage. The surrounding metal is the guide as to how low the lead should be filed, and if the area was tinned properly the lead will feather into the metal perfectly.

EPOXY FILLERS

More common with amateurs is the epoxy filler, normally called 'glass. There is nothing wrong with this type filler, although it is not as strong as lead and should not be used where a stress build-up is likely or at an edge where it can easily chip.

These plastic fillers, highly refined over the past 20 years, are popular because they are applied without heat and will not shrink or crack if properly mixed and applied. Always use the best epoxy fillers available as good insurance.

As with lead, the area to be treated with epoxy filler must be thoroughly cleaned. The filler is generally in a liquid form with a quick-setting hardener mixed just before application. Mixing must be thorough.

The mixture will set within 15-30 minutes, so work must go along quickly. Spread the mixture over the area with a wooden paddle or flexible rubber blade, as with putty.

The hardener added to the filler creates heat, and after an hour, the filler will be firm enough to be cheese-grated (roughly contoured with an open-cut plastic filler file).

After the rough shaping, which is easiest just before the filler gets superhard, the area is then sanded with a #80 paper, followed by 180 or 220 grit sandpaper, then cleaned and primed.

When either epoxy or lead has been used, always clean the area thoroughly with a cleaning compound such as

1. Bodywork Tools and Materials

2. Mixing Fiberglass Filler

1. Some of the common tools used in body repairs include spray gun, hand riveter, and various fiberglass fillers and repair materials.

2. Body fillers are made by mixing fiberglass filler with a small "dab" of hardening agent, which should be mixed in thoroughly. By varying the amount of hardener used, you can mix the filler to harden slowly or in a hurry. Don't add too much though, or the filler will actually heat up and crack off the repaired surface.

3. Never apply body fillers this thick! Road vibrations will cause it to crack and fall out. Instead, work the metal enough so little filler is required to make a smooth repair.

4. After sanding bare metal with a grinder or heavy sandpaper, deep scratches are sometimes left that cannot be concealed with primer. In this case, more sanding with a lighter paper is required.

5. Corvette makes a number of replacement panels as well as molds. Local independent fiberglass companies offer panels also. Surprisingly, panel replacement of fiberglass is quite similar to sheetmetal repair.

6. Repair of fiberglass follows a set pattern as shown in Figs. 1–4. When metal is repaired (Figs. 5–6), edges must be flanged as indicated, fiberglass patch laminated to lips.

3. Poor Bodywork

4. Grinding Marks

FIG. 1

20° BEVEL OUTSIDE EDGE OF HOLE

CLOTH (GRIND SMOOTH)   PLASTIC PUTTY

FIBERGLASS PANEL   MAT   FIG. 2

CLOTH   MAT (2 LAYERS)

POLYETHYLENE

FIG. 3

PLASTIC PUTTY   BEVEL EDGES IN A BROAD "V"

MAT   CLOTH   FIBERGLASS PANEL

FIG. 4

CLOTH   PLASTIC PUTTY

SHEET METAL   MAT   FIG. 5

POLYETHYLENE

PATCH UNDER POLYETHYLENE

FIG. 6

6. Glass Cloth Repairs

8-130 PANEL—UPPER GRILLE

8-130 PANEL—UPPER FENDER R & L

1-263 PANEL—LOWER GRILLE

8-130 PANEL—FRONT FENDER LOWER REAR   R & L '63 & '64

8-130 PANEL—LOWER FRONT FENDER   R & L

N.G.N. FLANGE PART

12-810 PANEL—BODY REAR UPPER R & L

8-130

12-986 BODY REAR LOWER PANEL

12-940 PANEL—REAR QUARTER R & L   R & L '65

5. Fiberglass Replacement Panels

Met-L-Prep, then apply primer.

Body glaze or putty comes in a tube and is actually like thick paint. It is extremely useful for covering small scratches, pinholes in epoxy fillers, and for filling small valleys in feather-edged areas. It isn't designed to be used like regular body filler, though, and should never be applied very thick. For best adhesion the area should be primered *before* applying putty. The putty flows on easily with a squeegee and watersands supersmooth.

REPLACING PANELS

It is often more expedient to remove and replace a badly damaged panel rather than straighten it. Because replacement panels from a junkyard sell for about 30% of new cost, exploring such a source makes sense economically. However, there are certain things to watch for during an R&R (remove and replace) operation.

Make sure the mounting area has been straightened and aligned, or the replacement panel will not fit.

Take that fender again. If the damage was heavy enough, the mounting near the door may have been bent. Surely the inner splash panel has been bent, and

the radiator-core support may also need straightening.

If the quarter panel must be replaced, then do a similar job to the crumpled panel. Often the replacement panel can be mated to the car beneath a beltline or fender molding.

If this is possible, overlap the top piece so water cannot slide down the joint and cause excessive rust, then braze each end of the mated joint. The overlap will be hidden by the chrome strip, so secure the joint with metal screws or (even better), use pop-rivets.

PAINTING

After all the bodywork has been completed, in preparation for a good paint job, every piece of chrome trim should be removed from the body. There are a few pieces that can't be taken off, for one reason or another, but the majority are removable. Reason for the extra work is to save extra work. That is, mask-taping the trim properly is a time-consuming project, and although it only takes about one-fourth the time of complete removal, there are other ramifications. In the first place, if you miscue with the tape, you can botch an otherwise good paint job. Secondly, if you

take the trim off, the entire body gets painted, under trim and all. Thirdly, the area around trim is a perfect place for wax and other types of film buildup, and if you're not very thorough with your preparation, this kind of film will ruin the paint. And finally, it's just a devil of a lot easier to prepare, paint, and finish a car that's minus trim. Incidentally, if the trim is held in place by stationary clips (the clip bolts to the body panel and the trim piece snaps away), don't go to great effort removing the clips. Just paint them.

In addition to the trim, take out the grille (so the cavity can be painted); remove the bumpers; remove the rubber bumpers from the hood, deck lid, and doors; and lastly, peel the rubber wind lacing seal away from the doors and deck lid. Be careful, for you'll want to reuse this seal if it's still good. If not, you can put on new rubber, either standard or universal type. In case you really want to be meticulous, remove the door upholstery panels and kick panels. These are difficult to tape off, and the little extra effort is worth it.

SANDING

It isn't important whether you feather-edge the repaired areas or sand the un-

Body & Paint

blemished paint first. Because water sanding is the fastest, cleanest, and easiest method of sanding, you'll probably do the overall sanding job first. This way, if the job stretches out over several days (nothing wrong with this), the slight surface rusting that's bound to cover the repaired areas will be taken off in the feather-edging step just before primer is applied.

Sandpaper for automotive use is available in both dry and wet-or-dry types, but for all practical purposes, the wet paper is far superior. The wet-or-dry type may be used either way, and costs about 10¢ per sheet, which means that you'll spend $1 for paper on the average job. Using water keeps the paper lubricated and the pores clean so that the paper will last much longer than if used dry. Wet-or-dry is available in a variety of grits, from 180 through 600, and you'll need several sheets of different rating. A couple of 180 grit, at least four of 220,

four of 320, and later some 600. In addition, pick up two sheets of dry #80, which is very coarse.

Obviously, it's wise to pick a place that will drain well for your sanding location. The residue from sanding actually acts like a mild stain, and it can discolor driveway concrete if left standing.

If possible, use a hose for water supply, with a bare trickle available at all times. If such is impractical, a bucket of water and good sponge will suffice. Thoroughly wet the surface before you start, and if possible, do the sanding in the shade, if for no other reason than comfort. Another hint, you might as well plan on getting wet, for you will before you're through.

The top is as good a starting place as any; work down to the hood and deck lid before attacking the side panels. Hold the hose in one hand, keeping the metal end from making new scratches, and sand with the other. Direct a small flow of water on the work as needed, which means a fine film of water at all times. You won't get too much water as far as

sanding is concerned, but too much will make it messier on you. When you're getting just enough water, the paper will glide without grabbing, but will have enough drag to tell you it's cutting.

The sanding pattern is extremely important and can have drastic effect upon the finished job. Work in one direction as much as possible, preferably lengthwise with the panel (much like the grain in wood), and never, never in circles. On many panels, such as the top rear windshield and rear windows, the lengthwise direction will not get around the windows well, so the direction must be changed to fit the circumstance, but the pattern here will be straight cross-grain effect.

The paper may be held either by hand or with a semi-flexible sanding block. The block is very good for large panels, but the hand conforms better to curves. If a block is used, tear strips from the sheet just wide enough for the block. Use 220, 280 or 320 for pre-primer sanding. If hand-held, the paper is torn differently. That is, the 9 × 11-in. sheet is

1. Repair Methods

2. Spraying Primer

3. Using a Sanding Block

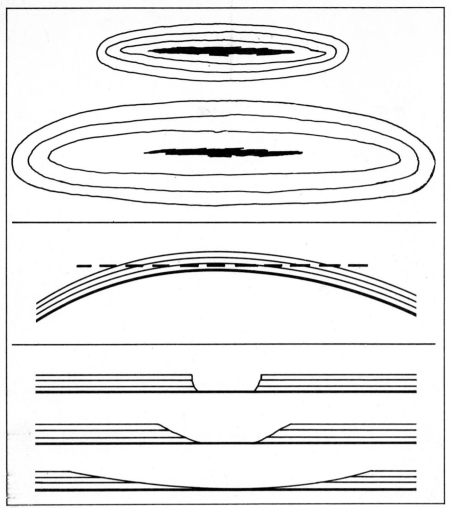

4. Featheredging

1. High-crown area damaged in collision can be replaced by using a supporting mold from inside. It may be necessary to bolt or rivet panels together to get them flush during initial repair.

2. When you think you have a panel pretty smooth, lay a coat of primer on it. Sanding the primer lightly will reveal if there are any high spots still left in the panel.

3. Sanding blocks like this made of hard rubber are inexpensive and do a much better job than using the flat of your hand.

4. These three drawings show how to featheredge sand a spot or chip. The larger the feathered circle. the better the result. Paint on a crowned surface will tend to sand flat, and must be radiused. Narrow scratches must be flared into area.

5. Thin putty or "glaze" spreads out almost like thick paint and is just the ticket for filling small sanding scratches or feathered-out nicks. The area must be primered before using putty, though.

6. Naturally, before any painting is done, the car must be masked off. This can be done for the most part with ¾-in. masking tape and sheets of newspaper. Narrow tape can be used on emblems like this, but the best results are obtained when all chrome is removed for preparation and paint.

5. Spreading "Glaze" Putty

6. Masking Off Trim

turned on its side, folded together, and torn down the center. Each piece is then folded triple, leaving one face toward the paint, one toward the hand, and one folded between the two exposed faces.

When sanding by hand, keep the entire hand in contact with the surface, not just the finger tips or side of the palm. However, for specific areas, these two pressure points may well be used to advantage.

After the entire area has been sanded, let it dry and check to make sure every inch has been covered. Any streaks or corners missed must be touched up.

With the biggest part of the surface sanded, attention can be directed toward the repaired areas, scratches, and chips. Getting these places feather-edged properly is vital to a good finished product! This cannot be over-stressed.

Feather-edging a large area, such as around a straightened place on a fender, is much simpler than small chipped spots. This is where those pieces of 80 grit dry sandpaper come in. To speed up the job, attach strips of the ¾-in. #80 to the sanding block (or to an electric or air-powered "jitterbug" sander) and do the rough-edging first. This paper cuts very fast, and leaves deep scratches, so use caution until you're familiar with it. With the rough production paper, it's best to sand with the edge, much like walking around the shore of a lake.

After this initial fast cut, switch to 220 and the block, plus water, and repeat. The idea is to feather the break between paint and metal over a wide area. There will be at least two paint layers showing, the color coat and the primer/surfacer, and on older cars the number can be as high as eight or nine layers. The wider the band of each paint layer showing, the better the feather-edging job! A 1-in. band means a much better job than a ¼-in. band. Finally, sand the feather-edged area in the direction of the overall panel sanding job.

The scratches are easy to remove if they're only one coat of paint thick. Just a little more localized pressure on the paper will do the job, but the "trough" should be feathered as much as possible. The little minute rock chips along the car front and around the wheel openings are harder to remove, and because of their sheer number, it's best to use a block or electric/air jitterbug. You can rent one of the handy gadgets, incidentally, for $3 a day. When the rock chips are really numerous and deep, resort to an initial attack with #100 paper, then follow up with the finer grits before priming. When this happens, the entire area of color coat is usually removed, but the effort is absolutely necessary.

Chips on the rest of the car, such as around exposed hinges or door openings, or what have you, are really the hardest of all to feather-edge. This is because their size means the feather-edging will leave a sort of smooth crater. Although the paint may be thin, the crater will really show up (even if properly feather-edged) in the finished job if you're not careful. The best route to follow when fixing up chipped places is to make the feather-edging area several times bigger than the chipped size. If

Body & Paint

there were several coats of paint on the car, the crater might best be filled with a thin coat of putty after the primer is applied. The important point is, make a chip crater as smooth as possible, flowing gradually into the surrounding paint.

Be careful when sanding next to chrome, aluminum or glass, as the paper will cut these surfaces quickly. Next to chrome, slide the index finger (or little finger) off the paper and use as a guide. The same goes for the other materials, too. With a block, just be careful.

The edges of all opening panels, such as hood, doors, ect., should be sanded to bare metal with the block. This won't be hard; paint here is usually minimal.

The door jambs and door edges should be washed clean of all accumulated dirt and grease, then thoroughly sanded with both paper and #00 steel wool. The steel wool gets down into all the little irregularities the paper can't reach, otherwise the final paint might not bond securely.

Fenders should be loosened and the fender welt removed, then the mating edges very carefully sanded, especially chipped places. This is one location where shoddy preparation will quickly show up. New fender welt, which only costs 20¢ per foot, may be added after the color is on. Don't try to tape it off!

Finally turn to the repaired areas again. If a spot has been worked, sand the bare area well with 220 or finer paper, until all rough file or grinder scratches are no longer rough to the touch. The jitterbug can be used here, also. Don't use rough paper, and don't lay on the pressure. Lead isn't nearly as hard as the surrounding metal, and neither is 'glass, so be careful.

FINAL PREPARATIONS

Should the fiberglass area have what appears to be blisters, some further repair is in order. This sometimes happens, so just peel out the blister air bubble with a knife blade and patch with more 'glass or resin.

Special attention is paid a repaired area before primer/surfacer is applied. If lead was used wash the entire area thoroughly with properly diluted Met-L-Prep, which removes the inherent acid and grease. Wash away the Met-L-Prep residue with water. With both 'glass and lead repaired areas, clean thoroughly with grease and wax remover (even though they've been well sanded), then spot with a good coat of primer.

At this stage of the game, a compressor is handy, which can be rented along with the paint gun for about $8 a day. You'll only need it for a day (actually much less). The compressor should be able to maintain a steady 60-80 lbs. pressure.

Build up a tank of pressure, drain the tank of any oil (the renter will show you how), then blow all the dirt and sanding residue from the car. Be especially careful to get all the little pieces of stuff in the cracks around windows, windshield, hood hinges, etc. Use a lint-free rag as you go along to clean the surfaces and all chrome and glass areas.

When the car is clean, tape off the trim, glass, and interior, and cover the

1. Paint Spray Booth

2. Gravity Feed Spray Gun

3. Marbles For Agitation

4. Proper Spray Pattern

5. Overlapping Each Pass

6. Testing Spray Pattern

7. Poor Pattern

1. You may not have a professional spray booth to paint in, but good jobs have been done by amateurs in a garage with floor wetted down, or outside on a calm day.

2. There are many kinds and brands of spray guns. Pressure, siphon and gravity feed (like this model) guns all have different capabilities.

3. When painting with metalflake or other metallic or iridescent paints, a few marbles or clean bolts in the paint gun will help to keep the metallic elements in suspension.

4. Spray gun pattern is critical in getting good results. Top pattern is too wide, gun needs adjusting. Middle pattern is just about right, at about 8 ins. from the gun. Bottom fan is much too narrow; this will load the paint on too heavily.

5. Practice making even strokes with paint gun, starting each pass "dry" and adding trigger at end of each stroke. Overlap must be just right or paint, especially any of the metallic types, will streak.

6. Before starting on the car, it's a good idea to test the spray pattern on something unimportant first.

7. This test spray pattern is too coarse or too wet, shows a need for an increase in air pressure of 5 lbs.

engine and the seats with an old piece of anything handy. Tape newspaper or wrapping paper around the engine compartment opening, and around entire door opening. Tape off the door upholstery panels and the glass molding if they haven't been removed. Keep all this paper as flat as possible, so debris can't fall into the folds and blow out later.

As you'll find, taping can be quite a maddening procedure. The best width to use on cars is ½ or ¾-in., which costs about 75¢ per roll. You'll need one or two rolls for the average car. When applying the tape, work over at least an arm-length stretch, rather than in short 3- and 4-in. distances. This makes following an edge infinitely easier, and the whole job much faster. For instance, to tape the long side molding, stick the tape end to one end of the molding, hold it there with the next finger, then unroll about 16 to 24 ins. of tape. Run the finger down this stretch, pushing the tape against the molding as you go. By sighting down the tape, you can get it exactly at the edge of the molding. If a little tape gets on the painted surface, run a razor blade parallel with the surface and cut away the offending tape. This tape must be removed, or an unpainted area, which shows up like a sore thumb, will be left!

When the entire car is taped, mix up the primer/surfacer. Always remember that neither lacquer nor acrylic will go

over enamel in color coat form! The only time this can be done is over a factory-baked enamel job, where the paint is dry clear through. Even baked enamel from local shops is likely to blister when covered with the hotter paints. This applies only to the color coats, and not to the primer, which will cover with no adverse effects.

SPRAY GUN TECHNIQUE

No matter what kind of paint will be finally used—enamel, lacquer, or acrylic—use a multi-purpose primer with the appropriate thinner. Mix according to the can directions, which is about two parts thinner to one part primer, and stir thoroughly. For primer, a good all-around spray gun head will do, something like a #30 on the DeVilbiss and #362 on the Binks. Adjust the gun so that the spray fan is about 8 ins. wide at a point 12 ins. from the gun head. If the fan is too wide, there will be a thin spot in the middle; if it's too narrow the pattern will appear as a tight band. The fan adjustment is the top knob above the handle. The second knob is for material adjustment, and won't concern you too much at this time.

Make several practice passes on a piece of cardboard, with the compressor setting at 60 lbs. constant. With the De-Vilbiss, keep the gun 8-12 ins. away from the surface; make it 10-12 ins. with the Binks. Notice that when the paint gun trigger is first depressed there is a moment when only air comes out. Following this, the paint comes. Practice making a smooth pass, keeping the gun a constant distance from the surface until the pass (which should average about 2 ft. per swing) is completed. Start the pass on one side, swing horizontally to the other limit, raise or lower the gun nearly a fan width and go back. Keep the gun parallel to the surface, so that one end of the fan isn't closer to the surface than the other.

As soon as you feel confident with the paint gun (don't worry too much, because primer dries relatively fast on the surface and it's easy to fix up a botched area), set it aside and get the car surface ready. Wash the entire car with a good wax/grease remover, then again blow away dirt, etc., from the cracks.

Start with the door, hood and deck lid openings. Spray the primer on evenly, in

Body & Paint

smooth strokes. When these are done, allow them to dry for 10 or 15 mins., then close the openings and start on the big outside metal.

The previously primed spots where metalwork was done must be sanded with 220 or finer paper, then wiped clean. Any small spots of putty should be treated likewise.

Start spraying on the top, which is the hardest to reach, and follow these handy hints. Throw the air hose over one shoulder and hold away from the car with your other hand; wrap a piece of rag around the gun/cap connection point to keep paint from dribbling out when painting with the gun in a horizontal position (such as for the top, hood, deck lid).

If the paint is going on right, it will appear smooth and wet for just a bit af-ter application. If it looks grainy, as if full of sand, the paint is too thick or you're holding the gun too far away from the surface. If the paint runs (you won't need anybody to show you what this panic is!), it is too thin or you are hold-ing the gun too close. If the patch alter-nates dry-wet-dry, or wet-runny-wet, your pass is not constant. And don't stay in one place too long. It's just like a dance step—1-2-3, 1-2-3, etc.

If the gun doesn't seem to be making a constant fan, it may be clogged up. If so, soak the head (which unscrews from the handle) and make sure all the little mixing holes are clear. Pour thinner through the handle part of the head (not through the air delivery hole), and make sure the pressure-equalizing hole in the cup lid is open. When all this has been done, spray a little clear thinner through the gun first to make sure it's really clean. As you use a primer gun, the primer—which is very thick anyway—tends to build up and close the cup lid vent, so poke this open occasionally.

Primer is the necessary good base for a fine paint job, so don't skimp. It takes about 1 gal. of unthinned primer/surfac-er for the average car, so keep going around the car until you're sure you've got it well covered. Cost is $10 per gal-lon for the primer, $3 per gallon for the thinner.

You don't need a special spray booth, so you can spray right out in the open. Naturally, don't spray next to a building, or in a windstorm, but don't worry about overspray. Primer dries before it's 5 ft. from the gun and will blow or wash off whatever it settles on. Don't spray under a tree that drips sap! Plan your time so that you're through spraying with at least 2 hrs. of sunlight left, and when the tem-perature is at least 40° or above. If spraying in the cold winter or inside when it's raining, use special thinner (the paint store will decide for you).

1. Proper Spray Pattern

2. Patterns for Spots and Panels

3. Holding Gun Properly

4. Cleaning Air Hole

5. Removing Masking Tape

1. This is a normal spray pattern. Do not use excessive air pressure as it wastes material in the form of overspray, and ruins paint surface.

2. The small spray pattern here is used for spot repairs. The larger pattern is used for panel repair and complete refinishing jobs.

3. A spray gun is nothing more than an air brush and must be held same distance from panel throughout stroke. When adjustments and stroke pattern are learned, most of the painting battle is won.

4. With guns that have an air hole at the top, it's important to keep the air hole free by poking a wire through it occasionally. The rag is tied around to catch any paint drips.

5. When removing masking tape from any surface, it's best to pull it back over itself like this, and always pull down away from newly painted panel or paint may chip.

Finally, if the car has slight waves in the panels that might be taken out by block sanding, a good trick is to spray a final coat of different colored primer. For instance, if the major primer color was light gray, finish with dark gray, or vice versa. Then, later on when you block sand, the thin top coat will come off but the other color will still show in low spots.

After the primer has dried for 20 to 30 mins., the tape can be removed. If you are painting over bleeders like maroon or red, the primer must be sprayed with a bleeder sealer to insure an even tone. Although it is possible to go right ahead and sand the car (dry) and follow with the color coats of paint, it is best to allow the primer to cure for several days, even weeks. The primer will dry and shrink, so allow about four weeks' time for a good quality job. You can drive the car meantime.

Scratches don't come in the paint can or from the gun. So, take it easy during the surfacer sanding operation. The surfacer will sand very easily, either dry or wet, and it's advisable to use 320 or 400 grit paper on surfacer. Remember this is the base for the color, and use of a coarser paper will leave scratches too deep for the color paint to cover.

Next, use the wax and grease remover solution, completely washing the car, even the smallest cracks. This is vital, for any foreign substance will invariably ruin an otherwise perfect job. For instance, just the marks left by your fingers will leave dark splotches under the final color. When washing the car with the cleaning solution, always use clean, lint-free rags (don't use shop towels, as they often are cleaned with low-grade solvents that contain contaminants bad for good paint adhesion). It's wise to use the special cleanser always, but in a pinch you can use lacquer thinner, applied with a very wet rag and immediately wiped off with a dry rag. Don't wait even a minute if you use thinner, as it is "hot" and will quickly soften the surfacer and may cause other damage to the paint below.

FINAL PAINT COAT

The car is now ready for the final color, and this is the precise moment most amateur painters get the jitters. It's also the time when one step must follow the other in rapid succession, so having the procedures well established in your mind will ensure best results.

What you do from now on depends a lot upon the paint you're using—the type, not the brand. Lacquer is the easiest to spray for the novice, followed by acrylic, then enamel. This is simply because the lacquer and acrylic dry much faster, compensating for many application errors—or at least, for a few.

Enamel paint, although hardest to actually apply, requires the least amount of overall effort, and is an excellent choice where maximum toughness is required. It gets its glossiness (shine) from a varnish used by the manufacturer. This varnish is made of a solution of resins with alcohol, turpentine, or amyl acetate. You must use enamel thinner with enamel paint. Although acrylic has received a big boost in use as standard finishes by several auto makers, at least one major

company still uses baked enamel. A baked enamel job is superior to an air-dry job and is very durable, but unless you have a bake oven available, you're stuck with air-dry. For years now auto enthusiasts have considered lacquer the only way to get a superb paint job, but such is not always the case. It depends generally upon the painter. For the average person unable to afford a good lacquer expert, and not wanting to take the extra preparation pains necessary for lacquer, enamel is an obvious answer. It will cover scratches well, and can be used almost anywhere you desire.

Acrylic is like lacquer, in that it dries right away, but it is plastic-based (lacquer is cotton-based) and undergoes a chemical change as the paint dries and unites with oxygen. Acrylic must be sprayed differently and will not dry to maximum gloss if put on in one heavy coat.

Before starting the color spraying, it's wise to completely clean the spraying equipment, especially if it has come from the local rental emporium. You can rent perfectly good equipment, but make sure the compressor is in good shape (not pumping oil). Paint guns will differ, but all you're interested in is a good all-around nozzle (head).

Clean the paint gun thoroughly before any use, either with acetone or lacquer thinner. Acetone works faster. Remove the pot and nozzle, then soak everything for 20 mins. or so. Follow by brushing the pot inside, the top sealing lip, the sealing area on the pot cap (the sealing gasket must be good), the nozzle, and the gun head. Make sure all mixing holes in the nozzle are clean.

If enamel is to be used, thin it with two parts thinner to one part paint, pouring the paint into the cup through a strainer which will trap bits of foreign matter. Tighten the pot until secure, as paint might otherwise drip from the connection (the shop rag tied around this connection point will prevent drips).

Before blowing color on the waiting car, test the gun pattern. Start by opening the gun up by turning the spreader adjustment (top thumb screw above handle) all the way out, and backing off the

Body & Paint

fluid screw (right beneath the spreader adjustment) until the first thread shows. Adjust the air pressure regulator to give a constant 40 lbs. pressure for lacquer and acrylics, or 60 lbs. for enamel. Hold the gun 6 to 8 ins. from the test surface, parallel to such surface, and give the trigger one full pull, then release.

The color coat is sprayed exactly like the primer/surfacer. However, some extra preparation might be needed if lacquer or acrylic is being applied over enamel. Just as a precaution, if the old paint is enamel, spray on a coat of Du-Pont #22 sealer, which will help keep the enamel from raising due to the hotter lacquer thinner. If you're not sure, always spray a test patch first. The sealer is always a good idea.

All the previous hard work will come to nothing if the final color coat is sprayed haphazardly. Before actually spraying any paint, practice the proper spraying swing. At all times, the nozzle should be from 8 to 12 ins. from the surface (individuals vary in technique, thus the difference in distances). Picture yourself facing the door of a car. You want to paint each individual panel, or panel group, with a full stroke, thereby reducing the number of overlaps to a minimum on each surface.

With the gun held at the left edge of the door, and the nozzle distance correct, twist the wrist so the gun is actually pointed lengthwise to the car. As the trigger is pulled, twist the wrist back toward the door. This makes the initial application of each stroke blend together at the overlap. As the gun comes to point directly at the surface, begin the smooth stroke across the panel. Not too fast, and not too slow. If you go too fast, the stroke will look misty; if too slow, the paint will pile up too heavy and try to run. Remember that it is easier to do a job with several thin coats than with one heavy coat. At the end of each stroke, twist the wrist away from the car in the opposite direction (or direction of the stroke).

Although the technique differs, most painters spray the door jambs, hood edge, trunk jambs, etc., before starting on the rest of the car. If you're careful during this phase, only a small amount of overspray will carry around the edge and onto the outside metal. If too much overspray gets around the opening, it may make the overall blending job too difficult. For lacquer or acrylic the area may be lightly sanded, for enamel the best procedure is a wash job with thinner before the paint hardens.

Because panels are sprayed one at a time, get into the habit of spraying consistently. Don't spray heavily in one place and lightly in another. As a panel is started, try starting the stroke slightly inboard from the panel edge and ending slightly short. As the next panel is started, the resulting overlap will keep the depth of paint constant.

The biggest single problem the amateur painter experiences is stroke inconsistency. The paint must overlap everywhere, otherwise it will appear streaked when it dries. It sometimes helps to

1. Taping for Pinstripes

2. Rubbing Compound

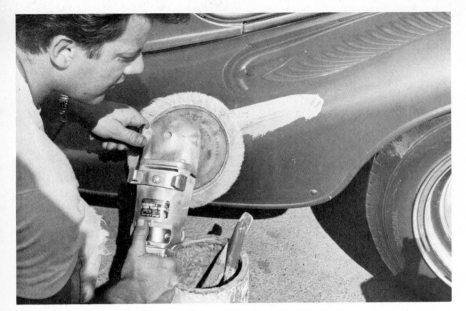

3. Buffing With Rubbing Compound

4. Cleaning Clogged Buffer

1. Pin striping is an art in itself, but if you lack a steady hand, you can make straight stripes with this special tape which is scored so strips can be pulled out to paint through.

2. After a new lacquer or acrylic paint job has cured (usually a week or two), the paint must be rubbed out to achieve its final high gloss. Be sure you are using the right rub compound for the type of paint used.

3. Paint can be rubbed out by hand or with a buffer. Go cautiously if you use a buffing machine or you may buff right down to the metal!

4. When compounding with a buffer, the fluffy sheepskin becomes matted with hardened compound and should be cleaned with a "ticking wheel."

5. Touch-up paints in all stock colors are available in most auto parts stores. For small nicks and scratches, tubes of touch-up paint with applicators can be bought at your dealer's parts counter.

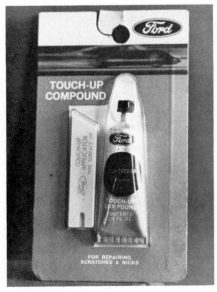

5. Ford Touch-Up Kit

make horizontal strokes first, then vertical strokes, etc. The idea is to apply the same amount of paint everywhere on the surface.

If lacquer is being used, the drying time is such that it may be applied at random. However, acrylic must be allowed to "flash" before the next coat is applied (surface harden). Enamel is a slow drier, therefore it should not be applied all at once. The first time around, a very light tack coat is applied. This will become sticky in a few minutes and helps make subsequent spraying easier by increasing adhesion. The second coat of enamel is sprayed normally, but the amateur should never try to get all the paint on the car in one pass (2 gals. required for the average sedan).

Starting with the top, spray each stroke evenly. If you load up a particular area, which is easy to do, the paint may sag or run. Don't panic, just continue with the spraying but stay away from that place. It is sometimes possible to stop a run in the early stages by simply backing away from the panel slightly and spraying nothing but air across the run. This will often give enough surface drying to hold the sag from advancing. When the first coat is dry, dip a tiny brush in enamel thinner and remove as much of the sag excess as possible. The idea is to soak up the excess rather than spread it around. After the sag has been carefully removed, fog a little paint over the area. If you do the job well, the little boo-boo won't be too apparent. On the next coat, go easy in the area of a run, again just spraying on a light fog coat.

An enamel job usually requires three coats—the tack coat, the first heavy color and the final color. After the last coat, wait a couple of minutes, check for sags and repair any if necessary, then leave the car to dry overnight. In fact, since enamel should be painted in a spray booth if possible, leave the car for a couple of hours before detailing.

A note about enamel and moisture. They just don't mix, so if the floor is washed down before painting to settle the dust, let it dry before spraying. Temperatures shouldn't be under 60° or over 100° F. when the car is being sprayed, otherwise special steps are required. Special additives are available to control the drying time, such as DuPont #3656 (rather than normal 366/g) for acrylic, which will slow drying if the temperature is too hot. If painting is done when the weather is wet or cold, the color can "blush." That is, moisture is trapped in the paint, so a slower thinner or special retarder may be needed. The paint store will guide you here. At all times, follow the mixing direction of the manufacturer explicitly!

Although the enamel job can be done at one spraying, lacquer and acrylic require more elapsed time for the best job. If you have the time, spray the latter in several good coats, then allow to dry for a couple of days. Water-sand with 600 sandpaper, then spray several more coats. Whereas enamel doesn't require any after-spray special attention, lacquer and acrylic must be color-sanded with 600 sandpaper before the final rubbing out process (buffing).

HOW-TO: Minor Fender Repair

1. Crease in '74 Pinto fender extends from headlight rim back beyond side lamp, with secondary damage in the form of a depression above the fenderwell. As a first step in spot repair procedure, Jim Bryam removes the rim.

2. Using a hammer and punch, Jim proceeds to make a series of holes in the damage area, spacing them 2-3 ins. apart until he's covered the primary damage area; experience tells you exactly how many you'll actually need.

3. Threading his body knocker into the holes, Jim begins to pull out the depression in the fender; periodically, he uses a body hammer along the edge beside the headlight to keep its countour from pulling out.

4. Once he's pulled the damaged area out, Jim uses the body hammer to take out the high spots. Educated sense of touch is important in this operation, as is the use of the proper dolly behind the fender while hammering.

5. Slight depressions can't be avoided, but high spots should be lowered to panel's shape before using the grinder. A #24 grit disc will do the trick nicely and is used to remove the paint, exposing the bare metal.

6. Body hammer and dolly are used to take the dent out of the headlight rim; body shops would simply replace it. Although the metal is torn, Jim is able to work it back close to its original shape with a little bit of patience.

7. After mixing body filler with catalyst, Jim applies it generously over the damaged area with a large rubber squeegee. The purpose here is to fill the low spots and provide a base for shaping the area to the fender contour.

8. While waiting for the filler to "flash off," Jim tackles the secondary damage area with a hammer and dolly; he then applies filler and begins to shape the contour of the fender using a "cheese grater" file.

9. An application of body filler to the damaged area of the headlight rim will fill the metal tear and provide a suitable surface for contour shaping. Cheese grater body file is also used here, but it's awkward going.

10. After a second light coat of filler has flashed off, Jim uses a power sander to restore the contour line. Fender damage in this area is a tricky proposition to repair on the Pinto because of prominent contour.

11. To match up the contour line perfectly, Jim replaces the headlight rim and uses a hand sanding block to carry the line through the rim. After it's been properly established, he'll finish up the job with the power sander.

12. After masking off the headlight and fender portion, Jim shoots a primer coat over the finished repair area, using a piece of cardboard to keep overspray to a minimum. When dry, he'll shoot the finish coat.

HOW-TO: Car Cosmetic Care

1. Maintaining the resale value of your car depends on taking proper cosmetic care of it, starting with regular, cold-water wash and rinse.

2. After a good driveway washing with as little detergent as possible, you can gently dry the paint with terry towels or a good, clean chamois.

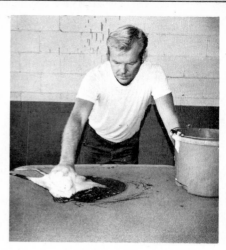

3. Don't neglect that vinyl roof! Use a mild detergent and scrub the roof with a brush. Let it dry, then apply a coat of protective Armor-All.

4. A light application of steel wool and cleansing powder is usually good enough to restore whitewalls and remove curb-caused scuff marks.

5. Don't overlook antenna. Chrome polish or Glass Wax not only cleans it for easier up/down operation, but removing oxidation improves reception.

6. Clean chrome areas with a chrome polish or Glass Wax. Remove any rust spots or pitting with steel wool and cover them with clear nail polish.

7. Brush touch-up kits are easiest to use. Build chip up to original finish thickness, then blend with light sanding or rubbing compound.

8. Touch-up compound is available at most dealers to match your paint. The thick compound is applied with supplied squeegee to chipped spot.

9. If you do use a spray bomb, use a cardboard mask with a small opening cut out. This keeps overspray down, and makes for a better paint blend.

10. Polishing with rubbing compound will restore new luster to oxidized paint jobs. Using rented machine for polishing saves lots of elbow grease.

11. Use care if you're a beginner at machine-polishing. Too much arm pressure on crown surfaces can cause pad to buckle, cutting through paint.

12. Stay away from chrome trim and hard-to-reach places with machine. Polish these areas yourself with some hand rubbing compound (coarser).

13. The inside of your car needs care too. Common household cleanser and sponge will remove smoke film and road dirt from headliner and seats.

14. Carpeting can be cleaned with a shampoo concentrate and a good scrub. Before carpet dries, vacuum rugs to remove the shampoo, dirt, and stains.

15. Tired of dirty, scuffed panels? Mask off everything else and shoot them with Vinyl Spray. You can even change your interior's color with it.

16. Vinyl Spray also works well on most vinyl dashes. Mask windshield and instrument panel well, though, as the overspray is hard to remove.

17. The metal part of your dash can be touched up with a pinstripe brush—but if nicks or chips are on a large area, overall refinishing is best.

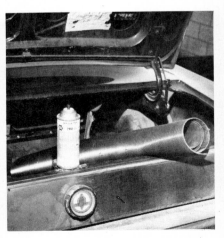

18. Trunk restoration is easy with a can of spatter-paint and a roll of black, ribbed rubber matting. Use your old trunk mat as a pattern.

Accessory Fix-it Tips

A car that doesn't have any of its accessories working is not much of a car. When the windshield wipers, the air conditioning, the heater, horns, or the cigarette lighter don't work, you really only have part of an automobile. A little knowledge of the weak points in accessory units will give you a pretty good clue as to where to look and what is required to fix them. In most cases, you can even fix them yourself.

There's one accessory, however, that you should not attempt to fix, because it can be dangerous. That is the air-conditioning unit. The liquid contained in an air-conditioning system can cause severe frostbite if it splashes on your skin; and if it hits you in the eye, it can freeze the eyeball and cause blindness. You can see why we don't recommend that you play around with your air-conditioning system, but it would be a good idea if you knew how it worked and perhaps were able to do a certain amount of diagnosis that you could pass on to the air-conditioning serviceman you choose to do the repairs. So let's take a look at air conditioning first.

AIR CONDITIONING

Nobody really knows how an air condi-tioner works; it works according to laws of nature. Water boils at 212° F., just because it does. It's one of those things that you can't explain, you just have to accept. The theory of air conditioning is based on a similar law of nature. You must accept the fact that when a substance evaporates—which, of course, means changing from a liquid to a gaseous state—it absorbs heat. Another way of stating this is that it takes a certain amount of heat to make a substance go from the liquid to the gaseous state. Either way you look at it, whenever a liquid evaporates and becomes a gas, a certain amount of heat is necessary to do the job. Pour some water on your hand and your skin will feel cool. It's because the water evaporates into the air, and in so doing, absorbs heat from your hand. Do it with alcohol and you will find that your skin becomes quite a bit cooler than with water. It's because the alcohol absorbs more heat when changing from a liquid to a gas.

If the absorption of heat will change a substance from liquid to gas, then it's reasonable to assume that if the substance gives up heat, it will change from a gas back to a liquid. About this time you should be getting a glimmer of how the air-conditioning system in your car works. All you need is some kind of liquid that you can evaporate in the passenger compartment. The liquid will, of course, pick up heat when it evaporates, thus cooling the air around the passengers. Then if you take the gas that results and cool it enough by blowing air over it so that it condenses back to a liquid, you have completed a full air-conditioning cycle and you can start all over again with the same liquid, evaporating it in the passenger compartment to cool the air.

The marvelous liquid that is used in an air-conditioning system to do this terrific job is called Refrigerant 12 or R-12. You have probably heard it referred to as Freon. Strictly speaking, Freon is only the trade name of the Refrigerant 12 that is sold by DuPont.

If you have the cycle of evaporation and condensation firmly in your mind—that the R-12 absorbs heat when it evaporates and gives off heat when it condenses—then we can take a look at the mechanical components of the air-conditioning system and see how they make the R-12 do its work. The R-12 is circulated through the air-conditioning system by the compressor that is mounted on the engine and driven by a belt from the engine crankshaft. You won't

1. Typical Air-Conditioning System

HIGH PRESSURE LIQUID
LOW PRESSURE LIQUID
HIGH PRESSURE GAS
LOW PRESSURE GAS

EVAPORATOR
EXPANSION VALVE
COMPRESSOR
CONDENSER
TO CONDENSER
OUT TO COMPRESSOR
RECEIVER
TO EXPANSION VALVE AND EVAPORATOR
OUT TO RECEIVER

2. Muffler on Olds Compressor

have any trouble recognizing the compressor on an engine. Just lift the hood and look for the biggest and ugliest hunk of iron that you can find.

The easiest way to understand the compressor is to consider it nothing more or less than a simple pump. From the compressor, the R-12 is pumped to the condenser, which is usually mounted in front of the radiator. From the condenser, the R-12 goes to the receiver-dryer, then to the expansion valve which controls the flow, then to the evaporator and back to the compressor. The evaporator is in the passenger compartment, of course, because that is where we want the R-12 to absorb heat when it evaporates. The condenser is out in front of the radiator in the main airflow, because we want it in the coolest place we can find, so that the R-12 can get rid of the heat.

When the R-12 comes out of the evaporator, it is a gas and it goes from there directly to the compressor. Therefore, the compressor is pumping gas only. It compresses the gas and forces it into the condenser, where the gas gives up heat to the air that is flowing through the

1. The refrigerant, called R-12, in a typical air-conditioning system is constantly changing from a liquid to a gas and back again under conditions of high and low pressure.

2. The large silver canister beside the compressor on this '72 Olds is a muffler. It helps cut down noises from the compressor and also helps minimize line vibrations.

3. Old-style GM compressor, with the piston rods connecting the socket plate to the pistons. Later models have longer pistons, without rods.

condenser fins. With this release of heat, the gas condenses to a liquid and flows to the receiver-dryer, the expansion valve, and into the evaporator again.

The expansion valve is necessary because there must be some way of controlling the flow of liquid into the evaporator. Without the control, liquid R-12 could flow through the evaporator faster than it could change from a liquid to a gas. The expansion valve controls the flow by sensing the temperature of the R-12 as it leaves the evaporator. A sensing bulb, connected to the expansion valve with a capillary tube, tells the expansion valve when to open and when to close. If the gas flowing out of the evaporator coil is too hot, the expansion valve will open and allow more R-12 to come in. If the gas is too cold, it means that the R-12 is flowing through so fast that it can't pick up the heat. In that case, the expansion valve cuts down the rate of flow.

If the expansion valve goes bad and allows liquid R-12 to flow out of the evaporator and get into the compressor, it can really ruin things. A liquid is not compressible, but the compressor does not know this and will try to compress it anyway. The result can be a mess and very expensive to fix.

When the expansion valve cuts down on the flow of liquid R-12, there has to be some place for the liquid to go, because the compressor is pumping continuously. This is where the receiver-dryer comes in. It is mounted between the condenser and the expansion valve. The receiver-dryer is a small tank with an inlet at the top and the outlet attached to a dip tube that goes to the bottom. When the expansion valve allows a lot of R-12 to pass, the level of liquid R-12 in the receiver-dryer goes down. The space

that was taken up by the liquid is now filled with gas. This situation occurs because the condenser cannot condense the gas into a liquid fast enough when the flow is too great.

The receiver-dryer takes care of the situation very well, however. When the expansion valve slows down the flow, the condenser will do its job better, and the gas in the receiver-dryer will be displaced by liquid R-12.

The basic air-conditioning system is really very simple. The controls that are added to the basic system to make it work better are where we run into some complication. Our air-conditioning units today use a clutch on the compressor pulley to turn the compressor on and off. The belt from the engine drives the pulley at all times, but the clutch is magnetically actuated so that it can engage or disengage the pulley from the compressor shaft. Occasionally the clutch plate will develop slippage—it moves into position when actuated and engages the pulley, but the pulley cannot drive it.

Some air-conditioning units use what is known as the clutch cycling method to control temperature. If the temperature gets too cold, they disengage the magnetic clutch so that the compressor shuts down. Of course, this stops the flow of R-12 so that nothing happens anymore. Other manufacturers leave the compressor clutch engaged anytime the air-conditioning unit is on. They control the flow of R-12 with additional valves that sense temperature and allow the R-12 to double back from the pressure to the suction side of the compressor.

The situation really gets complicated when the heater is hooked to the system for completely automatic temperature control. Those units will turn either the heater or air conditioner on or off when-

3. GM Compressor

Accessory Fix-it Tips

ever necessary to control the temperature in the car without any need for the driver to do anything except set the temperature he wants to maintain.

In checking out an air-conditioning system, the first thing to do is to have the engine running and observe the compressor while someone inside the car turns the air conditioner on and off. You should be able to see the compressor engage and disengage the pulley from the compressor shaft. If the compressor is working, look for the sight glass which is either on top of the receiver-dryer or in the line leading to it. The sight glass will probably be so covered with dust and dirt that you can't see anything. Wipe it off and observe the flow of liquid refrigerant.

Don't worry about any bubbles that appear when the compressor is first started; they should go away as the system gets operating. In fact, bubbles in the sight glass do not always indicate a low refrigerant level in the system. If the system is at a control point, bubbles may appear even when it's fully charged. A certain amount of foaming is also normal if the outside air temperature is 70°F or below. But if you do see bubbles in the sight glass, and they continue after the system has been in operation for several minutes, head for an air-conditioner service outlet and have it checked out—odds are that you will need an R-12 recharge and perhaps even repairs for minor leaks.

A system that is low on refrigerant does not necessarily mean that a leak has to be fixed somewhere. If you have to have the system charged once every five years, then it would be silly to look for such a minor leak. However, if every three months the system is bad because the refrigerant is leaking out, then you had better get your serviceman to find the leak or you might as well plan on doing a lot of recharging. Sometimes, the system works no better after servicing. In this case, it's likely that dirt, air, or moisture were allowed to get into the lines. As efficient air conditioner operation depends upon the pressure/temperature relationship of pure R-12, any contamination introduced alters this relationship and the system cannot function properly.

The electrical part of the air-conditioning system is the easiest to fix. If you don't get any air coming through the evaporator, look for a blower fuse that is burned out. It could even be a bad blower switch. If the compressor is not working, check for a blown fuse near the compressor on top of the engine. A check of a wiring diagram for your air-conditioning system will help you to locate fuses. The wiring diagram can be found in the shop manual for your car.

Many times a case of low cooling is not the fault of the air conditioner at all. Most cars have many air ducts or places where outside air can leak in. A leak in any location will allow hot outside air to enter, so that no matter how hard the air conditioner works, it can't keep up. To find leaks, drive at freeway speeds and have a friend put his hand in front of all the ducts and possible leaks. Fixing the leaks with tape is no problem, once you have located them.

CLOCK

Practically all modern automobile clocks are of the electrically wound, mechanical type. Late models are equipped with an adjustment feature that speeds up or slows down the clock whenever the time is reset by hand. Earlier models have an adjustment lever which can be moved slightly in the direction of "S" or "F". After a few such adjustments the clock should maintain reasonably accurate time.

Automotive clocks have been unfairly accused of being the most unreliable part of the car. We say "unfairly" because while no one seems to question the wisdom of taking his wristwatch to the jeweler once a year for a routine cleaning, equivalent care is rarely given the clock in a car. The lubricant in the mechanism has the same tendency to form gum after long periods, and the unit is subjected to road shocks and extremes of temperature. Thus, the automobile clock should be given routine service like any other timepiece.

The clock is always connected to the "hot" side of the ignition switch so that there is a current source for the winding mechanism whether the car is in use or not. If the unit is remote from the instrument cluster, there will be another wire leading from the illuminating bulb in the clock to the main light switch. Both of these circuits are grounded through the screws attaching the clock case to the

1. Setting Temperature Dial

2. Ford Sight Glass

3. Dust Cap on Plymouth Sight Glass

4. Charging the System

5. Printed Circuit Switch

1. Setting the temperature control dial on a GM Climate Control is done with a special tool that holds the shaft while you turn the dial.

2. Ford sight glass is in the line, instead of being on top of the dryer-receiver. A continuous stream of bubbles in the sight glass indicates the system needs a charge.

3. The sight glass on most cars gets covered with dirt in time, so you'll have to clean it off to check for bubbles in the system. This Plymouth, though, has a dust cap.

4. Your air-conditioning system can be recharged at any garage that does a.c. work. A checkout of the system and an R-12 recharge costs $10-$15.

5. Late-model Buicks have a printed circuit switch, controlled by a vacuum diaphragm working against a long spring (arrow).

panel so if the clock is inoperative, the tightness of these screws is the first item to check. The clock may be removed for repairs by unfastening these screws and the connecting wires. If the clock is part of the instrument cluster itself, the entire cluster must usually be removed to gain access to the clock. Some of the more modern clusters have printed or "bread board" circuitry, and the electrical connections are automatically made when the clock is positioned correctly in its mounting.

Generally speaking, two things can go wrong with an automotive clock. Either the clock movement stops operating, or the winding mechanism gets gummed up so that it doesn't work and blows a fuse. When you put a new fuse in, it will blow immediately. This is usually caused by a lack of lubrication or a gumming of the old lubrication in the winding mechanism. To fix the winding mechanism you will have to take the clock housing

itself apart, but it is not necessary to do anything to the works. A little oil in the right spot, which is obvious on inspection, and you will eliminate the fuse blowing. If it turns out that the clock problem is in the works itself, take it to a watchmaker so you can get professional repairs.

AUTOMATIC SPEED CONTROL

In a typical system, the desired speed is dialed on a gauge, sometimes incorporated in the speedometer. When the driver wishes this speed to be automatically maintained, he pushes the "speed set" button located in the tip of the turn indicator control on some cars. The unit will maintain this speed regardless of terrain, adding to or cutting back on the throttle opening automatically as is required. However, it has no way of telling that you are bearing down on a slow truck or coming up on an intersection. This information you feed into it by stepping lightly or otherwise on the brake. This action, sensed by an electro-vacuum switch in the system, deactivates the control until such time as you twirl the "resume-speed" switch.

Some older systems do not have the "resume-speed" switch. These return the car to automatic control as soon as the driver brings the vehicle back to the pre-selected speed. The tell-tale sign that the control has taken over is a pronounced stiffening of the accelerator pedal. You can override this to go faster, though the pressure on the pedal required is uncomfortable for any period longer than passing another car, but you cannot override it to go slower unless you de-activate the system with the brake.

Due to the safety hazard that could be created by any error in the adjustment or repair of a component in an automatic speed control system, it is recommended that this system be serviced only by a factory-trained mechanic.

AUTOMATIC HEADLIGHT DIMMERS

Headlight dimmers used to be very obvious. The photocell setup was on the top of the dash behind the windshield and looked very much like a gunsight or aiming device for the car. Late models all have the photo tube mounted in the grille or leading edge of the fender. It's not as prominent in that position but it is much more susceptible to dust and road grime. Many problems with the headlight dimmer can be solved simply by wiping off the front of the photocell.

Some cars have an on-off control in the headlight switch but in most models the only control is the foot-operated dimmer switch. One position of the dimmer switch puts the headlight control on automatic. The other position will keep the headlights on low beam at all times. There is a third position built into the foot switch which allows the driver to override the control and obtain high beam in bright areas or during daylight. This third position is activated by depressing the foot switch just until resistance is felt. When the driver takes his foot off

Accessory Fix-it Tips

the switch, the headlights will go back to low beam.

The system consists of a photoelectric cell and amplifier, usually housed as one unit on top of the instrument panel or on the left front fender; a power relay; a manual override foot switch to replace the conventional dimmer; and a vernier switch that lets the driver adjust sensitivity within the limits of the basic factory-set calibration. Horizontal aim on most dash-mounted models can be adjusted by turning the pivot pin on the outside of the case. The unit should be aimed as parallel to the centerline of the car as is visually possible. Vertical aiming requires removal of the case, which on some models exposes a bubble-type leveling gauge built into the sensing unit. While aiming vertically, the car must be on an absolutely level surface, the tires must be inflated to the proper pressure and the car should contain no load other than a half tank of gas.

HEATER/DEFROSTER

Basic differences in the design of relatively modern heaters and their associated defroster units are limited to the point of air intake and whether the various controls are actuated mechanically or by vacuum. All heaters except those on air-cooled cars utilize a core (basically a miniature radiator) to extract heat from the engine coolant and a fan to distribute the heated air through ducts. The desirable location for the fresh-air inlet is in the top surface of the cowl, just forward of the windshield. The alternate location, just behind the right side of the grille, is bad in heavy traffic because it picks up carbon monoxide and other noxious fumes from the car ahead. Though more expensive, vacuum-actuated controls are preferable to mechanical because their action is more precise and there is considerably less linkage to get out of adjustment.

HEATER SERVICING

Servicing any of the more modern heater/defroster designs is one of the meanest jobs (perhaps second only to windshield wiper linkage) on the car, helped in only a few rare instances where the blower motor and fan are accessible through the engine side of the cowl. Fortunately, very little goes wrong with the heater/defroster system.

There are two ways of controlling the heat: with a water valve or air doors. A water valve usually has a thermostat built into it. When you move the control valve to "hot," you are doing nothing more than turning up the thermostat. In the air-door system, water flows through the heater core at all times, and the doors direct the air through or around the heater or both. There is usually no thermostat in this system. You set the doors where you want them to get the right amount of heat.

Assuming the blower motor is working, heater malfunctions generally fall into these categories: 1) no heat, 2) heat all the time and 3) not enough heat. Let's deal with the last symptom first, because it is frequently caused by a malfunction outside the system or even by unfamiliarity on the part of the operator. Cable-actuated heating systems are found on most compact and intermediate-size cars. The somewhat more elaborate vacuum-actuated systems are used on more expensive cars.

In a cable-controlled model, a lever control actuates the air door in the ductwork to direct the airflow almost entirely to the interior of the car or almost entirely to the defroster outlets. The position marked "heat" usually routes 80% of the heated air to the interior and 20% to the

1. Getting at the clock's attaching screws will probably be the hardest part of removing your clock. On this Chrysler, as on most cars, the time spindle comes out the front, while the clock comes out of the back of the instrument panel.

2. Digital readout dash clocks first began to appear in 1975; they were common in luxury cars, as well as plusher full-size models, by '77. The unit's attachment in the dash is similar to conventional electric clocks. Inner "works," though, are too complex for the layman. Leave digital clock repair to a specialist, or simply buy a new one if the original goes bad.

3. Check your factory service manual before attempting this, but on older cars the clock's attaching screws often are exposed at the front of the dash once the dash trim is removed.

4. Cars with sporty interiors like Mustang and Cougar often have the clock mounted down on the console, which makes getting at the clock a little easier than working behind a cramped dashboard.

5. The brake switch and vacuum lines are important parts in an automatic speed control system. Malfunctions in these components can cause a runaway!

1. Typical Rear-Mounted Clock

2. Digital Clock

3. Front-Mounted Clock

defroster outlets. Another lever controls the degree of heat, from none to maximum, by actuating another door in the ductwork which determines how much of the incoming air is routed through the heater coil. A multi-position switch determines the speed of the fan. The fan is necessary in traffic but at highway speeds there is a ram effect from the incoming air and operation of the fan is no longer necessary.

Thus, the basics in operating this type of heater are deciding how you want to divide the incoming air, how hot it should be, and whether or not it needs a boost from the fan. Fresh-air ventilation is handled manually on either side, usually by direct controls mounted in the kickpads or under each side of the instrument panel. These outlets should not be used when heated air is desired. As to windows, you have to experiment with them or consult the operator's manual.

The vacuum control system works the same way except that you can't alter the heater-to-defroster airflow ratio of 80-20 or vice versa. The fresh-air vents are controlled by pushbutton and in most cases only one button may be operational at a time. The heat control and fan-speed selector are common to both systems. If pushbuttons are not present, check whether your system is vacuum or mechanical by looking for a vacuum line leading from the intake manifold to the general area of the heater. Make sure this line is free of cracks and securely seated on its nipples at both ends.

If it's not operation of the controls that

is causing the problem, it may be the thermostat or water pump in the cooling system. A thermostat stuck open will result in little heat from the heating system and little heat in the engine. Double-check this, plus your knowledge of the system's operational controls, before troubleshooting.

If the vacuum or mechanical valve that controls the flow of coolant through the heater coil is sticking in a partial or fully open position, the symptom is a constant flow of heat from the heater outlets. Conversely, if it is stuck closed, no heat can be obtained. A malfunction of the mechanical type of valve will almost always evidence itself in the form of stiff,

non-positive control operation. The operation of a vacuum valve is generally audible. You can turn off the engine to check its operation because there should be enough vacuum in reserve for one cycle. If you don't hear it click into position, suspect the valve. If the air-door valve is sticking open, there will be a flow of cold air from the heater or defroster outlets when the heater is turned off. If it is sticking in a partially or fully closed position, little or no heat will result. Symptoms of these valves sticking are the same as described above for both types of controls.

Unfortunately, replacement of either valve usually requires removal and disas-

4. Console Clock

5. Oldsmobile Cruise Control

Accessory Fix-it Tips

sembly of the entire heater. Except for noting that the engine coolant should first be drained below the level of the heater, it is impractical to give step-by-step procedures for removal of the heater due to the fact that the design for each make and model of car is different. You must first remove obvious obstructions such as the radio (see section in this chapter) and glove compartment box. Wires and cable leading to the system should be disconnected, and also the hoses at their attaching point on the engine side of the cowl. Note that in addition to the power lead to the fan, there will also be a separate wire to ground the fan motor to the car structure. A good trouble light will facilitate working under these cramped conditions and aid in locating the screws that attach the heater assembly to the car structure. Once the unit has been removed from the vehicle, its further disassembly should present no problem.

Prevention of air leaks in the system is important if maximum efficiency is to be obtained. Therefore, there will be one or more sequences in the assembly procedure where a caulking compound known as "body seal" must be used.

Heater motors are best repaired by a specialty shop, and a leaking or blocked core should be replaced. So, too, should malfunctioning vacuum valves. With mechanical valves, the trouble usually stems from a kinked cable which also must be replaced. Attempts to "unkink" these are usually unsuccessful. Adjustment is provided at the attaching points and may be made after the heater assembly has been installed. A rule of thumb for mechanical control action is that there should be between 1/16- and 1/8-in. clearance at either end of the lever travel when the applicable valve is in its extreme positions. When attaching the cable, the setting of the control lever and the valve should, of course, match.

HORNS

The horn system on a car consists of one or more horns, a relay and an actuating ring or button to complete the circuit. The function of the relay is to deliver a full ration of electric energy to the horn; without it, excessively large wires would have to be used in the system. All horn relays, except those on 1968 or later model General Motors cars, have three terminals marked "S," "B," and "H." The new GM relays have a fourth terminal for the ignition warning buzzer incorporated in the relay. The "S" terminal connects the horn ring or button into the circuit; the "B" terminal is the current source from the battery or actually, from the "hot" side of the voltage regulator; and the "H" terminal connects to the horn.

Usually one additional horn of the factory type may be added to an existing single- or dual-horn system without exceeding the capacity of the relay but an accessory horn, operated from its own switch, must be equipped with its own relay. The circuit is grounded through the horn mountings and at the steering wheel column. When the horn button or ring is pushed, it grounds or completes the circuit, the electromagnet in the relay is energized and makes contact, and the horns blow. When the circuit is not energized, a spring on the electromagnet keeps the contact open.

A horn with a harsh or tinny sound may only need adjustment. The method of adjustment varies by make. In the Sparton, Autolite and Prestolite horns used on Ford, American Motors and Chrysler cars, the adjusting screw or nut should be turned counterclockwise until no tone is heard. Then the adjustment is turned clockwise, ¼-turn at a time, until the desired mellow sound is achieved. In the Delco-Remy horns used on General Motors cars, the adjusting screw is more sensitive and should never be turned more than one full revolution in either direction. Otherwise, the procedure is the same. This adjustment is only to clear the horn's tone; it cannot raise or lower the pitch or change the basic note.

The horn circuit is simple to troubleshoot. If one or both horns won't blow, first bypass the relay and switch by running a jumper wire from the "B" post in the relay to the terminal in the horn. If the horn then blows, the trouble lies in the relay or switch. If the horn doesn't blow, try tapping it—dirt may have lodged in the contact. If it blows only when tapped, it may be badly out of adjustment and the procedures described above should be followed.

On older cars, the no-blow problem is usually caused by a bad ground from rust under the horn mounting. Cleaning the rust away until you get a bright metal mounting won't always cure it, either, because the fender panel that the horn is mounted to might have its own bad ground from rust. A quick way to find out if the horn is any good at all is to run a ground wire from the body of the horn back to the ground battery post. If the horn works, you know you have a ground problem and some cleanup work to do.

A faulty horn is easier to replace than to repair, but before this, isolate the relay from the switch. Connect the jumper wire from the "B" terminal to the "H" terminal. If the horn blows, the relay is defective and should be replaced. To check the switch on the steering wheel with a relay that is known to be functioning, run the jumper wire from the "S" terminal to ground. If the horns blow, the

1. Speed Control Servo Unit

1. We doubt you'll ever take one apart, but this shows how control is designed. This is a late GM type. Note governor weights (center) that maintain throttle opening once the system has been set.

2. Older GM system had phototube mounted above dash like gunsight.

3. Later GM models mount the tube behind the grille. The system often is combined with sentinel system that turns the headlights off.

2. Early-Model Headlight Dimmer

switch should be checked for dirt or faulty connections at the horn ring. Most rings may be removed by turning the decorative center plate to the left and removing it. This exposes the attaching screws for the ring which in turn may be removed for access to the switch. Switches, also, are easier to replace than repair.

ACCESSORY HORNS

There is a wide variety of accessory horns on the market, ranging from genuine, truck-type units actuated by compressed air to novelties that imitate such sounds as Bermuda bells and a mustang's whinny. The true compressed-air installation is relatively expensive as it requires a belt-driven compressor, smaller but similar to the ones used in air-conditioning systems. Somewhat cheaper are the electrically actuated compressors (or vacuum pumps, depending on the system), but some are a little short on power and consequently the note may be a rather poor imitation of the real thing. Still other accessory installations are operated by cylinders of compressed gas which must be replaced periodically. The latter two types are relatively easy to install as the system is completely sepa-

rate from the standard factory installation. Mail order houses like J. C. Whitney and Vilem B. Haan list all types of horns and the units come with complete installation instructions.

One particular type should be purchased with caution. This imitates the standard European "hee-haw" emergency signal which is now being adopted by some American police, fire, and ambulance operations. Any horn on a passenger car that even resembles an emergency warning is illegal in all states. A louder than normal sound, however, usually is not.

LOCKS

If you have to replace an ignition key lock or door lock, it's best to avoid buying a replacement lock cylinder that is already coded because you'll end up with the nuisance of a different set of keys for each lock. A locksmith can sometimes adapt a key to work in both the old and the new lock, but this makes them a lot less pick-proof. The best method is to buy an uncoded replacement cylinder and have the locksmith file the tumblers to fit the existing key.

A door lock is easy to remove and replace once access to it is gained by re-

3. Grille-Mounted Headlight Dimmer

Accessory Fix-it Tips

moving the door trim panel. In practically all designs, the panel is held by a retaining clip on the inside of the door sheet-metal which can be sprung off with a screwdriver. This clip will be found there whether the lock is in the door handle or separate from it. The lock assembly then slides out of its socket or housing in the door. The replacement assembly consists of a lock cylinder and a dust cover. The latter must be crimped to hold it in place before installation in the housing. A new cylinder should be lubricated, but this may be done after the job is buttoned up simply by coating the key with a light graphite and working the lock a few times.

Trunk lock replacement is done in the same manner, speeded, of course, by the lack of upholstery in that area. The lock in the tailgate of a station wagon may be reached by removing the window molding and trim panel and manipulating the glass electrically or by crank out of the way. Exercise caution here because when the glass is fully extended in a tailgate that is open, it is free to fall out of its retaining channels in most designs. To operate an electric window with the tailgate open, press the spring ground with your finger and have a partner actuate the control switch which is located in the driver's compartment.

Power locks, whether for the doors or trunk, are vacuum actuated. Although these locks may use the same vacuum source as other more commonly installed accessory components such as vacuum-controlled heater and air-conditioning valves—and the vacuum lines connecting these accessories may be shared in the interest of economy and saving clutter—each will have its own vacuum reservoir. These are usually located under the hood on the left fender. Most designs have a separate switch, usually in the glove compartment, through which the vacuum line for the trunk lock is routed.

Except for binding in the actuating cylinder, about the only malfunction possible in these systems is a crimped or leaking vacuum supply hose. It is easy to isolate the hose involved. With the engine idling, disconnect a vacuum supply hose to an accessory known to be working, place your fingertip over the end and feel the degree of suction. Anything less than full engine vacuum in the suspected hose indicates a crimp or leak. You may locate a crimp by observing the hose throughout its length; a leak may also be located by repeating this check at each connecting point or T-fitting. A leaking hose may be temporarily taped until replacement is convenient. If all vacuum-operated accessories are malfunctioning, the leak will be between the source of supply on the intake manifold and the first reservoir in the line. Further evidence can be found in a faster than usual, loping idle.

The simplest type of "power" trunk lock is a cable with one end attached to a pull knob located in the glove compartment and the other to a catch release on the trunk lid. Universal kits may be bought at most auto parts stores or through mail order houses. The regular trunk lock, of course, must either be left unlocked or removed entirely. Body shops will fill in the resulting hole for a very small charge. Hiding the trunk lock switch in the glove compartment delays even a serious thief because he has to jimmy one more lock.

CIGARETTE LIGHTER

A cigarette lighter consists of a removable element and a socket or plug. The plug is connected to the "hot" side of the ignition switch via the fuse box. In some installations, interior courtesy lights share the same 20-amp fuse, but in many designs there is a cartridge type fuse on the back of the lighter. As the plug is always "hot," it is a convenient source of power for accessories such as a trouble light, vacuum cleaner and coffee maker as well as the lighter element.

When the element is pushed in, the coiled resistance wire in it receives current and begins to heat. In 10 to 14 secs. the heat is sufficient to cause bimetallic grips in the socket to expand and release the element for use. They expand only a certain amount, however, because they also have a secondary gripping point to prevent the spring-loaded element from popping clear of its socket and causing a fire hazard. If this does occur, the socket is faulty and must be replaced as a unit.

The most common cause of lighter failure is a burned out fuse. If the fuse block has a slot marked "ltr" something similar, try putting in a new fuse that you know is good. If you still don't get current to the lighter, check at the back of the lighter socket for a cartridge fuse. If you have current to the lighter socket (check with a test light) but the lighter still won't work, the trouble is probably a burned out element. New elements are available, but be sure the prongs are the same as your old one, or it might not fit the socket. There are several different designs.

1. Coolant Circulation

HEATER CORE

RADIATOR

RADIO

There are four basic types of radios installed in modern cars, and in recent years they have been fully transistorized. These are AM with or without pushbuttons, AM/FM, AM/FM stereo and AM incorporating a stereo tape player. Repairing any of these receivers is beyond the scope of this book, but there are many checks and adjustments which may be made on items other than the receiver that are very often the cause of the trouble. If after these checks the trouble is pinpointed to the receiver, you can remove and install it yourself and save that labor cost. Receiver repairs and particularly warranty work should be done by an authorized shop. None of the car makers builds its own radio although it will put its own name on the unit. Usually, however, the actual maker will be noted on the receiver case or you can call the car dealer and ask for the name of the authorized repair station.

A basic adjustment is antenna trimming which must be done whenever the receiver is installed after removal for repairs. The serviceman trims to his own antenna which may not have the same characteristics as the one on your car. Locations of the trimming screw vary but it is often found hidden under the tuning knob, or on the side of the radio under the instrument panel. Let the radio play for 15 mins. to warm it, set the antenna between 31 and 40 ins. and select a weak but clear station as close as possible to 1400 kc. Remove the tuning knob or otherwise expose the trimming screw. With a screwdriver turn the trimming screw in small steps in both directions to where a setting is found with the strongest signal. Replace the knob and the job is done until the next time the receiver or antenna is disturbed.

NOISE SUPPRESSORS

Capacitors to suppress radio interference are normally located at or in the alternator or generator, on the "B" terminal of the ignition coil, on the voltage regulator, on the fuse block and some-

2. Heater Core

3. Electric Rear Window Defroster

4. Vacuum-Controlled Water Valve

1. Here's the flow in a typical heater system. Note that heater water flows from the bottom to the top of heater core. If your heater isn't working very well, you may have put the hoses on the wrong way.

2. A heater core is really just a small radiator. Very little ever goes wrong with one; being on the firewall or under the dash, it isn't subjected to the flying stones and careless wrench-handling that your regular radiator is. If you do start getting leaks in one, just take it out and bring it to a radiator shop.

3. Many new cars have an optional rear window defroster that is a set of wires built into the glass. There are no moving parts, and it does the job without any blower noises.

4. Vacuum-operated water valves like this '71 Plymouth unit are relatively trouble-free, as there are no cables to bind or need adjustment.

times on certain power accessories. The connections to these may corrode or come loose, but the capacitor itself seldom "wears out." If the capacitors are suspect, but you've determined that all of their connections are tight and clean, it is cheaper from a time standpoint to replace all of them rather than to try to isolate the offending item. Before doing this, however, inspect the spark plug wires. One or more old, leaking plug wires can cause radio static very similar in sound to a defective capacitor. Then determine if the static occurs only when the car is moving. In this case, the trouble is likely caused by either the front wheels or tires. To isolate one of these from the other, drive on a smooth road and drag the brakes slightly. If the static stops, the problem is in the front wheels; if it continues, it is the tires.

To cure front wheel static, install a collector spring and dust cap in each wheel. For tire static, radio shops have a powder available that must be injected into the tire with a special gun. Another cause of static when the car is in motion but not when standing still is a missing ball tip on the antenna.

ANTENNAS

A typical manual antenna may be readily removed for repair or replacement. Power antennas, except for tightening and cleaning, are best left to a specialized shop. Antennas should be kept clean at all times but not waxed. An occasional wipe with an oil moistened cloth is all that is necessary for lubrication of the power type. The quick check for antenna problems is to borrow one that is known to be good, plug it into the radio and hold it out the window of the car with, of course, a wire connection to any convenient ground. If the radio now plays, or plays better, the existing antenna should be repaired or replaced. If the radio gains volume when you touch an installed antenna, it is an indication of a poor ground.

RADIO REMOVAL

The receiver is supported primarily by attachment points at the two control knobs. There may be one or more supporting brackets at the rear of the unit. The attaching sleeve screws are behind the control knobs and of course the power, ground, speaker and antenna wires must be disconnected. On some air-conditioned cars it may be necessary to remove a portion of the duct work to allow clearance for radio removal. Repairs to the receiver should not be attempted by anyone but specially trained personnel.

Accessory Fix-it Tips

SEATS

Since the invention of the adjustable front seat, manual or power, the cushions of necessity became an integral part of the seat frame, which in turn is attached to the floorpan through the adjusting mechanism.

The adjuster is mounted to the floorpan by only two bolts, but alternate holes are provided in the adjuster for each of the bolts, one on either side of the center hole used by the factory. With the car on a hoist, these bolts may be removed and repositioned as desired to change the base of adjustment without removing the seat from the car. For changing the vertical base of adjustment, shims in these bolts may be removed or added as desired. For fore-and-aft change of permanent adjustment, the satellite track on the other side of the seat should use the same holes. In a change in the vertical, the number of shims on each side should match to prevent an uncomfortable tilt and possible binding of the seat in its slides.

Worn parts in the adjusting mechanism may be replaced by removal of the attaching bolts, which frees the assembly from the seat frame and allows it to be removed for bench maintenance. Each manufacturer's design varies in detail but the parts are straightforward and easy to work with.

Seatback latches are now required on all non-rigid seatbacks by the Federal government. Some use a much more elaborate mechanism that combines this latch with a reclining feature. In this design, the front seatback may be removed without disturbing the cushion or frame. The rear seat cushion is held in place by tabs and may be readily removed. The removal of the rear seatback may, in some cases, require loosening of the attaching points for the package shelf (accessible through the trunk) and possibly

1. Under-Dash Heater Installation

1. On most modern cars the heater is in combination with the defrosting and sometimes the air-conditioning systems. Some types, as here, mount under the dash, others on firewall.

2. Getting at the horn switch on most late cars with 2-spoke wheels means removing trim cover (usually padded).

3. About the only test you can make on a horn is for current draw. Hook up a voltmeter and ammeter as shown. The normal current draw for a dual-horn car is between 4 and 6 amps.

4. On most cars the door panel must be removed to get at the door lock, but on this '63 Ford you merely pry the retaining clip (arrow) out and pull the lock from the outside.

5. Once the lock is outside the door, a screwdriver can be used to pop off the retaining C-clip, and the lock is off and ready to be fixed or changed.

6. Cadillac has a vacuum-controlled trunk lock that shuts automatically when the lid is pushed down. Arrow points to roller that is the control mechanism. Trunk may be opened with key or by button in glove compartment.

2. Two-Spoke Wheel and Horn Switch

3. Testing Horn For Current Draw

rear window moldings. In either case, the procedures involve only the loosening of attaching screws.

The motor of an electric seat should be serviced by a specialized shop. The wiring here is uncomplicated because the switch is adjacent to the motor, but the circuit is routed through the fuse block from the power source.

MANUAL AND POWER WINDOWS

For economic and safety reasons, two types of "shatter-proof" glass are used in an automobile. The side and back windows are usually made from tempered glass which has the characteristic of fragmenting entirely into relatively harmless particles when broken. Sometimes the sheet doesn't disintegrate but visibility through it is reduced to near zero. For this reason another type of glass, called laminated, is used in windshields. As the name implies, this is a sandwich composed of two layers of glass separated by transparent plastic. The plastic isolates breaks, and visibility is maintained if the window is impacted.

Replacement glass for side windows may be of either type. Tempered glass must be cut to shape before the tempering process, so a glass shop will generally stock pre-cut forms for the most popular cars and cut laminated glass on a custom basis to fit rarer makes and body styles. Glass removal and replacement must be preceded by at least partial disassembly of the winding mechanism which, in turn, requires removal of the interior handles and upholstery trim panels.

WINDOW ADJUSTMENTS

There are adjustments you can make to compensate for normal wear. A common problem is a loose vent window (of the non-crank type) that won't keep its position against the airstream. A lower pivot nut at the bottom of the window regulates the tension, and you can get at this nut to tighten it by removing the inner window-to-door molding.

Adjustments to the regulating mechanism of any of the main side windows requires removal of the trim panel. First remove the window-to-door molding and the arm rest. Both of these items are attached with sheetmetal screws, although in the case of the arm rest, the screw heads may be hidden under plastic covers. Next, remove the inner door and window handles. Unfortunately, some of these require special tools. The trim itself is attached to the door struc-

4. Removing Lock Retaining Clip

5. Removing Lock Cylinder

6. Cadillac Trunk Latch

Accessory Fix-it Tips

ture by various types of clips that can be pried out with a screwdriver.

Most window adjustments can compensate for normal wear or correct leaks and wind whistle caused by misaligned glass, and are self-explanatory.

Anytime the trim panel is removed from the door, it is a good idea to lubricate the gears at various rubbing points of the window regulator with a heavy grease that will not run off and stain upholstery in hot weather.

1. If your doors don't fit or latch properly, the door may be just out of alignment. It can be realigned by loosening the screws on this striker plate for readjustment.

2. Some elements can be changed by unscrewing them from the knob, but you must push the sleeve back and grab the end of the element itself in order to unscrew it.

3. With the element unscrewed, the whole thing comes apart easily. The replacement element must be the same size and shape or it won't fit into the dash receptacle. Elements seldom go bad. Look for a blown fuse first, either at fuse block or lighter.

4. Cartridge fuse screws onto the rear of many lighters. Check for continuity with a test light. If it's blown, you have to replace it.

5. Removing lighter shell shows prongs that grab end of the element. Both the internal (top) and external types are used. They're not interchangeable.

6. Collar on this Ford lighter picks up light from behind the instrument panel to illuminate "lighter" sign. Element is covered by ash guard.

7. Here are several of the methods the factories use to eliminate static in radios. Suppression capacitors can be installed on the coil, generator and other electrical components; GM cars use a metal shield over the ignition points; spring-loaded dust caps can be used on the wheels; and most cars in recent years have used metal ground clips between the hood and the cowl.

8. Seats are hard to work on because the cushions cover up the works. If you remove the cushion, your chances of fixing the seat are better.

9. It's a sign of the times, but you see quite a few of these antennas made from coat hangers because someone vandalized the antenna. They work, but not too well.

10. Don't forget switch as a source of trouble on electric seats. If the seat works only when you wiggle the switch, you may have bad contacts.

11. At left is the mechanism for a GM 4-way power seat. For comparison, the model at right is a 6-way, which has the extra vertical gear nuts that raise and lower the seat.

1. Door Lock Striker Plate

2. Removing Element

3. Disassembled Lighter

4. Cartridge Fuse

5. Element Construction

6. Illuminating Collar

SHIELD

THREE GROUND CLIPS
LOCATED ON COWL
AT REAR OF HOOD

7. Static Suppressors

SEAT FRAME
ADJUSTER
ADJUSTER
RELEASE LEVER
KNOB
SET SCREW
SPACER
MANUAL BUCKET AND 50/50 BENCH
MANUAL BENCH
SEAT FRAME
ADJUSTER
FLOOR PAN
SUPPORT
ELECTRIC SEAT

8. Seat Mounting Mechanisms

ELECTRIC WINDOWS

Replacement or lubrication of the separate, permanent magnet-type motors that operate each window requires removal of the regulating mechanism. We have advised against the owner-mechanic attempting this for reasons described above. If you do go ahead, the regulator assembly must be held in a vise when the motor is removed from it to prevent the assist spring from unwinding. If the master switch is malfunctioning, it must be replaced as a unit. The window circuit utilizes a circuit breaker with the current source being the ammeter.

WINDSHIELD WASHERS AND WIPERS

Windshield washers fall into three general categories. The simplest type is a foot-operated pump mounted on the floorboard or cowl on the left side above the headlamp dimmer. It is connected by hoses to the fluid reservoir in the engine compartment and to the nozzles. The simplest electric type is at the bottom or adjacent to the fluid reservoir and is actuated by a switch incorporated in or adjacent to the wiper control. A "deluxe" type of pump is part of the windshield wiper motor and when actuated, also operates the wipers for a predetermined number of strokes.

Chemicals are sold in all service stations for mixing with water in the system. In winter the chemical acts as an antifreeze, with the degree of protection determined by the graduations on the bottle. The antifreeze not only keeps the solution from freezing in the bottle and breaking it, but prevents the solution from freezing solid when it hits the ice cold windshield. A partially frozen solution can create enough load to burn out the pump motor. In the summer, a solution of chemicals and water improves cleaning action to cut those bugs off the glass.

9. Homemade Antenna

10. Dash Control for Six-Way Seat

VERTICAL GEARNUT
JACKSCREW RIVET
JACKSCREW
HORIZONTAL ACTUATOR SCREWS
SHOULDER SCREW
HORIZONTAL ACTUATOR
GEARNUT ATTACHING NUTS
GEARNUT TENSION SPRINGS
UPPER CHANNEL
REAR VERTICAL GEARNUT
HORIZONTAL ACTUATOR
FRONT VERTICAL GEARNUT

11. Four-Way and Six-Way Adjusters

Accessory Fix-it Tips

In late-model cars, Rambler is alone in still using a vacuum-driven windshield wiper and this is only for 6-cylinder models. All others have a one- or multi-speed electrically driven system. A vacuum-driven system requires an auxiliary vacuum pump to keep the wipers moving steadily when the engine is under load. This pump is an integral part of the fuel pump on most cars equipped with vacuum wipers.

The location of the windshield wiper motor varies. Sometimes it is on the engine side of the firewall where it is readily accessible. In some other cars an access hole is provided in the firewall, and in others, the strip of body metal between the back end of the hood and the windshield can be removed to give working room. In some designs the entire instrument cluster must first be removed to gain access to the windshield wiper motor and linkage.

Foot pumps are inexpensive and should be replaced as an assembly. They are mounted to the floor pan with several screws with spacers and a retainer to give the mount rigidity in the soft carpet and mat. Replacement electric pumps are similarly easy to install and can generally be bought in rebuilt form. Ejection nozzles tend to corrode over a period of time and may be cleaned by a careful reaming with a hand-held drill bit. Aiming these nozzles is a "cut and try" operation and you should remember to aim low when the car is at rest because at speed, the fluid tends to carry up and over the windshield.

1. Power Window Mechanism

2. Window Adjustment Bolts

3. Window Channel Adjustment Points

4. Vent Window Assembly

5. Bayonet-Type Wiper Blades

WIPER MOTOR AND LINKAGE MAINTENANCE

Most wear in the linkage can fortunately be compensated for by adjusting the position of the wiper arms. Most are attached to their shafts by a conventional cap bolt. If no bolt is evident, a special tool, varying by the make of the car, is required to remove the wiper arm without damaging it.

Replacement wiper blades are obtainable in any service station. In newer designs only the rubber is replaced; older cars require a complete blade assembly. Extreme care should be taken not to bend the wiper arm when replacing a blade because it takes only a slight misalignment to cause metal to contact glass and the result is a permanently marred windshield.

The decision as to whether you should attempt to work on the linkage and motor or buy this service depends entirely upon its accessibility. Once you get at it, there is nothing very complicated about the assembly, and wear points are quite evident by their sloppiness. Unlike most other assemblies on the car, wiper linkage parts are sold separately. When you find the worn part, bring it with you to the dealer's parts counter so you can be sure you get the right replacement.

The easiest way to fix an electric wiper motor is by replacing it. New motors are rather expensive, but you can get good bargains on used ones in wrecking yards if you are willing to remove it from a wrecked car yourself. Vacuum wiper motors can usually be made to work, even though they haven't operated for years; simply squirt a little oil into the motor and work the shaft back and forth so that the oil lubricates the mechanism. A vacuum wiper rejuvenated by this method will certainly not have the power and speed of a completely overhauled or new unit, but at least it will work. ♛

6. Removing Wiper Arm

7. Wiper Shaft Spline

8. Windshield Washer Assembly

1. Take care in repairing a motor for a power window, as the spring in the regulator is extra powerful. Motor and regulator should be removed as a unit. The regulator should be clamped in a vise, so the gears can't move, before you loosen the motor.

2. If adjustment is not obvious, mark the position of the bolts as they are, then loosen them for adjustments.

3. Slotted hole behind clamp bolt is to allow adjustment of window channel. To get to these adjustments, you have to remove the interior trim panel.

4. Loose, floppy, hand-operated wind wings (vent windows) are usually a result of loose springs on post.

5. Two of the most common wiper blade types are the Trico (A) and the Anco (B). Both of those shown are bayonet type; there are pin-types also.

6,7. A little tab under the wiper arm must be lifted to remove the arm. You can slip it off with a screwdriver. Arms will go back on the splined part in any position. If the blades don't stop in the right position or hit the window frame, you can reposition arm.

8. A windshield washer consists of a reservoir for the water/detergent mix, usually a plastic bag or box, and a small motor which pumps the fluid up through the hoses onto the windshield.

9. Most wiper motors attach to the firewall, with the linkage to the wiper arms being under the dashboard.

10. This is a late Ford wiper motor, which has the park switch adjustment inside the wiper. You should have a shop manual to go by if you're going to disassemble an electric wiper.

9. Wiper Motor and Linkage

10. Disassembled Wiper Motor

Improving Fuel Economy

If you're not yet too sick of the nostalgia fads to think back a few years, remember when no one cared about gas mileage? It wasn't really that long ago that you could buy a gallon of the now-precious motor-nectar for 32¢—even less if there was a local price war amongst the stations. Of all the wars we've ever been in, one that most people would like to see revived is the old-fashioned "gas war," a healthy symptom of a functioning capitalist system but probably gone forever like nickel beer. While you're remembering the good old days, ask yourself whatever happened to that '57 Chevy with 283 engine, 2-bbl. carb and 3-speed standard trans that went 100,000 miles and still got 17 mpg—or better with overdrive. Then jolt yourself back to the present where a new, full-size car is lucky to get 12 mpg after only 10,000 miles.

Everyone today is gas-conscious, and well they should be with the cost of the deadly fuel what it is. Anything that focuses the attention of the public like the "energy crisis" is bound to bring out the hucksters who'll sell you the trick mileage device just like they've been selling those phony "spark intensifiers" for the last 30 years. The plain truth is that fantastic gas mileage is very difficult to come by, although respectable gains can be made simply by applying common sense in driving and maintenance.

DRIVING STYLE

You've probably already read several articles about how to drive with a soft-boiled egg on the gas pedal, but it is true that the difference between a good driver and a poor one is probably 50% in overall gas mileage. Fast takeoffs, high speeds, rapid decelerations and sharp turns all take their toll not only in gasoline but also in *tires*. In one *Motor Trend* test of a new Vega, hard driving netted 19 mpg while very careful driving brightened the picture to an incredible 33 mpg! That's dramatic proof of the difference driving style makes. Whatever your personal opinion of the recent 55-mph speed limits, it is true that driving a constant 50 mph will save over 10% in mileage over driving a steady 65-70 mph. The most important change you can make in your driving is the simplest, just keep an eye on your gas gauge and think about 60¢ a gallon every time you leave a stoplight!

There are other tips that can save you fuel in your driving habits. A very simple one is to always get your gas fillups early in the morning. The gasoline is cold from sitting all night and it's denser than it is later in the day when the storage tanks have warmed up. Being denser, it means that you'll get more gasoline for the same money. For the same reason, the expansion of gasoline, you shouldn't let your tank get below half-full, because the more air that is in your tank around the gasoline, the more the gas in the tank can vaporize. Also, a full tank left parked in the hot sun can overflow and waste precious fuel. So don't leave your car parked in the hot sun when the tank is full (it's not good for the paint job anyway). You've probably all seen a car in traffic which accelerates away from a stoplight with gasoline gushing out of the filler neck, even when the cap is in place. This is a horrible waste of resources and usually is due to a poor original design in Detroit. Cars whose filler cap is behind the license plate rather than up on the quarter-panel have *very* short filler pipes going into the tank, allowing gas to easily slosh out when accelerating. If you've got one of these cars, you might think seriously of adding a longer filler pipe and relocating the neck to the quarter-panel.

Smoothness is the key word in driving for better mileage. Avoid any sudden moves, whether they be sudden stops or sudden accelerations. Most drivers don't realize that every time they use the brakes, they're converting their fuel's energy into heat energy in the brakes. The more you use the brakes, the more your

1. No, we're not suggesting you do this, but we do want to emphasize that a careful right foot is one of the best tricks for better gas mileage.

2. Whether you install one in your dash permanently or just use it for tune-ups, a vacuum gauge is something every weekend mechanic should have. They can help in engine diagnosis—and driving by one teaches you to drive economically and consistently.

3. With a simple hookup to your fuel line and speedometer cable, this gas mileage meter by Spacekom reads mpg from 0-40 while you drive, to tell you just where your driving style is hurting you in the pocketbook.

4. It's been proven over and over again by hot rodders that relieving exhaust backpressure with a set of steel-tube headers is worth not only horsepower and torque, but mileage as well. Depending on how bad your stock system is, you can pick up from 2-6 mpg with headers and duals.

5. Fuel-pressure regulators aren't all that they may be claimed to be, but an adjustable one does seem to make sense. You can slow fuel pump pressure down on most cars to about 3 lbs. for improved mileage.

6. Along with headers, an efficient exhaust system should also have some large, straight pipes and free-flow mufflers like these Corvair turbo units which are street-quiet, too.

momentum is killed and the more gas you'll have to use to resume speed again. When driving in traffic, accelerate slowly and get into high gear as soon as possible without lugging the engine. Coast wherever it is legal and safe to do so, and when you see a red light ahead, don't buzz right up to it and slam on the brakes. If you can drive lazily up, so that the light changes before you get there, you'll have saved some energy by not destroying your forward momentum. When you *do* have to slow down or stop, use your brakes instead of downshifting a standard transmission. Downshifting makes the engine rev up and you're actually using more fuel to go slower.

INSTRUMENTATION

The energy crisis has been a real bonus to the aftermarket instrument people. Even Detroit is starting to offer vacuum gauges and such as options on new cars. Basic instruments that can prove helpful in driving for mileage are the good old tachometer and a vacuum gauge. The tach will tell you when you're lugging the engine or over-revving it, both undesirable conditions for economy. The tach and vacuum gauge are both valuable for engine tuning purposes, and if you're going after maximum economy you'll be doing some tuning for sure. Vacuum gauges have been referred to as "poor man's engine analyzers," because if you know just how to read one you can tell quite a bit about an engine through its vacuum readings under different conditions. Many vacuum gauges are marked with colored ranges that indicate "late timing," "bad plugs," etc., and these can be handy reference on all but the newest cars. New cars have such low vacuum readings to start with that the scales don't apply to them. Most gauges will also have power, cruise, and economy positions on the dial. Naturally, the idea is to drive so that the needle spends

most of its time pointing to the economy setting.

Another type of instrument being sold in droves now is the "mileage meter," a gauge to tell you how poor or how good your use of fuel is *while you drive.* The idea is that when you see the needle drop substantially every time you put your foot in it, you'll start driving in a more economical manner. Some good devices can be purchased for around $40 and installed without too much trouble. These mpg meters hook up to the speedometer to measure distance, and a sensor goes into the fuel line to read how much fuel is being consumed, with the gauge on the dash putting the info into mpg for you. Two of the devices introduced recently are by Aviatric Ltd., Box 7, Romsey S05 8XS, Hampshire, England, and Spacekom, Inc. of Goleta, Calif. The Spacekom unit is available through Sears automotive departments and through Hickey Enterprises, 1645 Callens Rd., Ventura, Calif. 93003. Spacekom's reads from 4 to 30 mpg and is said to be accurate within 3%.

EXHAUST SYSTEM

Of course, the sky's the limit in redesigning the internal combustion engine for greater efficiency and economy, but you're interested in what can be done at home, on a small budget and without an engineering department, right? Fortunately there *are* a number of things you can do at a reasonable cost. The first and most basic step would of course be to make certain the engine is in top stock tune to begin with. It's been estimated that if every car in America were in top tune, there would be no energy crisis at all, since a high percentage of the cars on the road today need at least some type of tuning or minor electrical parts that are robbing their owners of considerable mileage. Once you've tuned your engine for top economy in stock form, you have a baseline from which to

work in comparing the effects of any modifications you make after that.

The biggest overall improvements on most cars can be made in the exhaust system. For years, dual exhaust systems have been touted as producing more power and acceleration, but people are finding now that they make just as much sense as a mileage modification. Freeing up the backpressure in your exhaust system is one of the few modifications you can make to a car that will benefit both performance *and* economy. Switching from a restrictive, stock single-exhaust system to a dual setup with two low-restriction mufflers should be worth one or two mpg—at a very reasonable cost. And when we say low-restriction mufflers, we don't mean the noisy little glasspacks sold everywhere for $9.95. Tests have shown that there are some excellent stock-design mufflers which have less backpressure (and consequently more power and economy) than the small glasspacks, even though the latter are straight-through design and the stock type are generally baffled. The best muffler we've ever seen is the one made for the old turbocharged model of the Corvair. Most of the major muffler companies have a replacement for this item which is selling like proverbial hotcakes today. With a 2½-in. inlet, a 2¼-in. core and a 2¼-in. outlet, it will breathe as well as any other muffler and yet is as quiet as most stock mufflers and much quieter than the usual glasspack. The Chrysler Imperial, International Harvester (part No. 376607-C1) and Chevrolet L-88 mufflers are also excellent, free-flowing and quiet mufflers.

Something many of you may have shied away from is a set of steel tubing exhaust *headers.* Up till now, it's been only the hot rod set which has benefited from backpressure-reducing headers, but now it should be clear to even the transportation-only crowd that these are one of the best mileage-improving steps

4

5

6

Fuel Economy

you can take for the money invested. Most sets run $60 to $100 for a V-8 engine in a local speed shop or from a mail-order house, and on the average car they can pay for themselves in a year or so of driving. Our personal '66 Mustang with '71 302 engine (2-bbl.) went from 14.7 mpg with a stock single-exhaust system to an easy-on-the-pocketbook 20 mpg just by switching to headers and a pair of Corvair turbo mufflers! A gain like that would be hard to beat with any other single improvement at the same cost, and has the added benefit of more power and acceleration too. California Highway Patrol inspectors have remarked that the car is easily as quiet as many of the brand new cars they have inspected. Despite this rosy picture, advice on headers should not be without some cautions. In the East, where salts are used on winter roads, headers will rust out sooner than stock cast-iron manifolds, so replacement cost becomes a factor to weigh. Since the tubular headers do such a good job of scavenging the cylinders, they can create a *lean* condition; but on most cars a step up of one or two jet sizes in the carburetor cures this. Also, header bolts have a tendency to loosen up after awhile, and their tightness should be checked at normal underhood maintenance intervals.

OTHER ENGINE TIDBITS

We don't have the scope here to go into details of complicated internal modifications so we'll concentrate on the simpler steps to better mileage. If you feel confident that you can change a camshaft at home, then there are a number of new designs on the aftermarket by Isky, Crane, Racer Brown, Crower and others, profiled specifically to give better gas mileage and low-end torque. There is some sacrifice in top-end speed, but these cams provide more drivability than even stock profiles. You may realize gains of one or two mpg with one of these cams, but you'll have to weigh the mileage advantages against the cost and trouble of switching cams.

Since it is common sense that a hotter engine will better vaporize the fuel-air mixture in the intake manifold, just switching to a hotter thermostat may give you a slight mileage edge. This would apply to older cars with thermostats of 160°-180°, since newer cars already have 190°-205° thermostats. Just make sure that your cooling system is in good condition and is able to stand the extra heat.

Smaller carburetors, or smaller jets in your existing carburetor, have always been a popular subject area for mileage discussions. The carburetor companies have recently come out with what they call "emissions-mileage" carburetors, which are basically just leaned-out. Switching from a 4-bbl. carb to a 2-bbl. has always been a popular mileage trick, but you should measure both carburetors to be sure you're really gaining something. Some 4-bbl.'s get *better* gas mileage than some 2-bbl.'s because of very small primary throttle bores in the 4-bbl., especially with the modern "spread-bore" designs. By just keeping your foot out of the secondary side of the carburetor and perhaps installing jets one size smaller, your 4-bbl. should do as well as most other carbs you could replace it with—without spending any money. After all, what good are all these mileage tips if they all cost you more than the savings you'd make? When re-jetting your carburetor, make sure the engine is in tune, and keep going down in jet size until you get a noticeable lean-stumble condition while driving, then go back *up* one more jet size to eliminate the stumble. When driving at sustained freeway speeds, you might pay closer attention to the temp gauge now, since the leaner engine will run hotter. .

We've warned you about the hucksters with their sensationally advertised ignition goodies for $4.95, but there really are some things to be done in the spark department besides keeping the engine tuned and timed. Some good things always come out of a crisis, and the gas crisis and tough smog legislation have spurred Detroit to develop ignition systems that keep pollutant levels low over a long period of time. The best of these devices are the new electronic ignitions.

1. The new "spread-bore" carb designs can sometimes provide better mileage than a 2-bbl. carb because the small primaries are economical, yet the seldom-used secondaries give you the performance when you need it.

2. Water injectors have been around in one form or another since WW II, but APO's unit admits vapors from a liquid chemical to idle-air port on your carburetor. The manufacturer claims better mileage, more power and lower emissions, some of which has been backed up by independent magazine tests for mileage gains.

3. Aftermarket intake manifolds with the new single-plane designs like the Edelbrock Torker and Streetmaster, Weiand X-celerator, and Offenhauser Port-O-Sonic, coupled with emissions carbs like the Holley 6619, have shown significant improvements in late-model engine efficiency.

4. If your car doesn't already have a factory clutch fan, an investment in an aftermarket fiberglass or alloy fan can save up to one mpg by taking less horsepower to drive.

5. Two-barrel carbs can be adapted to most of the new mileage-emissions intake manifolds with a plate like this that locates the carb closer to the front than the rear. Some engines also show gains with a plenum divider plate like this under the carburetor.

6. Owners of Chrysler Corp. cars are lucky in the ignition department. The now-famous Chrysler electronic ignition is available from dealers in kit form for pre-'73 Mopars. At $68, it's a bargain in maintenance as well as emissions and mileage.

7. Even if you don't have a Mopar, you won't have to trade in your car to have the benefits of electronic ignition. Aftermarket units like this Hays Magna-Pulse breakerless are available in easily installed kits for Fords, GM, and even Mopars.

1

2

Chrysler was the first with a standard-equipment system and it has proven to be virtually maintenance-free. Some of the aftermarket companies are now making these systems too, and the best of them are *pointless* types like the Chrysler. By replacing the points with a magnetic pickup unit, the engine will stay in tune much longer (no point gaps to deteriorate), and the hotter spark keeps the plugs firing longer. Although there probably is no mileage gain over a perfectly tuned stock system, the pointless ignitions don't deteriorate between tune-ups;

so over the long run, emissions are down and mileage should be improved slightly. A good unit like the Hays Magna-Pulse (17905 Sky Park Blvd., Unit H, Irvine, Calif. 92664) will also improve cold starting and acceleration. Hays has units for converting your stock GM or Ford distributor, as well as a unit for Chryslers. Chrysler owners are advised, though, that they can update their older Mopars with a kit from their dealer for about the same price. Accel also has a breakerless electronic ignition kit for all popular cars. Bad plug wires are hard to

track down without special gear, and with today's hot underhood temperatures it's a good idea to replace your plug wires every 24,000 miles to be safe. When installing an electronic ignition, the manufacturers recommend installing new wires (preferably magnetic suppression wire with fiberglass core wrapped with monel wire) at the same time in order to ensure full efficiency.

Other mileage bolt-ons for the engine would have to include the new breed of lightweight cooling fans. Since it takes a certain amount of horsepower to drive a

3

4

5

7

6

Fuel Economy

stock steel fan, it makes sense that replacing it with a fiberglass or aluminum type would save some power. Many cars now have factory "clutch" fans that disengage at higher rpm to save power, and these work well also. The fiberglass and aluminum fans sold in speed shops and auto parts stores, in addition to being light, are supposed to flatten out at higher rpm to create less drag and soak up less horsepower. They also jazz up the engine compartment's looks, if that matters to you.

Fuel pressure regulators are now being touted as mileage tricks, but it's not that simple. Sure, if you cut down the fuel pressure to the carburetor you'll probably use less gas, but what about starving out when you're on the freeway? If for some reason your car has excessive fuel pump pressure, then by all means get an adjustable pressure regulator and cut down the flow. On most V-8 cars you can cut the fuel pressure down to about 3 lbs. and still have the car drivable.

While we're still on the subject of carburetion and fuel systems, this would be a good time to mention intake manifolds. The search for an intake manifold that can reduce exhaust emissions and still make power has spurred development of some new, single-plane aftermarket intake manifolds that work so well they may be copied by Detroit for '75 and '76 cars. The important thing to know about these manifolds, for you who are economy-minded, is that in addition to more drivability and lower emissions, they can also help the engine be a little more miserly with its petrol. An *efficient* engine should have a clean report card on emissions, power, *and* mileage—and that's just what these manifolds are designed to boost, efficiency. Edelbrock's new Streetmaster design is bringing a new breed of customer to speed shops—guys who never before would have bought a piece of speed equipment and now will buy anything to get decent gas mileage. Using a stock carburetor, cars whose manifolds are swapped for the Streetmaster consistently get better performance and improved economy by 10% or more. The other aftermarket manifold companies may also have something for you—and these parts are worth some investigation, if not from the mileage standpoint, at least from the "pre-smog motor" drivability they put back into a rough-running late-model car.

AN ECONOMICAL DRIVETRAIN

Everyone knows that a manual transmission provides for better gas mileage than an automatic transmission. Even though we have progressed out of the "slushbox" era to some really efficient 3-speed automatics, they still have some slippage, greater internal friction, and a hydraulic pump that takes extra power to drive. You probably knew there was a mpg or two difference when you bought your car, but you got the automatic anyway because you didn't know the energy crisis was coming, right? We're not going to suggest that you exchange your whole converter/trans package for the equivalent stick-shift pieces, because that's a lot of work—but some people are doing that today. Unless you're really attached to your car, it might be easier to trade yours in for a car that *has* standard-shift.

If you already have a standard transmission, good; but there is even more you can do. An overdrive unit is one of the best mileage goodies there is, and they're still available, both from the aftermarket and from any of those saviours of the backyard mechanic, the junkyards. Overdrive used to be a common factory option almost as long as cars have been built, but by the late '60's interest in the option had dwindled to the point where the manufacturers decided to drop it. Now that we are in an energy crisis, the importance of overdrive in fuel savings may bring it back again to the option list. Until then, you'll have to scour the wrecking yards to come up with a late-model overdrive for your make of car. If you already have a standard transmission, it won't be too difficult to make the conversion. You may have to change the driveshaft length to accommodate the new transmission and make the electrical or mechanical connections for the overdrive switch, but other than that it shouldn't be too difficult a job. One fellow we know of just did this with his 1972 Gremlin (304 V-8), and with no other changes to the car got 23 mpg on the highway!

If you have an automatic transmission, or can't find a rare overdrive unit in a wrecking yard, there is still a way out. The Hone Mfg. Co., 11748 E. Washington Blvd., Santa Fe Springs, Calif. 90670, makes 30% overdrive units to fit just about every kind of vehicle. Instead of attaching directly to the transmission, the Hone unit is installed in the driveline either just aft of the transmission or just ahead of the rear end, with its own crossmember. An added benefit of an

overdrive unit is potentially increased performance around town. For instance, if the present rear end gear ratio in your vehicle is 3.23, then in top gear and with overdrive engaged this ratio would drop to the Bonneville Salt Flat level of 2.26! This means that you could easily change your rear end gears for a 4.10 ratio for more acceleration and performance around town, and still have great economy in overdrive, where the ratio would drop to 2.87.

It should be obvious to you now that rear end gearing has a lot to do with gas mileage. A lower-numerical ratio allows the engine to just loaf along when cruising, and although it will reduce the low-speed acceleration and performance, a ratio change like this can definitely im-

1. If you can't afford an overdrive, just changing your basic final drive ratio in the rear end can prove of substantial benefit in mileage.

2. Few factory overdrives were made in the last 5 years, so chances of finding one may be slim, but whatever kind of vehicle you have, you can still have overdrive in the form of the Hone-O-Drive, which installs in the driveline between the rear end and transmission. Also a 30% unit, it'll drop a 3.23 gear to 2.26!

3. If you're lucky, like this 1972 Gremlin owner, you may find a late overdrive 3-speed for your car in a wrecking yard. With a 304 V-8, this setup produced 23 mpg on the road with 30% overdrive engaged.

4. If you have the know-how and the time to change a camshaft, some good gains in both mileage and low-end torque can be yours with one of the new RV cams like Isky's Mile-A-Mor or Crower's Gas-Stretcher. Like the single-plane intake manifolds, these cams can be worth the investment for drivability improvement alone.

5. Studying the economy results in this chart, you can see that just by juggling rear-end ratios, a car with a bigger engine can give the same performance with better mileage, even though with the same gear a smaller engine will always get better economy.

6. Some of the more commonly talked about mileage-improving steps are compared here with their actual gains on a typical big car, with surprising results. Almost all of the mileage modifications also improved the car's 0-60 mph performance times, too.

1

2

3

4

AXLE RATIO	3.23	2.93	2.56	2.29
390-CU.-IN. ENGINE Fuel Economy (mpg) Level Road—50 mph	17.4	18.2	19.7	21.1
Simulated City	13.7	14.0	14.6	15.0
Simulated Highway	15.0	15.9	16.5	17.7
Performance 0-60 Time (secs.)	9.42	9.88	10.41	10.77
420-CU.-IN. ENGINE Fuel Economy (mpg) Level Road—50 mph	16.6	18.0	19.1	20.7
Simulated City	13.6	13.8	14.1	14.9
Simulated Highway	14.6	15.5	16.4	17.4
Performance 0-60 Time (secs.)	9.02	9.05	9.35	9.99

5

ECONOMY AND PERFORMANCE	50 mph level road	Simulated city	Simulated highway	0-60 time
Base Line Run 420-cu.-in. engine 2.29 axle ratio	20.7	14.9	17.4	9.99
Same as above except: with radial-ply tires	21.1	14.7	17.5	—
Same as above except: with 10.5 to 1 compression ratio	21.4	15.2	17.6	9.22
Same as above except: with free flowing dual exhaust system	21.7	15.2	18.1	8.68
Same as above except: with fan clutch	22.2	15.7	18.4	8.36
Same as above except: with 4-bbl. carburetor	22.6	15.7	18.5	7.62

6

prove fuel mileage. Even a big car with a big engine can give better mileage than an intermediate car when equipped with the right ratio, and may still have better performance. Check the chart with this story for some suprising facts about big-car mileage. If you can't afford the overdrive route, then maybe what you should do is just change your rear end ratio to a lower-numerical one. It's not a job that is within the capabilities of every weekend mechanic, but most dealerships can do the job for you.

CHASSIS TUNING FOR ECONOMY

Tuning a car for economy can encompass many facets of a vehicle besides just the engine—there's some gasoline to be saved in the chassis, too. Your brakes, tires and front end alignment all have to do with the fuel that is consumed to power the car down the road. You can't "detune" your brakes the way you can your engine by switching to a smaller carburetor, but what you can do is eliminate some of the possible drag there that may be eating into your highway mileage. If you have front disc brakes, there's not much you can do with them, for they have a certain amount of drag inherent in their design and there are no adjustments for this, but you *can* do something with your drum brakes, which is why drum brakes are probably more economical in terms of mileage. Just switching to heavy-duty shoe-return springs and eliminating the self-adjusting mechanisms (there are kits for this job available in most auto parts stores) will ensure that there is no power-robbing rolling resistance in the braking system. If you're planning a brake overhaul anyway, then go one step further and make these changes too.

Since your tires are the final contact between your car and the road, they are very much a part of a car's fuel econo-

my picture. How they're inflated, aligned, and even what type of tire they are has a lot to do with the vehicle's rolling resistance. There has been considerable talk of late (spurred by heavy advertising programs from the tire companies) about how radial-ply tires will save you gasoline. It's true. Because of their more flexible sidewall construction, radial-ply tires offer less rolling resistance because there is less energy wasted on heat and friction between the plies than on a conventional or bias-belted tire. There should be at least a half-mpg to be saved on steady highway travel with radials, but less around town because the rolling resistance is less of a factor in stop-and-go driving. Because radials last longer than conventional tires (although they naturally cost more, too) they may also save you money in the long run of car ownership by reducing costs of tire rotating, mounting and balancing. It's false economy to run inexpensive tires if you do a lot of driving, because you'll be spending money for these tire services more often.

It goes without saying that your tires, of whatever construction, should be cared for regularly. Keeping the front end aligned properly and the tires at optimum inflation will not only assure you of the best possible fuel mileage but will also save money on the life of the tires themselves.

BUYING A CAR

We've shown you some of the things you can do with a car to improve fuel economy, but if you're not the home-mechanic type (then why are you reading this book?), then you can at least look for some of these econo-features in the next car you buy. Studying our chart will show you that small cars aren't the only ones capable of 20 mpg, so don't sell the intermediate cars short if you have a family that can use one. Some of the features or options to look for in a car would be radial tires, standard transmission, 5-speed or overdrive if available, de-clutching fan, dual exhausts, numerically low axle ratio, and a small engine. Don't purchase such options as air conditioning (eats at least one mpg or more), or power steering unless you really *need* them. Not all manufacturers offer them, but cruise control and electronic fuel injection are two options that are worth looking into for their savings in petrol.

Not all of the tips we've included in this story will give you the same results our tests have given, but the trends will be the same. A free-flowing exhaust system, for instance, will save in varying amounts depending upon how restrictive the car's stock system was. If this chapter doesn't give you information you can apply to your present car, at least you'll know what to look for when shopping for a new or used one. Not knowing where the price or availability of gasoline is going in the future, more and more, mileage-saving steps will be worth the initial investment cost compared to the long-run savings in fuel costs. And keeping the present environmental state in mind, what we do to save fuel ensures there'll be some around tomorrow.

Tune-Up Specifications

American Motors 4

YEAR	ENGINE		CARBURETOR		FLOAT LEVEL (INS.)	INITIAL TIMING		DISTRIBUTOR	
	CU. INS.	HP	MAKE	TYPE		STD. TRANS	AUTO. TRANS.	POINT GAP (INS.)	DWELL
1977	121	80	Holley	2-bbl.	.42	12° BTDC[2]	12° BTDC[3]	1	1

1 Electronic ignition standard. 2 10° BTDC on high-altitude cars. 3 8° BTDC on California cars.

American Motors 6

YEAR	CU. INS.	HP	MAKE	TYPE	FLOAT LEVEL	STD. TRANS	AUTO. TRANS.	POINT GAP (INS.)	DWELL
1977	232	90	Carter	1-bbl.	.476	8° BTDC[16]	10° BTDC	12	12
	258	95	Carter	1-bbl.	.476	6° BTDC[17]	8° BTDC[17]	12	12
	258	120	Carter	2-bbl.	.476	6° BTDC	8° BTDC	12	12
1976	232	90	Carter	1-bbl.	.476	8° BTDC	8° BTDC	12	12
	258	95	Carter	1-bbl.	.476	6° BTDC	8° BTDC	12	12
	258	120	Carter	2-bbl.	.250	6° BTDC	8° BTDC	12	12
1975	232	100	Carter	1-bbl.	15/32	5° BTDC[11]	5° BTDC[11]	12	-
	258	110	Carter	1-bbl.	15/32	5° BTDC[11]	5° BTDC[11]	12	-
1974	232	100	Carter	1-bbl.	15/32	5° BTDC[1]	5° BTDC[1]	.016	31°-34°
	258	110	Carter	1-bbl.	15/32	3° BTDC[1]	3° BTDC[1]	.016	31°-34°
1973	232	100	Carter	1-bbl.	29/64	5° BTDC[1]	5° BTDC[1]	.016	31°-34°
	258	110	Carter	1-bbl.	29/64	3° BTDC[1]	3° BTDC[1]	.016	31°-34°
1972	232	100	Carter	1-bbl.	29/64	5° BTDC[1]	5° BTDC[1]	.016	31°-34°
	258	110	Carter	1-bbl.	29/64	3° BTDC[1]	3° BTDC[1]	.016	31°-34°
1971	232	135	Carter	1-bbl.	29/64	3° BTDC[1]	5° BTDC[1]	.016	31°-34°
	258	150	Carter	1-bbl.	29/64	5° BTDC[1]	5° BTDC[1]	.016	31°-34°
1970	199	128	Carter	1-bbl.	29/64	3° ± 1° BTDC[1]	3° ± 1° BTDC[1]	.016	31°-34°
	232	145	Carter	1-bbl.	29/64	3° ± 1° BTDC[1]	3° ± 1° BTDC[1]	.016	31°-34°
	232	155	Autolite	2-bbl.	7/32	3° ± 1° BTDC[1]	3° ± 1° BTDC[1]	.016	31°-34°

1 At 500 rpm (vacuum advance hose disconnected).
2 600 with Exhaust Gas Recirculation (EGR).
3 550 with Exhaust Gas Recirculation (EGR).
4 California cars 700 rpm.
5 California cars 600 rpm.
6 Place in drive, set parking brake firmly, do not accelerate engine.
7 Lowest cylinder must be more than 75% of highest cylinder pressure.
8 Maximum variation 10 psi between cylinders.
9 Matador Wagons 600 rpm.
10 Matador 650 rpm.

American Motors V-8

YEAR	CU. INS.	HP	MAKE	TYPE	FLOAT LEVEL	STD. TRANS	AUTO. TRANS.	POINT GAP (INS.)	DWELL
1977	304	120	Motorcraft	2-bbl.	.78	—	10° BTDC[8]	7	7
	360	140	Motorcraft	2-bbl.	.78	—	10° BTDC[8]	7	7
1976	304	120	Motorcraft	2-bbl.	13/32	5° BTDC	10° BTDC[8]	7	7
	360	140	Motorcraft	2-bbl.	13/32	—	10° BTDC[8]	7	7
	360	180	Motorcraft	4-bbl.	.90	—	10° BTDC[8]	7	7
	401	N/A	Motorcraft	4-bbl.	.90	—	10° BTDC[8]	7	7
1975	304	150	Motorcraft	2-bbl.	13/32	5° BTDC	5° BTDC	7	—
	360	285	Motorcraft	2-bbl.	13/32	5° BTDC	5° BTDC	7	—
	360	295	Motorcraft	4-bbl.	9/100	—	5° BTDC	7	—
	401	345	Motorcraft	4-bbl.	9/100	—	5° BTDC	7	—
1974	304	150	Motorcraft	2-bbl.	13/32	5° BTDC[1]	5° BTDC[1]	.016	29°-31°
	360	175	Motorcraft	2-bbl.	13/32	5° BTDC[1]	5° BTDC[1]	.016	29°-31°
	360	195	Motorcraft	4-bbl.	13/16	5° BTDC[1]	5° BTDC[1]	.016	29°-31°
	360	220	Motorcraft	4-bbl.	13/16	5° BTDC[1]	5° BTDC[1]	.016	29°-31°
	401	235	Motorcraft	4-bbl.	13/16	5° BTDC[1]	5° BTDC[1]	.016	29°-31°
1973	304	150	Autolite	2-bbl.	3/8	5° BTDC[1]	5° BTDC[1]	.016	29°-31°
	360	175	Autolite	2-bbl.	3/8	5° BTDC[1]	5° BTDC[1]	.016	29°-31°
	360	195	Autolite	4-bbl.	13/16	5° BTDC[1]	5° BTDC[1]	.016	29°-31°
	401	255	Autolite	4-bbl.	13/16	5° BTDC[1]	5° BTDC[1]	.016	29°-31°
1972	304	150	Autolite	2-bbl.	3/8	5° BTDC[1]	5° BTDC[1]	.016	29°-31°
	360	175	Autolite	2-bbl.	3/8	5° BTDC[1]	5° BTDC[1]	.016	29°-31°
	360	175	Autolite	4-bbl.	13/16	5° BTDC[1]	5° BTDC[1]	.016	29°-31°
	401	175	Autolite	4-bbl.	13/16	5° BTDC[1]	5° BTDC[1]	.016	29°-31°
1971	304	210	Autolite	2-bbl.	3/8	2.5° BTDC[1]	2.5° BTDC[1]	.016	29°-31°
	360	245	Autolite	2-bbl.	3/8	2.5° BTDC[1]	2.5° BTDC[1]	.016	29°-31°
	360	285	Autolite	4-bbl.	13/16	2.5° BTDC[1]	2.5° BTDC[1]	.016	29°-31°
	401	330	Autolite	4-bbl.	13/16	2.5° BTDC[1]	2.5° BTDC[1]	.016	29°-31°
1970	304	210	Autolite	2-bbl.	3/8	5° ± 1° BTDC[1]	5° ± 1° BTDC[1]	.016	29°-31°
	360	245	Autolite	2-bbl.	3/8	5° ± 1° BTDC[1]	5° ± 1° BTDC[1]	.016	29°-31°
	360	290	Autolite	4-bbl.	13/16	5° ± 1° BTDC[1]	5° ± 1° BTDC[1]	.016	29°-31°
	390	325	Autolite	4-bbl.	13/16	5° ± 1° BTDC[1]	5° ± 1° BTDC[1]	.016	29°-31°
	390	340	Autolite	4-bbl.	13/16	TDC ± 1°[1,2]	TDC ± 1°[1,2]	.016	29°-31°

1 Set at 500 rpm with distributor vacuum advance hose disconnected and plugged.
2 390-cu.-in., 4-bbl.; effective with engine code 209x26 (type 2 distributor).
3 California cars—700 rpm.
4 Lowest cylinder pressure must be more than 75% of highest cylinder.

Buick, Oldsmobile, Pontiac V-6

YEAR	CU. INS.	HP	MAKE	TYPE	FLOAT LEVEL	STD. TRANS	AUTO. TRANS.	POINT GAP (INS.)	DWELL
1977	231	105	Roch.	2-bbl.	7/16[4]	12° BTDC	12° BTDC	1	—
1976	231	105	Roch.	2-bbl.	7/16[3]	12° BTDC	12° BTDC	1	—
1975	231	110	Roch.	2-bbl.	5/32	12° BTDC	12° BTDC	1	—

1 High Energy Ignition; no points used.
2 Skyhawk fuel pump is electric; psi should be 3.0-4.5.
3 Carburetor #17056143 is 15/32-in.
4 Carburetors #17057112 through 17057123 should be 19/32-in.; #17057404 & 05 should be 1/2-in.

Buick V-8

YEAR	CU. INS.	HP	MAKE	TYPE	FLOAT LEVEL	STD. TRANS	AUTO. TRANS.	POINT GAP (INS.)	DWELL
1977	301	135	Roch.	2-bbl.	11/32	—	12° BTDC	10	10
	305	145	Roch.	2-bbl.	19/32	—	8° BTDC	10	10
	350	135	Roch.	2-bbl.	15/32	—	12° BTDC	10	10
	350	155[11]	Roch.	4-bbl.	5/16[14]	—	12° BTDC	10	10
	403	185	Roch.	4-bbl.	13/32	—	12° BTDC	10	10
1976	260	110	Roch.	2-bbl.	1/8	—	12° BTDC	10	10
	350	140	Roch.	2-bbl.	15/32	—	12° BTDC	10	10

MAKE	SPARK PLUG			IDLE SPEED		FUEL PUMP PRESSURE	COMPRESSION
	TYPE	GAP (INS.)	TORQUE (FT.-LBS.)	STD. TRANS.†	AUTO. TRANS.††	(PSI)	(PSI)
CH.	N-8L	.033-.037	29	900	800	5.0-6.5	135

MAKE	SPARK PLUG			IDLE SPEED		FUEL PUMP PRESSURE	COMPRESSION
CH.	N12Y	.033-.037	25-30	600[15]	550[14]	4.0-5.0	140
CH.	N12Y	.033-.037	25-30	600	550[14]	4.0-5.0	150
CH.	N12Y	.033-.037	25-30	600	600[14]	4.0-5.0	150
CH.	N12Y	.033-.037	25-30	850	550[13,14]	4.0-5.0	140
CH.	N12Y	.033-.037	25-30	850[15]	550[13,14]	4.0-5.0	150
CH.	N12Y	.033-.037	25-30	600	700[13,14]	4.0-5.0	150
CH.	N12Y	.033-.037	25-30	600	550[13,14]	4-5	140
CH.	N12Y	.033-.037	25-30	600	550[13,14]	4-5	150
CH.	N12Y	.033-.037	25-30	700[2]	600[3]	4-5.5 @ 500 rpm	7
CH.	N12Y	.033-.037	25-30	700[2]	600[3]	4-5.5 @ 500 rpm	7
CH.	N12Y	.033-.037	25-30	700[9]	600[10]	4-5 @ 500 rpm	7
CH.	N12Y	.033-.037	25-30	700[9]	600[10]	4-5 @ 500 rpm	7
CH.	N12Y	.033-.037	25-30	600[4]	550[5,6]	4-5 @ 500 rpm	7
CH.	N12Y	.033-.037	25-30	600[4]	550[5,6]	4-5 @ 500 rpm	7
CH.	N12Y	.033-.037	25-30	700	600[2]	4-5 @ 500 rpm	185[8]
CH.	N12Y	.033-.037	25-30	700	600[2]	4-5 @ 500 rpm	185[8]
CH.	N14Y	.033-.037	25-30	600	550	4-5 @ 500 rpm	145[8]
CH.	N14Y	.033-.037	25-30	600	550	4-5 @ 500 rpm	145[8]
CH.	N14Y	.033-.037	25-30	600	550	4-5 @ 500 rpm	145[8]

11 3° BTDC on California cars.
12 Electronic ignition standard.
13 Set idle with transmission in drive and parking brake applied. Do not accelerate engine.
14 700 rpm on California cars.
15 850 rpm on California cars.
16 10° BTDC on California cars.
17 10° BTDC over 4000 ft.
†In neutral.
††In drive.

MAKE	SPARK PLUG			IDLE SPEED		FUEL PUMP PRESSURE	COMPRESSION
CH.	RN12Y	.033-.037	25-30	—	600[3]	5.0-6.5	140
CH.	RN12Y	.033-.037	25-30	—	600[3]	5.0-6.5	140
CH.	N12Y	.033-.037	25-30	750	700	5.0-6.5	140
CH.	N12Y	.033-.037	25-30	—	700	5.0-6.5	140
CH.	N12Y	.033-.037	25-30	—	700	5.0-6.5	140
CH.	N12Y	.033-.037	25-30	—	700	5.0-6.5	140
CH.	N12Y	.033-.037	25-30	750	700[6]	5-6.5 @ 500 rpm	140
CH.	N12Y	.033-.037	25-30	750	700[6]	5-6.5 @ 500 rpm	140
CH.	N12Y	.033-.037	25-30	—	700[6]	5-6.5 @ 500 rpm	140
CH.	N12Y	.033-.037	25-30	—	700[6]	5-6.5 @ 500 rpm	140
CH.	N12Y	.033-.037	25-30	750	700	5-6.5 @ 500 rpm	4
CH.	N12Y	.033-.037	25-30	700	750	5-6.5 @ 500 rpm	4
CH.	N12Y	.033-.037	25-30	700	750	5-6.5 @ 500 rpm	4
CH.	N12Y	.033-.037	25-30	750	700	5-6.5 @ 500 rpm	4
CH.	N12Y	.033-.037	25-30	750	700	5-6.5 @ 500 rpm	4
CH.	N12Y	.033-.037	25-30	750	700	5-6.5 @ 500 rpm	4
CH.	N12Y	.033-.037	25-30	750	700	5-6.5 @ 500 rpm	4
CH.	N12Y	.033-.037	25-30	750	650[3]	5-6.5 @ 500 rpm	4,5
CH.	N12Y	.033-.037	25-30	750	700	5-6.5 @ 500 rpm	4,5
CH.	N12Y	.033-.037	25-30	750	700	5-6.5 @ 500 rpm	4,5
CH.	N12Y	.033-.037	25-30	750	650[3]	5-6.5 @ 500 rpm	4,5
CH.	N12Y	.033-.037	25-30	750	650	5-6.5 @ 500 rpm	185[4,5]
CH.	N12Y	.033-.037	25-30	750	650	5-6.5 @ 500 rpm	185[4,5]
CH.	N12Y	.033-.037	25-30	750	650	5-6.5 @ 500 rpm	185[4,5]
CH.	N12Y	.033-.037	25-30	750	650	5-6.5 @ 500 rpm	200[4,5]
CH.	N12Y	.033-.037	25-30	650	600	5-6.5 @ 500 rpm	145[4,5]
CH.	N12Y	.033-.037	25-30	650	600	5-6.5 @ 500 rpm	145[4,5]
CH.	N12Y	.033-.037	25-30	650	600	5-6.5 @ 500 rpm	145[4,5]
CH.	N12Y	.033-.037	25-30	650	600	5-6.5 @ 500 rpm	145[4,5]
CH.	N12Y	.033-.037	25-30	650	600	5-6.5 @ 500 rpm	145[4,5]

5 Maximum variation: 10 psi between cylinders.
6 Set idle with transmission in drive and parking brake applied. Do not accelerate engine.
7 Electronic ignition standard.
8 5° BTDC on California cars.　†In neutral.　††In drive.

MAKE	SPARK PLUG			IDLE SPEED		FUEL PUMP PRESSURE	COMPRESSION
AC	R46TC[5]	.040	15-25	600	600	4.2-5.7[2]	N/A
AC	R44SX	.060	15-25	800	600	4.0-5.0[2]	N/A
AC	R445X	.060	15-25	600	600	3-4.5	N/A

5 Some cars may be equipped with R46TSX; if so, gap to .060-in.
†In neutral.　††In drive.

MAKE	SPARK PLUG			IDLE SPEED		FUEL PUMP PRESSURE	COMPRESSION
AC	R46TS	.040	15-25	—	600	4.25-5.75	2
AC	R45TS	.045	15-25	—	500	7.5-9.0	2
AC	R46TS	.040	15-25	—	600	5.0-6.5	2
AC	R46TS	.040	15-25	—	600[12]	5.0-6.5 [13]	2
AC	R46TS	.040	15-25	—	600[12]	4.25-5.75[13]	2
AC	R44SX	.060	15-25	—	600	4.0-5.0	2
AC	R45TSX	.060	15-25	—	600	5.0-6.5	2

Buick V-8

YEAR	CU. INS.	HP	MAKE	TYPE	FLOAT LEVEL (INS.)	STD. TRANS	AUTO. TRANS.	POINT GAP (INS.)	DWELL
	350	155	Roch.	4-bbl.	5/16	—	12° BTDC	[10]	[10]
	455	205	Roch.	4-bbl.	15/32	—	12° BTDC	[10]	[10]
1975	260	110	Roch.	2-bbl.	5/32	—	12° BTDC	[10]	—
	350	145	Roch.	2-bbl.	9/16	—	12° BTDC	[10]	—
	350	165	Roch.	4-bbl.	1/2	—	12° BTDC	[10]	—
	455	205	Roch.	4-bbl.	1/2	—	12° BTDC	[10]	—
1974	350	150	Roch.	2-bbl.	15/32	N/A	4° BTDC	.016	30° ± 1°
	350	175	Roch.	4-bbl.	15/32	N/A	4° BTDC	.016	30° ± 1°
	455	175	Roch.	2-bbl.	3/8	N/A	4° BTDC	.016	30° ± 1°
	455	210	Roch.	4-bbl.	3/8	N/A	4° BTDC	.016	30° ± 1°
	455	245[9]	Roch.	4-bbl.	3/8	N/A	4° BTDC	.016	30° ± 1°
1973	350	150	Roch.	2-bbl.	15/32	4° BTDC	4° BTDC	.016	30° ± 1°
	350	175	Roch.	4-bbl.	13/32[5]	4° BTDC	4° BTDC	.016	30° ± 1°
	455	225	Roch.	4-bbl.	3/8	4° BTDC	4° BTDC	.016	30° ± 1°
	455	Stage 1 260	Roch.	4-bbl.	15/32	10° BTDC	10° BTDC	.016	30° ± 1°
1972	350	150-155	Roch.	2-bbl.	15/32	4° BTDC[6]	4° BTDC[6]	.016	30° ± 2°
	350	175-195	Roch.	4-bbl.	15/32	—	4° BTDC[6]	.016	30° ± 2°
	455	225-260	Roch.	4-bbl.	13/32[5]	4° BTDC[6]	4° BTDC[6]	.016	30° ± 2°
	455	270 Stage 1	Roch.	4-bbl.	3/8	8° BTDC[6]	10° BTDC[6]	.016	30° ± 2°
1971	350	230	Roch.	2-bbl.	—	—	10° BTDC[6]	.016	30° ± 2°
	350	260	Roch.	4-bbl.	15/32	—	4° BTDC[6]	.016	30° ± 2°
	455	315	Roch.	4-bbl.	15/32	6° BTDC[6]	4° BTDC[6]	.016	30° ± 2°
	455	330	Roch.	4-bbl.	13/32[5]	6° BTDC[6]	4° BTDC[6]	.016	30° ± 2°
	455	345 Stage 1	Roch.	4-bbl.	3/8	10° BTDC[6]	10° BTDC[6]	.016	30° ± 2°
1970	350	260	Roch.	2-bbl.	15/32	6° BTDC[6]	6° BTDC[6]	.016	30° ± 1°
	350	285	Roch.	4-bbl.	5/16	6° BTDC[6]	6° BTDC[6]	.016	30° ± 1°
	350	315	Roch.	4-bbl.	5/16	6° BTDC[6]	6° BTDC[6]	.016	30° ± 1°
	455	350	Roch.	4-bbl.	3/8	6° BTDC[6]	6° BTDC[6]	.016	30° ± 1°
	455	360 Stage 1	Roch.	4-bbl.	5/16	10° BTDC[6]	10° BTDC[6]	.016	30° ± 1°

1 Lowest cylinder must be within 75% of highest cylinder.
2 Lowest cylinder must be within 70% of highest cylinder.
3 Air conditioning off.
4 LeSabre, Centurion 600 rpm.
5 Manual transmission only; automatic transmission float level is ⅜-in.
6 Set at idle with distributor vacuum advance hose disconnected and plugged.
7 600 rpm idle stop solenoid disconnected.
8 500 rpm idle stop solenoid disconnected.

Cadillac V-8

YEAR	CU. INS.	HP	MAKE	TYPE	FLOAT LEVEL (INS.)	STD. TRANS	AUTO. TRANS.	POINT GAP (INS.)	DWELL
1977	350	180	[7]	[7]	[7]	—	10° BTDC[10]	[6]	—
	425	N/A	[7]	[7]	[7]	—	18° BTDC	[6]	—
	425	180	Roch.	4-bbl.	13/32[11]	—	18° BTDC	[6]	—
1976	350	180	[7]	[7]	[7]	—	10° BTDC[9]	[6]	—
	500	200	[7]	[7]	[7]	—	12° BTDC	[6]	—
	500	190	Roch.	4-bbl.	13/32[8]	—	6° BTDC	[6]	—
1975	500	N/A	Roch.	4-bbl.	15/32	—	6° BTDC	[6]	—
1974	472	205	Roch.	4-bbl.	1/4	—	10° BTDC	.016	28°-32°
	500	210	Roch.	4-bbl.	23/64	—	10° BTDC	.016	28°-32°
1973	472	220	Roch.	4-bbl.	1/4	—	8° BTDC[5]	.016	28°-32°
	500	235	Roch.	4-bbl.	23/64	—	8° BTDC[5]	.016	28°-32°
1972	472	345	Roch.	4-bbl.	1/4	—	8° BTDC[5]	.016	28°-32°
	500	365	Roch.	4-bbl.	23/64	—	8° BTDC[5]	.016	28°-32°
1971	472	345	Roch.	4-bbl.	15/64	—	8° BTDC[5]	.016	28°-32°
	500	365	Roch.	4-bbl.	23/64	—	8° BTDC[5]	.016	28°-32°
1970	472	375	Roch.	4-bbl.	15/64	—	7.5° BTDC[5]	.016	28°-32°
	500	400	Roch.	4-bbl.	15/64	—	7.5° BTDC[5]	.016	28°-32°

2 Air conditioner off.
3 At engine cranking speed.
5 At 600 rpm with distributor vacuum advance hose disconnected and plugged.
6 High Energy Ignition, no points used.
7 Electronic fuel injection.
8 7/16-in. on California cars.

Chevy 4

YEAR	CU. INS.	HP	MAKE	TYPE	FLOAT LEVEL (INS.)	STD. TRANS	AUTO. TRANS.	POINT GAP (INS.)	DWELL
1977	140	84	Holley	2-bbl.	.46	0° BTDC	2° BTDC	[12]	[12]
	85	52	Roch.	1-bbl	5/32	12° BTDC	12° BTDC	[12]	[12]
	98	60	Roch.	1-bbl.	5/32	8° BTDC	8° BTDC	[12]	[12]
1976	122	110	[9]	[9]	[9]	12° BTDC	—	[12]	[12]
	140	70	Roch.	1-bbl.	11/32	8° BTDC	10° BTDC	[12]	[12]
	140	84	Holley	2-bbl.	.46	10° BTDC	12° BTDC	[12]	[12]
	85	52	Roch.	1-bbl.	5/32	10° BTDC	10° BTDC	[12]	[12]
	98	60	Roch.	1-bbl.	5/32	8° BTDC	10° BTDC	[12]	[12]
1975	140	78	Roch.	1-bbl.	1/16	8° BTDC	10° BTDC	[12]	—
	140	87	Holley	2-bbl.	13/32	10° BTDC	12° BTDC	[12]	—
	122	110	[9]	—	—	12° BTDC[10]	—	[12]	—
1974	140	75	Roch.	1-bbl.	1/16	10° BTDC	12° BTDC	.019	31°-34°
	140	85	Holley	2-bbl.	13/32	10° BTDC	12° BTDC	.019	31°-34°
1973	140	72	Roch.	1-bbl.	.06	8° BTDC[2]	8° BTDC[2]	.019	31°-34°
	140	85	Holley	2-bbl.	.42	10° BTDC[2]	12° BTDC[2]	.019	31°-34°
1972	140	80	Roch.	1-bbl.	1/8[7], 1/16[8]	8° BTDC[2]	6° BTDC[2,4]	.019	31°-34°
	140	90	Roch.	2-bbl.	19/32	8° BTDC[2]	8° BTDC[2]	.019	31°-34°
1971	140	90	Roch.	1-bbl.	1/4	6° BTDC[2]	10° BTDC[2]	.019	31°-34°
	140	110	Roch.	1-bbl.	19/32	6° BTDC[2]	10° BTDC[2]	.019	31°-34°

1 At cranking speed, throttle wide open; maximum variation is 20 psi between cylinders.
2 At idle with vacuum advance hose disconnected and plugged.
3 1200 rpm on 4-speed transmission cars.
4 California cars 4° BTDC.
5 California cars with 3-speed transmission, idle speed 850 rpm.
6 800 rpm on cars with air conditioning.
7 Manual transmission cars only.
8 Automatic transmission cars only.
9 Has Bendix fuel injection.

Chevy, Buick, Olds, Pontiac Inline-6

YEAR	CU. INS.	HP	MAKE	TYPE	FLOAT LEVEL (INS.)	STD. TRANS	AUTO. TRANS.	POINT GAP (INS.)	DWELL
1977	250	110	Roch.	1-bbl.	3/8	6° BTDC	8° BTDC	[12]	[12]
1976	250	105	Roch.	1-bbl.	11/32	6° BTDC	10° BTDC	[12]	[12]
1975	250	105	Roch.	1-bbl.	19/64	10° BTDC	10° BTDC	[12]	—
1974	250	100	Roch.	1-bbl.	19/64	8° BTDC	6° BTDC	.019	31°-34°

	SPARK PLUG			IDLE SPEED		FUEL PUMP PRESSURE	COMPRESSION
MAKE	TYPE	GAP (INS.)	TORQUE (FT.-LBS.)	STD. TRANS.†	AUTO. TRANS.††	(PSI)	(PSI)
AC	R45TSX	.060	15-25	—	600	5.0-6.5	2
AC	R45TSX	.060	15-25	—	600	7.5-9.0	2
AC	R45TSX	.060	15	—	600	3.5-4.5	2
AC	R45TSX	.060	15	—	600	4.25-5.75	2
AC	R45TSX	.060	15	—	600	4.25-5.75	2
AC	R45TSX	.060	15	—	600	4.25-5.75	2
AC	R45TS	.040	15	N/A	650_3	4.25-5.75	2
AC	R45TS	.040	15	N/A	650_3	4.25-5.75	2
AC	R45TS	.040	15	N/A	650_3	4.25-5.75	2
AC	R45TS	.040	15	N A	650_3	4.25-5.75	2
AC	R45TS	.040	15	N A	650_3	4.25-5.75	2
AC	R45TS	.040	15	800_7	650_8	4.25-5.75	2
AC	R45TS	.040	15	800_7	650_8	4.25-5.75	2
AC	R45TS	.040	15	900_7	650_8	4.25-5.75	2
AC	R45TS	.040	15	900_7	650_4	4.25-5.75	2
AC	R45TS	.040	15	800_7	650_8	3	2
AC	R45TS	.040	15	—	650_8	3	2
AC	R45TS	.040	15	900_7	650_8	4.5	2
AC	R45TS	.040	15	900_7	650_8	4.5	2
AC	R45TS	.030	15	800	—	3	1
AC	R45TS	.030	15	—	600	3	1
AC	R44TS	.030	15	700	600	4.5	1
AC	R44TS	.030	15	700	600	4.5	1
AC	R44TS	.030	15	700	600	4.5	1
AC	R45TS	.030	15	700_3	600_3	3	1
AC	R45TS	.030	15	700_3	600_3	3	1
AC	R45TS	.030	15	700_3	600_3	3	1
AC	R44TS	.030	15	700_3	600_3	4.5	1
AC	R44TS	.030	15	700_3	600_3	4.5	1

9 Stage 1 engine.
10 High Energy Ignition, no points used.
11 170 hp on California and high-altitude models.
12 550 on Riviera, Electra and Estate Wagon.
13 6-7.5 psi on Riviera, Electra and Estate Wagon.
14. Check fifth digit of engine code: "J" engines are 5/16-in.; "L" engines, 15/32-in.; "R" engines, 13/32-in.
†In neutral.
††In drive.

AC	R47SX	.080	25	—	650	39_7	N/A
AC	R45NSX	.060	25	—	650	39_7	140-165
AC	R45NSX	.060	25	—	650	5.25-6.5	140-165
AC	R46SX	.080	25	—	600	39_7	N/A
AC	R45NSX	.060	25	—	600	39_7	165-185
AC	R45NSX	.060	25	—	600	5.25-6.5	165-185
AC	R45NSX	.060	25	—	600	5.25-6.5 @ 1800	165-185
AC	R45NS	.035	25	—	600_2	5.25-6.5 @ 1800	165-185
AC	R45NS	.035	25	—	600_2	5.25-6.5 @ 1800	165-185
AC	R46N	.035	25	—	600_2	5.25-6.5 @ 500 rpm	165-185
AC	R46N	.035	25	—	600_2	5.25-6.5 @ 500 rpm	165-185
AC	R46N	.035	25	—	600_2	5.25-6.5 @ 600 rpm	165-185
AC	R46N	.035	25	—	600_2	5.25-6.5 @ 600 rpm	165-185
AC	R46N	.035	25	—	600_2	5.25-6.5 @ 600 rpm	165-185
AC	R46N	.035	25	—	600_2	5_3	165-185
AC	R46N	.035	25	—	600_2	5_3	165-185

9 6° BTDC on California cars.
10 8° BTDC on California cars.
11 17/32-in. on Eldorado.
†In neutral.
††In drive.

AC	R43TS	.035	15	700	750	3.0-4.5 @ 12.5V	140_1
AC	R43TS	.035	15	875	850	5.0-6.5	145
AC	R43TS	.035	15	$900_{16, 17}$	850	5.0-6.5	145
AC	R43LTS	.035	15	600	——	9, 11	N/A
AC	R43TSX	.035	15	700	750	3.0-4.5	140_1
AC	R43TSX	.035	15	700	750	3.0-4.5	140_1
AC	R43TS	.035	15	800_13	$800_{14, 15}$	5.0-6.5	145
AC	R43TS	.035	15	800_13	800_14	5.0-6.5	145
AC	R43TSX	.060	15	700	700	3-4.5	140_1
AC	R43TSX	.060	15	750	750_1	3-4.5	140_1
AC	R43LTS	.060	15	1600	—	$3-4.5_{11}$	N/A
AC	R42TS	.033-.038	15	700	750	3-4.5 @ 12.5 volts	140
AC	R42TS	.033-.038	15	700	750	3-4.5 @ 12.5 volts	140
AC	R42TS	.035	15	1000	750	3-4.5 @ 12.6 volts	140_1
AC	R42TS	.035	15	1200	750	3-4.5 @ 12.6 volts	140_1
AC	R42TS	.035	15	1200_5	700_6	3.5 @ 12.5 volts	140_1
AC	R42TS	.035	15	1200	1200	3.5 @ 12.5 volts	140_1
AC	R42TS	.035	15	750_3	650	3-4.5	140_1
AC	R42TS	.035	15	750_3	650	3-4.5	140_1

10 Retarded at 1600 rpm.
11 Additional in-line pump rated at 40 psi at 120 volts.
12 Transistor ignition, no points used.
13 1000 rpm on California cars.
14 950 rpm on cars with air conditioning.
15 850 rpm on California cars.
16 875 rpm on California cars.
17 900 rpm on high-altitude cars.
†In neutral.
††In drive.

AC	R46TS	.035	15	750	550	4.0-5.0	130
AC	R46TS	.035	25_{13}	850	550	5.5-6.5	130
AC	R46TX	.060	15	850	550	4.0-5.0	130_1
AC	R46T	.033-.038	15	850	600	4.0-5.0	130

Chevy, Buick, Olds, Pontiac Inline-6

YEAR	ENGINE CU. INS.	HP	CARBURETOR MAKE	TYPE	FLOAT LEVEL (INS.)	INITIAL TIMING STD. TRANS	AUTO. TRANS.	DISTRIBUTOR POINT GAP (INS.)	DWELL
1973	250[5]	100	Roch.	1-bbl.	1/4	6° BTDC[2]	6° BTDC[2]	.019	31°-34°
1972	250[6]	145	Roch.	1-bbl.	1/4	4° BTDC[2,4]	4° BTDC[2,4]	.019	31°-34°
1971	250	145	Roch.	1-bbl.	1/4	4° BTDC[2]	4° BTDC[2]	.019	31°-34°
1970	230[3]	140	Roch.	1-bbl.	1/4	TDC[2]	4° BTDC[2]	.019	31°-34°
	230	155	Roch.	1-bbl.	1/4	TDC[2]	4° BTDC[2]	.019	31°-34°

1 At cranking speed; throttle wide open—maximum variation 20 psi between cylinders.
2 At idle with distributor vacuum advance hose disconnected and plugged.
3 Only available in Chevrolet.

4 40° BTDC—K-20 Suburban models for California.
5 Not available in Buick in '73.
6 Not available in Buick/Olds in '72.
7 Idle solenoid disconnected/idle solenoid connected.

Chevy Small V-8

YEAR	ENGINE CU. INS.	HP	CARBURETOR MAKE	TYPE	FLOAT LEVEL (INS.)	INITIAL TIMING STD. TRANS	AUTO. TRANS.	DISTRIBUTOR POINT GAP (INS.)	DWELL
1977	305	145[8]	Roch.	2-bbl.	19/32	8° BTDC	8° BTDC[9]	7	7
	350	170[8]	Roch.	4-bbl.	15/32	8° BTDC	8° BTDC	7	7
	350	160[10]	Roch.	4-bbl.	15/32	8° BTDC	8° BTDC	7	7
	350 (L82)	210[11]	Roch.	4-bbl.	15/32	12° BTDC	12° BTDC	7	7
1976	305	140	Roch.	2-bbl.	19/32	6° BTDC	8° BTDC	7	7
	350	145	Roch.	2-bbl.	19/32	—	6° BTDC	7	7
	350	165	Roch.	4-bbl.	1/4	8° BTDC	8° BTDC	7	7
	350 (L48)	180	Roch.	4-bbl.	1/4	8° BTDC	8° BTDC	7	7
	350 (L82)	210	Roch.	4-bbl.	1/4	12° BTDC	12° BTDC	7	7
	400	175	Roch.	4-bbl.	1/4	—	8° BTDC	7	7
1975	262	110	Roch.	2-bbl.	19/64	8° BTDC	8° BTDC	7	—
	350	145	Roch.	2-bbl.	19/32	6° BTDC	6° BTDC	7	—
	350	155	Roch.	4-bbl.	1/4	6° BTDC	6° BTDC	7	—
	350	165	Roch.	4-bbl.	1/4	6° BTDC	12° BTDC	7	—
	350	205	Roch.	4-bbl.	1/4	6° BTDC	12° BTDC	7	—
	400	175	Roch.	4-bbl.	1/4	—	8° BTDC	7	—
1974	350	145	Roch.	2-bbl.	19/32	0° BTDC	8° BTDC	.019	29°-31°
	350	160	Roch.	4-bbl.	1/4	4° BTDC	8° BTDC	.019	29°-31°
	350	185/195	Roch.	4-bbl.	1/4	8° BTDC[6]	8° BTDC	.019	29°-31°
	350	245/250	Roch.	4-bbl.	1/4	8° BTDC	8° BTDC	.019	29°-31°
	400	150	Roch.	2-bbl.	19/32	N/A	8° BTDC	.019	29°-31°
	400	180	Roch.	4-bbl.	1/4	N/A	8° BTDC	.019	29°-31°
1973	307	115	Roch.	2-bbl.	21/32	4° BTDC	8° BTDC	.019	29°-31°
	350	145	Roch.	2-bbl.	19/32	8° BTDC	8° BTDC	.019	29°-31°
	350	175	Roch.	4-bbl.	7/32	8° BTDC	12° BTDC	.019	29°-31°
	350	190	Roch.	4-bbl.	7/32	12° BTDC	12° BTDC	.019	29°-31°
	350	245-250	Roch.	4-bbl.	7/32	8° BTDC	8° BTDC	.019	29°-31°
	350	255(Z-28)	Roch.	4-bbl.	7/32	8° BTDC	8° BTDC	.019	29°-31°
	400	150	Roch.	2-bbl.	19/32	—	6° BTDC	.019	29°-31°
1972	307	130	Roch.	2-bbl.	27/32	4° BTDC[2]	8° BTDC[2]	.019	29°-31°
	350	155	Roch.	2-bbl.	25/32	6° BTDC[2]	6° BTDC[2]	.019	29°-31°
	350	165	Roch.	4-bbl.	1/4	6° BTDC[2]	6° BTDC[2]	.019	29°-31°
	350	175	Holley	4-bbl.	4	4° BTDC[2,3]	8° BTDC[2]	.019	29°-31°
	350	255(Z-28)	Holley	4-bbl.	4	4° BTDC[2]	8° BTDC[2]	.019	29°-31°
	400	170	Roch.	4-bbl.	1/4	2° BTDC[2]	6° BTDC[2]	.019	29°-31°
1971	307	200	Roch.	2-bbl.	13/16	4° BTDC[2]	8° BTDC[2]	.019	29°-31°
	350	245	Roch.	2-bbl.	5	2° BTDC[2]	6° BTDC[2]	.019	29°-31°
	350	270	Roch.	4-bbl.	1/4	4° BTDC[2,3]	8° BTDC[2]	.019	29°-31°
	350	330	Holley	4-bbl.	4	8° BTDC[2]	12° BTDC[2]	.019	29°-31°
	400	225	Roch.	4-bbl.	23/32	4° BTDC[2]	8° BTDC[2]	.019	29°-31°
1970	302	290	Holley	4-bbl.	4	4° BTDC[2]	4° BTDC[2]	.019	28°-32°
	307	200	Roch.	2-bbl.	23/32	2° BTDC[2]	8° BTDC[2]	.019	28°-32°
	350	250	Roch.	2-bbl.	4	TDC[2,3]	4° BTDC[2]	.019	28°-32°
	350	300	Roch.	4-bbl.	27/32	TDC[2,3]	4° BTDC[2]	.019	28°-32°
	350	350	Roch.	4-bbl.	23/32	4° BTDC[2]	—	.019	28°-32°
	350	360	Holley	4-bbl.	1/4	14° BTDC[2]	—	.019	28°-32°
	350	370	Holley	4-bbl.	1/4	14° BTDC[2]	—	.019	28°-32°
	400	265	Roch.	2-bbl.	4	4° BTDC[2]	8° BTDC[2]	.019	28°-32°

1 At cranking speed; throttle wide open; spark plugs removed—maximum variation 20 psi between cylinders.
2 At idle with distributor vacuum advance hose disconnected and plugged.
3 8° BTDC on Corvette.

4 Wet fuel level; with float bowl sight plugs removed, fuel level should be at bottom edge of sight plug, but not overflowing.
5 23/32-in. on manual transmission cars; 25/32-in. on automatic transmission
6 Initial timing 4° BTDC in California.

Chevy Big V-8

YEAR	ENGINE CU. INS.	HP	CARBURETOR MAKE	TYPE	FLOAT LEVEL (INS.)	INITIAL TIMING STD. TRANS	AUTO. TRANS.	DISTRIBUTOR POINT GAP (INS.)	DWELL
1976	454	225	Roch.	4-bbl.	3/8	—	12° BTDC	8	8
1975	454	215	Roch.	4-bbl.	3/8	—	16° BTDC	8	
1974	454	235/270	Roch.	4-bbl.	3/8	10° BTDC	10° BTDC	.019	29°-31°
1973	454	245	Roch.	4-bbl.	1/4	10° BTDC[2]	10° BTDC[2]	.019	29°-31°
1972	402	210	Roch.	4-bbl.	1/4	8° BTDC[2]	8° BTDC[2]	.019	29°-31°
	402	240	Roch.	4-bbl.	1/4	8° BTDC[2]	8° BTDC[2]	.019	29°-31°
	454	270	Roch.	4-bbl.	1/4	8° BTDC[2]	8° BTDC[2]	.019	29°-31°
1971	402	300	Roch.	4-bbl.	1/4	8° BTDC[2]	8° BTDC[2]	.019	29°-31°
	454	365	Roch.	4-bbl.	1/4	8° BTDC[2]	8° BTDC[2]	.019	29°-31°
	454	425	Holley	4-bbl.	4	8° BTDC[2]	12° BTDC[2]	.019	29°-31°
1970	396	350[7]	Roch.	4-bbl.	1/4	TDC[2]	4° BTDC[2]	.019	28°-32°
	396	375[7]	Holley	4-bbl.	4	4° BTDC[2]	4° BTDC[2]	.019	28°-32°
	402	330[7]	Roch.	4-bbl.	1/4	4° BTDC[2]	4° BTDC[2]	.019	28°-32°
	427	390	Roch.	4-bbl.	1/4	4° BTDC[2]	4° BTDC[2]	.019	28°-32°
	427	400	Holley	3x2-bbl.	4	4° BTDC[2]	4° BTDC[2]	.019	28°-32°
	427	430	Holley	4-bbl.	4	12° BTDC[2,5]	—	.019	28°-32°
	427	435	Holley	3x2-bbl.	4	4° BTDC[2]	4° BTDC[2]	.019	28°-32°
	454	345	Roch.	4-bbl.	1/4	—	6° BTDC[2]	.019	28°-32°
	454	360	Roch.	4-bbl.	1/4	6° BTDC[2]	6° BTDC[2]	.019	28°-32°
	454	390	Roch.	4-bbl.	1/4	6° BTDC[2]	6° BTDC[2]	.019	28°-32°
	454	450	Holley	4-bbl.	4	4° BTDC[2]	4° BTDC[2]	.019	28°-32°

1 At cranking speed; throttle wide open; spark plugs removed—maximum variation 20 psi between cylinders.
2 Set at idle rpm with distributor vacuum advance hose disconnected and plugged.

4 Wet fuel level; with float bowl sight plug removed, fuel level should be at bottom edge of sight plug, but not overflowing.
5 Adjust timing at 800 rpm.

MAKE	TYPE	GAP (INS.)	TORQUE (FT.-LBS.)	IDLE SPEED STD. TRANS.†	IDLE SPEED AUTO. TRANS.††	FUEL PUMP PRESSURE (PSI)	COMPRESSION (PSI)
AC	R46T	.035	15	700/450 [7]	600/450 [7]	3.5-4.5	130 [1]
AC	R46T	.035	15	700/450 [7]	600/450 [7]	3.5-4.5	130 [1]
AC	R46TS	.035	15	550 [8]	500 [10]	3.5-4.5	130 [1]
AC	R46T	.035	15	750	600	3-4.5	130 [1]
AC	R46T	.035	15	750 [9]	600 [11]	3-4.5	130 [1]

[8] 600 rpm on cars equipped with air conditioning (air conditioning off).
[9] Idle solenoid connected, air conditioning off.
[10] 575 rpm on cars equipped with air conditioning (air conditioning off).
[11] Idle solenoid connected, air conditioning on.
[12] High Energy Ignition; no points used.
[13] 15 ft.-lbs. with tapered-seat plugs.
† In neutral.
†† In drive.

MAKE	TYPE	GAP (INS.)	TORQUE (FT.-LBS.)	IDLE SPEED STD. TRANS.†	IDLE SPEED AUTO. TRANS.††	FUEL PUMP PRESSURE (PSI)	COMPRESSION (PSI)
AC	R45TS	.045	15	600	500	7.5-9.0	160 [1]
AC	R45TS	.045	15	700	500	7.5-9.0	160 [1]
AC	R45TS	.045	15	700	500	7.5-9.0	160 [1]
AC	R45TS	.045	25	800	700	7.5-9.0	160 [1]
AC	R45TS	.045	15	800	600	7.5-9.0	160 [1]
AC	R45TS	.045	15	—	600	7.5-9.0	160 [1]
AC	R45TS	.045	15	800	800	7.5-9.0	160 [1]
AC	R45TS	.045	25	800	600	7.5-9.0	160 [1]
AC	R45TS	.045	25	1000	700	7.5-9.0	160 [1]
AC	R45TS	.045	15	—	600	7.5-9.0	160 [1]
AC	R44TX	.060	15	800	600	3.0-4.5	150 [1]
AC	R44TX	.060	15	800	600	7.5-9.0	150 [1]
AC	R44TX	.060	15	800	600	7.5-9.0	160 [1]
AC	R44TX	.060	15	800	900	7.5-9.0	160 [1]
AC	R44TX	.060	15	600	700	7.5-9.0	150 [1]
AC	R44TX	.060	15	—	600	7.5-9.0	160 [1]
AC	R44T	.033-.038	15	900	600	7.5-9.0	150
AC	R44T	.033-.038	15	900	600	7.5-9.0	160
AC	R44T	.033-.038	15	900	600	7.5-9.0	160
AC	R44T	.033-.038	15	900	700	7.5-9.0	150
AC	R44T	.033-.038	15	N A	600	7.5-9.0	160
AC	R44T	.033-.038	15	N A	600	7.5-9.0	160
AC	R44T	.035	15	900	600	5-6.5 @ Idle	150 [1]
AC	R44T	.035	15	900	600	7-8.5 @ Idle	160 [1]
AC	R44T	.035	15	900	600	7-8.5 @ Idle	160 [1]
AC	R44T	.035	15	900	600	7-8.5 @ Idle	160 [1]
AC	R44T	.035	15	900	700	7-8.5 @ Idle	160 [1]
AC	R44T	.035	15	900	600	7-8.5 @ Idle	150 [1]
AC	R44T	.035	15	—	600	7-8.5 @ Idle	160 [1]
AC	R44T	.033-.035	15	900	600	5-6.5 @ Idle	150 [1]
AC	R44T	.033-.035	15	900	600	7-8.5 @ 3600 rpm	160 [1]
AC	R44T	.033-.035	15	900	600	7-8.5 @ 3600 rpm	160 [1]
AC	R44T	.033-.035	15	800	600	7-8.5 @ 3600 rpm	160 [1]
AC	R44T	.033-.035	15	900	700	7-8.5 @ 3600 rpm	150 [1]
AC	R44T	.033-.035	15	900	600	7-8.5 @ 3600 rpm	160 [1]
AC	R46TS	.035	15	600	550	5-6.5 @ Idle	150 [1]
AC	R46TS	.035	15	600	550	7-8.5 @ 3600 rpm	160 [1]
AC	R44TS	.035	15	600	550	7-8.5 @ 3600 rpm	160 [1]
AC	R44TS	.035	15	700	700	7-8.5 @ 3600 rpm	150 [1]
AC	R44TS	.035	15	600	550	7-8.5 @ 3600 rpm	160 [1]
AC	R43	.035	25	900	750	5-6.5 @ Idle	190 [1]
AC	R43	.035	25	700	600	5-6.5 @ Idle	150 [1]
AC	R44	.035	25	750	600	5-6.5 @ Idle	160 [1]
AC	R44	.035	25	700	600	5-6.5 @ Idle	160 [1]
AC	R44	.035	25	750	—	5-6.5 @ Idle	160 [1]
AC	R43	.035	25	750	—	5-6.5 @ Idle	190 [1]
AC	R43	.035	25	750	—	5-6.5 @ Idle	190 [1]
AC	R44	.035	25	700	600	5-8 @ Idle	160 [1]

[7] High Energy Ignition; no points used.
[8] 10 hp less in California cars.
[9] 6° BTDC in California cars.
[10] L48 (Corvette) engine generates 180 hp.
[11] Not available in California.
† In neutral.
†† In drive.

MAKE	TYPE	GAP (INS.)	TORQUE (FT.-LBS.)	IDLE SPEED STD. TRANS.†	IDLE SPEED AUTO. TRANS.††	FUEL PUMP PRESSURE (PSI)	COMPRESSION (PSI)
AC	R45TSX	.060	15	—	600	7.5-9.0	160
AC	R44TX	.060	15	—	650	7.5-9.0	160 [1]
AC	R44T	.033-.038	15	800	600	7.5-9.0	160
AC	R44T	.035	15	900	600	7-8.5 @ Idle	160
AC	R44T	.033-.035	15	750	600	7-8.5 @ 3600 rpm	160
AC	R44T	.033-.035	15	750	600	7-8.5 @ 3600 rpm	160
AC	R44T	.033-.035	15	750	600	7-8.5 @ 3600 rpm	160
AC	R44TS	.035	15	600	600	7-8.5 @ 3600 rpm	160
AC	R42TS	.035	15	600	600	7-8.5 @ 3600 rpm	160
AC	R42TS	.035	15	700	700	7-8.5 @ 3600 rpm	150
AC	R44T	.035	15	700	600	5-8.5	160
AC	R43T	.035	15	750	700	5-8.5	160
AC	R44T	.035	15	700	700	5-8.5	160
AC	R43N	.035	25	800	600	5-8.5	160
AC	R43N	.035	25	750	600	5-8.5	160
AC	R43XL	.035	25	1000	—	5-8.5	150
AC	R43N [6]	.035	25	750	750	5-8.5	150
AC	44T	.035	15	—	600	5-8.5	160
AC	43T	.035	15	700	600	5-8.5	160
AC	43T	.035	15	700	700	5-8.5	150

[6] Use AC R43XL when equipped with RPO L89 engine.
[7] Actually 402-cu.-in. displacement, but engine is called "396" in Chevelle and Nova, and "400" in Chevrolet and Monte Carlo lines (not to be confused with 400/265 small-block V-8).
[8] High Energy Ignition; no points used.
† In neutral.
†† In drive.

Chrysler Slant-6

YEAR	ENGINE CU. INS.	HP	CARBURETOR MAKE	TYPE	FLOAT LEVEL (INS.)	INITIAL TIMING STD. TRANS.	AUTO. TRANS.	DISTRIBUTOR POINT GAP (INS.)	DWELL
1977	225	100[15]	Holley	1-bbl.	12	12° BTDC[16]	12° BTDC	11	11
	225	110	Carter	2-bbl.	1/4	12° BTDC	12° BTDC	11	11
1976	225	100	Holley	1-bbl.	12	6° BTDC[14]	2° BTDC	11	11
1975	225	95	Holley	1-bbl.	1/32	TDC	TDC	11	—
1974	198	95	Holley	1-bbl.	1/32	2.5° BTDC	2.5° BTDC	11	11
	225	105	Holley	1-bbl.	1/32	TDC	TDC	11	11
1973	198	95	Holley	1-bbl.	7	2.5° BTDC ± 2.5°[2]	TDC ± 2.5°[2]	11	11
	225	105	Holley	1-bbl.	7	TDC ± 2.5°[2,9]	TDC ± 2.5°[2]	11	11
1972	198	125	Holley	1-bbl.	7	2.5° BTDC ± 2.5°[2]	2.5° BTDC ± 2.5°[2]	.017-.023	41°-46°
	225	145	Holley	1-bbl.	7	TDC ± 2.5°[2]	TDC ± 2.5°[2]	.017-.023	41°-46°
1971	198	125	Carter	1-bbl.	1/4	2.5° BTDC ± 2.5°[2]	2.5° BTDC ± 2.5°[2]	.017-.023	41°-46°
	225	145	Holley	1-bbl.	7	2.5° BTDC ± 2.5°[2]	2.5° BTDC ± 2.5°[2]	.017-.023	41°-46°
1970	198	125	Carter	1-bbl.	1/4	TDC ± 2.5°[2]	TDC ± 2.5°[2]	.017-.023	41°-46°
	225	145	Holley	1-bbl.	7	TDC ± 2.5°[2]	TDC ± 2°[2]	.017-.023	41°-46°

[2] Set at curb idle with distributor vacuum advance hose disconnected and plugged.
[6] Set with headlights on and air conditioning on (if so equipped).
[7] Use float gauge.
[8] National. 700 rpm. California cars only.
[9] 2.5 BTDC · 2.5 on engines with distributor = 3438440 and =343842.
[10] 100 psi minimum; must not vary more than 25 psi between cylinders
[11] Electronic ignition system standard
[12] Flush with top of bowl cover gasket.

Chrysler Small V-8

YEAR	ENGINE CU. INS.	HP	CARBURETOR MAKE	TYPE	FLOAT LEVEL (INS.)	INITIAL TIMING STD. TRANS.	AUTO. TRANS.	DISTRIBUTOR POINT GAP (INS.)	DWELL
1977	318	145[19]	Carter	2-bbl.	1/4	—	8° BTDC	17	17
	360	155	Holley	2-bbl.	3/16[7]	—	10° BTDC	17	17
	360[20]	170	Carter	4-bbl.	27/32	—	6° BTDC	17	17
1976	318	150	Carter	2-bbl.	1/4	—	2° BTDC	17	17
	360	170	Holley	2-bbl.	3/16[7]	—	6° BTDC	17	17
	360	175	Carter	4-bbl.	29/32	—	6° BTDC	17	17
1975	318	145	Carter	2-bbl.	1/4	2° BTDC	2° BTDC	17	—
	318	150	Carter	2-bbl.	1/4	2° BTDC	2° BTDC	17	—
	360	180	Carter	2-bbl.	3/16	—	6° BTDC	17	—
	360	190	Carter	4-bbl.	1	—	6° BTDC	17	—
	360	230	Carter	4-bbl.	1	—	2° BTDC	17	—
1974	318	150	Carter	2-bbl.	1/4	TDC	TDC	17	17
	360	180	Holley	2-bbl.	3/16	N/A	5° BTDC	17	17
	360	200	Carter	4-bbl.	1	N/A	5° BTDC	17	17
	360	245	Carter	4-bbl.	1	5° BTDC[3]	5° BTDC	17	17
1973	318	150	Carter	2-bbl.	1/4	TDC ± 2.5°[2]	TDC ± 2.5°[2]	17	17
	340	240	Carter TQ	4-bbl.	1	5° ± 2.5°[2]	2.5° ± 2.5°[2]	17	17
	360	170	Holley	2-bbl.	.180[7]	—	TDC ± 2.5°[2]	17	17
1972	318	150	Carter	2-bbl.	1/4	TDC ± 2.5°[2]	TDC ± 2°[2]	.014-.019	30°-34°
	340	240	Carter TQ	4-bbl.	1	TDC ± 2.5°[2,3]	2.5° BTDC ± 2.5°[2]	4	4
	360	175	Holley	2-bbl.	.180[7]	TDC ± 2.5°[2]	2.5° BTDC ± 2.5°[2]	.014-.019	30°-34°
1971	318	230	Carter or Roch.	2-bbl.	1/4[9]	TDC ± 2.5°[2]	TDC ± 2.5°[2]	.014-.019	30°-34°
	340	275	Carter TQ	4-bbl.	1	5° BTDC ± 2.5°[2]	5° BTDC ± 2.5°[2]	.014-.019	10
1970	340	290	Holley	3x2-bbl.	12,13	2.5° BTDC ± 2.5°[2]	2.5° BTDC ± 2.5°[2]	.014-.019	10
	360	255	Holley	2-bbl.	14	2.5° BTDC ± 2.5°[2]	2.5° BTDC ± 2.5°[2]	.014-.019	30°-34°
	318	230	Carter	2-bbl.	1/4	TDC ± 2.5°[2]	TDC ± 2.5°[2]	.014-.019	30°-34°
	340	275	Carter	4-bbl.	7/32	5° BTDC ± 2.5°[2]	5° BTDC ± 2.5°[2]	.014-.019	30°-34°[10]

[1] 100 psi minimum per cylinder; must not vary more than 40 psi between cylinders.
[2] Set at curb idle, with distributor vacuum advance hose disconnected and plugged.
[3] 2.5° BTDC on California cars equipped with manual transmission.
[4] Point gap and dwell do not apply on cars equipped with electronic ignition systems.
[5] 700 rpm, manual transmission equipped cars, California only.
[6] Idle solenoid adjusted to obtain idle rpm.
[7] Dry float setting between toe of float and float stop.
[8] 110 psi minimum per cylinder; must not vary more than 40 psi between cylinders
[9] 21/32 on engines equipped with Rochester 2-bbl. carburetor.
[10] 27°-32° one set of points; 37°-42° both sets of points on dual point distributors.

Chrysler Big V-8

YEAR	ENGINE CU. INS.	HP	CARBURETOR MAKE	TYPE	FLOAT LEVEL (INS.)	INITIAL TIMING STD. TRANS.	AUTO. TRANS.	DISTRIBUTOR POINT GAP (INS.)	DWELL
1977	400	190	Carter	4-bbl.	27/32	—	10° BTDC	11	11
	400	195[33]	Carter	4-bbl.	27/32	—	8° BTDC	11	11
1976	400	175	Holley	2-bbl.	3/16	—	10° BTDC	11	11
	400	210[33]	Carter	4-bbl.	29/32	—	8° BTDC	11	11
	440	205[34]	Carter	4-bbl.	29/32	—	8° BTDC	11	11
1975	400	165	Holley	2-bbl.	3/16	—	10° BTDC	29	—
	400	175	Holley	2-bbl.	3/16	—	10° BTDC	29	—
	400	190	Carter	4-bbl.	1	—	8° BTDC	29	—
	400	235	Carter	4-bbl.	1	—	8° BTDC	29	—
	440	215	Carter	4-bbl.	1	—	8° BTDC	29	—
1974	400	185	Holley	2-bbl.	3/16	N/A	5° BTDC	29	29
	400	205	Carter	4-bbl.	1	N/A	5° BTDC	29	29
	400	250	Carter	4-bbl.	1	5° BTDC	5° BTDC[30]	29	29
	440	230	Carter	4-bbl.	1	N/A	10° BTDC	29	29
	440	275	Carter	4-bbl.	1	N/A	10° BTDC[10]	29	29
1973	400	185	Holley	2-bbl.	.180[13]	10° BTDC ± 2.5°	10° BTDC ± 2.5°	29	29
	400	220	Carter T9	4-bbl.	1	2.5° BTDC ± 2.5°	7.5° BTDC ± 2.5°	29	29
	440	220	Carter T9	4-bbl.	1	10° BTDC ± 2.5°	10° BTDC ± 2.5°	29	29
	440 hp	280	Carter T9	4-bbl.	1	10° BTDC ± 2.5°	10° BTDC ± 2.5°	29	29
1972	400	190	Holley	2-bbl.	.180[13]	5° BTDC ± 2.5°[9]	5° BTDC ± 2.5°[9]	.014-.019[11]	30°-34°
	400	265[1]	Carter	4-bbl.	1	TDC ± 2.5°[9,19]	10° BTDC ± 2.5°[9,10]	.014-.019[11]	30°-34°
	440	225[2,3,4]	Holley	4-bbl.	28	5° BTDC ± 2.5°[9]	10° BTDC ± 2.5°[9,10]	.014-.019[11]	30°-34°
	440	280[5,6]	Holley	4-bbl.	28	2.5° BTDC ± 2.5°[9]	5° BTDC ± 2.5°[9]	.014-.019[11]	30°-34°
	440	330	Holley	3x2-bbl.	18	2.5° BTDC ± 2.5°[9]	2.5° BTDC ± 2.5°[9]	11	11
1971	383	275	Carter	2-bbl.	5/16	TDC° ± 2.5°[9]	2.5° BTDC ± 2.5°[9]	.016-.021	28.5°-32.5°
	383	300	Holley or Carter	4-bbl.	21,24	TDC° ± 2.5°[9]	2.5° BTDC ± 2.5°[9]	.016-.021	28.5°-32.5°
	440	335	Carter	4-bbl.	7/32	—	5° BTDC ± 2.5°[9]	.016-.021	28.5°-32.5°
	440	370	Carter	4-bbl.	7/32	TDC° ± 2.5°[9]	2.5° BTDC ± 2.5°[9]	.016-.021	28.5°-32.5°
	440	385	Holley	3x2-bbl.	18	5° BTDC ± 2.5°[9]	5° BTDC ± 2.5°[9]	.014-.019	20
1970	383	290	Holley or Carter	2-bbl.	22	TDC ± 2.5°[9]	2.5° BTDC ± 2.5°[9]	.016-.019	28.5°-32.5°
	383	330	Carter	4-bbl.	5/16[23]	TDC ± 2.5°[9]	2.5° BTDC ± 2.5°[9]	.016-.019	28.5°-32.5°
	383	335	Holley	4-bbl.	24	TDC ± 2.5°[9]	2.5° BTDC ± 2.5°[9]	.016-.019	28.5°-32.5°
	440	350	Holley	4-bbl.	24	TDC ± 2.5°[9]	2.5° BTDC ± 2.5°[9]	.016-.019	28.5°-32.5°

| MAKE | SPARK PLUG | | | IDLE SPEED | | FUEL PUMP PRESSURE | COMPRESSION |
	TYPE	GAP (INS.)	TORQUE (FT.-LBS.)	STD. TRANS.†	AUTO. TRANS.††	(PSI)	(PSI)
CH.	RBL-15Y[17]	.035	25-35	700[18]	700[18]	4.0-5.5	10
CH.	RBL-15Y[17]	.035	25-35	700[18]	700[18]	4.0-5.5	10
CH.	RBL-13Y	.035	25-35	750[13]	750	4.0-5.5	10
CH.	BL13Y	.035	15	800	750	3.5-5 @ Idle	10
CH.	N14Y	.035	30	800	750	3.5-5 @ Idle	10
CH.	N14Y	.035	30	800	750	3.5-5 @ Idle	10
CH.	N14Y	.035	30	800	750	3.5-5 @ Idle	10
CH.	N14Y	.035	30	800	750	3.5-5 @ Idle	10
CH.	N14Y	.035	30	800	800	3.5-5 @ Idle	10
CH.	N14Y	.035	30	750[8]	750	3.5-5 @ Idle	10
CH.	N14Y	.035	30	800	800	3.5-5 @ Idle	10
CH.	N14Y	.035	30	750	750	3.5-5 @ Idle	10
CH.	N14Y	.035	30	750[6]	750[6]	3.5-5 @ 500 rpm	10
CH.	N14Y	.035	30	750[6]	650[6]	3.5-5 @ 500 rpm	10

13 800 rpm in California.
14 2° BTDC in California.
15 90 hp in California.
16 8° BTDC in California.
17 RBL-13Y in California.
18 750 rpm in California.
†In neutral.
††In drive.

CH.	RN-12Y	.035	25-35	—	700	5.75-7.25	1
CH.	RN-12Y	.035	25-35	—	700	5.75-7.25	1
CH.	RN-12Y	.035	25-35	—	750	5.75-7.25	1
CH.	RN-12Y	.035	25-35	—	750	6.0-7.5	1
CH.	RN-12Y	.035	25-35	—	700[18]	6.0-7.5	1
CH.	RN-12Y	.035	25-35	—	700[18]	6.0-7.5	1
CH.	N13Y	.035	30	750	750	5.0-7.0	1
CH.	N13Y	.035	30	750	750	5.0-7.0	1
CH.	N12Y	.035	30	—	650	5.0-7.0	1
CH.	N12Y	.035	30	—	650	5.0-7.0	1
CH.	N12Y	.035	30	—	650	5.0-7.0	1
CH.	N13Y	.035	30	750	750	5.0-7.0	1
CH.	N12Y	.035	30	—	750	5.0-7.0	1
CH.	N12Y	.035	30	—	750	5.0-7.0	1
CH.	N12Y	.035	30	850	850	5.0-7.0	1
CH.	N13Y	.035	30	750	750	5-7 @ Idle	1
CH.	N12Y	.035	30	900	750	5-7 @ Idle	1
CH.	N13Y	.035	30	—	750	5-7 @ Idle	1
CH.	N13Y	.035	30	750[5]	750	5-7 @ Idle	1
CH.	N9Y	.035	30	900[6]	750[6]	5-7 @ Idle	1
CH.	N13Y	.035	30	700	700	5-7 @ Idle	1
CH.	N14Y	.035	30	750	700	5-7 @ Idle	1
CH.	N9Y	.035	30	900[11]	900[11]	5-7 @ Idle	8
CH.	N9Y	.035	30	1000	950	5-7 @ Idle	8
CH.	N13Y	.035	30	750	700	5-7 @ Idle	1
CH.	N14Y	.035	30	750	700	5-7 @ 750 rpm	1
CH.	N9Y	.035	30	950	900	5-7 @ 750 rpm	8

11 Adjust with idle solenoid.
12 Center float bowl with fuel bowl inverted.
13 Wet fuel level; with bowl sight plugs removed, fuel level should be at bottom edge of sight plug hole.
14 No. 15 drill (.200-in.).
17 Electronic ignition system standard.
18 750 rpm in California.
19 135 hp in California.
20 360 4-bbl. engine available only in California.
†In neutral.   ††In drive.

CH.	RJ13Y	.035	25-35	—	750	5.75-7.25	7
CH.	RJ13Y	.035	25-35	—	750	5.75-7.25	7
CH.	J13Y	.035	25-35	—	700[31]	6.0-7.5	7
CH.	J13Y	.035	25-35	—	700[31]	6.0-7.5	7
CH.	RJ87P[35]	.035	25-35	—	750	6.0-7.5	7
CH.	J13Y	.035	30	—	750	4.0-5.5	7
CH.	J13Y	.035	30	—	750	4.0-5.5	7
CH.	J13Y	.035	30	—	750	4.0-5.5	7
CH.	J13Y	.035	30	—	750	4.0-5.5	7
CH.	RY87P	.040	30	—	750	4.0-5.5	7
CH.	J13Y	.035	30	N/A	750	4.0-5.5	7
CH.	J13Y	.035	30	N/A	900[31]	4.0-5.5	7
CH.	J11Y	.035	30	900	900[32]	4.0-5.5	7
CH.	J11Y	.035	30	N/A	750	4.0-5.5	7
CH.	J11Y	.035	30	N/A	800	7.0-8.2	7
CH.	J13Y	.035	30	—	700	3.5-5 @ Idle	100[7]
CH.	J11Y	.035	30	800	750	3.5-5 @ Idle	100[7]
CH.	J11Y	.035	30	—	700	3.5-5 @ Idle	100[7]
CH.	J11Y	.035	30	—	800	6-7.5 @ Idle	100[7]
CH.	J13Y	.035	30	700	700	3.5-5 @ Idle	100[7]
CH.	J11Y	.035	30	900[12,14]	750[12]	3.5-5 @ Idle	100[7]
CH.	J11Y	.035	30	900	750[15,16,17]	3.5-7.5 @ Idle	100[7]
CH.	J11Y	.035	30	900	900	3.5-7.5 @ Idle	100[7]
CH.	J14Y	.035	30	750	700	3.5-5 @ Idle	100[7]
CH.	J14Y	.035	30	900	800	3.5-5 @ Idle	110[8]
CH.	J13Y	.035	30	—	750	3.5-5 @ Idle	110[8]
CH.	J11Y	.035	30	900	900	3.5-5 @ Idle	110[8]
CH.	J11Y	.035	30	900	900	6-7.5 @ Idle	110[8]
CH.	N14Y	.035	30	750	650	3.5-5 @ 750 rpm	100[8]
CH.	J11Y	.035	30	700	900	3.5-5 @ 750 rpm	110[8]
CH.	J11Y	.035	30	750	750	3.5-5 @ 750 rpm	110[8]
CH.	J11Y	.035	30	650	650	3.5-5 @ 750 rpm	110[8]

Chrysler Big V-8

YEAR	ENGINE CU. INS.	HP	CARBURETOR MAKE	TYPE	FLOAT LEVEL (INS.)	INITIAL TIMING STD. TRANS	AUTO. TRANS.	DISTRIBUTOR POINT GAP (INS.)	DWELL
1970	440	375	Carter	4-bbl.	7/32	TDC ± 2.5°[9]	2.5° BTDC ± 2.5°[9]	.016-.019	28.5°-32.5°
	440	390	Holley	3x2-bbl.	18	5° BTDC ± 2.5°[9]	5° BTDC ± 2.5°[9]	.014-.019	20

[1] 255 hp when equipped with dual snorkel air cleaner.
[2] 225 hp when equipped with single snorkel air cleaner and single exhaust.
[3] 230 hp when equipped with single snorkel air cleaner and single exhaust.
[4] 245 hp when equipped with dual exhaust.
[5] 280 hp when equipped with dual snorkel air cleaner (high performance).
[6] 290 hp when equipped with air grabber (cold air package).
[7] 100 psi minimum per cylinder; must not vary more than 40 psi between cylinders.
[8] 110 psi minimum per cylinder; must not vary more than 40 psi between cylinders.
[9] Set at curb idle, with distributor vacuum disconnected and plugged.
[10] 5° BTDC California cars only.

[11] Point gap and dwell do not apply on cars equipped with electronic ignition system.
[12] Idle solenoid adjusted to obtain idle rpm.
[13] Dry float setting between toe of float and float stop.
[14] 800 rpm, manual transmission cars; California only.
[15] Standard air cleaner only; with high performance heated air: 900 rpm.
[16] U.S. only. California cars with R-6256-A Holley 4-bbl.: 800 rpm, except high performance heated air.
[17] U.S. only. California cars with R-690-A Holley 4-bbl.: 700 rpm, except high performance heated air.

Ford 4

1977	140	89[10]	Hol.-Web.	2-bbl.	15/32 dry	6° BTDC[12]	20° BTDC	9	9
1976	140	92	Hol.-Web.	2-bbl.	.460	6° BTDC	20° BTDC	9	9
1975	140	87	Hol.-Web.	2-bbl.	27/64	6° BTDC[8]	6° BTDC	9	—
1974	122	80	Hol.-Web.	2-bbl.	27/64	6° BTDC[7]	6° BTDC[7]	.025	37°-41°
	140	82/88[6]	Hol.-Web.	2-bbl.	27/64	6° BTDC	6° BTDC	.025	37°-41°
1973	98	50	Motorcraft	1-bbl.	1-13/64	12° BTDC[5]	—	.025	37°-41°
	122	80	Holley	2-bbl.	27/64	6° BTDC[5]	9° BTDC[5]	.025	37°-41°
1972	98	54	Motorcraft	1-bbl.	1-13/64	12° BTDC[2]	—	.025	36°-40°
	122	85	Motorcraft	2-bbl.	27/64	6° BTDC[2]	6° BTDC[2,3]	.025	36°-40°
1971	98	75	Autolite	1-bbl.	31/64	12° BTDC[2]	—	.025	38°-40°
	122	100	Autolite	2-bbl.	31/64	6° BTDC[2]	6° BTDC[2]	.025	48°-52°

[1] Lowest cylinder must be within 75% of highest cylinder.
[2] Set at 600 rpm with distributor vacuum advance hose(s) disconnected and plugged.
[3] 9° BTDC on California automatic transmission cars.

[4] Idle set with headlights on high beam and air conditioning on, throttle solenoid connected (higher rpm). Solenoid disconnected for lower rpm.
[5] Timing must be set to decal specs, if different from setting listed.
[6] Pinto—82 hp @ 4600 rpm; Mustang—88 hp @ 5000 rpm.

Ford Inline-6

1977	200	96[24]	Carter	1-bbl.	25/32	6° BTDC	6° BTDC	20	20
	250	98[25]	Carter	1-bbl.	25/32	4° BTDC	6° BTDC[26]	20	20
1976	200	81[21]	Carter	1-bbl.	25/32	10° BTDC	10° BTDC	20	20
	250	90[22]	Carter	1-bbl.	23/32	6° BTDC[23]	14° BTDC[23]	20	20
1975	200	75	Carter	2-bbl.	9/16	6° BTDC[19]	6° BTDC[19]	20	—
	250	72[18]	Carter	2-bbl.	9/16	6° BTDC[19]	6° BTDC[19]	20	—
1974	200	84	Carter	1-bbl.	9/16	6° BTDC	6° BTDC	.027[17]	33°-39°
	250	91	Carter	1-bbl.	9/16	6° BTDC	6° BTDC	.027[17]	35°-39°
1973	200	84	Carter	1-bbl.	3/8	6° BTDC[7,15]	6° BTDC[7,15]	.027	33°-39°
	250	99	Carter	1-bbl.	3/8	6° BTDC[7,15]	6° BTDC[7,15]	.027	33°-39°
1972	170	82	Motorcraft	1-bbl.	3/8	6° BTDC[7]	6° BTDC[7]	.027	35°-39°
	200	90	Motorcraft	1-bbl.	3/8	6° BTDC[7]	6° BTDC[7]	.027	35°-39°
	250	95	Motorcraft	1-bbl.	9/16	6° BTDC[7]	6° BTDC[7]	.027	35°-39°
1971	170	100	Carter	1-bbl.	3/8	6° BTDC[7]	6° BTDC[7]	.027	33°-38°
	200	115	Carter	1-bbl.	3/8	6° BTDC[7]	6° BTDC[7]	.027	33°-38°
	250	145	Carter	1-bbl.	9/16	6° BTDC[7]	6° BTDC[7]	.025[11]	34°-37.5°
1970	170	105	Carter	1-bbl.	7/32	6° BTDC[7]	6° BTDC[7]	.027	35°-40°
	200	120	Carter	1-bbl.	3/8	6° BTDC[7]	6° BTDC[7]	.027	35°-40°
	250	155	Carter	1-bbl.	9/16	6° BTDC[7]	6° BTDC[7]	.025	37°-42°

[3] Lowest cylinder must be within 75% of highest cylinder.
[5] Higher idle speed with solenoid energized and lower idle speed with solenoid de-energized.
[6] Set all idle speeds with headlights on high beam and air conditioning off.
[7] Set at 600 rpm with distributor vacuum advance hose(s) disconnected and plugged.
[8] No air conditioning. 800 rpm on cars with air conditioning.
[9] No air conditioning. 600 rpm on cars with air conditioning.

[10] No air conditioning. 600/500 idle rpm with headlights on high beam and air conditioning off; throttle solenoid connected (higher rpm), solenoid disconnected for lower rpm.
[11] Single diaphragm distributor only; .027-in. point gap, 33°-38° dwell on dual diaphragm distributor.
[12] Adjust idle speed with headlights on high beam and air conditioning off; throttle solenoid connected (higher rpm), solenoid disconnected for lower rpm.
[13] 750 rpm on engines not equipped with throttle solenoid.

Ford V-6

1977	170	93[9]	Ford[8]	2-bbl.[8]	3/8[8]	8° BTDC[7]	12° BTDC[7]	1	1
1976	170	103[4]	Motorcraft	2-bbl.	3/8	10° BTDC[2]	12° BTDC[5]	1	1
1975	170.8	97	Motorcraft	2-bbl.	7/16	6° BTDC	10° BTDC[2]	3	3
1974	170.8	105	Hol.-Web.	2-bbl.	27/64	12° BTDC	12° BTDC	.025	37°-41°

[1] Lowest cylinder must be within 75% of highest cylinder.
[2] 8° BTDC in California.
[3] Solid state ignition standard.

[4] 99 hp in California; 100 hp with automatic transmission in all states.
[5] 6° BTDC in California.
[6] 750 rpm in California.

Ford Windsor V-8

1977	302	139[23]	Ford 2150A[20]	2-bbl.[20]	7/16[20]	12° BTDC	8° BTDC[19]	18	18
	351	149[25]	Ford 2150A	2-bbl.	7/16	—	9° BTDC[19]	18	18
1976	302	134[21]	Ford 2150A	2-bbl.	7/16	12° BTDC[16]	8° BTDC[16]	18	18
	351	154	Ford 2150A	2-bbl.	7/16	—	12° BTDC	18	18
1975	302	129[17]	Motorcraft	2-bbl.	7/16	6° BTDC[19]	6° BTDC[19]	18	—
	351	154[17]	Motorcraft	2-bbl.	7/16	19	19	18	—
1974	302	140	Rawson	2-bbl.	7/16	6° BTDC	6° BTDC	.017	24°-30°
	351	162	Rawson	2-bbl.	7/16	N/A	6° BTDC	.017	24°-30°
1973	302	156	Motorcraft	2-bbl.	7/16	6° BTDC[2,14]	6° BTDC[2,14]	.017	24°-30°
	351	177	Motorcraft	2-bbl.	7/16	—	6° BTDC[2]	.017	24°-30°
1972	302	140	Motorcraft	2-bbl.	13/16	6° BTDC[2]	6° BTDC[2]	.017	26°-30°
	351W	266	Motorcraft	2-bbl.	7/16	6° BTDC[2]	6° BTDC[2]	.017	26°-30°
1971	302	210	Autolite	2-bbl.	7/16	6° BTDC[2]	6° BTDC[2]	.021[6]	24°-29°
	351	240	Autolite	4-bbl.	7/16	6° BTDC[2]	6° BTDC[2]	.021	24°-29°
1970	302	210	Autolite	2-bbl.	7/16	6° BTDC[2]	6° BTDC[2]	.021	24°-29°

SPARK PLUG				IDLE SPEED		FUEL PUMP PRESSURE	COMPRESSION
MAKE	TYPE	GAP (INS.)	TORQUE (FT.-LBS.)	STD. TRANS.†	AUTO. TRANS.††	(PSI)	(PSI)
CH.	J11Y	.035	30	900	800	3.5-5 @ 750 rpm	110[8]
CH.	J11Y	.035	30	900	900	6-7.5 @ 750 rpm	110[8]

18 Wet fuel level; with bowl sight plug removed, fuel level should be at the bottom edge of sight plug hole.
19 2.5° BTDC on California cars equipped with manual transmission.
20 Dwell on dual point distributor is 27°-32° when checking one set of points; 37°-42° when checking dwell with both sets of points operating.
21 7/32-in. on Carter 4-bbl. carburetors.
22 5/16-in. on Carter carburetors only; #7 drill (.200-in.) on Holley 2-bbl. carburetors.
23 7/32-in. float level on cars with manual transmissions.
24 15/64-in. on primary float level; 17/64-in. on secondary float level on Holley 4-bbl. carburetors.

28 .110-in. primary; 9204-in. secondary.
29 Electronic ignition system standard.
30 2.5° BTDC on California cars equipped with automatic transmission.
31 Idle speed 750 in California.
32 Idle speed 850 in California.
33 185 hp in California.
34 200 hp in California.
35 Those with Bosch plugs use WA95 gapped to .033-in.
† In neutral.
†† In drive.

MAKE	TYPE	GAP	TORQUE	STD. TRANS.†	AUTO. TRANS.††	FUEL PUMP (PSI)	COMPRESSION
Autolite	AWRF-42	.034	10-15	850	800[11]	5.5-6.5	1
Autolite	AGRF-52	.032-.036	10-15	750	650	5.5-6.5	1
MO.	AGRF-52	.034	15-25	550	550	3.5-4.5	1
MO.	BRF-42	.034	15-25	750	650	3.5-4.5	1
MO.	AGRF-52	.034	10-15	850	750	3.5-4.5	1
MO.	AGR-32	.030	10-15	750[4]	—	3.5-5.0	1
MO.	BRF-42	.034	15-20	750[4]	650	3.8-5.0	1
MO.	AGR-22	.030	10-15	750/500[4]	—	3.5-5.0	1
MO.	BRF-42	.034	15-20	750/500[4]	650/500[4]	3.0-5.0	1
Autolite	AGR-22	.030	10-15	750/500[4]	—	3.5-5.0	1
Autolite	BRF-32	.034	15-20	750/500[4]	650/500[4]	3.0-5.0	1

7 3° BTDC @ 650 rpm in California.
8 10° BTDC in California.
9 Breakerless ignition standard.
10 88 hp in California sedans, 85 hp in California wagons.
11 750 rpm in California.
12 20° BTDC in California.
† In neutral.
†† In drive.

MAKE	TYPE	GAP	TORQUE	STD. TRANS.†	AUTO. TRANS.††	FUEL PUMP (PSI)	COMPRESSION
Autolite	BRF-82	.050	15-20	800	650	5.5-6.5	3
Autolite	BRF-82	.050	15-20	850	600	5.5-6.5	3
Autolite	BRF-82	.044	15-20	800[19]	650[19]	5.5-6.5	3
Autolite	BRF-82	.044	15-20	850[19]	600[19]	5.5-6.5	3
Autolite	BRF-82	.044	15-20	750[19]	800[19]	4.5-5.5	3
Autolite	BRF-82	.044	15-20	800[19]	600[19]	4.5-5.5	3
MO.	BRF-82	.034	15-20	750	550	4.5-5.5	3
MO.	BRF-82	.044	15-20	500[16]	500[16]	4.5-5.5	3
Autolite	BRF-82	.034	15-20	750[2]	550[2]	4-6 @ 500 rpm	3
Autolite	BRF-82	.034	15-20	750[2]	600[2]	4-6 @ 500 rpm	3
Autolite	BRF-82	.034	15-20	750	—	4-6 @ 500 rpm	3
Autolite	BRF-82	.034	15-20	800/500[12,13]	600/500[12,14]	4-6 @ 500 rpm	3
Autolite	BRF-82	.034	15-20	750/500[12]	600/500[12]	4-6 @ 500 rpm	3
Autolite	BRF-82	.034	15-20	750	—	4-6 @ 500 rpm	3
Autolite	BRF-82	.034	15-20	750[8]	550[10]	4-6 @ 500 rpm	3
Autolite	BRF-82	.034	15-20	750	600	4-6 @ 500 rpm	3
Autolite	BF-82	.034	15-20	750[6,8]	550[9]	4-6 @ 500 rpm	3
Autolite	BF-82	.034	15-20	750[6,9]	550[9]	4-6 @ 500 rpm	3
Autolite	BF-82	.034	15-20	750/500[5,6]	600/500[5]	4-6 @ 500 rpm	3

14 550 rpm on engines not equipped with throttle solenoid.
15 Timing must be set to decal specs if different from setting listed.
16 With throttle solenoid off.
17 Solid state ignition (breakerless) in California.
18 Varies according to application, transmission and exhaust.
19 Varies according to emissions calibration; refer to emissions decal.
20 Solid state ignition standard.
21 78 hp with automatic transmission.

22 81 hp with automatic transmission; 78 hp with automatic transmission in California.
23 8° BTDC with air conditioning.
24 97 hp with automatic transmission.
25 86 hp in California.
26 8° BTDC in California.
† In neutral.
†† In drive.

MAKE	TYPE	GAP	TORQUE	STD. TRANS.†	AUTO. TRANS.††	FUEL PUMP (PSI)	COMPRESSION
MO.	AWSF-42	.034	15-20	850	700[6]	3.5-5.8	1
Autolite	AGR-42	.032-.036	15-20	850	700	3.5-5.8	1
MO.	AGR-42	.034	14-22	850	700	3.5-4.5	1
MO.	AGR-42	.044	14-22	750	650	3.5-4.5	1

7 On California models, refer to emissions decal.
8 California V-6 Pintos & Bobcats use Motorcraft 2700 Variable Venturi carburetor, with dry float setting of 1 3/64 ins.
9 On California models, 90 hp; 88 hp on California wagons.
† In neutral.
†† In drive.

MAKE	TYPE	GAP	TORQUE	STD. TRANS.†	AUTO. TRANS.††	FUEL PUMP (PSI)	COMPRESSION
MO.	ARF-52[24]	.050[24]	10-15	850	650	5.5-6.5	1
MO.	ARF-52[24]	.050[24]	10-15	—	625[19]	4.0-6.0	1
MO.	ARF-42	.042-.046	10-15	750	650[22]	5.5-6.5	1
MO.	ARF-42	.044	10-15	—	650	4.0-6.0	1
Auto.	ARF-42[19]	.044[19]	15-25	900[19]	650[19]	5.5-6.5	1
Auto.	ARF-42[19]	.044[19]	15-25	[19]	[19]	5.5-6.5	1
MO.	BRF-42	.044[15]	15-25	800	650	5.5-6.5	1
MO.	BRF-42	.034[16]	15-25	N A	600	5.5-6.5	1
Autolite	BRF-42	.034	15-20	850[3]	650[3]	4-6 @ 500 rpm	1
Autolite	BRF-42	.034	15-20	—	600[3]	5-7 @ 500 rpm	1
Autolite	BRF-42	.034	15-20	800 500[3]	600 500[3,4]	4-6 @ Idle	1
Autolite	ARF-42	.034	10-15	750 500[3]	575 500[3,4]	5.5-6.5 @ Idle	1
Autolite	BRF-42	.034	15-20	800 500[3]	600 500[3]	4-6 @ 500 rpm	1
Autolite	BRF-42	.034	15-20	775 500[3]	600 500[3]	5-7 @ 500 rpm	1
Autolite	BF-42	.035	15-20	800 500[3]	600 500[3,4]	4-6 @ 500 rpm	1

Ford Windsor V-8

YEAR	CU. INS.	HP	MAKE	TYPE	FLOAT LEVEL (INS.)	STD. TRANS.	AUTO. TRANS.	POINT GAP (INS.)	DWELL
1970	Boss 302	290	Holley	4-bbl.	9	16° BTDC[2]	16° BTDC[2]	.020[7]	30°-33°[8]
	351	250	Autolite	2-bbl.	7 16	10° BTDC[2]	10° BTDC[2]	.021	24°-29°

1 Lowest cylinder must be within 75% of highest cylinder.
2 Set at 600 rpm with distributor vacuum advance hose(s) disconnected and plugged.
3 Adjust idle speed with headlights on high beam and air conditioning off; throttle solenoid connected (higher rpm). solenoid disconnected for lower rpm.
4 575 rpm on engines not equipped with idle solenoid.
6 017-in. point gap and 26 -31 dwell on single diaphragm distributor.
7 Point gap each set of points.
8 Total dwell, dual point distributor.
9 Wet fuel level; with float bowl sight plugs removed. fuel level should be at bottom edge of sight plug, but not overflowing.
14 Timing must be set to decal specs if different from setting listed.
15 Spark plug gap .054 in California. or with solid state ignition.

Ford Cleveland V-8

YEAR	CU. INS.	HP	MAKE	TYPE	FLOAT LEVEL (INS.)	STD. TRANS.	AUTO. TRANS.	POINT GAP (INS.)	DWELL
1977	351M	161	Motorcraft	2-bbl.	3/8 [22]	—	8° BTDC	17	17
	400	173[20]	Motorcraft	2-bbl.	7/16	—	8° BTDC	17	17
1976	351M	152	Motorcraft	2-bbl.	7/16	—	12° BTDC[18]	17	17
	400	180	Motorcraft	2-bbl.	7/16	—	10° BTDC	17	17
1975	351M	148[15]	Motorcraft	2-bbl.	7/16	—	14° BTDC[16]	17	—
	400	158[15]	Motorcraft	2-bbl.	7/16	—	12° BTDC[16]	17	—
1974	351	163	Rawson	2-bbl.	7/16	N/A	14° BTDC	.017[14]	26°-30°
	351CJ	255	Rawson	4-bbl.	13/16	N/A	20° BTDC	.017	26°-30°
	400	170	Rawson	2-bbl.	7/16	N/A	12° BTDC	13	13
1973	351	159	Motorcraft	2-bbl.	7/16	—	14° BTDC[2,12]	.017	24°-30°
	351CJ	266	Motorcraft	4-bbl.	13/16	16° BTDC[2,12]	16° BTDC[2,12]	.017	24°-30°
	400	163	Motorcraft	2-bbl.	7/16	—	6° BTDC[2,12]	.017	24°-30°
1972	351	161-177	Motorcraft	2-bbl.	7/16	6° BTDC[2]	6° BTDC[2]	.017	26°-30°
	351CJ	248-266	Motorcraft	4-bbl.	13/16	16° BTDC[2,3]	16° BTDC[2,3]	.020[5]	26°-30°
	351HO	275	Motorcraft	4-bbl.	13/16	10° BTDC[2]	—	.020	26°-30°
	400	172	Motorcraft	2-bbl.	7/16	—	8° BTDC[2,4]	.017	26°-30°
1971	351	240	Autolite	2-bbl.	7/16	6° BTDC[2]	6° BTDC[2]	.021[8]	24°-29°
	351	285	Autolite	4-bbl.	13/16	6° BTDC[2]	6° BTDC[2]	.021	24°-29°
	Boss 351	330	Autolite	4-bbl.	13/16	6° BTDC[2]	6° BTDC[2]	.021	24°-29°
	400	260	Autolite	2-bbl.	7/16	—	10° BTDC[2,4]	.021[9]	24°-29°
1970	351	250	Autolite	2-bbl.	7/16	6° BTDC[2]	6° BTDC[2]	.021	24°-29°
	351	300	Autolite	4-bbl.	51/64-55/64	6° BTDC[2]	6° BTDC[2]	.021	24°-29°

1 Lowest cylinder must be within 75% of highest cylinder.
2 Set at 600 rpm with distributor vacuum advance hose(s) disconnected and plugged.
3 10° BTDC, 650 rpm curb idle speed on Cougars with 12-in. converter.
4 National only; 6° BTDC California cars.
5 Manual transmission only; .017-in. on automatic transmission cars.
6 Adjust idle speed with headlights on high beam and air conditioning off; throttle solenoid connected (higher rpm). Solenoid disconnected for lower rpm.
7 National only; 625/500 rpm California cars only.
8 California only; .017-in. point gap, 26°-31° dwell on automatic transmission cars (national).
9 Point gap (.017-in.) and 26°-31° dwell on single diaphragm distributor.
10 ARF-32 with manual transmission. ARF-42 with automatic transmission.
11 600 rpm on engines without throttle solenoid.
12 Timing must be set to decal specs if different from setting listed.
13 Solid state ignition is standard.

Ford Big V-8

YEAR	CU. INS.	HP	MAKE	TYPE	FLOAT LEVEL (INS.)	STD. TRANS.	AUTO. TRANS.	POINT GAP (INS.)	DWELL
1971	390	255	Autolite	2-bbl.	7/16	—	6° BTDC[2]	.021[3]	24°-29°
1970	390	270	Autolite	2-bbl.	7/16	10° BTDC[2]	6° BTDC[2]	.021[3]	24°-29°
	428CJ	335	Holley	4-bbl.	9	6° BTDC[2]	6° BTDC[2]	.020[5]	30°-33°[6]
	428SCJ	360	Holley	4-bbl.	9	6° BTDC[2]	6° BTDC[2]	.021[3]	24°-29°
1969	390	270	Autolite	2-bbl.	31/64	6° BTDC[11]	6° BTDC[11]	.017	26°-31°
	390	280[10]	Autolite	2-bbl.	31/64	6° BTDC[11]	6° BTDC[11]	.021	24°-29°
	390	320	Autolite	4-bbl.	13/16	6° BTDC[11]	6° BTDC[11]	.017	26°-31°
	428CJ	335	Holley	4-bbl.	9	6° BTDC[11]	6° BTDC[11]	.021	24°-29°
1968	390	270	Autolite	2-bbl.	31/64	6° BTDC[2]	6° BTDC[2]	.014-.016	26°-28.5°
	390	280[10]	Autolite	2-bbl.	31/64	—	6° BTDC[2]	.021	24°-29°
	390	315	Autolite	4-bbl.	25/32	6° BTDC[2]	6° BTDC[2]	.016	26°-31°
	390	325	Holley	4-bbl.	9	6° BTDC[2]	6° BTDC[2]	.019-.021	24°-29°
	390	335	Holley	4-bbl.	9	6° BTDC[2]	6° BTDC[2]	.014-.016	26°-28.5°
	427	390	Holley	4-bbl.	9	—	6° BTDC[2]	.017	26°-31°
	428	340	Autolite	4-bbl.	25/32	6° BTDC[2]	6° BTDC[2]	.017[12]	26°-31°
	428CJ	335	Holley	4-bbl.	9	6° BTDC[2]	6° BTDC[2]	.017	26°-31°

1 Lowest cylinder must be within 75% of highest cylinder.
2 Set at 600 rpm with distributor vacuum advance hose(s) disconnected and plugged.
3 .017-in. point gap and 26 -31 dwell on single diaphragm distributor.
4 Adjust idle speed with headlights on high beam and air conditioning off; throttle solenoid connected (higher rpm). solenoid disconnected for lower rpm.
5 Point gap, each set of points.
6 Total dwell, dual point distributor.
7 600/500 rpm with air conditioning.
8 Throttle solenoid energized.
9 Wet fuel level; with float bowl sight plugs removed, fuel level should be at bottom edge of sight plug hole.

Ford, Lincoln, Mercury Big V-8

YEAR	CU. INS.	HP	MAKE	TYPE	FLOAT LEVEL (INS.)	STD. TRANS.	AUTO. TRANS.	POINT GAP (INS.)	DWELL
1977	460	197[26]	Motorcraft	4-bbl.	1.0	—	16° BTDC	24	24
1976	460	202	Motorcraft	4-bbl.	1.0	—	8° BTDC[25]	24	24
1975	460	216[23]	Motorcraft	4-bbl.	3 4	—	14° BTDC	24	—
1974	460	195/220	Rawson [19]	4-bbl.	3 4	N A	14° BTDC	20	20
1973	429	201	Motorcraft	4-bbl.	49 64	—	10° BTDC[2]	.017	24°-30°
	460	208	Motorcraft	4-bbl.	49 64	—	14° BTDC[2]	.017	24°-30°
1972	429	205/212	Motorcraft	4-bbl.	49 64	—	10° BTDC[2]	.017	26°-30°
	460	200–224	Motorcraft	4-bbl.	49 64	—	10° BTDC[2,3]	.017	26°-30°
1971	429	320	Autolite	2-bbl.	49 64	—	6° BTDC[2]	.021[5]	24°-29°
	429	360	Autolite	4-bbl.	49 64	4° BTDC[2]	4° BTDC[2]	.021[5]	24°-29°
	429CJ	370	Roch.	4-bbl.	11 32	10° BTDC[2]	10° BTDC[2]	.020[5]	6,7
	429SCJ	375	Holley	4-bbl.	11	10° BTDC[2]	10° BTDC[2]	.020[5]	6,7
	460	365	Autolite	4-bbl.	49 64	—	5° BTDC[2]	.017	26°-31°
1970	429	320	Autolite	2-bbl.	7 16	6° BTDC[2]	6° BTDC[2]	.021[5]	24°-29°
	429	360[15]	Autolite	4-bbl.	25 32	6° BTDC[2]	6° BTDC[2]	.021[5]	24°-29°
	429CJ	360	Roch.	4-bbl.	5 8	10° BTDC[2]	10° BTDC[2]	.021[5]	24°-29°
	429SCJ	370	Holley	4-bbl.	11	10° BTDC[2]	10° BTDC[2]	.021[5]	24°-29°

	SPARK PLUG			IDLE SPEED		FUEL PUMP PRESSURE	COMPRESSION
MAKE	TYPE	GAP (INS.)	TORQUE (FT.-LBS.)	STD. TRANS.†	AUTO. TRANS.††	(PSI)	(PSI)
Autolite	AF-32	.035	10-15	800 500[3]	800 500[3]	4.5-6.5 @ 500 rpm	[1]
Autolite	AF-32	035	15-20	700 500[3]	600 500[3][4]	5-7 @ 500 rpm	[1]

16 Spark plug gap .044 with optional solid state ignition.
17 Varies according to application, transmission and exhaust.
18 Solid state ignition standard.
19 Varies according to emissions calibration; refer to emissions decal.
20 California models use Motorcraft 2700 Variable Venturi carburetor with dry float setting of 1 3/64 ins.

21 133 hp with automatic transmission; 130 hp with automatic in California.
22 700 rpm in California.
23 132 hp in California; 129 hp with 4-speed.
24 California models use ARF-52-6, gapped to .060-in.
25 135 hp in California.
†In neutral. ††In drive.

MO.	ARF-52[21]	.050[21]	10-15	—	16	6.5-7.5	[1]
MO.	ARF-52[21]	.050[21]	10-15	—	650[19]	6.5-7.5	[1]
MO.	ARF-52	.044	10-15	—	650[19]	6.5-7.5	[1]
MO.	ARF-52	.042-.046	10-15	—	650[19]	6.5-7.5	[1]
MO.	D4PF-CA[16]	.044[16]	15-25	—	650[16]	5.5-6.5	[1]
MO.	D4PF-CA[16]	.044[16]	15-25	—	625[16]	5.5-6.5	[1]
MO.	ARF-42	.044[14]	10-15	N A	700	5.5-6.5	[1]
MO.	ARF-42	.034	10-15	N A	800	5.5-6.5	[1]
MO.	ARF-42	.044	10-15	N A	625	5.5-6.5	[1]
Autolite	ARF-42	.034	10-15	—	700[6]	5-7 @ 500 rpm	[1]
Autolite	ARF-42	.034	10-15	1000[6]	800[6]	5-7 @ 500 rpm	[1]
Autolite	ARF-42	.034	10-15	—	625[6]	5-7 @ 500 rpm	[1]
Autolite	ARF-42	.034	10-15	750/500[6]	575/500[6][7]	5.5-6.5 @ Idle	[1]
Autolite	ARF-42	.034	10-15	1000/500[6]	700/500[6][3]	5.5-6.5 @ Idle	[1]
Autolite	ARF-42	.034	10-15	1000/500[6]	—	5.5-6.5 @ Idle	[1]
Autolite	ARF-42	.034	10-15	—	625/500[6]	5.5-6.5 @ Idle	[1]
Autolite	ARF-42	.034	10-15	700/500[6]	600/500[6]	5-7 @ 500 rpm	[1]
Autolite	10	.034	10-15	800/500[6]	600/500[6]	5-7 @ 500 rpm	[1]
Autolite	ARF-42	.034	10-15	825/500[6]	625/500[6]	5-7 @ 500 rpm	[1]
Autolite	ARF-42	.034	10-15	—	600/500[6]	5-7 @ 500 rpm	[1]
Autolite	AF-32	.034	10-15	700/500[6]	600/500[6][11]	5-7 @ 500 rpm	[1]
Autolite	BF-42	.034	10-15	700/500[6]	600/500[6][11]	5-7 @ 500 rpm	[1]

14 California engines have solid state ignitions, with .054-in. spark plug gap.
15 Varies according to application, transmission and exhaust.
16 Varies according to emissions calibration; refer to emissions decal.
17 Solid state ignition standard.
18 8° BTDC @ 650 rpm on California models.
19 625 rpm on California models.
20 168 hp on California models.
21 California models use AR52-6, gapped to .060-in.

22 7/16-in. on California models.
†In neutral.
††In drive.

Autolite	BF-32	.034	15-20	—	600/500[4]	5-7 @ 500 rpm	[1]
Autolite	BF-42	.035	15-20	750/500[4]	575[4][7]	5-7 @ 500 rpm	[1]
Autolite	BF-32	.035	15-20	725[8]	675[8]	4.5-6.5 @ 500 rpm	[1]
Autolite	BF-32	.035	15-20	725[8]	675[8]	4.5-6.5 @ 500 rpm	[1]
Autolite	BF-42	.035	15-20	650	550	4.5-6.5 @ Idle	[1]
Autolite	BF-42	.035	15-20	650	550	4.5-6.5 @ Idle	[1]
Autolite	BF-42	.035	15-20	700	550	4.5-6.5 @ Idle	[1]
Autolite	BF-32	.035	15-20	700	650	4.5-6.5 @ Idle	[1]
Autolite	BF-32	.034	15-20	625	550	4.5-6.5 @ 500 rpm	160-200
Autolite	BF-32	.034	15-20	—	550	4.5-6.5 @ 500 rpm	170-210
Autolite	BF-32	.034	15-20	625	550	4.5-6.5 @ 500 rpm	170-210
Autolite	BF-32	.034	15-20	625	550	4.5-6.5 @ 500 rpm	170-210
Autolite	BF-32	.034	15-20	625	550	4.5-6.5 @ 500 rpm	170-210
Autolite	BF-32	.034	15-20	—	600	4.5-6.5 @ 500 rpm	170-210
Autolite	BF-32	.034	15-20	625	550	4.5-6.5 @ 500 rpm	170-210
Autolite	BF-32	.034	15-20	625	550	4.5-6.5 @ 500 rpm	170-210

10 Premium fuel engine.
11 Set at idle rpm with distributor vacuum advance hose(s) disconnected and plugged.
12 IMCO air system only; .021-in. point gap and 24-29 dwell on engines equipped with Thermactor air system.

†In neutral.
††In drive.

MO.	ARF-52-6	.060	10-15	—	650	7.2-8.2	[1]
MO.	ARF-52	.042-.046	10-15	—	650	6.2-7.2	[1]
MO.	ARF-52	.044	10-15	—	650	5.5-6.5	[1]
MO.	ARF-52	.054[21]	10-15	N A	650	5.5-6.5[22]	[1]
Autolite	ARF-42	.034	10-15	—	650[4]	5-7 @ 500 rpm	[1]
Autolite	ARF-42	.034	10-15	—	625[4]	5-7 @ 500 rpm	[1]
Autolite	BRF-42	.034	15-20	—	600 500[4]	5.5-6.5 @ Idle	[1]
Autolite	BRF-42	.034	15-20	—	600 500[4]	5.5-6.5 @ Idle	[1]
Autolite	BRF-42	.034	10-15	—	590[4][8]	5-7 @ 500 rpm[10]	[1]
Autolite	BRF-42	.034	10-15	700[4]	600[4]	5-7 @ 500 rpm[10]	[1]
Autolite	AF-32	.034	10-15	700[4][9]	650[4][8]	6.5-8.5 @ 500 rpm[10]	[1]
Autolite	AF-32	.034	10-15	650/500[4]	700 500[4]	4.5-6.5 @ 500 rpm	[1]
Autolite	BF-42	.034	10-15	—	600[4]	5-7 @ 500 rpm[10]	[1]
Autolite	BF-42	.035	15-20	850/500[4]	600	5-7 @ 500 rpm	[1]
Autolite	BF-42[14]	.035	15-20	850/500[4]	600	5-7 @ 500 rpm	[1]
Autolite	AF-32	.035	10-15	850/500[4]	600	6.5-8.5 @ 500 rpm[10]	[1]
Autolite	AF-32	.035	10-15	850/500[4]	600	4.5-6.5 @ 500 rpm	[1]

Ford, Lincoln, Mercury Big V-8

YEAR	ENGINE CU. INS.	HP	CARBURETOR MAKE	TYPE	FLOAT LEVEL (INS.)	INITIAL TIMING STD. TRANS	AUTO. TRANS.	DISTRIBUTOR POINT GAP (INS.)	DWELL
1970	Boss 429	375	Holley	4-bbl.	11	10° BTDC[2]	10° BTDC[2]	.020	30°-33° [13]
	460	365	Autolite	4-bbl.	49 64	—	6° BTDC[2]	.017	26°-31°

1 Lowest cylinder must be within 75% of highest cylinder.
2 Set at 600 rpm with distributor vacuum advance hose(s) disconnected and plugged.
3 National only; 6° BTDC on California cars and all 3.00 rear axle ratios.
4 Adjust idle speed with headlights on high beam and air conditioning off; throttle solenoid connected (higher rpm), solenoid disconnected for lower rpm.
5 .017-in. gap and 26°-31° dwell on single diaphragm distributor.

6 Isolate and adjust individual points to 25°-25.5° dwell to obtain 30 -33 dwell combined; manual transmission cars only.
7 27.5°-29.5° dwell on automatic transmission cars only.
8 600/500 with air conditioning.
9 700/500 with air conditioning.
10 With fuel return plugged.

Oldsmobile V-8

YEAR	CU. INS.	HP	MAKE	TYPE	FLOAT LEVEL	STD. TRANS	AUTO. TRANS.	POINT GAP	DWELL
1977	260	105	Roch.	2-bbl.	1/8	16° BTDC	18° BTDC[19]	28	28
	305	145	Roch.	2-bbl.	7/16	8° BTDC	8° BTDC[20]	28	28
	350	160	Roch.	4-bbl.	15/32	—	8° BTDC[20]	28	28
	350	170	Roch.	4-bbl.	13/32	—	20° BTDC[21]	28	28
	403	200	Roch.	4-bbl.	13/32	—	20° BTDC[22]	28	28
1976	260	110	Roch.	2-bbl.	1/8	16° BTDC	18° BTDC	28	28
	260	110	Roch.	2-bbl.	1/8	14° BTDC	16° BTDC	28	28
	260	110	Roch.	2-bbl.	1/8	—	14° BTDC	28	28
	350	N/A	Roch.	2-bbl.	7/16	—	12° BTDC	28	28
	350	160	Roch.	4-bbl.	5/16	—	12° BTDC	28	28
	350	N/A	Roch.	4-bbl.	13/32	—	20° BTDC	28	28
	455	190	Roch.	4-bbl.	13/32	—	16° BTDC	28	28
	455	N/A	Roch.	4-bbl.	13/32	—	18° BTDC	28	28
	455	N/A	Roch.	4-bbl.	13/32	—	14° BTDC	28	28
	455	230	Roch.	4-bbl.	13/32	—	12° BTDC	28	28
1975	260	110	Roch.	2-bbl.	5/32	16° BTDC	18° BTDC	28	—
	350	170	Roch.	4-bbl.	9/16	—	12° BTDC	28	—
	350	180	Roch.	4-bbl.	9/16	—	20° BTDC	28	—
	455	190	Roch.	4-bbl.	1/2	—	16° BTDC	28	—
	455	215	Roch.	4-bbl.	1/2	—	12° BTDC	28	—
1974	350	180/200	Roch.	4-bbl.	1/4	N/A	12° BTDC	.016	30°
	455	210/230	Roch.	4-bbl.	1/4	N/A	8° BTDC	.016	30°
1973	350	160	Roch.	2-bbl.	17/32	—	12° BTDC[5]	.016	30°
	350	180	Roch.	4-bbl.	1/4	8° BTDC[5]	12° BTDC[5]	.016	30°
	455	225	Roch.	4-bbl.	1/4	10° BTDC[5]	8° BTDC[5]	.016	30°
1972	350	160[1]	Roch.	2-bbl.	17/32	8° BTDC[5]	8° BTDC[5]	.016	30°
	350	180[2]	Roch.	4-bbl.	1/4	—	12° BTDC[5]	.016	30°
	455	225	Roch.	4-bbl.	1/4	10° BTDC[5]	8° BTDC[5]	.016	30°
	455	250	Roch.	4-bbl.	1/4	10° BTDC[5]	8° BTDC[5]	.016	30°
	455	265	Roch.	4-bbl.	1/4	10° BTDC[5]	8° BTDC[5]	.016	30°
	455	270	Roch.	4-bbl.	1/4	10° BTDC[5]	8° BTDC[5]	.016	30°
	455	300 (W30)[3]	Roch.	4-bbl.	1/4	10° BTDC[5]	10° BTDC[6]	.016	30°
1971	350	240	Roch.	2-bbl.	17/32-18/32	10° BTDC[5]	10° BTDC[5]	.016	30°
	350	260	Roch.	4-bbl.	1/4	12° BTDC[5]	12° BTDC[5]	.016	30°
	455	280	Roch.	2-bbl.	17/32-18/32	8° BTDC[5]	8° BTDC[5]	.016	30°
	455	320	Roch.	4-bbl.	1/4	8° BTDC[5]	8° BTDC[5]	.016	30°
	455	340	Roch.	4-bbl.	1/4	10° BTDC[5]	10° BTDC[5]	.016	30°
	455	350 (W30)	Roch.	4-bbl.	1/4	12° BTDC[6,10]	10° BTDC[6]	.016	30°
	455	350	Roch.	4-bbl.	1/4	10° BTDC[5]	10° BTDC[5]	.016	30°
1970	350	250	Roch.	2-bbl.	9/16	10° BTDC[5,12]	10° BTDC[5,12]	.016	30°
	350	310	Roch.	4-bbl.	1/4	10° BTDC[5]	10° BTDC[5]	.016	30°
	350	325	Roch.	4-bbl.	1/4	14° BTDC[5]	14° BTDC[5]	.016	30°
	455	310	Roch.	2-bbl.	9/16	8° BTDC[5]	8° BTDC[5]	.016	30°
	455	320	Roch.	2-bbl.	9/16	—	8° BTDC[5]	.016	30°
	455	365	Roch.	4-bbl.	1/4	8° BTDC[5,13]	8° BTDC[5,13]	.016	30°
	455	370	Roch.	4-bbl.	1/4	8° BTDC[6,15]	8° BTDC[6,14]	.016	30°
	455	375	Roch.	4-bbl.	1/4	—	12° BTDC[5]	.016	30°
	455	390	Roch.	4-bbl.	1/4	—	8° BTDC[5]	.016	30°
	455	400	Roch.	4-bbl.	1/4	—	12° BTDC[5]	.016	30°

1 175 hp with dual exhaust.
2 200 hp with dual exhaust.
3 Ram Air.
4 Lowest cylinder must be 70% of highest, and not less than 100 psi.
5 Set at 1100 rpm with distributor and air cleaner vacuum hoses disconnected and plugged.
6 Set at 850 rpm with distributor and air cleaner vacuum hoses disconnected and plugged.

7 AC-R45S spark plugs used on manual transmission cars.
8 With throttle solenoid disconnected/throttle solenoid connected.
9 Lowest cylinder must be 80% of highest, and not less than 100 psi.
10 Set at 850 rpm on engines with W-30 option.
11 650 rpm on air conditioning equipped cars.
12 8° BTDC on engines coded TD, TC, TL.
13 12° BTDC on engines coded TW, TV, TU.
14 10° BTDC on super premium fuel engines.

Pontiac V-8

YEAR	CU. INS.	HP	MAKE	TYPE	FLOAT LEVEL	STD. TRANS	AUTO. TRANS.	POINT GAP	DWELL
1977	301	135	Roch.	2-bbl.	11/32	16° BTDC	12° BTDC	25	—
	305[15]	145	Roch.	2-bbl.	5/8	—	8° BTDC	25	—
	350	170	Roch.	4-bbl.	17/32	—	16° BTDC	25	—
	350	170	Roch.	4-bbl.	13/32	—	20° BTDC	25	—
	400	180	Roch.	4-bbl.	17/32	16° BTDC	16° BTDC	25	—
	400 (T/A)	200	Roch.	4-bbl.	17/32	16° BTDC	16° BTDC	25	—
	403	185	Roch.	4-bbl.	13/32	—	20° BTDC	25	—
1976	260	110	Roch.	2-bbl.	1/8	16° BTDC	18° BTDC	25	—
	350	155	Roch.	2-bbl.	9/16[11]	—	16° BTDC	25	—
	350	170	Roch.	4-bbl.	7/32[12]	—	16° BTDC	25	—
	400	175	Roch.	4-bbl.	9/16	—	16° BTDC	25	—
	400	200	Roch.	4-bbl.	17/32	12° BTDC	16° BTDC	25	—
	455	215	Roch.	4-bbl.	17/32	12° BTDC	16° BTDC	25	—
1975	140	78	Roch.	1-bbl.	11/32	10° BTDC	12° BTDC	25	—
	140	87	Holley	2-bbl.	13/32	10° BTDC	12° BTDC	25	—
	260	110	Roch.	2-bbl.	5/32	16° BTDC	18° BTDC	25	—
	350	170	Roch.	2-bbl.	9/16	—	12° BTDC	25	—
	350	185	Roch.	4-bbl.	9/16	12° BTDC	16° BTDC	25	—

MAKE	TYPE	GAP (INS.)	TORQUE (FT.-LBS.)	STD. TRANS.†	AUTO. TRANS.††	FUEL PUMP PRESSURE (PSI)	COMPRESSION (PSI)
Autolite	AF-32	.035	10-15	850/500[4]	600	4.5-6.5 @ 500 rpm	[1]
Autolite	BF-42	.035	15-20	—	600	5-7 @ 500 rpm	[1]

11 Wet fuel level; with float bowl sight plugs removed, fuel level should be at bottom edge of sight plug.
13 Total dwell, dual point distributor.
14 Mustang only. BRF-42 on Thunderbird engine.
15 Thunderbird option.
19 California engines have Carter carburetors.
20 Solid state ignition is standard, with .054-in. spark plug gap.

21 Spark plug gap .044-in. in California.
22 Fuel pump pressure range 6.2-7.2 in California.
23 Varies according to application, transmission and exhaust.
24 Solid state ignition standard.
25 14° BTDC in California.
26 208 hp on Mark V's.
†In neutral. ††In drive.

MAKE	TYPE	GAP (INS.)	TORQUE (FT.-LBS.)	STD. TRANS.†	AUTO. TRANS.††	FUEL PUMP PRESSURE (PSI)	COMPRESSION (PSI)
AC	R46SZ	.060	25	900	550	5.5-6.5	4
AC	R45TS	.045	15	600	500	5.5-6.5	4
AC	R45TS	.045	15	—	500	5.5-6.5	4
AC	R46SZ	.060	25	—	550	5.5-6.5	4
AC	R46SZ	.060	25	—	600	5.5-6.5	4
AC	R46SX	.080	25	750	550	5.5-6.5	4
AC	R46SX	.080	25	750	550	5.5-6.5	4
AC	R46SX	.080	25	—	550	5.5-6.5	4
AC	R45TSX	.060	25	—	600	5.5-6.5	4
AC	R45TSX	.060	25	—	600	5.5-6.5	4
AC	R46SX	.060	25	—	550	5.5-6.5	4
AC	R46SX	.060	25	—	550	5.5-6.5	4
AC	R46SX	.060	25	—	550	5.5-6.5	4
AC	R46SX	.060	25	—	600	5.5-6.5	4
AC	R46TX	.080	N/A	700	550	3.5-4.5	4
AC	R45TSX	.060	N/A	—	600	5.5-6.5	4
AC	R46SX	.080	N/A	—	600	5.5-6.5	4
AC	R46SX	.080	N/A	—	600	5.5-6.5	4
AC	R46SX	.080	N/A	—	550	5.5-6.5	4
AC	R46S[26]	.040	30	N/A	650	4.0-5.0	4
AC	R46S[27]	.040	30	N/A	650	5.5-6.5	4
AC	R46S	.040	35	—	700/550[8]	5.5-6.5 @ Idle	4
AC	R45S	.040	35	1100/650[8]	650/550[8]	5.5-6.5 @ Idle	4
AC	R46S[25]	.040	35	1000/750[8]	650/550[8]	5.5-6.5 @ Idle	4
AC	R46S	.040	35	600/750[8]	600/650[8]	5.5-6.5 @ Idle	4
AC	R46S[7]	.040	35	—	600/650[8]	5.5-6.5 @ Idle	4
AC	R46S	.040	35	550/750[8]	600	5.5-6.5 @ Idle	4
AC	R46S	.040	35	550/750[8]	600	5.5-6.5 @ Idle	4
AC	R46S[7]	.040	35	550/750[8]	550/650[8]	5.5-6.5 @ Idle	4
AC	R45S	.040	35	550/1000[8]	550/650[8]	5.5-6.5 @ Idle	4
AC	R46S	.040	35	750	600	5.5-6.5 @ Idle	9
AC	R46S[7]	.040	35	750	600	5.5-6.5 @ Idle	9
AC	R46S	.040	35	750	600	5.5-6.5 @ Idle	9
AC	R46S	.040	35	600	600	5.5-6.5 @ Idle	9
AC	R45S	.040	35	600	650	5.5-6.5 @ Idle	9
AC	R45S	.040	35	600	600[11]	5.5-6.5 @ Idle	9
AC	R46S	.040	35	600	600	5.5-6.5 @ Idle	9
AC	R46S	.030	35	750	575[18]	5-6 @ Idle	9
AC	R45S	.030	35	650	575	5-6 @ Idle	9
AC	R43S	.030	35	750	625	5-6 @ Idle	9
AC	R46S	.030	35	675	575	5-6 @ Idle	9
AC	R45S	.030	35	—	575	5-6 @ Idle	9
AC	R45S[16]	.030	35	675	650[17]	5-6 @ Idle	9
AC	R44S	.030	35	750	600	5-6 @ Idle	9
AC	R44S	.030	35	—	600	5-6 @ Idle	9
AC	R45S	.030	35	—	600	5-6 @ Idle	9
AC	R44S	.030	35	—	600	5-6 @ Idle	9

15 12° BTDC on super premium fuel engines.
16 AC-R44S on engines coded TW, TV, TU.
17 700 rpm on engines coded TW, TU.
18 675 rpm on engines coded TD, TC, TL.
19 20° BTDC for Omega and 88.
20 6° BTDC for California cars.
21 18° BTDC for Omega and 88 except wagon.
22 22° BTDC for Cutlass wagon.

23 Vista Cruiser; 10° BTDC.
25 Cutlass with manual transmission; R45S.
26 Cutlass models and station wagons use R45S.
27 Cutlass models with 230/275 hp, 455-cu.-in. engines use R45S.
28 High Energy Ignition; no points used.
†In neutral.
††In drive.

MAKE	TYPE	GAP (INS.)	TORQUE (FT.-LBS.)	STD. TRANS.†	AUTO. TRANS.††	FUEL PUMP PRESSURE (PSI)	COMPRESSION (PSI)
AC	R46TSX	.060	15	800	550	7.0-8.5	5
AC	R45TS	.045	25	800	600	7.5-9.0	5
AC	R45TSX	.060	15	—	575	7.0-8.5	5
AC	R46SZ[14]	.080	30	—	600[13]	5.5-6.5	5
AC	R45TSX	.060	15	800	575[13]	7.0-8.5	5
AC	R45TSX	.060	15	800	575[13]	7.0-8.5	5
AC	R46SZ[14]	.080	30	—	600[13]	5.5-6.5	5
AC	R44SX	.080	15	750	550	3.5-4.5	5
AC	R46TSX	.060	15	—	600	5.0-6.5	5
AC	R45TSX	.060	15	—	600	5.0-6.5	5
AC	R46TSX	.060	15	—	550	5.0-6.5	5
AC	R45TSX	.060	15	775	575	5.0-6.5	5
AC	R45TSX	.060	15	775	550	5.0-6.5	5
AC	R42TS	.035	15	700	750	3.0-4.5	5
AC	R42TS	.035	15	700	750	3.0-4.5	5
AC	R46TX	.060	15	700	550	3.5-4.5	5
AC	R45TSX	.060	15	—	600	5.0-6.5	5
AC	R45TSX	.060	15	700	600	5.0-6.5	5

Pontiac V-8

YEAR	ENGINE CU. INS.	HP	CARBURETOR MAKE	TYPE	FLOAT LEVEL (INS.)	INITIAL TIMING STD. TRANS	AUTO. TRANS.	DISTRIBUTOR POINT GAP (INS.)	DWELL
1975	400	180	Roch.	2-bbl.	1/2	—	16° BTDC	25	—
	400	190	Roch.	4-bbl.	1/2	12° BTDC	12° BTDC	25	—
	455	205	Roch.	4-bbl.	1/2	—	16° BTDC	25	—
1974	350	155/170	Roch.	2-bbl.	21/32	10° BTDC	12° BTDC	.016	30°
	350	170/200	Roch.	4-bbl.	3/8	10° BTDC	12° BTDC	.016	30°
	400	175/190	Roch.	2-bbl.	21/32	N/A	12° BTDC	.016	30°
	400	200/225	Roch.	4-bbl.	3/8	10° BTDC	12° BTDC	.016	30°
	455	215/250	Roch.	4-bbl.	3/8	N/A	12° BTDC	.016	30°
	455	290	Roch.	4-bbl.	3/8	10° BTDC	12° BTDC	.016	30°
1973	350	150	Roch.	2-bbl.	5/8	10° BTDC[6]	12° BTDC[6]	.019	30°
	400	170	Roch.	2-bbl.	5/8	—	12° BTDC[6]	.019	30°
	400	230	Roch.	4-bbl.	1/4	10° BTDC[6]	12° BTDC[6]	.019	30°
	455	250	Roch.	4-bbl.	1/4	10° BTDC[6]	12° BTDC[6]	.019	30°
1972	307	130	Roch.	2-bbl.	25/32	4° BTDC[6]	8° BTDC[6]	.019	30°
	350	160	Roch.	2-bbl.[4]	9/16[1]	8° BTDC[6]	10° BTDC[6]	.019	30°
	400	175[1]	Roch.	2 or 4-bbl.	22	8° BTDC[6]	10° BTDC[6]	.019	30°
	455	185[2,3]	Roch.	2 or 4-bbl.	22	8° BTDC[6]	10° BTDC[6]	.019	30°
1971	307	200	Roch.	2-bbl.	27/32	4° BTDC[6]	8° BTDC[6]	.019	30°
	350	250	Roch.	2-bbl.	9/16	8° BTDC[6]	8° BTDC[6]	.019	30°
	400	265	Roch.	2-bbl.	11/16	—	12° BTDC[6]	.019	30°
	400	300	Roch.	4-bbl.	9/32	8° BTDC[6]	8° BTDC[6]	.019	30°
	455	280	Roch.	2-bbl.	11/16	—	8° BTDC[6]	.019	30°
	455	325	Roch.	4-bbl.	9/32	—	8° BTDC[6]	.019	30°
	455	335	Roch.	4-bbl.	9/32	8° BTDC[6]	8° BTDC[6]	.019	30°
1970	350	255	Roch.	2-bbl.	9/16	9° BTDC[6]	9° BTDC[6]	.019	30°
	400	265	Roch.	2-bbl.	11/16	9° BTDC[6]	9° BTDC[6]	.019	30°
	400	290	Roch.	2-bbl.	11/16	9° BTDC[6]	9° BTDC[6]	.019	30°
	400	330	Roch.	4-bbl.	9/32	9° BTDC[6]	9° BTDC[6]	.019	30°
	400	345	Roch.	4-bbl.	9/32	9° BTDC[6]	9° BTDC[6]	.019	30°
	400	350	Roch.	4-bbl.	9/32	9° BTDC[6]	9° BTDC[6]	.019	30°
	400	366[2,3]	Roch.	4-bbl.	9/32	9° BTDC[6]	9° BTDC[6]	.019	30°
	400	370[2,4]	Roch.	4-bbl.	9/32	15° BTDC[6]	15° BTDC[6]	.019	30°
	455	360	Roch.	4-bbl.	9/32	9° BTDC[6]	9° BTDC[6]	.019	30°
	455	370	Roch.	4-bbl.	9/32	9° BTDC[6]	9° BTDC[6]	.019	30°

1 200 hp with dual exhaust and 4-bbl. carburetor.
2 220 hp with dual exhaust and 4-bbl. carbuetor.
3 300 hp with Ram Air.
4 Automatic transmission cars only. Manual transmission cars equipped with Carter 2-bbl. carburetor, float level 5/16-in.
5 No cylinder should be less than 80% of highest cylinder.
6 Set at idle rpm with distributor vacuum advance hose disconnected and plugged; idle solenoid disconnected.
7 Idle solenoid disconnected/idle solenoid connected.
8 625 rpm on 2-bbl. carburetors.
9 500/700 on 455 High Output engine (Ram Air).
10 Idle solenoid connected.

CYLINDER NUMBERING AND FIRING ORDER GUIDE

MAKE	CYLINDER NUMBERS (front to rear)	FIRING ORDER
AMERICAN MOTORS Inline-6's	1-2-3-4-5-6	1-5-3-6-2-4
AMERICAN MOTORS V-8's	L 1-3-5-7 R 2-4-6-8	1-8-4-3-6-5-7-2
BUICK Inline-6	1-2-3-4-5-6	1-5-3-6-2-4
BUICK V-6	L 1-3-5 R 2-4-6	1-6-5-4-3-2
BUICK V-8's	L 1-3-5-7 R 2-4-6-8	1-8-4-3-6-5-7-2
CADILLAC V-8's	L 1-3-5-7 R 2-4-6-8	1-5-6-3-4-2-7-8
CHEVROLET Inline-4's	1-2-3-4	1-3-4-2
CHEVROLET Inline-6	1-2-3-4-5-6	1-5-3-6-2-4
CHEVROLET V-8's	L 1-3-5-7 R 2-4-6-8	1-8-4-3-6-5-7-2
CHRYSLER CORP. Inline-6's	1-2-3-4-5-6	1-5-3-6-2-4
CHRYSLER CORP. V-8's	L 1-3-5-7 R 2-4-6-8	1-8-4-3-6-5-7-2
FORD MOTOR CO. Inline-4's	1-2-3-4	1-3-4-2
FORD MOTOR CO. Inline-6's	1-2-3-4-5-6	1-5-3-6-2-4
FORD MOTOR CO. V-6	L 1-2-3 R 2-4-6	1-4-2-5-3-6
FORD MOTOR CO. V-8 (302 only)	L 5-6-7-8 R 1-2-3-4	1-5-4-2-6-3-7-8
FORD MOTOR CO. V-8's (all others)	L 5-6-7-8 R 1-2-3-4	1-3-7-2-6-5-4-8
OLDSMOBILE Inline-6	1-2-3-4-5-6	1-5-3-6-2-4
OLDSMOBILE V-6	L 1-3-5 R 2-4-6	1-6-5-4-3-2
PONTIAC Inline-6	1-2-3-4-5-6	1-5-3-6-2-4
PONTIAC V-8's	L 1-3-5-7 R 2-4-6-8	1-8-4-3-6-5-7-2

MAKE	SPARK PLUG TYPE	GAP (INS.)	TORQUE (FT.-LBS.)	IDLE SPEED STD. TRANS.†	AUTO. TRANS.††	FUEL PUMP PRESSURE (PSI)	COMPRESSION (PSI)
AC	R46TSX	.060	15	—	750	5.0-6.5	5
AC	R45TSX	.060	15	750	750	5.0-6.5	5
AC	R45TSX	.060	15	—	750	5.0-6.5	5
AC	R46TS	.040	15	900	650	5.0-6.5	120-160 5
AC	R46TS	.040	15	1000	650	5.0-6.5	120-160 5
AC	R46TS	.040	15	N/A	650	5.0-6.5	120-160 5
AC	R45TS	.040	15	1000	650	5.0-6.5	120-160 5
AC	R45TS	.040	15	N/A	650	5.0-6.5	120-160 5
AC	R44TS	.040	15	1000	750	5.0-6.5	120-160 5
AC	R46TS	.040	15	900/600 7	650	3-6.5 @ Idle	120-160 5
AC	R46TS	.040	15		650	3-6.5 @ Idle	120-160 5
AC	R45TS	.040	15	1000/600 7	650	3-6.5 @ Idle	120-160 5
AC	R45TS	.040	15	1000/600 7	650	3-6.5 @ Idle	120-160 5
AC	R44T	.035	15	900/450 7	600/450 7	3-6.5 @ Idle	150 5
AC	R46TS	.035	15	800	625	3-6.5 @ Idle	120-160 5
AC	R46TS	.035	15	600/1000 7	500/700 7.8	3-6.5 @ Idle	120-160 5
AC	R45TS	.035	15	600/1000 7	500/600 7.9	3-6.5 @ Idle	120-160 5
AC	R45TS	.035	15	600/900 7	550/650 7	5-6.5 @ Idle	.150 5
AC	R47S	.035	25	800	600	5-6.5 @ Idle	120-160 5
AC	R47S	.035	25	—	600	5-6.5 @ Idle	120-160 5
AC	R47S	.035	25	600/1000 7	700	5-6.5 @ Idle	120-160 5
AC	R46S	.035	25	—	650	5-6.5 @ Idle	120-160 5
AC	R46S	.035	25	—	650	5-6.5 @ Idle	120-160 5
AC	R46S	.035	25	600/1000 7	700	5-6.5 @ Idle	120-160 5
AC	R46S	.035	25	800	650	5-8 @ 1000 rpm	150-170 5
AC	R46S	.035	25	800	650	5-8 @ 1000 rpm	150-170 5
AC	R46S	.035	25	800	650	5-8 @ 1000 rpm	185-210 5
AC	R45S	.035	25	950	650	5-8 @ 1000 rpm	185-210 5
AC	R45S	.035	25	950	650	5-8 @ 1000 rpm	185-210 5
AC	R45S	.035	25	950	650	5-8 @ 1000 rpm	185-210 5
AC	R44S	.035	25	1000 10	750 10	5-8 @ 1000 rpm	185-210 5
AC	R45S	.035	25	950	650	5-8 @ 1000 rpm	185-210 5

11 15/32-in. on the Ventura.
12 5/16-in. on the Ventura.
13 On air-conditioned cars, 550 rpm with A/C off, 650 rpm with A/C on.
14 R45SX for high-altitude engine.
15 Available in Ventura only.
22 ⅜-in. on 2-bbl. carburetor; ¼-in. on 4-bbl.

23 Ram Air III.
24 Ram Air IV.
25 High Energy Ignition, no points used.
† In neutral.
†† In drive.

Troubleshooting Guides

There are three ways that you can eliminate problems in an automobile. The first is to think about it, do a bit of testing and narrow the trouble down to one particular part or area. The second method is to replace everything on the car that might have anything to do with the problem in the hope that it can be eliminated. (A lot of shops do just this.) The third way is to sell the car. The first method is not used as much as it should be, as people just don't like to read. As they don't like to use their brains either, many jump quickly into the second method and start replacing everything on the car. There is one redeeming aspect to this approach—a lot of cars are eventually fixed that way.

We've seen complete rear axles replaced because there was a noise in the wheel bearing. We've also seen engines that wouldn't run correctly get loaded down with all new accessories—carburetor, distributor, spark plugs, wires, even the battery was changed because one of those units was probably the culprit. Unfortunately, you'll even find some mechanic among the pros who wants to replace a unit rather than analyze the problem. He's the one who'll accept any suggestion because he doesn't know what to do next. And then there's the poor soul, bless him, who will actually change the hood ornament or wheel covers to make the car run right, simply because these are the only parts he hasn't worked on already.

If you've got lots of money and time, that kind of hit-or-miss repairing is OK, but sadly, there's no guarantee of success, and you may end up with nothing else to do but sell the car. And if the fellow who buys it knows anything at all about making cars run, he's got the buy of a lifetime, because you've practically rebuilt it for him. That brings us full circle right back to method No. 1, where you have to find the part that is causing the problem and either fix or replace it.

Almost anybody knows where to start the search. If the engine dies, you look at the carburetor. If it misses, you suspect the spark plugs. For an overheating problem, you check the radiator. But after you've checked the obvious and found nothing wrong, you should go to this troubleshooting list where you'll find causes you hadn't thought of before.

Admittedly, the troubleshooting lists are not absolutely complete, and any attempt to make them so would more than fill this entire book. But we've tried to pick the most common problems (and some that aren't so common) and lay them out for you. Reading these, you'll soon conclude that everything is arranged in helter-skelter fashion, but that's deliberate on our part. We figure that this is one way of forcing you to think while you're reading. These troubleshooting lists are really like the starting switch on your car—they're the first step in a process that should result in a good running automobile.

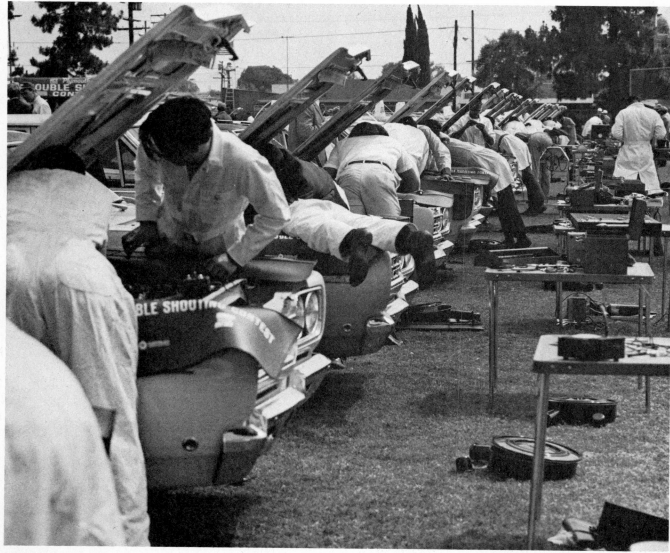

1. Engine

WILL NOT START

(a) Battery is weak.
(a) Test battery specific gravity, and recharge or replace if necessary.

(b) Battery terminals loose or corroded.
(b) Clean and tighten; apply coat of petroleum to terminals.

(c) Faulty ignition cables, wires, or distributor cap.
(c) Check wiring for cracks or shorting, and replace if necessary; replace distributor cap.

(d) Faulty coil.
(d) Test and replace if necessary.

(e) Spark plug gap incorrect.
(e) Remove and regap to specs.

(f) Ignition timing incorrect.
(f) Reset timing to specs.

(g) Dirt or moisture in fuel line or carburetor.
(g) Clean lines and carburetor.

(h) Carburetor flooded.
(h) Adjust float level and check seats.

(i) Carburetor float setting incorrect.
(i) Adjust float level and check seats.

(j) Fuel pump faulty.
(j) Test output and replace if necessary.

(k) Carburetor percolating; no fuel in carburetor.
(k) Measure float level, adjust bowl vent and inspect manifold control valve operation.

ENGINE STALLS

(a) Idle speed too low.
(a) Adjust carburetor.

(b) Choke adjustment incorrect.
(b) Adjust choke correctly.

(c) Idle mixture incorrect.
(c) Richen if too lean; lean if too rich. Use idle mixture screw on carburetor.

(d) Carburetor float setting incorrect.
(d) Adjust carburetor float level.

(e) Intake manifold has leak.
(e) Inspect intake manifold gasket; replace if necessary.

(f) Ignition wiring incorrect.
(f) Replace with correct wiring.

(g) Faulty coil.
(g) Test and replace if necessary.

(h) Burned or worn distributor rotor.
(h) Replace with new rotor.

(i) Tappet lash incorrect (6-cyl.)
(i) Adjust lash to specs.

LOSS OF ENGINE POWER

(a) Ignition timing incorrect.
(a) Reset timing to specs.

(b) Burned or worn distributor rotor.
(b) Replace with new rotor.

(c) Distributor shaft worn.
(c) Remove distributor and repair.

(d) Dirty spark plugs or incorrect gap.
(d) Remove, clean, and regap, or replace.

(e) Dirt or moisture in fuel line, carburetor, or filter.
(e) Clean lines and carburetor; replace filter.

(f) Carburetor float setting incorrect.
(f) Adjust float level.

(g) Fuel pump faulty.
(g) Test output and replace if necessary.

(h) Valve timing incorrect.
(h) Check and reset vave timing to specs.

(i) Cylinder head gasket faulty.
(i) Install new head gasket.

(j) Low cylinder compression.
(j) Remove plugs and test compression of each cylinder.

(k) Valves worn, pitted, or burned.
(k) Do valve job.

(l) Faulty TCS spark advance controls.
(l) Replace faulty components and replace.

(m) Faulty ignition cables, wires, or distributor cap.
(m) Check wiring for cracks or shorting, and replace if necessary; replace distributor cap.

(n) Faulty coil.
(n) Test and replace if necessary.

ENGINE MISSES ON ACCELERATION

(a) Dirty spark plugs or incorrect gap.
(a) Clean plugs and reset gap to specs.

(b) Dirt in carburetor.
(b) Remove and clean carburetor.

(c) Ignition timing incorrect.
(c) Reset timing to specs.

(d) Weak acceleration pump in carburetor.
(d) Replace with new pump.

(e) Valves worn, pitted, or burned.
(e) Do valve job.

(f) Faulty coil.
(f) Test and replace if necessary.

ENGINE MISSES AT HIGH RPM

(a) Dirty spark plugs or incorrect gap.
(a) Clean plugs and reset gap to specs.

(b) Distributor shaft worn.
(b) Remove distributor and repair.

(c) Distributor rotor worn or burned.
(c) Replace with new rotor.

(d) Faulty coil.
(d) Test, and replace if necessary.

(e) Ignition timing incorrect.
(e) Reset timing to specs.

(f) Dirt in carburetor jets.
(f) Clean jets thoroughly.

(g) Dirt or moisture in fuel line, carburetor, or fuel filter.
(g) Clean lines and carburetor; replace fuel filter.

NOISY VALVES

(a) Thin or diluted oil in crankcase.
(a) Change oil.

(b) Low oil pressure.
(b) Check engine oil level; inspect oil pump relief valve and spring.

(c) Dirt in tappets.
(c) Clean tappets.

(d) Bent pushrods.
(d) Install new pushrods.

(e) Rocker arms worn.
(e) Replace, and check oil supply to rockers.

(f) Tappets worn.
(f) Install new tappets.

(g) Valve guides worn.
(g) Ream, and install new valve guides.

(h) Run-out of valve seats or valve faces excessive.
(h) Grind valve seats and valves to specs.

(i) Tappet lash incorrect (6-cyl.)
(i) Adjust lash to specs.

CONNECTING ROD NOISE

(a) Oil supply insufficient.
(a) Check engine oil level.

(b) Low oil pressure.
(b) Check engine oil level; inspect oil pump relief valve and spring.

(c) Thin or diluted oil.
(c) Change oil.

(d) Bearing clearance excessive.
(d) Measure bearings for correct clearance.

(e) Connecting rod journals out-of-round.
(e) Replace crankshaft or regrind journals.

(f) Connecting rods misaligned.
(f) Replace bent connecting rods.

MAIN BEARING NOISE

(a)	Oil supply insufficient.	(a)	Check engine oil level.
(b)	Low oil pressure.	(b)	Check engine oil level, inspect oil pump relief valve and spring.
(c)	Thin or diluted oil.	(c)	Change oil.
(d)	Bearing clearance excessive.	(d)	Measure bearings for correct clearance.
(e)	Excessive end-play.	(e)	Check thrust main bearing for wear on flanges.
(f)	Crankshaft journal out-of-round.	(f)	Replace crankshaft or regrind journals.
(g)	Loose flywheel or torque converter.	(g)	Tighten to correct torque as per specs.

OIL PRESSURE DROP

(a)	Low oil level.	(a)	Check engine oil level.
(b)	Faulty oil pressure sending unit.	(b)	Replace with new sending unit.
(c)	Clogged oil filter.	(c)	Replace oil filter.
(d)	Oil pump worn.	(d)	Remove and replace worn parts or pump.
(e)	Thin or diluted oil.	(e)	Change oil.
(f)	Bearing clearance excessive.	(f)	Measure bearings for correct clearance.
(g)	Oil pump relief valve stuck.	(g)	Remove valve; inspect, clean, and reinstall.
(h)	Oil pump suction tube loose, bent, or cracked.	(h)	Remove oil pan, and install new tube if necessary.

OIL PUMPS AT RINGS

(a)	Worn, scuffed, or broken piston rings.	(a)	Hone cylinder bores and install new piston rings.
(b)	Carbon in oil ring slot.	(b)	Install new piston rings.
(c)	Rings too tight in grooves.	(c)	Remove rings and check grooves. If groove is not proper width, replace piston.

2. Starting System

STARTER WILL NOT OPERATE

(a)	Battery discharged or defective.	(a)	Check headlight operation; if dim or will not glow, charge battery. If battery cannot pass light-load test after charging, replace.
(b)	Poor cable wire connections.	(b)	Check connections at battery, solenoid, cowl connector, and ignition switch.
(c)	Neutral start switch out of adjustment or defective.	(c)	Move shift lever through all ranges with foot brake set and key in start position. If starter cranks in R and D, position shift lever in N with key off, remove neutral start switch, reinstall and try starting in N and P. If starter cranks in L2 and L1, replace switch.
(d)	Fusible link burned out.	(d)	Inspect condition of fusible link. If burned, replace and recheck starting.
(e)	Ignition switch defective.	(e)	Shift lever in neutral and turn ignition switch ON to see if wipers and turn signals operate. If not, check for disconnected cowl and/or ignition switch connector or burned fusible link. If all are OK, replace ignition switch.

(f) Solenoid defective.

(f) Connect voltmeter to solenoid "S" terminal and starter frame. Take reading when trying to start engine; if reading is 9 volts or more, replace solenoid.

(g) Seat belts not fastened.

(g) Fasten seat belts.

STARTER CLICKS BUT WILL NOT CRANK

(a) Poor connections at battery and/or starter.

(a) Check and retighten connections.

(b) Solenoid or starter motor defective.

(b) Remove starter motor, check solenoid and/or starter and repair or replace.

STARTER CRANKS ENGINE SLOWLY

(a) Battery discharged or defective.

(a) Check headlight operation as above.

(b) Poor connections at battery and/or starter.

(b) Check and retighten connections.

(c) Wrong starter motor on car.

(c) Check part numbers to insure that starter is correct for car; replace if incorrect.

(d) Starter is defective.

(d) Remove starter motor, inspect bushings and repair as necessary.

(e) Cranking voltage is low.

(e) Check cranking voltage at positive terminal of ignition coil; it should be at least 9.5 volts. If less, check condition of battery, cables and starter connections. If over 9.5 volts, low temperature or too heavy oil may be causing excessive drag.

STARTER SPINS BUT WILL NOT CRANK ENGINE

(a) Armature shaft dirty or corroded.

(a) Clean shaft and lubricate with lithium soap grease.

(b) Starter drive clutch defective.

(b) Check drive clutch. Replace if necessary.

(c) Missing teeth on flywheel ring gear.

(c) Replace flywheel ring gear and inspect teeth on drive pinion gear. Replace starter drive if necessary.

STARTER CRANKS ENGINE BUT IS EXCESSIVELY NOISY

(a) Drive pinion to ring gear clearance incorrect.

(a) Measure distance between tip of pinion tooth and root of two ring gear teeth with round feeler gauge at three locations around ring gear. Distance should be within .025 to .060-in. If distance is less than .025-in., shim starter away from engine block at both attaching bolts. If distance is greater than .060-in., shim to maximum of .30-in. at outboard attaching bolt. Recheck for correct clearance.

(b) Starter drive or ring gear is defective.

(b) Check drive and ring gear; replace if necessary.

(c) Starter bushing worn.

(c) Replace.

3. Fuel System

ENGINE CRANKS BUT WILL NOT START

(a) Car is out of gas.

(a) Add fuel to tank and check fuel gauge for proper operation.

(b) Choke valve does not close sufficiently when cold.

(b) Adjust the choke thermostatic coil.

(c) Choke valve or linkage binds or sticks.

(c) Realign or replace the choke valve or linkage as required. Clean but do not oil.

CONDITION	CORRECTION	CONDITION	CORRECTION
(d) No fuel in carburetor.	(d) Disconnect fuel line at tank and blow out with compressed air. Reconnect and check for proper operation. If not, replace fuel pump. Fuel filter may be plugged or carburetor float may require adjustment.	(d) Gasket between air horn and float bowl leaks.	(d) Torque air horn to float bowl to specs.
		(e) Carburetor loose on manifold.	(e) Tighten carburetor-to-manifold bolts to specs.
(e) Engine is flooded.	(e) Adjust throttle linkage and unloader if choke valve is not opening. If unloader works properly, disassemble and clean carburetor to remove dirt in carburetor float needle and seat. If engine still floods, check float for bent arm.	(f) Air valve sticks open.	(f) Free-up air valve shaft and align air valves. Check air valve spring for closing tension and replace if defective.
		(g) Secondary throttle valve lockout.	(g) Free-up and check for proper operation if binding, then adjust secondary throttle valve lockout.

ENGINE STARTS AND STALLS

NO POWER—HEAVY ACCELERATION OR HIGH SPEED

CONDITION	CORRECTION	CONDITION	CORRECTION
(a) Fast idle speed too low.	(a) Readjust fast idle to specs.	(a) Carburetor throttle valve not opening completely.	(a) Adjust linkage to obtain wide open throttle in carburetor.
(b) Choke vacuum break unit is defective.	(b) Replace diaphragm unit.	(b) Dirty or plugged fuel filters.	(b) Clean or replace filters.
(c) Choke coil rod out of adjustment.	(c) Adjust properly.	(c) Secondary throttle valves do not unlock once engine has warmed up.	(c) Free-up and adjust lockout.
(d) Choke valve or linkage binds or sticks.	(d) Realign or replace the choke valve or linkage as required. Clean but do not oil.	(d) Air valves bind, or are stuck open or closed.	(d) Free-up air valve shaft and align air valves. Check air valve spring for closing tension and replace if defective.
(e) Insufficient fuel in carburetor.	(e) Disconnect fuel line at tank and blow out with compressed air. Reconnect and check for proper operation. If not, replace fuel pump. Fuel filter may be plugged or carburetor float may need adjustment.	(e) Power system inoperative.	(e) Remove air horn and clean piston and cavity of dirt. Check power piston spring for distortion.
(f) Carburetor flooding.	(f) Check fuel filters and replace if necessary. If carburetor continues to flood, remove air horn and check float needle and seat for proper seal. If needle set leaks, replace.	(f) Float level too low.	(f) Check and reset float level to specs.
		(g) Float does not drop far enough in bowl.	(g) Check for bind in float hanger and arm; check float alignment in bowl.
		(h) Main metering jets or metering rods are dirty or plugged.	(h) Completely disassemble carburetor and clean thoroughly.

ENGINE IDLES ROUGH AND STALLS

ENGINE STARTS HARD WHEN HOT

CONDITION	CORRECTION	CONDITION	CORRECTION
(a) Idle speed setting incorrect.	(a) Readjust idle speed to specs.	(a) Choke valve does not open completely.	(a) As choke valve and/or linkage binds, clean or replace as required. Also check and adjust choke thermostatic coil.
(b) Manifold vacuum hoses disconnected, improperly installed or leak.	(b) Check all vacuum hoses, install or replace as required.		
(c) Carburetor loose on intake manifold.	(c) Tighten carburetor-to-manifold bolts to specs.	(b) No fuel in carburetor.	(b) Check fuel pump for proper operation and replace if necessary. Check and adjust float level.
(d) Dirt in idle channels.	(d) Clean fuel system and carburetor.	(c) Float bowl leaks.	(c) Locate leak and repair.
(e) Secondary throttle valve out of alignment.	(e) Loosen screws, align valves and tighten screws.		

ENGINE SURGES OR RUNS UNEVEN

CONDITION	CORRECTION	CONDITION	CORRECTION
(f) Defective intake manifold gasket.	(f) Replace manifold gasket.	(a) Fuel restriction.	(a) Check hoses and fuel lines for bends, kinks or leaks and straighten. Check fuel filter and replace if dirty or plugged.
(g) Defective carburetor base gasket.	(g) Replace gasket.		

ENGINE HESITATES ON ACCELERATION

CONDITION	CORRECTION	CONDITION	CORRECTION
(a) Accelerator pump system defective.	(a) Remove air horn and check pump cup. If cracked, scored or distorted, replace pump plunger. Check discharge ball for proper seating and location.	(b) Dirt or water in fuel.	(b) Clean fuel tank, lines and filters. Remove and clean carburetor.
		(c) Float level incorrect.	(c) Check for free float and float needle valve operation; free-up, adjust or replace as necessary.
(b) Dirt in pump passages or pump jet.	(b) Clean and blow out with compressed air.	(d) Main metering jets or metering rods are dirty, plugged or bent.	(d) Completely disassemble carburetor and clean thoroughly. Replace bent rods.
(c) Float level incorrect.	(c) Check and reset float level to specs. Make sure float needle is not sticking.	(e) Power system inoperative.	(e) Remove air horn and clean piston and cavity of dirt. Check power piston spring for distortion.

CONDITION	CORRECTION	CONDITION	CORRECTION

(f) Vacuum leakage.

(f) Tighten all hose connections. Torque carburetor to manifold to specs. Replace gasket if defective.

4. Emission System EGR

EGR VALVE STEM DOES NOT MOVE ON SYSTEM TEST

(a) Hoses may be cracked, leaking, disconnected or plugged.

(a) Inspect all hose connections and leakcheck to confirm hoses are open. If any defective hoses are found, replace.

(b) EGR valve is defective, ruptured diaphragm or valve stem frozen.

(b) Disconnect hose from EGR valve and connect external vacuum source of 10 Hg or more to valve diaphragm. If valve does not move, replace. If valve opens about 1/8-in., pinch off supply hose to check for diaphragm leakage—valve should remain open for 30 sec. or more. If leakage does occur, replace valve.

EGR VALVE STEM DOES NOT MOVE ON SYSTEM TEST BUT DOES ON EXTERNAL VACUUM SOURCE

(a) Temperature control valve is defective.

(a) Verify that temperature in vehicle area is above that specified for particular EGR system, then disconnect hose from temperature control valve and plug hose. If EGR valve stem operates normally, replace TC valve.

(b) Defective control system—plugged passages.

(b) Remove carburetor and check vacuum passages in throttle bore. Use suitable solvent to remove any deposits and check for flow with light air pressure. Do not use drills or wires to clean carburetor control passages as these can upset calibration of precision control orifices.

ENGINE WILL NOT IDLE, DIES OUT ON RETURN TO IDLE, IDLE IS SLOW AND ROUGH

(a) EGR valve is stuck open.

(a) Disconnect hose from EGR valve and plug hose. Check idle. If idle is satisfactory, amplifier unit is defective (Venturi Vacuum Control System only).

(b) EGR valve leakage in closed position.

(b) Remove EGR valve and inspect to insure poppet is seated. Replace if defective.

POOR ENGINE RESPONSE AT ROAD SPEEDS BELOW 40° F.

(a) Temperature control valve is defective.

(a) Replace TC valve.

5. Emission System Air Pump

EXCESSIVE BELT NOISE

(a) Loose belt.

(a) Tighten belt to specs.

(b) Seized pump.

(b) Replace pump.

EXCESSIVE PUMP NOISE—CHIRPING, RUMBLING OR KNOCKING

(a) Leak in hose.

(a) Locate leak using soap solution and correct.

(b) Loose hose.

(b) Tighten or replace hose clamp.

(c) Hose touches other engine parts.

(c) Change hose position.

(d) Diverter valve does not operate.

(d) Replace.

(e) Check valve does not operate.

(e) Replace.

(f) Pump mounting fasteners are loose.

(f) Tighten mounting screws to specs.

(g) Pump failure.

(g) Remove and replace pump.

NO AIR SUPPLY AS ENGINE ACCELERATES ABOVE 1500 RPM

(a) Loose drive belt.

(a) Tighten to specs.

(b) Supply hose leaks.

(b) Locate leak, repair or replace.

(c) Leak at fitting(s).

(c) Tighten or replace hose clamps.

(d) Diverter valve leaks.

(d) Run car at idle; if air is expelled through diverter exhaust, replace valve.

(e) Diverter valve does not operate.

(e) Replace.

(f) Check valve does not operate.

(f) Replace.

6. Fuel Pump

PUMP LEAKS FUEL

(a) Diaphragm is worn, ruptured or torn.

(a) Replace pump.

(b) Diaphragm mounting plates are loose.

(b) Replace pump.

(c) Loose inlet or outlet line fittings.

(c) Tighten line fittings.

PUMP LEAKS OIL

(a) Cracked or deteriorated pushrod oil seal.

(a) Replace pump.

(b) Rocker arm pivot pin is loose.

(b) Replace pump.

(c) Pump mounting bolts loose.

(c) Tighten mounting bolts securely.

(d) Pump to block gasket is defective.

(d) Install new gasket

INSUFFICIENT FUEL DELIVERY

(a) Vent in tank is restricted.

(a) Unplug vent and inspect tank for leaks.

(b) Leaks in fuel line or fittings.

(b) Tighten line fittings.

(c) Dirt or other restriction in fuel tank.

(c) Replace fuel filter and clean out tank.

(d) Diaphragm is worn, ruptured or torn.

(d) Replace pump.

(e) Gas lines frozen.

(e) Thaw lines and drain tank.

(f) Improperly seating valves.

(f) Replace pump.

(g) Pump pushrod worn.

(g) Replace pushrod.

(h) Vapor lock.

(h) Install a heat shield wherever lines or pump come near exhaust.

(i) Low pressure.

(i) Replace pump.

(j) Incorrect fuel pump affixed to car.

(j) Check part number and replace with correct pump unit.

CONDITION	CORRECTION
(k) Dirty or restricted fuel filter.	(k) Replace filter.

NOISY FUEL PUMP

CONDITION	CORRECTION
(a) Mounting bolts are loose.	(a) Tighten mounting bolts securely.
(b) Rocker arm scored or worn.	(b) Replace pump.
(c) Rocker arm spring weak or broken.	(c) Replace spring.
(d) Stiff inlet hose..	(d) Install new hose about 3 ins. longer than old hose.

7. Charging System

GENERATOR LIGHT STAYS ON WITH ENGINE RUNNING

CONDITION	CORRECTION
(a) Belt is loose or broken.	(a) Replace belt if necessary; tighten belt tension to specs.
(b) No generator output.	(b) Connect test lamp to generator No. 1 terminal. If lamp lights dimly, generator receives initial field current but has no output. Ground generator field. If light does not brighten, remove and repair generator. If light does brighten, the generator is OK and voltage regulator is defective.

GENERATOR LIGHT ON WITH IGNITION OFF

CONDITION	CORRECTION
(a) Positive diode shorted.	(a) Replace diode bridge.

GENERATOR LIGHT OFF WITH IGNITION ON BUT ENGINE NOT RUNNING

CONDITION	CORRECTION
(a) Indicator bulb burned out.	(a) Replace bulb and socket assembly.
(b) Blown fuse.	(b) Replace fuse controlling indicator lights if all are off. If indicator lights do not come on with new fuse, check for an open in indicator light feed wire and correct.
(c) Open between bulb and ground in generator.	(c) Ground No. 1 terminal wire. If bulb lights, remove generator for repair. If bulb still does not light, check further for an open between bulb and generator.

UNDERCHARGED BATTERY

CONDITION	CORRECTION
(a) Continuous small drain on battery.	(a) Disconnect positive cable from battery. Connect test light between cable and battery post. If test lamp lights, trace and correct source of drain.
(b) Belt is loose or broken.	(b) Replace belt if necessary; tighten belt tension to specs.
(c) Low generator output.	(c) Connect voltmeter across battery and record voltage reading. Set carburetor on high step of fast idle cam, start engine, and turn on all continuous use accessories. If voltage across battery reads lower than the open circuit voltage just recorded, generator current output is low. Remove unit and repair.

CONDITION	CORRECTION
(d) Low voltage regulator setting.	(d) Set up test as in (c) above but turn off all accessories. When engine is at normal operating temperature any reading between 13.5 and 15.0 volts indicates that regulator is OK.
(e) High resistance in starting circuit or ignition resistor bypass.	(e) Connect jumper from negative terminal of coil to ground to prevent starting engine. Connect voltmeter to positive coil terminal and ground. Crank engine. Any reading below 9.0 volts requires a further test. Check voltage across battery posts during cranking. If voltage reading is within .5 volt of that at coil, circuits are OK but battery is too low for proper test.

BATTERY OVERCHARGED

CONDITION	CORRECTION
(a) Shorted battery cell.	(a) Perform battery load test to determine if battery cell is at fault.
(b) Voltage regulator setting too high.	(b) See Undercharged Battery (c) above. Set up test as in (c) and perform as in (d). If voltage is over 15.0 volts, replace regulator.

8. Cooling System

ENGINE OVERHEATS

CONDITION	CORRECTION
(a) Belt tension is too low.	(a) Adjust belt tension to specs.
(b) Timing set incorrectly.	(b) Reset timing to specs.
(c) Timing retarded by faulty distributor vacuum advance unit or thermal vacuum switch.	(c) Check thermal advance for defective switch or distributor vacuum advance unit. Check hose for kinks, partial collapse or poor connections.
(d) Loss of system pressure.	(d) Test system and cap for pressure. If cap is not defective, inspect for leaks and repair when found.
(e) Radiator fins obstructed.	(e) Clean radiator fins of debris, bugs, etc.
(f) Cooling system passages blocked by rust or scale.	(f) Flush system and add fresh coolant.
(g) Reservoir hose is pinched or kinked.	(g) Replace hose and prevent kinking by rerouting if necessary.
(h) Lower radiator hose has collapsed.	(h) Replace.

COOLANT LOSS

CONDITION	CORRECTION
(a) Thermostat stuck in closed position.	(a) Replace thermostat.
(b) Leaking hoses or poor connections.	(b) Check hoses and connections. Tighten and/or replace if necessary.
(c) Heater core leaks.	(c) Replace heater core.
(d) Water temperature sending unit is leaking.	(d) Replace unit.
(e) Radiator leaks.	(e) Check radiator for leaks, especially bottom half.

ENGINE DOES NOT REACH NORMAL OPERATING TEMPERATURE

CONDITION	CORRECTION
(a) Radiator leaks.	(a) Check radiator for leaks, especially bottom half. Also check system for pressure.

CONDITION	CORRECTION
(b) Coolant reservoir/hose leaks.	(b) Replace reservoir or hose.
(c) Hoses or connections are loose or damaged.	(c) Reseat or replace hoses/clamps.
(d) Water pump seal leaks.	(d) Repair water pump or replace.
(e) Water pump gasket leaks.	(e) Replace gasket.
(f) Radiator cap defective.	(f) Test cap for pressure and replace.
(g) Radiator filler neck distorted.	(g) Use wooden block and mallet to reform neck evenly to fit cap.
(h) Cylinder head gasket leaks.	(h) Replace gasket.
(i) Improper cylinder head screw torque.	(i) Retorque screws to specs.
(j) Cylinder block core plug leaks.	(j) Replace core plug.
(k) Cracked cylinder head/block, or warped cylinder head/block gasket surface.	(k) Resurface if possible; replace if not.
(l) Heater core leaks.	(l) Replace core.
(m) Thermostat stuck open.	(m) Install new thermostat—make sure it's correct type and heat range.
(n) Heater water control valve leaks.	(n) Replace valve.
(o) Coolant level too low.	(o) Add coolant.

9. Turbo Hydra-Matic

NO DRIVE IN DRIVE RANGE

CONDITION	CORRECTION
(a) Oil level low.	(a) Top up to correct level. Check for external leaks or defective vacuum modulator. Leaking diaphragm will evacuate oil from unit.
(b) Oil pressure is low.	(b) Check filter assembly as O-ring may be missing or damaged; neck weld may leak or filter might be blocked. Check pump assembly for damage by converter. In rare cases, there might be porosity in intake bore of unit.
(c) Manual linkage is out of adjustment.	(c) Check and adjust linkage.
(d) Faulty control valve assembly.	(d) Reconnect manual valve to manual lever.
(e) Forward clutch not working properly.	(e) Check for cracked piston, missing or damaged seals, or burned clutch plates.
(f) Pump feed circuit to forward clutch faulty.	(f) Check for missing or broken oil seal rings, leak in feed circuits, pump-to-case gasket out of position or damaged. Clutch drum ball check may be stuck or missing.
(g) Broken spring or damaged cage in roller clutch assembly.	(g) Replace.

OIL PRESSURE TOO HIGH OR TOO LOW

CONDITION	CORRECTION
(a) High oil pressure.	(a) Vacuum line or fittings may leak; also check vacuum modulator, modulator valve, pressure regulator and oil pump for correct operation.
(b) Low oil pressure.	(b) Vacuum line or fittings may be obstructed; also check vacuum modulator, modulator valve, pressure regulator, governor and oil pump for correct operation.

1-2 SHIFT: FULL THROTTLE ONLY

CONDITION	CORRECTION
(a) Sticking or defective detent switch.	(a) Replace.
(b) Detent solenoid is loose, has leaking gasket or sticks open.	(b) Repair and/or replace as necessary.
(c) Control valve assembly faulty.	(c) Valve body spacer plate to cover gasket may leak. It can also be damaged or incorrectly installed. Check detent valve train for sticking and 3-2 valve for same.
(d) Porosity in case assembly.	(d) Replace.

NO 1-2 SHIFT: FIRST SPEED ONLY

CONDITION	CORRECTION
(a) Governor assembly faulty.	(a) Governor valve sticks. Driven gear may also be loose, damaged or worn. If driven gear shows signs of damage, check output shaft drive gear for nicks or rough finish.
(b) Control valve assembly faulty.	(b) Check 1-2 shift valve train to see if it's closed. Governor feed channels may be blocked, leaking or pipes out of position. Check valve body spacer plate-to-cover gasket as it may be leaking, damaged or incorrectly installed.
(c) Defective case.	(c) Replace leaking or blown-out intermediate clutch plug. Governor feed channel may also be blocked or governor bore could be scored or worn causing cross pressure leak.
(d) Intermediate clutch not working correctly.	(d) Replace clutch piston seals. Check center support oil rings as they may be missing or broken. Orifice plug could also be missing.

FIRST & SECOND SPEEDS ONLY, NO 2-3 SHIFT

CONDITION	CORRECTION
(a) Detent solenoid stuck open.	(a) Replace.
(b) Detent switch faulty.	(b) Replace.
(c) Control valve assembly faulty.	(c) Check 2-3 shift train to see if it's stuck. Also check valve body spacer plate-to-cover gasket as it may be leaking, damaged or incorrectly installed.
(d) Direct clutch defective.	(d) Replace center support oil rings. Also check clutch piston seals for damage and make sure that piston ball check is not stuck or missing.

DRIVE IN NEUTRAL

CONDITION	CORRECTION
(a) Manual linkage out of adjustment.	(a) Adjust linkage.
(b) Forward clutch does not release.	(b) Replace.

NO DRIVE OR SLIPS IN REVERSE

CONDITION	CORRECTION
(a) Oil level low.	(a) Top up oil to proper level.
(b) Manual linkage out of adjustment.	(b) Adjust linkage.

CONDITION	CORRECTION
(c) Incorrect oil pressure.	(c) Replace vacuum modulator assembly.
(d) Control valve assembly faulty.	(d) Replace valve body spacer plate-to-gasket. Check 2-3 valve train to see if it's stuck open. Make sure low reverse ball is not missing from case and that reverse feed passage is correctly installed.
(e) Rear servo piston seal ring damaged or missing.	(e) Replace ring.
(f) Reverse or low band defective or burned.	(f) Replace band.
(g) Direct clutch—clutch plates burned or damaged.	(g) Replace clutch plates. Check to see if caused by stuck ball check in piston. Also check outer seal as it may be damaged too.

SLIPS IN ALL RANGES

CONDITION	CORRECTION
(a) Oil level low.	(a) Top up oil to proper level.
(b) Incorrect oil pressure.	(b) Replace vacuum modulator assembly. Also check for plugged or leaking filter assembly, especially a damaged O-ring.
(c) Forward and direct clutches burned.	(c) Replace burned clutches and locate cause.

1-2 SHIFT SLIPS

CONDITION	CORRECTION
(a) Oil level low.	(a) Top up oil to proper level.
(b) Incorrect oil pressure.	(b) Replace vacuum modulator assembly. Check pump pressure regulator valve at same time for correct operation.
(c) Front accumulator oil ring damaged or missing.	(c) Replace.
(d) Control valve assembly bolts are loose.	(d) Torque valve body attaching bolts to correct specs if 1-2 accumulator valve train is not sticking. If valve sticks, replace.
(e) Rear accumulator oil ring damaged or missing.	(e) Replace.
(f) Mispositioned pump-to-case gasket.	(f) Replace gasket correctly.
(g) Intermediate clutch plug in case leaking excessively.	(g) Replace. If leak continues, there may be porosity between channels.
(h) Intermediate clutch piston seals damaged.	(h) Replace. Clutch plates may also be burned and should be replaced if necessary.

ROUGH 1-2 SHIFT

CONDITION	CORRECTION
(a) Incorrect oil pressure.	(a) Replace vacuum modulator assembly. Check for loose fittings or restrictions in line.
(b) Control valve assembly bolts loose.	(b) Torque valve body to case bolts to specs.
(c) Valve body spacer plate-to-cover gasket damaged or mispositioned.	(c) Replace gasket.
(d) Intermediate clutch ball missing or not sealing.	(d) Replace or ascertain why sealing is not taking place.
(e) Rear servo accumulator assembly faulty.	(e) Remove unit and check for damaged oil rings, stuck piston, broken or missing spring or damaged bore. Repair accordingly.

2-3 SHIFT SLIPS

CONDITION	CORRECTION
(a) Oil level low.	(a) Top up oil to proper level.
(b) Incorrect oil pressure.	(b) Replace vacuum modulator assembly. Check for mislocated pump-to-case gasket and replace correctly if necessary.
(c) Accumulator piston pin leaks at swedge end.	(c) Replace.
(d) Direct clutch—piston seals leak.	(d) Replace seals and check for leak from center support oil seal rings.

ROUGH 2-3 SHIFT

CONDITION	CORRECTION
(a) Oil pressure is too high.	(a) Modulator valve sticks or assembly is defective. Determine which and repair accordingly.
(b) Front servo accumulator spring missing or broken.	(b) Replace. Check for stuck piston.

NO ENGINE BRAKING—2ND GEAR

CONDITION	CORRECTION
(a) Front band broken or burned.	(a) Replace and determine cause.

NO ENGINE BRAKING—1ST GEAR

CONDITION	CORRECTION
(a) Low-reverse check ball missing from case.	(a) Replace.
(b) Rear servo oil seal ring, bore or piston damaged.	(b) Replace.
(c) Rear band apply pin is short or improperly assembled.	(c) Replace correctly.
(d) Rear band is broken or burned.	(d) Replace and determine cause.

NO PART-THROTTLE DOWNSHIFT

CONDITION	CORRECTION
(a) 3-2 valve stuck, spring missing or broken.	(a) Free valve and/or replace spring.
(b) Oil pressure incorrect.	(b) Check operation of vacuum modulator assembly and replace if necessary.

NO DETENT DOWNSHIFTS

CONDITION	CORRECTION
(a) 3-2 valve stuck, spring missing or broken.	(a) Free valve and/or replace spring.
(b) Detent switch out of adjustment.	(b) Adjust.
(c) Solenoid inoperative.	(c) Replace.
(d) Detent valve train sticking.	(d) Replace.

WILL NOT HOLD IN PARK

CONDITION	CORRECTION
(a) Linkage needs adjustment.	(a) Adjust linkage.
(b) Defective parking brake lever and actuator assembly.	(b) Replace.
(c) Parking pawl broken.	(c) Replace.

10. 3-Speed Manual Transmission

NOISY IN FORWARD SPEEDS

CONDITION	CORRECTION
(a) Low lubricant level.	(a) Top up as required.
(b) Incorrect lubricant in use.	(b) Drain and refill with correct lubricant.
(c) Transmission loose or incorrectly aligned.	(c) Tighten attachment bolts and check alignment.

CONDITION	CORRECTION
(d) Main drive gear or drive gear bearing worn or damaged.	(d) Disassemble transmission and replace drive gear or bearing as required.
(e) Countergear or needle roller bearings worn or damaged.	(e) Disassemble transmission and replace as necessary.

NOISY IN REVERSE GEAR

CONDITION	CORRECTION
(a) Reverse gear, reverse idler gear or shaft worn or damaged.	(a) Disassemble transmission and replace gears or shaft as necessary.

SHIFTS HARD

CONDITION	CORRECTION
(a) Clutch improperly adjusted.	(a) Adjust clutch correctly.
(b) Shift linkage out of adjustment.	(b) Check linkage and adjust for smooth operation.
(c) Shift linkage bent; loose or damaged linkage.	(c) Replace damaged linkage; tighten loose linkage.
(d) Shift levers, shafts or forks worn.	(d) Disassemble transmission and replace components as required.
(e) Blocking rings worn or broken.	(e) Disassemble transmission and replace rings.

JUMPS OUT OF GEAR

CONDITION	CORRECTION
(a) Shift linkage loose, worn or needs adjustment.	(a) Tighten loose linkage. Replace worn linkage, adjust.
(b) Transmission loose or incorrectly aligned.	(b) Tighten attachment bolts and check alignment.
(c) Bent or worn shift fork, lever and/or shaft.	(c) Disassemble transmission and replace parts as necessary for this and remaining causes.
(d) Pilot bearing worn.	
(e) Detent cam spring weak or notches worn.	
(f) Loose or broken bearing retainer, bearings on main drive gear and output shaft.	
(g) Worn or broken blocking ring.	
(h) Bent output shaft.	

STICKS IN GEAR

CONDITION	CORRECTION
(a) Clutch does not release fully.	(a) Adjust clutch properly.
(b) Low lubricant level.	(b) Top up as required.
(c) Incorrect lubricant in use.	(c) Drain and refill with correct lubricant.
(d) Tight main drive gear pilot bearing.	(d) Disassemble transmission and replace parts as necessary for this and remaining causes.
(e) Frozen synchronizing blocking ring on main drive gear cone.	
(f) Damaged teeth on synchronizer sleeve and/or main drive gear.	

FORWARD GEARS CLASH

CONDITION	CORRECTION
(a) Clutch does not release fully.	(a) Adjust clutch to release fully.
(b) Springs in synchronizer assembly are weak or broken.	(b) Disassemble transmission and replace springs as required.
(c) Blocking rings and/or cone surfaces are worn.	(c) Disassemble transmission and replace worn components.

REVERSE GEAR CLASH

CONDITION	CORRECTION
(a) Engine idle is set too high.	(a) Reset engine idle.
(b) Clutch needs adjustment.	(b) Adjust clutch.

CONDITION	CORRECTION
(c) Clutch driven plate drags or is distorted.	(c) Adjust if possible; replace if necessary.
(d) Main drive gear bearing is tight or frozen.	(d) Disassemble transmission and replace bearing.

11. 4-Speed Manual Transmission

SHIFTS HARD ON DOWNSHIFT

CONDITION	CORRECTION
(a) Downshifting at too great rpms.	(a) Shifting into low gear above 45 mph and second above 65 mph makes extra work for synchronizing assemblies. If low or 2nd is used constantly at high speeds, there is the danger of damage from overspeeding the engine.

DISENGAGES FROM GEAR

CONDITION	CORRECTION
(a) Dirt between transmission case and clutch housing.	(a) Clean mating surfaces involved.
(b) Does not engage fully.	(b) Check linkage for interference and adjust or replace if damaged.
(c) Clutching teeth worn or defective and/or clutch hub spline worn.	(c) Replace gear, clutch hub and sleeve.

NOISY OPERATION

CONDITION	CORRECTION
(a) Worn, scored or broken gears.	(a) Replace gears.
(b) Dirty or worn bearing.	(b) Flush transmission with kerosene. If noise is still there, replace bearings and examine gears—replace if worn or damaged.
(c) Clutch sleeve interferes with countergear.	(c) Replace worn shift forks, countergear and idler gear thrust washers to restore gears and clutch sleeve to proper location. Thrust faces on these gears should be checked for wear and replaced if necessary.

LEAKS LUBRICANT

CONDITION	CORRECTION
(a) Too much lubricant in transmission.	(a) Drain to correct level.
(b) Main drive gear bearing retainer loose or broken.	(b) Tighten or replace retainer.
(c) Front main bearing retainer gasket damaged.	(c) Replace gasket.
(d) Cover loose or gasket damaged.	(d) Tighten cover or replace gasket.
(e) Operating shaft seal leaks.	(e) Replace operating shaft seal.
(f) Countershaft loose in case.	(f) Replace case.
(g) Lack of sealant on bolts.	(g) Coat bolts with sealant.
(h) Extension oil seal worn.	(h) Replace seal.

BACKLASH IN ALL REDUCTION GEARS IS EXCESSIVE

CONDITION	CORRECTION
(a) Countergear bearings worn.	(a) Replace bearings and shaft.
(b) Too much end-play in countergear.	(b) Replace countergear thrust washers.

NOISY IN ALL REDUCTION GEARS

CONDITION	CORRECTION
(a) Insufficient lubricant.	(a) Check and top up to correct level.
(b) Main drive gear or countergear worn or damaged.	(b) Replace gears.

SHIFTS HARD, UP OR DOWN

(a) Clutch binds or releases too slowly.

(a) Adjust or repair clutch.

(b) Shift linkage binds.

(b) Free linkage, lubricate and adjust if necessary.

NOISY IN ALL GEARS

(a) Insufficient lubricant.

(a) Check and top up to correct level.

(b) Countergear bearings worn.

(b) Replace bearings and shaft.

(c) Main drive gear and countershaft drive gear worn or damaged.

(c) Replace gears.

(d) Main drive gear or mainshaft ball bearings damaged.

(d) Replace bearings.

(e) Speedometer gears damaged.

(e) Replace gears.

NOISY IN HIGH GEAR

(a) Front main bearing damaged.

(a) Replace bearing.

(b) Rear bearing damaged.

(b) Replace bearing.

(c) Speedometer gears damaged.

(c) Replace gears.

NOISY IN NEUTRAL WITH ENGINE RUNNING

(a) Front main bearing damaged.

(a) Replace bearing.

(b) Mainshaft pilot bearing damaged.

(b) Replace bearing.

12. Clutch

FAILS TO RELEASE

(a) Linkage adjustment is incorrect.

(a) Adjust linkage correctly.

(b) Pedal travel is wrong.

(b) Trim bumper stop and adjust linkage.

(c) Linkage is loose.

(c) Replace bushings.

(d) Pilot bearing is worn or damaged.

(d) Replace bearing.

(e) Faulty driven plate.

(e) Replace driven plate.

(f) Fork off ball stud.

(f) Install correctly.

(g) Clutch driven plate hub binds on main drive gear spline.

(g) Repair or replace main drive.

CLUTCH SLIPS

(a) No lash.

(a) Adjust linkage.

(b) Driven plate contaminated with oil.

(b) Install new driven plate; locate and correct oil leak.

(c) Driven plate facing worn or torn.

(c) Replace driven plate.

(d) Pressure plate or flywheel warped.

(d) Replace.

(e) Weak diaphragm spring.

(e) Replace cover assembly.

(f) Driven plate not seated correctly.

(f) Make 15-45 starts.

(g) Driven plate overheated.

(g) Let cool then check lash.

CLUTCH GRABS

(a) Driven plate facing glazed, burned or oil contaminated.

(a) Replace with new driven plate.

(b) Main drive gear splines worn.

(b) Replace transmission main drive gear.

(c) Engine mountings loose.

(c) Check and tighten or replace mountings.

(d) Pressure plate or flywheel warped.

(d) Replace.

(e) Flywheel or pressure plate burned or resin-smeared.

(e) Sand off if superficial but replace burned or heat checked parts.

RATTLING OR TRANSMISSION CLICK

(a) Clutch fork is loose on ball stud or in bearing groove.

(a) Check ball stud and retaining spring—replace if necessary.

(b) Oil in driven plate damper.

(b) Replace driven plate.

(c) Driven plate damper spring fails.

(c) Replace driven plate.

THROWOUT BEARING NOISE WHEN CLUTCH IS FULL ENGAGED

(a) Improperly adjusted linkage.

(a) Check and adjust linkage properly.

(b) Throwout bearing binds on transmission bearing retainer.

(b) Clean, relubricate and check for nicks, burrs, etc.

(c) Tension between clutch fork spring and ball stud is not sufficient.

(c) Replace fork.

(d) Fork improperly installed.

(d) Remove and reinstall properly.

(e) Linkage return spring is weak.

(e) Replace spring.

CLUTCH IS NOISY

(a) Throwout bearing is worn.

(a) Replace.

(b) Fork is off ball stud causing a heavy clicking noise.

(b) Remove and reinstall properly.

PEDAL DOES NOT RETURN WHEN CLUTCH IS DISENGAGED

(a) Linkage is binding.

(a) Free linkage; adjust if necessary and lubricate.

(b) Pressure plate spring is weak.

(b) Replace spring.

(c) Linkage return spring is weak.

(c) Replace spring.

REQUIRES HIGH PEDAL EFFORT

(a) Linkage is binding.

(a) Free linkage; adjust if necessary and lubricate.

(b) Driven plate is worn excessively.

(b) Replace with new driven plate.

13. Front Suspension

POOR DIRECTIONAL STABILITY

(a) Stabilizer bar broken or missing link.

(a) Remove and replace stabilizer and/or link.

(b) Shock absorber defective.

(b) Install new shock absorber.

(c) Front wheel alignment (caster) is incorrect.

(c) Align front wheels.

(d) Loose wheel bearings.

(d) Adjust wheel bearings to specs.

(e) Ball joints and/or steering linkage need lubrication.

(e) Lubricate suspension components.

(f) Steering gear not on high point.

(f) Adjust steering gear on high point.

HARD STEERING

(a) Ball joints and/or steering linkage need lubrication.

(a) Lubricate suspension components.

(b) Front tire pressure low or uneven.

(b) Inflate tires to proper pressure.

CONDITION	CORRECTION	CONDITION	CORRECTION

(c) Power steering unit partially or completely inoperative.

(c) Check power steering unit for proper operation (See Power Steering).

(d) Front wheel alignment is incorrect (manual steering only).

(d) Check and align front wheels.

FRONT WHEEL SHIMMY

(a) Tire and wheel out-of-round, or out-of-balance.

(a) Check runout and balance tires.

(b) Wheel bearings worn or too loose.

(b) Adjust wheel bearings to specs.

(c) Tie-rod ends worn.

(c) Replace tie-rod end(s).

(d) Ball joints worn.

(d) Replace ball joints.

(e) Defective shock absorber.

(e) Install new shock absorber.

CAR PULLS TO ONE SIDE

(a) Tire pressure low or uneven.

(a) Inflate tires to proper pressure.

(b) Front or rear brake drag.

(b) Check brake adjustment.

(c) Front spring broken or sagging.

(c) Replace spring.

(d) Front wheel alignment (camber) is incorrect.

(d) Align front wheels.

TOO MUCH PLAY IN STEERING

(a) Steering gear parts worn.

(a) Overhaul gear and replace worn components.

(b) Steering gear incorrectly adjusted.

(b) Adjust steering gear.

WHEEL TRAMP

(a) Tire and wheel out-of-balance.

(a) Balance wheels.

(b) Tire and wheel out-of-round.

(b) Replace tire.

(c) Bump or blister on tire.

(c) Replace tire.

(d) Defective shock absorber.

(d) Install new shock absorber.

FRONT END NOISE

(a) Ball joints and/or steering linkage need lubrication.

(a) Lubricate suspension components.

(b) Worn or loose shock absorber bushings.

(b) Tighten bolts and/or replace bushings.

(c) Control arm bushings worn.

(c) Replace bushings.

(d) Stabilizer bar loose.

(d) Tighten stabilizer bar attachments.

(e) Tie-rod ends worn.

(e) Replace tie-rod end(s).

(f) Wheel bearings worn or too loose.

(f) Check wheel bearings and adjust to specs or replace.

(g) Suspension bolts loose.

(g) Torque to specs or replace.

(h) Wheel nuts loose.

(h) Tighten wheel nuts.

TIRE WEAR EXCESSIVE OR UNEVEN

(a) Tires improperly inflated.

(a) Inflate tires to proper pressure.

(b) Toe-in adjustment is incorrect.

(b) Adjust toe-in to specs.

(c) Wheels out-of-balance.

(c) Balance wheels.

SCUFFED TIRES

(a) Toe-in adjustment is incorrect.

(a) Adjust toe-in to specs.

(b) Tires improperly inflated.

(b) Inflate tires to proper pressure.

(c) Suspension arm is bent or twisted.

(c) Replace arm.

CUPPED TIRES

(a) Tire or wheel runout is excessive.

(a) Adjust or compensate for runout.

(b) Wheel and tire out-of-balance.

(b) Balance wheels.

(c) Wheel bearings worn or out of adjustment.

(c) Adjust wheel bearings to specs or replace.

(d) Ball joints worn excessively.

(d) Replace ball joints.

(e) Defective front shock absorbers.

(e) Install new shock absorbers.

ERRATIC STEERING WHEN BRAKING

(a) Tires improperly inflated.

(a) Inflate tires to proper pressure.

(b) Front wheel bearings worn or incorrectly adjusted.

(b) Adjust bearings to specs or replace.

(c) Brakes need adjustment.

(c) Check brakes for uneven or incorrect adjustment.

(d) Caster adjustment incorrect or uneven.

(d) Check and adjust caster to specs.

RETURNABILITY POOR

(a) Improper caster setting (negative).

(a) Check and adjust caster to specs.

(b) Power steering gear unit binding internally.

(b) Remove and overhaul steering gear.

(c) Steering gear out of adjustment.

(c) Adjust steering gear to specs.

(d) Worn idler arm bushing.

(d) Replace idler arm.

(e) Steering linkage needs lubrication.

(e) Lubricate linkage.

14. Driveline and Universal Joint

ROUGHNESS OR VIBRATION AT ANY SPEED

(a) Dented or bent driveshaft.

(a) Replace driveshaft.

(b) Undercoating on driveshaft.

(b) Clean driveshaft.

(c) Tires are out-of-balance.

(c) Balance.

(d) Universal joints are tight.

(d) Hit yokes with a hammer to free up. If it's impossible to free, or if joint feels rough when rotated by hand, overhaul.

(e) U-bolt torque excessive.

(e) Adjust to specified torque.

(f) Universal joints are worn.

(f) Overhaul and replace necessary parts.

(g) Companion flange has burrs or gouges. Check snap ring locating surfaces on flange yoke.

(g) Rework or replace companion flange.

(h) Unbalanced driveshaft or companion flange.

(h) Check to see if balance weights on driveshaft are missing. Remove and reassemble driveshaft to companion shaft 180° from original position.

(i) Slip yoke spline is too loose.

(i) Replace necessary parts.

(j) Driveshaft runout.

(j) Check runout at front and rear. This should be less than specified by manufacturer. If not, rotate shaft 180° and recheck. If still too much, replace shaft.

ROUGHNESS AT LOW SPEEDS WITH LIGHT LOAD

(a) U-bolt clamp nuts too tight.

(a) Check and torque to specs. If torque was too great and brinelled pattern is evident on trunnions, replace joints.

SCRAPING NOISE

(a) Companion flange, slinger or end yoke rubs on rear axle carrier.

(a) Remove interference by straightening slinger.

LEAK AT FRONT SLIP YOKE

(a) Splined yoke has rough outside surface.

(a) Replace seal if cut. Replace yoke if outside surface is badly burred; hone or smooth with crocus cloth if burring is slight.

(b) Transmission rear oil seal is defective.

(b) Replace seal. Top up transmission to proper level.

DRIVELINE KNOCK OR CLUNK WHEN OPERATED AT 10 MPH IN HIGH GEAR OR NEUTRAL

(a) Universal joints worn or damaged.

(a) Disassemble universal joints and replace worn or damaged parts.

(b) Side-gear hub counterbore in differential worn oversize.

(b) Replace differential case and/or side gears as necessary.

PINGING OR CLICKING IN DRIVELINE

(a) Upper or lower control arm bushing bolts are loose.

(a) Tighten bolts to specified torque.

(b) Companion flange is loose.

(b) Remove and turn 180° from its original position, then apply white lead to splines and reinstall. Tighten pinion nut to specified torque.

15. Power Steering System

HISSING NOISE IN STEERING GEAR

(a) There's some noise in all power steering systems, one of the most common of which is a slight hiss evident at standstill or park.

(a) A slight hiss is normal and in no way affects steering.

RATTLE OR CHUCKLE NOISE IN STEERING GEAR

(a) Gearbox is loose on frame.

(a) Check gear-to-frame mounting and tighten bolts to 70 ft.-lbs.

(b) Steering linkage is loose.

(b) Check linkage pivot points for wear and replace if necessary.

(c) Pressure hose is touching another part of car.

(c) Adjust hose position but do not bend steel tubing by hand.

(d) Loose pitman shaft over center adjustment.

(d) Adjust to specs.

SQUAWK NOISE IN STEERING GEAR DURING TURN MANEUVER

(a) Dampener "O" ring on valve spool cut.

(a) Replace O-ring.

CHIRP NOISE IN PUMP OR BELT SQUEAL

(a) Loose belt.

(a) Adjust belt tension to specs.

GROWL NOISE IN STEERING PUMP

(a) Restriction in hoses or steering gear causing excessive back pressure.

(a) Locate restriction and correct, replacing part or hose if necessary.

(b) Scored pressure plates, thrust plate or rotor.

(b) Replace damaged parts and flush system.

(c) Cam ring extremely worn.

(c) Replace cam ring.

GROAN NOISE IN STEERING PUMP

(a) Low lubricant level.

(a) Fill reservoir to proper level.

(b) Air in the lubricant or a poor pressure hose connection.

(b) Tighten connector to specified torque. Bleed system by operating steering from right to left full turn.

RATTLE OR KNOCK IN STEERING PUMP

(a) Loose pump pulley nut.

(a) Tighten nut to specified torque.

(b) Vanes not properly installed.

(b) Remove and replace correctly.

(c) Vanes sticking in rotor slots.

(c) Free by removing dirt, varnish or burrs that act as a restriction.

SWISH NOISE IN STEERING PUMP

(a) Defective flow control valve.

(a) Replace valve.

WHINE NOISE IN STEERING PUMP

(a) Pump shaft bearing is scored.

(a) Replace housing and shaft and flush system.

POOR STEERING WHEEL RETURN TO CENTER

(a) Lack of lubrication in linkage and ball joints.

(a) Lubricate linkage and ball joints.

(b) Lower coupling flange rubs against steering gear adjuster plug.

(b) Loosen the pinch bolt and assemble correctly.

(c) Misalignment of steering gear to column.

(c) Align steering column.

(d) Tires improperly inflated.

(d) Inflate to specified pressure.

(e) Front wheel alignment incorrect.

(e) Check alignment and adjust to specs. Before aligning, disconnect pitman arm of linkage from pitman shaft of gear and turn front wheels by hand. If wheels will not turn easily, linkage or ball joints are also at fault.

(f) Steering linkage binds.

(f) Replace pivots.

(g) Ball joints bind.

(g) Replace ball joints.

(h) Steering wheel rubs against directional signal housing.

(h) Adjust steering jacket.

(i) Steering shaft bearings are tight or frozen.

(i) Replace bearings.

CAR WANDERS FROM ONE SIDE OF ROAD TO THE OTHER

(a) Front end out of alignment.

(a) Check front end and align to specs.

(b) Unbalanced steering gear valve, requires light effort in direction of lead and heavy in opposite direction.

(b) Replace valve.

MOMENTARY INCREASE IN EFFORT WHEN TURNING WHEEL FAST

(a) Low lubricant level in pump.

(a) Top up with power steering fluid as necessary.

(b) Pump belt slips.

(b) Check belt for wear; tighten or replace, and adjust to tension specs.

(c) High internal leakage.

(c) Check pump pressure; repair or replace.

CONDITION	CORRECTION

STEERING WHEEL SURGES WHEN TURNING

	CONDITION		CORRECTION
(a)	Low lubricant level.	(a)	Top up as required.
(b)	Loose pump belt.	(b)	Adjust belt tension to specs.
(c)	Steering linkage hits oil pan at full turn position.	(c)	Correct clearance.
(d)	Pump pressure is insufficient.	(d)	Check pump pressure and replace relief valve if defective.
(e)	Flow control valve sticks.	(e)	Check for varnish or damage and replace if necessary.

EXCESSIVE WHEEL KICK-BACK OR LOOSE STEERING

	CONDITION		CORRECTION
(a)	Air in system.	(a)	Add power steering fluid to pump reservoir and bleed by operating steering, then check hose connectors for proper torque and adjust as required.
(b)	Steering gear loose on frame.	(b)	Tighten attaching bolts to specified torque.
(c)	Steering gear flexible coupling loose on shaft; rubber disc mounting screws loose.	(c)	Tighten flange pinch bolts to 30 ft.-lbs., if serrations are undamaged. Tighten upper flange to coupling nuts to specified torque.
(d)	Excess wear in steering linkage.	(d)	Replace loose pivots.
(e)	Front wheel bearings worn or incorrectly adjusted.	(e)	Adjust bearings or replace.
(f)	Poppet valve (gear) worn.	(f)	Replace.
(g)	Thrust bearing preload adjustment (gear) loose.	(g)	Adjust to specs with gear out of car.
(h)	Excessive over-center lash.	(h)	Adjust to specs with gear out of car.

HARD STEERING OR LACK OF ASSIST

	CONDITION		CORRECTION
(a)	Loose pump belt.	(a)	Adjust belt tension to specs.
(b)	Low oil in reservoir.	(b)	Top up to proper level. If excessively low, check lines and joints for evidence of external leakage. Tighten any loose connectors to 30 ft.-lbs.
(c)	Steering gear to column misalignment.	(c)	Align steering column.
(d)	Lower coupling flange rubs against steering gear adjuster plug.	(d)	Loosen pinch bolt and assemble correctly.
(e)	Tires not properly inflated.	(e)	Inflate to recommended pressure.

16. Drum Brakes

PEDAL GOES TO FLOOR

	CONDITION		CORRECTION
(a)	Fluid level low in reservoir.	(a)	Fill and bleed master cylinder.
(b)	Air in hydraulic system.	(b)	Fill and bleed system.
(c)	Brakes improperly adjusted.	(c)	Repair or replace self-adjuster.
(d)	Wheel cylinders leaking.	(d)	Recondition or replace wheel cylinder. It may be necessary to replace brake shoes.
(e)	Loose or broken brake lines.	(e)	Tighten all brake fittings or replace brake line.
(f)	Worn or leaking master cylinder.	(f)	Recondition or replace master cylinder and bleed system.
(g)	Brake lining excessively worn.	(g)	Reline and adjust brakes.

BRAKE PEDAL IS SPONGY

	CONDITION		CORRECTION
(a)	Air in hydraulic system.	(a)	Fill master cylinder and bleed hydraulic system.
(b)	Contaminated or incorrect brake fluid.	(b)	Drain, flush and refill with proper brake fluid.
(c)	Brake drums excessively worn or cracked.	(c)	Replace drums.

BRAKES PULL WHEN APPLIED

	CONDITION		CORRECTION
(a)	Contaminated lining.	(a)	Replace with new lining of original quality.
(b)	Front end needs alignment.	(b)	Check and align front end.
(c)	Brake adjustment incorrect.	(c)	Adjust brakes and check fluid.
(d)	Unmatched brake linings.	(d)	Match primary and secondary linings with same type on all wheels.
(e)	Brake shoes are distorted.	(e)	Replace shoes.
(f)	Restriction in brake hose or line.	(f)	Locate and replace plugged hose or brake line.
(g)	Rear spring broken.	(g)	Replace.

BRAKES SQUEAL OR CHIRP

	CONDITION		CORRECTION
(a)	Brake lining glazed or saturated.	(a)	Cam grind (glazed only) or replace lining.
(b)	Brake shoe retaining spring weak or broken.	(b)	Replace with new retaining spring.
(c)	Brake shoe return spring weak or broken.	(c)	Replace with new return spring.
(d)	Brake shoes are distorted.	(d)	Replace shoes.
(e)	Support plate is bent.	(e)	Replace with new support plate.
(f)	Dust in brakes or scored brake drums.	(f)	Blow out brake assembly with compressed air and reface drums—machine, do not grind.
(g)	Drum or eccentric axle flange pilot out-of-round.	(g)	Remove and replace—lubricate support plate contact areas.

BRAKES DRAG

	CONDITION		CORRECTION
(a)	Wheel or parking brake adjustment incorrect.	(a)	Adjust brakes and check fluid level.
(b)	Parking brake engaged.	(b)	Release parking brake.
(c)	Brake shoe return spring weak or broken.	(c)	Replace with new shoe return spring.
(d)	Brake pedal binds.	(d)	Free pedal and lubricate linkage.
(e)	Master cylinder cup sticks.	(e)	Recondition master cylinder.
(f)	Master cylinder relief port is obstructed.	(f)	Use compressed air to blow out relief port.
(g)	Brake drum is bent or out-of-round.	(g)	Reface or replace drum.
(h)	Stop light switch needs adjustment.	(h)	Adjust switch to allow for full return of pedal.

HARD PEDAL

	CONDITION		CORRECTION
(a)	Brake booster is not working.	(a)	Replace unit.
(b)	Restriction in brake line or hose.	(b)	Clean out or replace brake line or hose.
(c)	Frozen brake pedal linkage.	(c)	Free and lubricate linkage.

WHEEL LOCKS

	CONDITION		CORRECTION
(a)	Brake lining is contaminated with oil or grease.	(a)	Reline all brakes.
(b)	Brake lining is loose or torn.	(b)	Replace damaged linings.

CONDITION	CORRECTION
(c) Wheel cylinder cups stick.	(c) Recondition or replace wheel cylinders.
(d) Wheel bearings out of adjustment.	(d) Clean, pack and adjust wheel bearings to specs.

BRAKES FADE

CONDITION	CORRECTION
(a) Use of inferior linings.	(a) Replace with original quality linings.
(b) Brake drums overheat.	(b) Check for dragging brakes.
(c) Contaminated or incorrect brake fluid.	(c) Drain, flush, refill and bleed hydraulic brake system.
(d) Saturated brake lining.	(d) Reline all brakes.

SURGE BELOW 15 MPH

CONDITION	CORRECTION
(a) Rear brake drum bent or out-of-round.	(a) Reface or replace drum.

CHATTER FROM 40 TO 80 MPH

CONDITION	CORRECTION
(a) Front brake drum bent or out-of-round.	(a) Reface or replace drum.

SHOE KNOCK

CONDITION	CORRECTION
(a) Machine grooves in contact face of brake drum.	(a) Sand, reface or replace brake drum.
(b) Hold-down springs are weak.	(b) Replace with new springs.

BRAKES DO NOT SELF-ADJUST

CONDITION	CORRECTION
(a) Adjuster screw is frozen in thread.	(a) Clean and free all thread areas.
(b) Adjuster screw is corroded at thrust washer.	(b) Clean threads and replace thrust washer.
(c) Adjuster lever does not engage star wheel properly.	(c) Repair, free up or replace adjuster.
(d) Adjuster incorrectly installed.	(d) Check and reinstall correctly.

17. Disc Brakes

PEDAL TRAVEL IS EXCESSIVE

CONDITION	CORRECTION
(a) Air leak or insufficient fluid in hydraulic system or caliper.	(a) Check system for leaks and bleed.
(b) Shoe and lining assembly warped or excessively tapered.	(b) Install new shoe and linings.
(c) Disc runout excessive.	(c) Check disc for runout with dial indicator. Install a new or refinished disc.
(d) Rear brake needs adjustment.	(d) Adjust and check rear brakes.
(e) Wheel bearing adjustment is too loose.	(e) Readjust wheel bearing to specified torque.
(f) Caliper piston seal damaged.	(f) Install new piston seal.
(g) Contaminated or incorrect brake fluid.	(g) Drain and replace with correct fluid.
(h) Power brake unit malfunction.	(h) Replace unit.

BRAKE CHATTER

CONDITION	CORRECTION
(a) Braking disc has excessive thickness variation.	(a) Check disc for thickness variation with a micrometer.
(b) Lateral runout of braking disc is excessive.	(b) Check disc for lateral runout with a dial indicator; replace with new or refaced disc.
(c) Front bearing clearance is too great.	(c) Readjust wheel bearings to specified torque.

REQUIRES EXCESSIVE PEDAL EFFORT

CONDITION	CORRECTION
(a) Brake fluid, oil or grease on linings.	(a) Replace with new linings.
(b) Incorrect or faulty lining.	(b) Remove and replace lining with original quality lining.
(c) Seized or frozen piston(s).	(c) Disassemble caliper and free up piston(s).
(d) Power brake malfunction.	(d) Replace unit.

PULL, GRABBING OR UNEVEN BRAKING ACTION

CONDITION	CORRECTION
(a) Brake fluid, oil or grease on linings.	(a) Replace with new linings.
(b) Linings unmatched.	(b) Replace with correct lining.
(c) Seized or frozen piston(s).	(c) Disassemble caliper and free up piston(s).
(d) Tire pressure insufficient.	(d) Check and inflate tires to recommended pressures.
(e) Front end needs alignment.	(e) Check and align front end to specs.
(f) Rear spring broken.	(f) Replace.
(g) Restriction in hose or line.	(g) Check hoses and lines and replace.
(h) Caliper incorrectly aligned with braking disc.	(h) Check alignment and remove caliper if necessary to correct alignment when replacing.

BRAKE RATTLE AT LOW SPEEDS ON ROUGH ROADS

CONDITION	CORRECTION
(a) Inboard shoe anti-rattle spring either missing or not properly positioned.	(a) Install new anti-rattle spring or position properly.
(b) Clearance between shoe and caliper is too great.	(b) Replace shoe and lining assemblies.

SCRAPING

CONDITION	CORRECTION
(a) Mounting bolts are too long.	(a) Replace with mounting bolts of correct length.
(b) Wheel bearings are loose.	(b) Readjust wheel bearings to correct specs.
(c) Splash shield is deformed and rubs on rotor.	(c) Bend shield to provide proper clearance.

FRONT BRAKES HEAT UP AND FAIL TO RELEASE

CONDITION	CORRECTION
(a) Pedal linkage sticks.	(a) Free sticking linkage and lubricate.
(b) Seized or frozen piston(s).	(b) Disassemble caliper and free piston(s).
(c) Power brake unit malfunction.	(c) Replace unit.

LEAKING WHEEL CYLINDER

CONDITION	CORRECTION
(a) Worn or damaged caliper piston seal.	(a) Remove and disassemble caliper; install new seal.
(b) Scoring or corrosion on surface of cylinder bore.	(b) Remove and disassemble caliper; hone cylinder bore and install new seal.

PEDAL GOES TO FLOOR—NO BRAKING ACTION

CONDITION	CORRECTION
(a) Air in hydraulic system.	(a) Bleed hydraulic system correctly.
(b) Fluid leak past primary cup in master cylinder.	(b) Recondition master cylinder.
(c) Hose or line leak in system.	(c) Check hoses and lines for leak and repair or replace as required.
(d) Rear brakes need adjustment.	(d) Adjust rear brakes.
(e) Bleeder screw open.	(e) Close bleeder screw and bleed entire system.